W9-AXK-090

United States Edition

2018 Year B

Workbook for **Lectors,** **Gospel Readers,** and **Proclaimers** of the **Word**®

Elaine Park, SSL, STD

Konrad Schaefer, OSB, SSD

Douglas Leal

LTP
LITURGY
TRAINING
PUBLICATIONS

CONTENTS

New American Bible readings are taken from *Lectionary for Mass* for Use in the Dioceses of the United States of America, second typical edition © 1998, 1997, 1970 by the Confraternity of Christian Doctrine, Washington, DC, and are reproduced herein by license of the copyright owner. All rights reserved. No part of *Lectionary for Mass* may be reproduced in any form without permission in writing from the Confraternity of Christian Doctrine, Washington, DC.

Excerpts from the English translation of the Psalm Responses, Titles of the Readings from *Lectionary for Mass* © 1969, 1981, 1997, International Commission on English in the Liturgy Corporation (ICEL). All rights reserved. Texts contained in this work derived whole or in part from liturgical texts copyrighted by the International Commission on English in the Liturgy (ICEL)have been published here with the confirmation of the Committee on Divine Worship, United States Conference of Catholic Bishops. No other texts in this work have been formally reviewed or approved by the United States Conference of Catholic Bishops.

WORKBOOK FOR LECTORS, GOSPEL READERS, AND PROCLAIMERS OF THE WORD® 2018, United States Edition © 2017 Archdiocese of Chicago. All rights reserved.

Liturgy Training Publications, 3949 South Racine Avenue, Chicago, IL 60609, 800-933-1800, fax 800-933-7094, orders@ltp.org, www.LTP.org.

Cover art: Barbara Simcoe

This book was edited by Lorie Simmons. Christian Rocha was the production editor, Anna Manhart was the designer, and Luis Leal was the production artist.

(continues on next page)

Ordinary Time

Printed in the United States of
America.
ISBN: 978-1-61671-347-8
WL18

In accordance with c. 827,
permission to publish was granted
on March 29, 2017, by Reverend
Monsignor John F. Canary, Vicar
General of the Archdiocese of
Chicago. Permission to publish is
an official declaration of ecclesiasti-
cal authority that the material is
free from doctrinal and moral error.
No legal responsibility is assumed
by the grant of this permission.

(see endnotes on page x)

The Authors

Two Scripture scholars wrote the
commentaries (see their initials
after each one).

Elaine Park has a licentiate in
sacred Scripture (SSL) from the
Pontifical Biblical Institute (1987)
and a doctorate in sacred theology
(STD) from the Gregorian University
(1995), both in Rome. She has been
a professor of biblical studies and
academic dean at Mt. Angel
Seminary in St. Benedict, Oregon.
She frequently gives talks and
retreats on biblical topics.

Fr. Konrad Schaefer, OSB, a monk of
Mount Angel Abbey, Oregon,
received the SSL from the Pontifical
Biblical Institute in Rome and a
doctorate in Sacred Scripture from
the École Biblique in Jerusalem. He
teaches at the Pontifical University
of Mexico and resides at Our Lady
of the Angels Priory in Cuernavaca,
Mexico, where he also writes and
offers retreats. He is the author of
Psalms, from Liturgical Press (2001).

Douglas Leal has written all of the
margin notes. He holds an MA in
pastoral ministry from the Boston
College School of Theology and
Ministry. He has written, directed,
and acted in numerous theater
productions, conducts lector
training workshops nationwide, and
is the author of *Stop Reading and
Start Proclaiming!*, available from
LTP at http://www.ltp.org.

MINISTRY OF THE WORD BASICS

The Word of God in the Liturgy

The Word of God proclaimed in the Liturgy is a living Word with power to nourish and transform both those who proclaim it and those who hear it. In the words of the Second Vatican Council's *Constitution on Divine Revelation* (*Dei Verbum*), "The Church has always venerated the divine Scriptures just as she venerates the body of the Lord, since, especially in the sacred liturgy, she unceasingly receives and offers to the faithful the bread of life from the table both of God's word and of Christ's body" (DV, 21).

Throughout its history, the Church has affirmed over and over the close tie between the Word proclaimed in the Liturgy and the Word made flesh received in the Eucharist, recognizing both as Christ present to give himself as food. Pope Francis, in his Apostolic Exhortation *Evangelii gaudium*, writes that the hearts of the faithful who gather on the Lord's Day are nourished both by his Word and by the bread of eternal life (EG, 15). He emphasizes as well that being fed at both tables gives strength for the whole journey: "God's word, listened to and celebrated, above all in the Eucharist, nourishes and inwardly strengthens Christians, enabling them to offer an authentic witness to the Gospel in daily life. . . . The preaching of the word, living and effective, prepares for the reception of the sacrament, and in the sacrament that word attains its maximum efficacy" (EG, 174).

The image of food to refer to God's Word has a strong foundation in the Hebrew Scriptures. Moses tells the people prior to their entering the land, "it is not by bread alone that people live, but by all that comes forth from the mouth of the LORD" (Deuteronomy 8:3). The prophet Jeremiah, commanded to proclaim God's Word, cried out, "When I found your words, I devoured them; your words were my joy, the happiness of my heart" (Jeremiah 15:16). And God later instructed Ezekiel to open his mouth and eat the scroll. Ezekiel recounts the episode: "Feed your stomach and fill your belly with this scroll I am giving you. I ate it, and it was as sweet as honey in my mouth" (Ezekiel 3:1–3). Each of these passages, and many more, highlight God's gift of satisfying our deepest hungers with a Word that is life-giving.

How does this Word of God actually feed us with joy, happiness, sweetness, and an abundance of life? Think of what goes into a lavishly prepared feast that gives delight and nourishment to guests. In the same way, the Word of God proclaimed in the liturgy also requires careful selection and preparation. Those proclaiming the Word are like good chefs who have done everything needed to present a nourishing meal. The Lectionary provides the selection of the food set at the table of the Word. Its design offers a rich variety, much like a well-chosen

> **In the beginning was the Word, and the Word was with God, and the Word was God.**

menu. The variety of fare means that the readings provide, as fully as possible, an overview of the biblical story and its great themes, even when they might not be people's favorite menu items. Although it isn't the role of the reader to make the selection, it is important for those who proclaim to see where particular texts fit into the broad sweep of the biblical story (our salvation history), how it harmonizes with the season or feast we are celebrating, and how it can offer insights for their particular community at this particular moment. Some questions we might ask are: Why was this text selected? How does it relate to the other readings of the day? How does it provide the variety of nourishment essential for a mature faith? Was the passage selected because of the season or feast, or as part of a continuous reading of a book, letter, or Gospel? How do we hear it echoed in the images and words of the prayers, music, liturgical environment, and ritual actions of this specific liturgy?

In addition to being nourishing food, the Word in the liturgy is also a very personal communication from God to his people: "When the Sacred Scriptures are read in the Church, God himself speaks to his people, and Christ, present in his word, proclaims the Gospel" (*General Instruction of the Roman Missal*, 29). Proclaimers of the Word, then, lend their voices for this personal communication, preparing themselves with sincere humility, through prayer, study, and practice to faithfully convey to the people what God intends.

Understanding the Word We Proclaim

Preparation for reading at the table of the Word can be just as multifaceted as preparing for a family feast. Consider the story of Philip and the Ethiopian eunuch, in which Philip asked the eunuch who was reading from Isaiah, "Do you understand what you are reading?" (Acts 8:30), a question that we should ask ourselves in preparing for liturgical proclamation. If we who proclaim do not understand our reading, how can we help the assembly understand it? In his Apostolic Exhortation *Verbum Domini*, Pope Benedict XVI commented: "Word and Eucharist are so deeply bound together that we cannot understand one without the other: the word of God sacramentally takes flesh in the event of the Eucharist. The Eucharist opens us to an understanding of Scripture, just as Scripture for its part illumines and explains the mystery of the Eucharist" (VD, 55).

Understanding Word and Sacrament comes partly through research that draws on the wisdom of others, and also through prayer that relies on the inspiration of the Holy Spirit. The wisdom of others may be both from written sources and from discussion and prayer flowing from the readings, perhaps with people from the parish. The biblical texts themselves, as well as prayers used in the liturgy of the day, are rich sources that can prepare one's mind and heart. Such careful reading, research, and prayer comprise the preparation we do in the days prior to our proclamation. Some additional quiet reflection immediately before the celebration of the liturgy is the final preparation.

Good preparation for proclamation aims at unleashing the power of the Word for the whole assembly. As at a festive meal, a hospitable attitude welcomes all who are gathered and also welcomes the Word that will be proclaimed. We taste, we chew, we savor, we digest and absorb the Word so that it becomes a part of us, going forth with the energy of the Holy Spirit. It is most particularly in the liturgy that God's Word becomes bread plentiful enough to feed five thousand and more, becoming an abundant source of nourishment. This is beautifully expressed by St. Ambrose: "This bread which Jesus breaks is, according to the mystery, the Word of God and a teaching about Christ. When this bread is distributed, it multiplies. . . . Jesus gives his words as bread" (*Treatise on Luke's Gospel*, 6:86).

Elaine Park

Proclaiming Effectively: The Art of the Storyteller

Jesus was an excellent storyteller. The evidence of his skill is right there in the Gospels. Everyone was "astonished" at his "gracious words" which had authority and impact (Matthew 7:28; Mark 11:18; Luke 4:22, 32). You don't attract more than five thousand people to a hillside on a hot day if you don't know how to tell a good story! His skills allowed the Word that he preached to touch the hearts and minds of those gathered. Isn't that what we hope to do with our proclamation?

Listen closely to the good storytellers you know. See how the stories they tell appear on their face, are colored by their voice, seem to flow from their whole being. These people are full of energy as they tell their stories; they work to connect with the family or community that listens; they have a desire, a need, to communicate well. We have the same desire to communicate that Word of God well, so these same skills

This is my commandment: love one another as I love you.

will be crucial to our proclamation of the Word. This book is designed to help you develop those skills.

The commentaries on each reading are written by Scripture scholars who share their insights. The margin notes give you advice on proclaiming the readings, helping you incorporate essential skills into your ministry of the Word. Those notes are intended to coach you as you prepare for your proclamation. Think of them as comments from a guide or mentor, standing alongside you as you practice, throwing out helpful ideas, hints, strategies, questions, cautions, and encouragements.

Preparing the Text

The ministry of a proclaimer is rooted in the text, so begin there. Read the Scripture commentary that accompanies each reading to help you understand what you're proclaiming. No matter how skilled a proclaimer you are, you can't proclaim what you can't understand! It's also helpful to read the passages from your Bible that come before and after the text, so you have a better idea of its context. For the same reason, it's important to read the other readings of the day, including the Responsorial Psalm. As you gain experience you'll also become interested in how your reading relates to the readings of the weeks prior, and following, and to the season as a whole.

Form or Purpose

The margin notes identify the *form* or *purpose* of each reading, which tells us a lot about how best to proclaim it. Different forms require different emphases, and different ways of proclaiming. Those who study Scripture classify texts into many different forms, but for the purposes of proclaiming, we will use three: *narrative*, *didactic*, and *exhortatory*.

A **narrative** text reads like a story and may include characters, dialogue, a setting, and action. The point of view may be that of the narrator or any character in the story. Scripture is full of narratives—stories about creation, our ancestors in faith, the history of Israel, the life of Jesus, or the ministries of the first Apostles.

When proclaiming a narrative, strive to help your assembly know what's happening in the story. Keep characters distinct. Be clear about shifts in setting. Allow the community to *see* the story unfold as you proclaim. Some stories may be very familiar to your community through years of repetition. Your goal is to bring back a sense of wonder and anticipation to these stories, so they maintain their power to amaze. Avoid *telegraphing*—that is, resist allowing the end of the story to color how you proclaim the entire reading.

A **didactic** text makes a point or teaches something. The author may lay out an argument or make a case to support the point. The letters of Paul contain mostly didactic text, as do some of the history books, prophets, and wisdom books. The texts describing Jesus' teachings in the Gospel accounts are usually didactic. It's important to understand the author's point and the flow of any supporting argument or logic. Your goal is to help your community follow the argument and understand what's being taught.

Exhortatory texts make an urgent appeal to listeners. They may encourage, warn, or challenge, and often include a call to action. In these texts the emotions are heightened and the stakes are high. Sometimes, the exhortation is directed to God, pleading for mercy or justice or praising God's goodness and love. The speaker is sometimes the author; other times God directly addresses the people. They are most often found in the prophets and the epistles, or letters, but there is also exhortatory text in the Gospels, especially John. In an exhortatory text, it's essential to convey the urgency and passion behind the words.

Although most readings are primarily one of these three styles, some may combine styles. The notes will identify places where the style of the reading changes.

Literary Devices

As you study your text, identify any literary devices. The notes will point out some of these. They can reveal much about the meaning of the passage, so pay attention and make a choice about how they will affect your proclamation. The most common devices are *parallelism*, *thought rhyme*, *paradox*, and *repetition*.

Parallelism refers to phrases or sentences that have a similar structure or express a similar idea, as in these examples:

> for he has clothed me with a robe of salvation,
> and wrapped me in a mantle of justice.
> (Isaiah 61:10)

> I will bless those who bless you
> and curse those who curse you. (Genesis 12:3)

> Remain in me, as I remain in you. (John 15:4)

The rhythm of our proclamation—the words we choose to stress—will help the community hear the parallelism in these lines. If we disregard the parallel structure in our proclamation, we will obscure the meaning. Parallelism is one of the most frequently used literary devices in both testaments.

Thought rhyme is a form of parallelism used in Hebrew poetry. Hebrew poets showed their skill not in the cleverness of their rhymes but in their ability to be deeply descriptive of a thing or idea. Consider this passage from Sirach (15:18–20):

> Immense is the wisdom of the Lord;
>   he is mighty in power, and all-seeing.
> The eyes of God are on those who fear him;
>   he understands man's every deed.
> No one does he command to act unjustly,
>   To none does he give license to sin.

Notice that both lines of each couplet say the same thing, but each line says it in a different way. Thought rhyme occurs throughout wisdom literature and the prophets. When proclaiming, use care to keep the two lines together and use emphasis to show the parallelism.

Paradox uses parallelism to express an idea that seems to contradict itself. Jesus often employs paradox to show that the reign of God will turn our expectations upside down:

> Thus, the last will be first, and the first will
> be last. (Matthew 20:16)

> For every one who exalts himself will be
> humbled,
> but the one who humbles himself will be
> exalted. (Luke 14:11)

Again, use the rhythm of your proclamation to make the parallelism evident, with some extra emphasis on the contradictory phrase.

Repetition of the same word or phrase over the course of a reading emphasizes a point. Sometimes a word is doubled ("Amen, amen"). More often, a word, phrase, or idea is repeated a few times throughout a reading. When you proclaim, make each instance distinct, and build your intensity with each repetition.

Tools: Voice and Body

Studying the text is only the beginning of our work as proclaimers. Our ministry has a significant *physical* aspect—it requires the use of our bodies as well as our minds. Simply reading the words clearly from the ambo so they can be heard and understood is not enough for effective proclamation; we must also pay attention to what we are communicating with our tone, pace, volume, eyes, face, even our posture. In fact, those who study communication tell us that we read meaning more from nonverbal cues than from spoken words.

If I were to approach you with a concerned look and say, slowly, in a low tone and with sadness in my voice, "I have some news for you," you'd likely be very worried about this news. But if I were to run up to you excitedly, with eyes shining, energy in my voice, and quickly say, "I have some news for you," you'd probably be eager to hear the news. Notice that the words were exactly the same in both situations, yet the meaning was completely different. The difference was conveyed entirely through nonverbal cues. Nonverbal expression is critical to our ministry; without the right cues the community will never understand what we proclaim. The notes will help you work on this.

Pace refers to the speed of your proclamation—how fast you speak. The most common problem for proclaimers new to the ministry is going too fast to be understood. More important than finding the right pace, however, is making sure to *vary* your pace, since pace gives clues to the *meaning* of a reading. We express joy or anxiety at a faster pace and sorrow or sadness at a slower pace.

Volume pertains both to being heard (loudness or softness) and to *vocal energy* (the direction and strength of your intention to speak). The notes will suggest places where you might raise or lower your volume, but you should still have good vocal energy even when your volume is low. It's also important to

Magnify the LORD with me; let us exalt his name together.

articulate well so you can be clearly understood; the notes will warn you about any tricky phrases that might require extra attention to articulate correctly.

Inflection refers to the pitch or tone of our voice (high or low). It conveys attitude and feeling. The high end of our range of inflection might be used to express intensity and excitement, while the low end could express sadness or contrition. Find places to vary your inflection throughout your proclamation.

The notes will point out words or phrases in danger of being "swallowed"—that is, words which could be mumbled, and thus lost to the assembly. Make sure you articulate these so they are clearly heard.

Pauses are critical cues that allow your listeners to follow the sense of a text, especially one laying out an argument. Pause in order to break up separate thoughts, set apart significant statements, or indicate major shifts of thought. Never pause in the middle of a single thought. Your primary guide for pauses is punctuation. In general, pause and take a full breath at periods, question marks, exclamation points, and sometimes at semicolons and colons. Don't come to a full stop at commas; rather, break your speech briefly (and take a short, catch-up breath if needed).

There should always be a pause at the end of the reading, before you proclaim the closing dialogue ("The Word of the Lord" or "The Gospel of the Lord"). The notes will indicate when a reading might require a longer pause than usual.

Choice Words. Some words in the readings in this book are printed in bold. These are *choice words*. They're the key words that an effective proclaimer will use to convey the meaning, emotion, and intent of the reading. *They are not necessarily meant to be stressed.* Rather, they are flagged to encourage you to make some *choice* about them. They're significant words, so take some time in your preparation to consider how you will proclaim them.

Eye contact with the community is necessary for effective proclamation. You wouldn't trust someone who didn't make eye contact with you while they were speaking; you'd either dismiss or quickly lose interest in what they were saying. Making eye contact with the assembly connects us with them and connects them to the reading more deeply than using our voice alone. This helps the assembly stay with the story and keeps them engaged.

Except in a few instances, the notes don't indicate where you should be making eye contact in your proclamation because you are encouraged to do so *throughout* the text. Experienced proclaimers look down and scan the next part of the text quickly, then look up and proclaim it. They may make eye contact for as much as seventy-five percent of a reading, particularly on the more significant lines. Of course, this takes practice and experience to do well! If you're new to this skill, set modest goals at first, then increase steadily. Your skill with eye contact will grow over time as your confidence as a proclaimer increases.

Whenever you look up, include everyone in the assembly with your glance, looking most often at (or just above) the people farthest away from you. Link your vocal energy to eye contact; that is, direct your voice to where you look. This will help keep your vocal energy up so you can be both seen *and* heard by the whole assembly.

The notes will indicate difficult or awkward phrases which you might want to proclaim looking directly at the text. Apart from these, however, aim to make eye contact with the assembly as much as you comfortably can.

Posture and Facial Expression. Stand at the ambo in a relaxed posture, with your hands on the Lectionary or the ambo. Don't hunch over, hiding your face from the assembly. Share yourself freely.

Your face will communicate much to the assembly about the reading. It will especially tell them that you're proclaiming "Good News"—the meaning of the word "Gospel." When we share Good News from the ambo we should also share our joy—with a *smile* on our face (and in our eyes and voice). Our smile tells the assembly that we proclaim news of joy, love, mercy, forgiveness, and compassion. Without this cue, they may miss it, so allow yourself to smile when it's appropriate to the reading.

Intention

Our *need* to communicate *something in particular* gives our communication urgency and drive. One of the pitfalls of proclamation is that we don't always have a clear reason to communicate, other than "now it's time for the Liturgy of the Word." The result is a reading that's flat and unfocused. For our proclamation to be effective, we have to rediscover our reason to communicate, our *intention*.

The Scripture commentary will help you understand the original purpose for the text—a good starting point for discerning an intention. What does the reading ask your assembly to *do* or to *be* after hearing your proclamation? After all, we are to "be doers of the word and not hearers only" (James 1:22). Choosing an intention like, "This reading gives the origin of Passover" or "This reading tells about the Annunciation" is a weaker choice than "This reading shows that God will set you free" or "This reading urges you to trust God as Mary did." It's an even stronger choice to shorten the intention into a brief command: "Be free!" or "Trust God!"

Focus on an intention every time you proclaim. (The notes will offer suggestions for some of the readings.) An intention helps pull together all the necessary elements of good proclamation because when we have a *need* to communicate, we work hard to use all our skills to make sure our communication is clear. Of course, you are an *instrument* of the Holy Spirit. Your intention helps you focus your proclamation, but the effect of your proclamation on your listeners is always the work of the Holy Spirit, who gives to "each person individually everything that in the proclamation of the word of God is spoken for the good of the whole gathering of the faithful" (Introduction to the Lectionary, 9).

Expressive Proclamation

Although the Liturgy of the Word is not intended to be theatrical, proclamation cannot be effective unless it is expressive. Readers have little time and few words with which to convey the meaning of a Lectionary passage, and the judicious expression of emotion aids that process greatly. We read emotions very quickly. In the example given earlier, you would have determined a great deal of meaning in my approaching you with excitement or with sadness, before I even said, "I have some news for you." Emotion is a powerful nonverbal communicator, and thus a central element in proclamation.

As we prepare our proclamation we need to make choices about expression. Some choices are

The LORD's word is true; all his works are trustworthy.

already evident in the text. If it says Paul is rejoicing, or Jeremiah is grumbling, or God is acting with compassion, then the emotion we need to express is clear. In other cases, we must make our own choice. The notes offer some suggestions. In a narrative, find an emotion or point of view for each character, keeping in mind that these might change during the reading. In an exhortatory text, all the emotions are heightened, so make bold choices and practice conveying them with your voice, eyes, and face. A didactic text might seem emotion*less*, but assuredly there is emotion present. A teaching is usually given out of *love* for the community being taught.

Admittedly, proclaiming expressively can be a challenge. Many people aren't comfortable showing emotions in public. But the Scriptures we proclaim are not sterile, cold stories; they're dynamic and full of passion. If we fail to include emotion in our proclamation, we're leaving out meaning, thus making it even more difficult for our assembly to understand and connect with the Word. Of course, we shouldn't

proclaim with exaggerated emotion so that we draw attention to ourselves and away from the text. Rather we are called to faithfully proclaim the emotion as it is present in the text.

Pray the Text

You may have a favorite method of praying with Scripture; if so, use it with your text. If not, you can read and meditate on your text during prayer. If you proclaim a narrative text, you could imagine yourself in the story as one of the characters or as an onlooker. If you proclaim a didactic or exhortatory text, you could imagine yourself as the original writer of the text, or as one of the first hearers. If your text speaks directly to God, you can use it *as* your prayer. In your prayer you may discern an intention for your text, or certain emotions may arise that you'll want to use in your proclamation. Take note of these or any other insights.

Recognize That the Stakes Are High

Would you work harder to tell someone that they had a loose thread on their shirt or that their hair was on fire? Likely the latter! When the *stakes are high,* all your communication skills are heightened without your even thinking about them. That's why it's important to recognize how significant your ministry is to the community. The Word that you have the privilege of proclaiming is a Word that desperately needs to be heard by your community, and if you don't proclaim it well, an opportunity is lost. Remind yourself of this awesome responsibility each time you proclaim, and you'll be inspired to work hard to help the Word of God come alive for the community.

Douglas Leal

An Option to Consider

The third edition of *The Roman Missal* encourages ministers of the Word to chant the introduction and conclusion to the readings ("A reading from . . . "; "The word of the Lord"). For those parishes wishing to use these chants, they are demonstrated in audio files that may be accessed either through the QR codes given here (with a smartphone) or through the URL indicated beneath the code. This URL is case sensitive, so be careful to distinguish between the letter l (lowercase L) and the numeral 1.

The first QR code contains the tones for the First Reading in both a male and a female voice.

http://bit.ly/l2mjeG

The second QR code contains the tones for the Second Reading in both a male and a female voice.

http://bit.ly/krwEYy

The third QR code contains the simple tone for the Gospel.

http://bit.ly/iZZvSg

The fourth QR code contains the solemn tone for the Gospel.

http://bit.ly/lwf6Hh

A fuller explanation of this new practice, along with musical notation for the chants, is provided in a downloadable PDF file found at http://www.ltp.org/t-productsupplements.aspx. Once you arrive at this web page, scroll until you find the image of the cover of Workbook, click on it, and the PDF file will appear.

Pronunciation Key

bait = bayt	thin = thin
cat = kat	vision = VIZH⋆n
sang = sang	ship = ship
father = FAH-ther	sir = ser
care = kayr	gloat = gloht
paw = paw	cot = kot
jar = jahr	noise = noyz
easy = EE-zee	poison = POY-z⋆n
her = her	plow = plow
let = let	although = ahl-THOH
queen = kween	church = cherch
delude = deh-LOOD	fun = fuhn
when = hwen	fur = fer
ice = īs	flute = floot
if = if	foot = foot
finesse = fih-NES	

Recommended Works

Find a list of recommended reading in a downloadable PDF file at http://www.ltp.org/t-product supplements.aspx.

Shorter Readings

In the Scripture readings reproduced in this book, shorter readings are indicated by brackets and also by a citation given at the end of the reading.

Endnotes

(continued from page iii)

Quotations from *Verbum Domini* by Pope Benedict XVI and from *Evangelii gaudium* by Pope Francis, © LIBRERIA EDITRICE VATICANA.

Excerpts from the English translation of the Introduction from *Lectionary for Mass* © 1969, 1981, 1997, International Commission on English in the Liturgy Corporation (ICEL); excerpts from the English translation of *The Roman Missal* © 2010, ICEL. All rights reserved.

Texts contained in this work derived whole or in part from liturgical texts copyrighted by the International Commission on English in the Liturgy (ICEL) have been published here with the confirmation of the Committee on Divine Worship, United States Conference of Catholic Bishops. No other texts in this work have been formally reviewed or approved by the United States Conference of Catholic Bishops.

FIRST SUNDAY OF ADVENT

LECTIONARY #2

READING I   Isaiah 63:16b–17, 19b; 64:2–7

A reading from the Book of the Prophet Isaiah

> **You**, LORD, are our **father**,
>   our **redeemer** you are named **forever**.
> **Why** do you let us **wander**, O LORD, from your ways,
>   and **harden** our hearts so that we fear you **not**?
> **Return** for the **sake** of your servants,
>   the tribes of **your** heritage.
> **Oh**, that you would **rend** the heavens and come down,
>   with the mountains **quaking** before you,
> while you wrought **awesome** deeds we could not **hope** for,
>   such as they had not **heard** of from of old.
> No ear has ever **heard**, no eye ever **seen**, any God but **you**
>   doing such deeds for those who **wait** for him.
> Would that you might meet us doing **right**,
>   that we were **mindful** of you in our ways!
> **Behold**, you are **angry**, and we are **sinful**;
>   **all** of us have become like **unclean** people,
>   **all** our good deeds are like polluted **rags**;
> we have all **withered** like leaves,
>   and our **guilt** carries us away like the **wind**.
> There is **none** who calls upon your name,
>   who **rouses** himself to **cling** to you;
> for you have **hidden** your face from us
>   and have delivered us up to our **guilt**.

An exhortatory prayer to God, full of strong, sometimes contradictory emotions. Practice changing quickly between these intense feelings.
Isaiah = ī-ZAY-uh
Assert these opening lines confidently.

In a pleading tone.

Pause at the end of this line.
Fill the word "Oh" with a longing for God.
Speak with excitement about the strength of God.

In a hopeful voice. Keep your energy up!

Shift to penitence. Soften your tone and speak the truth: we have all fallen short.

An embarrassing admission. Don't swallow "rags."

Drop your intensity slightly to convey the weakness of dried leaves.
In a hopeless tone.

Pause.

READING I The liturgical year opens with a reading from Isaiah, the prophet most often quoted and liturgically proclaimed in both Judaism and Christianity. The historical context of the First Reading is most likely the time of return and reconstruction after the exile in Babylon in the sixth century BC. Those who returned from exile expected to experience again the glory of the idyllic land promised to their ancestors. When the reality turned out to be starkly different—with the Temple and cities in ruins, the economy and legal systems fractured, and justice unheeded—Isaiah cried out in lamentation to God.

The prophet speaks for the whole community, calling on the God who performed awesome deeds in the past to once again come to their assistance. God should save them, since they maintain that the Lord is actually the cause for some of their distress. They claim that God let them wander and hardened their hearts so that the people no longer fear him. Yet interwoven into the complaints against God, Isaiah expresses some of the richest affirmations of God's power and goodness. God is father and redeemer, and has wrought awesome deeds even beyond what they could hope for. Following the exalted language for God, we may be jolted by the graphic and grim descriptions of the people: sinful, unclean, polluted, withered, guilty. Only a God who is so powerful, and who is a father to the people, can restore them to health and wholeness. There is a sense of hopeful longing for people who are clay in the hands of the potter, the very work of God's hands.

Use "Yet" to quickly switch to confidence and firm conviction. Despite everything, God is in control and will not abandon us.

Slowly and with great assurance.

Yet, O LORD, you **are** our father;
  we are the **clay** and you the **potter**:
  we are **all** the **work** of your **hands**.

For meditation and context:

RESPONSORIAL PSALM   Psalm 80:2–3, 15–16, 18–19 (4)

R. Lord, make us turn to you; let us see your face and we shall be saved.

O shepherd of Israel, hearken,
  from your throne upon the cherubim,
    shine forth.
Rouse your power,
  and come to save us.

Once again, O LORD of hosts,
  look down from heaven, and see;
take care of this vine,
  and protect what your right hand
    has planted,
  the son of man whom you yourself
    made strong.

May your help be with the man of your
    right hand,
  with the son of man whom you yourself
    made strong.
Then we will no more withdraw from you;
  give us new life, and we will call upon
    your name.

TO KEEP IN MIND
Exhortatory texts make an urgent appeal to listeners. They may encourage, warn, or challenge, and often include a call to action. You must convey the urgency and passion behind the words.

An exhortatory reading. This is all good news. Praise and encourage the assembly for their faithfulness.

Corinthians = kohr-IN-thee-uhnz

Linger over this phrase; they really are your brothers and sisters!

Smile with your voice, eyes, and face!

Keep this long thought together, pausing only briefly at commas (except as noted).

No pause at this comma.

Who in your life embodies these qualities? Proclaim as if speaking to that person.

Pause.

READING II   1 Corinthians 1:3–9

A reading from the first Letter of Saint Paul to the Corinthians

Brothers and **sisters**:
Grace to you and **peace** from God our Father
  and the Lord Jesus **Christ**.

I give **thanks** to my God **always** on your account
  for the **grace** of **God bestowed** on you in Christ **Jesus**,
  that in **him** you were **enriched** in **every** way,
  with all **discourse** and all **knowledge**,
  as the testimony to Christ was **confirmed** among you,
  so that you are not **lacking** in **any** spiritual **gift**
  as you wait for the **revelation** of our Lord Jesus **Christ**.

READING II Paul ordinarily begins his letters with greetings to the community and a prayer of thanksgiving to God, as he does here in his First Letter to the Corinthians. The brief greeting expresses Paul's desire that God's freely given grace and abiding peace may be with the believers. He immediately follows the greeting with thanksgiving that God's grace has in fact already been given to the community, enriching them with speech, knowledge, and boundless spiritual gifts. Such graces are not temporary or fleeting, but will be continued even to the end.

Although phrased as a thanksgiving prayer, there is an implicit appeal to the Corinthians to live in accordance with the grace received. Every gift given by God through Christ is for the building up of the community. There are great varieties of gifts, and they are the source of unity in the Church. Having begun with thanks to God for the abundant graces for the community, Paul will explain later in the letter how all of these gifts come from the same Spirit, given individually according to God's will.

In the final sentence of the thanksgiving, Paul offers an initial description of the

Church. The life of the community begins with and is sustained by the faithful God who calls the members into fellowship. "Fellowship," in Greek *koinonia*, means a deep and abiding communion with Christ and one another. Thus, Paul's first description of the Church for the Corinthians is not about doctrine or behavior, but about relationship—an important insight for believers of every time and place.

GOSPEL Advent is a season of watchfulness—being alert as Jesus instructs in today's Gospel. Both

irreproachable = without blame

Deliberately and with firm conviction.

Slow down a bit.

He will keep you **firm** to the **end**,
 irreproachable on the day of our Lord Jesus Christ.
God is **faithful**,
 and by **him** you were called to **fellowship** with his **Son**,
 Jesus **Christ** our **Lord**.

An exhortatory parable on being always prepared—important advice. Be eager in your sharing rather than demanding.

Start strong! These lines summarize the entire reading.

Drop your intensity a bit with this example.

The words "watch" and "watchful" occur four times. Heighten each successive occurrence.

Really encourage watchfulness.

Pray this for the assembly.

Slight pause at the colon, then raise your voice to reach "all. "

GOSPEL   Mark 13:33–37

A reading from the holy Gospel according to Mark

Jesus said to his disciples:
"Be **watchful**! Be **alert**!
You do not **know** when the time will **come**.
It is like a man traveling **abroad**.
He **leaves** home and places his **servants** in charge,
 each with his own **work**,
 and orders the gatekeeper to be on the **watch**.
Watch, therefore;
 you do not **know** when the lord of the house is **coming,**
 whether in the **evening**, or at **midnight**,
 or at **cockcrow**, or in the **morning**.
May he not come **suddenly** and find you **sleeping**.
What I say to **you**, I say to **all**: '**Watch**!'"

TO KEEP IN MIND
Repetition of the same word or phrase over the course of a reading emphasizes a point. Make each instance distinct, and build your intensity with each repetition.

---

before and after his parable about being watchful for the return of a householder who travels abroad, Jesus tells his listeners to watch. The word for "watch" (*gregoreo*) is the action of a sentinel or sentry, a person who remains always attentive, always vigilant, waiting sometimes for the arrival of someone expected, even while remaining alert for someone or something sudden and unexpected.

The reading from Mark's Gospel is the last part of an address Jesus gives about the "last things": the signs of the end, persecutions, and the coming of the Son of Man. It occurs just before the Passover that will begin Jesus' Passion. Jesus will repeat the injunction to watch when he is in the garden with Peter, James, and John. Through this repeated urging of watchfulness, Jesus reminds his disciples that their attentiveness must be a constant habit, whether they are with Jesus in the garden, or living as his disciples after his Death and Resurrection. The careful watchfulness in Jesus' instruction enables sentinels not only to see the arrival of the householder (Jesus himself), but also to understand, at least in part, the significance of the arrival.

This is the watchfulness of Advent. We remember the waiting of our ancestors, watching for God's sending of the messiah, fulfilled in Jesus' coming. We watch and wait for Jesus' coming again in glory. We are attentive to his presence each day, especially as we meet him in the Eucharist. During this season, we are all sentinels, watching for the coming of the Lord, and rejoicing in his presence. E.P.

THE IMMACULATE CONCEPTION OF THE BLESSED VIRGIN MARY

LECTIONARY #689

This narrative is mostly dialogue. Understand the different intentions and emotions of each character: Adam, Eve, and God.

Start slowly, reminding the assembly where we are in the story.

God begins with questions.

Express Adam's fear in your voice and face.

God sees no shame in their nakedness.

Proclaim God's lines with the feeling of betrayal.

Adam shifts blame from himself to Eve to God.

Is she being honest, or evading blame? Let your choice come through in the proclamation.

Pause before God turns to the serpent; gather your energy before delivering God's condemnation.

Keep pace and energy up; make eye contact with the assembly.

Make this sound as distasteful as it is!

READING I   Genesis 3:9–15, 20

A reading from the Book of Genesis

After the man, **Adam**, had **eaten** of the **tree**,
   the Lord God **called** to the man and **asked** him,
      "Where **are** you?"
He answered, "I **heard** you in the garden;
   but I was **afraid**, because I was **naked**,
   so I **hid** myself."
Then he asked, "**Who** told you that you were naked?
You have **eaten**, then,
   from the **tree** of which I had **forbidden** you to eat!"
The man replied, "The **woman** whom **you** put here with me—
   she gave me fruit from the tree, and so I **ate** it."
The Lord God then asked the **woman**,
   "Why did you **do** such a thing?"
The woman **answered**, "The **serpent tricked** me into it,
   so I **ate** it."

Then the Lord God said to the **serpent**:
   "Because you have **done** this, you shall be **banned**
      from all the **animals**
      and from **all** the wild creatures;
   on your **belly** shall you crawl,
      and **dirt** shall you eat
      all the **days** of your life.

READING I The reading from Genesis is part of a longer narrative that stretches from Genesis 2:25 through 3:24. It begins by stating that the man and his wife were naked, but that they felt no shame. Their nakedness signifies both their innocence and their ignorance. They seem easy prey for the serpent, whose temptation leads them to eat of the forbidden fruit. Today's reading begins after their eating from the tree, with God's call to them, "Where are you?" Adam and his wife Eve are hiding, attempting to evade God, and also to hide their nakedness, which they

have covered with fig leaves. They have lost their innocence and their ignorance of sin. God continues to ask questions of the couple: "Who told you that you were naked?" and "Why did you do such a thing?"—queries for which God already knows the answer. The questions provide the opportunity for the man and woman to admit what they have done, even as they attempt to place the blame on someone else, from wife to serpent. Adam even tries to blame God, since God put the woman in the garden with him. The blaming does not fool God, who delineates the consequences

for all the characters in the story, beginning with the serpent. Cursed and banned from being with other animals, the serpent will be forced to crawl on his belly. The punishment suggests that the serpent formerly had legs like other wild creatures, but will now be demeaned, forced to crawl and eat the dirt of the earth. No longer will the serpent be able to tempt woman, for there will be an eternal enmity between the serpent's offspring and those of the woman. The punishment meted out to the couple is described in verses just after the reading, including the pain of childbirth for the

4

enmity = mutual hatred

Pause to allow the "storm" to subside and God to disappear from the scene.

Naming is an act of love.

This blessing results from an otherwise bad situation: Eve is the mother of us all.

For meditation and context:

> **TO KEEP IN MIND**
> *Exhortatory* texts make an urgent appeal to listeners. They may encourage, warn, or challenge, and often include a call to action. You must convey the urgency and passion behind the words.

An exhortatory reading. Keep energy up; smile so your assembly knows this is good news! There are four main thoughts; pause between them. Keep your voice up at the commas and drop only slightly at the periods.

Ephesians = ee-FEE-zhuhnz

Blessed = BLES-uhd

Blessed = blesd

First, Paul praises God.

Second, Paul reminds us we were chosen as children of God.

Third, our choice was God's will. Pause before this line and take time with its complex phrasing.

Drop your voice slightly on this parenthetical phrase.

I will put **enmity** between you and the **woman**,
   and between **your** offspring and **hers**;
he will strike at your **head**,
   while **you** strike at his **heel**."

The man called his wife **Eve**,
   because she became the **mother** of **all** the **living**.

RESPONSORIAL PSALM   Psalm 98:1, 2–3ab, 3cd–4 (1a)

R. Sing to the Lord a new song, for he has done marvelous deeds.

Sing to the LORD a new song,
   for he has done wondrous deeds;
His right hand has won victory for him,
   his holy arm.

The LORD has made his salvation known:
   in the sight of the nations he has revealed
      his justice.
He has remembered his kindness and his
      faithfulness
   toward the house of Israel.

All the ends of the earth have seen
   the salvation by our God.
Sing joyfully to the LORD, all you lands;
   break into song; sing praise.

READING II   Ephesians 1:3–6, 11–12

A reading from the Letter of Saint Paul to the Ephesians

Brothers and **sisters**:
Blessed be the **God** and **Father** of our Lord Jesus **Christ**,
   who has **blessed** us in Christ
   with every spiritual **blessing** in the heavens,
      as he **chose** us in him, before the **foundation** of the world,
   to be **holy** and without **blemish** before him.
In **love** he destined us for **adoption** to himself through
      Jesus **Christ**,
   in accord with the favor of his **will**,
   for the **praise** of the **glory** of his **grace**
      that he **granted** us in the **beloved**.

---

woman, and being ruled by her husband. The punishment for the man is his toiling over land that is cursed—filled with thorns and thistles. And both of them are expelled from the garden.

This ancient story describes original relationships fractured by sin, and the ongoing consequences. Questions and answers, along with consequences of sin, are intended to draw readers into the story. The questions are addressed to everyone who hears the account: "Where are you?" "Why did you [you who hear this story] do such a thing?" Admission of guilt, accepting

the consequences, and hope for newness are part of our human story, beginning with this account from Genesis.

READING II It is appropriate that this reading from Ephesians be used in the liturgy, since the original usage was likely liturgical, proclaimed when the nascent communities gathered for worship or Baptism. Such blessings of God, called *berakah*, were hymns of extended praise in the Jewish tradition (for example, Psalms 41:13; 72:18, 19). The early Church adapted these praises, transforming them by

emphasizing God's salvific work in Christ (2 Corinthians 1: 3–5; 1 Peter 1: 3–12). In this blessing, we praise God who has extended blessings to embrace all who are "in Christ," a shorthand phrase to refer to the baptized. Paul's use of "us" and "we" as recipients of God's saving blessings connects his own life with the community of believers.

The focus of the hymn is on blessings given through the myriad actions of God that reach through all times and places, as far as the heavens and begun before the foundation of the world. "Every spiritual

Fourth, we were chosen to praise God.
No pause between "destined" and "will."

In **him** we were also **chosen**,
  destined in accord with the purpose of the One
  who accomplishes **all** things according to the intention
    of his **will**,
so that we might **exist** for the praise of his **glory**,
we who **first** hoped in **Christ**.

Slow down and speak this final line directly to your assembly with love and joy.

GOSPEL   Luke 1:26–38

A reading from the holy Gospel according to Luke

A narrative, mostly dialogue. Practice changing emotions noticeably as you switch between the words of Gabriel and Mary.

The angel **Gabriel** was sent from **God**
  to a town of Galilee called **Nazareth**,
  to a **virgin** betrothed to a man named **Joseph**,
  of the house of **David**,
  and the virgin's name was **Mary**.

Don't lose the phrase "sent from God."

No pause after "Joseph."

And coming to her, he said,
  "**Hail**, **full** of **grace**! The **Lord** is **with** you."
But she was greatly **troubled** at what was said
  and **pondered** what sort of greeting this might be.
Then the angel said to her,
  "**Do not be afraid**, Mary,
  for you have found **favor** with God.

Proclaim this greeting with much joy.
Proclaim these lines with Mary's fear.

Gabriel isn't here to make speeches! He must help Mary understand. Notice how he comforts her.

> **TO KEEP IN MIND**
> A *narrative* has characters, dialogue, a setting, and action. Help your listeners see the story unfold, keep characters distinct, and be clear about shifts in setting.

blessing" is best understood as the power and presence of the Holy Spirit in each of the blessings. The first blessing is God's choosing of us, announced two times in the reading. Associated with God's choice or election in Christ is that of being destined in accord with God's purpose. Predestination occurs in other places in Paul's writings as well (for example, 1 Corinthians 2:7; Romans 8:29–30), and has given rise to the notion of some people being predestined for salvation and others for damnation. Paul's view of predestination, however, is that blessing, not condemnation, has been

God's plan from the beginning, a plan flowing from his love. The intention of choosing us is to make us holy, so we may live as God's adopted, beloved children, beloved as is Christ himself. Being chosen or elected by God is not based on any prior good deeds, but simply because of God's abiding love. The final words of the reading highlight the very purpose of our existence: that we who have hoped in Christ might praise God's glory. This liturgical hymn thus begins and ends with praise of God, as do all of our liturgical gatherings.

GOSPEL   In the First Reading we heard a story of the first acts of disobedience, followed by a proclamation of God's blessings given in love. Here in the Gospel we hear a contrasting story of perfect obedience and the fulfillment of God's promise of divine blessings, now bestowed on God's chosen one, the mother of Jesus. Her portrait is beautifully and skillfully drawn. She is a virgin named Mary, or Miriam, after her Jewish ancestor. All that she does and says in the opening chapters of Luke's Gospel show her as a woman steeped in the Jewish tradition.

This is great news!

Four phrases describe the child; make each distinct.

Switch back to Mary's fear and confusion.

Gabriel comforts again.

Take your time with "Son of God."
Again, news of great joy!

Best news of all! Keep your energy up, then pause.
Quiet but confident tone.

Pause after this line to let the significance of Mary's response ring in your assembly's hearts, then conclude with the angel's departure.

TO KEEP IN MIND
Making eye contact with the assembly connects you with them and connects them to the reading more deeply than using your voice alone. This helps the assembly stay with the story and keeps them engaged.

Behold, you will **conceive** in your womb and bear a **son**,
and you shall name him **Jesus**.
He will be **great** and will be called **Son** of the Most **High**,
and the Lord God will give him the **throne** of David
his **father**,
and he will **rule** over the house of Jacob **forever**,
and of his **Kingdom** there will be **no end**."
But Mary said to the angel,
"How can this **be**,
since I have no **relations** with a man?"
And the angel said to her in reply,
"The Holy **Spirit** will come **upon** you,
and the power of the Most **High** will **overshadow** you.
Therefore the child to be born
will be called **holy**, the Son of **God**.
And **behold**, **Elizabeth**, your relative,
has **also** conceived a son in her old **age**,
and this is the **sixth** month for her who was called **barren**;
for **nothing** will be **impossible** for God."
Mary said, "**Behold**, I am the **handmaid** of the Lord.
May it be **done** to me according to **your** word."
Then the angel **departed** from her.

This scene even echoes other stories from the Old Testament in which an angel announces a coming birth through the power of God (for example, Judges 13:2–7). Gabriel addresses the young woman from Nazareth as "full of grace," almost as if that were her name. Based on the root word for "grace," her new name is *kecharitomene*, indicating that she has been exceedingly favored, or abundantly graced. The grace, given long ago, is God's freely-bestowed blessing, assured by the divine presence: "the Lord is with you." The angel promises Mary that, though a virgin, she will con-ceive and bear a son. Her child will be great, will be given the throne of his ancestor David, will be holy, and will be the Son of God. The identity of Mary in this scene is intimately connected with the identity of her son.

Although Mary questions, "How can this be?" her response is an unequivocal yes to whatever God asks of her. She identifies herself as a "handmaid of the Lord," perhaps better translated as "slave (*doule*) of the Lord," the same designation that St. Paul uses for himself. With her self-identification, Mary states both her humility before God, and that she is in God's service without reservation. She promises obedience, not only to what God asks of her through the angel, but also yes to whatever God may ask in the future. Far from being a passive acceptance, Mary's answer is a courageous, freely exercised eagerness. E.P.

SECOND SUNDAY OF ADVENT

LECTIONARY #5

An exhortatory reading full of good news. Smile with your voice, eyes, and face.

Isaiah = ī-ZAY-uh

The lines themselves tell you how to proclaim: tenderly, giving comfort to your assembly.

expiated = EK-spee-ayt-*d (paid for)
Raise your energy slightly.

Pause at the colon.
Keep your energy up for the rest of the reading. This is *awesome* news! Let your excitement come through!

Slow a little but keep your excitement up for the appearance of the Lord.

> **TO KEEP IN MIND**
> *Exhortatory* texts make an urgent appeal to listeners. They may encourage, warn, or challenge, and often include a call to action. You must convey the urgency and passion behind the words.

READING I   Isaiah 40:1–5, 9–11

A reading from the Book of the Prophet Isaiah

Comfort, give **comfort** to my people,
  says your God.
Speak **tenderly** to Jerusalem, and **proclaim** to her
  that her **service** is at an **end**,
  her **guilt** is **expiated**;
indeed, she has received from the hand of the LORD
  double for all her sins.

  A voice **cries** out:
In the desert **prepare** the way of the LORD!
  Make **straight** in the wasteland a **highway** for our **God**!
Every **valley** shall be filled **in**,
  every **mountain** and **hill** shall be made **low**;
the **rugged** land shall be made a **plain**,
  the **rough** country, a broad **valley**.
Then the **glory** of the LORD shall be **revealed**,
  and **all** people shall see it **together**;
  for the mouth of the LORD has **spoken**.

READING I   The Book of Isaiah is a compilation of over two centuries of prophecies from three distinct periods in Israel's history. Today's reading comes from the second of these periods, the sixth century BC, at the end of the exile in Babylon. This part of Isaiah extends from chapter 40 through 55, and is usually referred to as Deutero (or Second)-Isaiah. Today's reading from chapter 40 is the beginning of Deutero-Isaiah, offering the people in exile words of hope and comfort. Whether heard as Handel's familiar "Comfort ye, my people," or as it sounds in Hebrew, an almost lullaby-like alliteration (nahamu nahamu ami omar elohekem), the works convey a profound, reassuring intimacy. Such comfort was surely needed by the exiles, who had endured years of separation from the land God had promised their ancestors. These words convey to the people that their time of punishment in Babylon has come to an end. Now that their guilt has been expiated, the prophet announces to them that God is about to do new things—extraordinary deeds comparable to the signs and wonders of old. The God who had brought their ancestors to freedom by a journey through the desert is about to lead the exiles back through the desert to their own land.

Deutero-Isaiah calls on messengers to tell the people to prepare for their great trek. Their path through the desert will be no ordinary highway, but will be "the way of the LORD" and "a highway for our God." Both phrases suggest that the returning exiles will not be traveling alone, but that their God will make the journey with them. The image of filled-in valleys, lowered mountains, and all the rough and rugged places made smooth describes the perfect

"Zion" is not the name of the mountain; it is the "person" being commanded to go up. Same with "Jerusalem."

Do not fear to proclaim with full enthusiasm!

As if you see God coming near.

recompense = reward for wrongs suffered

Keep your energy up but drop your voice slightly to convey this tender and intimate image.

For meditation and context:

Go up onto a **high** mountain,
    Zion, **herald** of glad tidings;
cry out at the **top** of your voice,
    Jerusalem, herald of **good** news!
Fear **not** to cry out
    and **say** to the cities of Judah:
    Here is your **God**!
Here comes with **power**
    the Lord **God**,
    who **rules** by his strong arm;
here is his **reward** with him,
    his **recompense** before him.
Like a **shepherd** he **feeds** his **flock**;
    in his **arms** he **gathers** the **lambs**,
    carrying them in his **bosom**,
    and **leading** the ewes with **care**.

RESPONSORIAL PSALM   Psalm 85:9–10, 11–12, 13–14 (8)

R. Lord, let us see your kindness, and grant us your salvation.

I will hear what God proclaims;
    the LORD—for he proclaims peace to
      his people.
Near indeed is his salvation to those who
    fear him,
    glory dwelling in our land.

Kindness and truth shall meet;
    justice and peace shall kiss.
Truth shall spring out of the earth,
    and justice shall look down from heaven.

The LORD himself will give his benefits;
    our land shall yield its increase.
Justice shall walk before him,
    and prepare the way of his steps.

TO KEEP IN MIND
Pause in order to break up separate thoughts, set apart significant statements, or indicate major shifts. Never pause in the middle of a single thought. Your primary guide for pauses is punctuation.

---

road on which a powerful king or military leader would return home in triumph. This is the path for God who comes with power, "who rules by his strong arm." God will return in majesty. However, the final image of God in the reading is not that of a powerful, triumphant warrior, but of a shepherd who feeds the flock, carries the lambs in his bosom, and leads with care. The reading ends as it began—with words of great tenderness.

READING II Written late in the first century or early second

century, 2 Peter may be the last New Testament book to be written. By the time of its circulation, the Church had been waiting well over a half century for Christ to return. Later in Mark's Gospel, Jesus will tell his disciples that people "will see the Son of Man coming in the clouds with great power and glory" (13:26). In last week's Gospel, we heard the parable of the householder whose return was certain, but when it would occur was not known. So too is the return of the Son of Man. Until he returns, believers are to remain attentive. He tells them repeatedly to watch.

Such teaching led to the expectation that Christ's return would be soon, certainly in the lifetime of his first disciples. The author of 2 Peter writes in part to assure the next generations of believers that what we consider "delay" is not so with God: "with the Lord one day is like a thousand years and a thousand years like one day," paraphrasing Psalm 90:4 . Since, from a human perspective, the waiting has been long and filled with uncertainly, we could well expect an exhortation for patience. Instead, it is God who is patient,

A didactic passage; make Peter's teaching clear. He makes four points.

Proclaim this first point with tender concern for the assembly. Don't swallow "beloved." beloved = bee LUHV-hud

Convey the gentle patience of God in your voice.

Pause at the end of this line.

Raise your intensity on this second point to convey the surprise and intensity of the day of the Lord.

Pause.
The third point: So what does this mean for us?
This phrase can sound like a question.
Here is the answer.

This is merely the necessary set-up for a new creation.
Pause.

The final point. We have nothing to worry about—*good news!* With excitement.

Proclaim this line (especially "beloved") with loving, calming concern.
Slow down and set apart "at peace."

TO KEEP IN MIND
A *didactic* text makes a point or teaches something. Help your assembly to follow the argument and understand what's being taught.

READING II   2 Peter 3:8–14

A reading from the second Letter of Saint Peter

Do not ignore this **one** fact, **beloved**,
    that with the Lord one **day** is like a thousand **years**
    and a **thousand** years like one **day**.
The Lord does not **delay** his promise, as **some** regard "delay,"
    but he is **patient** with you,
    not wishing that **any** should perish
    but that **all** should come to **repentance**.
But the **day** of the Lord will come like a **thief**,
    and then the heavens will pass **away** with a mighty **roar**
    and the **elements** will be dissolved by **fire**,
    and the **earth** and everything **done** on it will be found **out**.

Since **everything** is to be dissolved in this way,
    what sort of **persons** ought you **to be**,
    conducting yourselves in **holiness** and **devotion**,
    waiting for and **hastening** the coming of the **day** of God,
    because of which the **heavens** will be dissolved in **flames**
    and the elements melted by **fire**.
But according to his **promise**
    we await **new** heavens and **a new** earth
    in which **righteousness** dwells.
Therefore, **beloved**, since you **await** these things,
    be **eager** to be found without **spot** or **blemish** before him,
        at **peace**.

"patient with you," adding that God wishes all to come to repentance.

When the day of the Lord ultimately comes, it will arrive like a thief, an image found in the Gospel accounts (Matthew 24:43–44; Luke 12:39); Paul also uses the image to allay the anxiety of the community in Thessalonika (1 Thessalonians 5:2). Along with examples from parables, the New Testament is filled with other imagery to describe coming apocalyptic events. Sights and sounds that are familiar point to future events that have never been seen or heard, but that will certainly come about.

Whether Jesus' discourses, Paul's letters, or other apocalyptic passages in the Bible, the intent is not to describe a literal scenario of what will occur, but to urge righteous living in the present. Coupled with the message of the coming day of the Lord with power and might, the author instructs people how they are to live in the here and now. They should conduct themselves with holiness and devotion, waiting without spot or blemish, and being at peace. These ancient instructions remain sound advice as we continue to wait for the day of the Lord.

GOSPEL   Three biblical figures express in different ways the spirit of the season of Advent: the prophet Isaiah, whose words create hope and expectation; Mary, the mother of Jesus, whose obedience opened the door to the Incarnation; and John the Baptist, whose ministry was to prepare the way of the Lord. Each of them points to Jesus, as does Mark in the opening verse of his Gospel. His account is the beginning of the Good News of Jesus, who is the Christ and Son of God. In introducing both John and

GOSPEL   Mark 1:1–8

A reading from the holy Gospel according to Mark

The **beginning** of the gospel of Jesus **Christ** the Son of **God**.

As it is **written** in Isaiah the **prophet**:
*Behold, I am sending my messenger **ahead** of you;*
*he will **prepare** your way.*
*A voice of one **crying out** in the desert:*
*"Prepare the **way** of the **Lord**,*
*make **straight** his paths."*
John the **Baptist** appeared in the **desert**
proclaiming a baptism of **repentance** for the forgiveness of **sins**.
People of the **whole** Judean countryside
and **all** the inhabitants of Jerusalem
were going **out** to him
and were being **baptized** by him in the Jordan **River**
as they **acknowledged** their sins.
John was clothed in **camel's** hair,
with a leather **belt** around his waist.
He fed on **locusts** and wild **honey**.
And **this** is what he proclaimed:
"One **mightier** than **I** is coming **after** me.
I am not **worthy** to stoop and loosen the thongs of his **sandals**.
I have baptized you with **water**;
he will baptize you with the Holy **Spirit**."

A narrative reading with some exhortatory lines.
Don't swallow "beginning."

The whole quote is exhortatory. Keep your energy up.

Pause before shifting to the narrative about John.

See the crowds streaming from everywhere as you describe the scene. Don't pause until the period.

Don't gloss over these attributes; they're a little strange and should sound so.

Proclaim this exhortation with John's passion.

John is not dismissing the significance of his baptism; baptism with the Holy Spirit completes it.
Keep your voice *up* on "Holy Spirit."

Jesus, today's reading serves as a prologue to Mark's whole Gospel.

A verse from the Advent prophet, Isaiah, introduces us to the mission of John—a portion of the prophecy we heard in the First Reading. Sent by God as a messenger, John is the voice crying out in the desert, "Prepare the way of the LORD." The way of the Lord was Israel's path to freedom from slavery in Egypt and from exile in Babylon. Now John is preparing people for a new path to freedom that will begin with a baptism of repentance and forgiveness of sin.

John's strange attire is reminiscent of that of the prophet Elijah, thereby portraying John as another desert prophet. John's promise of forgiveness of sins drew large crowds of people waiting for a new manifestation of God's power. The origin of John's baptism is uncertain, perhaps related to the ritual cleansings of Judaism or the ceremonial washing of initiation, symbolizing conversion. Whatever its origin, John's baptism calls those who are immersed in the water to repentance (metanoia), to change of mind, heart, and behavior. While the ancestors followed the desert way of the Lord to return to the Promised Land, those baptized by John follow the way of the Lord to return to right relationship with God. Even though John attracted a large following, he was only a messenger, a herald for the one mightier than himself. The way of the Lord proclaimed by John is a journey of discipleship to Jesus Christ, Son of God.

THIRD SUNDAY OF ADVENT

LECTIONARY #8

READING I   Isaiah 61:1–2a, 10–11

A reading from the Book of the Prophet Isaiah

This exhortation is all good news, so smile with your voice, eyes, and face throughout.

Isaiah = ī-ZAY-uh

With excitement and energy, using mostly the higher part of your range of inflection or pitch.
Stress the words in bold.

> The **spirit** of the Lord GOD is upon me,
>   because the LORD has **anointed** me;
> he has **sent** me to bring **glad tidings** to the poor,
>   to **heal** the brokenhearted,
> to proclaim **liberty** to the captives
>   and **release** to the **prisoners**,
> to announce a year of **favor** from the LORD
>   and a day of **vindication** by our God.

Announce this directly to your assembly.

> I rejoice **heartily** in the LORD,
>   in my **God** is the **joy** of my soul;
> for he has **clothed** me with a **robe** of **salvation**
>   and **wrapped** me in a **mantle** of **justice**,
> like a **bridegroom** adorned with a **diadem**,
>   like a **bride** bedecked with her **jewels**.
> As the **earth** brings forth its **plants**,
>   and a **garden** makes its **growth** spring **up**,
> so will the Lord GOD make **justice** and **praise**
>   **spring** up before all the **nations**.

From here on keep each parallel couplet together and use rhythm to stress the parallelism.

Really see the beauty of the bride and groom.

Pause at the end of this line.

Slow down a bit to the end, but don't drop your energy.

Drop your inflection or pitch only slightly at the end.

READING I Written when Israel had returned from exile to find the land in ruins and the community living in rampant injustice and poverty, Isaiah's prophecy is directed to a people who longs for God to restore both land and people. According to today's reading, restoration will come about, not by a grand theophany, but through the prophet, who is empowered by God's Spirit, anointed, and sent to bring good news to the poor. Isaiah's audience would clearly see themselves among the poor and brokenhearted, eager for healing. The prophet's mission is to proclaim liberty and release to them, announcing a year of the Lord's favor, reminding them of the jubilee year, as described in Leviticus (25:8–55). There, legal norms required return of property to its original owner, release of slaves, and cancellation of debts. In Deuteronomy 15, jubilee is based on the covenant between Israel and God that requires a fresh start for those who have suffered loss of land and liberty. The wealthy are to forgive the debts of the poor. To ensure that people will know what God asks, the jubilee year must be proclaimed. In fact, the Hebrew name may be derived from the ram's horn, the yubal, used to call people to listen. Isaiah's mission is to broadcast glad tidings, proclaim liberty, and announce a year of favor. Isaiah's words of restoration are not empty promises, but are assured by the presence of God's Spirit and Isaiah's prophetic anointing.

The prescriptions of the jubilee year were probably more of an ideal than a practiced reality. Yet Isaiah's reference to the jubilee year tradition had an important sig-

For meditation and context:

TO KEEP IN MIND

Exhortatory texts make an urgent appeal to listeners. They may encourage, warn, or challenge, and often include a call to action. You must convey the urgency and passion behind the words.

At first this reading is didactic, then exhortatory; proclaim with love and a desire for your assembly to grow in faith.
Thessalonians = thes-uh-LOH-nee-uhnz

Smile and invite, rather than demand, with these short teachings. Keep each separate.

As if to say, who would do this?

Pause at the end of this line.

Pray this line over the community.
Set apart the phrase "spirit, soul, and body."

With confidence.
Slowly and deliberately.

RESPONSORIAL PSALM   Luke 1:46–48, 49–50, 53–54 (Isaiah 61:10b)

R. My soul rejoices in my God.

My soul proclaims the greatness of the Lord;
  my spirit rejoices in God my Savior,
for he has looked upon his lowly servant.
  From this day all generations will call
  me blessed.

The Almighty has done great things for me,
  and holy is his Name.
He has mercy on those who fear him
  in every generation.

He has filled the hungry with good things,
  and the rich he has sent away empty.
He has come to the help of his servant Israel
  for he has remembered his promise
  of mercy.

READING II   1 Thessalonians 5:16–24

A reading from the first Letter of Saint Paul to the Thessalonians

Brothers and sisters:
Rejoice **always**. **Pray** without **ceasing**.
In **all** circumstances give **thanks**,
  for **this** is the will of God for you in Christ Jesus.
Do not **quench** the Spirit.
Do not **despise** prophetic utterances.
Test **everything**; **retain** what is **good**.
Refrain from every kind of **evil**.

May the God of **peace** make you perfectly **holy**
  and may you **entirely**, **spirit**, **soul**, and **body**,
    be preserved **blameless** for the coming of our Lord
      Jesus Christ.
The one who **calls** you is **faithful**,
  and he will also **accomplish** it.

---

nificance for the returned exiles. The promise is now given, not to individual owners who had lost their land, but to the whole nation. All the impoverished, captive, and imprisoned hear the good news. The whole nation must join in restoring the fortunes of their fellow citizens, creating a renewed jubilee society. The second part of the reading is an apt, joyful response to God's jubilee promise. The prophet sees that promise already fulfilled, with the whole earth joining in praise. God's justice will

ultimately prevail and be manifest before all the nations.

READING II In the last part of his First Letter to the Thessalonians, Paul exhorts the community to live in fidelity to Christ. He begins by telling the people they are to respect their leaders and then tells the leaders how they ought to minister to various members of the body, being patient with all. In this reading, Paul continues his exhortation, speaking to the whole community. His message to them urges

constancy. Their joy, prayer, and thanksgiving should extend to every moment: "always . . . without ceasing . . . in all circumstances," because this is God's will for them. What a positive and vibrant notion of God's will, focusing on continually living in joy, prayer, and thanksgiving!

Because Paul is well aware of difficulties that are part of every community, his exhortation also includes warnings: do not "quench the Spirit" nor "despise prophetic utterances." Rather, they should test them, and whatever is good, they should retain.

A narrative with exhortatory passages. What does the reading want the assembly to take from it? Keep that thought in your mind throughout.

Exhortatory; raise your energy.

Pause.

Narrative; the questioners sound anxious and combative; John sounds secure and confident in his identity.

A triple repetition of John's admission; heighten each one.

Increase their irritation on each question.

Complete frustration and anger.

TO KEEP IN MIND

A *narrative* has characters, dialogue, a setting, and action. Help your listeners see the story unfold, keep characters distinct, and be clear about shifts in setting.

GOSPEL   John 1:6–8, 19–28

A reading from the holy Gospel according to John

A man named **John** was sent from God.
He came for **testimony**, to testify to the **light**,
    so that **all** might **believe** through him.
He was **not** the light,
    but came to testify **to** the light.

And **this** is the testimony of John.
When the Jews from Jerusalem sent priests and Levites to him
    to ask him, "Who **are** you?"
    he **admitted** and did not **deny** it,
    but **admitted**, "I am **not** the Christ."
So they asked him,
    "What **are** you then? Are you **Elijah**?"
And he said, "I am **not**."
"Are you the **Prophet**?"
He answered, "**No**."
So they said to him,
    "Who **are** you, so we can give an **answer** to those who sent us?

Whatever kind of prophetic activity may have been present in the church, Paul advises that care should be taken. On the one hand, they must not automatically reject prophecy, which may be an authentic manifestation of God's Spirit and offer needed guidance for the community. On the other hand, they must carefully test what is being said, so that good and not evil is furthered. In the context of this letter, in which people are anxious about the parousia, authentic, Spirit-inspired prophecy can preserve them from needless anxiety, laxity of morals, or misguided understanding.

Paul concludes with prayer, exemplifying the holistic vision that he encouraged in the community. He prays that God will be the abiding source of holiness in every dimension of their lives. When Christ comes again, each person should be found blameless. Paul is certain that God will accomplish what he asks because God has called the Church into being, and God is faithful.

GOSPEL Again we see John the Baptist as one who leads us to Jesus. Today's portrait of John the Baptist is taken from the opening chapter of the Fourth Gospel, where major themes and images of John the Evangelist's account are introduced. John the Baptist himself becomes the means of introducing Jesus. His role is clear: he came for testimony, to testify to the light. He is to give witness (*martyria*), stating unambiguously who he is, as well as who he is not, always pointing away from himself toward the light. An image closely associated with life and God's presence, light radiates to bring knowledge and belief. Its opposite, darkness, can neither understand nor overcome light (John 1:5). The priests and

Pause at the end of this line.

Exhortatory.
Raise your energy.
Pause.
Narrative.

Even more questions! With suspicion; they are looking to trap John.

Exhortatory.

Pause at the end of the line.
Narrative. Drop your volume slightly.

TO KEEP IN MIND
Use inflection (the high or low pitch of your voice) to convey attitude and feeling. High pitch expresses intensity and excitement; low pitch expresses sadness, contrition, or solemnity.

What do you have to **say** for yourself?"
He said:
   "I am *the **voice** of one* **crying** *out in the desert,*
   'Make **straight** *the way of the* **Lord**,'
   as Isaiah the **prophet** said."
Some Pharisees were **also** sent.
They asked him,
   "**Why** then do you **baptize**
   if you are not the **Christ** or **Elijah** or the **Prophet**?"
John answered them,
   "**I** baptize with **water**;
   but there is one **among** you whom you do not **recognize**,
   the one who is coming **after** me,
   whose **sandal** strap I am not **worthy** to untie."
This happened in Bethany across the Jordan,
   where John was **baptizing**.

Levites give John the opening he needs, first to clarify his own identify, and then to turn their attention toward Jesus, the light of the world.

Although John himself does not say it, the first way he is described is as one "sent from God." His status is given to us, who hear the Gospel, although it is not known by John's interrogators. Even before they ask him, John states that he is not the Christ, leading them to question him further. He is not Elijah, nor "the" prophet, probably referring to the prophet like Moses whom God promised to raise up

(Deuteronomy 18:15, 18). Each of these denials shows that John is not the one the Jews have been waiting for. With mounting impatience, the priests and Levites ask directly, "What do you have to say for yourself?" John's answer, like the description in last week's Gospel, is taken from the prophet Isaiah. John is only the voice, the one who cries out: "Make straight the way of the Lord." The level path through the desert foretold by Isaiah is the background for the path of the Lord that John announces. He prepares this roadway not

only for the people, but also so that the Lord may now come to them.

Widely known as "the Baptist," in fact John's primary role is not baptizing. All his words and his actions, including baptism, are to prepare the people for one whose sandals he is unworthy to untie. But they do not recognize him; they are still lacking the light needed for understanding and faith. E.P.

FOURTH SUNDAY
OF ADVENT

LECTIONARY #11

READING I   2 Samuel 7:1–5, 8b–12, 14a, 16

A reading from the second Book of Samuel

When King **David** was **settled** in his palace,
    and the LORD had given him **rest** from his enemies
        on every side,
    he said to **Nathan** the prophet,
    "Here **I** am living in a house of **cedar**,
    while the ark of **God** dwells in a **tent**!"
Nathan answered the king,
    "**Go**, do **whatever** you have in mind,
    for the LORD is **with** you."
But that night the LORD **spoke** to Nathan and said:
    "**Go**, tell my servant **David**, 'Thus says the LORD:
    Should you build **me** a house to dwell in?

"'It was **I** who took you from the **pasture**
    and from the care of the **flock**
    to be **commander** of my people Israel.
I have been **with** you **wherever** you went,
    and I have **destroyed** all your enemies before you.
And I will make you **famous** like the **great** ones of the earth.
I will fix a **place** for my people Israel;
    I will **plant** them so that they may **dwell** in their place
    without further **disturbance**.

A narrative that is also exhortatory. David wants to build a house for God, but it's God who will build up David's house. Help your assembly hear this call to trust in God more than in their own achievements.
Convey David's calm and comfort in your voice.

Scandalous! (at least in David's mind)

With confidence. Nathan has it wrong, but doesn't know it yet.

Make it clear that the answer to this question is "no." (See 2 Samuel 7:5–7)
Exhortatory. In this part, how does God feel having to remind David of what he should already know? Exasperated, patient, consoling?

Remind your assembly: rely on God, not your own power.

God will always care for the people.

READING I King David, idealized in later generations, ruled over the newly unified nation of Israel from about 1000 to 960 BC. He was a strong military commander and shrewd political strategist. One of his most brilliant moves, both militarily and politically, was to make Jerusalem his capital city. The setting of today's First Reading is Jerusalem in a time of peace, regarded as a gift from the Lord. David is living securely and comfortably in a house (*bayit*) of cedar. Having been so blessed with peace by the Lord, he now wants to build a house for the ark of God.

During the years of desert wanderings in the time of Moses, the dwelling place for the ark had been a tent, and even in David's time it remained in a tent. When David tells Nathan the prophet his desire to build a house for the ark, Nathan's initial response is one of support: David should go forward with his plan, "for the LORD is with you."

Nathan soon learns, however, that the LORD has other plans. God gives Nathan a lengthy message for David, beginning with a question: "Should you build me a house to dwell in?" David, the military commander and political strategist, sees himself as the one who devises and executes his plans, but now God reminds him that it is God, not David, who has been the one devising and executing all along. I "took you from the pasture. . . . I have been with you wherever you went. . . . I destroyed all your enemies." The God who was so active in David's life and the life of the whole nation in the past will continue to act for them in the future. Again, we hear God speaking, this time telling what he will do: "I will make you famous. . . . I will fix a place for my people. . . . I will plant them. . . . I will give you rest from all your

16

Speak directly to the assembly, encouraging them with this promise. Pause
Even better news! Be excited to share your plans with David!

Gently.

With bold confidence and reassurance.
Keep your voice up through to the end.

For meditation and context:

TO KEEP IN MIND
A *narrative* has characters, dialogue, a setting, and action. Help your listeners see the story unfold, keep characters distinct, and be clear about shifts in setting.

TO KEEP IN MIND
Exhortatory texts make an urgent appeal to listeners. They may encourage, warn, or challenge, and often include a call to action. You must convey the urgency and passion behind the words.

Neither shall the wicked continue to **afflict** them as they did
    of **old**,
  since the time I first appointed **judges** over my people Israel.
I will give you **rest** from all your enemies.
The Lord **also** reveals to you
  that he will establish a house for **you**.
And when your **time** comes and you **rest** with your ancestors,
  I will **raise up** your **heir** after you, **sprung** from your loins,
  and I will make his kingdom **firm**.
I will be a **father** to him,
  and he shall be a **son** to me.
Your **house** and your **kingdom** shall endure **forever** before me;
  your **throne** shall stand firm **forever**.'"

RESPONSORIAL PSALM   Psalm 89:2–3, 4–5, 27, 29 (2a)

R. For ever I will sing the goodness of the Lord.

The promises of the Lord I will sing forever;
  through all generations my mouth shall
    proclaim your faithfulness.
For you have said, "My kindness is
    established forever";
  in heaven you have confirmed your
    faithfulness.

"I have made a covenant with my chosen one,
  I have sworn to David my servant:
forever will I confirm your posterity
  and establish your throne for all
    generations."

"He shall say of me, 'You are my father,
  my God, the rock, my savior.'
Forever I will maintain my kindness
    toward him,
  and my covenant with him stands firm."

---

enemies." Then God turns to David's hope of building a house for God, again declaring that he is the one who will act. God, not David, will be the one to build a house. But this will not be the kind of house that David envisioned. The house (*bayit*) that God will build begins with God raising up an heir, whose kingdom God will make firm. The house that David envisioned was a building, a temple; the house that God will build is a dynasty and a kingdom that will endure forever.

During Advent, we remember the long wait for God's fulfillment of this promise, one we see fulfilled in Jesus, son of David.

READING II At the conclusion to his Letter to the Romans, Paul sums up some of his core teachings in a prayer of praise. He develops this one sentence around key concepts and terminology that he first used in the opening verses of the letter, and developed throughout. Since Paul had not yet been to Rome when he wrote to the church there, the letter serves as a means of introducing himself as

well as his theology. Called to be an Apostle, Paul writes that he has been set apart for the Gospel, which was promised through the prophets and centered on God's son. "Gospel" is a key concept of the letter, with all of the other terms seen as aspects of the Gospel. Early in the letter Paul outlined his understanding of the Gospel: "it is the power of God for the salvation of everyone who believes: for the Jew first, and then Greek. For in it is revealed the righteousness of God from faith to faith" (1:16–17). In his concluding prayer, Paul reiterates this teaching,

Exhortatory—one long sentence of praise to God. Proclaim in the higher part of your pitch range throughout. Take a quick breath at each comma.

Keep your pace up so as not to lose the train of thought.

Raise your intensity with each succeeding "according to . . . " phrase.

Take a quick breath here.

Brief pause.

With grandeur. Begin slowing.

Keep your voice up all the way to the end.

READING II   Romans 16:25–27

A reading from the Letter of Saint Paul to the Romans

Brothers and sisters:
To **him** who can **strengthen** you,
   according to my **gospel** and the **proclamation** of Jesus Christ,
   according to the **revelation** of the mystery kept **secret**
      for long ages
but now **manifested** through the prophetic writings and,
   according to the **command** of the eternal God,
made known to **all** nations to bring about the **obedience**
      of **faith**,
   to the **only** wise God, through Jesus **Christ**
be **glory forever** and **ever**. **Amen**.

A narrative that is mostly dialogue. Practice changing emotions noticeably as you switch between the words of Gabriel and Mary.

Don't lose the phrase "sent from God."

No pause after "Joseph."

Proclaim this greeting with much joy.
Proclaim these lines with Mary's fear.

Gabriel isn't here to make speeches! He must help Mary understand. Notice how he comforts her.

GOSPEL   Luke 1:26–38

A reading from the holy Gospel according to Luke

The angel **Gabriel** was sent from **God**
   to a town of Galilee called **Nazareth**,
   to a **virgin** betrothed to a man named **Joseph**,
   of the house of **David**,
   and the virgin's name was **Mary**.
And **coming** to her, he said,
   "**Hail**, **full** of **grace**! The **Lord** is **with** you."
But she was **greatly** troubled at what was said
   and **pondered** what sort of greeting this might be.
Then the angel said to her,
   "Do **not** be **afraid**, Mary,
   for you have found **favor** with God.

thereby framing his letter with a focus on Gospel. The center and meaning of the Good News is Jesus himself, proclaimed as salvation for all who believe.

   This Good News was foretold through the prophets, was proclaimed by Jesus, and is now brought by Paul to the community in Rome. In every instance, the Gospel is revelation (*apocalypsis*), a disclosing of mysteries long hidden but now made manifest to believers. More than simple communication of facts or concepts, revelation is also a powerful manifestation of God's

in-breaking into the world to conquer evil and bring salvation.

   In his own day as well as subsequent centuries, Paul has often been seen as one bringing bad news because of his sometimes harsh condemnations and demands. Yet everything that Paul announces is part of the Gospel of God, the Good News of God's saving plan fulfilled in Jesus. Paul's exhortations are the logical response of those who hear and believe the Good News. Obedience springs from faith. Paul's final praise is to the God who is wise, for God's

wisdom had revealed the saving Gospel to all nations. To God be glory forever!

GOSPEL   One of the most beautiful and frequently illustrated religious scenes is that of the angel Gabriel's Annunciation to Mary. Sometimes we see Mary elegantly clothed, seated as if on a royal throne in a beautifully frescoed room. Although such artistic renderings present a profound insight into Mary's glory in eternity, other artists draw her as young maiden who lived in simplicity, even poverty. In Mary's village of Nazareth, there

This is great news!

Set these lines apart; it's the fulfillment of the promises we heard in Reading I.

Switch back to Mary's fear and confusion.

Gabriel comforts again.

Take your time with "Son of God."

Again, news of great joy!

Best news of all! Keep your energy up, then pause.

Quiet but confident tone.

Pause after this line to let the significance of Mary's response ring in your assembly's hearts, then conclude with the angel's departure.

TO KEEP IN MIND
Proclamation cannot be effective unless it is expressive. As you prepare your proclamation, make choices about emotions. Some choices are already evident in the text.

"**Behold**, you will **conceive** in your womb and bear a **son**,
　　and you shall name him **Jesus**.
He will be **great** and will be called **Son** of the Most **High**,
　　and the Lord **God** will give him the **throne** of David
　　　　his **father**,
　　and he will **rule** over the house of Jacob **forever**,
　　and of his **kingdom** there will be no **end**."
But Mary said to the angel,
　　"How can this **be**,
　　since I have no relations with a **man**?"
And the angel said to her in reply,
　　"The Holy **Spirit** will come **upon** you,
　　and the power of the Most **High** will **overshadow** you.
Therefore the **child** to be born
　　will be called **holy**, the Son of **God**.
　　And behold, **Elizabeth**, your relative,
　　has **also** conceived a son in her old **age**,
　　and this is the **sixth** month for her who was called **barren**;
　　for **nothing** will be **impossible** for God."
Mary said, "**Behold**, I am the **handmaid** of the Lord.
May it be **done** to me according to **your** word."
Then the angel **departed** from her.

---

were no magnificent buildings, mosaics, or frescoes. Mary's clothing would have been homespun. Mary would have gone with other women to the town's single well to draw water. In her home, she would have been engaged in cleaning, gardening, cooking, and sewing. The angel Gabriel brought the announcement to Mary in this humble setting.

　　Gabriel's announcement to Mary is the second of angelic messages of pending birth. The first was given to the priestly Zechariah in the Jerusalem Temple: to an important person, in the city of kings, at the house of God's dwelling. By juxtaposing the Annunciation to Mary with that to Zechariah, the evangelist Luke highlights the insignificance of the young woman and her village. A second juxtaposition, the child to be born of Zechariah and Elizabeth and the son to be born of Mary, reverses the expected status. In every way, Jesus will be greater than John the Baptist. John is filled with the Holy Spirit in his mother's womb, while Jesus' very conception is by the power of the Spirit. John will be prophet of the Most High, and Jesus is Son of the Most High. John will give knowledge of sal-vation, while Jesus is the Savior who brings salvation. At the birth of his son, Zechariah proclaims "you will go before the Lord to prepare his ways." John's role is to prepare the path for the son of Mary, Jesus, who will rule over the house of Jacob, and his kingdom will have no end. The two annunciations in Luke's Gospel prepare us for the celebration of the birth of God's Son who will bring salvation to a waiting world. E.P.

THE NATIVITY OF THE LORD (CHRISTMAS): VIGIL

LECTIONARY #13

READING I   Isaiah 62:1–5

A reading from the Book of the Prophet Isaiah

Exhortatory. Keep your energy up throughout. Note the couplets of thought rhyme: the same idea expressed twice using different images. Keep the couplets together; let their structure dictate your rhythm.
Isaiah = Ī-ZAY-uh
Proclaim as if you had no choice but to proclaim!

For **Zion's** sake I will **not** be **silent**,
   for **Jerusalem's** sake I will **not** be **quiet**,
until her **vindication** shines **forth** like the **dawn**
   and her **victory** like a burning **torch**.

Make eye contact throughout the reading. Maintain a sense of urgency: persuade your assembly of how much God loves them. Imagine telling someone suffering that the bad times are all over. How would you look and sound? How would you feel?

Nations shall **behold** your vindication,
   and all the **kings** your **glory**;
you shall be called by a **new** name
   pronounced by the mouth of the **Lord**.
You shall be a glorious **crown** in the hand of the LORD,
   a royal **diadem** held by your God.

Contrast the shame of the old names with the joy of the new names.

No **more** shall people call you "**Forsaken**,"
   or your land "**Desolate**,"
but you shall be called "My **Delight**,"
   and your land "**Espoused**."
For the LORD **delights** in you
   and makes your land his **spouse**.

Emphasize the metaphors of marriage. God wants to be as close to us as a married couple is to each other!

As a young **man** marries a **virgin**,
   your **Builder** shall marry **you**;
and as a bridegroom **rejoices** in his **bride**
   so shall your **God** rejoice in **you**.

Slow down, smile, and maintain eye contact through this final line.

READING I   The readings for the four Sundays of Advent spoke of longing and expectation for the coming of the Savior. Isaiah contributed to the atmosphere of waiting by expressing the people's intense desire for restoration of land and people. In the face of suffering and disillusionment, Isaiah gave the people grounds for hope that God would again come to save them. Today's reading from Isaiah comes from the same historical period as the one from the Third Sunday of Advent: the people have returned to a ruined Jerusalem from exile in Babylon in the sixth century BC.

Today, we first hear that Isaiah cannot keep silent about Israel's vindication—its release from captivity in Babylon. So wondrous is Israel's victory that neither the voice of the prophet nor the voice of God can be silenced. In the opening verse, Isaiah seems to be addressing the nations who witness Israel's victorious liberation that shines forth like the dawn. As dawn breaks forth with suddenness and certainty, so too is Israel's release from captivity sudden and certain after seventy long years. Isaiah then turns to Israel herself, declaring to the people that nations and kings will see their freedom. Because they have been freed, they will be signs of God's own glory. In this part of Isaiah, "glory" (cabod) is repeated over and over, signifying God's radiant presence that is seen in the people themselves.

As the prophet announces what is in store for them, he emphasizes the new things that God will accomplish. So different will be their lives that God will give them another name. When they were in exile, they were called "Forsaken" and their

For meditation and context:

TO KEEP IN MIND

Exhortatory texts make an urgent appeal to listeners. They may encourage, warn, or challenge, and often include a call to action. You must convey the urgency and passion behind the words.

Didactic. Proclaim it with the love teachers have for their students or parents have for their children.

Antioch = AN-tee-ahk

Pisidia = pih-SID-ee-uh

Don't swallow "synagogue." Paul is speaking to fellow Jews and doesn't assume everyone knows who Jesus is; neither should you.

He motions for silence.

The "God-fearing" = Gentiles attracted to the teachings of Judaism.

Joyfully recall God's great care for Israel!

sojourn = SOH-jern (exile)

The reading omits a few verses of the story to go quickly to David. Let that be your emphasis.

Proclaim with God's voice of pleased satisfaction.

RESPONSORIAL PSALM   Psalm 89:4–5, 16–17, 27, 29 (2a)

R. For ever I will sing the goodness of the Lord.

I have made a covenant with my chosen one,
  I have sworn to David my servant:
forever will I confirm your posterity
  and establish your throne for all
    generations.

Blessed the people who know the
    joyful shout;
  in the light of your countenance, O LORD,
    they walk.
At your name they rejoice all the day,
  and through your justice they are exalted.

He shall say of me, "You are my father,
  my God, the rock, my savior."
Forever I will maintain my kindness
    toward him,
  and my covenant with him stands firm.

READING II   Acts of the Apostles 13:16–17, 22–25

A reading from the Acts of the Apostles

When **Paul** reached Antioch in Pisidia and entered the **synagogue**,
  he **stood** up, motioned with his **hand**, and said,
    "Fellow **Israelites** and you **others** who are God-fearing, **listen**.
The God of this people Israel **chose** our ancestors
  and **exalted** the people during their **sojourn** in the land
      of Egypt.
With uplifted arm he led them **out** of it.
Then he removed **Saul** and raised up **David** as king;
  of **him** he testified,
    'I have found **David**, son of **Jesse**, a man after my own **heart**;
    he will carry out my **every** wish.'

land was called "Desolate." Since names were considered to express a person or nation's identity, their previous names expressed the depth of their loss. They sound as if their relationship with God has been severed. The new names of people and land are not only about their changed situation, but are about the intimate relationship that God will have with them. "My Delight" expresses well the love relationship of husband and wife. The land itself will be called "Espoused." These two identities reveal that the strained relationship between God and the people, developed

earlier by the prophet Hosea (in Hosea 2:18) has been forgotten. God will take Israel as a bride, rejoicing in her as if he were a newly married bridegroom.

The future which Isaiah announced to the returned exiles was vastly different from what they actually experienced when they came back to the Promised Land. His proclamation of salvation and of God's abiding love for them was basis for hope, and an implicit exhortation to remain faithful to the covenant relationship. On this Vigil of Christmas, it remains cause for our own hope and calls us anew to fidelity to

the one who fulfilled Isaiah's prophecy of salvation far beyond expectations.

READING II Many of the speeches in Acts of the Apostles delivered by Peter, Stephen, and Paul review the history of Israel that leads to the culmination of the covenant and fulfillment of promises in Jesus. They illustrate how the story of Jesus is in continuity with the story of Israel. In this speech, delivered by Paul in Pisidian Antioch during his first missionary journey, he addresses his fellow Jews and God-fearers (Gentiles interested in Judaism)

Here's Paul's whole point.

Paul is quoting John. Don't let it sound like he's referring to himself.

This ending is slightly awkward since we're left with John's words and not Paul's. Take a longer pause than usual to let the community process this before "The word of the Lord."

Two readings in one; the first is didactic, the second narrative.

The steady rhythm conveys a sense of security and comfort: through all these generations, God was preparing the world for Jesus. Let the rhythm come naturally, but notice where it is broken; something significant is being said! Do your best with the pronunciations, but don't lose the easy flow. If you make a mistake, go right back into the rhythm. Use the periods as places to briefly stop, then increase energy as you begin again.

geneology = jee-nee-OL-uh-jee
Abraham = AY-bruh-ham; Isaac – Ī-zik
Judah = JOO-duh
Perez = PAYR-ez; Zerah = ZEE-rah
Only five women are included in this list.
Tamar= TAY-mahr
Hezron = HEZ-ruhn
Ram = ram
Amminadab =uh-MIN-uh-dab
Nahshon = NAH-shon
Salmon = SAL-muhn
Boaz = BOH-az
Rahab = RAY-hab
Obed = OH-bed
Jesse = JES-ee
Pause before reciting the next fourteen generations.

From **this** man's descendants **God**, according to his **promise**,
    has brought to Israel a **savior**, **Jesus**.
John **heralded** his coming by proclaiming a baptism of **repentance**
    to **all** the people of Israel;
    and as John was **completing** his course, he would say,
    'What do you suppose that I **am**? I am not **he**.
Behold, one is coming **after** me;
    I am not **worthy** to unfasten the **sandals** of his feet.'"

GOSPEL   Matthew 1:1–25

A reading from the holy Gospel according to Matthew

The book of the **genealogy** of Jesus **Christ**,
    the son of **David**, the son of **Abraham**.

Abraham became the father of **Isaac**,
    Isaac the father of **Jacob**,
    Jacob the father of **Judah** and his brothers.
Judah became the father of **Perez** and **Zerah**,
    whose **mother** was **Tamar**.
Perez became the father of **Hezron**,
    Hezron the father of **Ram**,
    Ram the father of **Amminadab**.
Amminadab became the father of **Nahshon**,
    Nahshon the father of **Salmon**,
    Salmon the father of **Boaz**,
    whose **mother** was **Rahab**.
Boaz became the father of **Obed**,
    whose **mother** was **Ruth**.
Obed became the father of **Jesse**,
    Jesse the father of **David** the **king**.

---

in the synagogue. He begins by first recalling God's choice of their ancestors, making of them a great people during their enslavement in Egypt. God's uplifted arm, symbol of God's great power, led them out of Egypt.

Our reading omits several verses in which Paul reviews their wilderness journey, entrance into the land of Canaan, and his appointing of judges who led them until they asked for a king. Their first king was Saul, whose reign ended disastrously when he was killed in battle. Paul interprets this event as God's doing so that David could become king.

The speech, recounting the history of Israel in broad strokes, is leading up to David, "a man after my own heart." God's promise to David, as we heard in the reading from 2 Samuel on the Fourth Sunday of Advent, was to build him a house, referring to David's descendants. Paul explains that this promise was fulfilled in Jesus, descendant of David and savior to Israel.

Paul's address in the synagogue has the same view of John the Baptist as we heard in the Advent Gospel accounts. John was a herald, the one preparing the way of the Lord, and was not the one to fulfill the

Davidic promise. He attests, "I am not he." John's preaching and his baptism of repentance were directed "to all the people of Israel" in order to ready them for the one whose sandals John was not worthy to unfasten.

The remainder of Paul's speech (Acts 13:26–41) is about Jesus, the one promised to the fathers, and the one whom God raised up. The preparation is completed. While John's mission was to Israel, Jesus' salvific mission extends beyond that of John to everyone who believes. Israel's hopes centered on God sending a savior to

Uriah's wife, Bathsheba, is unnamed.

Uriah = yoo-RI-uh

Rehoboam = ree-huh-BOH-uhm

Abijah = uh-BĪ-juh

Asaph = AY-saf

Jehoshaphat = jeh-HOH-shuh-fat

Joram = JOHR-uhm

Uzziah = yuh-ZĪ-uh

Jotham = JOH-thuhm

Ahaz = AY-haz

Hezekiah = hez-eh-KĪ-uh

Manasseh = muh-NAS-uh

Amos = AY-m*s

Josiah = joh-SĪ-uh

Jechoniah = jek-oh-NĪ-uh

Pause before reciting the last fourteen generations.

Shealtiel = shee-AL-tee-uhl

Zerubbabel = zuh-ROOB-uh-b*l

Abiud = uh-BĪ-uhd

Eliakim = ee-LĪ-uh-kim

Azor = AY-sohr

Zadok = ZAD-uhk

Achim = AH-kim

Eliud = ee-LĪ-uhd

Eleazar = el-ee-AY-zer

Matthan = MATH-uhn

David became the father of **Solomon,**
  whose **mother** had been the wife of **Uriah.**
Solomon became the father of **Rehoboam,**
  Rehoboam the father of **Abijah,**
  Abijah the father of **Asaph.**
Asaph became the father of **Jehoshaphat,**
  Jehoshaphat the father of **Joram,**
  Joram the father of **Uzziah.**
Uzziah became the father of **Jotham,**
  Jotham the father of **Ahaz,**
  Ahaz the father of **Hezekiah.**
Hezekiah became the father of **Manasseh,**
  Manasseh the father of **Amos,**
  Amos the father of **Josiah.**
Josiah became the father of **Jechoniah** and his brothers
  at the time of the Babylonian **exile.**

After the Babylonian exile,
  Jechoniah became the father of **Shealtiel,**
  Shealtiel the father of **Zerubbabel,**
  Zerubbabel the father of **Abiud.**
Abiud became the father of **Eliakim,**
  Eliakim the father of **Azor,**
  Azor the father of **Zadok.**
Zadok became the father of **Achim,**
  Achim the father of **Eliud,**
  Eliud the father of **Eleazar.**
Eleazar became the father of **Matthan,**
  Matthan the father of **Jacob,**
  Jacob the father of **Joseph,** the husband of **Mary.**
Of her was born **Jesus** who is called the **Christ.**

---

them. The fulfillment brought the savior to all people.

The readings of Advent repeatedly pointed to the future. Promises were made. Hope was stimulated. The image of God was of one who would remain faithful, and would at some unknown time act to restore his people. Paul's speech is about fulfillment of those promises and hope. The story of Israel has been preparing for the advent of Jesus, whose birth we celebrate.

GOSPEL Paul's speech in the synagogue of Pisidian Antioch reviewed the history of Israel quickly, moving through centuries with bare mention of significant names, so that he could race to the account of Jesus. The reading from Matthew, the first twenty-five verses of his Gospel, goes very slowly, in what some consider an agonizing recital of unfamiliar names, through the same history. Yet, whether a rapid summary or a slow recital, both readings take us to the same person: Jesus, the son of David.

Matthew wrote his Gospel for a predominantly Jewish Christian audience. In the decade between 80 and 90, when Matthew was probably written, many Jews who believed in Jesus were torn between fidelity to their ancient beliefs and practices and their new belief in Jesus. One of Matthew's intentions was to show this young community that Jesus was the fulfillment of their tradition. Admittedly, Jesus brought unexpected newness, but he was always faithful to the covenant and God of his ancestors. In speaking to his disciples, Jesus reminds them of these two dimensions: "Every scribe who has been instructed in the kingdom of heaven is like the head of a

Matthew has gone to great lengths to show the parallelism of generations during each of the great epochs of Jewish history. End with a satisfied tone: "See how everything comes out right!"

Try to recapture all the drama, conflict, and wonder in the story, as if the outcome were in doubt until the very end. You're answering an important question: where did this amazing Jesus Christ come from?
The conflict in these lines reflects the conflict in Joseph's heart as he decides what to do.

Express sadness in your voice at this choice.

Bring a sense of wonder and awe to your proclamation of the angel's visit.
Soothingly; the angel tries to calm Joseph's fear about honoring his commitment to Mary.

"God saves" is the meaning of the name "Jesus." Pause to let the angel disappear from the scene.

Another name for Jesus with another meaning. Take your time with each.

There's a satisfied feel to this conclusion: Joseph has made the right choice.

Let Joseph's love for the child come through as you describe his naming.

Thus the total number of **generations**
 from **Abraham** to **David**
 is **fourteen** generations;
 from **David** to the Babylonian **exile**,
 fourteen generations;
 from the Babylonian **exile** to the **Christ**,
 fourteen generations.

[**Now** this is how the **birth** of Jesus Christ came about.
When his mother **Mary** was betrothed to **Joseph**,
 but before they **lived** together,
 she was found with **child** through the Holy **Spirit**.
Joseph her **husband**, since he was a **righteous** man,
 yet unwilling to expose her to **shame**,
 decided to **divorce** her quietly.
Such was his **intention** when, **behold**,
 the **angel** of the Lord appeared to him in a **dream** and said,
 "**Joseph**, son of David,
 do not be **afraid** to take Mary your **wife** into your **home**.
For it is through the Holy **Spirit**
 that this child has been **conceived** in her.
She will bear a **son** and you are to name him **Jesus**,
 because he will **save** his people from their **sins**."
All this took place to **fulfill**
 what the Lord had said through the **prophet**:
 *Behold, the **virgin** shall **conceive** and bear a **son**,*
 *and they shall name him **Emmanuel**,*
 which means "**God** is **with** us."
When Joseph **awoke**,
 he **did** as the angel of the Lord had **commanded** him
 and took his **wife** into his **home**.
He had no **relations** with her until she bore a **son**,
 and he **named** him Jesus.]

[Shorter: Matthew 1:18–25 (see brackets)]

household who brings from his storeroom both the new and the old" (13:52).
 The opening verses of Matthew do precisely that: they bring together the old—the ancestors of Jesus—even as they are progressing steadily toward the new: Jesus who is called the Christ. Matthew begins, "The genealogy of Jesus Christ," echoing genealogies found in the Old Testament (for example, in Genesis 5:1). The names of Jesus' ancestors include some well known and some obscure; they include more people remembered for their sins than their holiness. Yet the promises of

descendants made to Abraham and to David were ultimately fulfilled even when repeatedly threatened by human sin and misfortunes. Matthew also includes the names of five women, a new feature embedded into the old. Each of these women overcame obstacles and gave birth in unusual and unexpected circumstances. They alert those who listen to the genealogy to expect surprises to unfold in the story of Jesus.
 The "genealogy" (*genesis*) of Jesus Christ opens Matthew's Gospel. Immediately after the genealogy, Matthew tells how the

"birth" (*genesis*) of Jesus came about. Both genealogy and birth tell about the genesis of Jesus. The ancestors as well as Mary and Joseph exemplify how God's plan linked the old and new in Jesus. Isaiah's prophecy of old that a virgin would give birth to a son called Emmanuel will be fulfilled in a new way in Mary's son. E.P.

THE NATIVITY OF THE LORD (CHRISTMAS): NIGHT

LECTIONARY #14

READING I   Isaiah 9:1–6

A reading from the Book of the Prophet Isaiah

The people who walked in **darkness**
    have seen a great **light**;
upon those who dwelt in the land of **gloom**
    a **light** has shone.
You have brought them abundant **joy**
    and great **rejoicing**,
as they **rejoice** before you as at the **harvest**,
    as people make **merry** when dividing **spoils**.
For the **yoke** that **burdened** them,
    the **pole** on their **shoulder**,
and the **rod** of their **taskmaster**
    you have **smashed**, as on the day of **Midian**.
For every **boot** that tramped in **battle**,
    every **cloak** rolled in **blood**,
    will be **burned** as fuel for **flames**.
For a **child** is born to us, a **son** is given us;
    upon his shoulder **dominion** rests.
They name him **Wonder-Counselor**, **God-Hero**,
    Father-Forever, **Prince** of **Peace**.

An exhortatory hymn of praise. Give voice to the exuberant joy of this night! Keep your pace up (but not *too* fast). Pause only at punctuation.

Isaiah = Ī-ZAY-uh
Emphasize the contrasts between darkness and light.

Although you're speaking to God, make eye contact with the community.

"See" the people rejoicing!

A triple thought rhyme; intensify with each line.

Midian = MID-ee-uhn
Use a quiet tone on images of war. Note that it's *tramped* (one syllable, meaning marched), not *trampled*.
The cloak is a gruesome image, but sorrow has turned to joy. Pause.
Revive your energy here. This is good news!

Give each name its emphasis.

READING I Isaiah, the Advent prophet of hope, is also the Christmas prophet of fulfillment. He exercised his ministry for about forty years, prophesying during the reign of three kings of Judah. Tonight's reading is from the reign of the second of these kings, Ahaz, who ruled from 735 to 715 BC. Like most of the kings of Israel and Judah, Ahaz did not govern in accordance with the covenant between God and his people. He was weak and vacillating and relied on foreign alliances rather than on God's power to save. With a weak king and powerful enemies on

every side, the historical situation of Judah was so often characterized by darkness and gloom that the precise background for this prophecy is not certain. What is certain is the transformation of darkness into a great light, and gloom replaced by abundant joy. The burdens and violence of foreign oppressors have ended, and symbols of their armies burned as fuel for fire. Even if we knew for sure the historical setting, we could still read this prophecy as a proclamation of God's power to change every situation of darkness and gloom into one of light and joy. In his joy at this radiance, Isaiah

addresses God: "You have brought them abundant joy . . . they rejoice before you."

Then he speaks to the people. The cause for joy is a child who is born "to us"; he will be born for the sake of the people who hear Isaiah's prophecy. This newborn son will be the source of the great transformation of darkness to light that Isaiah proclaims. Isaiah may have been thinking of the son born to King Ahaz, Hezekiah, one of the few kings of Judah who did rule with righteousness. However, even though Hezekiah was a far better king than his father, he did not measure up to the glorious

How do you feel imagining such a world?

His dominion is **vast**
  and forever **peaceful**,
from **David's** throne, and over his **kingdom**,
  which he **confirms** and **sustains**
by **judgment** and **justice**,
  both **now** and **forever**.
The **zeal** of the LORD of hosts will **do** this!

Pause.

With deliberate finality.

For meditation and context:

RESPONSORIAL PSALM   Psalm 96:1–2, 2–3, 11–12, 13 (Luke 2:11)

R. Today is born our Savior, Christ the Lord.

Sing to the LORD a new song;
  sing to the LORD, all you lands.
Sing to the LORD; bless his name.

Announce his salvation, day after day.
  Tell his glory among the nations;
  among all peoples, his wondrous deeds.

Let the heavens be glad and the
    earth rejoice;
  let the sea and what fills it resound;
  let the plains be joyful and all that is
    in them!
Then shall all the trees of the forest exult.

They shall exult before the LORD,
    for he comes;
  for he comes to rule the earth.
He shall rule the world with justice
    and the peoples with his constancy.

TO KEEP IN MIND

Exhortatory texts make an urgent appeal to listeners. They may encourage, warn, or challenge, and often include a call to action. You must convey the urgency and passion behind the words.

An exhortatory reading. All *good news!* Smile with your voice, eyes, and face!

Titus = TĪ-tuhs

Proclaim so that the community will live as those who know they are loved.
The reading is only one sentence, but don't rush. Pause at commas and at the end of the printed lines (except where noted), but keep your voice up.
You are praising your community for how well they live!

Don't pause at the end of this line.

Use the eagerness in your voice to convey your community's desire to do good.

READING II   Titus 2:11–14

A reading from the Letter of Saint Paul to Titus

Beloved:
The **grace** of God has **appeared,** saving **all**
  and training us to **reject** godless ways and **worldly** desires
  and to live **temperately**, **justly**, and **devoutly** in this age,
  as we **await** the blessed **hope**,
  the appearance of the **glory** of our great **God**
  and **savior** Jesus **Christ**,
  who **gave** himself for us to **deliver** us from all **lawlessness**
  and to **cleanse** for himself a people as his **own**,
  eager to do what is **good**.

description of the prophecy. The titles given to the child express an extraordinary scope; he will be a military hero, a father to the people, a bringer of peace; his rule will bring peace and harmony not only "to us," but will have a vast reach; his justice will be both now and forever. Though he will rule from David's throne, he is more than any earthly king could ever be. Isaiah's prophecy, along with other prophecies in the Old Testament, gave rise to expectations of an ideal king through whom God would transform darkness to light, and gloom into joy.

READING II In the Letter to Titus, Paul offers pastoral guidance to Titus, whom he addresses as "my true child in our common faith" (1:4). All of the counsel that Paul gives Titus is for the sake of their common faith. As Titus' spiritual father, Paul outlines for him his roles and responsibilities, the requirements for other church leaders, and the expected behavior of all its members. After giving his initial advice, Paul presents the theological foundation for his exhortation, and then continues with additional advice and further theology. We hear his first theological

insights in tonight's reading, and the second one will be read at the Christmas Mass at dawn.

He begins: "The grace of God has appeared" (*epiphaino*), referring to the "epiphany" of God's grace already manifest in Jesus for the salvation of all people. Paul had just explained to Titus how people in the church are expected to live. Here he elucidates that the grace of God gives them the ability to live in accord with his teaching. He says that God's grace "trains" us (*paideuo*), a verb that was used to describe upbringing of children, including education,

A narrative reading. Proclaim simply, like a bedtime story. What effect do you want this story to have on the assembly? Keep that intention in mind as you proclaim.

Caesar Augustus = SEE-zer aw-GUHS-tuhs

Careful not to swallow "enrolled." It refers to the census, but that might not be clear to the assembly.

Quirinius = kwih-RIN-ee-uhs

Emphasize "city of David."
Judea = joo-dee-uh
Drop your voice slightly on this parenthetical phrase.

Begin to slow down from here to "inn."

Proclaim with the tenderness of a mother caring for her newborn.
Proclaim this as a simple fact without "comment."
Pause as the scene shifts to the shepherds, then pick up your pace again.

Bring a feeling of wonder and surprise to the angel's appearance. This is not an everyday occurrence; it shouldn't sound like one!

You've been selected to deliver good news that will bring great joy tonight, so let your feeling come through in the words of the angel!

GOSPEL   Luke 2:1–14

A reading from the holy Gospel according to Luke

In those days a **decree** went out from **Caesar Augustus**
    that the whole **world** should be **enrolled**.
This was the **first** enrollment,
    when Quirinius was governor of Syria.
So **all** went to be **enrolled**, **each** to his own **town**.
And **Joseph** too went up from **Galilee** from the town
        of **Nazareth**
    to **Judea**, to the city of **David** that is called **Bethlehem**,
    because he was of the **house** and **family** of David,
    to be enrolled with **Mary**, his **betrothed**, who was with **child**.
While they were there,
    the **time** came for her to have her **child**,
    and she gave **birth** to her firstborn **son**.
She **wrapped** him in **swaddling** clothes and **laid** him in a **manger**,
    because there was no **room** for them in the **inn**.

Now there were **shepherds** in that region living in the **fields**
    and keeping the **night** watch over their flock.
The **angel** of the Lord **appeared** to them
    and the **glory** of the Lord **shone** around them,
    and they were **struck** with great **fear**.
The angel **said** to them,
    "Do **not** be **afraid**;
    for **behold**, I proclaim to you good **news** of great **joy**
    that will be for **all** the people.
For **today** in the city of **David**
    a **savior** has been **born** for you who is **Christ** and **Lord**.

---

discipline, and correcting, so that they reach maturity. The training provided by God's grace guides us in two directions: rejecting what is godless and worldly, and taking on what is temperate, just, and devout. This rejection of evil and acceptance of good is a brief summary of the lengthier exhortations that Paul develops throughout the letter.

The grace of God has already appeared in Christ. Now believers wait in blessed hope for a future epiphany: "the glory of our great God and savior Jesus Christ." All of the actions of the one who gave himself for us, Jesus the Savior, are meant to make us a people who belong to him, ever eager to do what is good, living faithfully by the power of God's grace.

GOSPEL   We can view Luke's narrative of the birth of Jesus through many different lenses, seeing the account as one that embraces all times, peoples, and places, often in sharp contrasts. Luke brings together history and theology, the power of Rome and the insignificance of Nazareth, earth and heaven, shepherds and angels—and at the center of it all: mother and child.

From the opening verse, Luke establishes the historicity of the event. By naming the rulers and their cities, he tells us that the story of Jesus' birth took place in history, not in some mythological past. The powerful Augustus and his census of "the whole world" soon move off the stage, to be replaced by Nazareth, an insignificant Galilean village. From that inconsequential Galilean hamlet, a humble couple makes their way to Judah and the city of David, Bethlehem. When Luke recounts the actual

Quicken your energy with "suddenly."
Amazement has been taken to a whole new
level!

Although this is the last line, keep your voice
and energy up throughout. Then pause before
"The word of the Lord."

And this will be a **sign** for you:
>   you will find an **infant** wrapped in **swaddling** clothes
>   and lying in a **manger**."
And **suddenly** there was a **multitude** of the heavenly host with
>   the angel,
> **praising** God and saying:
>   "**Glory** to God in the **highest**
>   and on **earth peace** to those on whom his **favor** rests."

THE 4 STEPS OF *LECTIO DIVINA* OR PRAYERFUL READING

1. *Lectio:* Read a Scripture passage aloud slowly. Notice what phrase captures your attention and be attentive to its meaning. Silent pause.

2. *Meditatio:* Read the passage aloud slowly again, reflecting on the passage, allowing God to speak to you through it. Silent pause.

3. *Oratio:* Read it aloud slowly a third time, allowing it to be your prayer or response to God's gift of insight to you. Silent pause.

4. *Contemplatio:* Read it aloud slowly a fourth time, now resting in God's word.

---

birth of the child, he does so briefly: Mary gave birth to her firstborn son, wrapped him in swaddling clothes and laid him in a manger. The recounting of the birth is almost as hidden, as quiet and tucked away, as the place of the birth.

Then Luke develops another scene, this one involving lowly shepherds and a multitude of angels. The scene is replete with details, unlike the short account of the birth. Here Luke's theology takes center stage. The angel announces the good news of great joy that is for all people. The one

born in the city of David is a Savior, Christ and Lord. These are exalted titles, but confirmed by a lowly sign: a child in swaddling clothes lying in a manger. Simple as is the sign, there may be an allusion to Solomon, a king likewise wrapped as any other infant in swaddling clothes (Wisdom 7:4–6). From the earthly sign, we are taken again to heavenly heights as the angels praise God, with a prayer that also becomes our own. Luke will develop each of the elements of the angelic announcements throughout his Gospel. We already know who Jesus is, but

the characters in the Gospel story will only gradually learn how Jesus is Savior, Christ, and Lord.

By weaving together history and theology, heaven and earth, highborn and lowly, Luke shows us that the child born in Bethlehem is for all times, peoples, and places. He continues to bring peace on earth to those on whom his favor rests. E.P.

THE NATIVITY OF THE LORD (CHRISTMAS): DAWN

An exhortatory reading. It's short, so don't rush. Isaiah calls the people to hope in a God who will restore Zion to its glory. Proclaim this as if to someone you know who needs to hear a message of hope.

Isaiah = ī-ZAY-uh

Keep your voice and energy up throughout!

Announce his coming as if you were on a watchtower, alerting the whole city that you've spotted him from a long way off.

recompense = REK-uhm-pens (compensation for wrongs suffered)

Smile with your face, eyes, and voice so your community knows this is *good news!*

Make sure "Frequented" (= FREE-kwen-t*d) sounds like a proper name; it will not be a word the community expects here.

For meditation and context:

TO KEEP IN MIND
Be careful not to "swallow" words by mumbling. Articulate carefully so that every word is clearly heard, especially at the end of lines.

LECTIONARY #15

READING I   Isaiah 62:11–12

A reading from the Book of the Prophet Isaiah

See, the LORD **proclaims**
  to the **ends** of the **earth**:
say to daughter **Zion**,
  your savior **comes!**
Here is his **reward** with him,
  his **recompense** before him.
They shall be called the **holy** people,
  the **redeemed** of the LORD,
and you shall be called "**Frequented**,"
  a city that is **not forsaken**.

RESPONSORIAL PSALM   Psalm 97:1, 6, 11–12
R. A light will shine on us this day: the Lord is born for us.

The LORD is king; let the earth rejoice;
  let the many isles be glad.
The heavens proclaim his justice,
  and all peoples see his glory.

Light dawns for the just;
  and gladness, for the upright of heart.
Be glad in the LORD, you just,
  and give thanks to his holy name.

READING I   At the Christmas Vigil Mass, we heard the first part of Isaiah's prophecy of transformation. At this Christmas Mass at dawn, Isaiah's promise rings out with even greater joy. The Lord now proclaims, even to the ends of the earth, what is in store for daughter Zion. The whole world saw the captivity and loss of God's own people, and now they are to hear of their salvation. Even though the entire earth is to hear of God's rescue, daughter Zion, Jerusalem, is the primary recipient of the Good News: "Your savior comes!" As the people had made a journey to return to their land, now their savior is making a journey toward them. The prophet had commanded the people to "build up the highway," (Isaiah 62:10) a road not only for themselves, but also for God's own presence.

Through Isaiah, God adds to the new name of "My Delight" already promised to the people. They will be called "the holy people," a designation reminiscent of the identity Moses used for God's people (for example, Deuteronomy 7:6), meaning they have been set apart as a people consecrated to God. They will also be called "the redeemed of the Lord," for God has acted as their closest kinsman by rescuing them from destitution. The response of a redeemed people is one of gratitude, awe, and fidelity; even more, they are in a loving and intimate relationship with the God who is their closest relative. The land that had been called "Desolate" also receives a new name. God's own people had not inhabited the land, but now it will be called "Frequented," again populated by a holy and redeemed nation.

A didactic reading, but it still requires energy and enthusiasm. Keep the phrases together, and pause a little more than usual at the commas.

Titus = TĪ-tuhs

First thought: "When the kindness . . . his mercy."
Drop your voice slightly on this parenthetical phrase.
Second thought: "he saved us . . . our savior." Make "bath of rebirth and renewal" one phrase; it refers to Baptism.
Let the word "richly" sound like what it means.
Third thought: "so that we . . . eternal life." Slight pause after grace.
Slow down and let the gift of our inheritance really sink in.

TO KEEP IN MIND
A *didactic* text makes a point or teaches something. Help your assembly to follow the argument and understand what's being taught.

TO KEEP IN MIND
Pay attention to the pace of your reading. Varying the pace gives listeners clues to the meaning of the text. The most common problem for proclaimers new to the ministry is going too fast to be understood.

READING II   Titus 3:4–7

A reading from the Letter of Saint Paul to Titus

Beloved:
When the **kindness** and generous **love**
  of God our savior **appeared**,
not because of any righteous deeds **we** had done
  but because of his **mercy**,
he **saved** us through the **bath** of **rebirth**
  and **renewal** by the Holy **Spirit**,
whom he **richly** poured out on us
  through Jesus **Christ** our **savior**,
so that we might be **justified** by his **grace**
  and become **heirs** in **hope** of eternal **life**.

Today we celebrate that the Savior promised by Isaiah has made the longest of journeys to come among us!

READING II The reading from Titus is the second of Paul's theological explanations that are foundational for life in Christ. In his pastoral guidance to Titus, as in other of Paul's letters, he roots moral teaching, or the behavior and relationships expected of Christians, in theology. This pattern of teaching is sometimes referred to as "indicative-imperative." The "indicative" is the statement of our faith;

the "imperative" is the behavior that flows from our belief. As in the reading for Mass during the Night, we hear brief expositions of the faith of the early Church, the "indicative" that inspires living in accordance with what we profess.

"The kindness and generous love of God our savior" is almost a name for Jesus. He is the one whose appearance (literally his "epiphany") is a personal manifestation of God's kindness and love. His appearance among us is based not on anything we have done, but on God's mercy. Through Baptism, "the bath of rebirth" we are immersed into

God's saving love. In Baptism, the Holy Spirit is poured out on us through Christ. God, Christ, Holy Spirit: the later Trinitarian language and understanding of God as One-in-Three, has a foundation in the context of Baptism. This short but profound text was likely a baptismal hymn, instructing believers that the kindness and generous love of God is still available to us through Baptism. God's grace in Baptism justifies us, brings us into right relationship with God and God's people. Together we become hope-filled heirs of eternal life. All who are baptized are expected to respond

A narrative reading concluding the Christmas story; it assumes the assembly knows the story up to this point, and they probably do, but your tone will have to remind them that this is a story of joy and excitement.

Start slowly to let the community catch up to where we are in the story.
Proclaim with the eager enthusiasm of those about to leave their flocks (their entire livelihood!) unguarded to check out this amazing thing.
Don't let it sound like Mary and Joseph are in the manger! Pause after "manger" to let the scene settle. manger = MAYN-jer

You also should be amazed as you proclaim!

Pause before and after these lines about Mary; proclaim with the reflective tone Mary assumes.
Raise your energy. Use the words "glorifying and praising God" to do just that!

There's a tone of satisfaction to Luke's words here: You can trust what you've been told.

TO KEEP IN MIND
In a narrative, find an emotion or point of view for each character, keeping in mind that these might change during the reading.

TO KEEP IN MIND
Pray the text, using your favorite method of praying with Scripture.

GOSPEL   Luke 2:15–20

A reading from the holy Gospel according to Luke

When the angels went **away** from them to **heaven**,
    the **shepherds** said to one another,
    "Let us **go**, then, to **Bethlehem**
    to **see** this thing that has taken place,
    which the Lord has made **known** to us."
So they went in **haste** and found **Mary** and **Joseph**,
    and the **infant** lying in the manger.
When they **saw** this,
    they made **known** the message
    that had been **told** them about this child.
All who heard it were **amazed**
    by what had been told them by the shepherds.
And Mary **kept** all these things,
    reflecting on them in her **heart**.
Then the shepherds returned,
    glorifying and **praising** God
    for **all** they had **heard** and **seen**,
    just as it had been told to them.

---

to the gift of God's grace by lives that exhibit godly kindness and generous love.

GOSPEL Isaiah announced, "Your savior comes," and Paul wrote to Titus that God's kindness and love have already appeared. Now we hear Luke's narrative that tells how people responded to the birth of this Savior, this epiphany of love found in an infant lying in a manger. The shepherds, lowly Judeans considered unworthy by the Jerusalem elite, are eager to see what the angels had proclaimed to them. Their journeying "in haste" echoes Mary's traveling "in haste" to her cousin Elizabeth (Luke 1:39). God's revelation inspires both Mary and the shepherds to hurry forward to experience the wonders God has done. As soon as the shepherds see the child in the manger, they become bearers of the Good News, becoming the first evangelists to announce the birth of the Savior. Those who hear their message are amazed, a response that often includes astonishment along with puzzlement. (See for example Luke 1:21, 63 and 2:33.) After the exuberant broadcasting by the shepherds, we hear of Mary's quiet contemplation. She is reflecting on "all these things " interiorly, beginning with the Annunciation of Jesus' birth. After Jesus is found in the Temple, she will again keep "all these things" in her heart, becoming a model for prayerfully pondering the great mysteries.

The reading that opened with the shepherds hastening to see the child concludes with their returning to their flocks, glorifying and praising God. Back at their humble occupation, they are changed by what they have seen and heard. E.P.

THE NATIVITY OF THE LORD (CHRISTMAS): DAY

LECTIONARY #16

READING I   Isaiah 52:7–10

A reading from the Book of the Prophet Isaiah

How **beautiful** upon the **mountains**
   are the **feet** of him who brings **glad tidings**,
announcing **peace**, bearing good **news**,
   announcing **salvation**, and saying to **Zion**,
   "Your **God** is **King**!"

Hark! Your sentinels raise a **cry**,
   together they **shout** for joy,
for they see **directly**, before their **eyes**,
   the LORD **restoring** Zion.
Break **out** together in **song**,
   O ruins of Jerusalem!
For the LORD **comforts** his people,
   he **redeems** Jerusalem.
The LORD has **bared** his holy arm
   in the sight of all the **nations**;
all the **ends** of the earth will **behold**
   the **salvation** of our **God**.

An exhortatory reading of joyous news! Be sure to smile with your face, eyes, and voice.

Isaiah = ī-ZAY-uh

Lovingly describe this bearer of good news (today this is you!), then be delighted with the news itself.
Four similar actions, but make each one distinct.

Practice a few different ways of proclaiming "Your God is King" until you've captured all its inherent conviction and exhilaration.

With the word "Hark" stop and listen for yourself. Then hear the news from the sentinels and relay it to the assembly.
Convince the community that breaking out in song is the only appropriate response to this news!

Don't gloss over "O"; fill it with emotion.

Reassure your community—all will be well with the Lord.

Rolling up one's sleeves is a sign of strength and commitment to the task.

A grand, sweeping conclusion. Proclaim slowly and with amazement, satisfaction, joy, pride, or an appropriate emotion of your choice.

READING I   In the readings of Advent and Christmas, a variety of characters announce good news. The prophet Isaiah declares that God will comfort his people, will transform the desolate nation, and give them new names. Angels announce to Zechariah and Mary the miraculous births of sons, and other angels sing to shepherds that the promised son of Mary can be found in a manger. Then the shepherds themselves become bearers of the Good News of Jesus' birth. Today's First Reading, from Isaiah, crackles with energy as he brings the good news to the people in exile.

The glad tidings are especially strong because immediately before this reading, God instructs, "Shake off the dust . . . loose the bonds from your neck, captive daughter Zion!" God is telling the people to prepare for the end of their exile. The greatest assurance of the promise is God's own declaration in verse six: "Here I am!"

Following that assurance, Isaiah's prophecy continues with the portrait of an energetic runner announcing the glad tidings for which the people have been waiting. The God who just told them, "Here I am!" will bring peace and salvation. The glad tiding that God is coming to Jerusalem signifies that the promise is already being fulfilled, even as the people continue in exile. The sentinels on Jerusalem's heights are the first to experience the good news. They see right before their eyes, "the LORD restoring Zion." So great are the glad tidings that even the ruins of Jerusalem will join in festive song.

The good news proclaimed in Isaiah's prophecy brings comfort to the people, and all the nations who had seen Israel con-

For meditation and context:

TO KEEP IN MIND

A *didactic* text makes a point or teaches something. Help your assembly to follow the argument and understand what's being taught.

RESPONSORIAL PSALM   Psalm 98:1, 2–3, 3–4, 5–6 (3c)

R. All the ends of the earth have seen the saving power of God.

Sing to the LORD a new song,
   for he has done wondrous deeds;
his right hand has won victory for him,
   his holy arm.

The LORD has made his salvation known:
   in the sight of the nations he has revealed
      his justice.
He has remembered his kindness and his
      faithfulness
   toward the house of Israel.

All the ends of the earth have seen
   the salvation by our God.
Sing joyfully to the LORD, all you lands;
   break into song; sing praise.

Sing praise to the LORD with the harp,
   with the harp and melodious song.
With trumpets and the sound of the horn
   sing joyfully before the King, the LORD.

A didactic reading showing the unique status of Jesus as Son of God. What does the reading call your community to do after hearing this? Make that the reason you proclaim, and keep that intention uppermost in your mind.

God spoke once through words and actions; now, words and actions are one in Jesus.

Increase your energy as you begin each of the three clauses that describe the Son: "whom he . . . ," "who is . . . ," "who sustains . . . "

refulgence = ree-FUHL-j*nts (radiance or brilliance)

You might show disdain for the "lowly" position of the angels, since Jesus' position is "far superior." The community knows the answers to these rhetorical questions. It's as if you're sharing an inside joke: Can you imagine anyone thinking they're as special as Jesus?

This is the right relationship between Jesus and the angels, and God sees to it.

READING II   Hebrews 1:1–6

A reading from the Letter to the Hebrews

Brothers and sisters:
In times **past**, God spoke in **partial** and **various** ways
   to our ancestors through the **prophets**;
   in these **last** days, he has spoken to **us** through the **Son**,
   whom he made **heir** of all things
   and **through** whom he created the **universe**,
      who is the **refulgence** of his **glory**,
         the very **imprint** of his **being**,
      and who **sustains** all things by his mighty **word**.
      When he had accomplished **purification** from sins,
      he took his **seat** at the **right** hand of the Majesty on **high**,
      as **far** superior to the **angels**
      as the **name** he has inherited is more **excellent** than theirs.

For to **which** of the angels did God ever say:
   You are my **son***; this day I have* **begotten** *you*?
Or again:
   I will be a **father** *to him, and he shall be a* **son** *to me*?
And **again**, when he leads the **firstborn** into the world, he says:
   Let all the **angels** *of God* **worship** *him*.

quered, exiled, and shamed now see the Lord's mighty power in redeeming his people. All the ends of the earth will see God's salvation. This hope-filled news of peace and salvation announced in the sixth century BC was ultimately fulfilled in the birth of the infant king, the prince of peace, the savior. In him, God again says, "Here I am!"

READING II   Letters in the New Testament, like other letters in the first century, ordinarily begin with a salutation identifying the sender and recipients. The Letter to the Hebrews

opens without such a greeting, beginning instead with a theological reflection. The title "to the Hebrews" suggests that this document, whether a real letter or a theological treatise, was directed to Christians of Jewish background. The first words presume knowledge of the Hebrew Scriptures (what we call the Old Testament), reminding the audience how God has spoken to their ancestors through the prophets. In the past, God communicated only in partial and varied ways; we hear many of these prophetic testimonies throughout the liturgical year. Rich and important as they are,

the author of Hebrews says that the prophetic words provide only limited revelation. In these last days, the time in which we are now living, God has spoken definitively and personally through his Son.

   After this introduction, all attention moves to this Son in a hymn that confesses faith, possibly sung in early liturgies. Because God has spoken through the Son, everything that the Son is and does is seen in his relationship to God. God has made him "heir of all things," portraying a privileged Father-Son relationship. The Jewish Christian audience knows well that God

An exhortatory reading which might be best proclaimed with an increasingly quiet intensity rather than exuberant energy—although either could work.

Look carefully at the words in bold. The key to this reading is how you proclaim these operative words; make an intentional choice about each of them.

Emphasize the images of life, light, and darkness.

Pause at the end of this line.

Drop your voice slightly as you describe John in these lines.

Pause at the end of this line.

Raise your voice again as you return to Jesus.

Don't overemphasize the aspects of rejection. Keep it simple, in line with the rest of the reading.

TO KEEP IN MIND

A *narrative* has characters, dialogue, a setting, and action. Help your listeners see the story unfold, keep characters distinct, and be clear about shifts in setting.

GOSPEL   John 1:1–18

A reading from the holy Gospel according to John

[In the **beginning** was the **Word**,
    and the **Word** was with **God**,
    and the Word **was** God.
He was in the beginning **with** God.
All things came to be **through** him,
    and **without** him **nothing** came to be.
What came to be through him was **life**,
    and this life was the **light** of the human race;
the light **shines** in the **darkness**,
    and the darkness has not **overcome** it.]
A man named **John** was sent from **God**.
He came for **testimony**, to testify to the **light**,
    so that all might **believe** through him.
He was **not** the light,
    but came to testify **to** the light.
[The **true** light, which enlightens **everyone**,
    was coming into the world.
He was **in** the world,
    and the world came to be **through** him,
    but the world did not **know** him.
He came to what was his **own**,
    but his own people did not **accept** him.

---

created the universe; now they learn that the Son is God's agent in creating. We see God's own glory in the Son who is "the very imprint of his being." This description of the Son is reminiscent of personified wisdom who possessed divine attributes and participated in creation (Wisdom 7:26), a background that a Jewish Christian audience would recognize.

In addition to personified wisdom imagery, the hymn draws on psalms and prophets to show that the Son is far superior to the angels. Only to his Son does God say, "this day I have begotten you." In its

original context (for example in Psalm 2:7), the word "son" refers to an earthly king, either David or one of his descendants, but in the hymn, it can refer only to Christ, the Son of God. He is so far superior to angels that all the angels are to worship him. Although the word "Gospel" doesn't occur in the hymn, the text is a profound proclamation of the Good News embodied in the Son of God.

GOSPEL   John begins his Gospel with a soaring hymn, one we could consider a musical introduction to his

whole account. Like musical overtures, the opening verses present themes that will be repeated, developed, and varied throughout the symphony of his Gospel. It is a summary of John's Good News and a key to understanding it.

The Letter to the Hebrews began with God speaking of old through the prophets. John's poetry begins long eons before: "In the beginning." The Word that in time was spoken through the prophets existed before all time with God. In Hebrews, we saw the Son as God's agent in creation. John's portrait of the Word is more expan-

Amazing! You are describing us: children of God, born of God.

The climax of the reading—God chooses to take on "flesh," all the messiness of being human. Yet the statement is simple and elegant. Try proclaiming slowly, with a quiet wonder in your voice and face.

You can pick up your pace and energy again here.

Careful with this awkward construction.

Pause briefly to indicate the end of John's quote.

The grace of the new Covenant builds on the grace of the old.

The Good News of today is that the birth of Jesus reveals the unseen God to us all!

> But to those who **did** accept him
>   he gave **power** to become **children** of **God**,
>   to those who **believe** in his name,
>   who were born not by **natural** generation
>   nor by human **choice** nor by a **man's** decision
>   but of **God**.
>   And the **Word** became **flesh**
>   and made his **dwelling** among us,
>   and we **saw** his **glory**,
>   the glory as of the Father's only **Son**,
>   full of **grace** and **truth**.]
> John **testified** to him and **cried** out, saying,
>   "This was **he** of whom I said,
>   'The one who is coming **after** me ranks **ahead** of me
>   because he existed **before** me.'"
> From his **fullness** we have all received,
>   **grace** in place of **grace**,
>   because while the **law** was given through **Moses**,
>   **grace** and **truth** came through Jesus **Christ**.
> No one has ever **seen** God.
> The only **Son**, **God**, who is at the Father's side,
>   has **revealed** him.

[Shorter: John 1:1–5, 9–14 (see brackets)]

TO KEEP IN MIND
Use inflection (the high or low pitch of your voice) to convey attitude and feeling. High pitch expresses intensity and excitement; low pitch expresses sadness, contrition, or solemnity.

---

sive, for all things came to be through him; in him is light and life. Throughout his Gospel, John sets up contrasts, images, and terms with more than one meaning that he first introduces in these opening verses. Light, sometimes synonymous with life, and at other times indicating knowledge and God's presence, is contrasted with darkness, the realm of sin, death, and dearth of knowledge. Darkness is unable to overcome light. The first of his many words with twofold meanings, "overcome" (*katalambano*), can also mean "comprehend."

Darkness is neither able to overcome the light, nor able to understand it.

After the opening poetry, a brief narrative introduces John the Baptist. His role as forerunner to the Messiah (similar to his depiction in the synoptic Gospels) follows immediately after the prologue. John himself is not the light, but his mission is to be a witness to the light. Light is clearly referring to a person, to Jesus who is both Life and Light, accepted by some, but rejected by his own. He is the Word personified who "became flesh and made his dwelling among us"; literally, he "pitched his tent among us." The exalted, eternal Word has entered our world in the humblest of ways. When he proclaims the enfleshment of the Word, John refers to "us" for the first time in his overture. The Word has made his dwelling "among us," and "we saw his glory." God's glory, a radiance of divine presence, shines forth in the Father's only Son, and we have seen God's glory. We have received from his fullness of grace and truth, and received it in abundance. E.P.

THE HOLY FAMILY OF JESUS, MARY, AND JOSEPH

LECTIONARY #17

READING I   Genesis 15:1–6; 21:1–3

A reading from the Book of Genesis

A narrative reading. Recall a time when it was difficult for you to trust God, and bring those emotions to Abram.

The **word** of the Lord came to Abram in a **vision**, saying:
  "Fear **not**, Abram!
    I am your shield;
    I will make your reward **very** great."

With an air of mystery. This is not an everyday occurrence.

But Abram said,
  "**O** Lord GOD, what **good** will your gifts be,
  if I keep on being **childless**

Good news. Make sure Abram knows you care.

  and have as my heir the **steward** of my house, Eliezer?"

With bold confidence. Make this a promise.

Despondent. Abram sees no way out.

Abram continued,
  "**See**, you have given me no **offspring**,

Eliezer = el-ee-AY-zer

  and so one of my **servants** will be my heir."
Then the word of the LORD came to him:
  "**No**, that one shall **not** be your heir;

He repeats his complaint. Increase your intensity, with anger or frustration.

  your **own** issue shall be your heir."
The Lord took Abram **outside** and said,

Console Abram with this promise.

  "**Look** up at the sky and **count** the stars, if you **can**.

This is amazing considering Abram and Sarah's age.

Just **so**," he added, "shall your **descendants** be."

Be expansive in your proclamation to convey the vastness of the sky.

Abram put his **faith** in the LORD,

Speak this line with Abram's feelings—"Ok, I'll trust you."

  who credited it to him as an act of **righteousness**.

Good news.

Today, options are given for the readings. Contact your parish staff to learn which readings will be used.

READING I **Genesis.** The saga of Abram begins when the Lord tells him to leave his native land and go to the land God will show him. He will become a great nation, God promises, even though Abram and his wife Sarai have no children. Their journey takes them from Ur to Canaan, the land God promised to Abram. But still there was no son, no heir. It seemed that God's promise of making Abram a great nation would not be fulfilled. But in today's reading, the Lord renews the promise: Abram receives a prophetic revelation, one that will certainly be fulfilled. The command, "Fear not," and God's words, "I am your shield," are intended to reassure Abram of the vision's authenticity.

Abram, accustomed to being in charge, maintains his authoritative voice even when addressing God, who had said, "Fear not." Abram shows no fear in accusing God! "What good will your gifts be if I keep on being childless?" Since God has given him no children, Abram has chosen Eliezer, his steward, as his heir, a not-very-subtle indictment of God's delay in providing Abram with a son. God's reply is to renew the original promise, amplifying it. More than a single heir, Abram's descendants will be as numerous as the stars that are too vast to count. Now Abram lets go of his questions and accusations, and he puts his faith in the Lord. Faith, in this context, implies trusting the God who has spoken, confident in God's promises. God regards such faith as righteousness, for Abram has placed himself in right relationship to God.

The Lord took **note** of Sarah as he had **said** he would;
>   he **did** for her as he had **promised**.
Sarah became **pregnant** and bore Abraham a **son** in his old age,
>   at the **set** time that God had **stated**.
Abraham gave the name **Isaac** to this son of his
>   whom Sarah bore him.

Or:

READING I   Sirach 3:2–6, 12–14

A reading from the Book of Sirach

God sets a father in **honor** over his children;
>   a mother's authority he **confirms** over her sons.
Whoever **honors** his father **atones** for sins,
>   and **preserves** himself from them.
When he **prays**, he is **heard**;
>   he stores up **riches** who reveres his mother.
Whoever honors his **father** is **gladdened** by children,
>   and, when he **prays**, is **heard**.
Whoever **reveres** his father will live a **long** life;
>   he who **obeys** his father brings **comfort** to his mother.

My **son**, take **care** of your father when he is **old**;
>   grieve him **not** as **long** as he lives.
Even if his **mind** fail, be **considerate** of him;
>   revile him **not** all the days of his **life**;
kindness to a father will not be **forgotten**,
>   **firmly** planted against the **debt** of your sins
>   —a house raised in **justice** to you.

Margin notes:

Share Sarah's joy, and satisfaction that everything turns out as promised!

Slight emphasis on "Abraham"; God has given him a new name for his new destiny (Genesis 17:3–5).

A didactic reading. Proclaim simply, with gentleness and love.

Sirach = SEER-ak; SĪ-ruhk

Honoring one's parents has rewards for one's self as well. Emphasize those rewards (atonement, answered prayer, treasure, children, long life).

The second occurrence of this idea; slowly and deliberately.

Pause after this line.

Proclaim this section as if you are the father, asking your child to be kind to you as you age.

Pause slightly after this line.

Keep your voice up to the end.

The second part of the reading is from several chapters later in Genesis. When the son is finally born to the couple in their old age, Abraham names their son "Isaac," which means "He laughed," perhaps referring to Sarai's laughter when she heard she would have a son (Genesis 18:15).

Sirach. Sirach, also called Ecclesiasticus, was written in Hebrew around 200 BC by Jesus Ben Sira, a teacher who wrote to instruct young men in living wisely. Sirach advises on practical aspects of daily living.

In today's reading, Sirach explains the practical application of how to live in fear of the Lord in family relationships. Advising adult sons, Sirach begins with a statement of God's overall plan in which God sets the father over his children, and the mother has authority over her sons. Following the biblical command to honor your father and your mother (Exodus 20:12; Deuteronomy 5:16) will ensure family harmony and prosperity. Sirach also explains the advantages given to those who keep this commandment: atonement and preservation from sins, prayers that are heard, being gladdened by one's own children, and a long life. In his instruction, we can see Sirach's underlying appreciation of the loving relationship between father and mother.

Although we can easily discern the patriarchal cultural perspective in Sirach's advice, particularly in the final verses, we can expand his teaching regarding honor to fathers to include equally the respect and obedience owed to mothers. His instruction to adult children to care for their aging parents is as relevant today as in the ancient world. Sirach seems to be speaking from experience, the source for much of wisdom instruction. No matter how a parent's physical and mental health may fail,

For meditation and context:

TO KEEP IN MIND

Pause in order to break up separate thoughts, set apart significant statements, or indicate major shifts. Never pause in the middle of a single thought. Your primary guide for pauses is punctuation.

RESPONSORIAL PSALM   Psalm 105:1–2, 3–4, 5–6, 8–9 (7a , 8a)

R. The Lord remembers his covenant for ever.

Give thanks to the LORD, invoke his name;
   make known among the nations
     his deeds.
Sing to him, sing his praise,
   proclaim all his wondrous deeds.

Glory in his holy name;
   rejoice, O hearts that seek the LORD!
Look to the LORD in his strength;
   constantly seek his face.

You descendants of Abraham, his servants,
   sons of Jacob, his chosen ones!
He, the LORD, is our God;
   throughout the earth his
     judgments prevail.

He remembers forever his covenant
   which he made binding for a thousand
     generations
which he entered into with Abraham
   and by his oath to Isaac.

Or:

For meditation and context:

RESPONSORIAL PSALM   Psalm 128:1–2, 3, 4–5 (1)

R. Blessed are those who fear the Lord and walk in his ways.

Blessed is everyone who fears the LORD,
   who walks in his ways!
For you shall eat the fruit of your handiwork;
   blessed shall you be, and favored.

Your wife shall be like a fruitful vine
   in the recesses of your home;
your children like olive plants
   around your table.

Behold, thus is the man blessed
   who fears the LORD.
The LORD bless you from Zion:
   may you see the prosperity of Jerusalem
     all the days of your life.

TO KEEP IN MIND

A *didactic* text makes a point or teaches something. Help your assembly to follow the argument and understand what's being taught.

A didactic reading; proclaim it to help your assembly trust God despite all odds. Keep the phrase "Trust God" in mind throughout.

READING II   Hebrews 11:8, 11–12, 17–19

A reading from the Letter to the Hebrews

Brothers and sisters:
By **faith** Abraham obeyed when he was **called** to go out to a place
   that he was to receive as an **inheritance**;
   he went **out**, not **knowing** where he was to go.
By **faith** he received power to **generate**,
   even though he was **past** the normal age
   —and Sarah **herself** was sterile—
   for he thought that the one who had **made** the promise
     was **trustworthy**.

Emphasize "By faith."

Pause at the comma, as if to say *"although not knowing . . . "*

"By faith" appears again. Heighten this occurrence.

Amazing.

Even more amazing!

care, consideration, and kindness remain ever the responsibility of their children. The benefits of living in wise relationships and showing reverence and obedience to parents is founded on reverence and obedience to God. It will enhance every member of the family and God will never forget.

READING II | **Hebrews.** "Faith is the realization of what is hoped for and evidence of things not seen" (Hebrews 11:1). Beginning with Abel, the author of Hebrews presents people from the Old Testament who are models of such

faith in God. Today's reading centers on the faith of Abraham, whose saga extends from Genesis 12–25. It draws on three episodes in Abraham's story to illustrate his great faith—his trust, obedience, and courage.

The Abraham tradition begins in Genesis 12 with God's call to him to "go forth . . ." and Abraham responded by going "as the LORD directed him." The Letter to the Hebrews emphasizes his faith. Since he didn't know where to go, he had to trust in God. The second example of Abraham's faith is taken from Genesis 15; there, after initially questioning God, he believed that

his elderly, barren wife would conceive a son, as God had promised, even though without a son Abraham was "as good as dead." Abraham's faith is in a person, the God of the promise, as much as in the promise itself. In the third episode, a severe test, Abraham is asked to sacrifice his son Isaac, the child of the promise (Genesis 22). How could Abraham obey and kill the very one who fulfilled the promise? Yet he "offers" (*prosphero*) his son. Although his his sacrifice on the altar was not completed, Abraham had indeed made a true offering by his obedience. This reading

As an aside.

Convey vastness by slowing slightly and emphasizing "numerous" and "countless."

Heighten "By faith" one final time.

Be impressed with Abraham's bold choice.

So it **was** that there came forth from **one man**,
　　himself as good as **dead**,
　　　descendants as **numerous** as the **stars** in the **sky**
　　and as **countless** as the **sands** on the **seashore**.

By **faith** Abraham, when put to the **test**, offered up **Isaac**,
　　and he who had received the **promises** was ready to offer his
　　　only **son**,
　　of **whom** it was said,
　　"Through **Isaac** descendants shall bear your **name**."
He reasoned that **God** was able to raise **even** from the **dead**,
　　and he received Isaac **back** as a **symbol**.

Or:

A didactic reading that gives advice on creating community. Take your time; there's a lot packed in this reading.

Colossians = kuh-LOSH-uhnz

Drop your voice on the parenthetical ("as . . . beloved").

No pause at this comma.

"Even better!" Be eager to share this advice.

Slowly; the last piece which brings it all together. Pause.

Don't lose "richly," a wonderful image.

READING II   Colossians 3:12–21

A reading from the Letter of Saint Paul to the Colossians

[Brothers and sisters:
Put on, as God's **chosen** ones, **holy** and **beloved**,
　　heartfelt **compassion**, **kindness**, **humility**, **gentleness**,
　　　and **patience**,
　　bearing with one another and **forgiving** one another,
　　if one has a grievance against another;
　　as the Lord has forgiven **you**, so must you **also** do.
And over **all** these put on **love**,
　　that is, the bond of **perfection**.
And let the **peace** of Christ **control** your hearts,
　　the **peace** into which you were **also** called in one **body**.
And be **thankful**.
Let the **word** of Christ dwell in you **richly**,
　　as in all **wisdom** you teach and **admonish** one another,
　　singing **psalms**, **hymns**, and spiritual **songs**
　　with **gratitude** in your hearts to God.

looks inside Abraham's mind: if God could bring life to the barren Sarah, Abraham reasoned, when he "was as good as dead," couldn't God also raise his son Isaac from the dead? The letter's author regards Isaac himself as a "symbol" (*parabole*) to Christians who see in it a foreshadowing of Christ's Resurrection. Abraham's faith is a model for our own trusting and obedient faith in the God who fulfills promises, who does the seemingly impossible, and who can "raise even from the dead."

Colossians Paul's exhortation in the reading from Colossians begins with the image of putting on clothing so as to be attired as God's chosen ones. Paul views Baptism as the moment when believers first put on the clothing of Christ. Just before this reading begins he tells the community, "you have taken off the old self . . . and have put on the new self, which is being renewed" (Colossians 3:9–10). Their clothing is thus more than an outer garment that they can easily change, but a sign of their inner and ongoing transformation in Christ. The garments they are now to wear express their conversion from the old way of life to the new. The virtues in which they are clothed are those that Christ himself manifested. As he acted with compassion, kindness, and the whole array of virtues that prefers the good of other people, so too must they. Over all the other garments they put on love, for it creates the bond of perfection, completion, and harmony. Living in Christ's own peace, the believing community is called to form one body, with each one clothed in Christ himself (see also Galatians 3:27).

As Paul used baptismal imagery with reference to clothing, he is likely providing further baptismal instruction in what he

Imagine your community rejoicing together. Convey how that makes you feel.

A grand conclusion.

Pause.

A difficult passage; proclaim out of love for the assembly. Work hard to show that love with your face and voice.

A longer pause than usual before "The Word of the Lord."

And **whatever** you do, in **word** or in **deed**,
    do **everything** in the name of the Lord **Jesus**,
    giving **thanks** to God the Father through him.]

Wives, be subordinate to your husbands,
    as is **proper** in the Lord.
Husbands, **love** your wives,
    and avoid any **bitterness** toward them.
Children, **obey** your parents in **everything**,
    for this is **pleasing** to the Lord.
Fathers, do not **provoke** your children,
    so they may not become **discouraged**.

[Shorter: Colossians 3:12–17 (see brackets)]

This narrative reading contains exhortatory passages.

Be pleased to share this intriguing story. Maintain your pace through this lengthy set-up. Pause at commas except as noted.

No pause here.
Don't emphasize this quote or the flow of the sentence will be obscured.

A slight stress on "and" will keep this phrase connected to the beginning of the sentence. Don't pause until the period.
Pause after this line.

Slow down in this section. Simeon = SIM-ee-uhn

Let your admiration for Simeon show as you describe him.

With an air of mystery.

GOSPEL   Luke 2:22–40

A reading from the holy Gospel according to Luke

[When the days were completed for their **purification**
    according to the law of Moses,
    they took him up to **Jerusalem**
    to **present** him to the **Lord**,]
    just as it is written in the **law** of the Lord,
*Every **male** that opens the **womb** shall be **consecrated**
        to the **Lord**,*
    and to offer the **sacrifice** of
    *a pair of **turtledoves** or two young **pigeons**,*
    in accordance with the **dictate** in the law of the Lord.

Now there was a man in Jerusalem whose name was **Simeon**.
This man was **righteous** and **devout**,
    awaiting the **consolation** of Israel,
    and the Holy Spirit was **upon** him.
It had been **revealed** to him by the Holy Spirit
    that he should not see **death**
    before he had seen the **Christ** of the **Lord**.

---

writes about prayer. When the community gathers for worship, they do so in thanksgiving, letting the Word of Christ make a home in them. The Word "of Christ" has several possible meanings. It can refer to the words about Christ, the words that Christ himself taught; and it can refer to Christ himself, the Word-made-flesh. Three times in this instruction, Paul reminds the baptized to be thankful, a virtue at the heart of Christian prayer and relationships.

The final exhortation is similar to other household codes in the Greco-Roman world of the first century. The relationship

between husbands and wives and children and their parents is standard in household codes, with the normative understanding that the husband is the head. While influenced by the patriarchal milieu, Paul's code goes beyond it. Husbands are to put on the garment of love, not bitterness or excessive control, exhibiting in their homes the transformation expected of the baptized, showing compassion, kindness, and the virtues of Christ himself.

| GOSPEL |
From the opening words of this account of the

Presentation of the Lord, we are in a first-century Jewish milieu. Mary and Joseph act "according to the law of Moses." They travel from Galilee to the holy city Jerusalem to fulfill the requirements of sacrifice dictated in the Law. They bring the offering expected of their social class: two turtle doves or young pigeons.

In the Temple, they meet two other Jewish figures: the righteous and devout Simeon, and the prophetess Anna, who worshiped God night and day with fasting and prayer. The Spirit of God who filled Israel's prophets is present with Simeon, as

He came in the **Spirit** into the temple;
> and when the parents brought in the child **Jesus**
> to perform the custom of the **law** in regard to him,
> he **took** him into his arms and **blessed** God, saying:
>> "**Now**, Master, you may let your servant **go**
>>> in **peace**, according to your **word**,
>> for my eyes have **seen** your **salvation**,
>>> which you prepared in **sight** of all the **peoples**,
>> **a light** for **revelation** to the **Gentiles**,
>>> and **glory** for your people **Israel**."

The child's father and mother were **amazed** at what was said
> about him;
> and Simeon **blessed** them and said to **Mary** his mother,
> "**Behold**, this child is destined
> for the **fall** and **rise** of **many** in Israel,
> and to be a **sign** that will be **contradicted**
> —and you **yourself** a **sword** will pierce—
> so that the thoughts of **many** hearts may be **revealed**."

There was also a **prophetess**, **Anna**,
> the daughter of **Phanuel**, of the tribe of Asher.

She was **advanced** in years,
> having lived **seven** years with her husband after her **marriage**,
> and then as a **widow** until she was **eighty-four**.

She never **left** the temple,
> but worshiped **night** and **day** with **fasting** and **prayer**.

And coming **forward** at that very **time**,
> she gave **thanks** to God and **spoke** about the child
> to **all** who were awaiting the **redemption** of **Jerusalem**.

[When they had **fulfilled** all the prescriptions
> of the law of the Lord,
> they returned to **Galilee**,
> to their own town of **Nazareth**.

The child **grew** and became **strong**, filled with **wisdom**;
> and the favor of **God** was **upon** him.]

[Shorter: Luke 2:22, 39–40 (see brackets)]

Left margin annotations:

Gently; as if speaking to the child. How does Simeon feel?

Raise your energy slowly.

Pause after this line.

With their amazement.

Slight pause before "and."

Slowly; with great importance and enthusiasm.

With some sadness.

A long pause.

Eagerly; the story gets even better!

Phanuel = FAN-yoo-el

Pick up your pace again.

With Anna's energy and excitement.

Pause after this line.

Simply; after all that excitement, they return to family life.

Slowly, with a parent's pride!

---

is noted three times, thereby emphasizing the prophetic character of Simeon's words. As were so many Jews of the first century, Simeon was "awaiting the consolation of the Israel," most likely referring to the Messiah, since the Holy Spirit had revealed that Simeon wouldn't die before he had seen the Christ (Messiah). Simeon's blessing is a canticle, filled with echoes of the Old testament, such as Psalm 98:2: "The Lord has made his victory known; has revealed his triumph in the sight of the nations." When Simeon, inspired by the Spirit, proclaims that the child is "salvation, . . . light for revelation to the Gentiles, and glory for your people Israel," he is announcing that God's promises made through the prophet Isaiah are now fulfilled in the child (for example, see Isaiah 42:6; 4:6). After blessing Mary, Simeon adds a prophecy about future controversy, the division over Jesus that will divide his own people, and that will be a source of sorrow for his mother. The scene then shifts to Anna. Like Simeon, she plays a prophetic role when she announces the advent of "the redemption of Jerusalem" to all who were awaiting it, as was Anna herself.

The account that began with the humble family, faithful to their Jewish traditions, concludes on a similar note. Mary and Joseph have fulfilled everything that the Lord required of them. Jesus himself will grow to maturity in their home in the insignificant town of Nazareth, learning from his Jewish parents, filled with wisdom and God's favor or grace (*charis*). God's favor, manifest in the family of Jesus, Mary, and Joseph, extends far beyond their home, becoming a grace for Jews and Gentiles alike. E.P.

THE EPIPHANY
OF THE LORD

An exhortatory reading; proclaim with heightened emotions. Imagine speaking to someone whose life has been full of darkness and struggle. You are announcing the bad times are over, persuading this person to rejoice.

A very strong opening. Be vigorous as you proclaim this Good News! Contrast the images of light and dark in these lines.

They are so full of the light of the Lord that other nations are naturally attracted to them.

You're telling someone whose eyes have been downcast that they can now look up, and they will see what the Lord has done!

A tender image; soften here.

Renew your energy and really see this rich (literally!) vision unfold before you. Rejoice *with* the listener at their salvation.

Be amazed at the outpouring of wealth and treasure, each greater than the last.

dromedaries = single-humped camels; Midian = MID-ee-uhn; Ephah = EE-fuh

Pause to let the image really sink in before "The word of the Lord."

LECTIONARY #20

READING I   Isaiah 60:1–6

A reading from the Book of the Prophet Isaiah

Rise **up** in splendor, Jerusalem! Your **light** has **come**,
  the **glory** of the Lord **shines** upon you.
See, **darkness** covers the earth,
  and thick **clouds** cover the **peoples**;
but upon **you** the LORD **shines**,
  and **over** you appears his **glory**.
Nations shall walk by your **light**,
  and **kings** by your shining **radiance**.
Raise your eyes and **look** about;
  they all **gather** and **come** to you:
your **sons** come from **afar**,
  and your **daughters** in the arms of their **nurses**.

Then you shall be **radiant** at what you see,
  your heart shall **throb** and **overflow**,
for the **riches** of the sea shall be **emptied** out before you,
  the **wealth** of nations shall be **brought** to you.
Caravans of **camels** shall **fill** you,
  dromedaries from **Midian** and **Ephah**;
all from **Sheba** shall come
  bearing **gold** and **frankincense**,
  and proclaiming the **praises** of the LORD.

READING I The reading from Isaiah introduces a beautiful proclamation of salvation that continues for three chapters (Isaiah 60–62). Isaiah's promise of a future filled with abundance begins with a command to those who will experience it: "Rise up in splendor, Jerusalem!" The imperative is literally twofold, as if to say: "Arise!" and "Be light!" Jerusalem itself is to become light because the Lord's own glory has risen upon them. Glory is a tangible epiphany, or showing of God's presence—all-encompassing, more penetrating and powerful than darkness.

Glory, light, and shining radiance throughout this prophecy symbolize the dawn of a new age of salvation in which the darkness of exile, loss, and even sin, will be transformed.

After Isaiah's initial command, "Rise up in splendor!" he adds more imperatives: "See. . . . Raise your eyes and look about." In order to experience God's radiance, Jerusalem's inhabitants must not focus on the darkness of past exile and present devastation of the land, but raise their eyes to see God's glory appearing over them. Jerusalem will be light because God's own light is shining upon them, creating an

image of reflected light. Shining radiance from Jerusalem means that nations and kings will also see and experience God's radiance. God's graciousness to Jerusalem is thus not solely for their own benefit, but has a universal perspective. God has chosen them so that they may bring God's light to others. The wealth that the nations bring will overflow, as everyone joins in joyful praise of the Lord of light and glory.

READING II In the opening sentence of the reading from Ephesians, Paul, or someone writing in his name,

For meditation and context:

TO KEEP IN MIND
Pay attention to the pace of your reading. Varying the pace gives listeners clues to the meaning of the text. The most common problem for proclaimers new to the ministry is going too fast to be understood.

A didactic reading in which Paul shares the Good News that the whole world, Jews and Gentiles, shares in the promise of Jesus.
Ephesians = ee-FEE=zhuhnz

Paul lays a foundation of credibility before making his point.
Be sure you know the "mystery" he's referring to: that we are all members of the body of Christ.
No pause between "It" and "Spirit."

This is the point; give it importance, and smile with your voice, eyes, and face.

gospel = good news!

A narrative reading with multiple characters and settings. Know each character's feelings and desires and use them in your proclamation. Pause between the many scenes to help the assembly follow the story.

Behold = something amazing is about to happen!
Convey the excitement in the voices of the Magi.

RESPONSORIAL PSALM   Psalm 72:1–2, 7–8, 10–11, 12–13 (11)

R. Lord, every nation on earth will adore you.

O God, with your judgment endow the king,
    and with your justice, the king's son;
he shall govern your people with justice
    and your afflicted ones with judgment.

Justice shall flower in his days,
    and profound peace, till the moon
        be no more.
May he rule from sea to sea,
    and from the River to the ends of the earth.

The kings of Tarshish and the Isles shall
        offer gifts;
    the kings of Arabia and Seba shall bring
        tribute.
All kings shall pay him homage,
    all nations shall serve him.

For he shall rescue the poor when he cries out,
    and the afflicted when he has no one to
        help him.
He shall have pity for the lowly and the poor;
    the lives of the poor he shall save.

READING II   Ephesians 3:2–3a, 5–6

A reading from the Letter of Saint Paul to the Ephesians

Brothers and sisters:
You have heard of the stewardship of God's **grace**
    that was **given** to me for your **benefit**,
    namely, that the **mystery** was made **known** to me by **revelation**.
It was not made known to people in **other** generations
    as it has **now** been revealed
    to his holy **apostles** and **prophets** by the **Spirit**:
    that the **Gentiles** are **coheirs**, **members** of the **same** body,
    and **copartners** in the **promise** in Christ **Jesus** through
        the **gospel**.

GOSPEL   Matthew 2:1–12

A reading from the holy Gospel according to Matthew

When **Jesus** was born in **Bethlehem** of **Judea**,
    in the days of King Herod,
    behold, **magi** from the **east** arrived in Jerusalem, saying,
    "**Where** is the newborn **king** of the **Jews**?

---

explains his ministry through the lens of four theological terms: stewardship (*oikonomia*), grace (*charis*), mystery (*mysterion*), and revelation (*apocalypsis*). *Oikonomia* sometimes refers to Paul's commission to preach to the Gentiles, and more broadly to God's plan of salvation; here, both meanings are woven together, since Paul's ministry is to bring God's plan for the Gentiles to fulfillment, accomplished by God's grace. *Charis*, as Paul explains elsewhere, is given to each member of the body for the common good (1 Corinthians 12:7). Paul's grace is "given [to him] for your benefit." His stew-

ardship of grace entails proclaiming the mystery, Good News previously hidden, but now made known to Paul by revelation. Revelation has a rational content: truth that is uncovered or unveiled. It is also an experience of God's pervasive grace, having a relational as well as intellectual dimension.

As Paul announces the specific content of the revelation, he expands Isaiah's prophecy of universalism. The Gentiles not only walk by the light; they become equal members of the body of Christ. Paul's terminology is creative and emphatic in expressing this mystery revealed by the

Spirit. Three times he uses the prefix *syn* – (co-, indicating "with-ness") with the nouns referring to the Gentiles: they are coheirs, comembers of the body, cosharers in the promise. The new reality requires new language that expresses God's plan being brought to fulfillment.

| GOSPEL | Matthew's Gospel account was written for a primarily |

Christian-Jewish audience, people who needed to understand how Jesus brought their hopes to fulfillment, and also that his story was in continuity with their tradition.

We saw his **star** at its **rising**
　and have **come** to do him **homage**."
When King Herod heard this,
　he was greatly **troubled**,
　and **all Jerusalem** with him.
Assembling all the chief priests and the scribes of the people,
　he **inquired** of them where the Christ was to be **born**.
They said to him, "In **Bethlehem** of **Judea**,
　for **thus** it has been written through the prophet:
　　And **you**, **Bethlehem**, *land of* **Judah**,
　　　are **by no means least** *among the rulers of Judah;*
　　since from you shall come a **ruler**,
　　　who is to **shepherd** *my people* **Israel**."
Then Herod called the magi **secretly**
　and ascertained from them the time of the star's appearance.
He sent them to **Bethlehem** and said,
　"**Go** and search **diligently** for the child.
When you have **found** him, bring me **word**,
　that I **too** may go and do him homage."
After their **audience** with the king they **set** out.
And **behold**, the **star** that they had seen at its rising
　　preceded them,
　until it came and **stopped** over the place where the **child** was.
They were **overjoyed** at seeing the star,
　and on entering the **house**
　they saw the **child** with **Mary** his mother.
They **prostrated** themselves and did him **homage**.
Then they opened their **treasures**
　and offered him gifts of **gold**, **frankincense**, and **myrrh**.
And having been warned in a **dream** not to **return** to Herod,
　they **departed** for their country by **another** way.

homage = HOM-ij

Pause before switching to Herod.
Proclaim these lines with Herod's anxiety.

Let the prophet's joy come through in your voice.
Be sure you emphasize "by no means."

Pause again as Herod returns to the Magi.
Bring an air of conspiracy to his voice, as he tries to hide his actions from the people.

Although we know Herod is insincere, don't make him sound so. He would be very good at hiding it!

Pause as the scene shifts.

You, too, should be overjoyed as you proclaim this meeting!

*prostrated = PROS-trayt*d*
Slight pause after "homage."

List the gifts slowly, with a sense of grandeur, then pause to let the scene settle.
Don't make too much of this dream, lest the story end with a focus on Herod rather than the encounter with Jesus.

Throughout his Gospel, Matthew frequently shows that fulfillment and continuity occurred in a surprising, unexpected way. Sometimes he uses direct citations from the Old Testament, and other times through allusion and imagery. The magi in today's Gospel, following the light of the star, can easily be seen as a fulfillment of Isaiah's prophecy that assures Jerusalem that nations and kings will walk in shining radiance. They are Gentiles seeking the newborn Jewish king, signs both of fulfillment of the prophecy and foreshadowing of mission to the Gentiles. Matthew shows explicitly that Jesus fulfills Jewish expectations by citing the prophet Micah (5:1, 3), combined with 2 Samuel 5:2. For Herod, the prophecy is a means of thwarting God's plan, while the Gentile magi continue their search for the child so they may do him homage. The contrast between their joy and homage and Herod's scheming displays further that God's plans will be fulfilled.

The magi also show fulfillment of Isaiah's prophecy heard in the First Reading, as well as Psalm 72:10–11, with their gifts of gold and frankincense. The gift of myrrh, not included in the prophecies, has long been interpreted as pointing to Christ's future suffering, since it was an aromatic substance used in embalming (see John 19:39).

Through this account, Matthew provides a sense of continuity with the past as well as anticipation for the future. Whether in the ancient story of the Jews, or in the ongoing life of the followers of Jesus, God's plan will be fulfilled. E.P.

SECOND SUNDAY IN ORDINARY TIME

LECTIONARY #65

READING I   1 Samuel 3:3b–10, 19

A reading from the first Book of Samuel

Samuel was **sleeping** in the **temple** of the LORD
   where the **ark** of **God** was.
The LORD **called** to Samuel, who answered, "**Here** I am."
Samuel ran to **Eli** and said, "**Here** I am. You **called** me."
"I did not **call** you," Eli said. "Go back to **sleep**."
So he went back to **sleep.**
Again the LORD called Samuel, who **rose** and went to **Eli.**
"**Here** I am," he said. "You **called** me."
But Eli answered, "I did **not** call you, my **son**. Go back to **sleep**."

At that time Samuel was not **familiar** with the LORD,
   because the LORD had not **revealed** anything to him as yet.
The LORD called Samuel **again**, for the **third** time.
Getting **up** and going to **Eli**, he said, "Here I **am**. You **called** me."
Then Eli **understood** that the LORD was calling the youth.
So he said to Samuel, "Go to **sleep**, and **if** you are **called**, reply,
   '**Speak**, LORD, for your servant is **listening**.'"
When Samuel went to **sleep** in his place,
   the LORD **came** and revealed his **presence**,
   calling out as before, "Samuel, **Samuel**!"
Samuel answered, "**Speak**, for your servant is **listening**."

Samuel **grew** up, and the LORD was **with** him,
   not permitting any **word** of his to be without **effect.**

A narrative. Do you want your assembly to listen as intently, or respond to God as eagerly as Samuel did? Make that the purpose of your proclamation.

With great eagerness.

Eli = EE-lī

This is not a rebuke. Eli states the facts.

As if to calm him from a fitful sleep.

He's certain Eli has been calling him.

In the "voice" of Eli, slowly recognizing what's happening.

Quietly, with gentle care and concern.

Raise your energy; heighten the second "Samuel."

With the same eagerness as before. Pause.

Smile, as if Eli were sharing his pride in Samuel.

READING I The story of Samuel begins long before his call in today's reading. He was the child promised to the barren woman Hannah. In gratitude, she brought him to the temple when he was a boy to serve the Lord under the guidance of the high priest Eli. He even wore the priestly garment called an ephod. While Eli's own sons were described as scoundrels because of their sinful lives, Samuel "was growing in stature and in worth in the estimation of the LORD and the people" (1 Samuel 2:26).

When today's reading begins, the high priest Eli was old and nearly blind, so Samuel attended to Eli's needs as part of his service in the temple. Because prophecy and divine revelation were not common in Samuel's day, it is not surprising that neither Eli nor Samuel immediately recognized that God was speaking to the young man. We can easily imagine Eli calling to Samuel at night, asking if everything is in order in the temple, or requesting personal assistance. The only voice that Samuel expects is Eli's. Each time Samuel hears the call, he immediately answers "Here I am." Although

Samuel at first believes Eli is calling, the young man is humbly obedient. He will display the same humility and obedience in his relationship with the Lord. Following Eli's instructions, Samuel identifies himself as the Lord's servant who is listening. The Word of God that had been so rarely spoken directly to people prior to Samuel's call becomes effective and bears fruit as Samuel takes on his role as judge and prophet. Unlike earlier judges who had more limited sway, "all Israel . . . came to know that Samuel was a trustworthy prophet of the LORD" (1 Samuel 3:20).

For meditation and context:

TO KEEP IN MIND

A didactic reading is usually given out of love for the community. Make sure that love is evident in your proclamation.

A didactic reading In which Paul teaches clearly that the body is good! Keep this in mind throughout your proclamation.

Corinthians = kohr-IN-thee-uhnz

Don't chide; remind us what we should already know.

Don't gloss over this; it's significant that the Lord is not just for the spirit, but also for the body.

"You know this, right?"

Pause after this line.

A simple instruction; state it simply.

This is good news. Smile with your voice, eyes, and face.

Slowly; slight pause after "therefore."

RESPONSORIAL PSALM   Psalm 40:2, 4, 7–8, 8–9, 10 (8a and 9a)

R. Here am I, Lord; I come to do your will.

I have waited, waited for the LORD,
   and he stooped toward me and heard
     my cry.
And he put a new song into my mouth,
   a hymn to our God.

Sacrifice or offering you wished not,
   but ears open to obedience you gave me.
Holocausts or sin-offerings you sought not;
   then said I, "Behold I come."

"In the written scroll it is prescribed for me,
to do your will, O my God, is my delight,
   and your law is within my heart!"

I announced your justice in the vast
   assembly;
   I did not restrain my lips, as you,
     O LORD, know.

READING II   1 Corinthians 6:13c–15a, 17–20

A reading from the first Letter of Saint Paul to the Corinthians

Brothers and sisters:
The body is not for **immorality**, but for the **Lord**,
   and the **Lord** is for the **body**;
   God **raised** the Lord and will also raise **us** by his power.

Do you not **know** that your bodies are members of **Christ**?
But whoever is **joined** to the Lord becomes one **Spirit** with him.
Avoid immorality.
Every **other** sin a person commits is **outside** the body,
   but the **immoral** person sins against his **own** body.
Do you not know that your **body**
   is a **temple** of the Holy **Spirit** within you,
   whom you have from **God**, and that you are not your **own**?
For you have been purchased at a **price**.
Therefore **glorify** God in your **body**.

READING II Corinth was an important city in Paul's mission. He probably spent about a year and a half there, and wrote several letters to the church when he heard about erroneous teaching and immoral behavior occurring in his absence. In today's reading, the problem he addresses is "immorality," *porneia*, a broad term that can refer to any kind of unlawful sexual activity. In order to move the Corinthians to change their behavior, Paul begins by trying to change their understanding, specifically their understanding of the body. Throughout the letter, Paul writes repeatedly about the body, *soma*, expanding and reinterpreting what body means for one's belief and behavior. *Soma* denotes a person as a whole, complex being, and is another way of saying "self." In addition to his explanation regarding sexual immorality, Paul develops the meaning of *soma* in addressing abuses at the Eucharist, factions, exercise of charisms in the church, and the denial of the Resurrection.

Many in Corinth seem to have had little regard for the body, either their own or that of another person. In contrast, Paul explains that the human body is made to be in relationship with the Lord—so closely joined to Christ that each person, each *soma*, becomes one Spirit with him. The body is a temple, a dwelling place of the Holy Spirit. If the Corinthians understand this fundamental identity, then reverence for the body should follow. Rather than defiling the body through sexual immorality, those who are intimately united with Christ glorify God in their bodies.

GOSPEL The prologue of John's Gospel is a poetic introduction to Jesus, John the Baptist, and major

A narrative reading. No one is preaching in this text; it's a series of intimate conversations among two or three. Match your overall intensity with those conversations.

What does John feel? Amazement, awe, excitement? Bring your choice to your proclamation.

Drop your voice on the parenthetical phrase.

Invite, with a welcoming smile.

Pause after this line.

With energy and excitement!

Pleased, and welcoming.

Cephas = SEE-fuhs

TO KEEP IN MIND

In a narrative, find an emotion or point of view for each character, keeping in mind that these might change during the reading.

GOSPEL   John 1:35–42

A reading from the holy Gospel according to John

John was standing with two of his disciples,
    and as he watched **Jesus** walk by, he said,
    "**Behold**, the **Lamb** of **God**."
The two disciples **heard** what he said and **followed** Jesus.
Jesus **turned** and saw them following him and said to them,
    "What are you **looking** for?"
They said to him, "**Rabbi**"—which translated means **Teacher**—,
    "where are you **staying**?"
He said to them, "**Come**, and you will **see**."
So they **went** and saw where Jesus was staying,
    and they **stayed** with him that day.
It was about four in the afternoon.
Andrew, the brother of Simon **Peter**,
    was **one** of the two who **heard** John and **followed** Jesus.
He **first** found his own brother **Simon** and told him,
    "We have found the **Messiah**" —which is translated **Christ**—.
Then he **brought** him to Jesus.
Jesus **looked** at him and said,
    "You are **Simon** the son of **John**;
    you will be called **Cephas**"—which is translated **Peter**.

---

theological themes of John's account. The narrative that follows serves similarly as a prose introduction. Both poetry and prose are directed to all who hear the Good News in order to draw them into the story of Jesus and elicit a response of faith.

Today's reading is the dramatic encounter of Jesus with his first followers. It begins with John the Baptist's directing his disciples to Jesus as the Lamb of God, a designation that may refer to the paschal Lamb, the gentle lamb led to slaughter, the suffering servant of Isaiah, or the apocalyptic lamb who will destroy evil. The

symbolism in John's Gospel often has multiple layers of meaning.

Jesus asks John's curious disciples, "What are you looking for?" These are Jesus' first words in the Gospel; he addresses his question to everyone who would follow him. "To look for" or "to seek" (*zeteo*) is a motif in John's Gospel signifying both an intense search and deep desire. Jesus invites those who are genuine searchers, "Come, and you will see." The two verbs combined indicate the process of coming to faith in Jesus.

Andrew, one of John's disciples who followed Jesus, has begun his faith journey of coming after Jesus, for he tells his brother Simon Peter, "We have found the Messiah." Our attention immediately shifts to Simon, given his new name Cephas by Jesus. Jesus' initial question "What are you looking for?" means that Cephas, and anyone who seeks Jesus, must "come and see" to gain a fuller understanding of Jesus' messiahship. E.P.

THIRD SUNDAY
IN ORDINARY TIME

LECTIONARY #68

A narrative with a point, not a history lesson. Proclaim this to encourage your assembly to respond just as eagerly to the Word proclaimed to them as Nineveh responds to Jonah.
Jonah = JOH-nuh

This should sound like a very important assignment.
Nineveh = NIN-uh-vuh

Don't throw away this line; stress that it's a big city.
Emphasize the immediacy of their response.

Don't make too much of this line, since it comes in the context of the city's decision to repent.
Slow down, and be pleased to report this good news!

Pause after this line.

How does God feel? Compassionate, pleased, surprised? Proclaim this line with God's emotion.

A happy ending!

READING I   Jonah 3:1–5, 10

A reading from the Book of the Prophet Jonah

The **word** of the L ORD came to **Jonah**, saying:
    "**Set** out for the great city of **Nineveh**,
    and **announce** to it the message that I will **tell** you."
So Jonah made **ready** and **went** to Nineveh,
    according to the L ORD's **bidding**.
Now Nineveh was an **enormously large** city;
    it took **three** days to go through it.
Jonah began his **journey** through the city,
    and had gone but a **single** day's walk announcing,
    "**Forty** days more and Nineveh shall be **destroyed**,"
when the people of Nineveh **believed** God;
    they proclaimed a **fast**
    and **all** of them, **great** and **small**, put on **sackcloth**.

When God **saw** by their actions how they **turned** from their
        evil way,
    he **repented** of the evil that he had **threatened** to do to them;
    he did **not** carry it out.

READING I   "The word of the L ORD came to Jonah," is a typical introduction to a divinely inspired message to a prophet of Israel. The rest of the story of Jonah is anything but typical, making the book and the prophet unique in the prophetic tradition. More narrative than other prophetic books, the Book of Jonah describes the most reluctant of prophets; further, God calls him not to preach to his own people but to those of the great city of Nineveh, known in the ancient world for its brutality.

Our reading omits an important phrase in the introduction: God's word came to Jonah "a second time." The first time, Jonah attempted to flee the divine commission, resulting in the well-known story of Jonah and the great fish. When the second call comes, Jonah "went to Nineveh, according to the L ORD's bidding." The rapidity of his response seems like an attempt to get the unpleasant task quickly completed. Reluctant though he is, Jonah does seem content to announce Nineveh's impending doom. Surprisingly, all the people of Nineveh repent and believe in God.

The verses omitted in today's reading describe the extent of their conversion, which includes a royal decree commanding that all must turn from their evil and violence. Their turning from evil moves God to turn away from the threat that Jonah had proclaimed. The brief description of God refraining from punishing Nineveh reveals God's mercy that extends beyond Israel to one of their greatest enemies. Jonah is not so forgiving! He was "greatly displeased" and became angry.

The strangeness of Jonah's story has led to a wide diversity of interpretations.

For meditation and context:

TO KEEP IN MIND

Pay attention to the pace of your reading. Varying the pace gives listeners clues to the meaning of the text. The most common problem for proclaimers new to the ministry is going too fast to be understood.

An exhortatory reading. Proclaim so as to help your assembly focus on what's important.

Corinthians = kohr-IN-thee-uhnz

Match your energy with Paul's sense of urgency.

Slowly increase your intensity through these lines.

Pause after this line.

Put a hint of joy in this line, since what comes after the world passes away is even better than the world we know now.

A reading with both narrative and exhortatory elements, this is really two readings in one. Decide what they ask of your listeners and proclaim toward those intentions—perhaps "Repent and believe," or "Follow Jesus."

Slowly and distinctly; John's arrest is an abrupt start.
Exhortatory. Raise your voice and energy so this sounds like a quote. These lines summarize the theme of Jesus' ministry. Pause after this line.

RESPONSORIAL PSALM   Psalm 25:4–5, 6–7, 8–9 (4a)

R. Teach me your ways, O Lord.

Your ways, O Lord, make known to me;
    teach me your paths,
guide me in your truth and teach me,
    for you are God my savior.

Remember that your compassion, O Lord,
    and your love are from of old.
In your kindness remember me,
    because of your goodness, O Lord.

Good and upright is the Lord;
    thus he shows sinners the way.
He guides the humble to justice
    and teaches the humble his way.

READING II   1 Corinthians 7:29–31

A reading from the first Letter of Saint Paul to the Corinthians

I **tell** you, brothers and sisters, the time is running **out**.
From **now** on, let those having **wives** act as **not** having them,
    those **weeping** as **not** weeping,
    those **rejoicing** as **not** rejoicing,
    those **buying** as **not** owning,
    those **using** the world as not using it **fully**.
For the world in its **present** form is **passing away**.

GOSPEL   Mark 1:14–20

A reading from the holy Gospel according to Mark

After **John** had been **arrested**,
    Jesus came to **Galilee** proclaiming the **gospel** of God:
    "**This** is the time of **fulfillment**.
The kingdom of **God** is at **hand**.
Repent, and **believe** in the **gospel**."

Some scholars see the whole book as a parable, rather than a historical narrative. Jonah's humorous attempt to escape God's call is characteristic of a work of fiction intended to teach moral and spiritual lessons. Whatever its genre, the book has important theological messages: the power of God's Word; the universal call to repentance; and the vastness of God's compassion.

 READING II In the verses just before today's reading from First Corinthians, Paul writes to the church about how to live in the present age with the understanding that there will be an age to come. Throughout all his letters, the church's belief in this future age underlies Paul's teaching and his exhortations. Today's text begins with his explanation that the time until God's arrival to bring the age to come is very short. The word he uses for "time" is *kairos*, indicating the time designated by God, the appointed time of fulfilling God's promises and will. In the context of today's reading, the *kairos* refers to Christ's coming in glory at his *parousia*. Yet those who believe in Christ have already experienced God's *kairos*. Christ's coming at the Incarnation was a *kairos*, as was his proclamation of the reign of God, his Death, and his Resurrection. The Christ who will come in the future has already come among us, as we await his future coming. That imbues all realities of this present life with an already-and-not-yet tension—whether we are marrying, weeping, rejoicing, buying, or engaged in any other activities of daily life. Paul writes of these present experiences with a poetic cadence that opens up another way of looking at our ordinary existence. The

Narrative. Slowly; the line is full of important details.

As he passed by the Sea of **Galilee**,
    he saw **Simon** and his brother **Andrew** casting their **nets**
        into the sea;
    they were **fishermen**.
Jesus said to them,

Make it an attractive offer, with an inviting smile and Jesus' excitement to share his mission.

    "Come after **me**, and I will make you fishers of **men**."
Then they **abandoned** their nets and **followed** him.

Pause after this line.

Zebedee = ZEB-uh-dee

He walked along a little **farther**
    and saw **James**, the son of **Zebedee**, and his brother **John**.

The emphasis is on "them" rather than "called."

They **too** were in a boat mending their **nets**.
Then he called **them**.

No pause here.

So they **left** their father Zebedee in the boat

Slight pause after "hired men."

    along with the hired men and **followed** him.

THE 4 STEPS OF *LECTIO DIVINA* OR PRAYERFUL READING

1. *Lectio:* Read a Scripture passage aloud slowly. Notice what phrase captures your attention and be attentive to its meaning. Silent pause.

2. *Meditatio:* Read the passage aloud slowly again, reflecting on the passage, allowing God to speak to you through it. Silent pause.

3. *Oratio:* Read it aloud slowly a third time, allowing it to be your prayer or response to God's gift of insight to you. Silent pause.

4. *Contemplatio:* Read it aloud slowly a fourth time, now resting in God's word.

---

things of the present age to which people cling, the world even with its grandeur and loveliness, are only a glimpse and a beginning of the glory of the age to come.

GOSPEL | Jesus' first words in Mark's Gospel are a proclamation of his own Good News: the appointed time (*kairos*) of God's in-breaking is fulfilled; God's kingdom has drawn near, is right on the point of being inaugurated. That the proclamation of God's kingdom is Good News means that God's reign is not like the kingdoms that Jesus' audience knew. The

Roman Empire of that day stretched throughout the Mediterranean world, and exercised political, military, and economic control over all the peoples within its boundaries. Besides the emperor Augustus, there were lesser kings, such as King Herod. When Jesus begins his ministry with the proclamation of God's kingdom, John the Baptist has already been arrested. King Herod will have John beheaded, one of the many tangible signs of the brutality and injustice of Herod's kingdom. What a contrast is the Kingdom of God that Jesus proclaims! The response to Herod's kingdom is

fear and cringing compliance. The response to God's kingdom is repentance (*metanoia*, or conversion of heart) and belief in his Good News.

Immediately after announcing the Kingdom of God, Jesus calls his first disciples. Without using the words "repentance" or "belief," Mark shows that Simon, Andrew, James, and John exhibited both repentance and belief, albeit in the very initial stages of their lifelong response to Jesus and the Good News of the Kingdom of God. E.P.

FOURTH SUNDAY IN ORDINARY TIME

An exhortatory reading. Decide what intentions and emotions the story implies for Moses, God, and the people. What do they want and how do they feel?

Deuteronomy = doo-ter-AH-nuh-mee

Good news. Moses wants to reassure the people that God's care is unending.

Horeb = HOHR-eb; no pause here.

Quickly, with some fear and anxiety.

Pause after this line.

"Good idea!"

How does God feel sharing these plans? Confident, pleased, excited? Make your choice clear in your voice and face.

Don't stress "him" or it will sound like the line refers to the prophet rather than the one who will not listen.

Proclaim "he shall die" slowly and with deliberate finality.

LECTIONARY #71

READING I Deuteronomy 18:15–20

A reading from the Book of Deuteronomy

Moses spoke to all the people, saying:
    "A **prophet** like **me** will the LORD, your God, raise **up** for you
    from among your **own kin**;
    to **him** you shall listen.
This is **exactly** what you **requested** of the LORD, your God,
      at **Horeb**
    on the day of the **assembly**, when you said,
    'Let us not **again** hear the **voice** of the LORD, our God,
    nor see this great **fire** any more, lest we **die**.'
And the LORD said to me, 'This was **well** said.
I will **raise** up for them a **prophet** like you from among their **kin**,
    and will put **my** words into his mouth;
    he shall tell them **all** that I **command** him.
Whoever will not **listen** to my words which he speaks
     in my name,
    I **myself** will make him answer for it.
But if a prophet **presumes** to speak in my name
    an oracle that I have **not** commanded him to speak,
    or speaks in the name of **other** gods, **he** shall **die**.'"

READING I Throughout the Torah, Moses is the leader chosen by God to bring the people out of Egypt and to communicate God's Law to them. Besides being the leader and lawgiver, Moses is a prophet; he is in fact a paradigmatic prophet for later prophets in Israel. When Moses tells the people that God will raise up another prophet like him, he gives a brief summary of essential characteristics of a prophet. First, unlike other offices for which people were trained, appointed, or gained through a dynasty, a prophet is raised up by God. Since God alone is the one who creates a prophet, the prophet is independent of institutions such as kingship or priesthood. Prophets often are a lonely voice challenging accepted practices and ways of thinking. In that sense, the prophet seems to be an outsider. Yet, God raises prophets "from among your own kin." Coming from within Israel, the prophet also has an insider perspective in calling his own people to repentance. The people themselves wanted such a prophet, and even requested it at Horeb (Deuteronomy 5:23–26), though they repeatedly failed to heed the prophetic message. Moses exhorts them to listen, for it is God's own words, not those of the prophet that come forth from his mouth—another essential quality of authentic prophecy.

We can see Moses' prophecy fulfilled in two ways. God did repeatedly send prophets like Moses throughout their history. Their frequent declaration, "the word of the LORD," assures their audience that God is speaking through them. An even greater fulfillment is found in Jesus. A prophet like Moses, Jesus was raised up by God from among his own kin. He communicated God's Word so perfectly that he was

For meditation and context:

TO KEEP IN MIND
Use inflection (the high or low pitch of your voice) to convey attitude and feeling. High pitch expresses intensity and excitement; low pitch expresses sadness, contrition, or solemnity.

A didactic reading, continuing from last Sunday's Reading II. Proclaim so as to help your assembly stay focused on what's important.

Corinthians = kohr-IN-thee-uhnz

Paul gives this instruction out of love. Do the same for your assembly.

anxious about = focused on

Keep your pace up so these thoughts stay together.
Be single-minded!

Pause after this line.
Slower from here to the end.

Here is good advice for all, regardless of marital state. Slowly and deliberately.

RESPONSORIAL PSALM   Psalm 95:1–2, 6–7, 7–9 (8)

R. If today you hear his voice, harden not your hearts.

Come, let us sing joyfully to the LORD;
    let us acclaim the rock of our salvation.
Let us come into his presence with
        thanksgiving;
    let us joyfully sing psalms to him.

Come, let us bow down in worship;
    let us kneel before the LORD who made us.
For he is our God,
    and we are the people he shepherds,
        the flock he guides.

Oh, that today you would hear his voice:
    "Harden not your hearts as at Meribah,
        as in the day of Massah in the desert,
    where your fathers tempted me;
        they tested me though they had seen
            my works."

READING II   1 Corinthians 7:32–35

A reading from the first Letter of Saint Paul to the Corinthians

Brothers and sisters:
I should like you to be **free** of **anxieties**.
An **unmarried** man is anxious about the things of the **Lord**,
    how he may **please** the Lord.
But a **married** man is anxious about the things of the **world**,
    how he may please his **wife**, and he is **divided**.
An unmarried **woman** or a **virgin** is anxious about the things
        of the **Lord**,
    so that she may be **holy** in both **body** and **spirit**.
A **married** woman, on the other hand,
    is anxious about the things of the **world**,
    how she may please her **husband**.
I am telling you this for your own **benefit**,
    not to impose a **restraint** upon you,
    but for the sake of **propriety**
    and adherence to the Lord without **distraction**.

himself the Word made flesh, the very embodiment of God's prophetic Word.

READING II Paul's commentary on being married or unmarried is best understood in the context of his expectation of the Lord's coming again, expressed in the verse just before our reading begins: "the world in its present form is passing away," and that includes institutions such as marriage and slavery. If the world we have known and experienced is soon to be gone, being anxious about "the things of the world" is a misplaced anxiety.

Although Paul begins by saying he would like the Corinthians to be free from anxiety, he goes on to describe the anxiety that everyone, married or unmarried, male or female, experiences. Paul wants people to be anxious about the right things. In his view, both married men and married women are anxious to please their spouse. They thus divide their concerns between devotion to their spouse and devotion to the Lord, or between "the things of the world" and "the things of the Lord." On the other hand, unmarried women and men are anxious about the things of the Lord, and

have undivided hearts. Their adherence to the Lord means that unmarried women and men prepare for his coming without the distraction and responsibilities of marriage.

Paul is sometimes accused of having a bias against women. However in this passage, the observations that he makes about men and women are comparable. A married man is concerned how he may please his wife, and a married woman how to please her husband. We see a mutuality in their relationship that remains valid and positive.

A narrative reading in which a lot is happening; take your time.

Capernaum = kuh-PER-nee-*m; kuh-PER-n*m

Proclaim this line as if the people were speaking.

Pause after this line.

As if in pain.

With a sinister tone.

Proclaim the word "rebuked" sharply.

With real force.

Quickly; slight pause after "cry."

Convey the crowd's amazement and excitement.

Impressed.

Incredulous! Pause.

Don't drop your energy; reflect the excitement of the people about Jesus.

TO KEEP IN MIND

Pause in order to break up separate thoughts, set apart significant statements, or indicate major shifts. Never pause in the middle of a single thought. Your primary guide for pauses is punctuation.

GOSPEL   Mark 1:21–28

A reading from the holy Gospel according to Mark

Then they came to Capernaum,
    and on the sabbath **Jesus** entered the synagogue and **taught**.
The people were **astonished** at his teaching,
    for he taught them as one having **authority** and not as
        the **scribes**.
In their synagogue was a man with an **unclean spirit**;
    he **cried** out, "What have you to **do** with us, Jesus of Nazareth?
Have you come to **destroy** us?
I **know** who you are—the **Holy** One of **God**!"
Jesus **rebuked** him and said,
    "**Quiet**! Come **out** of him!"
The unclean spirit **convulsed** him and with a loud **cry** came out
    of him.
All were **amazed** and asked one another,
    "What **is** this?
A **new** teaching with **authority**.
He commands even the unclean **spirits** and they **obey** him."
His **fame** spread **everywhere** throughout the **whole** region
    of Galilee.

GOSPEL   After Jesus announces the advent of the Kingdom of God, he begins his public ministry in Galilee. Capernaum is the center of Jesus' ministry in Galilee, the city of his first teaching and miracles in Mark's Gospel. The Greek text introducing today's reading says that Jesus immediately (*euthus*) entered the synagogue; "immediately" is a favorite word in Mark's Gospel that highlights the urgency of Jesus' mission. This first miracle introduces us to important features of Jesus' ministry that occur over and over in all of the Gospels: Sabbath, teaching, healing,

and authority. The first action of Jesus is teaching; the custom was for an adult male to teach on the Sabbath in the synagogue. Jesus' teaching was extraordinary in that he taught with authority, rather than relying on the opinions and interpretations of others. He continues to exhibit his authority by rebuking an unclean spirit. Those gathered in the synagogue would have been shocked by the presence of the man with an unclean spirit, for such an unholy, defiled person would not be allowed in synagogue or Temple. Rather than expelling the man, Jesus expels the demon. The

unclean sprit knows Jesus' identity and calls out his name and title, for it recognizes a power and authority far superior to its own. The command of Jesus, "Quiet! Come out of him!" is sufficient to conquer the evil force within the man.

Then the synagogue crowd recognizes Jesus' authority on a deeper level. His authority is more than powerful Sabbath teaching; Jesus' authority extends to his power over evil. His authority is evidence that the Kingdom of God has indeed come near. E.P.

FIFTH SUNDAY
IN ORDINARY TIME

An exhortatory reading, and definitely not good news. Don't be afraid to fully express Job's misery and hopelessness. Use the same energy you'd use for any exhortatory reading.

Job = johb

Ask the assembly, "Don't you agree?" Use care not to drop your voice at the end of these lines.
Don't let your intensity fade; there is a tinge of anger that drives this lament.

Quicken your pace to convey restlessness.

Emphasize the images of the shuttle and the wind. Slowly and with a wistful melancholy.

Drop your tone slowly to the end.

TO KEEP IN MIND
Exhortatory texts make an urgent appeal to listeners. They may encourage, warn, or challenge, and often include a call to action. You must convey the urgency and passion behind the words.

LECTIONARY #74

READING I   Job 7:1–4, 6–7

A reading from the Book of Job

Job spoke, saying:
>   Is not man's life on earth a **drudgery**?
>>   Are not his days those of **hirelings**?
>   He is a **slave** who longs for the **shade**,
>>   a **hireling** who waits for his **wages**.
>   So **I** have been assigned **months** of misery,
>>   and **troubled** nights have been **allotted** to me.
>   If in **bed** I say, "**When** shall I arise?"
>>   then the night **drags** on;
>>   I am filled with **restlessness** until the dawn.
>   My days are **swifter** than a weaver's **shuttle**;
>>   they come to an **end** without **hope**.
>   **Remember** that my life is like the **wind**;
>>   I shall not see **happiness** again.

READING I   Most people know of Job, a man afflicted by extreme sufferings, described in the opening scenes of the book. There we learn that Job's suffering came about because "Satan," the adversary, protested that Job was righteous only because he was prosperous in every way. If his fortune were reversed, surely Job would curse God. Let him suffer, and see what happens!

As Job's friends see his horrendous change of fortune, they give lengthy explanations for the cause, which only amplifies Job's suffering. The long complaint we hear in today's reading is, in part, Job's response to his friend Eliphaz, who suggested that Job must have brought the suffering upon himself; it is God's way of punishing and disciplining the guilty Job. In reply, Job looks at the plight of all humanity as little more than the life of a hireling or a slave. Although he addresses his agonized complaint to the pompous Eliphaz, Job is really speaking so that God will know that Job is innocent.

Days, months, nights, dawn: with the time-focused terminology, Job laments that there is no moment in which he can be free from his agony. His inescapable troubles have simply "been assigned" and "allotted" to him. He doesn't need to say who has done the assigning, for it is only God who has such power. Even in the vigorous complaint in today's reading, Job does not curse God. Like lamenters in the psalms, Job pours out his agony before God. Job's anguish and the unsatisfactory lectures of his friends are attempts from Israel's wisdom tradition to find reasons for human suffering, for which they find no easy explanation.

READING II   Most of Paul's First Letter to the Corinthians consists

54

For meditation and context:

TO KEEP IN MIND

A *didactic* text makes a point or teaches something. Help your assembly to follow the argument and understand what's being taught.

A didactic reading in which Paul stresses his own sense of obligation and privilege as a preacher of the Gospel as he tries to reassert his authority as their teacher.

Corinthians = kohr-IN-thee-uhnz

Bring Paul's passion for the Gospel to your proclamation.

recompense = REK-uhm-pens
Sometimes we do our job willingly; but even when we're not willing, we know we still have to do our job.

Be eager to share the Gospel with the assembly.
The Gospel is so valuable, Paul could easily demand "payment" for sharing it.

"I am free to do as I wish."

You, too, "become" someone else when you proclaim, for the sake of your assembly!
The Word of God you proclaim to the assembly is also a source of life for you. How does that enhance your proclamation?

RESPONSORIAL PSALM   Psalm 147:1–2, 3–4, 5–6 (3a)

R. Praise the Lord, who heals the brokenhearted.
or
R. Alleluia.

Praise the LORD, for he is good;
　　sing praise to our God, for he is gracious;
　　it is fitting to praise him.
The LORD rebuilds Jerusalem;
　　the dispersed of Israel he gathers.

He heals the brokenhearted
　　and binds up their wounds.
He tells the number of the stars;
　　he calls each by name.

Great is our Lord and mighty in power;
　　to his wisdom there is no limit.
The LORD sustains the lowly;
　　the wicked he casts to the ground.

READING II   1 Corinthians 9:16–19, 22–23

A reading from the first Letter of Saint Paul to the Corinthians

Brothers and sisters:
If I preach the **gospel**, this is no reason for me to **boast**,
　　for an **obligation** has been **imposed** on me,
　　and **woe** to me if I do **not** preach it!
If I do so **willingly**, I have a **recompense**,
　　but if **unwillingly**, then I have been entrusted with
　　　a **stewardship**.
What then is my recompense?
That, when I **preach**,
　　I offer the gospel **free** of charge
　　so as not to make full use of my **right** in the gospel.

Although I am **free** in regard to all,
　　I have made myself a **slave** to all
　　so as to win over as **many** as possible.
To the **weak** I became **weak**, to win **over** the weak.
I have become **all** things to **all**, to save at least **some**.
All this I do for the sake of the **gospel**,
　　so that I **too** may have a **share** in it.

of teaching and exhortation to correct Corinthian misbelief and misbehavior. In today's reading, Paul changes focus as he writes about himself. Everything he says throughout this reading is in the first person singular in which Paul provides an emphatic, passionate explanation of his vocation. He says that the very core of his ministry is to preach the Gospel, that is, to be an evangelist announcing the Good News of Jesus. He does not boast about his preaching, for he received his call as an obligation or necessity, *anagke*, indicating the condition under which slaves work.

Paul repeatedly identifies himself as a slave (*doulos*) to Christ, not in a servile status, but as one whose whole life and obedience is given to his Lord. Being a slave for Christ is paradoxical, for there is a profound freedom in fulfilling the assigned tasks. Paul extends the dual status of being free and being a slave to his relationship with the Corinthian community. He explains that he has made himself a slave to those to whom he brings the Gospel. He identifies himself with the weak for the same reason. Paul has freely "become all things to all" for the sake of the Gospel. Given widespread divi-

sions in the Corinthian community, Paul presents himself as an evangelist who works for the benefit of everyone, with no distinctions. Paul has preached his Gospel free of charge, but the preaching itself has its own reward. Paul's recompense is to share in the power of the Good News he has been bringing to others.

GOSPEL The rapid pace of Mark's Gospel continues as Jesus' disciples immediately tell him about the fever afflicting Simon's mother-in-law. In a tender gesture that ignores any fear of

A narrative reading. Contrast Jesus' calm and focus with the excitement and anxiety of those around him.

Slight pause after "Andrew."

Slowly and simply.

Amazed! Pause.

Keep your pace up to convey the busyness of this scene.

Pause after this line.

A bit quieter, to suggest the hour and solitude.

Immediately raise your energy and pace on this interruption.

Frustrated.

Jesus is calm and dedicated to his mission.

Good news. Smile with your voice, eyes, and face.

Emphasize the expansiveness of his ministry.

TO KEEP IN MIND

Be careful not to "swallow" words by mumbling. Articulate carefully so that every word is clearly heard, especially at the end of lines.

GOSPEL   Mark 1:29–39

A reading from the holy Gospel according to Mark

On leaving the **synagogue**
   Jesus entered the house of **Simon** and **Andrew** with **James**
      and **John**.
Simon's **mother-in-law** lay sick with a **fever**.
They **immediately** told him about her.
He **approached**, **grasped** her hand, and helped her **up**.
Then the fever **left** her and she **waited** on them.

When it was **evening**, after sunset,
   they brought to him all who were **ill** or possessed by **demons**.
The **whole** town was gathered at the door.
He cured **many** who were **sick** with various **diseases**,
   and he drove out many **demons**,
      not permitting them to **speak** because they **knew** him.

Rising very early before dawn, he **left**
   and went off to a **deserted** place, where he **prayed**.
Simon and those who were with him **pursued** him
   and on **finding** him said, "Everyone is **looking** for you."
He told them, "Let us go **on** to the nearby **villages**
   that I may preach there **also**.
For **this purpose** have I come."
So he went into their **synagogues**,
   preaching and driving out **demons** throughout the **whole**
      of Galilee.

---

touching the ill, Jesus grasps her hand. Then he "helped her up"; literally, he "raised her up" (*egeiro*), a verb used in Resurrection accounts. Her healing is a sign of the fullness of life in the Kingdom of God and foreshadows the Resurrection. Once healed, she "waited on them." Here Mark uses another verb rich in meaning; her action is one of service (*diakoneo*) that describes Christian ministry. Once healed, she participates in the mission of Jesus' disciples.

   After the quiet event of the cure of Simon's mother-in-law, Mark presents a crowded, noisy scene of the "whole town"

seeking healing from various diseases and demon possession. Only the demons cast out by Jesus know him, for he has shown a power greater than their own. Jesus' forbidding the demons to speak, like his telling people not to proclaim his identity, occurs elsewhere in Mark's Gospel. The time has not yet arrived for anyone to announce his identity. Only when Jesus has completed his life, Death, and Resurrection will people realize the full meaning of Jesus as Messiah and Son of God.

   After his strenuous actions in these scenes, Jesus withdraws to the desert to

pray. Mark briefly narrates Jesus' time alone, and brief must have been his respite. His own disciples track him down, and remind him that people are looking for him. Jesus then continues his ministry, preaching and driving out demons in fulfillment of the purpose for which he came. E.P.

SIXTH SUNDAY IN ORDINARY TIME

LECTIONARY #77

READING I   Leviticus 13:1–2, 44–46

A reading from the Book of Leviticus

The LORD said to **Moses** and **Aaron**,
   "If someone has on his skin a **scab** or **pustule** or **blotch**
   which appears to be the sore of **leprosy**,
   he shall be brought to **Aaron**, the **priest**,
   or to one of the priests among his **descendants**.
If the man **is** leprous and unclean,
   the priest shall **declare** him unclean
   by reason of the **sore** on his head.

"The one who **bears** the sore of leprosy
   shall keep his garments **rent** and his head **bare**,
   and shall muffle his **beard**;
   he shall cry out, '**Unclean, unclean!**'
As long as the sore is on him he shall **declare** himself unclean,
   since he is in **fact** unclean.
He shall dwell **apart**, making his abode **outside** the camp."

RESPONSORIAL PSALM   Psalm 32:1–2, 5, 11 (7)

R. I turn to you, Lord, in time of trouble, and you fill me with the joy of salvation.

Blessed is he whose fault is taken away,
   whose sin is covered.
Blessed the man to whom the LORD imputes
   not guilt,
   in whose spirit there is no guile.

Then I acknowledged my sin to you,
   my guilt I covered not.
I said, "I confess my faults to the LORD,"
   and you took away the guilt of my sin.

Be glad in the LORD and rejoice, you just;
   exult, all you upright of heart.

A didactic reading. These laws may sound harsh, but they are designed to protect the community from contagious disease. Keep your tone light so God doesn't sound angry or judgmental.
Leviticus = lih-VIT-ih-kuhs

Aaron = AYR-uhn
Convey God's concern about the seriousness of this.

leprous = LEP-ruhs

Keep the instructions simple, with no disdain.

Raise your voice but don't shout.

Imagine how difficult it would be to send someone away from the community, even for its protection. Put a hint of sadness in your tone.

For meditation and context:

TO KEEP IN MIND
Pray the text, using your favorite method of praying with Scripture.

READING I Though set during the time of wandering in the desert before entering the Promised Land, Leviticus is in effect a code of conduct particularly for the priests and Levites who later served in the Jerusalem Temple. The name of the book was assigned by the Greek translators because so much of the book deals with priests from the tribe of Levi. The book is intended as Moses' instruction for the children of Israel.

Today's reading is from a portion of the book that deals with the laws of purity, whether in daily life or ritual actions (chapters 11–16). Following after the discussion of clean and unclean animals and the purity laws associated with childbirth, today's text deals with the norms when someone is afflicted with leprosy. The separation of lepers from the rest of the community reflected a legitimate concern about the spread of the disease. The unfortunate consequence is that sufferers were isolated from family and were excluded from worshiping with the community. In addition, they were burdened by the widespread thinking that the disease was a divine punishment.

READING II In First Corinthians, Paul addresses many questions posed to him by the Christian community about marriage and virginity, idolatry, and practical situations such as buying meat that had been offered in a pagan sacrifice, and whether they should accept dinner invitations from unbelievers. In today's short reading, Paul concludes his advice, giving it a strong theological foundation. He begins by telling his audience, "whatever you do, do everything for the glory of God." He had already told them that while certain actions might not be morally wrong, they

A didactic reading In which Paul encourages moderation—for the glory of God and also to avoid unwelcome attention to the community.
Corinthians = kohr-IN-thee-uhnz

Encourage your assembly to glorify God with their whole lives!

Keep your energy and pace up; pause briefly at the commas to keep the meaning clear.

Pause after this line.
Slow on this last line.

READING II   1 Corinthians 10:31—11:1

A reading from the first Letter of Saint Paul to the Corinthians

Brothers and sisters,
Whether you **eat** or **drink**, or **whatever** you do,
  do **everything** for the glory of **God**.
Avoid giving **offense**, whether to the **Jews** or **Greeks** or the
    church of **God**,
  just as **I** try to please **everyone** in every **way**,
  not seeking my **own** benefit but that of the **many**,
  that they may be **saved**.
Be **imitators** of **me**, as **I** am of **Christ**.

A narrative reading. From Reading I, we know what a difficult life this leper has faced. Let his joy at being healed burst forth in your proclamation.

With anguish.
Show Jesus' compassion in your voice and face.

Quicken suddenly.

Firmly.

Raise your volume and energy. Smile—the man can't contain his happiness!

Keep your energy up to convey the excitement of the crowds.

GOSPEL   Mark 1:40–45

A reading from the holy Gospel according to Mark

A **leper** came to **Jesus** and kneeling down **begged** him and said,
  "If you **wish**, you can make me **clean**."
Moved with **pity**, he stretched out his **hand**,
  touched him, and **said** to him,
  "I **do** will it. Be made **clean**."
The leprosy left him **immediately**, and he was made **clean**.
Then, warning him **sternly**, he **dismissed** him at once.

He **said** to him, "See that you tell **no** one **anything**,
  but **go**, show yourself to the **priest**
  and **offer** for your cleansing what Moses **prescribed**;
  that will be **proof** for them."

The man went away and began to **publicize** the whole matter.
He **spread** the report abroad
  so that it was **impossible** for Jesus to enter a town **openly**.
He remained **outside** in **deserted** places,
  and people kept **coming** to him from **everywhere**.

---

should be guided by how the action would affect their neighbors. Even if a certain action is allowed, will someone be scandalized by it? The glory of God is the first motivation, followed by considering the impact of one's actions on others. These take precedence over one's own benefit or desires and can result in many being saved. When Paul says "be imitators of me, as I am of Christ," he is encouraging the Corinthians to join him in making Christ the standard for everything they do. Christ himself did all for God's glory, and for the benefit of both Jews and Greeks, that all might be saved.

GOSPEL   As the First Reading showed, since lepers were unclean, they could not associate with others. Yet this leper crosses a boundary in kneeling before Jesus and begging for healing. He expects that Jesus can do what only God could: heal one who is unclean. Jesus responds with compassion, also crossing a boundary by touching the leper, making himself unclean according to purity laws.

True to the rapid pace of Mark's account, healing is immediate. Jesus' warning that the healed leper "tell no one anything" seems surprising. Since people are already well aware of Jesus' healing activity, why make this healing secret? The reason for Jesus' instruction for silence is not certain here, nor in other instances throughout the Gospel. He most likely wants to wait until people have a fuller and correct understanding of his person and mission and suffering. In any event, the man does not obey Jesus, but tells of the whole matter far and wide, adding to the sense of rapid movement. Trying to slow down the pace, Jesus remains in deserted places while the people keep coming to him. E.P.

ASH WEDNESDAY

An exhortatory reading that mixes good news with challenge. Desire is the key to this reading. How will you express both the Lord's desire for us to repent and our desire for God?

Joel = JOH-*l

Start with strength. It's not too late! Let your assembly hear God yearning for them!

rend = tear
Tearing of one's garments showed grief and sorrow. God desires an open heart more than showy signs.

This is good news. How does it feel to know God waits with open arms, ready to bless us despite our mistakes? Bring that emotion to this proclamation.

Linger over these phases describing the great mercy of God.

Spoken with gratitude for God's for mercy.

Paul could not be clearer. The time is now!

Now, pick up your pace and keep your voice and energy up as you issue these calls. They should sound like calls to action and not a to-do list.

The assembly should know by your attitude that this is urgent!

This is serious business!

LECTIONARY #219

READING I   Joel 2:12–18

A reading from the Book of the Prophet Joel

Even **now**, says the LORD,
    return to me with your **whole** heart,
    with **fasting**, and **weeping**, and **mourning**;
Rend your **hearts,** not your **garments**,
    and **return** to the LORD, your God.
For **gracious** and **merciful** is he,
    slow to anger, **rich** in kindness,
    and **relenting** in punishment.
Perhaps he will **again** relent
    and leave behind him a **blessing**,
Offerings and **libations**
    for the LORD, your God.

Blow the **trumpet** in Zion!
    proclaim a fast,
    call an assembly;
Gather the people,
    notify the congregation;
Assemble the elders,
    gather the children
    and the **infants** at the breast;
Let the **bridegroom** quit his room
    and the **bride** her chamber.

READING I The lenten season begins with a prophetic call to repentance. Through the prophet Joel, the Lord urges the people to "return to me with your whole heart." The call of people to repentance is an ancient and often repeated admonition in the biblical tradition: "Return, O Israelites, to him whom you have utterly deserted" (Isaiah 31:6). The verb "return" (*shub*) occurs in various forms over a thousand times in the Old Testament. Often used to refer to individuals and the whole nation turning back to God, it has a practical dimension of turning away from evil and turning toward good. So universal is the need for repentance that Joel's oracle has a timeless quality. It is not associated with any specific time or historical situation, and pleads with people of every age and circumstance to repent.

As Joel's prophecy continues, we see another use of the verb *shub*, this time in reference to God's restoring people to favor and turning away from punishing them: "Perhaps he will again relent (*shub*), and leave behind a blessing." The divine relenting flows from God's very nature that Joel describes beautifully. God is "gracious and merciful," "slow to anger," and "rich in kindness." A similar description for God occurs in the Torah and the Psalms (for example, Exodus 34:6–7; Psalm 86:15), presenting the God of Israel as profoundly relational and merciful. The people of the covenant rightly have confidence that God will indeed turn away from punishing them, will restore and renew them.

Joel outlines for the people important signs of their repentance: fasting, mourning, and weeping over their sinfulness, bringing offerings and libations for God, blowing the ram's horn (the shofar), as a

Between the **porch** and the **altar**
  let the **priests**, the **ministers** of the LORD, **weep**,
And say, "**Spare**, **O** LORD, your people,
  and make not your heritage a **reproach**,
  with the nations **ruling** over them!
Why should they say among the peoples,
  '**Where** is their God?' "

Then the LORD was **stirred** to concern for his land
  and took **pity** on his people.

RESPONSORIAL PSALM   Psalm 51:3–4, 5–6ab, 12–13, 14 and 17 (3a)
R. Be merciful, O Lord, for we have sinned.

Have mercy on me, O God, in your goodness;
  in the greatness of your compassion wipe
    out my offense.
Thoroughly wash me from my guilt
  and of my sin cleanse me.

For I acknowledge my offense,
  and my sin is before me always:
"Against you only have I sinned,
  and done what is evil in your sight."

A clean heart create for me, O God,
  and a steadfast spirit renew within me.
Cast me not out from your presence,
  and your Holy Spirit take not from me.

Give me back the joy of your salvation,
  and a willing spirit sustain in me.
O Lord, open my lips,
  and my mouth shall proclaim your praise.

READING II   2 Corinthians 5:20—6:2

A reading from the second Letter of Saint Paul to the Corinthians

Brothers and sisters:
We are **ambassadors** for **Christ**,
  as if **God** were **appealing** through **us**.
We **implore** you on behalf of Christ,
  be **reconciled** to God.
For **our** sake he made him to **be** sin who did not **know** sin,
  so that we might become the **righteousness** of God in him.

Careful not to swallow "weep."

Now the pleading comes from the people. You are voicing the assembly's desire for God. Fill the word "O" with this desire.

No pause at this comma.

Take a long pause before revealing the Lord's response, and proclaim it gently, with tenderness and love.

For meditation and context:

TO KEEP IN MIND
Making eye contact with the assembly connects you with them and connects them to the reading more deeply than using your voice alone. This helps the assembly stay with the story and keeps them engaged.

An exhortatory reading with a sense of urgency. Be an agent of reconciliation through your proclamation.
Corinthians = kohr-IN-thee-uhnz

Notice the repeated idea of "appeal" and "implore." Heighten each occurrence.

Christ appeals through your proclamation.

Here is the point of the whole passage: speak deliberately and with intensity, then pause to let it sink in.

---

loud call to all the people to repent, and prayer of the whole assembly—from infants to elders, even brides and grooms. The priests in charge of the liturgical gathering then call out to God, "Spare, O LORD, your people."

The final movement of the reading announces God's compassion in relenting from punishing Israel, a joyful conclusion to the mutual "turning" of God and people.

READING II In Second Corinthians, Paul frequently uses first person plural words, ("we" and "us") to refer to himself and Timothy, the cosender of the letter. Today's reading begins with "We are ambassadors for Christ," likely designating Paul and Timothy, and perhaps other Apostles. Their role as ambassadors has a political origin that denotes people appointed to represent the government, people who could speak for it. As ambassadors for Christ, Paul and other ambassadors similarly represent Christ and teach according to the mind of Christ. Paul logically explains that the appeal they make is as if God were appealing through them. Their plea is that the Corinthians be reconciled to God. In this part of the letter, reconciliation is a major theme, with forms of the word "reconcile" (*katallasso*) used five times from 2 Corinthians 5:18–20. The term means "a thorough change" that most often involves a return to a favorable relationship. In the military sphere of the time, it indicated an end to hostilities and forging of peace. God initiates this change in relationship, assigning to Paul and his companions the ministry (*diakonia*) and message (*logos*) of reconciliation. Their role as ambassadors who represent Christ is to bring about God's

"Together" refers to Paul, Timothy, and Christ.

It would be a tragedy to receive God's grace and not respond to it.

Capture the tenderness in God's response.

Paul could not be clearer. The time is now!

A didactic reading: proclaim out of love and a desire to help your assembly get the most out of Lent. It concerns the three Lenten practices: almsgiving, prayer, and fasting. Note that Jesus' emphasis is not on what you do, but how you do it.
This is the point of the whole passage.

Pause before the teaching on almsgiving.
Jesus is using hyperbole with some humor.

Contrast being seen by others (useless) with being seen by the Father.

And what a small reward it is!

Don't scold; rather, teach out of love. Jesus suggests a better way, which pleases God more.

Pause again before this teaching on prayer.

TO KEEP IN MIND
A didactic reading is usually given out of love for the community. Make sure that love is evident in your proclamation.

Working **together**, then,
   we **appeal** to you **not** to receive the grace of God in **vain**.
For he says:

   In an acceptable time I **heard** you,
      and on the day of salvation I **helped** you.

Behold, **now** is a **very** acceptable time;
   behold, **now** is the day of **salvation**.

GOSPEL   Matthew 6:1–6, 16–18

A reading from the holy Gospel according to Matthew

Jesus said to his disciples:
   "Take **care** not to perform righteous deeds
   in order that people may **see** them;
      otherwise, you will have no **recompense** from your heavenly
         Father.
When you give **alms**,
   do not blow a **trumpet** before you,
   as the **hypocrites** do in the synagogues and in the streets
   to win the praise of **others**.
Amen, I say to you,
   they have **received** their reward.
But when **you** give alms,
   do not let your **left** hand know what your **right** is doing,
   so that your almsgiving may be **secret**.
And your Father who sees in secret will **repay** you.

---

reconciliation to the Corinthians through service and proclamation.
   Paul then expands the "we" references to include the whole Christian community: "For our sake he [God] made him to be sin who did not know sin, so that we might become the righteousness of God in him." Here Paul is saying that Christ, though sinless himself, takes our place in his sacrificial Death on the Cross. Because of his reconciling act, our status is changed. Paul uses an emphatic "we," telling his entire audience that we now have both the power and the responsibility of living

according to God's own righteousness: right relationship with God and one another. Paul urges the community not to receive the grace of God in vain. Further, he says that the day of salvation has already begun in Christ's saving Death. He is thus exhorting us to receive God's abundant grace and live in its power.

GOSPEL   Today's Gospel from Matthew provides a strong foundation for the traditional lenten practices of almsgiving, prayer, and fasting. The reading is taken from the Sermon on the

Mount, Jesus' first sermon in Matthew's Gospel. According to Saint Augustine, this discourse presents the perfect standard of Christian life. In this great sermon, Jesus presents the fundamentals of life and belief for those who follow him. What he says about almsgiving, prayer, and fasting is a significant part of this teaching that describes how to live in right relationship with God and one another.
   For all three of these acts of piety, an essential principle applies: they cannot be performed in order that people may see them. Jesus contrasts disciples' lack of

It is the secrets of your heart that the Father wants you to share.

Pause before this final teaching on fasting.

This behavior is not only hypocritical but somewhat ridiculous!

Given this teaching, there's some irony in leaving the Mass with ashes on our foreheads. But the point is that outward signs of repentance are worthless without an inward change of heart.

TO KEEP IN MIND
Always pause at the end of the reading, before you proclaim the closing dialogue ("The Word of the Lord" or "The Gospel of the Lord").

"When you **pray,**
  do not be like the **hypocrites,**
  who **love** to stand and pray in the synagogues and on street
    corners
  so that **others** may see them.
Amen, I say to you,
  they have **received** their reward.
But when **you** pray, go to your **inner** room,
  close the door, and pray to your Father in **secret.**
And your Father who **sees** in secret will **repay** you.

"When you **fast,**
  do not look **gloomy** like the hypocrites.
They **neglect** their appearance,
  so that they may appea**r** to **others** to be fasting.
Amen, I say to you, they have **received** their reward.
But when **you** fast,
  anoint your head and **wash** your face,
  so that you may not **appear** to be fasting,
  except to your Father who is **hidden.**
And your Father who **sees** what is hidden will **repay** you."

---

ostentation with the hypocrites' showy pretentiousness. Jesus' audience would understand the meaning of "hypocrites" as actors who pretend to be something they are not. Their masked performances in synagogues and in the streets are meant to win human praise and reward. "Amen," Jesus says regarding each of the three performances, "they have received their reward." Jesus' "amen" makes his statements emphatic and authoritative—a forceful reminder to his disciples to avoid such behavior.

Because almsgiving, prayer, and fasting are acts that express one's relationship with God, they should be done quietly, without any of the fanfare of the hypocrites. Jesus is speaking against neither the daily public liturgical prayers, nor the public fasting that was sometimes called for at times of great need or national disasters. Such practices enhance the faith of the community. His critique is against turning private acts of piety into public spectacles for the sake of reward. Jesus' words to his disciples resonate with Joel's prophecy

calling the people to turn to God "with your whole heart." Like the compassionate God of Joel's prophecy, the Father will reward with mercy and compassion the humble acts of devotion that rise from one's heart. E.P.

FIRST SUNDAY OF LENT

LECTIONARY #23

READING I Genesis 9:8–15

A reading from the Book of Genesis

God said to **Noah** and to his sons with him:
"**See**, I am now establishing my **covenant** with **you**
and your **descendants** after you
and with **every** living creature that was with you:
all the birds, and the various tame and wild **animals**
that were with you and came out of the **ark**.
I will establish my **covenant** with you,
that **never** again shall all bodily creatures be destroyed
by the waters of a **flood**;
there shall not be **another** flood to devastate the earth."
God added:
"**This** is the **sign** that I am giving for all ages to come,
of the covenant between me and you
and every living creature with you:
I set my **bow** in the clouds to serve as a **sign**
of the covenant between **me** and the **earth**.
When I bring **clouds** over the earth,
and the bow **appears** in the clouds,
I will **recall** the covenant I have made
between me and you and all living beings,
so that the waters shall **never** again become a flood
to destroy all mortal beings."

A narrative reading telling a very familiar story. This reading is all good news. Imagine God's joy in sharing this promise of love and care, and bring that energy to your proclamation.

Use the word "see" to convey your eagerness.

Be expansive as you include all of creation in this covenant.

Speak slowly and deliberately here.

As if the covenant weren't enough, God's abundant love adds this beautiful sign. Raise your energy and excitement as you describe the sign.

Again, the sign extends to all creation.

The rainbow reminds us as well as God of this covenant. Smile as you recall it.

READING I The dramatic narrative of Noah and the flood began "when the LORD saw how great was man's wickedness on earth" (Genesis 6:5). In the midst of widespread sin, God decided to "wipe out" all mortals, doing so with a great flood. Only Noah, his family, and the creatures he put into the ark were saved.

When the floodwaters recede, Noah and all in the ark emerge on dry land and build an altar to the Lord. After God smells the sweet odor of Noah's sacrifice, he promises never to doom the earth again because of human sin. Our reading opens when God makes a covenant that restores the lost relationship with humankind. Not simply repeating the original blessing given to the first man and woman, God expands it. In the beginning, God had blessed the couple; now God establishes a covenant, not only with Noah, but also with his descendants, and even with every living creature that comes out of the ark. Most fully, God says the covenant is "between me and the earth." The repeated words "every" and "all" emphasize the extent of the covenant, both temporally and spatially. This covenant, like others made with individuals and peoples, is a solemn agreement that forges a bond between the parties. In establishing the covenant, God promises there shall not be another devastating flood. God will set a bow in the clouds as a sign of divine fidelity.

Many stories in the ancient world tell of a great flood, but only the biblical version weaves into it the profound theology of God's mercy that far exceeds human sinfulness. This first covenant establishes the pattern of God's repeated covenant making that renews over and over the bond between God and the covenant partners.

For meditation and context:

TO KEEP IN MIND

Pay attention to the pace of your reading. Varying the pace gives listeners clues to the meaning of the text. The most common problem for proclaimers new to the ministry is going too fast to be understood.

RESPONSORIAL PSALM   Psalm 25:4–5, 6–7, 8–9 (10)

R. Your ways, O Lord, are love and truth to those who keep your covenant.

Your ways, O LORD, make known to me;
    teach me your paths,
guide me in your truth and teach me,
    for you are God my savior.

Remember that your compassion, O LORD,
    and your love are from of old.
In your kindness remember me,
    because of your goodness, O LORD.

Good and upright is the LORD,
    thus he shows sinners the way.
He guides the humble to justice,
    and he teaches the humble his way.

A didactic reading. Peter teaches that Christ brings us life through our Baptism. Help your assembly recognize the difference Christ makes in their lives and to fully embrace the joy of their Baptism.

Emphasize the contrasts: righteous and unrighteous, death and life, flesh and Spirt.

This is good news!

Pause at the end of this line.

Keep this long sentence together, pausing only at the commas.

Drop your voice on the parenthetical phrase, "eight in all."

Underscore the idea that water is the instrument of salvation.

More good news!

READING II   1 Peter 3:18–22

A reading from the first Letter of Saint Peter

Beloved:
Christ **suffered** for sins **once**,
    the **righteous** for the sake of the **unrighteous**,
    that he might lead you to **God**.
Put to **death** in the **flesh**,
    he was brought to **life** in the **Spirit**.
In it he also went to preach to the spirits in **prison**,
    who had **once** been **disobedient**
    while God **patiently** waited in the days of **Noah**
    during the building of the **ark**,
    in which a **few** persons, eight in all,
    were saved through **water.**
This prefigured **baptism**, which saves you **now**.

READING II   The First Letter of Peter is probably a circular letter sent to the numerous cities mentioned in the letter's address. In that context, today's reading provided for the communities of Asia Minor essential teachings about Christ, to whom believers are incorporated through Baptism. The theology we hear today, and in all of 1 Peter, has many parallels with other New Testament writings, each presenting the faith of mainstream Christianity in the early Church. As a succinct summary of the meaning of Christ's suffering and

Death, this passage could well have been used both in liturgy and catechesis.

In the verses just before our reading, Peter wrote about the suffering believers experience, particularly suffering because of righteousness. When he begins his teaching about Christ's suffering, Peter reminds his audience that Christ, the righteous one, suffered for the sake of the unrighteous. Christians who are themselves suffering because of the unrighteous should feel a strong union with Christ, who suffered similarly, "that he might lead you to God."

Baptism is the means by which believers enter into the mystery of Christ's suffering, Death, and Resurrection. With the story of Noah as background, Peter focuses on the image of water by which the righteous in Noah's own day were saved. Using typical Jewish exegesis, Peter explains that the ancient account of being saved through water prefigured Baptism. The prayer of blessing of the water in the font at the Easter Vigil expresses a rich understanding of the symbolism of water. That understanding begins on this first Sunday of Lent,

Of course not!

Raise your energy from here through the end.

Give each of these three its own emphasis.
Don't swallow "him."

It is not a removal of dirt from the body
　　but an **appeal** to God for a clear **conscience**,
　　through the **resurrection** of Jesus Christ,
　　who has gone into **heaven**
　　and is at the right hand of **God**,
　　with **angels**, **authorities**, and **powers subject** to him.

GOSPEL   Mark 1:12–15

A reading from the holy Gospel according to Mark

The Spirit **drove** Jesus out into the **desert**,
　　and he **remained** in the desert for **forty** days, **tempted**
　　　　by Satan.
He was among **wild** beasts,
　　and the **angels** ministered to him.

After John had been **arrested**,
　　Jesus came to **Galilee** proclaiming the **gospel** of God:
　　"**This** is the time of **fulfillment**.
The kingdom of God is at **hand**.
　　Repent, and **believe** in the gospel."

A narrative with an exhortatory proclamation at the end. Although brief, this Reading is packed with significance. Take your time.

Convey the urgency of the Spirit's action (especially in the word "drove").

Bring a sense of wonder to this strange but comforting scene.
Pause.
Change your tone to indicate the transition from the mystical setting of the desert to the quotidian setting of Galilee.
Jesus' proclamation is exhortatory. Raise your energy and volume.

TO KEEP IN MIND
Making eye contact with the assembly connects you with them and connects them to the reading more deeply than using your voice alone. This helps the assembly stay with the story and keeps them engaged.

and will prepare the elect for their own immersion into the baptismal waters.

GOSPEL Matthew, Mark, and Luke each tell of Jesus' temptation before he begins his public ministry. The account in Mark is by far the shortest of these temptation accounts. Without describing how Satan tempted Jesus, as Matthew and Luke do, Mark's brief scene sets the stage for what will happen later in the life of Jesus. Most explicitly, Satan, the tempter in the wilderness, is not the only one who will try to turn Jesus aside from

his mission. Another individual, called "Satan" by Jesus, tempts him later in the Gospel. "Get behind me, Satan," Jesus says to Peter when he tries to keep Jesus from completing his journey to Jerusalem. As Jesus resisted the tempter in the wilderness, he will resist Peter's misguided urging, and every other temptation to turn aside from his Father's will.

After the temptation, Jesus begins his ministry by proclaiming the Kingdom of God. His opening words are best understood in light of the Jewish hope for the coming of God's reign. Throughout their

history, they repeatedly wondered, "Is this the time of fulfillment?" As the story unfolds in Mark's Gospel, the answer becomes clearer: the Kingdom of God is manifest in Jesus' words and actions. The response to the presence of God's kingdom, so different from what they were expecting, is repentance and belief. Repentance and belief are more than momentary or merely intellectual responses, for they entail lifelong conversion and enduring fidelity to Jesus. E.P.

SECOND SUNDAY OF LENT

LECTIONARY #26

READING I   Genesis 22:1–2, 9a, 10–13, 15–18

A reading from the Book of Genesis

God put **Abraham** to the **test**.
He called to him, "**Abraham**!"
"**Here** I am!" he replied.
Then God said:
  "Take your son **Isaac**, your **only** one, whom you **love**,
    and go to the land of Moriah.
There you shall **offer** him up as a **holocaust**
  on a height that I will point out to you."

When they came to the place of which God had told him,
  Abraham built an **altar** there and arranged the **wood** on it.
Then he **reached** out and took the **knife** to **slaughter** his son.
But the LORD's messenger **called** to him from heaven,
  "Abraham, **Abraham**!"
"**Here** I am!" he answered.
"Do not lay your **hand** on the boy," said the messenger.
"Do not do the **least** thing to him.
I know **now** how **devoted** you are to God,
  since you did not **withhold** from me your **own** beloved son."
As Abraham looked about,
  he spied a **ram** caught by its horns in the thicket.
So he went and **took** the ram
  and offered it up as a **holocaust** in place of his **son**.

A narrative we know well, but don't telegraph the end. The scene is full of drama and the stakes are very high: both Isaac's life and the promise made to Abraham that he would have many descendants are in jeopardy.

Abraham has an intimate relationship with God.

Moriah = moh-RĪ-uh

Pause to let this sink in.
Convey the sense of dread and horror that Abraham must feel as he does these things. Pause at the end of this line.

A sudden, last-second intervention!
Raise your voice as if you had to stay Abraham's hand.

Quicken your pace; the scene's tension is released.

READING I | The story of Abraham began when God told him to go forth (*lekh-lekha*) from his native land on an unknown journey, demanding faith in facing the unknown. In the story of Abraham's testing, God again calls him to go forth (*lekh-lekha*) on an unknown journey, requiring an even greater faith. In Jewish tradition, this is the tenth and final trial that Abraham faces. Not only does God test Abraham by telling him to offer his son as a holocaust, but in doing so puts the promise to make of Abraham a great nation in jeopardy. In sacrificing Isaac, Abraham would also be sacrificing his own hope for numerous descendants.

The brevity of God's command makes the description of Isaac stand out painfully: "your son Isaac, your only son, whom you love." Isaac is more than hope for the future, for he is also a beloved son. The whole account swiftly moves forward with the same brevity of expression, almost as if the narrator must rush through the horror of the planned sacrifice. We can sense Abraham's relief when the Lord's messenger stops him, even as he is holding the knife in his hand.

Throughout the narrative, the lack of emotion on the part of both Abraham and Isaac adds to the sense of numbing shock. After the angel's rescue, the story moves quickly to the theological point: Abraham's total devotion to God. He trusted that God would ultimately be faithful to the promise, but not knowing how. Because of such devotion, God blessed Abraham abundantly. Following the rapid narrative of the scene on Mount Moriah, the blessing is richly and slowly developed, emphasizing God's gracious response to Abraham's obedience.

Again the Lord's messenger called to Abraham from heaven
    and said:
  "I **swear** by **myself**, declares the Lord,
  that because you **acted** as you did
  in not **withholding** from me your beloved **son,**
  I will **bless** you **abundantly**
  and make your **descendants** as countless
  as the **stars** of the sky and the **sands** of the seashore;
  your descendants shall take **possession**
  of the gates of their **enemies**,
  and in **your** descendants **all** the nations of the earth shall
    find **blessing—**
  all this because you **obeyed** my command."

The reward is as great as the test was demanding. Keep your pace up to the end.

Emphasize the universality of Abraham's blessing.

For meditation and context:

TO KEEP IN MIND

You can't proclaim what you don't understand. Read the Scripture passage and its commentary in *Workbook*. Then read it from your Bible, including what comes before and after it so that you understand the context.

RESPONSORIAL PSALM   Psalm 116:10, 15, 16–17, 18–19 (9)

R. I will walk before the Lord, in the land of the living.

I believed, even when I said,
  "I am greatly afflicted."
Precious in the eyes of the Lord
  is the death of his faithful ones.

O Lord, I am your servant;
  I am your servant, the son of your
    handmaid;
  you have loosed my bonds.
To you will I offer sacrifice of thanksgiving,
  and I will call upon the name of the Lord.

My vows to the Lord I will pay
  in the presence of all his people,
in the courts of the house of the Lord,
  in your midst, O Jerusalem.

A bracing, exhortatory reading that is all good news. Keep your energy up throughout, and smile with your voice, eyes, and face.

READING II   Romans 8:31b–34

A reading from the Letter of Saint Paul to the Romans

Brothers and sisters:
If **God** is **for** us, **who** can be **against** us?
He who did not spare his own **Son**
  but handed him over for us **all**,
  how will he not also give us everything **else** along with him?

Use the rhetorical questions in this reading to challenge and reassure the assembly at the same time: How can you not trust in God? God's care for you is steadfast and everlasting!

READING II Paul is a master of rhetorical questions. As he asks a series of questions, we hear only Paul, and not how his audience might respond. When Paul asks, "If God is for us, who can be against us?" the Roman Christians could well ask, "Then why are we being persecuted?" Paul's second question seems to answer that unspoken rejoinder. God who did not spare his own Son will give us everything along with Christ. Since God handed over his own Son for all of us, God will, logically, give us everything else "along with him." "Along with him" is an ambiguous phrase with several possible meanings. First, suffering is given to us along with the suffering given to Christ. "Along with him" can also mean that God, with Christ, will give us everything we need. The phrase can mean further that the greatest gift that God gives to us is Christ himself. We can rightfully keep all these meanings in mind.

Paul's next questions about charges, acquittal and condemnation have the sound of a courtroom. Clearly, the God who will "give us everything else" will not be a judge who will condemn us. After the series of questions, Paul moves to the single declarative statement about Christ's Death, Resurrection, and exaltation. Paul in effect answers his courtroom questions: no matter the circumstances, the risen, exalted Christ will intercede for us.

GOSPEL The account of the Transfiguration is a key passage in portraying the identity of Jesus. It begins with Jesus leading Peter, James, and John to a high mountain, immediately evoking the multiple mountain images of Scripture as places of revelation. Before his friends, Jesus is transfigured (*metamorphoo*),

The answer to each question is "no one!"

Slight pause here, to make sure it doesn't sound like the next line is the answer to the question.

Paul wants to focus on Christ's Resurrection, not his Death.

The best news of all! Keep your energy up to the end.

Who will bring a charge against God's chosen ones?
  It is **God** who **acquits** us, **who** will condemn?
Christ Jesus it is who **died**—or, rather, was **raised**—
  who also is at the **right** hand of God,
  who **indeed** intercedes for us.

A familiar narrative. Encourage a sense of wonder and awe in your assembly as they hear it. Take your time; much happens here quickly, but keep all the events distinct.

Make sure this doesn't sound like an everyday occurrence, but like the surprising and mysterious event it is. Proclaim with the amazement of the three onlookers.

fuller = a person who cleans wool to prepare it to be made into cloth

Elijah = ee-Lī-juh

Pause.

GOSPEL   Mark 9:2–10

A reading from the holy Gospel according to Mark

Jesus took **Peter**, **James**, and **John**
  and led them up a high **mountain** apart by themselves.
And he was **transfigured** before them,
  and his clothes became **dazzling** white,
  such as no **fuller** on earth could bleach them.
Then **Elijah** appeared to them along with **Moses**,
  and they were **conversing** with Jesus.
Then **Peter** said to Jesus in reply,
  "**Rabbi**, it is **good** that we are here!

With Peter's confused excitement.

Let us make three **tents**:
  one for **you**, one for **Moses**, and one for **Elijah**."
He **hardly** knew what to say, they were so **terrified**.

This shouldn't sound ominous but mysterious.

Then a **cloud** came, casting a **shadow** over them;
  from the cloud came a **voice**,

With great love. Pause.

Quickly.

Pause.

  "This is my **beloved** Son. **Listen** to him."
Suddenly, looking around, they no longer saw **anyone**
  but Jesus alone with them.

As they were coming down from the mountain,
  he charged them **not** to relate what they had seen to **anyone**,
  except when the Son of Man had **risen** from the **dead**.
So they kept the matter to themselves,

With the Apostles' puzzled curiosity.

  questioning what **rising** from the dead meant.

indicating a transformation of what is outwardly visible to show his inward, divine form. The appearance of Moses, the Lawgiver, and Elijah, the prophet, insert Jesus into the Jewish tradition. Then, Peter's suggestion of making three tents is reminiscent of the tabernacles during the Old Testament harvest festival. The mountain of revelation, the figures of Moses and Elijah, and the hoped-for tents all identity Jesus in continuity with the Jewish tradition. When the voice from the heavens proclaims him as the beloved Son, we hear an echo of another Jewish story, that of

Abraham and Isaac, the beloved son who was about to be sacrificed. Such a resonance points ahead to the coming sacrifice of Jesus, which he refers to when he tells his disciples not to tell anyone until the Son of Man has risen from the dead.

There is only one command from the heavenly voice: "Listen to him." Jesus' disciples must be attentive to all that he tells them, particularly as they make their way to Jerusalem. With the multiple allusions to Jewish traditions, the presence of the three bewildered disciples, and a foreshadowing of Jesus' sacrifice, the Transfiguration

account weaves together past, present, and future. In every age, Jesus is God's beloved Son. E.P.

THIRD SUNDAY OF LENT

This didactic passage is one of the best known in Scripture. Let your assembly hear it afresh by conveying God's great love in showing us how to be in relationship with God and each other.

Exodus = EK-suh-duhs

The Israelites owe their freedom to God, who will not abandon them to chaos. He continues to care for them—and us.

Good news!

LECTIONARY #29

READING I Exodus 20:1–17

A reading from the Book of Exodus

[In those days, **God** delivered all these **commandments**:
"**I**, the LORD, am your **God**,
who brought you out of the land of **Egypt**, that place of **slavery**.
You shall not have **other** gods besides me.]
You shall not carve **idols** for yourselves
in the shape of **anything** in the sky **above**
or on the earth **below** or in the waters **beneath** the earth;
you shall not **bow** down before them or **worship** them.
For **I**, the LORD, your **God**, am a **jealous** God,
inflicting **punishment** for their fathers' wickedness
on the children of those who hate me,
down to the third and fourth generation;
but bestowing **mercy** down to the **thousandth** generation
on the children of those who **love** me and **keep**
my commandments.

This may seem cruel, but it reflects the reality that our sinful choices often have consequences for those near to us as well.

Note that God's mercy is so much greater than God's punishment.

Pause at the end of this line.

["You shall not take the **name** of the LORD, your God, in **vain**.
For the LORD will not leave **unpunished**
the one who **takes** his name in vain.

Pause at the end of this line.

"**Remember** to keep **holy** the **sabbath** day.]
Six days you may labor and do all your work,
but the **seventh** day is the **sabbath** of the LORD, your God.

This is good news—God demands that we care for ourselves by balancing action with rest. Proclaim gently, with the joy that the sabbath brings.

Today, options are given for the readings: Year A or Year B. Contact your parish staff to learn which readings will be used.

READING I Of the numerous laws and ordinances in the Torah, surely the Ten Commandments are the most familiar. Yet they are introduced in today's reading not as "commandments," but literally as the "words" (*devarim*) that God spoke. The focus is thus on God's personal communication to Israel, through which God provides instruction that is foundational to their covenant relationship. God's opening words are not about the Law, or the consequences if the Law is not followed, but they present God's identity as a personal God who has chosen Israel as covenant partner: "I, the LORD, [Yahweh] am your God." God is already known to Israel, having brought them out of Egypt where they were enslaved. God's words spoken to Israel through Moses all flow from the covenant relationship and Israel's identity as God's people.

The first three commandments express the absolute fidelity that Israel owes to God. The bond between God and Israel is so fundamental that adherence to any other god would be an unthinkable violation, tantamount to denying the identity of both God and Israel. Unlike the widespread polytheism in the ancient world that tolerated worship of a variety of gods, the God of Israel prohibited carving idols of other gods and worshiping them. The covenant and God's deliverance of Israel implied an exclusive bond characterized by mercy on God's part, and obedient love on Israel's part. Taking the Lord's name "in vain," is the next commandment. This included taking false oaths or even use of

No **work** may be done then either by you, or your son or daughter,
  or your male or female slave, or your beast,
  or by the alien who lives with you.
In **six** days the LORD made the **heavens** and the **earth**,
  the **sea** and **all** that is in them;
  but on the **seventh** day he **rested**.
That is why the LORD has **blessed** the sabbath day and made
  it **holy**.

["**Honor** your **father** and your **mother**,
  that you may have a long **life** in the land
  which the LORD, your God, is giving you.
You shall not **kill**.
You shall not commit **adultery**.
You shall not **steal**.
You shall not bear **false** witness against your neighbor.
You shall not **covet** your neighbor's **house**.
You shall not **covet** your neighbor's **wife**,
  nor his male or female **slave**, nor his **ox** or **ass**,
  nor anything **else** that belongs to him."]

[Shorter: Exodus 20:1–3, 7–8, 12–17 (see brackets)]

RESPONSORIAL PSALM   Psalm 19:8, 9, 10, 11 (John 6:68c)

R. Lord, you have the words of everlasting life.

The law of the LORD is perfect,
  refreshing the soul;
the decree of the LORD is trustworthy,
  giving wisdom to the simple.

The precepts of the LORD are right,
  rejoicing the heart;
the command of the LORD is clear,
  enlightening the eye.

The fear of the LORD is pure,
  enduring forever;
the ordinances of the LORD are true,
  all of them just.

They are more precious than gold,
  than a heap of purest gold;
sweeter also than syrup
  or honey from the comb.

Pause before the final seven commandments about community life.

These will not be new information for your assembly; anyone who has ever lived in any community would agree with these rules. Proclaim with an attitude of "Isn't life better for us when we all live together like this?"

Avoid a stern tone; all these commandments are given out of love.

Take a longer pause than usual before "The Word of the Lord."

For meditation and context:

TO KEEP IN MIND
Pause in order to break up separate thoughts, set apart significant statements, or indicate major shifts. Never pause in the middle of a single thought. Your primary guide for pauses is punctuation.

---

magic rituals using God's name, thereby showing contempt for God. Keeping the Sabbath holy is an essential practice of Israel's tradition and worship; everyone, including slaves and animals, dedicated the day to God, emulating God's own rest on the seventh day of creation.

Having established the right relationship between God and Israel, the rest of God's words show the right relationship among the people themselves. All of the commandments are considered apodictic; that is, ways of life that apply to all times and circumstances: honoring parents,

refraining from killing, adultery, stealing, bearing false witness and having designs on a desired object or person belonging to another. Living in accord with these norms maintains a society in which people can live in harmony with God and one another.

READING II   "Christ crucified." In two words, Paul announces the paradoxical proclamation that was (and is) often a stumbling block to faith. The image of a stumbling block (*skandalon*) occurs frequently in the Gospel accounts and Paul's letters as a metaphor for something that

causes people to trip and fall. Jesus even calls Simon Peter a *skandalon* when Peter tries to prevent Jesus from going to Jerusalem where the Cross awaits him (Matthew 16:23). Jews and Gentile Greeks, Apostles and Pharisees, friends and opponents, people past and present, all have difficulty understanding and accepting the scandal, the stumbling block, of the Cross. For Jews, one hung on a tree was cursed (Deuteronomy 21:23); for Greeks, accepting one who had undergone such a disgraceful death as a messiah was utter foolishness.

A didactic reading. A crucified savior is hard to accept, especially if you're looking for a different sort of savior. But God turns human expectations upside down. When has that happened to you? Bring that emotion to this proclamation.

Corinthians = kohr-IN-thee-uhnz

Dismiss both pursuits as folly. Greeks = Gentiles

Slow on "Christ crucified."

Brief pause at this comma.

Good news!

Encourage your assembly: Put your trust in God, not in your own wisdom or strength!

READING II   1 Corinthians 1:22–25

A reading from the first Letter of Saint Paul to the Corinthians

Brothers and sisters:
Jews demand **signs** and **Greeks** look for **wisdom**,
 but **we** proclaim Christ **crucified**,
 a **stumbling** block to Jews and **foolishness** to Gentiles,
 but to those who are **called**, Jews and Greeks **alike**,
 Christ the **power** of God and the **wisdom** of God.
For the **foolishness** of God is **wiser** than human wisdom,
 and the **weakness** of God is **stronger** than human strength.

A powerful narrative. Don't shy away from proclaiming with the full force of Jesus' anger.

Jesus' anger rises slowly as he surveys the scene.

Quicken your pace and heighten your intensity.
Use the verbs to drive the action.

You needn't shout but you must raise your volume and energy.
At the end of this line pause, and let it resound for a moment.
Quieter, as if the disciples are talking amongst themselves.
Return to normal volume and pace.

GOSPEL   John 2:13–25

A reading from the holy Gospel according to John

Since the **Passover** of the Jews was near,
 Jesus went up to **Jerusalem**.
He found in the **temple** area those who sold **oxen**, **sheep**,
 and **doves**,
 as well as the **money changers** seated there.
He made a **whip** out of cords
 and **drove** them all out of the temple area, with the **sheep**
 and **oxen**,
 and **spilled** the **coins** of the money changers
 and **overturned** their **tables**,
 and to those who sold **doves** he said,
 "Take these **out** of here,
 and **stop** making my Father's house a **marketplace**."
His **disciples** recalled the words of **Scripture**,
 Zeal for your house will **consume** *me.*
At this the Jews answered and said to him,
 "What **sign** can you show us for **doing** this?"

Throughout his letters, Paul provides theological, pastoral, and spiritual insights into this paradoxical mystery of Christ crucified. The *"kenosis* hymn" (*kenosis* meaning "emptying") in Philippians, for example, is a poetic and profound exposition of Christ who emptied himself and was crucified (Philippians 2:5–11). In today's short pericope, Paul does not develop the account of Jesus' Death on the Cross, or offer theological reasoning, but simply sets up a contrast between accepted human judgments and God's reversal of them. What appears as foolishness from a human perspective is in reality divine wisdom; what looks like divine weakness from a human viewpoint is actually a manifestation of God's power and wisdom. In spite of the appearance of the weakness and folly of the Cross, Paul announces Christ crucified as the heart of his Gospel. Paul's emphasis on Christ crucified extends beyond the past event, for the crucified one is now alive and living in the believers. Moreover, Christ's Crucifixion, his emptying himself for the sake of others, became a pattern for Paul's own life and ministry. What Paul had once considered to be power and wisdom, he came to regard as "so much rubbish" (Philippians 3:8), as he accepted the Cross of Christ in his own body. "Christ crucified" remains for everyone God's power and wisdom.

GOSPEL   John the Evangelist is a master of symbolism, foreshadowing, and words that have double and deeper meanings. We see John's multifaceted literary expertise in today's account of Jesus in the Jerusalem Temple at the time of Passover. The Passover context is the first clue that what is taking

Calmer than before, but still with conviction.

Scoffing. "Seriously?"

This is not news to your assembly. Connect with them as you share this understanding.

Pause.

Convey a hint of danger.

> **TO KEEP IN MIND**
> In a narrative, find an emotion or point of view for each character, keeping in mind that these might change during the reading.

> **TO KEEP IN MIND**
> Making eye contact with the assembly connects you with them and connects them to the reading more deeply than using your voice alone. This helps the assembly stay with the story and keeps them engaged.

Jesus answered and said to them,
   "**Destroy** this temple and in **three days** I will raise it **up**."
The Jews said,
   "This **temple** has been under construction for forty-six **years**,
   and **you** will raise it up in three **days**?"
But he was speaking about the temple of his **body**.
Therefore, when he was **raised** from the dead,
   his disciples **remembered** that he had said this,
   and they came to **believe** the Scripture
   and the word Jesus had spoken.

While he was in Jerusalem for the feast of **Passover**,
   many began to believe in his name
   when they saw the **signs** he was doing.
But Jesus would not **trust** himself to them because he **knew** them all,
   and did not need **anyone** to testify about human nature.
He himself understood it **well**.

place is pointing ahead to Jesus' own future Passover that will also take place in Jerusalem. His conflict with the money changers also foreshadows his future, final conflict with the Jerusalem authorities. All four canonical Gospels have an account of Jesus driving out the money-changers, but only in John is it placed at the beginning, rather than at the end, of his ministry. The early placement of the scene serves as an introduction and foreshadowing to the Death and Resurrection of Jesus.

After Jesus' conflict with the money changers, the dialogue moves to a conver-

sation with the Jews who ask him for a sign. Like other characters in John's Gospel, such as Nicodemus and the Samaritan woman, the Jews misunderstand Jesus' words. In all these cases, the misunderstanding is the evangelist's opportunity for Jesus to explain himself and his mission to people who are mystified, often vacillating between confusion and hostility. The Jews totally misunderstand Jesus when he says that he will raise up the Temple in three days. They understand Jesus to be referring to the Temple building, the *naos*, meaning the Temple sanctuary. Jesus uses

the same word to refer to himself, the temple of his body that is the sanctuary where God dwells. The scene taking place on a certain Passover at the beginning of Jesus' ministry prepares us for another Passover when the temple of Jesus' body will be (temporarily) destroyed, only to be raised up. Looking even farther into the future, the evangelist tells us that Jesus' disciples remembered this episode when he rose from the dead. Then the misunderstanding is finally made clear. E.P.

THIRD SUNDAY OF LENT, YEAR A

A narrative reading that is all conversation. Give each speaker (the people, Moses, God) a distinct emotion. Look at "grumbled," "cried out," and the simple "answered" for clues. Express the feelings in narrative lines as well as dialogue.

Exodus = EK-suh-duhs

The word "grumbled" sounds like what it means.

Proclaim as if one person speaks for all. Are they furious? Annoyed? Terrified? Anxious? Choose and proclaim from that perspective.

Pause before introducing Moses' response.

Moses has reached his limit!

Speak Moses' words with a sense of desperation and fear.

Pause again before introducing God's response.

God's answer is as calm as Moses' plea is anxious. "Don't worry; I've got this!"

Horeb = HOHR-eb

Pause again.

The story ends here. Pause before giving the origin of the place names.

Massah = MAS-uh

Meribah = MAYR-ih-bah

Again, proclaim with the emotion of the people.

LECTIONARY #28

READING I   Exodus 17:3–7

A reading from the Book of Exodus

In those days, in their **thirst** for water,
    the people **grumbled** against Moses,
    saying, "**Why** did you ever make us **leave** Egypt?
Was it just to have us **die** here of **thirst**
    with our children and our livestock?"
So Moses **cried** out to the LORD,
    "What shall I **do** with this people?
A little more and they will **stone** me!"
The LORD **answered** Moses,
    "Go over there in front of the people,
    along with some of the elders of Israel,
    holding in your hand, as you go,
    the **staff** with which you struck the **river**.
I will be **standing** there in front of you on the **rock** in Horeb.
Strike the rock, and the water will **flow** from it
    for the people to **drink**."
This Moses **did**, in the presence of the elders of Israel.
The place was called **Massah** and **Meribah**,
    because the Israelites **quarreled** there
    and **tested** the LORD, saying,
    "Is the LORD in our **midst** or **not**?"

Today, options are given for the readings: Year A or Year B. Contact your parish staff to learn which readings will be used.

READING I   The people of Israel are on the first stages of their desert journey, in the second month after their departure from Egypt, and are near Mount Sinai. Already at this early stage of their forty-year trek, God has repeatedly shown great signs and wonders that first freed the Israelites from Egypt, then led them through the waters of the Red Sea, and then fed them with a mysterious bread in the wilderness. Now, facing another situation of need, thirsting for water, the people respond not with faith or hope that God would again come to their rescue, but with loud, insistent grumbling. "Why did you ever make us leave Egypt? Was it just to have us die here of thirst?" Grumbling has already been a pattern of the once-enslaved people. At the edge of the Red Sea, they had complained, "Were there no burial places in Egypt that you brought us out here to die in the wilderness?" (Exodus 14:11). When they were hungry in the desert, they complained against Moses and Aaron that they had led them into the wilderness to make the whole community die of famine (Exodus 16:3). Moses says to the people that their murmuring is not against him, but against the Lord. When they again grumble against Moses in this scene, it is clear that in their growling complaint they are putting God to the test. In the verse just before today's reading, Moses had challenged the people specifically, "Why do you quarrel with me? Why do you put the LORD to a test?" The people are demanding tangible signs that God is with

For meditation and context:

TO KEEP IN MIND
Pay attention to the pace of your reading. Varying the pace gives listeners clues to the meaning of the text. The most common problem for proclaimers new to the ministry is going too fast to be understood.

RESPONSORIAL PSALM   Psalm 95:1–2, 6–7, 8–9 (8)

R. If today you hear his voice, harden not your hearts.

Come, let us sing joyfully to the LORD;
   let us acclaim the Rock of our salvation.
Let us come into his presence with
      thanksgiving;
   let us joyfully sing psalms to him.

Come, let us bow down in worship;
   let us kneel before the LORD who made us.
For he is our God,
   and we are the people he shepherds,
      the flock he guides.

Oh, that today you would hear his voice:
   "Harden not your hearts as at Meribah,
      as in the day of Massah in the desert.
Where your fathers tempted me;
   they tested me though they had seen
      my works."

An exhortatory reading. Resist the temptation to rush to the final passage about Christ's Death. Emphasize the progression Paul sets up in the first part: faith leads to peace which leads to grace which leads to hope which leads to love. Only then does the final point make sense.

You're telling the community what they already have through their faith.

Good news!
Linger over this phrase describing God's overflowing love!

"Ungodly" is a surprise; don't swallow it.
This is an aside; pick up the pace a bit.

Don't stress "proves," as if God's love needs proof; here, it simply means "shows."

God's gift of love is free, for sinner and saint alike. This is indeed good news. Keep your voice up to the end.

READING II   Romans 5:1–2, 5–8

A reading from the Letter of Saint Paul to the Romans

Brothers and sisters:
Since we have been justified by **faith**,
   we have **peace** with God through our Lord Jesus **Christ**,
   through whom we have gained **access** by faith
   to this **grace** in which we stand,
   and we boast in **hope** of the **glory** of God.

And hope does not **disappoint**,
   because the love of God has been **poured** out into our hearts
   through the Holy Spirit who has been given to us.
For **Christ**, while we were still **helpless**,
   died at the appointed time for the **ungodly**.
Indeed, only with **difficulty** does one die for a **just** person,
   though perhaps for a **good** person one might even find courage
      to die.
But God proves his **love** for us
   in that while we were still **sinners** Christ **died** for us.

---

them, insisting that the Lord act in accordance with their demands.

Throughout this reading, the words between Moses and the people are mostly in the form of questions. The people question Moses, "Why did you ever make us leave Egypt?" and then Moses questions God, "What shall I do with this people?" Such questions are a means of drawing all who later read the account to get involved in the dialogue. What are the questions they ask? Are their questions ones of complaint, or of hope? Are they putting God to the test?

Throughout the whole story of the desert wandering, Moses stands as the intermediary between God and the people, and in this scene it is to Moses that God answers with words that contain both command and promise. God directs Moses to take some of the elders with him; those chosen will be witnesses for the sign God will perform. The Lord directs Moses to hold the staff he had already used in striking the river (the Red Sea) that enabled the people to cross dry-shod and escape the Egyptian pursuers. Now Moses is to stand in front of the people, and God promises to

stand in front of Moses. As Moses had earlier struck the river at God's command, resulting in a great sign of passing through the water, now Moses is to strike the rock for another sign of live-saving water. The new event on Mount Horeb is an audio-visual reminder of the earlier miracle and assurance of God's abiding power and presence. The names that are given to the place have a legendary character: "Massah" which means "testing," and "Meribah," signifying "quarreling," became bywords for Israel's repeated testing and quarreling with God, and with his servant

What makes a narrative interesting is the "character arc"—how a character changes significantly over the course of the story. The woman has a great character arc. She grows from skeptic to inquirer to disciple. Make strong choices about the woman's feelings so that the change is evident.

Samaria = suh-MAYR-ee-uh

Sychar = SĪ-kahr

Let some tiredness come through in your voice.

Slight pause to let the scene settle.

How would Jesus sound? Remember his tiredness.

Drop your voice slightly on this aside.

Samaritan = suh-MAYR-uh-tuhn

She is unafraid to challenge Jesus.

Drop your voice again; another aside.

Jesus is not chastising the woman. How could she have known? He appreciates the opportunity to teach. (Later, he says that this ministry nourishes him.)

Let her sarcasm come through.

cistern = SIS-tern

That this well was built by Jacob is a source of pride for the town.

Use care with this sentence's construction: water taken in becomes a self-sustaining source of water.

GOSPEL   John 4:5–42

A reading from the holy Gospel according to John

[Jesus came to a town of **Samaria** called Sychar,
    near the plot of land that **Jacob** had given to his son Joseph.
Jacob's **well** was there.
Jesus, **tired** from his journey, sat down there at the **well.**
It was about **noon.**

A **woman** of Samaria came to draw **water.**
Jesus said to her,
    "Give me a **drink.**"
His disciples had gone into the town to buy food.
The Samaritan woman said to him,
    "How can **you**, a **Jew**, ask me, a **Samaritan woman**, for a **drink**?"
—For Jews use nothing in common with Samaritans.—
Jesus answered and said to her,
    "If you **knew** the gift of God
    and **who** is saying to you, 'Give me a drink,'
    you would have asked **him**
    and he would have given you **living** water."
The woman said to him,
    "Sir, you do not even have a **bucket** and the cistern is **deep**;
    where then can you get this living water?
Are you **greater** than our father Jacob,
    who **gave** us this cistern and drank from it **himself**
    with his children and his flocks?"
Jesus answered and said to her,
    "Everyone who drinks **this** water will be **thirsty** again;
    but whoever drinks the water **I** shall give will **never** thirst;
    the water I shall give will become in him
    a **spring** of water **welling** up to eternal **life.**"

Moses. Moses' final question to Israel, "Is the Lord in our midst or not?" should now get a resounding yes from the desert wanderers as well as from all who reflect on this story.

READING II Beginning with this passage in Romans 5, Paul explains the meaning of justification that extends through Romans 8. As a central theme of his Letter to the Romans, Paul has already written about justification from several perspectives, and here looks at how justification results in a life of grace in Christ.

Examining the terms Paul uses helps us understand what he says here.

"We have been justified by faith." The word "justified" is a passive form of the verb *dikaioo*, which means "to make a person righteous, just, or innocent." Since the verb is passive, being justified is not something that people accomplish themselves, but people are justified by someone else. God is the one who justifies, doing so by freely given grace (Romans 3:24). While believers look forward to being eternally justified by God, Paul explains that God's saving gift of justification has already

begun. Such an already-and-not-yet perspective is typical of Paul's understanding of God's saving actions. We are already being transformed through God's power, are already incorporated into Christ, even as we look forward in hope to life in fullness. God's saving act of justifying flows from God's very nature, for God is just (*dikaios*; 3:26), ever acting to establish, maintain, and restore right relationships.

Throughout Romans and other letters, Paul combines justification with faith, (*pistis*). The very limited notion that justification by faith means accepting a body of

Is the woman sincere, or still a little sarcastic? Perhaps she's intrigued by this man and starting to wonder who he might be. Express the choice in your delivery.

Give the woman a moment before introducing her response.

What is the woman feeling? Shame? Anger? Sadness?

Jesus states the truth simply.

"Good for you for telling the truth!"

She acknowledges Jesus as a prophet, but immediately challenges him again.

Soon, distinctions like Jew and Samaritan will be meaningless.

> **TO KEEP IN MIND**
> In a narrative, find an emotion or point of view for each character, keeping in mind that these might change during the reading.

The woman said to him,
　"Sir, **give** me this water, so that I may not be **thirsty**
　or have to keep **coming** here to draw water."]

Jesus said to her,
　"**Go** call your **husband** and come **back**."
The woman answered and said to him,
　"I do not **have** a husband."
Jesus answered her,
　"You are **right** in saying, 'I do not have a husband.'
For you have had **five** husbands,
　and the one you have **now** is **not** your husband.
What you have said is **true**."
The woman said to him,
　"Sir, [I can see that you are a **prophet**.
Our ancestors worshiped on this **mountain**;
　but you people say that the place to worship is in **Jerusalem**."
Jesus said to her,
　"**Believe** me, woman, the hour is **coming**
　when you will worship the Father
　neither on this mountain **nor** in Jerusalem.
You people worship what you do not **understand**;
　we worship what we **understand**,
　because **salvation** is from the **Jews**.
But the hour is **coming**, and is now **here**,
　when **true** worshipers will worship the Father in **Spirit**
　　and **truth**;
　and indeed the Father **seeks** such people to worship him.
God is **Spirit**, and those who **worship** him
　must worship in **Spirit** and **truth**."

belief is far from Paul's understanding. *Pistis* entails trust in the God who saves and obedient fidelity to the relationship. Further, justification by faith is rooted in God's own fidelity, for both justice and fidelity are characteristic of God. Christ is a full manifestation of God's fidelity, the one who was always faithful both to God and to humankind. Our own faith or fidelity is both a gift from God and a response to God's own faithfulness.

"We have been justified by faith" is thus both a present and a future saving transformation; it is both divine grace and human response. The fruits of justification that Paul explains in today's reading are likewise both present and future—gift as well as response. First, we are at peace with God through Christ. The biblical concept of peace is that of fullness, soundness, or wholeness. Even now, at peace with God, we have access to God's grace; "standing" in God's grace is a present reality giving us confidence to boast in the hope we have for God's glory in the future. Having begun with reference to faith, then to hope, Paul then speaks of love. The love of God poured into our hearts is another

Pauline phrase that can be understood in two ways. God's own love, the love that comes from God, has been poured by God into our hearts. From another angle, the love that we have for God is both our response to God's love and a gift that God has given us.

Without using either the words "faith" or "justification," everything that Paul says about Christ in the final portion of our reading is a vivid example of God's fidelity and saving justice. Christ died for us when we were helpless, giving his life even for the ungodly. What greater proof could we want

Notice that Jesus has said nothing about the Messiah. Why does the woman bring up the subject? Does she, a Samaritan woman, suspect Jesus might be the Christ? Could she be hoping he will confirm her suspicion? Let that come through in your proclamation.

A long pause here; the woman is awed into silence.

Emphasize "woman" as the source of the disciples' amazement.

The disciples are so confused by Jesus' actions they don't know what to say.

Proclaim her actions with excitement; she leaves in such haste she abandons her jar.

Speak this directly to your assembly; encourage them with the woman's amazement.

The disciples are really concerned about Jesus (perhaps because of his seemingly strange behavior?).

His ministry—such as this conversation with the woman—sustains him.

Drop your volume as if the disciples are whispering to each other.

Jesus tries to refocus the disciples on ministering to the community.

Speak these lines with some urgency.

TO KEEP IN MIND

Pause in order to break up separate thoughts, set apart significant statements, or indicate major shifts. Never pause in the middle of a single thought. Your primary guide for pauses is punctuation.

The woman said to him,
  "I know that the **Messiah** is coming, the one called the **Christ**;
  when he **comes**, he will tell us **everything**."
Jesus said to her,
  "**I** am **he**, the one **speaking** with you."]

At that moment his disciples **returned**,
  and were **amazed** that he was talking with a **woman**,
  but still no one said, "What are you **looking** for?"
  or "Why are you **talking** with her?"
The woman **left** her water jar
  and went into the town and said to the people,
  "**Come** see a man who told me **everything** I have done.
Could he possibly be the **Christ**?"
They went out of the town and **came** to him.
Meanwhile, the disciples **urged** him, "Rabbi, **eat**."
But he said to them,
  "I have **food** to eat of which you do not **know**."
So the disciples **said** to one another,
  "Could someone have **brought** him something to eat?"
Jesus said to them,
  "My **food** is to do the **will** of the one who **sent** me
  and to **finish** his work.
Do you not **say**, 'In four months the **harvest** will be here'?
I tell you, look **up** and see the fields **ripe** for the harvest.
The reaper is **already** receiving payment
  and gathering crops for eternal **life**,
  so that the **sower** and **reaper** can **rejoice** together.
For here the saying is verified that 'One **sows** and another **reaps**.'

---

of God justifying us through Christ—a sign of God's abiding love and fidelity!

GOSPEL In all of the Gospels, Jesus does what is shocking and controversial, always reversing widespread expectations. He associates with people deemed unacceptable, challenges the established practices of the day, and does so with confident authority. Even his closest disciples do not understand him. In today's Gospel story of Jesus and the Samaritan woman, the portrait of Jesus acting outside the norm is on full display.

The unnamed Samaritan woman comes to the well at noon, in the heat of the day. This is the first of her actions that, like those of Jesus, is unexpected. Since women would typically come to draw water early in the morning before the heat of the day, we have a hint that she may be an outcast among her own people. Yet John the evangelist may also be contrasting her encounter with Jesus with that of Nicodemus, who came at night. The woman is meeting Jesus in the light of day, openly and unafraid.

Jesus' disciples having gone into the town, he meets the woman alone. Asking any Samaritan for a drink would be surprising, for the long history of enmity between Jews and Samaritans means that even drinking from the same cup would be forbidden, resulting in ritual impurity. Asking a woman, one suspiciously alone, is even more shocking. Her questioning of Jesus is the opening he needs to teach her about living water. The woman would naturally understand living water as running water that would bubble up from a spring. Jesus' teaching moves her understanding from

Pause.

Speak the line with the woman's excitement.

Here is the point of the whole story. Maintain eye contact with the community and speak slowly and deliberately.

TO KEEP IN MIND
Always pause at the end of the reading, before you proclaim the closing dialogue ("The Word of the Lord" or "The Gospel of the Lord").

TO KEEP IN MIND
What does the reading ask your assembly to do or to be after hearing your proclamation? Focus on an intention every time you proclaim.

I sent you to **reap** what you have not **worked** for;
    others have done the work,
    and **you** are sharing the **fruits** of their work."

[Many of the **Samaritans** of that town began to **believe** in him]
    because of the word of the **woman** who testified,
    "He told me everything I have done."
[When the Samaritans **came** to him,
    they invited him to **stay** with them;
    and he stayed there two days.
Many **more** began to believe in him because of his word,
    and they said to the woman,
    "We no longer believe because of **your** word;
    for we have heard for **ourselves**,
    and we know that this is **truly** the savior of the world."]

[Shorter: John 4:5–15, 19b–26, 39a, 40–42 (see brackets)]

earthly water to a heavenly "gift of God." Further, having initially asked her for a drink, he now inspires her to ask him for a drink of this water that is "welling up to eternal life."

Jesus abruptly tells the woman to call her husband, and knows even before she speaks that she has had five "husbands." Just as living water has a symbolic meaning, so too may Jesus' reference to her five husbands. After they were conquered by Assyria, the Samaritans had intermarried with five foreign nations and worshiped their gods (2 Kings 17:30–31) Such idolatry was comparable to marital infidelity, and those other gods were regarded as unlawful husbands. The woman may thus represent the Samaritan people, to whom Jesus now offers living water. The woman readily acknowledges Jesus as prophet and speaks knowledgably with him about Samaritan theology, further suggesting her symbolic role. She speaks for her whole people.

When Jesus' disciples return from their shopping, the account moves rapidly. The disciples are amazed because Jesus is doing the unexpected in talking with a Samaritan woman, and she hurries from the scene to tell her people to come see a man who could be the Christ. The author concludes by saying that her witness brought many Samaritans to believe in Jesus, and many more believed because of Jesus' own words. Including the Samaritans among Jesus' followers reversed widespread expectations. Jesus is "savior of the world," even of the idolatrous Samaritans. E.P.

FOURTH SUNDAY OF LENT

A narrative reading in which the entire drama of the Babylonian exile is related, but this is not a mere history lesson. How does the reading want your assembly to be or to act after hearing this? Keep that intention uppermost in your mind throughout.

Chronicles = KRAH-nih-k*ls

Judah = JOO -duh

How do you feel knowing your ancestors in faith behaved this way? Bring your choice to this proclamation.

And how do you feel about God's faithfulness and care? Let that feeling come through here.

Hit the verbs in the sentence with the force of the people's rejection.

Don't swallow "remedy." Pause.

It is God who is acting here through the people's enemies.

With sadness; the beginning of the exile.

Chaldeans = kahl-DEE-uhnz; kal-DEE-unhz

LECTIONARY #32

READING I   2 Chronicles 36:14–16, 19–23

A reading from the second Book of Chronicles

In those days, **all** the **princes** of Judah, the **priests**, and the **people**
    added infidelity to **infidelity**,
    practicing all the **abominations** of the nations
    and **polluting** the LORD's **temple**
    which he had **consecrated** in Jerusalem.

Early and **often** did the LORD, the God of their fathers,
    send his **messengers** to them,
    for he had **compassion** on his people and his **dwelling** place.
But they **mocked** the messengers of God,
    despised his warnings, and **scoffed** at his prophets,
    until the **anger** of the LORD against his people was so **inflamed**
    that there was no **remedy**.
Their enemies **burnt** the house of God,
    tore down the walls of Jerusalem,
    set all its palaces **afire**,
    and **destroyed** all its precious objects.
Those who **escaped** the **sword** were carried **captive** to **Babylon**,
    where they became **servants** of the king of the Chaldeans and
        his sons
    until the kingdom of the **Persians** came to power.

Today, options are given for the readings: Year A or Year B. Contact your parish staff to learn which readings will be used.

READING I The reading from Chronicles is from the last chapter of the two-volume theological history that begins with Adam and concludes with the declarations of Cyrus the Persian. Today's text is a window that offers a glimpse into the entire history of Israel from the chronicler's perspective. The leadership of princes and priests was sometimes lax and other times blatantly sinful as they added infidelity to infidelity, and their people followed. The chronicler reports that they polluted the Lord's Temple in Jerusalem, worshiped idols, and were unjust to each other. In spite of their sinfulness, God did not abandon them, but sent prophets as messengers. God's motivation was compassion, an essential characteristic of the God of the covenant (see Psalm 103:8). Yet the people met God's merciful compassion with three repeated responses: they mocked God's messengers, they despised God's warnings, and they scoffed at the prophets. Then God's anger against the people was so inflamed that he allowed hostile nations to attack the people in order to punish them. Weakened by their sin, the people were prey to enemies who burnt the house of God, tore down walls, destroyed palaces, killed many people, and sent others into exile in Babylon. In these few verses, we hear a summary of the history that was repeated over and over: the people's sin; God's compassion in drawing them back; the people's continued sin; and divine punishment, often through foreign nations.

Quietly. God "rests" the land so, like the people, it can be renewed.

A longer pause to indicate the passage of time.

Quickly change your tone as the story shifts dramatically from God's punishment to God's salvation of the people.

Jeremiah = jayr-uh-MĪ-uh

Cyrus = SĪ-ruhs

God frees the people from slavery through Cyrus's action. Your assembly will only know this is good news (incredible news!) by your nonverbal expression, so make sure you smile with your voice, eyes, and face through to the end.

Slowly and with finality.

For meditation and context:

TO KEEP IN MIND

Proclamation cannot be effective unless it is expressive. As you prepare your proclamation, make choices about emotions. Some choices are already evident in the text.

All this was to fulfill the **word** of the Lord spoken by **Jeremiah:**
   "Until the land has **retrieved** its lost **sabbaths,**
   during all the time it lies **waste** it shall have **rest**
   while **seventy** years are fulfilled."

In the first year of **Cyrus,** king of **Persia,**
   in order to **fulfill** the word of the Lord spoken by Jeremiah,
   the Lord **inspired** King Cyrus of **Persia**
   to issue this **proclamation** throughout his kingdom,
   both by word of **mouth** and in **writing:**
   "Thus says **Cyrus,** king of **Persia:**
   All the kingdoms of the **earth**
   the Lord, the God of heaven, has **given** to me,
   and he has **also charged** me to build him a **house**
   in **Jerusalem,** which is in **Judah.**
Whoever, therefore, among you **belongs** to any part
    of **his** people,
   let him go **up,** and may his God be **with** him!"

RESPONSORIAL PSALM   Psalm 137:1–2, 3, 4–5, 6 (6ab)

R. Let my tongue be silenced, if I ever forget you!

By the streams of Babylon
   we sat and wept when we
     remembered Zion.
On the aspens of that land
   we hung up our harps.

For there our captors asked of us
   the lyrics of our songs,
and our despoilers urged us to be joyous:
   "Sing for us the songs of Zion!"

How could we sing a song of the Lord
   in a foreign land?
If I forget you, Jerusalem,
   may my right hand be forgotten!

May my tongue cleave to my palate
   if I remember you not,
if I place not Jerusalem
   ahead of my joy.

The prophets had warned of the consequences of such wickedness. Jeremiah in particular prophesied that their failure to respect the Sabbath would result in the land itself being laid waste in a kind of prolonged Sabbath rest: a seventy year exile in Babylon. Yet that is not the end of the story. The conclusion of the chronicler's history is filled with promise. God did not only use foreign nations to punish. Here God uses Cyrus, king of Persia, to offer the people another chance at life in their own land. In fulfillment of Jeremiah's prophecy, Cyrus announces that the Lord has charged him to build him a house in Jerusalem. Cyrus prays for whoever goes up to Jerusalem: "may his God be with him!" Such hope after a turbulent history ends the book, and is in fact the final chapter of "the TaNaK," the Hebrew Bible.

READING II In the First Reading, from Chronicles, we heard that God acted with compassion when Israel had sinned. In the Letter to the Ephesians, we hear a corresponding depiction: God is rich in mercy, and that mercy and compassion are particularly evident when people have sinned. Whether it be the infidelities of the past or the transgressions in Paul's day, God reaches out to sinners with unbounded mercy as a manifestation of divine love. In Christ, we can see how active that divine mercy is. God brings people to life with Christ and saves them by grace, and both expressions indicate a transformation. Those dead through sin now have life. Sinners in need of rescue from the slavery and imprisonment of sin have been brought to safety.

Paul says we have already been raised with Christ, and are seated with Christ in the

This exhortatory reading appears complex, but the idea is simple: we are saved by grace. Make sure your assembly knows this is good news by smiling with your voice, eyes, and face throughout.

Ephesians = ee-FEE-zhuhnz

The main idea of this long sentence is "God, because of great love, brought us to life, raised us up, and seated us with him." Pause at each comma; keep your voice up on the main idea, and drop it on the parentheticals.

"By grace you have been saved" is an exclamation—like "Praise God!"

Pause as if this comma were a period.

Start with your voice up to connect to what came before.

Pause at the end of this line.

Contrast our work with God's work.

TO KEEP IN MIND
Pause in order to break up separate thoughts, set apart significant statements, or indicate major shifts. Never pause in the middle of a single thought. Your primary guide for pauses is punctuation.

READING II   Ephesians 2:4–10

A reading from the Letter of Saint Paul to the Ephesians

Brothers and sisters:
God, who is **rich** in mercy,
    because of the great **love** he had for us,
    even when we were **dead** in our transgressions,
    brought us to **life** with Christ—by **grace** you have
        been **saved**—,
    raised us up **with** him,
    and **seated** us with him in the **heavens** in Christ Jesus,
    that in the ages to come
    He might show the immeasurable **riches** of his **grace**
    in his **kindness** to us in Christ **Jesus**.
For by **grace** you have been **saved** through **faith**,
    and this is not from **you**; it is the **gift** of **God**;
    it is not from **works**, so no one may **boast**.
For we are his **handiwork**, created in Christ **Jesus** for the
        good works
    that God has prepared in **advance**,
    that we should **live** in them.

---

heavenly places, proclaiming that believers already share in Christ's exaltation. Three times Paul attaches the prefix *syn –* (with) to verbs to express how intimate is the relationship we have with Christ. We might translate the verbs as colive, be coraised and be coseated. Elsewhere Paul uses a collection of verbs with the *syn –* prefix in a baptismal context, and he is likely doing so here as well. Paul creates new words to express the extraordinary newness created by God's mercy. Baptism is the immersion into the grace of God by which

we, even now, share in Christ's life, Death, Resurrection, and exaltation.

Paul adds to his description of God's abundant mercy by writing of God's immeasurable riches, acting in kindness, and ever bestowing the gift of grace. Lest believers think that their own actions bring about the transformation Paul has been describing, he insists that salvation is the work of God's grace. The final image used to describer a person transformed by grace is "work of art." Each person immersed into Christ's life is a stunning creation made by the divine craftsman. To see a believer is to

see God's own handiwork. People doing good works and living the new life in Christ are living testimony to the God who is rich in mercy.

| GOSPEL | In the Gospel, Jesus is continuing to teach Nicodemus, the Pharisee who came to him in darkness. Reminding Nicodemus of the story of Moses lifting a bronze serpent in the desert, Jesus looks ahead to the Son of Man also being lifted up. In the desert, the bronze serpent, lifted up on a pole, was a source of healing from poisonous snakes.

Think of someone specific you know who needs to hear that God loves them. Proclaim this exhortatory reading as if speaking to that one person. Encourage them; really convince them of God's great love for them.

Nicodemus = nik-uh-DEE-muhs

This whole first section is good news. Smile with your voice, eyes, and face.

Don't gloss over "God so loved the world." Make sure your assembly knows how much God loves them!

Keep your voice up to the end of the line.

Be emphatic: Jesus did not come to condemn!

We condemn ourselves if we refuse to accept God's gift of love in Jesus.

Pause at the end of this line.

The verdict by which we are saved or condemned.

How does Jesus feel about those who prefer darkness? Sad? Frustrated? Angry?

Urge your assembly to "come to the light!"

Don't swallow "in God."

TO KEEP IN MIND
Words in bold are significant words about which you must make a choice to help their meaning stand out. You may (or may not) choose to stress them.

GOSPEL   John 3:14–21

A reading from the holy Gospel according to John

Jesus said to Nicodemus:
"Just as Moses lifted up the **serpent** in the desert,
so must the Son of **Man** be lifted up,
so that everyone who **believes** in him may have eternal **life**."

For God **so loved** the world that he **gave** his **only** Son,
so that **everyone** who believes in him might not **perish**
but might have eternal **life**.
For God did not send his Son into the world to **condemn**
the world,
but that the world might be **saved** through him.
Whoever **believes** in him will **not** be condemned,
but whoever does **not** believe has **already** been condemned,
because he has not believed in the name of the only Son
of **God**.
And **this** is the verdict,
that the **light** came into the **world**,
but people preferred **darkness** to light,
because their works were **evil**.
For **everyone** who does **wicked** things **hates** the light
and does not come **toward** the light,
so that his works might not be **exposed**.
But whoever lives the **truth comes** to the light,
so that his works may be **clearly** seen as done in **God**.

The Son of Man, Jesus himself, will also be lifted up on a pole, the Cross, and so become a source of healing, even to eternal life. As John the evangelist does elsewhere, he uses a term with a double meaning: "lifted up" (hypsothenai). The meaning that Nicodemus would assume is a physical lifting up to be seen, a meaning that is true both for the bronze serpent and for Jesus. When Jesus is lifted up on the Cross, he will bring greater healing than the bronze serpent, for he will give eternal life. The second meaning of the verb hypsothenai is "to exalt," indicating that the Cross is

also a manifestation of God's glory and majesty. This is the first of three passages in which John uses the verb (also 8:28 and 12:32, 34). John teaches that, lifted up on the Cross, Jesus is also glorified. The paradox of the Cross comes to the fore as the two meanings are brought together.

The motivation for God giving his Son is love (agapao), a saving love leading to eternal life. The discourse reveals Jesus' identity and his relationship with the world he came to save, not to condemn. He comes as light in the darkness; he reveals truth, and is himself the truth. Everyone in

the world has a choice to believe in Jesus, to choose either light or darkness. Condemnation comes for those who freely and deliberately choose evil, darkness, and falsehood. Having come as Savior and light for the world, Jesus is telling Nicodemus to come out of the darkness into the light of Jesus and his saving love. Directed to Nicodemus, the discourse is also addressed to all who hear Jesus' words. E.P.

FOURTH SUNDAY OF LENT, YEAR A

LECTIONARY #31

READING I   1 Samuel 16:1b, 6–7, 10–13a

A narrative that teaches us about "seeing." God, Samuel, and Jesse see a person's worthiness to be "anointed" very differently. Let their unique perspectives come through in your proclamation.

Samuel = SAM-yoo-uhl

We jump right into the action. God is decisive.

Jesse = JES-ee

Why doesn't God simply tell Samuel which son is chosen? Does God want Samuel to learn something too?

Eliab = ee-LĪ-uhb

Samuel is confident that he knows what God wants.

The moral of this story. Speak these lines slowly and deliberately.

Now Samuel understands.

Samuel has an idea!

A reading from the first Book of Samuel

The LORD said to **Samuel**:
   "Fill your horn with **oil**, and be on your **way**.
I am sending you to **Jesse** of **Bethlehem**,
   for I have chosen my **king** from among his sons."

As Jesse and his sons came to the **sacrifice**,
   Samuel looked at **Eliab** and thought,
   "**Surely** the LORD's anointed is here before him."
But the LORD said to Samuel:
   "Do not judge from his **appearance** or from his lofty **stature**,
   because I have **rejected** him.
Not as **man** sees does **God** see,
   because man sees the **appearance**
   but the LORD looks into the **heart**."
In the **same** way Jesse presented **seven** sons before Samuel,
   but Samuel said to Jesse,
   "The **Lord** has not chosen any **one** of these."
Then Samuel asked Jesse,
   "Are these **all** the sons you have?"
Jesse replied,
   "There is still the **youngest**, who is tending the sheep."
Samuel said to Jesse,
   "**Send** for him;
   we will not begin the sacrificial banquet until he **arrives** here."

Today, options are given for the readings: Year A or Year B. Contact your parish staff to learn which readings will be used.

| READING I | God's choice of people throughout the biblical tradition is often surprising. Beginning with God's favor of Abel over Cain and Jacob over Esau, God often chose the younger son over the expected elder one. The choice of Israel, a people seen as small and insignificant, is the same motif on a larger scale. In today's reading, when God tells

the judge and prophet Samuel to go to Bethlehem to anoint the one God has chosen as king, we hear another story of God's electing the younger, seemingly inconsequential son. Those familiar with this biblical motif are not surprised at the choice of young David, even though in the story Samuel is slow to grasp God's intentions.

The account begins after Saul, the first anointed king, is rejected by God. Saul, "who was head and shoulders above all the crowd" (1 Samuel 10:23), accorded well with expectations for kingly countenance. But Saul proved an unworthy king. Even

before God rejected Saul, Saul himself had "rejected the command of the LORD" (1 Samuel 15:23). Because of Saul's unworthiness as king, God assigns to Samuel the task of finding the next chosen king. Samuel is to fill his horn with oil and anoint him. Such pouring of oil on the head was part of a rite of inauguration for priests, kings, and sometimes for prophets. It was a sign of God's choice, and consecrated a person for office. So important was anointing that the king was sometimes referred to simply as "the LORD's anointed" (as in 1 Samuel 24:6), and was considered inviolable.

Jesse is a bit incredulous. "David couldn't possibly be the one!"

ruddy = having a healthy, reddish complexion

There's an eagerness in God's command.

Jesse **sent** and had the young man **brought** to them.
He was **ruddy**, a youth **handsome** to behold
     and making a **splendid** appearance.
The LORD said,
     "**There**—**anoint** him, for **this** is the one!"
Then Samuel, with the horn of oil in hand,
     anointed David in the presence of his **brothers**;
     and from **that** day **on**, the **spirit** of the LORD **rushed**
          upon David.

For meditation and context:

RESPONSORIAL PSALM   Psalm 23:1–3a, 3b–4, 5, 6 (1)
R. The Lord is my shepherd; there is nothing I shall want.

The LORD is my shepherd; I shall not want.
     In verdant pastures he gives me repose;
beside restful waters he leads me;
     he refreshes my soul.

He guides me in right paths
     for his name's sake.
Even though I walk in the dark valley
     I fear no evil; for you are at my side
with your rod and your staff
     that give me courage.

You spread the table before me
     in the sight of my foes;
you anoint my head with oil;
     my cup overflows.

Only goodness and kindness follow me
     all the days of my life;
and I shall dwell in the house of the LORD
     for years to come.

TO KEEP IN MIND
Use inflection (the high or low pitch of your voice) to convey attitude and feeling. High pitch expresses intensity and excitement; low pitch expresses sadness, contrition, or solemnity.

An exhortatory reading, encouraging us to live as "children of light." Have strong opinions about the value of light versus dark, and let your attitude toward each come through as you proclaim.

Ephesians = ee-FEE-shuhnz

Good news! Smile with your voice, eyes, and face.

READING II   Ephesians 5:8–14

A reading from the Letter of Saint Paul to the Ephesians

Brothers and sisters:
You were once **darkness**,
     but now you are **light** in the Lord.
Live as **children** of light,
     for **light** produces every kind of **goodness**
          and **righteousness** and **truth**.
Try to learn what is **pleasing** to the Lord.

The first of Jesse's sons that Samuel sees is Eliab, the eldest. At sight of him, with fine appearance and lofty stature, Samuel immediately thinks that he is the Lord's anointed. Eliab's appearance is similar to that of the rejected Saul, a connection lost on Samuel. Just as God had rejected the towering Saul, so too does God reject Eliab. Before Samuel looks at the remaining sons, God warns him not to be swayed by appearances: "Not as man sees does God see, because man sees the appearance but the Lord looks into the heart." Six more sons are brought before

Samuel, and with God's words ringing in his ears, Samuel knows that God has not chosen any of them. Seven sons would seem to be the whole list, particularly with the symbolic meaning of seven as whole or complete. The last son is too insignificant to be counted among the seven. Samuel seems puzzled, since God had sent him to Jesse's house where he would find the one God had chosen as king. As if he had forgotten the youngest son tending the sheep, Jesse admits to having one more. He sends for the young man, "ruddy" and "handsome." This time the well-formed appear-

ance matches God's preference. Samuel immediately anoints the youth as God commands him, "There—anoint him, for this is the one!" By leaving David's name unmentioned until the last verse, the narrator reinforces the unlikely choice of David.

Several images of the passage became important traditions about King David. The Lord who looks into the heart found in David "a man after his own heart" (1 Samuel 13:14). And the boy tending the sheep became the king tending his people.

Be dismissive of these "fruitless" works.

Any part of our lives we try to keep secret needs to be healed in the light.

Take your time with this final quote, and let the community see your joy in this promise:

Take no part in the **fruitless** works of darkness;
    rather **expose** them, for it is shameful even to **mention**
    the things done by them in **secret**;
    but everything **exposed** by the light becomes **visible**,
    for everything that **becomes** visible is **light**.
Therefore, it says:
    "**Awake**, O sleeper,
    and **arise** from the dead,
    and Christ will give you **light**."

A narrative with many characters, much action, and multiple scene changes. Vary your pace, inflection, and volume in this long reading. Know each character's intention and emotion so you can keep your assembly engaged.

Don't swallow "blind from birth"; Rabbi = RAB-ī

This traditional teaching—that blindness is punishment for sin—bothers the disciples.

GOSPEL   John 9:1–41

A reading from the holy Gospel according to John

[As Jesus passed by he saw a man **blind** from **birth**.]
His **disciples** asked him,
    "**Rabbi**, who **sinned**, **this** man or his **parents**,
    that he was born **blind**?"
Jesus answered,
    "Neither **he** nor his **parents** sinned;
    it is so that the works of God might be made **visible**
        through him.
We have to do the works of the one who sent me while it is **day**.
Night is coming when no one can work.
While I am in the **world**, I am the **light** of the world."
When he had said this, [he **spat** on the ground
    and made **clay** with the **saliva**,
    and **smeared** the clay on his **eyes**, and said to him,
    "Go **wash** in the Pool of Siloam"—which means Sent—.
So he went and washed, and came back able to **see**.

His neighbors and those who had seen him earlier
    as a beggar said,
    "Isn't this the one who used to sit and **beg**?"

Following Jesus enables one to see rightly.

Take your time describing Jesus' action, and don't be afraid of its earthiness. Use the words "spat" and "smeared" to give it energy.

Siloam = sih-LOH-uhm
Drop your voice slightly on the parenthetical phrase.
Bring the man's amazement to this line.
Give this exchange a lot of energy; the dissention caused by Jesus' healing begins here. Make sure the different voices in these few lines sound distinct.

READING II | Throughout this exhortation we find vivid contrasts: life in the past and life now, darkness and light, sleeping and waking. Paul uses them to urge believers to live in accordance with the faith they now profess and to reject their past way of life. The first image is stark: "you were once darkness," using darkness as a personification of the ignorance, shame, wickedness, and fruitless works that characterized their former life. But now, "you are light" signals a total transformation of the person. They are light "in the Lord" because they have been plunged into Christ's life and transforming light through Baptism.

Today's reading is part of a longer exhortation in which the author, either Paul or someone writing in his name, provides instruction on how believers are to live in the world. To describe the visible, active way of life believers should practice, Paul uses the verb "walk" (*peripateo*), translated here and elsewhere as "live." He uses the verb seven times in Ephesians (2:2,10; 4:1; 4:17; 5:2, 8, 15), sometimes to denote the unwise manner of past life, and other times as the realm in which they now live. When Paul says "Live (walk) as children of the light," he uses a verb form that means to do so in a sustained basis. Walking in the Lord's light is no temporary activity, but encompasses everything that believers do. The light in which they walk is effective. Goodness, righteousness, and truth are visible manifestations, open to scrutiny in the light of day. Goodness (*agathosyne*) refers to an intrinsic quality of heart and mind that is manifest is deeds of kindness. The word does not occur in secular Greek, highlighting the fact that such goodness is from God, and is one of the fruits of the Spirit

Some said, "It **is**,"
    but **others** said, "**No**, he just **looks** like him."
He said, "I **am**."]
So they said to him, "**How** were your eyes opened?"
He replied,
    "The man called **Jesus** made **clay** and **anointed** my eyes
    and told me, 'Go to Siloam and **wash**.'
So I went there and washed and was able to **see**."
And they said to him, "Where **is** he?"
He said, "I don't **know**."

[They brought the one who was once blind to the **Pharisees**.
Now Jesus had made clay and opened his eyes on a **sabbath**.
So then the Pharisees **also** asked him how he was able to see.
He said to them,
    "He put **clay** on my eyes, and I **washed**, and now I can **see**."
So some of the Pharisees said,
    "This man is not from **God**,
    because he does not keep the **sabbath**."
But **others** said,
    "How can a **sinful** man do such **signs**?"
And there was a **division** among them.
So they said to the blind man **again**,
    "What do **you** have to say about him,
    since he opened your eyes?"
He said, "He is a **prophet**."]

Now the Jews did not **believe**
    that he had been **blind** and gained his **sight**
    until they summoned the **parents** of the one who had gained
        his sight.
They asked them,
    "Is this your **son**, who you say was **born** blind?
How does he now **see**?"
His parents answered and said,
    "We **know** that this is our **son** and that he was born **blind**.

Margin notes (left column):

Pick up the pace and let the man's natural excitement at being healed come through in his words.

The man's responses are simple and honest.

Pause before this scene shift.

Don't swallow "sabbath."

Keep the energy up as the arguing continues, and make sure it sounds like arguing.

Pause here to let his statement settle.

Proclaim these lines with the suspicion of the Pharisees.

Imagine the fright of his parents being brought before the Pharisees and risking expulsion. The stakes are high! Proclaim their lines with anxiety and a desire to get this over with quickly!

(Galatians 5:22). Righteousness (*dikaiosyne*), like goodness, is a divine attribute in which we share. It refers to being in right relationship in every sphere. The third quality produced by light is truth (*aletheia*). Truth, another divine characteristic, includes both what is spoken and what is done. It includes constancy, sincerity, freedom from falsehood, and is trustworthy and reliable. Truth can be exposed to the light, whereas deceit remains always in the dark.

The final verse of our reading is likely from an early Christian hymn used in Baptism. Awaking from sleep and rising

from the dead continue the emphasis on transformation found throughout the exhortation. Christ, who is himself light, gives light to those who have awakened from sleep, no longer living in darkness. The verse following our reading reiterates Paul's emphasis on how believers are to conduct their lives: "Watch carefully how you live (walk), not as foolish persons, but as wise." Originally addressed to an early Christian community in Ephesus, the appeal to manifest goodness, righteousness, and truth, ever walking in the light of

the Lord, remains a clear and vital instruction to people of every time and place.

GOSPEL The Gospel begins with Jesus seeing a man (*anthropos*) blind from birth. The noun *anthropos* means a human person, and according to St. Augustine, the blind man stands for the human race, blind from birth. Regarding the blind man from a cultural perspective, Jesus' disciples ask him whose sin was responsible for his blindness. A common notion of the time was that illness of any kind was caused by sinfulness. They pre-

We do **not** know how he **sees** now,
    nor do we know **who** opened his eyes.
Ask **him**, he is of age;
    he can speak for **himself**."
His parents said this because they were **afraid**
    of the Jews, for the Jews had already agreed
    that if anyone **acknowledged** him as the Christ,
    he would be **expelled** from the synagogue.
For this reason his parents said,
    "He is of **age**; question **him**."

So a **second** time they called the man who had been blind
    and said to him, "Give **God** the praise!
We **know** that this man is a **sinner**."
He replied,
    "If he is a **sinner**, I do not **know**.
One thing I **do** know is that I was **blind** and now I **see**."
So they said to him,
    "What did he **do** to you?
    How did he open your eyes?"
He answered them,
    "I told you **already** and you did not **listen**.
Why do you want to hear it **again**?
Do **you** want to become his disciples, **too**?"
They **ridiculed** him and said,
    "**You** are that man's disciple;
    we are disciples of **Moses**!
We **know** that God spoke to **Moses**,
    but we do **not** know where this one is from."
The man answered and said to them,
    "This is what is so **amazing**,
    that you do not know where he is **from**, yet he **opened** my **eyes**.
We **know** that God does not listen to **sinners**,
    but if one is **devout** and does his **will**, he **listens** to him.
It is **unheard** of that anyone **ever** opened the eyes of a person
    born blind.

Proclaim these lines with the same anxiety as the parents' response, as if they were speaking their thoughts.

Notice the play on who "knows" what. The Pharisees are sure about their judgments.

The man refuses to conjecture about another person's heart.

Be insistent! This doesn't make any sense to the Pharisees. It must be a trick!

With some sarcasm.

The man has made fun of them and now the Pharisees are really angry!

Again, note the play on who thinks *they know and who* really *knows.*

To the man it's perfectly clear where Jesus is from, and he can't understand the Pharisees' inability to see.

---

sumed that the person had either inherited blindness due to the parents' sin, or that persons born blind were guilty themselves—an unusual, otherwise unattested notion. Their question and misunderstanding, frequent in the Fourth Gospel, is an occasion for Jesus to teach. On this occasion, he will teach not only by his words, but also by his act of healing. In both ways, he reveals his identity as the light of the world, transforming blindness to sight, darkness to light, ignorance to understanding.

Sometimes Jesus heals people simply by a word. This time, he does several

actions, and even gets the blind man involved in the healing. First, Jesus spits on the ground, and makes clay with the saliva. Turning around the Jewish understanding that any bodily fluid, including saliva, was unclean (as in Leviticus 15:8), Jesus uses it for healing. He makes something "unclean" into a new substance that heals. The evangelist says that Jesus then "smeared" the clay on the man's eyes; the word he uses here is *epichrio*, based on the word "anoint" (*chrio*), giving a possible baptismal symbolism, as does the man's washing in the pool of Siloam. The pool's symbolic

meaning, "Sent," means that the man is be washed in the "One-who-is-Sent," washed in Jesus himself, the living water.

The healing in this story has long been interpreted as a new act of creation; Irenaeus, for example, wrote that it was the same hand of God in Jesus' actions that had formed humanity in the beginning. Jesus had told his disciples that he did the work of God, and in his actions is displaying God's own work. The clay Jesus uses in his work has a striking biblical resonance: "O LORD, you are our father; we are the clay

This is too much! This is the high point of the Pharisees' anger.

Describe this action with their outrage.

Expelled, he is again an outcast. Jesus comes to invite him into the community of the Reign of God.

Drop your volume a bit as if this were an intimate conversation between the two.

If this man were **not** from God,
    he would not be able to **do** anything."
[They answered and said to him,
    "You were born **totally** in sin,
    and are **you** trying to teach **us**?"
Then they **threw** him out.

When Jesus heard that they had thrown him out,
    he **found** him and said, "Do you **believe** in the Son of Man?"
He answered and said,
    "Who **is** he, sir, that I may **believe** in him?"
Jesus said to him,
    "You have **seen** him,
    and the one **speaking** with you is **he**."
He said,
    "I **do** believe, Lord," and he worshiped him.]
Then Jesus said,
    "I came into this world for **judgment**,
    so that those who do **not** see **might** see,
    and those who **do** see might become **blind**."

Some of the **Pharisees** who were with him **heard** this
    and said to him, "Surely **we** are not also blind, **are** we?"
Jesus said to them,
    "If you **were** blind, you would have no **sin**;
    but now you are saying, 'We **see**,' so your sin **remains**."

[Shorter: John 9:1, 6–9, 13–17, 34–38 (see brackets)]

Not seeing rightly is not a sin if you acknowledge that your sight is imperfect. But when you think your way of seeing is the *only* right way, then your sin remains.

TO KEEP IN MIND
In a narrative, find an emotion or point of view for each character, keeping in mind that these might change during the reading.

---

and you the potter: we are the work of your hands" (Isaiah 64:7).

As the Gospel continues, the man having received his physical sight continues to develop his insight, his eyes of faith. When he is first questioned about who has cured him, he replies simply "the man called Jesus." Questioned further, he identifies Jesus as a prophet, later affirming that Jesus must be from God, or he could do nothing. The man is not afraid to admit what he doesn't know, and to ask questions. In the final scene, the man has another encounter with Jesus, and identifies him as *kyrios*, "Lord," professes "I do believe," and worships him.

As the once-blind man gains deeper insight, the evangelist sets up an intriguing contrast. The Pharisees, who think that they can see, grow more and more blind. They state confidently that Jesus is not from God, and that they know he is a sinner. They do ironically hit on the truth when they ridicule the newly sighted man. After telling him that they are disciples of Moses, they say of Jesus, "we do not know where this one is from." Yet the *anthropos* knows that Jesus is from God, while the Pharisees remain in blindness and sin. E.P.

FIFTH SUNDAY OF LENT

A beautiful exhortatory reading of good news. How does the reading want your assembly to respond to this news? Keep that intention in mind as you proclaim.

Jeremiah = jayr-uh-MĪ-uh
Don't make this sound ominous; these are good days that are coming.
Emphasize the distinctions between the old and new covenants.

How does God feel about this broken covenant?
How does God feel about this new covenant? Change your expression immediately to reflect this new emotion.

Slowly, with great joy and solemnity.

Smile with your voice, eyes, and face as you share God's joy in making this covenant.

TO KEEP IN MIND

You can't proclaim what you don't understand. Read the Scripture passage and its commentary in *Workbook*. Then read it from your Bible, including what comes before and after it so that you understand the context.

LECTIONARY #35

READING I   Jeremiah 31:31–34

A reading from the Book of the Prophet Jeremiah

The days are **coming**, says the LORD,
   when I will make a **new** covenant with the house of Israel
   and the house of Judah.
It will not be like the covenant I made with their **fathers**
   the day I **took** them by the **hand**
   to lead them **forth** from the land of Egypt;
   for they **broke** my covenant,
   and I had to show myself their **master**, says the LORD.
But **this** is the covenant that I will **make**
   with the house of Israel after those days, says the LORD.
I will place my law **within** them and **write** it upon their **hearts**;
   I will be their **God**, and **they** shall be my **people**.
No **longer** will they have need to **teach** their friends and relatives
   how to know the LORD.
All, from **least** to **greatest**, shall **know** me, says the LORD,
   for I will **forgive** their **evildoing** and **remember** their sin
      no **more**.

Today, options are given for the readings: Year A or Year B. Contact your parish staff to learn which readings will be used.

READING I | Jeremiah's historical context was one of political and religious turmoil, reflected in his personal life. The northern kingdom had been devastated by Assyria, and Babylon attacked his homeland of Judah, sending many into exile. In the midst of this devastation and personal anguish is one of the most beautiful of biblical prophecies: chapters 30–31, usually referred to as Jeremiah's "book of consolation." In contrast to the darkness of much of his prophecy, his "book of consolation" soars with the poetry of healing, hope, and newness. Perhaps written near the end of the exile, chapters 30–31 look forward to restoration and the reuniting of Israel and Judah.

Today's reading is a promise of the coming days in which the covenant of old will be transformed. Although Jeremiah saw the exile as God's punishment for the sins of leaders and people, his proclamation of the new covenant is not based on their repentance, but simply on God's choice. We can see both continuity and newness in this promised covenant. The continuity stems from God's abiding choice of the house of Israel: "I will be their God, and they shall be my people." In spite of their repeated rebellion, they are still God's treasured possession. The newness is interior and individual. Since the Law that had been written on stone had not forged their fidelity, the new covenant will be written on their hearts, allowing all to know the God who will forgive their sins.

For meditation and context:

TO KEEP IN MIND

Pay attention to the pace of your reading. Varying the pace gives listeners clues to the meaning of the text. The most common problem for proclaimers new to the ministry is going too fast to be understood.

This didactic reading teaches that Christ is our model of prayer. We are permitted—encouraged even—to cry out to God in our pain. Do you know someone who needs this permission? Proclaim as if you were speaking to that person.

Don't swallow "flesh."

This is a visceral image; give it energy.

Good news!

Emphasize the progression: through fidelity to God Jesus received life; through fidelity to Jesus we receive life.

A narrative with exhortatory passages. Although Jesus is speaking about his impending death, he is clear that this is ultimately good news: learning to give our lives is a difficult but essential part of our faith that the Father will honor.

Bethsaida = beth-SAY-uh-duh

With eagerness and excitement.

RESPONSORIAL PSALM   Psalm 51:3–4, 12–13, 14–15 (12a)

R. Create a clean heart in me, O God.

Have mercy on me, O God, in your goodness;
    in the greatness of your compassion wipe
        out my offense.
Thoroughly wash me from my guilt
    and of my sin cleanse me.

A clean heart create for me, O God,
    and a steadfast spirit renew within me.
Cast me not out from your presence,
    and your Holy Spirit take not from me.

Give me back the joy of your salvation,
    and a willing spirit sustain in me.
I will teach transgressors your ways,
    and sinners shall return to you.

READING II   Hebrews 5:7–9

A reading from the Letter to the Hebrews

In the days when Christ Jesus was in the **flesh**,
    he offered **prayers** and **supplications** with loud **cries** and **tears**
    to the one who was able to **save** him from death,
    and he was **heard** because of his reverence.
Son though he **was**, he learned **obedience** from what he **suffered**;
    and when he was made **perfect**,
    he became the source of eternal **salvation** for **all** who
        obey him.

GOSPEL   John 12:20–33

A reading from the holy Gospel according to John

Some **Greeks** who had come to worship at the Passover Feast
        came to **Philip**, who was from Bethsaida in Galilee,
    and asked him, "Sir, we would like to see **Jesus**."

READING II The beautiful text from Hebrews begins with a portrayal of Jesus "in the flesh," presenting him in the human status he shares with all people. When he was in the flesh, Jesus did what other human beings do: he prayed, he cried out to God, he wept, he suffered. This description brings to mind Jesus in the Garden of Gethsemane. There he cried out to God in his agony, and he shed tears.

This Jesus is not only "in the flesh," but he is also "Son," a christological affirmation that he is Son of God. The Letter to the Hebrews as a whole emphasizes Jesus' divine sonship, giving a multifaceted depiction of him in its opening verses. The Son is "heir of all things and through whom he created the universe, who is the refulgence of his glory, the very imprint his being, and who sustains all things by his mighty word" (1:2–3). In today's reading, the author says that even though Jesus is Son, with all the glory that entails, he learned obedience through suffering. We see this paradoxical pairing of divine sonship and suffering in the "*kenosis* hymn" of Philippians as well: "Though he was in the form of God . . . [Jesus] emptied himself . . . he hum-bled himself, becoming obedient to death" (Philippians 2:6–8).

Since Jesus was sinless, what does it mean that he was "made perfect"? Though the term perfection (*teleios*) can connote moral purity, the perfection of Christ refers to completion, to fulfillment. Having completed the purpose for which he came into the world, Christ Jesus in glory is the source of salvation for those who obey him. In the final verse, believers are subtly enjoined to be obedient as was Christ, the font of eternal salvation.

This is how Jesus answers their question: If you want to "see" Jesus you must be willing to become like him—in death but also in glory.
"Pay attention!"

Dismiss the smallness of this outcome.
With exuberance reflecting the bounty one grain produces.

This is all good news. Make sure it sounds that way!
Pause.

Jesus acknowledges his very human feelings.

This is a solemn pronouncement, but should resonate with vigor and life!
Quickly.
With amazement. Drop your voice to convey the whisperings of the crowd.

Good news!

Fear not! Jesus' Death brings life to you!
Pause.
Drop your voice slightly but not so much that this line is lost.

> **TO KEEP IN MIND**
> A didactic reading is usually given out of love for the community. Make sure that love is evident in your proclamation.

Philip went and told **Andrew**;
    then Andrew and Philip went and told **Jesus**.
Jesus answered them,
    "The hour has **come** for the Son of Man to be **glorified**.
Amen, **amen**, I say to you,
    unless a grain of wheat falls to the ground and **dies**,
    it **remains** just a **grain** of wheat;
    but if it **dies**, it produces **much** fruit.
Whoever **loves** his life **loses** it,
    and whoever **hates** his life in **this** world
    will **preserve** it for **eternal** life.
Whoever **serves** me must **follow** me,
    and where **I** am, there **also** will my servant be.
The Father will **honor** whoever serves me.

"I am **troubled** now. Yet what should I say,
'Father, **save** me from this hour'?
But it was for **this** purpose that I **came** to this hour.
Father, **glorify** your name."
Then a **voice** came from heaven,
    "I **have** glorified it and will glorify it **again**."
The crowd there heard it and said it was **thunder**;
    but **others** said, "An **angel** has spoken to him."
Jesus answered and said,
    "This voice did not come for **my** sake but for **yours**.
Now is the time of **judgment** on this world;
    now the **ruler** of this world will be **driven** out.
And when I am **lifted** up from the **earth**,
    I will draw **everyone** to **myself**."
He said this indicating the kind of **death** he would die.

GOSPEL | The Gospel opens with some Greeks, probably Gentiles, wanting to see Jesus. The plotting of Jesus' opponents, the gathering of Jews and Greeks, and the setting in Jerusalem have led Jesus to announce, "the hour has come for the Son of Man to be glorified." At the wedding feast at Cana, Jesus said that his hour had not yet come, but did not explain what he meant. Now he tells his disciples succinctly that the hour means his glorification. Glory, (*doxa*) first introduced in the prologue (1:14) is a visible manifestation of God's presence revealed to humanity. In this scene, before anyone can conclude that Jesus will immediately show forth his glory, he uses a metaphor of the seed that must die. As an image of his own impending Death, the grain that "falls to the ground" in order to produce fruit tells his disciples that his hour of glorification must include his Death. Only through losing his life in this world will Jesus' glorification be accomplished. All who want to come to eternal life must likewise be willing to lay down their lives; they must follow Jesus, must lose life in order to save it.

Since the hour of his glorification is also the hour of his agony, Jesus is troubled. Only his Father can save him from this hour. With a divine voice heard only here in John's Gospel, Jesus' Father announces that he has already glorified Jesus, and will do so yet again, referring to the coming hour of glory accomplished through Jesus' Death. A final way Jesus refers to this mysterious hour is his being "lifted up." The term simultaneously means Jesus' being lifted up on the Cross, and his exaltation, the hour of his glorification. E.P.

FIFTH SUNDAY
OF LENT, YEAR A

An exhortatory reading that should be proclaimed with great intensity and love. God's promise of restoration is good news.

Ezekiel = ee-ZEE-kee-uhl

Fill these lines (and especially the word "O") with God's love for the people: "I can't wait to bring you life!"

This shouldn't sound like, "Then you'll be sorry!" Rather, "Then you'll know how much I love you!"

The second time this phrase appears; look directly at the assembly as you express God's love and longing for his people.

These lines restate the same ideas as above; slow down to let them sink in more deeply. What does God sound like as he makes these promises?

Pause after this line.

Take significant pauses at each comma; slow down on "I will do it," and proclaim with steadfast assurance.

For meditation and context:

LECTIONARY #34

READING I Ezekiel 37:12–14

A reading from the Book of the Prophet Ezekiel

Thus says the Lord **God**:
　O my people, I will **open** your graves
　and have you **rise** from them,
　and bring you **back** to the land of **Israel**.
Then you shall **know** that **I** am the Lord,
　when I **open** your graves and have you **rise** from them,
　O my **people**!
I will put my **spirit** in you that you may **live**,
　and I will settle you upon your **land;**
　thus you shall **know** that I am the **Lord**.
I have **promised**, and I will **do** it, says the Lord.

RESPONSORIAL PSALM Psalm 130:1–2, 3–4, 5–6, 7–8 (7)

R. With the Lord there is mercy and fullness of redemption.

Out of the depths I cry to you, O Lord;
　Lord, hear my voice!
Let your ears be attentive
　to my voice in supplication.

If you, O Lord, mark iniquities,
　Lord, who can stand?
But with you is forgiveness,
　that you may be revered.

I trust in the Lord;
　my soul trusts in his word.
More than sentinels wait for the dawn,
　let Israel wait for the Lord.

For with the Lord is kindness
　and with him is plenteous redemption;
and he will redeem Israel
　from all their iniquities.

TO KEEP IN MIND

Exhortatory texts make an urgent appeal to listeners. They may encourage, warn, or challenge, and often include a call to action. You must convey the urgency and passion behind the words.

Today, options are given for the readings: Year A or Year B. Contact your parish staff to learn which readings will be used.

READING I Ezekiel, priest and prophet, lived through Babylon's destruction of Jerusalem and its Temple in 586 BC, and was later taken into exile. While in Babylon, Ezekiel received his call to be a prophet. From the beginning, Ezekiel had numerous divinely inspired, often bizarre, visions that accompanied the more typical "Thus says the Lord God" prophetic mes-

sages. The prophecy in today's reading took place in the third of four vision narratives. Ezekiel says that the hand of the Lord "led me out in the spirit of the Lord and set me in the center of the broad valley. It was now filled with bones" (37:1). In this massive graveyard, the bones are dry, without any possibility of life. God commanded Ezekiel to prophecy over the bones, promising to bring them back to life. When Ezekiel does as God had commanded, he hears a rattling as the dry bones come together. Then God commands Ezekiel to say to the spirit (*ruah*), "breathe into these

slain that they may come to life" (37:9). When the spirit came into them, the bones did come alive and stood up. God tells the prophet, "These bones are the whole house of Israel" (37:11). They had been thinking that they were as good as dead, their bones dried up, and their hope lost.

At this point, today's reading begins. Through the prophet, God again speaks, announcing great promises to the people. The promise to open graves and have the people rise from them has already been foreshadowed in the previous scene of dry bones. Exile in Babylon is comparable to a

Make sure you understand Paul's reasoning in this didactic reading; keep separate thoughts separate by pausing at the periods. Note the contrast Paul sets up between flesh/body and spirit, between death and life.

Those still bound to sin are "in the flesh." Remind your assembly that they are not in the flesh.

This actually means "since Christ is in you." Use a dismissive tone in this parenthetical phrase: Don't worry about the sinful body. Keep the pace up from here to the end, pausing briefly at commas, so as not to lose the train of thought.
The same spirit brings the same Resurrection.

The body is not evil! It will be redeemed as well and come to life.

READING II   Romans 8:8–11

A reading from the Letter of Saint Paul to the Romans

Brothers and sisters:
Those who are in the **flesh** cannot please God.
But **you** are **not** in the flesh;
    on the **contrary**, you are in the **spirit**,
    if only the Spirit of God **dwells** in you.
Whoever does not have the Spirit of Christ does not **belong**
        to him.
But if Christ is **in** you,
    although the **body** is dead because of **sin**,
    the spirit is **alive** because of **righteousness**.
If the **Spirit** of the one who raised Jesus from the dead **dwells**
        in you,
    the One who raised **Christ** from the dead
    will give **life** to your mortal bodies **also**,
    through his **Spirit dwelling** in **you**.

TO KEEP IN MIND
A *didactic* text makes a point or teaches something. Help your assembly to follow the argument and understand what's being taught.

TO KEEP IN MIND
Making eye contact with the assembly connects you with them and connects them to the reading more deeply than using your voice alone. This helps the assembly stay with the story and keeps them engaged.

---

grave that God assures will be opened; the entombed people will be brought back to life. For people in exile, the only life that matters is life in their own land. Their hopelessness can be transformed by God's promise to bring them back to the land of Israel. The Lord who speaks through Ezekiel is the God of life who originally breathed a life-giving spirit (*ruah*) into Adam. God's giving of the spirit's breath by freeing the people from exile is analogous to a new creation.

When the people are settled again in their own land, God says that the result will

be "you shall know that I am the Lord." The promise of knowing the Lord occurs seventy-two times in Ezekiel, signifying the people's listening, recognition, and right relationship with God. Their lack of knowledge, indicating their rebellion and refusal to listen and obey, had resulted in the punishment of exile. God's message to the people expects an appropriate response of obedience so that they will know the God who has brought them back to life.

The ancient promise of making the people rise from their graves, a metaphor referring to the promise of restoration from

exile, is later interpreted as the promise of a literal risen life beyond death. Christians see Jesus' Resurrection as the first sign of fulfillment of Ezekiel's prophecy of rising from the grave. Whether referring to restoration to their land or restoration to life-after-death, this prophecy concludes with absolute assurance that all the promises will be fulfilled. "I have promised, and I will do it, says the Lord."

READING II   In Paul's exhortation to the Roman Christians, he contrasts living "in the flesh" and living "in the

A narrative in which all the emotions are heightened. We know this story, but don't telegraph the ending. Rather, keep the emotions authentic to what is happening at each point in the story.

Lazarus = LAZ-uh-ruhs

Bethany = BETH-uh-nee

"You remember Mary, don't you?"

Jesus has complete confidence that, whatever happens, God will be glorified. His disciples aren't so sure.

Again, it's Jesus' trust in God that allows him to delay his departure. Rabbi = RAB-ī

Make sure the disciples' anxiety and concern come through.

Jesus remains calm and confident.

GOSPEL   John 11:1–45

A reading from the holy Gospel according to John

Now a man was **ill**, **Lazarus** from Bethany,
    the village of **Mary** and her sister **Martha**.
Mary was the one who had **anointed** the Lord with perfumed oil
    and dried his feet with her **hair**;
    it was her **brother** Lazarus who was ill.
So [the sisters sent word to Jesus saying,
    "Master, the one you **love** is **ill**."
When Jesus heard this he said,
    "This illness is **not** to end in **death**,
    but is for the **glory** of God,
    that the Son of God may be **glorified** through it."
Now Jesus **loved** Martha and her sister and Lazarus.
So when he heard that he was ill,
    he **remained** for two days in the place where he was.
Then **after** this he said to his disciples,
    "Let us go back to **Judea**."]
The disciples said to him,
    "Rabbi, the Jews were just trying to **stone** you,
    and you want to go **back** there?"
Jesus answered,
    "Are there not twelve hours in a **day**?
If one walks during the **day**, he does not **stumble**,
    because he sees the **light** of this world.
But if one walks at **night**, he **stumbles**,
    because the light is not **in** him."
He said this, and then told them,
    "Our friend Lazarus is **asleep**,
    but I am going to **awaken** him."

spirit." Both words, flesh and spirit, have several meanings. Sometimes being in the flesh simply refers to the human condition, as we hear in the Letter to the Hebrews, "when Christ Jesus was in the flesh" (5:7). Flesh in this sense is the whole human person, observable and able to relate to others. At other times, being in the flesh has a negative connotation, indicating a person in a limited, earthbound existence, closed in to selfish desires, and resistant to God. In verse 7, just before today's reading, Paul summarizes, "the concern of the flesh is

hostility toward God; it does not submit to the law of God, nor can it."

"Spirit" has diverse meanings as well. It can refer to the life principle that animates a person, giving the capacity to think and to exercise the will. In today's pericope, living in the spirit presents a manner of life opposite to living in the flesh: a person open to God, acting in accordance with God's will, and pleasing to God. In the letter to the Romans, the first mention Paul makes of Spirit is "Spirit of holiness" (1:4), God's own Spirit, the divine presence and power. A person living "in the spirit" is

receptive to this animating divine Spirit. Paul tells the Roman community that if the Spirit dwells in them they belong to Christ. Shortly after this passage, Paul writes further on the communion between the human spirit and the divine Spirit, telling his audience they have received a spirit of adoption, making them children of God, and joint heirs with Christ (8:15–17).

Using the designations "the Spirit of God," and "the Spirit of Christ," Paul explains that the Spirit raised Christ from the dead. The Spirit can likewise give life to those who are dead because of sin. We heard in the

"Good, then we don't have to go to Bethany!"

Simply; no drama.

Didymus = DID-uh-muhs (meaning twin)

Thomas recognizes that Jesus has a connection with God that gives him confidence and peace, even unto death, and he wants it too! But this statement is really for us. Use eye contact to invite listeners into this intimate relationship with God.
Bethany = BETH-uh-nee

What is Martha feeling toward Jesus? Don't deny her a very human response.

She catches herself, and affirms her trust in Jesus and God.

This statement shouldn't sound grandiose. Jesus is having a very intimate conversation with a grieving friend, trying to console her.

So the disciples said to him,
    "Master, if he is **asleep**, he will be **saved**."
But Jesus was talking about his **death**,
    while **they** thought that he meant ordinary sleep.
So then Jesus said to them **clearly**,
    "Lazarus has **died**.
And I am **glad** for you that I was not there,
    that you may **believe**.
Let us **go** to him."
So **Thomas**, called Didymus, said to his fellow disciples,
    "Let us **also** go to **die** with him."

[When Jesus arrived, he found that Lazarus
    had already been in the tomb for **four** days.]
Now Bethany was near Jerusalem, only about two miles away.
And many of the Jews had come to Martha and Mary
    to **comfort** them about their brother.
[When Martha heard that **Jesus** was coming,
    she went to **meet** him;
    but **Mary** sat at home.
Martha said to Jesus,
    "Lord, if you had **been** here,
    my brother would not have **died**.
But even **now** I know that **whatever** you ask of God,
    God will **give** you."
Jesus said to her,
    "Your brother will **rise**."
Martha said to him,
    "I **know** he will rise,
    in the **resurrection** on the last day."
Jesus told her,
    "**I** am the **resurrection** and the **life**;
    whoever **believes** in me, even if he **dies**, will **live**,
    and everyone who **lives** and **believes** in me will **never** die.

First Reading from Ezekiel that return to the land was analogous to being raised from the dead. Now what was only a metaphor is fulfilled in Jesus' being raised from the dead. The Spirit dwelling in us will also give life to our mortal bodies after death.

| GOSPEL | In John's Gospel, the portrait of Jesus is more majestic and exalted than in the Synoptic Gospels (Matthew, Mark, and Luke). He and the Father are one, and that intimate relationship pervades the Gospel. Yet in the account of the raising of Lazarus, Jesus'

human emotions come to the fore, displaying his deep love for Lazarus and his sisters and the pain he feels at Lazarus' death. Lazarus' sisters, Mary and Martha, send a brief message to Jesus, "Master (*kyrios*), the one you love is ill." Before making the journey to their home in Bethany, Jesus explains to his disciples that his friend's illness will not end in death, but for the glory of God, and that he will waken Lazarus, who has fallen asleep. Using the image of sleep, misunderstood by his disciples, (a frequent catalyst for teaching in John's Gospel) the disciples say that if he is only

asleep, he will be saved (*sothesetai*), using a verb that can mean either "recover" or "be saved." Ironically, in their misunderstanding they have spoken the truth that Lazarus will be saved to eternal life.

Jesus' disciples are fearful about entering Judea, where Jesus' opponents will be waiting, perhaps to stone him. Demonstrating a combination of fear and desperation at Jesus' determination to go to Judea, his disciple Thomas cries out, "Let us also go to die with him." Lazarus' death, the presence of Jesus' enemies in Judea, and Thomas' outcry are foreboding signs of

With simple confidence.

Do **you** believe this?"
She said to him, "**Yes**, Lord.
I have come to believe that **you** are the **Christ**, the Son of God,
   the one who is coming into the world."]

There's excitement mixed in her grief.

When she had said this,
   she went and called her sister Mary **secretly**, saying,
     "The **teacher** is here and is **asking** for you."
As soon as she heard this,
   she rose **quickly** and went to him.

Keep the scene moving; no need to linger on these details.

For Jesus had not yet come into the village,
   but was still where Martha had **met** him.
So when the Jews who were with her in the house comforting her
   saw Mary get up quickly and go out,
     they **followed** her,
   presuming that she was going to the tomb to **weep** there.
When Mary came to where Jesus was and **saw** him,
   she fell at his **feet** and said to him,
     "**Lord**, if you had **been** here,
   my brother would not have **died**."

Mary makes the same statement as Martha. Is she expressing her anger, her trust, or a little of both?

The human Jesus is clearly overwhelmed by the very human emotions around him.

perturbed = per-TERBD (agitated and upset)

When Jesus saw her **weeping** and the **Jews** who had come with
    her weeping,
   [he became **perturbed** and **deeply** troubled, and said,
   "**Where** have you laid him?"
They said to him, "Sir, come and **see**."
And Jesus **wept**.
So the Jews said, "See how he **loved** him."

Let Jesus' grief come through as you describe his emotions.

Articulate this short line carefully and with all of Jesus' sadness. Pause before and after.

Is the crowd angry too? Disappointed?

But some of them said,
   "Could not the one who **opened** the **eyes** of the blind man
   have **done** something so that this man would not have **died**?"

Note Jesus is still upset.

So Jesus, perturbed **again**, came to the **tomb**.
It was a cave, and a **stone** lay across it.
Jesus said, "**Take away** the stone."

Jesus' Passion that will soon take place, just as his disciples feared.

    Because Jesus had waited two days, and then made the journey to Bethany, Lazarus had not only died, but had even been in the tomb for four days. In the Judaism of the time, there was a common belief that a person's soul remained near the body for three days; by the fourth day, it was certain that the person had died. Even before Jesus arrives at the tomb, Martha hurries out to meet him. The conversation between Jesus and Martha is more than a personal dialogue. Woven into

it is the faith-filled proclamation of the Church. With Martha, the Church believes, "Whatever you ask of God, God will give you." In the narrative and theological context of John's Gospel, Martha's statement reinforces the portrait of Jesus as the only Son of the Father, and looks ahead to Jesus' priestly prayer at the final supper with his disciples (John 17).

    As their dialogue continues, Martha speaks as a Jew who believes in the resurrection of the dead. Not all Jews believed in the resurrection, but those who did looked for it only on the last day. Jesus moves

Martha from this belief to a new revelation, an unveiling about Jesus himself as the Resurrection and the Life. He begins with "I am" (*ego eimi*), as he does elsewhere in John's Gospel: I am the bread of life, the light of the world, the sheep-gate, the good shepherd. Jesus' "I am" statements resonate with the divine "I am" announced to Moses (Exodus 3:14). Not only does Jesus' "I am" relate him to his Father, but the "I am" statements also present his saving relationship with those who believe in him, as bread, as shepherd, and as life. In response to Jesus' question, "Do you

Martha, the dead man's sister, said to him,
  "Lord, by now there will be a **stench**;
  he has been dead for four **days**."
Jesus said to her,
  "Did I not tell you that if you **believe**
  you will see the **glory** of God?"
So they took **away** the stone.
And Jesus **raised** his eyes and said,
  "**Father**, I **thank** you for **hearing** me.
I know that you **always** hear me;
  but because of the **crowd** here I have said this,
  that they may believe that you **sent** me."
And when he had said this,
  he **cried** out in a **loud** voice,
  "**Lazarus**, come **out**!"
The **dead** man **came** out,
  tied hand and foot with burial bands,
  and his face was **wrapped** in a **cloth**.
So Jesus said to them,
  "**Untie** him and let him **go**."

Now **many** of the Jews who had come to Mary
  and **seen** what he had done began to **believe** in him.}

[Shorter: John 11:3–7, 17, 20–27, 33b–45 (see brackets)]

Pour all of Jesus' emotion into this prayer: he's seen two close friends in grief; he himself is agitated and sad; and, on top of it all, it seems the crowd still doesn't believe he was sent by God.

You needn't shout but you must raise your volume here.

More quietly, exhausted with emotion.

Slow down on this conclusion.

> **TO KEEP IN MIND**
> Proclamation cannot be effective unless it is expressive. As you prepare your proclamation, make choices about emotions. Some choices are already evident in the text.

believe this?" Martha responds with the most fully developed confession of faith in John's Gospel: Jesus is Christ, Son of God, the one coming into the world.

As soon as Martha expresses her belief, she calls her sister Mary, who enters the scene along with Jews who had come to comfort her. Repeating Martha's greeting that Jesus could have saved her brother, Mary weeps. So too does Jesus, showing to all present how much he loved Lazarus. With words and actions that display the truth that Jesus is "the resurrection and the life," he orders the stone to be removed. He promises Martha that if she believes, she will see the glory of God, reiterating what he had told his disciples when first hearing of Lazarus' illness. Jesus then prays aloud to his Father in a prayer of thanksgiving, for he knows, far more than Martha does, that God will do whatever he asks.

"Lazarus, come out!" Sometimes Jesus completes his signs with touching and other actions, and at other times with words alone. Jesus' words in this scene are brief and effective, as Lazarus immediately comes forth to be untied from the bands of death. In response to this last and greatest sign foreshadowing Jesus' own rising from the dead, some come to believe in him. Others determine that both Jesus and Lazarus must be put to death. E.P.

PALM SUNDAY OF THE PASSION OF THE LORD

A simple narrative with an unexpected ending. The more attention you bring to the details the richer the images will be for your assembly, and the better they will be able to enter the experience themselves a few moments later in the procession.

Bethphage = BETH-fuh-jee;
Bethany = BETH-uh-nee

Jesus is speaking to two disciples. This should sound like simple conversation and not preaching.

There's a hint of a threat here. Jesus' disciples know that danger might await him in Jerusalem; Jesus tries to calm them.

With suspicion.
A little anxious.
Now the danger has passed.

LECTIONARY #37

GOSPEL AT THE PROCESSION   Mark 11:1–10

A reading from the holy Gospel according to Mark

When Jesus and his disciples drew near to **Jerusalem**,
    to Bethphage and Bethany at the Mount of **Olives**,
    he sent two of his **disciples** and said to them,
    "**Go** into the village **opposite** you,
    and immediately on **entering** it,
    you will find a **colt** tethered on which no one has ever sat.
Untie it and **bring** it here.
If anyone should say to you,
    '**Why** are you **doing** this?' reply,
    'The Master has **need** of it
    and will send it back here at **once**.'"
So they **went** off
    and **found** a colt tethered at a gate outside on the street,
    and they **untied** it.
Some of the **bystanders** said to them,
    "What are you **doing**, untying the colt?"
They answered them **just** as Jesus had **told** them to,
    and they **permitted** them to do it.
So they **brought** the colt to Jesus
    and put their **cloaks** over it.
And he **sat** on it.

PROCESSION GOSPEL | **Mark.** On the Sunday before his Death, Jesus made a symbolic entry into Jerusalem, portrayed in each of the Gospel accounts. After the rapid pace of Mark's story of Jesus' ministry, he slows the narrative here, attending to details that convey symbolism and theological meaning.

A prophecy from Zechariah provides the image for Jesus' entry: "Shout for joy, O daughter Jerusalem! Behold, your king is coming to you, a just savior is he, humble and riding on a donkey, on a colt, the foal of a donkey" (9:9). This paradoxical picture of a king entering the city humbly, rather than as a conquering warrior is a clue.

When Jesus instructs his disciples with so much detail, we get a glimpse into his identity and purpose. His instructions have a prophetic tone, and he is clearly acting as their *kyrios*, which can mean simply their master, but also points to Jesus' relationship with the Lord God. Jesus' directions also indicate that he is acting according to a predetermined plan. Everything happens as Jesus anticipates, for he acts in accord with the will of his Father.

As people see Jesus, some spread their cloaks on the road, and others put down leafy branches. Throughout Mark's Gospel, neither the crowds nor Jesus' own disciples understand him, his teaching, or his actions. Their cries of "Hosanna!" and proclaiming that he is coming in the name of the Lord would suggest that they have finally understood him. Yet, as the Passion story unfolds, it is clear that the crowds were looking at him more as an exalted king than as a humble savior. The kingdom that he will bring can be established only through his suffering and death.

Quicken your pace; proclaim with the excitement of the crowds.

> Many people spread their cloaks on the road,
>   and others spread leafy branches
>   that they had cut from the fields.
> Those preceding him as well as those following kept crying out:
>   "Hosanna!
>   Blessed is he who comes in the name of the Lord!
>   Blessed is the kingdom of our father David that is to come!
>   Hosanna in the highest!"

An exhortatory conclusion. Raise your voice (and your eyes and face) and proclaim with exuberant joy!

Take a longer pause than usual before "The Gospel of the Lord."

Or

GOSPEL AT THE PROCESSION   John 12:12–16

A narrative with exhortatory passages. This text is brief but demands a dynamic proclamation.

A reading from the holy Gospel according to John

No time for warm-ups! Bring the energy and excitement of the crowd to the proclamation right away.

> When the great crowd that had come to the feast heard
>   that Jesus was coming to Jerusalem,
>   they took palm branches and went out to meet him, and
>   cried out:
>   "Hosanna!
>   Blessed is he who comes in the name of the Lord, the king
>   of Israel."

Exhortatory. Raise your voice (and your eyes and face) and proclaim with exuberant joy!

> Jesus found an ass and sat upon it, as is written:
>   *Fear no more, O daughter Zion;*
>   *see, your king comes, seated upon an ass's colt.*

Another exhortatory quote.

Use the word "see" to urge your assembly to imagine this scene. Pause.

Drop your intensity only slightly on this narrative conclusion.

> His disciples did not understand this at first,
>   but when Jesus had been glorified
>   they remembered that these things were written about him
>   and that they had done this for him.

John. The account of Jesus' entry in John's Gospel shares features with the synoptic versions but includes some significant differences. The context is unique to John. After Jesus had raised Lazarus from the dead (followed by Mary's anointing of Jesus' feet at Bethany), the crowds in Jerusalem were eager to see Jesus as well as Lazarus. John creates an atmosphere of foreboding. describing the chief priests' fear that the crowd's belief in Jesus would weaken the Jews' status with the Romans.

The crowds gathered for Passover set into motion the events leading to Jesus'

Passion. The Pharisees opposed to Jesus would hear the raised voices along the road and see people meeting Jesus with palm branches, a symbol of victory and honor. Even more alarming would be the cry, "Hosanna! Blessed is he who comes in the name of the Lord," quoted from Psalm 118:26. It showed that the crowds were looking to Jesus as a messiah who would usher in God's reign. Only after Jesus is glorified, having been raised from the dead, will his disciples remember and finally understand what had been written and brought to fulfillment in him. Although nei-

ther his disciples nor the crowd grasp what kind of messiah and king Jesus is before he has completed his hour, the crowd's acclamation would have further frightened and enraged Jesus' opponents. Such public enthusiasm for Jesus would certainly come to the notice of the Roman officials, and would cause loss of the power and prestige of the Pharisees and chief priests. Shortly after this scene, the evangelist notes the Pharisees' heightened apprehension: "Look, the whole world has gone after him" (12:19). They know that they must put the plot to kill Jesus into effect.

LECTIONARY #37

An exhortatory reading in which the prophet affirms his strength through adversity and his unwavering trust in God.

Isaiah = Ī-ZAY-uh

Proclaim this phrase slowly and distinctly, with a "well-trained tongue."
Speak with tenderness to the weary in your assembly.

Imagine and express how this intimate relationship with God might feel.

"I've done what I was asked to do."
How does the prophet feel about the abuse he's suffered? In the context of this reading, it's unlikely that he's angry. He stands his ground, doesn't submit but also doesn't fight back.
buffets = BUF-its (slaps)

"No human insults can hurt me."

Raise your face to the community, and proclaim confidently—with God, nothing can harm you.

For meditation and context:

TO KEEP IN MIND
You can't proclaim what you don't understand. Read the Scripture passage and its commentary in *Workbook*. Then read it from your Bible, including what comes before and after it so that you understand the context.

READING I   Isaiah 50:4–7

A reading from the Book of the Prophet Isaiah

The Lord GOD has **given** me
   a **well**-trained **tongue**,
that I might **know** how to speak to the **weary**
   a word that will **rouse** them.
Morning after **morning**
   he **opens** my ear that I may **hear**;
and I have not **rebelled**,
   have **not** turned back.
I gave my **back** to those who **beat** me,
   my **cheeks** to those who **plucked** my **beard**;
my **face** I did not **shield**
   from **buffets** and **spitting**.

The Lord **God** is my **help**,
   therefore I am **not disgraced**;
I have **set** my face like **flint**,
   knowing that I shall **not** be put to shame.

RESPONSORIAL PSALM   Psalm 22:8–9, 17–18, 19–20, 23–24 (2a)

R. My God, my God, why have you abandoned me?

All who see me scoff at me;
   they mock me with parted lips, they wag
      their heads:
"He relied on the LORD; let him deliver him,
   let him rescue him, if he loves him."

Indeed, many dogs surround me,
   a pack of evildoers closes in upon me;
they have pierced my hands and my feet;
   I can count all my bones.

They divide my garments among them,
   and for my vesture they cast lots.
But you, O LORD, be not far from me;
   O my help, hasten to aid me.

I will proclaim your name to my brethren;
   in the midst of the assembly I will
      praise you:
"You who fear the LORD, praise him;
   all you descendants of Jacob, give glory
      to him;
   revere him, all you descendants of Israel!"

READING I   Today's First Reading is one of four prophecies of Isaiah referred to collectively as "Servant Songs." Probably written in the sixth century BC during the last years of the Jews' exile in Babylon, they speak of a servant of God who is unjustly and brutally persecuted as he selflessly fulfills his mission. The identity of this servant is mysterious. Many possibilities have been suggested, such as Isaiah himself, Moses, King Hezekiah, and Cyrus of Persia. For some, the servant refers to the people of Israel, presented with ideal virtues. Others believe that the identity of the servant was deliberately veiled to leave open possibilities of future fulfillment.

Today's reading is the third of these Servant Songs; the prophet himself seems to be speaking. God has given him a well-trained tongue so that he may give solace to the weary. He is beaten, his beard is plucked, and he endures insults and even spitting. In the face of such harsh treatment, the prophet remains faithful, for "the Lord GOD is my help." While this may be the prophet himself speaking, the writer may be using the first person voice to speak of someone else, either an individual or a whole group of people such as those exiled in Babylon. Christian readers, and even some among the Jews, interpret all of the Servant Songs as referring to the messiah, and the Christian tradition finds the servant portrait fulfilled in Jesus. In his suffering, humiliating and undeserved, Jesus did not rebel. Not even the Cross, the worst form of execution, put Jesus to shame. He relied on the Lord God as his help.

READING II   Some of the earliest hymns, rich in poetic imagery, are embedded in Paul's letters. By putting

Exhortatory. This hymn starts strong, diminishing to a quiet middle, then rising again to the great proclamation at the end. Use pacing and volume to signal changes in intensity.

Philippians = fih-LIP-ee-uhnz

There's no warm up: we jump right in, so make eye contact with the community right from beginning.

Begin to diminish your energy slightly.

Arrive here with quiet intensity and slow down, but don't lose contact with the assembly.
Pause before this line.
Gradually pick up pace and energy from here to the end. It's one long sentence; pause only at the commas.

Keep building your energy.

Keep your energy up; slow down just a bit and proclaim this final line deliberately and with great joy.

READING II   Philippians 2:6–11

A reading from the Letter of Saint Paul to the Philippians

Christ **Jesus**, though he was in the form of **God**,
    did not regard **equality** with God
    something to be **grasped**.
Rather, he **emptied** himself,
    taking the form of a **slave**,
    coming in **human** likeness;
    and found human in **appearance**,
    he **humbled** himself,
    becoming **obedient** to the point of **death**,
    even death on a **cross**.
Because of this, God greatly **exalted** him
    and **bestowed** on him the **name**
    which is above **every** name,
    that at the name of **Jesus**
    every **knee** should **bend**,
    of those in **heaven** and on **earth** and **under** the earth,
    and every **tongue confess** that
    Jesus Christ is **Lord**,
    to the **glory** of God the **Father**.

This familiar narrative is full of drama and quickly changing, intense emotions. Keep your assembly engaged by varying your pace. Practice making clear and strong emotional choices. Focus, as Mark does, on keeping the story moving.

Don't dismiss this line too quickly.
Drop your voice as they discuss their plot.

GOSPEL   MARK 14:1—15:47

The Passion of our Lord Jesus Christ according to Mark

The **Passover** and the Feast of Unleavened **Bread**
    were to take **place** in **two** days' time.
So the chief **priests** and the **scribes** were seeking a way
    to **arrest** him by **treachery** and put him to **death**.
They said, "**Not** during the **festival**,
    for fear that there may be a **riot** among the people."

---

these hymns in a new context, Paul adds to their original meaning, as seen in today's beautiful hymn. He introduces the hymn by telling the Philippian community, "Have among yourselves the same attitude that is also yours in Christ Jesus" (2:5). Thus as the hymn teaches about Christ, it also encourages believers to live in the same way.

So central to the hymn is the proclamation that Christ emptied himself (*ekenosen*) that it is often entitled "The *Kenosis* Hymn." In emptying himself, Christ chose to renounce his divine status, freely giving up the equality to God that is eter-

nally his. The first dimension of Jesus' *kenosis* is his taking on human likeness: the *kenosis* of the Incarnation. And in his human form, he emptied himself still further by taking on the form of a slave. His life was not one of privilege or power, but of lowliness: the *kenosis* of humility. The third movement in the drama is his obedience even to death on a Cross: the *kenosis* of his self-emptying Death.

Because of Christ's total obedience in emptying himself, God exalted him. The second part of the hymn reverses the emptying motif to its total opposite. Christ is

now exalted, raised again to the status that rightfully belongs to him. We can well imagine the early Christians' exuberant singing at the verse: "God greatly exalted him"; the verb might be translated "superexalted," indicating the heights of glory after the depths of emptying.

Immediately after the hymn, Paul uses the word "therefore," (translated "So, then,") reminding his audience that what they proclaim about Christ has implications for their own lives. The same obedience that characterized Christ's emptying should be evident in their own lives.

Bethany = BETH-uh-nee

spikenard = SPĪK-nahrd

Linger over the phrase "poured it on his head" to express the lavishness of the gesture.

Pause after this line.

With calm assurance.

Slowly. You are fulfilling this prophecy of Jesus right now.

Pause as the scene shifts.

Iscariot = ih-SKAYR-ee-uht

Smile.

Pause after this line.

When he was in **Bethany** reclining at table
　　in the house of **Simon** the **leper**,
　　a **woman** came with an **alabaster** jar of perfumed **oil**,
　　costly genuine spikenard.
She **broke** the alabaster jar and **poured** it on his **head**.
There were some who were **indignant**.
"Why has there been this **waste** of perfumed oil?
It could have been **sold** for more than three **hundred** days' wages
　　and the money given to the **poor**."
They were **infuriated** with her.
Jesus said, "Let her **alone**.
Why do you make **trouble** for her?
She has done a **good** thing for me.
The **poor** you will **always** have with you,
　　and whenever you **wish** you can do **good** to them,
　　but you will **not** always have **me**.
She has done what she **could**.
She has **anticipated** anointing my body for **burial**.
Amen, I **say** to you,
　　wherever the **gospel** is **proclaimed** to the whole **world**,
　　what she has **done** will be told in **memory** of her."

Then **Judas Iscariot**, one of the **Twelve**,
　　went off to the chief **priests** to hand him **over** to them.
When they **heard** him they were **pleased**
　　and promised to pay him **money**.
Then he looked for an **opportunity** to hand him **over**.
On the **first day** of the Feast of Unleavened Bread,
　　when they **sacrificed** the Passover **lamb**,
　　his disciples said to him,
　　"Where do you want us to **go**
　　and **prepare** for you to eat the Passover?"

GOSPEL Mark set the stage for the events of the last week of Jesus' life in the opening chapters of his Gospel account: the arrest of John the Baptist, soon followed by escalating criticism and controversy, plotting between the Pharisees and Herodians about how to destroy Jesus, and one of Jesus' disciples identified as the one "who betrayed him" (3:19). As Mark tells the story of Jesus' ministry, he anticipates the Passion more explicitly. Jesus tells his disciples three times that he must suffer, and like John the Baptist, be handed over and put to death.

After his ministry of healing and teaching, Jesus arrives in Jerusalem. In the scene just before this Gospel reading, Jesus gives an apocalyptic discourse to his disciples, speaking about the future, both earthly and cosmic. Jesus says that they too, like the Baptist and like Jesus, will be handed over and be beaten. His final word to them before the beginning of the Passion narrative is "Watch" (*gregoreite*). The word Jesus uses urges his disciples to be vigilant, attentive, and to stay alert. His followers will need such vigilance as they witness what happens to him. Today everyone who

hears the account of Jesus' Passion and Death needs a similar attentiveness ito hear anew the story of his suffering for us.

The setting for the final week of Jesus' life is the upcoming feast of Passover when many Jews made pilgrimage to Jerusalem. The scene is set two days before the feast, which places it on Wednesday, the day before Jesus' last supper that would inaugurate the Passover feast. With so many people in the holy city, the chief priests and scribes plan to arrest Jesus and put him to death by stealth, fearing an uprising from the throngs who had just welcomed him

A man carrying a water jar (as opposed to a woman) would be an unusual sight.

He sent two of his disciples and said to them,
    "Go into the **city** and a **man** will meet you,
    carrying a **jar** of **water**.
Follow him.
Wherever he **enters**, say to the master of the house,
    'The Teacher says, "Where is my **guest** room
    where I may eat the **Passover** with my **disciples**?"'
Then he will show you a large **upper** room **furnished** and **ready**.
Make the preparations for us **there**."
The disciples then **went** off, **entered** the city,
    and found it **just** as he had told them;
    and they **prepared** the Passover.

Convey the disciples' amazement at how events unfold exactly as Jesus described. Pause after this line.

When it was **evening**, he came with the **Twelve**.
And as they reclined at table and were **eating**, Jesus said,
    "**Amen**, I say to you, **one** of you will **betray** me,
    one who is **eating** with me."
They began to be **distressed** and to say to him, one by one,
    "**Surely** it is not **I**?"
He said to them,
    "One of the **Twelve**, the one who **dips** with me
        into the **dish**.

How would Jesus feel knowing he was to be betrayed by a friend? Bring that emotion to this line.

With real surprise and concern.

Return to Jesus' emotion.

"One whom I eat with everyday."

For the Son of Man indeed **goes**, as it is written of him,
    but **woe** to that man by **whom** the Son of Man is **betrayed**.
It would be **better** for that man if he had **never** been **born**."

Is Jesus angry or sad, seeking vengeance or expressing his love for his betrayer? Pause.

While they were **eating**,
    he **took** bread, said the **blessing**,
    broke it, and **gave** it to them, and said,
    "**Take** it; this is my **body**."
Then he took a **cup**, gave **thanks**, and **gave** it to them,
    and they all **drank** from it.
He said to them,
    "This is my **blood** of the **covenant**,
    which will be **shed** for **many**.

Four actions; slow down and make each one distinct.

Again, keep the four actions distinct.

with cries of "Hosanna!" A disturbance from uncontrolled crowds would result in disgrace and loss of power for the Jewish leaders from the Roman government.

Meanwhile, Jesus is in the small village of Bethany outside Jerusalem. When an unknown woman pours costly oil on Jesus' head, some are angry, claiming that the money would be better spent on the poor. Jesus accepts her act as a gesture of compassion. She may have anointed his head to recognize him as messiah or to honor him as a descendant of King David. That she broke the alabaster jar suggests another

meaning: jars used to anoint the dead were often shattered and left in their coffin.

Jesus' rebuke to her critics turns their criticism onto themselves. The woman alone has performed a good, even beautiful (*kalos*), action, showing extravagant kindness to Jesus. Even if the woman is unaware of the deeper meaning of her anointing, Jesus sees it as preparation of his body for burial. In response to the supposed concern about the poor, Jesus teaches that the obligation to care for the poor will remain even after he is not with them. Since the poor will always be "with

you," you yourselves must care for them. Contrasted with the inauthentic concern for the poor, the woman has shown authentic discipleship. What she has done will be proclaimed to the whole world.

The plot of the chief priest and scribes initiated early in Jesus' ministry is put into play by one of Jesus' closest disciples, Judas. The repeated identity of Judas as "one of the Twelve" emphasizes the bond that he had shared with Jesus. As the account continues, the evangelist emphasizes the depth of Judas' betrayal

"Listen!"

Pause after this line.

Express Jesus' feeling, knowing he will soon be abandoned and alone. But note how quickly he turns to reassure his friends that though they leave him, he will not leave them.

Peter is certain.

Raise your intensity and volume.

Gethsemane = geth-SEM-uh-nee

Jesus' emotions are plainly stated: trouble, distress, sorrow. Make sure these come through in your proclamation, not only of his words, but of his actions as well.

TO KEEP IN MIND

In a narrative, find an emotion or point of view for each character, keeping in mind that these might change during the reading.

Amen, I say to you,
  I shall not drink **again** the fruit of the **vine**
  until the day when I drink it **new** in the **kingdom** of God."
Then, after singing a **hymn**,
  they went out to the Mount of **Olives**.

Then Jesus said to them,
  "**All** of you will have your faith **shaken**, for it is written:
    *I will **strike** the shepherd,*
      *and the **sheep** will be **dispersed**.*
But after I have been **raised** up,
  I shall go **before** you to **Galilee**."
Peter said to him,
  "Even though **all** should have their faith **shaken**,
  mine will **not** be."
Then Jesus said to him,
  "**Amen**, I say to you,
  this **very** night before the cock crows **twice**
  you will **deny** me **three** times."
But he **vehemently** replied,
  "Even though I should have to **die** with you,
  I will not **deny** you."
And they **all** spoke similarly.

Then they came to a place named **Gethsemane**,
  and he said to his disciples,
  "**Sit** here while I **pray**."
He took with him **Peter**, **James**, and **John**,
  and began to be **troubled** and **distressed**.
Then he said to them, "My soul is **sorrowful** even to **death**.
Remain here and keep **watch**."

---

that severs the fellowship not only with Jesus but with the other disciples as well.

At the Passover meal, those gathered retell the story of the Exodus, of God freeing their ancestors from slavery; they sing psalms and pray in thanksgiving. Filled with symbolic foods and actions, the meal rituals at Passover strengthen community identity among the people of Israel. Jesus will use the meal with its compelling symbolism to again foretell what is to happen and to give new meaning to the symbols and table fellowship with his disciples.

The instructions that Jesus gives to his disciples in preparation for the meal are reminiscent of the orders he had given prior to his entry into Jerusalem (11:1–7). In both scenes, Jesus acts with prophetic authority as he moves deliberately to fulfill all he had foretold. He dispatches two disciples to assure that the room for the Passover meal is in readiness. The room is spacious enough for Jesus, the Twelve, and other disciples such as those sent ahead. Located on an upper story, the room is well away from the noisy crowds below. The evangelist has developed the scene with

vivid detail; the feast will take place in a peaceful, well-furnished atmosphere.

However, expectations are quickly turned around. Although Jesus had three times told his disciples about the suffering to come, they were not ready to hear how it would be accomplished. They must have been shocked to hear, "One of you will betray me, one who is eating with me." His disciples, who so often misunderstood him, would surely have grasped the allusion to Psalm 41: "Even my trusted friend, who ate my bread, has raised his heel against me."

This scene is called the "agony in the garden" for a reason. Don't make this sound like a pious prayer. Expressing Jesus' real agony will help the assembly understand how Jesus is with them in their own moments of agony.

What is Jesus feeling as he asks this question? His comment seems to indicate that he understands Peter's struggle.

Slowly; with greater intensity as he prays a second time.

Proclaim the first half of this line from Jesus' perspective.

Pray the second half from the disciples' perspective.

Return to Jesus' emotions. His triple prayer shows how intense his feelings are.

The struggle is over. All that remains is to bring it to fulfillment.

Quicken your pace.

Keep the pace up.

Drop your voice (but not your pace) to a conspiratorial whisper.

A moment of quiet intimacy.

Immediately step up your pace and energy again to convey the confusion and violence.

He advanced a little and **fell** to the ground and **prayed**
  that if it were **possible** the hour might **pass** by him;
  he said, "**Abba, Father, all** things are possible to **you**.
Take this cup **away** from me,
  but not what **I** will but what **you** will."
When he returned he found them **asleep**.
He said to Peter, "Simon, are you **asleep**?
Could you not keep **watch** for one hour?
Watch and **pray** that you may not undergo the **test**.
The **spirit** is **willing** but the **flesh** is **weak**."
Withdrawing **again**, he **prayed**, saying the **same** thing.
Then he returned once **more** and found them **asleep**,
  for they could not keep their **eyes** open
  and did not know what to **answer** him.
He returned a **third** time and said to them,
  "Are you **still** sleeping and taking your **rest**?
It is **enough**. The hour has **come**.
Behold, the Son of Man is to be handed over to **sinners**.
Get **up**, let us **go**.
See, my **betrayer** is at hand."

Then, while he was still **speaking**,
  Judas, one of the Twelve, **arrived**,
  accompanied by a **crowd** with **swords** and **clubs**
  who had come from the chief **priests**,
  the **scribes**, and the **elders**.
His betrayer had arranged a **signal** with them, saying,
  "The man I shall **kiss** is the one;
  arrest him and **lead** him away securely."
He came and **immediately** went over to him and said,
  "**Rabbi**." And he **kissed** him.
At this they laid **hands** on him and **arrested** him.

Thus even the one who will betray him remains at the meal when Jesus gives to his disciples the gift of himself. His words and actions over bread and cup of wine have a liturgical feel that stretches far beyond the meal itself. The ordinary bread and wine become the very presence of Jesus to those who share in the meal. The evangelist underscores the depth of Jesus' gift to his disciples by inserting this scene between the prediction of Judas' betrayal and Peter's triple denial. Jesus remains faithful, while his closest disciples do not. Jesus' predictions further develop his por-

trait as a prophet. The prophecy of Peter's denial is one more certain to be fulfilled.

Having left the meal, Jesus and his disciples make their way to the Mount of Olives, to Gethsemane. Withdrawing, he takes with him Peter, James, and John, the three who were with him at his Transfiguration. While Jesus prays in anguish, his three friends are to watch, as he had exhorted them at the end of his apocalyptic discourse. Jesus' prayer is made intimate and poignant with one word, "Abba," the loving address of son to father. Jesus combines his personal prayer with

words from the psalms, making the laments of his ancestors his own (for example, Psalm 42:5, 11 and 55:4).

In contrast to Jesus' intense prayer, the disciples' sleeping shows their failure in the simple task of keeping vigil and foreshadows Peter's more blatant denial just hours ahead. After their third failure to keep awake, Jesus tells them that the hour has come. Although John's Gospel stresses "the hour" (13:1) to indicate Jesus' passing over from this world to the Father, a similar notion is implied here. The hour in

One of the bystanders **drew** his sword,
     struck the high priest's servant, and **cut** off his ear.
Jesus said to them in reply,
     "Have you come out as against a **robber**,
     with swords and clubs, to **seize** me?
Day after day I was with you **teaching** in the temple area,
     yet you did not **arrest** me;
     but that the Scriptures may be **fulfilled**."
And they all **left** him and **fled**.
Now a young man followed him
     wearing **nothing** but a linen cloth about his body.
They **seized** him,
     but he left the cloth **behind** and ran off **naked**.

They led Jesus away to the high priest,
     and all the **chief** priests and the **elders** and the **scribes**
          came **together**.
Peter followed him at a **distance** into the high priest's **courtyard**
     and was seated with the guards, **warming** himself at the fire.
The chief **priests** and the entire **Sanhedrin**
     kept trying to obtain **testimony** against Jesus
     in order to put him to **death**, but they found **none**.
Many gave false witness against him,
     but their testimony did not **agree**.
Some took the stand and testified **falsely** against him,
     alleging, "We heard him say,
     'I will **destroy** this temple made with **hands**
     and within **three days** I will build **another**
     not made with hands.'"
Even **so** their testimony did **not** agree.
The **high** priest **rose** before the assembly and questioned Jesus,
     saying, "Have you no **answer**?
What are these men **testifying** against you?"
But he was **silent** and answered **nothing**.
Again the high priest asked him and said to him,
     "Are you the **Christ**, the **son** of the **Blessed** One?"

Pause at the end of this line.

Incredulous.

This line is easily lost; slowly and deliberately.

Don't swallow "naked." Pause.

With energy; this is a very important assembly.

Drop your energy slightly to distinguish the intimacy of this outdoor scene from the official formality of the indoor scene.

Raise your energy through "death," then drop with disappointment.

With haughtiness.

With volume and intensity.

Quietly.

Even greater energy and volume.

Gethsemane is the beginning of Jesus being handed over to be put to death.

In the next scene, Judas, identified as "the betrayer" (14:42, 44), is the only one of the Twelve named. He hands Jesus over. Forms of the verb *paradidomai* appear frequently in the Passion; it underlies both the words "hand over" and "betray." As one of the Twelve at the supper, Judas exploited a sign of friendship by sharing a meal with them; now he uses a kiss, a sign of respect and affection, in the act of betrayal.

The chief priests, scribes and elders had plotted to arrest Jesus away from the crowds gathered for Passover, lest there be violence. In another ironic twist, they bring the very instruments of violence: a crowd armed with swords and clubs. When one of the bystanders (identified in John's Gospel as Peter) uses a sword to strike the high priest's servant, Jesus asks why they have come with such weapons to seize him when he had taught openly in the Temple. In the dark garden, Jesus exposes their plot to arrest him out of sight of the crowds. Jesus' disciples, who seem to be in the shadows of the scene, now flee. Mark also tells of a mysterious young man wearing only a linen cloth. When the soldiers seize him he leaves the cloth behind and flees naked. He may represent all who abandoned Jesus.

When Jesus is led away to the high priest, Peter again appears, but only at a distance, warming himself at the fire, probably trying to overhear what happened to Jesus without attracting attention to himself. Throughout the Passion narrative, the evangelist alludes to psalms and prophets that are brought to fulfillment. Peter's distant presence brings to mind the lament:

Calmly; with the confidence of someone who knows exactly who he is.

Proclaim the high priest's horror in his actions and words.

Keep your energy up.
Quicken your pace. Convey the anger of the bystanders and give force to the words of violence: "spit," "struck," "blows."
Prophesy = PROF-uh-sī (the verb; not the noun, which would be PROF-uh-see)
Pause after this line.

Slow your pace as you leave the scene of violence and return to the outdoors.

The suspense builds slowly in this scene. Your energy should do the same.

A bit casually.

Nazarene = NAZ-uh-reen

Offhandedly.

A casual action to deflect suspicion.

Don't make too much of this (yet).

Insist.

More forcefully; Peter is a getting anxious.

Hit the words "curse" and "swear."
With real panic. No pause at the end of this line.
The climax of the scene.

Then Jesus answered, "I **am**;
   and 'you will see the Son of Man
      seated at the **right** hand of the **Power**
      and **coming** with the **clouds** of **heaven**.'"
At **that** the high priest **tore** his garments and said,
   "What **further** need have we of **witnesses**?
You have **heard** the **blasphemy**.
What do you **think**?"
They all **condemned** him as deserving to **die**.
Some began to **spit** on him.
They **blindfolded** him and **struck** him and said to him,
   "**Prophesy!**"
And the guards greeted him with **blows**.

While **Peter** was below in the **courtyard**,
   one of the high priest's maids came along.
Seeing Peter warming himself,
   she looked **intently** at him and said,
   "You **too** were with the Nazarene, **Jesus**."
But he **denied** it saying,
   "I neither **know** nor **understand** what you are talking about."
So he went out into the **outer** court.
Then the **cock** crowed.
The maid saw him and began **again** to say to the bystanders,
   "This man is **one** of them."
Once **again** he denied it.
A little **later** the bystanders said to Peter once more,
   "**Surely** you are one of them; for you **too** are a **Galilean**."
He began to **curse** and to **swear**,
   "I do not **know** this man about whom you are talking."
And **immediately** a cock crowed a **second** time.

"Friends and companions shun my disease; my neighbors stand far off" (Psalm 38:12).

   Before the entire Sanhedrin, the ruling council of the Jews, Jesus meets the repeated false testimony with silence until he is asked, "Are you the Christ, the son of the Blessed one?" Earlier in the Gospel, when Peter correctly identified Jesus as messiah, he warned him not to tell anyone. Jesus' reluctance to let people know his identity was most likely because their understanding of messiah did not include suffering. Now as he begins that suffering, Jesus openly declares who he is. In his own

words, Jesus confirms that he is indeed the Christ, Son of God, and Son of Man, bringing the drama of the Gospel to a high point. Jesus' "I am" (*ego eimi*) gives his statement solemnity, emphasis, and certainty. In the face of his accusers, Jesus doesn't hesitate to claim his authority and ultimate triumph "at the right hand of the Power." Even before this, the Sanhedrin had determined to obtain testimony to put him to death. Now the chief priest claims to have found it from Jesus himself. Blasphemy! In the Torah, the one who blasphemed the name of the LORD was to be put to death

(Leviticus 24:16). Blasphemy could mean deriding or insulting God, even if the name of God was not used. The high priest claims that Jesus' statement is an arrogant application to himself of what belongs to God alone, an insult to God deserving of death.

   After the entire Sanhedrin finds Jesus guilty, the actions against him are rapid and brutal. Spitting, blindfolding, striking him with blows. Jesus' treatment is like that inflicted on the servant described centuries earlier by Isaiah, "I gave my back to those who beat me . . . my face I did not hide from insults and spitting" (Isaiah 50:6). Even

Simply; a fact stated without recrimination.

Slowly; with Peter's regret. Pause.

The story drives forward again; pick up your pace.

What does Pilate think of Jesus? Is he curious, amused, anxious? Make a strong choice.

Calmly.

With urgency. Pilate needs to make a decision.

Barabbas = buh-RAB-uhs

Raise your voice as Pilate addresses the noisy crowd.

Drop your voice here on Pilate's internal thoughts.

Build the intensity with each exchange.

> **TO KEEP IN MIND**
> Use inflection (the high or low pitch of your voice) to convey attitude and feeling. High pitch expresses intensity and excitement; low pitch expresses sadness, contrition, or solemnity.

Then Peter **remembered** the word that Jesus had said to him,
  "Before the cock crows **twice** you will deny me **three** times."
He broke **down** and **wept**.

[As soon as **morning** came,
  the chief priests with the elders and the scribes,
    that is, the whole **Sanhedrin**, held a council.
They **bound** Jesus, led him **away**, and handed him **over** to **Pilate**.
Pilate questioned him,
  "Are you the **king** of the **Jews**?"
He said to him in reply, "**You** say so."
The chief priests accused him of **many** things.
Again Pilate questioned him,
  "Have you no **answer**?
See how **many** things they **accuse** you of."
Jesus gave him no further **answer**, so that Pilate was **amazed**.

Now on the occasion of the feast he used to **release** to them
  one prisoner whom they requested.
A man called **Barabbas** was then in prison
  along with the rebels who had committed **murder**
    in a rebellion.
The crowd came forward and began to **ask** him
  to do for them as he was accustomed.
Pilate answered,
  "Do you want me to **release** to you the **king** of the Jews?"
For he knew that it was out of **envy**
  that the chief priests had handed him over.
But the chief priests **stirred** up the crowd
  to have him release **Barabbas** for them **instead**.

as Jesus' tormentors mock him by telling him, "Prophesy!" the evangelist develops an ironic portrait of Jesus as a true prophet. His prophecy about Peter's triple denial begins to be fulfilled at that very moment. Not only does Peter deny Jesus, he says finally that he doesn't even know the man, distancing himself from any relationship. At hearing the second crowing of the cock in the hours before dawn, Peter's remorse is immediate and deep. He remembers, he breaks down, and he weeps.

The scene changes again, moving from the house of the high priest to the court of Pilate. Mark uses one of his favorite phrases, "and immediately" (*kai euthus*), translated in the Lectionary "As soon as," for the last time here, indicating the rapidity with which Jesus' opponents transfer him to the Roman prefect. Their hasty action is another fulfillment of Jesus' prophecy that the chief priests would "hand him over to the Gentiles" (10:33). Put into power by Rome, Pilate was in Jerusalem for Passover, his presence needed to assist in keeping peace when crowds are gathered. Although sources outside the New Testament describe Pilate as a cruel, relentless Roman puppet, he seems in this scene to be sincerely questioning Jesus, unconvinced of his guilt, weak rather than malicious. Ultimately, the legal responsibility for Jesus' death lies with Pilate, who apparently wants to avoid condemning him. At the same time, Pilate was undoubtedly concerned about the crowds—particularly if Jesus was regarded as a political leader, the "king of the Jews," one who could stir the people against Rome. Determining that Jesus is no such threat, and recognizing the plot of the chief priests, Pilate attempts to get the crowd to

Raise your volume.

Pilate is afraid—of the crowd or perhaps of making the wrong decision.

Even louder. Slight pause.

Drop your intensity. How do you, as the narrator, feel about this action?

Now quicken your pace again.

praetorium = prih-TOHR-ee-uhm

This is a scene of violence; make it sound so.

Hit the words "striking," "spitting," "mocking," and "stripping."

Cyrenian = si-REE-nee-uhn

Rufus = ROO-fuhs

Golgotha = GAWL-huh-thuh

Drop your voice on the parenthetical phrase.

myrrh = mer (a sedative)

Don't let a tone of sadness take over this section. Keep the focus where Mark does: on the actions and emotions of those involved.

Pilate **again** said to them in reply,
  "Then **what** do you want me to do
  with the man you call the **king** of the **Jews**?"
They **shouted** again, "**Crucify** him."
Pilate said to them, "**Why**? What **evil** has he done?"
They only shouted the **louder**, "**Crucify** him."
So Pilate, wishing to **satisfy** the crowd,
  released **Barabbas** to them and, after he had Jesus **scourged**,
  handed him over to be **crucified**.

The **soldiers** led him away inside the **palace**,
  that is, the **praetorium**, and **assembled** the whole **cohort**.
They **clothed** him in **purple** and,
  weaving a crown of **thorns**, **placed** it on him.
They began to **salute** him with, "**Hail**, **King** of the Jews!"
  and kept **striking** his head with a **reed** and **spitting** upon him.
They **knelt** before him in **homage**.
And when they had **mocked** him,
  they **stripped** him of the purple cloak,
  dressed him in his **own** clothes,
  and led him out to **crucify** him.

(16) They **pressed** into service a passer-by, **Simon**,
  a Cyrenian, who was coming in from the country,
  the father of Alexander and Rufus,
  to carry his **cross**.

They **brought** him to the place of **Golgotha**
  —which is translated Place of the **Skull**—.
They gave him wine drugged with **myrrh**,
  but he did not take it.
Then they **crucified** him and divided his **garments**
  by casting **lots** for them to see what each should **take**.
It was **nine** o'clock in the morning when they **crucified** him.

call for his release. When the crowd refuses the suggestion, demanding instead that Jesus be crucified, Pilate asks, sounding pathetically hopeless, "Why? What evil has he done?" In his weakness after continued attempts to placate the Jewish leaders, the crowds, and the Roman authority, Pilate gives in. Once more Jesus is "handed over," as Pilate hands Jesus over to be crucified.

At the house of the high priest, Jesus had been shown to be a true prophet, even as the people yelled at him derisively to prophecy. Now they mock Jesus as a king, clothing him in royal purple, pressing a

crown of thorns on his head, and kneeling before him. All the trappings of kingship, inflicted on Jesus with derision, create an ironic portrait of the one who is in fact a king. Unlike kings of this world, Jesus rules as a servant of all (Mark 10:45).

Each time Jesus has been handed over, he is treated more like an inanimate object than as a living person who feels the pain of scourging and battering. All through the Passion account, the only person who has shown any tenderness to Jesus is the woman who anointed him. While Jesus is on his way to Golgotha, the soldiers compel

one other person, Simon of Cyrene, to help him. Even though Simon did not volunteer his service, he did fulfill a significant quality of discipleship. Taking up the Cross, he followed Jesus (8:34). When Jesus finally arrives at Golgotha, all the actions against him contribute to another image: Jesus is the righteous one unjustly persecuted. Multiple allusions to the psalms and prophets underlie the scene. In particular we hear echoes of Psalm 22, a lament of an innocent person harshly treated. First, the soldiers divide Jesus' garments and cast lots for them (22:18) and then continue

Don't gloss over this; slowly and distinctly.

The **inscription** of the charge against him read,
  "The **King** of the **Jews**."
With him they crucified two **revolutionaries**,
  one on his **right** and one on his **left**.
Those passing by **reviled** him,
  shaking their **heads** and saying,

"Aha" = "Now we see who you really are!"

  "**Aha**! You who would destroy the temple
  and **rebuild** it in three **days**,
  save **yourself** by coming **down** from the cross."
Likewise the chief **priests**, with the **scribes**,
  mocked him among themselves and said,

With heavy sarcasm.

  "He saved **others**; he cannot save **himself**.
Let the **Christ**, the **King** of Israel,
  come down now from the cross
  that we may **see** and **believe**."
Those who were **crucified** with him **also** kept abusing him.

At **noon darkness** came over the whole land
  until **three** in the afternoon.

Give full voice to Jesus' feeling of abandonment.

Eloi, Eloi, lema sabachthani = el-oh-ee, el-oh-ee, luh-MAH sah-bahk-tah-nee

And at three o'clock Jesus **cried out** in **a loud** voice,
  "*Eloi, Eloi, lema sabachthani?*"
  which is translated,

Use the translation to convey a quieter, more intimate cry to God.

  "My **God**, my **God**, **why** have you **forsaken** me?"
Some of the bystanders who heard it said,

Elijah = ee-LĪ-juh

  "**Look**, he is calling **Elijah**."
One of them **ran**, soaked a sponge with **wine**, put it on a reed
  and **gave** it to him to drink saying,
  "**Wait**, let us **see** if Elijah comes to take him down."

Raise your volume and intensity quickly through "cry," then drop it slowly to the end.

Jesus gave a **loud cry** and **breathed** his **last**.

  [Here all kneel and pause for a short time.]

Immediately return to the proclamation with energy.

centurion = sen-TOOR-ee-uhn

The **veil** of the **sanctuary** was torn in **two** from **top** to **bottom**.
When the **centurion** who stood facing him
  saw how he breathed his last he said,

Quietly; awed and amazed.

  "**Truly** this man **was** the Son of **God**!"]
There were also **women** looking on from a distance.

their mockery, as in the psalm, "All who see me mock me" (22:8). Crucified with two others, revolutionaries, calls to mind Isaiah's description of the suffering servant who "was counted among the wicked" (53:12). Even the darkness over the whole land resonates with biblical imagery: "I will make the sun set at midday and cover the earth with darkness in broad daylight" (Amos 8:9). In Jesus' cry from the Cross, he prays the first words of Psalm 22: "My God, my God, why have you forsaken me?" These are the only words Jesus utters according to Mark's account. Barely able to

breathe, Jesus manages to raise a loud voice. Though his words are a genuine cry of agony, they are not a sign of despair. Rather, they express profound faith in the only one who can hear and save him. Jesus would know the entirety of the psalm, with its hopeful, triumphant concluding verses: "All the ends of the earth will worship and turn to the LORD . . . the generation to come will be told of the LORD, that they may proclaim to a people yet unborn the deliverance you have brought" (22:28, 32).

The tapestry of allusions weaves an intricate image of Jesus on Golgotha. He is

innocent and righteous, unjustly condemned, abandoned by friends and mocked by strangers. In his agony he remains faithful, crying out to God, his Abba, as in Gethsemane. Creation itself is affected by the drama, first by darkness over the land, and then by the ripping of the Temple curtain. The tearing of the veil of the sanctuary has opened up for all people the place that signifies God's presence.

After the ripping of the curtain, the final words spoken in the Passion come from a Roman centurion: "Truly this man was the Son of God!" The title "Son of God,"

Magdalene = MAG-duh-leen
Joses = JOH-seez; JOH-sez
Salome = suh-LOH-mee

Among them were Mary **Magdalene**,
    Mary the mother of the younger **James** and of **Joses**,
        and **Salome**.
These women had **followed** him when he was in Galilee
    and **ministered** to him.
There were also many **other** women
    who had come up **with** him to Jerusalem.

When it was already **evening**,
    since it was the day of **preparation**,
    the day before the **sabbath**, **Joseph** of **Arimathea**,
    a distinguished member of the **council**,
    who was **himself** awaiting the kingdom of God,
    came and **courageously** went to Pilate
    and **asked** for the body of Jesus.
Pilate was **amazed** that he was already dead.
He summoned the centurion
    and **asked** him if Jesus had already died.
And when he **learned** of it from the centurion,
    he **gave** the body to Joseph.
Having bought a linen **cloth**, he took him **down**,
    wrapped him in the linen cloth,
    and **laid** him in a **tomb** that had been **hewn** out of the **rock**.
Then he rolled a **stone** against the entrance to the tomb.
Mary Magdalene and Mary the mother of Joses
    watched where he was **laid**.

[Shorter: Mark 15:1–39 (see brackets)]

Arimathea = ayr-ih-muh-THEE-uh
No pause here.

Proclaim this action with Joseph's conviction.

Let your voice and face echo Joseph's gentle care for Jesus' body. This is the first sign of tenderness in the story since the woman's anointing.

TO KEEP IN MIND
Pay attention to the pace of your reading. Varying the pace gives listeners clues to the meaning of the text. The most common problem for proclaimers new to the ministry is going too fast to be understood.

given to Jesus in the opening verse of the Gospel, can only be understood through his Passion and Death. At his Crucifixion, Jesus' identity is revealed to Jew and Gentile alike: the Son of God, prophet and king, Messiah and Suffering Servant.

Since their fleeing when Jesus was arrested at Gethsemane, his disciples have been absent throughout his entire Passion. We have seen only Peter with his threefold denial and Judas with his betrayal. There are, however, other disciples mentioned by name who are present at the last. Beginning with Mary Magdalene, Mark names the women who were counted among his disciples. They had followed him and served him from the beginning in Galilee. Whether the evangelist's description of the women "from a distance" means that they were looking on from a distance, or that they had traveled from a distance, their presence is an unmistakable sign of their faithful discipleship. After Jesus' Death, another disciple comes to the fore: Joseph of Arimathea. First introduced here, Joseph, a member of the Sanhedrin and a faithful Jew, shows more courage than Jesus' closest disciples. He is a man "await-ing the kingdom of God," but Mark does not suggest he was a disciple of Jesus. Without explaining a motive for Joseph's actions, Mark simply presents him as an observant Jew who acts with compassion. After Pilate has made certain that Jesus has died, he releases the body to Joseph, who honors Jesus with the sensitive attention denied him in his final hours. The stone rolled against the entrance of the tomb, witnessed by Mary Magdalene, ends the drama of Jesus' Passion and Death even as it sets the stage for Mary returning to the tomb on the first day of the week. E.P.

THURSDAY OF HOLY WEEK (HOLY THURSDAY): EVENING MASS OF THE LORD'S SUPPER

LECTIONARY #39

READING I   Exodus 12:1–8, 11–14

A reading from the Book of Exodus

The LORD said to Moses and Aaron in the land of **Egypt**,
"This **month** shall stand at the **head** of your calendar;
you shall reckon it the **first** month of the year.
Tell the whole **community** of Israel:
On the **tenth** of this month **every** one of your families
must procure for itself a **lamb**, one apiece for each household.
If a family is too **small** for a whole lamb,
it shall join the **nearest** household in procuring one
and shall **share** in the lamb
in **proportion** to the number of persons who **partake** of it.
The lamb must be a year-old **male** and without **blemish**.
You may **take** it from either the **sheep** or the **goats**.
You shall **keep** it until the fourteenth day of this month,
and **then**, with the whole assembly of Israel **present**,
it shall be **slaughtered** during the evening twilight.
They shall take some of its **blood**
and apply it to the two **doorposts** and the **lintel**
of every **house** in which they **partake** of the lamb.
That **same** night they shall eat its roasted flesh
with **unleavened** bread and bitter **herbs**.

This narrative reading is one long set of specific instructions from God. It could sound dry without the dramatic story behind the instructions. How would God sound delivering this plan?

Exodus = EK-suh-duhs

Don't lose "land of Egypt"; it reminds us that the people are enslaved.

The event is so significant the whole year will be reckoned from it.

Keep your pace up.

The celebration is not to be a financial burden on anyone.

Slow down; this is a very strange request.

READING I The Passover is so central to the identity of the Israelites and their relationship with God that they remember it in multiple ways. Throughout the Torah, brief statements of belief identify the Lord as the one who delivered them from slavery: "I, the LORD, am your God who brought you out of the land of Egypt to be your God" (Numbers 15:41; compare with Exodus 20:2, Deuteronomy 26:6–10). These creedal statements are often embedded in longer stories that recount how God set the people free. The story begins when "a new

king, who knew nothing of Joseph, rose to power in Egypt" (Exodus 1:8) and quickly moves to the account of Moses' encounter with God who tells him, "I have witnessed the affliction of my people in Egypt and . . . have come down to rescue them from the power of the Egyptians" (Exodus 3:7, 8). The divine deliverance of Israel reaches a highpoint in the instructions God gives to Moses and Aaron recounted in today's reading. Along with creed and story, another way to forge community identity is through ritual celebrations that involve the whole community at set times,

with prescribed actions and prayers. Creed, story, ritual: three essential ways to remember God's acts of deliverance of those enslaved in Egypt.

At the heart of the Passover story and ritual is the meal, described in detail. The time of year, the actions, and foods have significance for coming generations who will celebrate it as a perpetual institution. Ever after, the month of the Passover is to be the beginning of the liturgical year. In fact, the directions for the meal sound much like instructions for a liturgical celebration. People are to gather, prepare everything for

girt = belted

Another odd set of instructions.

"This is **how** you are to eat it:
 with your loins **girt**, **sandals** on your feet and your staff
  in **hand**,
 you shall eat like those who are in **flight**.
It is the **Passover** of the Lord.

Don't shy away from these violent actions of God, but don't overplay them either.

"See how much I care for you!"

For on this **same** night I will go through **Egypt**,
 striking down every **firstborn** of the land, both **man** and **beast**,
 and executing **judgment** on all the gods of Egypt—**I**, the **Lord**!
But the **blood** will mark the houses where **you** are.

No need to point up the phrase "pass over."

Seeing the blood, I will pass **over** you;
 thus, when I **strike** the land of Egypt,
 no destructive blow will come upon you.

Let the joy of the future celebrations come through in your proclamation.

"**This** day shall be a **memorial feast** for you,
 which **all** your generations shall **celebrate**
 with **pilgrimage** to the Lord, as a **perpetual** institution."

For meditation and context:

RESPONSORIAL PSALM Psalm 116:12–13, 15–16bc, 17–18
(1 Corinthians 10:16)

R. Our blessing-cup is a communion with the Blood of Christ.

How shall I make a return to the Lord
 for all the good he has done for me?
The cup of salvation I will take up,
 and I will call upon the name of the Lord.

Precious in the eyes of the Lord
 is the death of his faithful ones.
I am your servant, the son of your handmaid;
 you have loosed my bonds.

To you will I offer sacrifice of thanksgiving,
 and I will call upon the name of the Lord.
My vows to the Lord I will pay
 in the presence of all his people.

TO KEEP IN MIND

A *narrative* has characters, dialogue, a setting, and action. Help your listeners see the story unfold, keep characters distinct, and be clear about shifts in setting.

---

the meal, eat and dress in a certain way, and keep the feast as a memorial celebration. All who gather for the meal are to share in the lamb procured ahead of time. It must have no blemish, since it is set aside as a sacrifice to God. Applying the blood of the lamb to the doorposts may be an adaptation of an ancient pastoral practice of spreading the blood of a lamb to ward off evil. Whatever the origin, the blood attains a new meaning on this night. The Lord will pass over any houses marked with the blood of the lamb, initiating the beginning of the Lord bringing them out of Egypt.

READING II Today's reading from First Corinthians is the oldest written account of the Last Supper. Although it is the oldest written account, dating from the midfifties, Paul says that he received it, indicating that it was a tradition passed on to him orally and through the celebration of the Lord's Supper itself. In using the language of receiving and handing on, Paul is implying that he is faithful to a living tradition rooted in Jesus' own actions on the night he was betrayed. It was important for the Corinthians to be reminded anew of Jesus' words and actions

because, as Paul had just chastised them, their own gatherings "are doing more harm than good" (11:17). The divisions in the community are evident when "one goes hungry while another gets drunk" (11:22). Instead of sharing in the Lord's supper, each one is eating his own supper, making the meal a sign of division rather than communion. Their individualistic, selfish behavior is, in effect, another instance of betrayal of Jesus.

 The meal that Jesus shared with his disciples was, in contrast, one of intimacy. Jesus begins in a manner typical of a Jewish

The words in this narrative will be very familiar to your assembly. Take time and let them hear it afresh.

Corinthians = kohr-IN-thee-uhnz

Note the progression: from the Lord to Paul to you. Tonight you are another link in that chain.

Be slow and deliberate.

Let the immense love of Jesus come through these words.

Pause.

Again, take your time.

This is not a history lesson. This action will happen shortly right here in your assembly.

READING II   1 Corinthians 11:23–26

A reading from the first Letter of Saint Paul to the Corinthians

Brothers and sisters:
I received from the **Lord** what I also handed on to **you**,
    that the Lord **Jesus**, on the **night** he was handed over,
    took bread, and, after he had given **thanks**,
    broke it and said, "This is my **body** that is for **you**.
Do this in **remembrance** of me."
In the **same** way also the **cup**, after supper, saying,
    "This **cup** is the **new** covenant in my **blood**.
Do this, as often as you **drink** it, in **remembrance** of me."
For as often as you **eat** this bread and **drink** the cup,
    you proclaim the **death** of the Lord until he **comes**.

A narrative. The intention is clearly stated in the last lines: be servants to each other. Keep that purpose in mind throughout your proclamation.

Don't stress the word "pass."
A significant statement! Linger over it.
Iscariot = ih-SKAYR-ee-uht
Lower your volume on this aside.

He knows who he is and where his true identity comes from, so he loses nothing by taking the role of a servant.

This is very unexpected. Let the disciples' amazement at this action come through in your proclamation.

GOSPEL   John 13:1–15

A reading from the holy Gospel according to John

Before the feast of **Passover**, Jesus **knew** that his hour had come
    to pass from **this** world to the **Father**.
He loved his **own** in the world and he loved them to the **end**.
The **devil** had already induced **Judas**, son of Simon the Iscariot,
        to hand him **over**.
So, during supper,
    fully **aware** that the Father had put **everything** into his power
    and that he had **come** from God and was **returning** to God,
    he **rose** from supper and took off his outer garments.
He took a towel and **tied** it around his waist.
Then he poured **water** into a basin
    and began to **wash** the disciples' **feet**
    and **dry** them with the towel around his waist.

meal. His thanksgiving draws the participants together before God. When Jesus gives his body "for you," "you" includes more than the first disciples gathered in Jerusalem, but embraces all who gather in remembrance of him. Both bread and cup are a participation in the very body and blood of Christ, in his very life. Sharing in Christ's own body makes the community "though many . . . one body" (10:17). Jesus binds the community through a new covenant in his blood. His language is reminiscent of that of the prophet Jeremiah (31:31), thereby fulfilling the ancient promise.

The wording in Paul's account is close to that in Luke's Gospel. Only Luke and Paul include the command to "do this in remembrance of me." The verb form for "do in remembrance" means to keep on doing this, not do it as a one-time action, but as one that is repeated. Like the Passover, Jesus' supper is a new memorial; "doing in remembrance" means that Jesus' self-gift is present at each celebration of the Lord's supper.

| GOSPEL | The hour of Jesus has been long anticipated in John's |

Gospel. Now that the hour has come, John finally makes clear what the hour means: passing from this world to the Father. John says that Jesus was aware "that he had come from God and was returning to God." It is the hour of Jesus' own Passover, from this world to the Father, from death to life. As he gathers with his disciples for a final supper, Jesus prepares them for the coming hour. All that he will do is a sign of his loving them "to the end" (*eis telos*). As the evangelist has done many times throughout his Gospel, he uses a phrase with a double meaning. *Eis telos* can have a tem-

"I can't believe you're going to do this."

Jesus doesn't expect Peter to understand.

Peter is very confused, but if being washed is good, then he wants as much as he can get!

Drop your voice slightly on this aside.
Pause at the end of this line.

Pause after the question; Jesus doesn't expect an answer, but give the disciples a moment to consider before explaining.
Be slow and deliberate; here is the whole point of the story.

> **TO KEEP IN MIND**
> Smile when you share good news in a reading. Nonverbal cues like a smile help your assembly better understand your reading.

He came to Simon **Peter**, who said to him,
  "Master, are **you** going to wash **my** feet?"
Jesus **answered** and said to him,
  "What I am **doing**, you do not understand **now**,
  but you will understand **later**."
Peter said to him, "You will **never** wash my feet."
Jesus answered him,
  "Unless I **wash** you, you will have **no** inheritance with me."
Simon Peter said to him,
  "Master, then not only my **feet**, but my **hands** and **head**
    as well."
Jesus said to him,
  "Whoever has bathed has no **need** except to have his
    feet washed,
  for he is clean all **over**;
  so **you** are clean, but not **all**."
For he knew who would **betray** him;
  for this reason, he said, "Not **all** of you are clean."

So when he had **washed** their feet
  and put his **garments** back on and reclined at **table** again,
  he said to them, "Do you **realize** what I have **done** for you?
You call me '**teacher**' and '**master**,' and **rightly** so, for indeed I **am**.
If **I**, therefore, the **master** and **teacher**, have washed **your** feet,
  you ought to wash one **another's** feet.
I have given you a **model** to follow,
  so that as **I** have done for **you**, you should **also** do."

poral meaning, meaning that Jesus loves his own until the very last moment. It also means "to the uttermost;" Jesus loved to the greatest degree possible.

The scene according to John is very different from the synoptic accounts, where the meal seems to be a Passover celebration. In John, it occurs before the Passover. Even more distinctive is the washing of the feet, whereas the other Gospel accounts include Jesus' institution of the Eucharist. The action of foot washing is rich in symbolism. In the cultural context, the expression "with unwashed feet"

meant that someone was without sufficient preparation. Thus Jesus' washing of his disciples' feet is a means of preparing them for his coming hour. In the washing, we see another symbol: Jesus takes on the role of a servant. With a towel around his waist, he appears as a typical household slave, acting freely, motivated by love. Peter's resistance to Jesus' action is understandable; Jesus is his "Master" (*kyrios*), not a slave. Washing the feet of guests was also an act of hospitality, an expected sign of respect. Jesus is offering hospitality to all, even as he is about to be rejected—a development

highlighted by the presence of Judas. In the brief account of the last supper in Corinthians, Jesus told his followers to "do this in remembrance of me." In a similar way, he now tells his disciples that his washing of their feet is a model for them: "As I have done for you, you should also do." E.P.

FRIDAY OF THE PASSION OF THE LORD (GOOD FRIDAY)

LECTIONARY #40

READING I   Isaiah 52:13—53:12

A reading from the Book of the Prophet Isaiah

See, my servant shall **prosper**,
    he shall be raised **high** and greatly **exalted**.
Even as **many** were **amazed** at him—
    so **marred** was his look beyond human semblance
    and his **appearance** beyond that of the sons of man—
so shall he **startle** many nations,
    because of him **kings** shall stand **speechless**;
for those who have not been **told** shall **see**,
    those who have not **heard** shall **ponder** it.

Who would **believe** what we have heard?
    To **whom** has the arm of the LORD been **revealed**?
He grew up like a **sapling** before him,
    like a **shoot** from the parched earth;
there was in him no **stately** bearing to make us **look** at him,
    nor **appearance** that would **attract** us to him.
He was **spurned** and **avoided** by people,
    a man of **suffering**, accustomed to **infirmity**,
one of those from whom people **hide** their faces,
    spurned, and we held him in no **esteem**.

An exhortatory reading, much of it in thought rhyme. Don't let a somber mood overtake this story of good news. Though poignant, it tells of triumph, not defeat. The servant's sufferings contrast with what he accomplishes: he "prospers," is "exalted," placed among "the great."

Isaiah = Ī-ZAY-uh

Open strong! Make eye contact with your assembly from the start, and set the tone for the reading. This is good news!

True, he doesn't look like someone you'd expect to be "exalted."

Be amazed, like speechless kings!

Pause at the end of this line.

We know a secret: this story doesn't end with suffering, but with life!

Such things happen in every community. Think of the suffering servants in yours.

Whom do we hide our faces from today? Whom do we spurn?

READING I On Palm Sunday, we heard the third of the poems from Isaiah commonly referred to as "servant songs," prophecies that describe an unidentified servant of God. Though righteous, the servant suffers and remains faithful no matter how harshly he is treated. Today's reading is the fourth and final of these "servant songs." In the opening and closing parts of the poem, we hear the voice of God, both times speaking of "my servant." The repeated designation emphasizes the personal and abiding relationship between the servant and God.

The opening Hebrew word of the prophecy is *hinneh*, "behold," or "see," a term that urges everyone to give careful attention to what follows. "See, my servant shall prosper." This is God's own servant who will ultimately flourish and be greatly exalted even though his appearance suggests just the opposite. Such a startling paradox will require careful attention and leave people speechless. God's concluding words expand the initial portrait of one marred in appearance, adding to the enigma. The very suffering of the servant will be a source of justification and

pardon for others. Such an interpretation of anguish runs counter to the commonly held notion that suffering was the result of personal sinfulness. Yet it is the sin, injustice, and wickedness of others that is inflicted on God's servant; it is their guilt, not his own, that he bears—another paradox to be pondered.

God's words frame those of the community that relate what has been revealed to them. While the initial words of God referred only briefly to the marred appearance of his servant, the community develops the portrait in detail. The people begin

Slow down; you've just learned that those you have dismissed as worthless are actually bearing your own sufferings. How do you feel about this? Let that emotional choice come through in these lines.

How have our communities gone astray? What is our guilt and sorrow?

Pause at the end of this line.

Avoid a tone of pity or sadness as you describe the servant's attitude in these lines; his silence is a sign of his strength and trust in God. Proclaim with that steadfast conviction.

Because God knows what plans are in store for the servant.
Here is the servant's reward for his suffering.

This is good news!

More good news!

Yet it was **our** infirmities that he bore,
   our sufferings that he endured,
while we thought of him as **stricken**,
   as one **smitten** by God and **afflicted**.
But he was **pierced** for our **offenses**,
   crushed for our **sins**;
upon **him** was the chastisement that makes us **whole**,
   by his **stripes** we were **healed**.
We had **all** gone astray like **sheep**,
   each following his **own** way;
but the LORD laid upon **him**
   the guilt of us **all**.

Though he was **harshly** treated, he **submitted**
   and opened **not** his mouth;
like a lamb led to the **slaughter**
   or a sheep before the **shearers**,
he was **silent** and opened not his mouth.
Oppressed and **condemned**, he was taken **away**,
   and **who** would have thought any more of his **destiny**?
When he was cut **off** from the land of the **living**,
   and **smitten** for the sin of his **people**,
a **grave** was assigned him among the **wicked**
   and a **burial** place with **evildoers**,
though he had done **no wrong**
   nor spoken any **falsehood**.
But the LORD was **pleased**
   to **crush** him in infirmity.

If he gives his **life** as an offering for sin,
   he shall see his descendants in a **long** life,
   and the will of the LORD shall be **accomplished**
      through him.

Because of his **affliction**
   he shall see the **light** in fullness of days;

with questions that express their own grappling with their experience of this mysterious servant, using first person plural pronouns. They admit that we held him in no esteem, and we thought of him as stricken. It is incomprehensible that he bore our infirmities, endured our sufferings. Coupled with the servant's physical suffering is his total rejection by the people for whom he suffered. Yet, he never retaliated, submitting like a lamb led to the slaughter.

There is nothing in the servant songs that made the servant's identity clear, nor was it obvious if the servant referred to an individual or stood for a whole group, such as the Jewish people in exile. Only in light of Christ's redemptive suffering, his surrendering of himself to death for the sake of others, has the identity of the unnamed servant been able to shine forth with clarity. Jesus is God's servant, the one who took upon himself the guilt of us all, taking away our sins, and winning pardon for our offenses.

READING II Jesus is a great high priest and Son of God! In the reading from Hebrews, this twofold proclamation not only offers insights into Jesus' identity but is also the basis for steadfast faith in him. The author of Hebrews exhorts us to hold fast to our confession, probably referring to baptismal faith and commitment.

A central theme in Hebrews is Jesus' role as high priest, first described as "a merciful and faithful high priest" (2:17), two qualities that characterize Jesus' priestly ministry. The portrait of Jesus as high priest in Hebrews draws on the Jewish tradition, where the high priest was regarded as the mediator between God and the people. On the Day of Atonement, the high priest would pass through the veil of the Temple

The final triumph!

Slow down on this final line, and maintain eye contact with the assembly.

For meditation and context:

TO KEEP IN MIND
Proclamation cannot be effective unless it is expressive. As you prepare your proclamation, make choices about emotions. Some choices are already evident in the text.

through his **suffering**, my servant shall justify **many**,
    and their **guilt** he shall bear.
Therefore I will give him his portion among the **great**,
    and he shall divide the spoils with the **mighty**,
because he **surrendered** himself to death
    and was counted among the **wicked**;
and he shall take **away** the sins of **many**,
    and win **pardon** for their **offenses**.

RESPONSORIAL PSALM · Psalm 31:2, 6, 12–13, 15–16, 17, 25 (Luke 23:46)

R. Father, into your hands I commend my spirit.

In you, O LORD, I take refuge;
    let me never be put to shame.
In your justice rescue me.
Into your hands I commend my spirit;
    you will redeem me, O LORD,
        O faithful God.

For all my foes I am an object of reproach,
    a laughingstock to my neighbors,
        and a dread to my friends;
    they who see me abroad flee from me.
I am forgotten like the unremembered dead;
    I am like a dish that is broken.

But my trust is in you, O LORD;
    I say, "You are my God.
In your hands is my destiny; rescue me
    from the clutches of my enemies and
        my persecutors."

Let your face shine upon your servant;
    save me in your kindness.
Take courage and be stouthearted,
    all you who hope in the LORD.

An exhortatory reading. Think of someone you know who is struggling with their faith, especially one who is suffering and in need of encouragement. Proclaim this reading as if you were speaking to that one person.

The challenge of holding onto our faith is easier because we have someone like us who, like a high priest, leads us on the path to God.

our confession = our faith

Our priest not only goes before us but also stands beside us, and enters into all our suffering.

Don't swallow "sin."

READING II   Hebrews 4:14–16; 5:7–9

A reading from the Letter to the Hebrews

Brothers and sisters:
Since we have a **great** high priest who has passed through
    the **heavens**,
    Jesus, the **Son** of **God**,
    let us hold **fast** to our **confession**.
For we do not have a high priest
    who is unable to **sympathize** with our **weaknesses**,
    but one who has similarly been tested in **every** way,
    yet without **sin**.

to enter the Holy of Holies, the very presence of God. There, he would sprinkle the blood of a sacrificial animal as expiation for sin. The designation "great high priest" presents Jesus as one greatly exalted, even more than the Jewish high priest who only passed through the curtain of the Temple, while Jesus passed into the heavenly presence of God. Not the blood of a sacrificial animal, but the pouring out of his own blood was the means of mercy. Though high priest is a lofty title, ordinarily suggesting a distance from those who are sinful and weak, Hebrews emphasizes that Jesus

the high priest is intimately connected with us. He sympathizes with our weakness, having similarly been tested in every way. His high priesthood is ever exercised in mercy and grace.

The second part of the reading (heard also on the Fifth Sunday of Lent) brings together Jesus' divine sonship and his humanity, the "days when [he] was in the flesh." Like the designation "high priest," that of Son is an exalted title. Yet Jesus' sonship is exercised in lowliness, in suffering, and obedience. As Son, he shares with us our human condition, remaining faithful

even as he cries out to God in his agony. Our response to Jesus, the Son of God, is to live in similar lowliness, obedience, and reliance on God.

GOSPEL   Each of the Gospel accounts has a long Passion narrative that tells of Jesus' betrayal, mock trial, suffering, and Death. While it is clearly the same story, the portraits of Jesus are somewhat different in each version, developed along the same lines that the four evangelists already began to sketch in the earlier parts of their accounts. For example, in

So why wouldn't we ask for mercy and grace from such a person? This is good news! Maintain eye contact with your assembly on this line, and invite them to throw all their cares upon Jesus.

There is nothing wrong with crying out to God in our need like Jesus did.

Suffering, though painful in the moment, can lead to learning and growth.

So let us **confidently** approach the throne of **grace**
to receive **mercy** and to find **grace** for timely help.

In the days when Christ was in the **flesh**,
he offered **prayers** and **supplications** with loud **cries** and **tears**
to the one who was able to **save** him from death,
and he was **heard** because of his **reverence**.
Son though he was, he learned **obedience** from what he suffered;
and when he was made **perfect**,
he became the **source** of eternal salvation for **all** who
obey him.

In John's Passion narrative, Jesus is completely in control of all that happens to him. He's not emotionless, but has a centered intensity, while all those around him are frantic and unbalanced. Keep that contrast evident in your pacing and volume.

Kidron = KID-ruhn

Judas is expecting a fight. Might this tell us something about his intention?

Jesus goes out to them; he is in control.

Nazorean = naz-uh-REE-uhn

Jesus uses the name of God revealed to Moses.

The crowd falls to the ground at the name of God.

GOSPEL   John 18:1—19:42

The Passion of our Lord Jesus Christ according to John

Jesus went out with his disciples across the Kidron valley
to where there was a **garden**,
into which he and his disciples entered.
Judas his **betrayer also** knew the place,
because Jesus had **often** met there with his disciples.
So Judas got a band of **soldiers** and **guards**
from the chief **priests** and the **Pharisees**
and went there with **lanterns**, **torches**, and **weapons**.
Jesus, knowing **everything** that was going to happen to him,
went **out** and said to them, "**Whom** are you **looking** for?"
They **answered** him, "**Jesus** the **Nazorean**."
He said to them, "**I AM**."
Judas his betrayer was **also** with them.
When he said to them, "**I AM**,"
they turned away and **fell** to the ground.
So he **again** asked them,
"**Whom** are you looking for?"
They said, "**Jesus** the **Nazorean**."

Luke's Gospel, Jesus began his ministry by announcing his release to captives and liberty to prisoners; from the Cross, he offers release and liberty in the form of forgiveness to a thief crucified with him, and even asks for mercy on those who crucified him. In John's Gospel, the narrative we hear on this Good Friday, Jesus knows everything that is about to happen, displaying the same knowledge that was his throughout the Gospel. His portrait displays a king, majestically lifted up on the Cross, just as he had told Nicodemus early in the Gospel: "So must the Son of Man be lifted up"

(3:14). As we listen to John's account, we will hear and see Jesus moving deliberately and serenely to fulfill what he knows must happen. All of Jesus' words and actions throughout the Passion account flow from his having loved his own, and loved them to the end (13:1). Beginning with the betrayal in the garden and concluding with his handing over the spirit from the Cross, Jesus shows compassion and infinite love for those who are his disciples.

Our reading begins with Jesus and his disciples going to a garden, a place familiar to Judas as well. As he has done through-

out his Gospel, the evangelist uses symbolism and paradox in the Passion narrative. His symbolic universe is rich and multi-faceted, able to embrace diverse imagery throughout the narrative: Jesus will be portrayed as king, priest, the Lamb of sacrifice, and the righteous sufferer, opening the account to a wide variety of interpretations and insights.

John has already used darkness and night as symbolic of ignorance and evil, and does so in the garden scene as well. Jesus, the light of the world, simply entered the garden with his disciples, but Judas and

Proclaim this moment of sudden violence quickly.

Obviously a threat that, next time, it will be someone's head.

Malchus = MAL-kuhs

Speak with force and authority. There will be no violence from Jesus or on his behalf.

Annas = AN-uhs

Caiaphas = KĪ-uh fuhs

Getting rid of one troublemaker might keep the Romans from punishing the whole city for his actions.

Offhandedly.

Jesus answered,
  "I **told** you that **I AM**.
So if you are looking for **me**, let these men **go**."
This was to fulfill what he had said,
  "I have not lost **any** of those you gave me."
Then Simon **Peter**, who had a **sword**, **drew** it,
  struck the high priest's slave, and **cut** off his right ear.
The slave's name was Malchus.
Jesus said to Peter,
  "Put your **sword** into its **scabbard**.
Shall I not drink the **cup** that the Father gave me?"

So the band of soldiers, the tribune, and the Jewish guards
    seized Jesus,
  bound him, and brought him to **Annas** first.
He was the father-in-law of Caiaphas,
  who was high **priest** that year.
It was **Caiaphas** who had counseled the Jews
  that it was better that **one** man should die rather than
    the **people**.

Simon Peter and another disciple **followed** Jesus.
Now the other disciple was **known** to the high **priest**,
  and he entered the **courtyard** of the high priest with Jesus.
But Peter stood at the gate **outside**.
So the other **disciple**, the **acquaintance** of the high priest,
  went out and **spoke** to the gatekeeper and brought Peter **in**.
Then the **maid** who was the gatekeeper said to Peter,
  "**You** are not one of this man's **disciples**, are you?"
He said, "I am **not**."
Now the slaves and the guards were standing around a char-
    coal **fire**
  that they had made, because it was cold,
  and were **warming** themselves.
Peter was **also** standing there keeping warm.

those who will arrest Jesus need lanterns and torches since they are walking in the darkness. Jesus meets them calmly, already knowing all that will happen. Unlike the garden scene in the synoptic Gospels, Jesus is not crying out in agony, since this is the hour for which he came (12:27). His apparently simple answer identifies himself as the one they are seeking, "I AM," as he has done so often throughout the gospel. Yet as the "I AM," Jesus is intimately identified with the great "I AM" of the Torah, the name God gave to Moses (Exodus 3:14). The reaction of falling to the ground highlights

the power of the name in the face of enemies. Judas and company have come prepared for violence, carrying weapons along with their lanterns. When Simon Peter meets violence with violence, Jesus uses the moment to again teach the necessity of drinking of the cup that the Father gave him. His disciples must share in his suffering. With no sign of resistance on his part, Jesus is seized, bound, and brought to trial.

  While Jesus is brought before Annas, Simon Peter and another disciple cautiously enter the courtyard. This is the second appearance of Peter in the account,

having just cut off the ear of the high priest's slave. Peter's first denial is that he is not one of "this man's" disciples, putting a distance between himself and the group of Jesus' followers. While Jesus had readily acknowledged his identity in the garden, Peter denies who he is. Ironically, Peter's denial that he is a disciple appears to be true as he distances himself from Jesus and his companions. He is standing with the slaves and guards, warming himself by the fire, seeming to belong more to that group than to Jesus.

Jesus gives a reasoned response, but also implies that the chief priest already knows exactly what Jesus taught. Jesus refuses to play the game the chief priest is setting up.

Speak "struck" sharply to convey the blow.

Keep the guard's anger in his response.

Jesus remains calm and will not return anger with anger. Again, his response is simple and reasoned.

Speak this second denial with more firmness.

Give this description the intensity of Peter's response.

Peter recognizes what he's done.

Pause for a scene shift.

praetorium = prih-TOHR-ee-uhm

John contrasts action inside the praetorium between Pilate and Jesus, and action outside between Pilate and the high priests. The "internal" conversation is about identity and truth. The "external" conversation is about guilt and power and is antagonistic. Change your tone as the scene alternates between inside and outside.

They stick to the minor details of the Law while doing violence to its intent.

The high priest questioned Jesus
    about his **disciples** and about his **doctrine**.
Jesus answered him,
    "I have spoken **publicly** to the **world.**
I have always taught in a **synagogue**
    or in the **temple** area where all the Jews gather,
    and in secret I have said **nothing**. Why ask **me**?
Ask those who **heard** me what I said to them.
They know what I said."
When he had said this,
    one of the temple guards standing there **struck** Jesus and said,
    "Is **this** the way you answer the high priest?"
Jesus answered him,
    "If I have spoken **wrongly**, **testify** to the wrong;
    but if I have spoken **rightly**, why do you **strike** me?"
Then Annas sent him **bound** to **Caiaphas** the high priest.

Now Simon **Peter** was standing there keeping **warm.**
And they said to him,
    "**You** are not one of his disciples, **are** you?"
He **denied** it and said,
    "I am **not**."
One of the **slaves** of the high priest,
    a relative of the one whose ear Peter had cut off, said,
    "Didn't I **see** you in the garden **with** him?"
Again Peter denied it.
And **immediately** the **cock** crowed.

Then they brought Jesus from Caiaphas to the **praetorium**.
It was morning.
And they themselves did not **enter** the praetorium,
    in order not to be **defiled** so that they could eat the **Passover**.
So **Pilate** came out to them and said,
    "What **charge** do you bring against this man?"

Between Peter's first denial and the second, the narrative again focuses on Jesus, appearing in sharp contrast to Peter. Annas, his interrogator, asks Jesus about two things: his disciples, and his doctrine. Jesus' answers are straightforward and fearless. Jesus tells Annas that he has spoken publicly (*parresia*), a term often used to describe prophetic speech, including both frankness and boldness. His teaching has not been in secret, as those who have heard him can testify. Jesus seems to be saying that Annas should ask his disciples about him and his teaching. Peter, warming him-

self along with Jesus' opponents, has failed even to admit being one of Jesus' disciples. Before the scene switches again to the fearful Peter, we see Jesus facing his accusers with prophetic assurance. Then he is led, bound, to Caiaphas the high priest.

The contrast between Jesus and Peter continues, with two more denials. Even the mention of the garden, where Peter had cut off the ear of Malchus, brings another denial. This is Peter's trial, where his guilt is heard in the crowing of the cock, bringing to fulfillment Jesus' prophecy: "The cock will not crow before you deny me three times"

(13:38). The evangelist creates another irony: even as Jesus had been questioned as a false prophet and messianic pretender, he is shown to be a true prophet.

The Jewish leaders now hand Jesus over to the Roman authority, the governor Pilate. Only Rome would have power to condemn anyone to death, the outcome hoped for by the Jewish authorities. There is dynamic movement in the trial before Pilate, with scene changes alternating between inside and outside the *praetorium*. While Pilate hurries back and forth, from one setting to another, Jesus continues to be

The chief priests must get Pilate to condemn Jesus to death. Their response here is matter-of-fact, but their desperation increases as the scene progresses.

Pilate doesn't want to be bothered.

Keep your voice low throughout the conversations between Pilate and Jesus, as if they were standing very close.

He knows Jesus is no king. What does Pilate want from Jesus? Pilate's power comes solely from his position; perhaps he wants to understand how someone with no position can still hold power.
"Speak for yourself!"

Pilate is puzzled. How could the chief priests be threatened by a nobody like Jesus?

Jesus remains calm in his response: Kingdoms of this world fight; his kingdom is one of peace.

"My truth comes from within, not from what others think of me."

How does Pilate feel about Jesus at this point? Is he intrigued? Dismissive? Frightened?

They answered and said to him,
    "If he were **not** a criminal,
    we would not have handed him **over** to you."
At this, Pilate said to them,
    "Take him **yourselves**, and **judge** him according to your law."
The Jews answered him,
    "We do not have the right to **execute** anyone,"
    in order that the word of Jesus might be fulfilled
    that he said indicating the **kind** of death he would die.
So Pilate went back into the praetorium
    and **summoned** Jesus and said to him,
    "Are **you** the **King** of the Jews?"
Jesus answered,
    "Do you say this on your **own**
    or have **others** told you about me?"
Pilate answered,
    "I am not a **Jew**, am I?
Your own **nation** and the chief **priests** handed you over to me.
What have you **done**?"
Jesus answered,
    "My kingdom does not belong to **this** world.
If my kingdom **did** belong to this world,
    my attendants would be **fighting**
    to keep me from being handed over to the Jews.
But as it **is**, my kingdom is not **here**."
So Pilate said to him,
    "Then you **are** a king?"
Jesus answered,
    "**You** say I am a king.
For **this** I was **born** and for **this** I came into the **world**,
    to **testify** to the **truth**.
Everyone who **belongs** to the truth **listens** to my voice."
Pilate said to him, "What is **truth**?"

unafraid; Pilate's scurrying back and forth from Jesus inside the *praetorium* to the priests and crowds outside exhibits his growing fear. His question to Jesus, "Are you the King of the Jews?" initiates a thematic emphasis that will continue through the rest of the Passion narrative. In delving into the mystery of Jesus' kingship, the Fourth Gospel combines history and theology, paradox and irony.

From a historical perspective, Pilate's question to Jesus is a political one. Anyone claiming kingship would be regarded as a threat to Rome, guilty of insurrection or

attempting to seize power. Pilate's fear was likely complicated. He was fearful of alienating Caiaphas with whom he collaborated, since Caiaphas was a reliable supporter of Pilate, useful in keeping the Jewish populace under control. Pilate wouldn't want to alienate such a powerful ally. He was also fearful of the crowds from all over the empire, greatly increased in size because of the Passover feast. Going against their wishes could well lead to the kind of chaos that Pilate wanted desperately to avoid. And then there is Jesus. For Pilate, Jesus could be the kind of subversive so feared

by Rome. Is he in fact claiming to be a king? Pilate is not interested in Jesus' teaching, but in the political consequences, the threat that he poses to Pilate's power, and ultimately to that of Rome. His movement from one place to another reflects well the uncertainty and fear that must have motivated his actions.

While Pilate's question on whether Jesus is a king is based on political and practical concerns, Jesus' answer moves outside of such earthly concerns. His kingdom is not of this world. Unlike the kings and kingdoms with which Plate is familiar,

When he had said this,
he **again** went out to the Jews and said to them,
"I find no **guilt** in him.
But you have a custom that I release one **prisoner** to you
at Passover.
Do you want me to release to you the **King** of the Jews?"
They cried out again,
"Not **this** one but **Barabbas**!"
Now Barabbas was a **revolutionary**.

Barabbas = buh-RAB-uhs

Then Pilate took Jesus and had him **scourged**.
And the soldiers wove a crown out of **thorns** and placed it
on his **head**,
and **clothed** him in a **purple** cloak,
and they came to him and said,
"**Hail**, **King** of the Jews!"
And they **struck** him **repeatedly**.
Once **more** Pilate went out and said to them,
"**Look**, I am bringing him out to you,
so that you may **know** that I find no **guilt** in him."
So Jesus came out,
wearing the crown of **thorns** and the purple **cloak**.
And he said to them, "**Behold**, the man!"
When the chief priests and the guards saw him they **cried** out,
"**Crucify** him, **crucify** him!"
Pilate said to them,
"Take him **yourselves** and crucify him.
I find no **guilt** in him."
The Jews answered,
"We have a **law**, and according to that law he ought to **die**,
because he made himself the **Son** of God."
Now when Pilate heard this statement,
he became even **more** afraid,
and went back into the praetorium and said to Jesus,
"Where are you **from**?"

This should sound like mocking.

Pilate still doesn't understand why Jesus would be a threat.

The chief priests and guards are becoming frenzied.

Pilate is completely unnerved by Jesus.

Jesus' kingship is in another realm. His mission is to testify to the truth, a concept totally lost on Pilate. "What is truth?" is a question that sounds more dismissive than probing. Pilate is interested in getting the case resolved before the situation gets out of control. Though he finds no guilt in Jesus, the fearful Pilate leaves the decision to others. His question, in which he refers to Jesus as "king of the Jews," is another case of irony: unrecognized by Pilate, Caiaphas, the soldiers, or crowds, Jesus is indeed a king. The trappings of kingship, including a crown of thorns on his head and purple

clothing, continue the ironic portrait of Jesus as king. In their mockery, they have correctly identified Jesus, who will make his way to the Cross still wearing the signs of kingship.

Twice Pilate presents Jesus to the crowd, first saying, "Behold the man," and later "Behold your king." This first time, Pilate seems to be calling attention to Jesus' humanity, weak and humiliated. The second time, identifying Jesus as "your king," Pilate has again, ironically, correctly identified Jesus, although the volatile crowd rejects the title. Spurred on by the

chief priests, the people react by attacking Pilate at his weakest point: his fear of Rome. They accuse him of being no friend of Caesar, and that their only king is Caesar, a jarring admission at the holy time of Passover. The combination of fear of the crowds and fear of Rome overcomes Pilate's fear of Jesus. No longer vacillating, Pilate hands him over to be crucified.

Unlike the synoptic Gospels in which Simon of Cyrene is forced to help Jesus carry his Cross, in John's Gospel he carries the Cross himself. Paradoxically, he is acting as the one in control, even majestic, as

Pilate is getting desperate. Raise your energy here. Only Jesus remains outside the storm of violence and intrigues swirling about.

Jesus did not **answer** him.
So Pilate said to him,
    "Do you not **speak** to me?
Do you not **know** that I have power to **release** you
    and I have power to **crucify** you?"
Jesus answered him,
    "You would have **no** power over me
    if it had not been **given** to you from **above**.
For this reason the one who handed me **over** to you
    has the **greater** sin."
Consequently, Pilate tried to **release** him; but the **Jews** cried out,
    "If you **release** him, you are not a **Friend** of **Caesar**.
Everyone who makes himself a **king** opposes Caesar."

Speak "Friend of Caesar" like a title.

When Pilate heard these words he brought Jesus out
    and seated him on the judge's bench
    in the place called **Stone Pavement**, in Hebrew, **Gabbatha**.

Gabbatha = GAB-uh-thuh

It was **preparation** day for Passover, and it was about **noon**.
And he said to the Jews,
    "**Behold**, your **king**!"

The rest of this exchange intensifies very quickly in both pace and energy.

They **cried** out,
    "Take him **away**, take him **away**! **Crucify** him!"
Pilate said to them,
    "Shall I **crucify** your **king**?"

It should sound like a riot is about to break out.

The chief priests have blasphemed (the very charge they brought against Jesus) by claiming Caesar as their king over God. Stop, and let this sink in.

The chief priests answered,
    "We have no king but **Caesar**."
Then he handed him over to them to be **crucified**.

More quietly, then take a significant pause to let the scene subside.

Jesus remains in control; no one helps him and it seems no one needs to.

So they **took** Jesus, and, **carrying** the cross **himself**,
    he went out to what is called the Place of the **Skull**,
    in Hebrew, **Golgotha**.

Golgotha = GAWL-guh-thuh

Take your time setting this scene.

There they **crucified** him, and with him two others,
    one on either side, with Jesus in the middle.

---

he is led to his Crucifixion. Ancient sources attest to the horror of death by crucifixion. The Jewish author Josephus called it "the most miserable of all deaths," and Cicero described it as "the cruelest, most terrible punishment." The evangelist omits all the shock of crucifixion, focusing instead on Jesus' identity and final words. Pilate's inscription, "Jesus the Nazorean, the King of the Jews," correctly identifies Jesus, is angrily objected to by the chief priests. In an act in which he finally opposes the Jewish leadership, Pilate remains steadfast, stating for all to see who Jesus is, even on

the Cross. The inscription in Hebrew, Greek, and Latin proclaims him as king for the whole world.

The Jewish crowd, so adamant in forcing Jesus' Crucifixion, is no longer mentioned, for the Roman soldiers are now overseeing his Death. Their dividing of Jesus' garments and casting lots for his seamless tunic seem an odd interruption to the narrative. Such details must be included for symbolic value. In addition to the scriptural fulfillment noted by the evangelist are other possible meanings. Not tearing the garment may symbolize the

unity of Jesus and his Father, a unity not broken by Jesus' Death; some patristic authors interpreted the untorn tunic as symbolic of the unity of Jesus' followers. Others have seen the seamless tunic as an allusion to the garment of the high priest, thereby presenting Jesus as both king and high priest.

Those standing by the Cross, according to John, include Jesus' mother, other women, and the disciple whom Jesus loved. Only in John are the mother and Beloved Disciple mentioned. The mother of Jesus first appeared at the wedding

Perhaps Pilate realized that Jesus had the makings of a king.

Pilate also had an **inscription** written and put on the cross.
It read,
> "**Jesus** the **Nazorean**, the **King** of the **Jews**."

Now many of the Jews **read** this inscription,
> because the place where Jesus was crucified was near the **city**;
> and it was written in **Hebrew**, **Latin**, and **Greek**.

So the chief **priests** of the Jews said to Pilate,
> "Do not write 'The **King** of the Jews,'
> but that he **said**, 'I am the King of the Jews.'"

Pilate answered,
> "What I have **written**, I have **written**."

When the soldiers had **crucified** Jesus,
> they took his clothes and divided them into four shares,
> a share for each **soldier**.

They also took his **tunic**, but the tunic was **seamless**,
> woven in one **piece** from the top down.

So they said to one another,
> "Let's not **tear** it, but cast **lots** for it to see whose it will be,"
> in order that the passage of Scripture might be **fulfilled**
> > that says:
> > > *They divided my garments among them,*
> > > *and for my* vesture *they cast* **lots**.

This is what the soldiers **did**.
Standing by the cross of Jesus were his **mother**
> and his mother's **sister**, **Mary** the wife of Clopas,
> and Mary of **Magdala**.

Pause.
There are four women at the cross. Make sure each is distinct.

When Jesus saw his **mother** and the **disciple** there whom
> he **loved**
he said to his mother, "**Woman**, behold, your **son**."
Then he said to the **disciple**,
> "**Behold**, your **mother**."

And from that hour the **disciple** took her into his **home**.

A woman without a husband or son would struggle to survive, so Jesus gives her into the disciple's care.

feast at Cana, when Jesus addressed her as "woman." Again, he speaks to her as "woman," an unusual way for a son to address his mother, immediately suggesting a symbolic meaning. In addition to being a real historical person, the mother of Jesus, the "woman" brings to mind another woman mentioned in the book of Revelation. In both places the woman is a representative of the Church. Standing faithfully at the Cross, the woman and the Beloved Disciple—those who remain faithful to Jesus—are to "behold" each other, signifying a new relationship in which the

family of Jesus will continue beyond his Death. As we look at these two figures, both real and symbolic, we can meditate on their continuing significance for believers.

Jesus has two additional words from the Cross: "I thirst" and "It is finished." In response to Jesus' cry of thirsting, they offer him a sponge of wine on a sprig of hyssop. The evangelist is likely suggesting the hyssop used for sprinkling the blood of the paschal lamb (Exodus 12:22). First proclaimed as "Lamb of God" by John the Baptist (1:29), Jesus is the lamb of sacrifice on the Cross. His thirsting, according to

John, fulfills the Scripture. Though he doesn't cite the passage, a likely candidate is Psalm 69:4: "I am weary with crying out; my throat is parched."

Jesus' final word, "It is finished," connects his Death with the introduction to the Passion account: having "loved his own, . . . he loved them to the end" (13:1). We can hear his final word addressed to his Father with whom he is always united, to those who stand at the Cross, and to all who hear the Gospel. Jesus' death exhibits the totality of his love for his own. His kingship, his offering of himself as lamb of

Begin to slow down and lower your volume.

After this, aware that everything was now **finished**,
    in order that the Scripture might be **fulfilled**,
    Jesus said, "I **thirst**."
There was a vessel filled with common wine.

hyssop = HIS-uhp

So they put a sponge soaked in **wine** on a sprig of hyssop
    and put it up to his **mouth**.
When Jesus had **taken** the wine, he said,

There's a tired but satisfied tone here.

    "It is **finished**."
And bowing his **head**, he handed over the **spirit**.

[Here all kneel and pause for a short time.]

Pick up your pace.

Now since it was **preparation** day,
    in order that the bodies might not **remain**
    on the cross on the sabbath,
    for the sabbath day of that week was a **solemn** one,
    the Jews asked Pilate that their legs be **broken**
    and that they be taken **down**.
So the soldiers came and broke the legs of the **first**
    and then of the **other** one who was crucified with Jesus.
But when they came to Jesus and saw that he was **already** dead,
    they did **not** break **his** legs,
    but one soldier **thrust** his **lance** into his **side**,
    and immediately **blood** and **water** flowed out.

An amazing sight!
Lower your voice on this aside.

An eyewitness has **testified**, and his testimony is **true**;
    he **knows** that he is speaking the **truth**,
    so that you **also** may come to believe.
For this happened so that the Scripture passage might
    be fulfilled:
    *Not a **bone** of it will be **broken**.*
And again **another** passage says:
    *They will **look** upon him whom they have **pierced**.*

---

sacrifice, and his priestly mission are brought to completion at his Death. Having been handed over in betrayal and arrest, Jesus now hands over his spirit, his final gift from the Cross.

After Jesus' Death, John's symbolism continues. Jesus' unbroken legs are evocative of the paschal lamb, for the lamb must be unblemished and perfect. In addition, the image of the righteous sufferer may be implied: "Many are the troubles of the righteous, but the Lord delivers him from them all. He watches over all his bones; not one of them shall be broken" (Psalm 34:20–21).

Blood and water reflect more than the historical reality of Jesus' Death on the Cross, suggesting further symbolism. The water flowing from Jesus' side brings to mind Jesus' own words when he offered life-giving water to the Samaritan woman (4:14), as well as his promise of fulfilling the Scripture that says "Rivers of living water will flow from within him" (7:38). Blood as well has symbolic value, particularly related to the blood of the paschal lamb that delivers the Hebrews from the final plague in Egypt. Associated with birth, the blood and water flowing from the side may also point

to new birth offered through the Eucharist and Baptism, now flowing from Jesus to the believing community.

The Passion account began in a garden, and concludes in another garden. The first was a garden of betrayal, and the final one, of burial. There, Jesus is buried with honor and attentiveness by two secret disciples. The disciples who were with Jesus throughout his ministry, the Twelve, were sadly absent in his Passion. They are also absent at his burial. Joseph of Arimathea and Nicodemus come forth to claim his body, tending it with spices and burial

Arimathea = ayr-ih-muh-THEE-uh

Nicodemus = nik-uh-DEE-muhs (see John 3:1)

myrrh = mer; aloes = AL-ohz (spices to anoint the body)

Truly a burial fit for a king.

You might bring a hint of joy into your mention of the garden, the place of the Resurrection.

After this, **Joseph** of **Arimathea**,
    secretly a disciple of Jesus for **fear** of the **Jews**,
    asked Pilate if he could **remove** the body of Jesus.
And Pilate **permitted** it.
So he came and **took** his body.
Nicodemus, the one who had first come to him at night,
    also came bringing a mixture of myrrh and aloes
    weighing about one hundred pounds.
They **took** the body of Jesus
    and **bound** it with burial cloths along with the **spices**,
    according to the Jewish burial custom.
Now in the place where he had been crucified there was
        a **garden**,
    and in the garden a **new tomb**, in which no one had yet
        been buried.
So they laid Jesus **there** because of the Jewish preparation day;
    for the tomb was close by.

THE 4 STEPS OF *LECTIO DIVINA* OR PRAYERFUL READING

1. *Lectio:* Read a Scripture passage aloud slowly. Notice what phrase captures your attention and be attentive to its meaning. Silent pause.

2. *Meditatio:* Read the passage aloud slowly again, reflecting on the passage, allowing God to speak to you through it. Silent pause.

3. *Oratio:* Read it aloud slowly a third time, allowing it to be your prayer or response to God's gift of insight to you. Silent pause.

4. *Contemplatio:* Read it aloud slowly a fourth time, now resting in God's word.

---

cloths. The burial is extravagant, one appropriate for a king, with a hundred pounds of myrrh and aloes. Final mention of the tomb sets the stage for finding it empty on the first day of the week. E.P.

HOLY SATURDAY: EASTER VIGIL

LECTIONARY #41

READING I   Genesis 1:1—2:2

A reading from the Book of Genesis

[In the **beginning**, when God **created** the heavens and the earth,]
    the earth was a formless **wasteland**, and **darkness** covered
        the **abyss**,
while a mighty wind **swept** over the waters.

Then God **said**,
    "Let there be **light**," and there **was** light.
God saw how **good** the light was.
God then **separated** the light from the **darkness**.
God called the light "**day**," and the darkness he called "**night**."
Thus **evening** came, and **morning** followed—the **first** day.

Then God said,
    "Let there be a **dome** in the middle of the waters,
    to **separate** one body of water from the other."
And so it **happened**:
    God **made** the dome,
    and it separated the water **above** the dome from the water
        below it.
God called the dome "the **sky**."
Evening came, and **morning** followed—the **second** day.

Then God said,
    "Let the **water** under the sky be gathered into a single **basin**,
    so that the dry **land** may appear."

A narrative; don't shy away from the rhythm created by the repeated phrasing. It creates the feeling of an unfolding ritual. Let your pacing and intensity increase a bit with each day, like a sunrise.

Use a hushed tone and take your time describing this opening scene.

Let the scene settle a moment.

Keep the volume low, even on God's lines, as if God were almost breathing creation into being.

Speak all these names as if they are brand new.

Raise the volume on God's voice just a bit with each day.

READING I The readings of the Easter Vigil move from the poetic account of creation to the testing of Abraham, to Israel's deliverance from Egypt, and to beautiful hope-filled prophetic promises. The readings immerse us in the great moments in the story of salvation. After these dramatic traditions from the Old Testament, the New Testament readings culminate in the Gospel, long prepared for and wondrously fulfilled in Jesus' Passover from death to life. The readings that begin with creation conclude with the new creation manifest in Jesus' Resurrection.

The First Reading is rhythmically ordered around six days of creation and a final day of divine rest. Like other ancient creation accounts, this one is not a scientific or historical treatise. It is a sacred text, an expression of the faith of Israel that announces the sovereignty and uniqueness of God. In contrast with the myths of other cultures, there is no cosmic battle, no pantheon of competing gods, no evil. The distinctiveness of the first chapter of Genesis is the power of the one God who has made all of creation—both time and space—and has made it good. The account is designed

so that every generation can learn of a God who accomplishes everything simply by divine speech, is infinitely creative and powerful, and brings about only what is good. For their part, people are to recognize their duty of reverence to this God, their responsibility of stewardship over creation, the dignity that God has given to them, and their sharing in God's own rest on the seventh day. This poetic opening chapter of the Old Testament enhances the atmosphere of wonder and awe, so fitting for the Easter Vigil.

And so it **happened**:
    the water under the sky was **gathered** into its basin,
    and the dry land **appeared.**
God called the **dry land** "the **earth**,"
    and the **basin** of the **water** he called "the **sea.**"
God saw how **good** it was.
Then God said,
    "Let the **earth** bring **forth** vegetation:
    every kind of **plant** that bears **seed**
    and every kind of **fruit** tree on earth
    that bears fruit with its **seed** in it."
And so it **happened**:
    the earth brought **forth** every kind of **plant** that bears **seed**
    and every kind of **fruit** tree on earth
    that bears fruit with its **seed** in it.
God saw how **good** it was.
Evening came, and morning **followed**—the **third** day.

Then God said:
    "Let there be **lights** in the dome of the sky,
    to separate **day** from **night**.
Let them mark the fixed **times**, the days and the years,
    and serve as **luminaries** in the dome of the sky,
    to shed **light** upon the earth."
And so it **happened**:
    God made the **two** great lights,
    the **greater** one to govern the **day**,
    and the **lesser** one to govern the **night**;
    and he made the **stars**.
God **set** them in the dome of the sky,
    to shed **light** upon the earth,
    to **govern** the day and the night,
    and to **separate** the light from the darkness.
God saw how **good** it was.
Evening came, and **morning** followed—the **fourth** day.

Now God invites the earth to join with God in bringing life.

Pick up your pacing.

Don't swallow "stars."

The structure of the story contributes to the image of a God who orders creation according to a plan, establishing everything in harmony. Each day begins with God speaking: "Then God said," followed by God's command, accomplished immediately. God says only "Let there be light," and there was light! For each element of creation, God sees that it is good, and then gives a name to the newly created reality, beginning with the names "day" and "night." Then, almost as a musical antiphon, God's creative act is concluded, "Evening came, and morning followed—the first day." The pattern creates a peaceful rhythm.

Along with other biblical texts that reflect on creation (for example, Proverbs 8 and psalms such as 33 and 104), Genesis 1 explains that God is the cause of all of the rhythms and diversity of life that we see and experience: night and day, rain water and sea water, plants and animals, sun and moon, and humanity itself. God's actions on the first five days create a world of time and space filled with God's own goodness. On the sixth day God creates male and female in the divine image, and gives to them both blessing and responsibility. Thus, before the entry of sin and hostility into the world, God entrusts to humanity the task of keeping the world in the divinely established harmony.

Then God rests, creating rest itself on the seventh day. Since men and women are created in God's image, the seventh day is to be a day of rest for them as well. On the Sabbath, humanity is to share in God's own peace, serenity and tranquility. Creation itself, both time and space, is ordered to this day of rest. So important is this day that the creation account concludes with

Let your vocal energy reflect the energy of all the animals. Use the words "teem" and "fly" to emphasize the movement.

Then God said,
"Let the water **teem** with an **abundance** of living **creatures**,
and on the earth let birds **fly** beneath the dome of the sky."
And so it **happened**:
God created the great **sea** monsters
and **all** kinds of swimming creatures with which the
water **teems**,
and all kinds of winged **birds**.

God's first blessing is for the animals.

God saw how **good** it was, and God **blessed** them, saying,
"Be **fertile**, **multiply**, and **fill** the water of the seas;
and let the birds **multiply** on the earth."
Evening came, and morning **followed**—the **fifth** day.

The earth is becoming a busy place!

Then God said,
"Let the **earth** bring forth all kinds of living **creatures**:
cattle, **creeping** things, and wild **animals** of **all** kinds."
And so it **happened**:
God made all kinds of wild **animals**, all kinds of **cattle**,
and all kinds of **creeping** things of the earth.
God saw how **good** it was.

Pause here.

Your tone should change to indicate something significant is about to happen. Slow down.

Then [God said:
"Let us make **man** in our **image**, after our **likeness**.
Let them have **dominion** over the fish of the sea,
the birds of the air, and the cattle,
and over **all** the wild animals
and all the creatures that crawl on the ground."

Speak these lines slowly and deliberately. Our creation is good news, so smile with your voice, eyes, and face!

God created **man** in his **image**;
in the image of **God** he created him;
male and **female** he created them.
God **blessed** them, saying:
"Be **fertile** and **multiply**;
fill the earth and **subdue** it.

Pick up your pace again here.

Have **dominion** over the fish of the sea, the birds of the air,
and **all** the living things that move on the earth."

God blessing the day (a verse unfortunately not included in the Lectionary): "God blessed the seventh day and made it holy" (Genesis 2:3). This final blessing is the culmination of the creation account.

 READING II Omitted from the readings on this night are a few other episodes in the history of salvation. After the creation account, characterized by harmony and goodness, the next chapters of Genesis present a world increasingly

filled with sin and estrangement from God. Though created in God's image and likeness, men and women did not reflect God's own goodness. In this context of alienation, God steps into the story. The LORD speaks to a seventy-five-year-old childless man named Abram: "I will make of you a great nation, and I will bless you" (12:2). This call initiates the saga of Abram, whose name God will change to Abraham, "father of a multitude." He is to be the means of God extending the divine blessing: "All the fami-

lies of the earth shall find blessing in you" (12:3). This promise appears with no strings attached; God does not ask Abram to perform specific acts or rituals, but simply to trust in the promise. Trust will be needed, since Abram and his wife Sarai continue to wait for the promised descendant. When God again comes to Abram in a vision, Abram moans, "What good will your gifts be, if I keep on being childless?" (15:2). Expanding on the original promise, God makes a covenant with Abram, announcing

Keep your pace up. God cares for all creation, making sure every creature has what it needs to thrive.

Everything together is very good.

For meditation and context:

TO KEEP IN MIND

A *narrative* has characters, dialogue, a setting, and action. Help your listeners see the story unfold, keep characters distinct, and be clear about shifts in setting.

God **also** said:

"**See**, I give you every **seed**-bearing plant all over the earth
and every **tree** that has seed-bearing **fruit** on it to be your **food**;
and to all the **animals** of the land, all the **birds** of the air,
and all the living creatures that crawl on the **ground**,
I give all the **green** plants for food."
And so it **happened**.
God looked at **everything** he had made, and he found it
very good.]
Evening came, and **morning** followed—the **sixth** day.

Thus the **heavens** and the **earth** and all their array
were **completed**.
Since on the **seventh** day God was finished
with the **work** he had been doing,
he **rested** on the seventh day from all the work he
had undertaken.

[Shorter: Genesis 1:1, 26–31a (see brackets)]

RESPONSORIAL PSALM   Psalm 104:1–2, 5–6, 10, 12, 13–14, 24, 35 (30)
R. **Lord, send out your Spirit, and renew the face of the earth.**

Bless the LORD, O my soul!
  O LORD, my God, you are great indeed!
You are clothed with majesty and glory,
  robed in light as with a cloak.

You fixed the earth upon its foundation,
  not to be moved forever;
with the ocean, as with a garment, you
    covered it;
  above the mountains the waters stood.

You send forth springs into the watercourses
  that wind among the mountains.
Beside them the birds of heaven dwell;
  from among the branches they send forth
    their song.

You water the mountains from your palace;
  the earth is replete with the fruit
    of your works.
You raise grass for the cattle,
  and vegetation for man's use,
producing bread from the earth.

How manifold are your works, O LORD!
  In wisdom you have wrought them all—
the earth is full of your creatures.
  Bless the LORD, O my soul!

Or:

that his descendants will be as numerous as the stars. Trusting in the promise, Abram puts his faith in God, who does fulfill the promise, giving a son, Isaac, to Abram and Sara in their old age.

In the Second Reading for the Easter Vigil, God puts Abraham to the test. Throughout the Abraham cycle, he faces numerous tests, with this account, regarded in the Jewish tradition as the tenth and final test of Abraham's faith. Having waited so long to bring about the

promise of a descendant, now God commands Abraham to take his beloved son and sacrifice him as a burnt offering. Abraham's response sounds almost wooden as he rises early, saddles a donkey, and even cuts wood for the sacrifice, careful actions performed with a kind of numbness and shock.

We hear nothing of Isaac's reaction to his father's actions, until, having the altar of sacrifice prepared, he asks, "Father . . . where is the sheep for the holocaust?"

Abraham sorrowfully tells him. "God himself will provide (*elohim yir'e*) the sheep for the holocaust." The God who had provided a son to the elderly couple will, somehow, again provide the animal of sacrifice. When they reach their destination, Abraham continues his numbed actions: he builds an altar, lays the wood, binds his son, lays him on the altar, and takes a knife to kill his son. Anyone hearing the story must feel the same horror at his actions. The intervention of an angel stops the sacrifice at the last

For meditation and context:

TO KEEP IN MIND

In a narrative, find an emotion or
point of view for each character,
keeping in mind that these might
change during the reading.

RESPONSORIAL PSALM   Psalm 33:4–5, 6–7, 12–13, 20 and 22 (5b)

R. The earth is full of the goodness of the Lord.

Upright is the word of the LORD,
  and all his works are trustworthy.
He loves justice and right;
  of the kindness of the LORD the earth
    is full.

By the word of the LORD the heavens
    were made;
  by the breath of his mouth all their host.
He gathers the waters of the sea as in a flask;
  in cellars he confines the deep.

Blessed the nation whose God is the LORD,
  the people he has chosen for his own
    inheritance.
From heaven the LORD looks down;
  he sees all mankind.

Our soul waits for the LORD,
  who is our help and our shield.
May your kindness, O LORD, be upon us
  who have put our hope in you.

A well-known narrative, but don't telegraph
the end. The scene is full of drama and the
stakes are very high—Isaac's life and the
promise made to Abraham that he would
have many descendants are both in jeopardy.

Abraham has an intimate relationship with
God.

Moriah = moh-RĪ-uh

Pause to let this sink in.

READING II   Genesis 22:1–18

A reading from the Book of Genesis

[God put **Abraham** to the **test**.
He called to him, "**Abraham**!"
"**Here** I am," he replied.
Then God said:
  "Take your son **Isaac**, your **only** one, whom you **love**,
    and go to the land of Moriah.
There you shall offer him up as a **holocaust**
    on a height that **I** will point out to you."]
Early the next morning Abraham saddled his donkey,
    took with him his son **Isaac** and two of his servants as well,
    and with the wood that he had cut for the **holocaust**,
    set out for the place of which God had told him.

On the third day Abraham got **sight** of the place from afar.
Then he said to his servants:
    "Both of you stay **here** with the donkey,
      while the **boy** and I go on over **yonder**.
We will **worship** and then come **back** to you."

We should hear the seriousness of the
situation in Abraham's voice.

moment, when he points out a ram in a
nearby thicket. The angel tells Abraham
that he has shown his fear of God, and his
total obedience. He has passed the test.
Then Abraham names the place for God's
providence: *Yahweh-yir'eh*, which means
"the Lord will provide." The term, *yir'e* can
be translated either "provide" or "see"; the
two meanings together suggest that whatever God sees, God will watch over provi-
dently. Abraham affirmed his trust that God
would see/provide even before the divine

intervention. Faith in divine providence,
particularly in the face of the inexplicable
or seemingly impossible, is one of the theological teachings of the story. Not only has
God provided the animal of sacrifice, but
God provides an abundant blessing in
renewing the promise that Abraham will
have numerous offspring and that all
nations of the earth will find blessing
because of his obedience.

  This is a difficult story to hear and to
understand. Many attempts have arisen to

mitigate the incomprehensible command of
God that Abraham sacrifice his own son.
Although the biblical account focuses on
Abraham rather than Isaac, many rabbinic
commentators regard Isaac as an adult, a
willing participant in the sacrifice. He
thereby became a prototype of a martyr in
Judaism, and an image of Christ in
Christianity. In one paraphrase of the story,
an Aramaic version, Isaac himself asks his
father to bind him securely to that he not
kick and make the sacrifice unworthy.

Thereupon Abraham took the wood for the holocaust
    and **laid** it on his son **Isaac's** shoulders,
  while he himself carried the **fire** and the **knife**.
As the two walked on together, Isaac **spoke** to his
    father Abraham:
  "**Father!**" Isaac said.
"**Yes**, son," he replied.
Isaac continued, "Here are the **fire** and the **wood**,
  but where is the **sheep** for the holocaust?"
"**Son**," Abraham answered,
  "God **himself** will provide the sheep for the holocaust."
Then the two continued going forward.

[When they **came** to the place of which God had told him,
  Abraham built an **altar** there and arranged the **wood** on it.]
Next he **tied** up his son **Isaac**,
  and put him on **top** of the wood on the altar.
[Then he **reached** out and took the **knife** to **slaughter** his son.
But the LORD's messenger **called** to him from heaven,
  "Abraham, **Abraham!**"
"**Here** I am," he answered.
"Do not lay your **hand** on the boy," said the messenger.
"Do not do the least **thing** to him.
I know **now** how **devoted** you are to God,
  since you did not **withhold** from me your own beloved **son**."
As Abraham looked **about**,
  he spied a **ram** caught by its horns in the thicket.
So he went and **took** the ram
  and offered **it** up as a **holocaust** in **place** of his son.]
Abraham named the site **Yahweh-yireh**;
  hence people now say, "On the mountain the LORD will **see**."

A typical father-son exchange; don't make it sound foreboding.

An honest question.

Convey the sense of dread and horror that Abraham must feel as he does these things.

Pause at the end of this line.

Sudden intervention!

Raise your voice as if you had to stay Abraham's hand.

Quicken your pace; the scene's tension is released.

Yahweh-yireh = YAH-way-YEER-ay

Other interpretations also present Isaac as willing victim, ready to participate in whatever God asks.

READING III The Third Reading of the Easter Vigil is central to the traditions of both Jews and Christians. The account of the passing through the waters of the sea is rich in literary skill and forceful symbols, told both in prose and poetry. It is yet one more manifestation of the Lord's power over Egypt, particularly over the obstinate Pharaoh who refused to let the people go. Even after the Pharaoh had finally released the enslaved people following the tenth plague, he changed his mind and pursued them with an army, with horses, chariots, and charioteers. While the people were encamped by the sea and they saw the Egyptians on the march in pursuit, they immediately complained to Moses, "Were there no burial places in Egypt that you brought us to die in the wilderness?" (14:11). In response, Moses assures the people, "The LORD will fight for you" (14:14). This is the point where our reading begins, when the Lord commands Moses to stretch his hand over the sea to divide it. In the creation account heard in the first reading, God had similarly separated the waters, gathering them into one place so that dry land appeared. Now Moses' action at God's command also makes dry land appear from the separated water. Repetition of "divided waters" and "dry land" emphasizes the connection with Genesis. Moreover, as at

The reward is as great as the test was demanding. Keep your pace up to the end.

Emphasize the universality of Abraham's blessing.

[**Again** the LORD's messenger **called** to Abraham from heaven
and said:
"I **swear** by myself, declares the LORD,
that because you acted as you **did**
in not **withholding** from me your beloved **son**,
I will bless you **abundantly**
and make your descendants as **countless**
as the **stars** of the sky and the **sands** of the seashore;
your descendants shall take possession
of the gates of their **enemies**,
and in your descendants **all** the nations of the earth shall
find **blessing**—
all this because you **obeyed** my **command**."]

[Shorter: Genesis 22:1–2, 9a, 10–13, 15–18 (see brackets)]

For meditation and context:

RESPONSORIAL PSALM   Psalm 16:5, 8, 9–10, 11 (1)

R. You are my inheritance, O Lord.

O LORD, my allotted portion and my cup,
    you it is who hold fast my lot.
I set the LORD ever before me;
    with him at my right hand I shall not
    be disturbed.

Therefore my heart is glad and my soul
    rejoices,
    my body, too, abides in confidence;
because you will not abandon my soul to the
    netherworld,
    nor will you suffer your faithful one to
    undergo corruption.

You will show me the path to life,
    fullness of joys in your presence,
    the delights at your right hand forever.

TO KEEP IN MIND
Proclamation cannot be effective unless it is expressive. As you prepare your proclamation, make choices about emotions. Some choices are already evident in the text.

---

the narrative of creation, the Lord has power over all the elements of nature: darkness, light, and over the winds and waters. The passing through the waters of the sea is portrayed as a new creation!

The presence and power of God dominate the event. An angel of God and a pillar of cloud are images associated with theophanies (appearances of God to humankind) in the biblical tradition. In addition to such well-known symbols, we hear over and over of the Lord's actions and

presence. The Lord drove the sea back; the Lord in the pillar of fire and cloud looked down. The Egyptians retreated when they saw that the Lord was fighting with the Israelites against them. Then as the water moves back into place the Egyptians are thrown into the midst of the sea. In these ways the Lord saved Israel, and they saw the great work the Lord had done. Each time we hear "the LORD," the Hebrew text uses the sacred name "Yahweh." This is the God revealed to Moses on Mount Horeb,

who promised to rescue the suffering people from the hands of the Egyptians. Now that promise is being fulfilled, with no doubt about who is accomplishing the wonder.

Although the dramatic tale of the Egyptian pursuit results in the drowning of the Egyptians in the sea, the greatest result is God's glory. This glory is the LORD's weighty magnificence, observable in the works of creation, new creation and redemption, and in all of the divine acts of deliverance and compassion. God also dis-

Another well-known narrative. Keep the story fresh by proclaiming as if the end were in doubt. Your own excitement will keep the assembly engaged.

Exodus = EK-suh-duhs

We start in the middle of the story: The Israelites have been complaining against God that they are about to be slaughtered by the Egyptians. God's response is, "Don't you trust me?"

Be deliberate with this line; it would have seemed like a very odd command at first hearing to Moses.

How does God feel revealing this plan?

Pause at the end of this line.

Proclaim these amazing events with excitement and energy, as if they were unfolding right before your eyes. Don't read like a dispassionate news reporter, but convey all the intensity, anticipation, danger, and triumph inherent in the story.

What would you feel if you were watching this happen? Bring that emotion to your proclamation.

READING III   Exodus 14:15—15:1

A reading from the Book of Exodus

The LORD said to **Moses**, "**Why** are you crying **out** to me?
Tell the Israelites to go **forward**.
And **you**, **lift up** your staff and, with hand **outstretched**
    over the sea,
  split the sea in two,
   that the Israelites may pass **through** it on **dry** land.
But I will make the Egyptians so **obstinate**
  that they will go in **after** them.
Then I will receive **glory** through Pharaoh and all his army,
  his chariots and charioteers.
The Egyptians shall **know** that **I** am the Lord,
  when I receive glory through Pharaoh
  and his chariots and charioteers."

The **angel** of God, who had been **leading** Israel's camp,
  now **moved** and went around **behind** them.
The column of **cloud** also, leaving the **front**,
  took up its place **behind** them,
  so that it came **between** the camp of the **Egyptians**
  and that of **Israel**.
But the cloud now became **dark**, and thus the **night** passed
  without the rival camps coming any closer together all
   night long.
Then Moses **stretched** out his hand over the **sea**,
  and the LORD **swept** the sea
  with a **strong** east **wind** throughout the night
  and so **turned** it into **dry** land.
When the **water** was thus **divided**,
  the Israelites marched into the **midst** of the sea on dry land,
  with the water like a **wall** to their **right** and to their **left**.

---

plays glory in the conquering of evil and destruction of injustice. God's glory means that the God of Moses is more powerful than Pharaoh and the gods of Egypt, powerful over nature and over intractable evil. When God shows forth glory even the Egyptians will know that the Lord is God. When God saved the people, they feared him, and they believed in the Lord and his servant Moses. The joy and celebration of the whole people follows the story, bothin the book of Exodus and in this lit-

urgy. The Responsorial Psalm is the poetic complement to the narrative in which the Lord accomplishes the wondrous passage through the sea, showing forth majestic glory.

| READING IV | When the people of Israel were in exile in Babylon, the words of divinely-inspired prophets gave them hope that God had not abandoned them. Today's Fourth Reading comes near the end of the exile in the sixth

century BC in a part of the book of Isaiah usually referred to as Second-Isaiah. Whoever the author was, he continued the tradition that was begun by Isaiah of Jerusalem long before the exile. Faced with the apparently powerful gods of Babylon, particularly Marduk, the exiles needed a deeper understanding and relationship with their God. The prophet thus gives them a rich and personal collection of images for God: LORD, God of hosts, your maker, your husband, the Holy One of

Proclaim this action quickly.

Careful with this awkward construction, and make sure it's clear that "the Lord cast . . . a glance" upon the Egyptians.

The Egyptians **followed** in pursuit;
  all Pharaoh's horses and chariots and charioteers went
    after them
  right into the **midst** of the sea.
In the night watch just before dawn
  the LORD **cast** through the column of the **fiery** cloud
  upon the Egyptian force a **glance** that threw it into a **panic**;
  and he so **clogged** their chariot wheels
  that they could hardly drive.
With **that** the Egyptians sounded the **retreat** before Israel,
  because the LORD was fighting for them **against** the Egyptians.

Then the LORD told Moses, "**Stretch** out your **hand** over the sea,
  that the water may flow **back** upon the Egyptians,
  upon their chariots and their charioteers."
So Moses **stretched** out his hand over the sea,
  and at dawn the sea flowed **back** to its normal depth.
The Egyptians were fleeing head **on** toward the **sea**,
  when the LORD **hurled** them into its midst.
As the water flowed **back**,
  it **covered** the chariots and the charioteers of Pharaoh's
    whole army
  which had followed the Israelites into the sea.
Not a single **one** of them escaped.
But the Israelites had marched on dry **land**
  through the **midst** of the sea,
  with the water like a **wall** to their **right** and to their **left**.
Thus the LORD **saved** Israel on that day
  from the power of the Egyptians.

Keep the sense of amazement in all these actions.

Here is the victorious conclusion.

TO KEEP IN MIND
Pay attention to the pace of your reading. Varying the pace gives listeners clues to the meaning of the text. The most common problem for proclaimers new to the ministry is going too fast to be understood.

Israel, your Redeemer. The guiding image in this passage is God as husband, and Israel, as well as Jerusalem itself, as the wife. In the verses just before today's reading, Isaiah offered astounding words of hope: "Enlarge the space for your tent, spread out your tent cloths unsparingly" (54:2). The prophet was telling Israel, portrayed as the once abandoned wife, that she will again have a tent to live in, and she will even need to enlarge it for her numerous offspring. Once shamed because of sin, she was like a wife forsaken and grieved, cast off like the wife of a man's youth. We can

well imagine the collective shame felt by the people, who regarded their exile as punishment for their betrayal. In particular, their idolatry was akin to adultery, blatant unfaithfulness to the covenant they had with their God.

Because of Israel's faithlessness, God abandoned her in wrath, but only for a moment. In contrast to the brief punishment, God's compassion will be everlasting, his steadfast love will never depart, and his covenant of peace will not be removed. Divine compassion (*rehem*) appears three times in this passage,

emphasized as an abiding characteristic of God toward Israel. Rooted in the word *raham*, "womb," it signifies a deep, intimate, unshakable feeling, like the love of a mother for the child in the womb. Along with *rehem* is another repeated divine quality, *hesed*, love that is everlasting and steadfast, often associated with God's covenant fidelity. *Hesed* is love that is manifest in action.

Finally, the prophetic promise presents to the people still in exile a vision of a renewed city. The prophecy has an immediacy about it; this isn't a vision of some

Pause after "his servant Moses."

When Israel **saw** the Egyptians lying **dead** on the seashore
and beheld the great **power** that the LORD
had shown against the Egyptians,
they **feared** the LORD and **believed** in him and in his
servant Moses.

With great joy! Smile with your voice, eyes, and face!

Then **Moses** and the **Israelites** sang this **song** to the LORD:
I will **sing** to the **LORD**, for he is **gloriously triumphant**;
horse and chariot he has **cast** into the **sea.**

For meditation and context:

RESPONSORIAL PSALM   Exodus 15:1–2, 3–4, 5–6, 17–18 (1b)

R. Let us sing to the Lord; he has covered himself in glory.

I will sing to the LORD, for he is gloriously
   triumphant;
   horse and chariot he has cast into the sea.
My strength and my courage is the LORD,
   and he has been my savior.
He is my God, I praise him;
   the God of my father, I extol him.

The LORD is a warrior,
   LORD is his name!
Pharaoh's chariots and army he hurled into
   the sea;
   the elite of his officers were submerged
   in the Red Sea.

The flood waters covered them,
   they sank into the depths like a stone.
Your right hand, O LORD, magnificent
   in power,
   your right hand, O LORD, has shattered
   the enemy.

You brought in the people you redeemed
   and planted them on the mountain of
   your inheritance—
the place where you made your seat,
   O LORD,
   the sanctuary, LORD, which your hands
   established.
The LORD shall reign forever and ever.

An exhortatory reading in which God describes the desire to be in intimate relationship with us.

Isaiah = Ī-ZAY-uh

God wants to be as close to us as a married couple is to each other.

READING IV   Isaiah 54:5–14

A reading from the Book of the Prophet Isaiah

The One who has become your **husband** is your **Maker**;
his **name** is the **LORD** of **hosts**;
your **redeemer** is the **Holy** One of Israel,
called **God** of all the **earth.**

far-distant future, but reveals something that God is about to do. Their exile will soon end. No longer in ruins, Jerusalem will shine with precious stones, from the foundations to the pinnacles, with jewels embedded in the walls and on the gates. It is almost as if Jerusalem itself is a bride bedecked with myriad treasures that a loving bridegroom can bestow. All of the oppression, fear, and terror of the present will be transformed. In newly re-created Zion, the Lord himself will teach the children, and all will once again experience God's bountiful prosperity.

READING IV Like the Fourth Reading, from Isaiah 54, the reading from Isaiah 55 is a prophecy of hope and fulfillment. While Isaiah 54 promises a renewed Jerusalem to the exiles in Babylon, the assurances in the next chapter are more expansive, directed to "everyone who thirsts." The wide-open invitation to come and receive water and bread without cost is applicable to all individuals and nations, and in every historical circumstance. It resonates with the invitation of Wisdom to be guests at her feast: "Come, eat of my food, and drink of the wine I have mixed"

(Proverbs 9:5). The biblical writers develop the imagery of food and drink with multivalent possibilities. Some rabbinic commentators interpreted water as a metaphor for Torah, and in the Wisdom tradition, bread and water together symbolize wise teaching: "She will feed him with the bread of learning, and give him the water of understanding to drink" (Sirach 15:3). Thirsting for water is also a metaphor for people yearning for a relationship with God: "Those who drink of me will thirst for more" (Sirach 24:21). Isaiah doesn't limit his food and drink imagery to the basic necessities of

Imagine trying to convince a very skeptical person about God's great love. Imagine that this reading is your only chance to do so.

How does God feel reviewing these past actions? How do you sound when you regret the way you treated someone and you try to win them back?

The centerpiece of the reading; proclaim slowly and deliberately.

Pause.

Now raise your intensity and convince your assembly of your sincerity.
carnelians = kahr-NEEL-yuhnz (red semi-precious stones)

carbuncles = KAHR-bung-k*lz (bright red gems)

God takes great joy in securing our peace and our future.

The LORD calls you **back**,
　　like a wife **forsaken** and grieved in **spirit**,
　　a wife married in **youth** and then cast **off**,
　　says your God.
For a **brief moment** I **abandoned** you,
　　but with great **tenderness** I will take you **back**.
In an outburst of **wrath**, for a **moment**
　　I **hid** my face from you;
but with enduring **love** I take **pity** on you,
　　says the LORD, your **redeemer**.
This is for me like the days of **Noah**,
　　when I **swore** that the waters of Noah
　　should never **again** deluge the earth;
so I have sworn not to be **angry** with you,
　　or to **rebuke** you.
Though the mountains **leave** their place
　　and the hills be **shaken**,
my **love** shall **never** leave you
　　nor my covenant of **peace** be **shaken**,
　　says the LORD, who has **mercy** on you.
O **afflicted** one, **storm-battered** and **unconsoled**,
　　I lay your pavements in **carnelians**,
　　and your foundations in **sapphires**;
I will make your battlements of **rubies**,
　　your gates of **carbuncles**,
　　and all your walls of precious **stones**.
All your **children** shall be taught by the LORD,
　　and **great** shall be the **peace** of your children.
In **justice** shall you be established,
　　far from the fear of oppression,
　　where destruction cannot come **near** you.

life, but presents a picture of a banquet where people will delight in rich food. The banquet imagery highlights God's abundant care for Israel and evokes the hope of a new age of fulfillment. Isaiah of Jerusalem created a beautiful scene that is a background for today's reading: "On this mountain the LORD of hosts will provide for all peoples a feast of rich food and choice wines" (Isaiah 25:6).

Isaiah's prophecy makes a universal appeal to respond to the divine invitation:

come, eat, listen, delight, seek, forsake evil, return to the Lord. Such apparently ordinary human acts bring people into God's presence to receive the promised rich fare. The divine bounty includes life, an everlasting covenant, and steadfast love, *hesed*. The promise of *hesed* goes beyond David and his descendants, and even beyond the Jewish people to embrace the nations. Isaiah declares that the nations unknown to the exiles will run to them because God "has glorified you." The wording of the

promise brings the future glory into the present. What God has promised is so certain that it is as if already accomplished.

The invitation continues: "seek the LORD," used elsewhere to exhort people to the sanctuary, often understood as the Jerusalem Temple. In this prophecy, Isaiah tells everyone to find the Lord whenever and wherever God may be present. Those who respond to this gentle invitation, who turn away from evil ways and even unrighteous thoughts, will know God's mercy. The

For meditation and context:

TO KEEP IN MIND
Parallelism refers to phrases or
sentences that have a similar
structure or express a similar idea.
Use emphasis and rhythm to make
sure any parallelism stands out.

RESPONSORIAL PSALM   Psalm 30:2, 4, 5–6, 11–12, 13 (2a)

R. I will praise you, Lord, for you have rescued me.

I will extol you, O LORD, for you drew
    me clear
  and did not let my enemies rejoice over me.
O LORD, you brought me up from the
    netherworld;
  you preserved me from among those
    going down into the pit.

Sing praise to the LORD, you his faithful ones,
  and give thanks to his holy name.
For his anger lasts but a moment;
  a lifetime, his good will.
At nightfall, weeping enters in,
  but with the dawn, rejoicing.

Hear, O LORD, and have pity on me;
  O LORD, be my helper.
You changed my mourning into dancing;
  O LORD, my God, forever will I give
    you thanks.

An exhortatory reading. Think of a specific
person you know who is weary and needs a
message of hope; proclaim as if speaking to
that person. This is in God's voice and is all
good news, so decide how you will maintain
that energy throughout.

Isaiah = ī-ZAY-uh

Make this a strong invitation. Use direct your
eye contact and vocal energy toward those
farthest from you. Take time with this section.

How does God sound conveying this
invitation? Make a strong choice.

Insist that they come!

How silly!

You will not only be fed, but fed well.

Listening to God brings life!

Pick up your pace here to the end of this
section.

READING V   Isaiah 55:1–11

A reading from the Book of the Prophet Isaiah

Thus says the LORD:
All you who are thirsty,
  come to the water!
You who have no **money**,
  come, receive **grain** and **eat**;
come, without **paying** and without **cost**,
  drink **wine** and **milk**!
Why spend your money for what is not **bread**,
  your **wages** for what fails to **satisfy**?
Heed me, and you shall eat **well**,
  you shall **delight** in **rich** fare.
Come to me **heedfully**,
  listen, that you may have **life**.
I will **renew** with you the **everlasting** covenant,
  the benefits assured to David.

reading concludes with another water
image: the rain and snow that come down
from heaven soak into the earth, bringing
about seed and bread. So too is God's
Word. It soaks down deeply into the human
spirit, and accomplishes God's purpose.

    Isaiah's promise of life-giving waters,
bread that is freely given, and a rich banquet is particularly appropriate at the
Easter Vigil. The waters of Baptism, the
bountiful proclamation of God's Word, and
the eucharistic feast provide a banquet far

richer than any envisioned by Isaiah. This
night everyone is invited: come, eat, listen,
and delight in the Lord's rich fare.

READING VI The sixth Easter Vigil reading, a poem from Baruch, is
a beautiful hymn that praises Wisdom, not
as an abstract reality but as a personified
and relational entity. Although ascribed to
Baruch, a scribe of the prophet Jeremiah,
the hymn to Wisdom (along with the rest of
the book) was perhaps written long after

the life of Jeremiah and the Babylonian
exile. Yet the reality of the exile remained a
forceful example of the consequences of
disobedience and the necessity of repentance. The whole book can be read as a
perennial exhortation to see God's Law as
the source of life and well-being. Just
before today's hymn to Wisdom is a prayer
of supplication (2:11—3:8) that is a helpful
theological context for understanding the
hymn. In the prayer, the people with
"anguished soul, the dismayed spirit" (3:1)

As I made him a **witness** to the peoples,
    a **leader** and **commander** of nations,
so shall you **summon** a nation you knew **not**,
    and nations that knew you not shall **run** to you,
because of the **LORD**, your God,
    the **Holy** One of Israel, who has **glorified** you.

Seek the LORD while he may be **found**,
    call him while he is **near**.
Let the scoundrel **forsake** his way,
    and the **wicked** man his thoughts;
let him turn to the LORD for **mercy**;
    to our **God**, who is **generous** in forgiving.
For **my** thoughts are not **your** thoughts,
    nor are **your** ways **my** ways, says the LORD.
As **high** as the **heavens** are **above** the **earth**,
    so high are **my** ways above **your** ways
    and **my** thoughts above **your** thoughts.

For just as from the **heavens**
    the **rain** and **snow** come down
and do not **return** there
    till they have **watered** the earth,
    making it **fertile** and **fruitful**,
giving **seed** to the one who **sows**
    and **bread** to the one who **eats**,
so shall my **word** be
    that goes **forth** from my mouth;
my **word** shall not return to me **void**,
    but shall do my **will**,
    achieving the **end** for which I **sent** it.

Pause before the next section, a new thought.

Encourage your assembly to sincerely seek out God.

This is not a rebuke, but a declaration of amnesty for all!

"I am more ready to forgive than you are."

How glad we are that God doesn't act as we might!

Pause before the final section.

God uses these metaphors to assure us that the promises made will be fulfilled. Here is your last chance to convince those still skeptical of God's great mercy!
These are images of generosity and plenty.

The word you proclaim is a living word, and demands a proclamation worthy of it.

Proclaim with confident assurance: "I will do what I say."

TO KEEP IN MIND
What does the reading ask your assembly to do or to be after hearing your proclamation? Focus on an intention every time you proclaim.

call out to God to save them, and to again show mercy on them, even though their sins are many. They are impious, and have violated all God's statutes; they did not heed the voice of the Lord. Although the exile is their rightful punishment, they remind God that they are God's own people, and the Lord is able to turn them back from their "stiff-necked stubbornness and from their evil deeds" (2:33). The prayer, in which Israel admitted its disobedience, opens the possibility of restoration if they turn away from their sinful deeds and are obedient to God's commandments.

After this plea to God, Baruch addresses the people: "Hear, O Israel, the commandments of life: listen, and know prudence!" The essential way to learn Wisdom is through the "commandments of life," the very law that Israel had disobeyed. Prayer and hymn each emphasize the necessity of adherence to God's statutes if the people are to live. The Mosaic Law, equated with Wisdom, gives life in all its dimensions, both individually and collectively. But Israel has forsaken the fountain of Wisdom, bringing about their exile in the land of their enemies, and they have

grown old in a foreign country. Now if they are to learn anew the depth and richness of God's Wisdom, they must listen and walk in the way of God through adherence to God's commandments.

Throughout the hymn, as elsewhere in Wisdom writings, Wisdom is personified as a woman with quasidivine qualities. Those who find her will find strength and understanding, and will discern where there is life, light, and peace. In this text, as well as elsewhere in Wisdom literature (for example Proverbs 8:22–31 and Wisdom 8:1), Wisdom was present at creation; she

For meditation and context:

TO KEEP IN MIND

You can't proclaim what you don't understand. Read the Scripture passage and its commentary in *Workbook*. Then read it from your Bible, including what comes before and after it so that you understand the context.

An exhortatory reading; encourage your community to seek wisdom.

Baruch = buh-ROOK

Start strong! Call out to your assembly to pay attention!

"Why do you think you are suffering?"

Here's the answer!
A life of peace is still available to us.

Invite the assembly to grow in their search for wisdom.

The answer to these questions is "God," and by extension, all of us who are in relationship with God.

RESPONSORIAL PSALM   Isaiah 12:2–3, 4, 5–6 (3)

R. You will draw water joyfully from the springs of salvation.

God indeed is my savior;
  I am confident and unafraid.
My strength and my courage is the LORD,
  and he has been my savior.
With joy you will draw water
  at the fountain of salvation.

Give thanks to the LORD, acclaim his name;
  among the nations make known his deeds,
  proclaim how exalted is his name.

Sing praise to the LORD for his glorious
    achievement;
  let this be known throughout all the earth.
Shout with exultation, O city of Zion,
  for great in your midst
  is the Holy One of Israel!

READING VI   Baruch 3:9–15, 32—4:4

A reading from the Book of the Prophet Baruch

Hear, O Israel, the commandments of **life**:
  listen, and know **prudence**!
How **is** it, Israel,
  that you are in the land of your **foes**,
  grown old in a **foreign** land,
defiled with the dead,
  accounted with those destined for the **netherworld**?
You have **forsaken** the fountain of **wisdom**!
  Had you walked in the way of **God**,
  you would have dwelt in **enduring peace**.
Learn where **prudence** is,
  where **strength**, where **understanding**;
that you may know also
  where are length of **days**, and **life**,
  where light of the **eyes**, and **peace**.
Who has **found** the place of wisdom,
  who has **entered** into her treasuries?

was present as well in the history of God's people. The Lord gave her to Jacob and to Israel, and ultimately Wisdom lived with humanity.

Having begun the poem with an exhortation to hear the commandments, Baruch continues, "She [Wisdom] is the book of the precepts of God, the law that endures forever." Though the figure of Wisdom is mysterious, she will be found in the Law. This understanding of Wisdom should lead the exiles to obey the ancient commandments that they had so often abandoned. Holding fast to Wisdom is equivalent to obeying the

commandments. Holding fast to Wisdom, to the Law itself, will give life. Forsaking Wisdom, forsaking the commandments, will result in death. The hymn concludes with a hope-filled invitation to turn toward Wisdom and walk in her shining light. Embracing Wisdom by keeping the commandments is not a burden, but a means of life, light, glory, and happiness.

READING VII Like the Easter Vigil readings from Isaiah and Baruch, the setting for the reading from the prophet Ezekiel is the exile in Babylon. With

language reminiscent of that of the other prophets, Ezekiel begins by delineating the sins of the people that led to their exile. They defiled their own land with their deeds, their conduct was unclean, they shed blood on the land, and they polluted it with idols. The verbs describing their actions create a sharp sense of putrid contamination; we can visualize and even smell death throughout the land. God's response is severe: "I scattered them among the nations, dispersing them over foreign lands."

These lines echo tonight's Reading I
from Genesis.

The stars are joyous in their response!

Show your excitement in having access to
such a God.

God's wisdom isn't just for God; rather, God
shares this wisdom with all of us tonight
through Jesus Christ.
she = wisdom
Wisdom is available to everyone; this is good
news!

Wisdom is the true Law.

Again, invite your assembly to turn to
wisdom.

Good news! We know what pleases God!
Smile with your voice, eyes, and face.

The One who knows **all** things knows **her**;
  he has probed her by his **knowledge**—
the One who **established** the earth for all time,
  and **filled** it with four-footed beasts;
he who **dismisses** the light, and it **departs**,
  calls it, and it obeys him **trembling**;
before whom the stars at their posts
  shine and **rejoice**;
when he **calls** them, they answer, "Here we **are**!"
  shining with **joy** for their Maker.
Such is our God;
  no **other** is to be compared to him:
he has traced out the whole **way** of understanding,
  and has given her to **Jacob**, his servant,
  to **Israel**, his beloved son.

Since then she has **appeared** on earth,
  and **moved** among people.
She is the book of the **precepts** of God,
  the law that endures **forever**;
all who **cling** to her will **live**,
  but those will **die** who **forsake** her.
Turn, **O** Jacob, and **receive** her:
  walk by her **light** toward **splendor**.
Give not your glory to **another**,
  your **privileges** to an **alien** race.
Blessed are **we**, O Israel;
  for what pleases God is **known** to us!

In all of their sinful, death-dealing actions, Israel did more than pollute the land. They profaned God's holy name. For Ezekiel, this is the most serious of sins, clearly indicated by his use of the word "profane" (*halal*) five times in this passage. Something profane is the polar opposite of what is holy; to make profane is to cheapen what is esteemed, to violate what is perfect, to demean what is exalted, to be impious before One who should be worshiped. And Israel profaned what is most esteemed, perfect, and exalted: God's holy name. In the biblical idiom, a name (*shem*)

refers to the identity, the reputation, the presence, the true reality of who a person is. God's name is holy (*qadosh*), meaning that the identity of God is One set apart from what is commonplace; God's holy name is splendid and majestic, to be recognized with reverence and awe.

In the face of Israel's profaning God's holy name, God tells the prophet, "Not for your sakes do I act, house of Israel, but for the sake of my holy name." The multiple actions that God does for Israel are therefore first and foremost so that the holiness of God's name will be known, not only in

Israel, but also among the nations. The Lord will display his radiant holiness before their very eyes. For God's sinful people, along with the foreign nations, to know the name of God implies more than recognizing or understanding God; knowing God's name means to have an intimate relationship with God, expressed in fidelity, obedience, and reverent worship.

The divine actions that transform the profanation of God's holy name will at the same time transform Israel itself. The first actions in Ezekiel's prophecy were about God's punishment in scattering and dis-

For meditation and context:

TO KEEP IN MIND

Always pause at the end of the reading, before you proclaim the closing dialogue ("The Word of the Lord" or "The Gospel of the Lord").

An exhortatory prophecy of salvation for Ezekiel's audience and for your assembly. Except for the first line, the entire reading is in God's voice. How does God sound as he makes these promises of salvation—to Israel and to us? Make a strong choice and bring it to your proclamation.

Ezekiel = ee-ZEE-kee-uhl

"Son of man" refers to Ezekiel.

Although these lines speak of God's "fury," "wrath," and punishment, God is not angry now. Still, God wants faithful behavior.

The people's sins and punishment made God appear weak.

Pause at the end of this line.

Note that our salvation doesn't depend on anything *we* have done. God gives freely because that's who God is.

RESPONSORIAL PSALM Psalm 19:8, 9, 10, 11 (John 6:68c)

R. Lord, you have the words of everlasting life.

The law of the LORD is perfect,
  refreshing the soul;
the decree of the LORD is trustworthy,
  giving wisdom to the simple.

The precepts of the LORD are right,
  rejoicing the heart;
the command of the LORD is clear,
  enlightening the eye.

The fear of the LORD is pure,
  enduring forever;
the ordinances of the LORD are true,
  all of them just.

They are more precious than gold,
  than a heap of purest gold;
sweeter also than syrup
  or honey from the comb.

READING VII Ezekiel 36:16–17a, 18–28

A reading from the Book of the Prophet Ezekiel

The word of the LORD came to me, saying:
  Son of **man**, when the house of Israel lived in their **land**,
  they **defiled** it by their conduct and deeds.
Therefore I **poured** out my **fury** upon them
  because of the **blood** that they poured out on the ground,
  and because they **defiled** it with **idols**.
I **scattered** them among the nations,
  dispersing them over foreign lands;
  according to their conduct and deeds I **judged** them.
But when they came among the nations **wherever** they came,
  they served to **profane** my holy name,
  because it was said of them: "These are the people of the **LORD**,
  yet they had to **leave** their land."
So I have **relented** because of my holy name
  which the house of Israel profaned
  among the nations where they came.
Therefore say to the house of Israel: **Thus** says the Lord **God**:
  Not for **your** sakes do I act, house of Israel,
  but for the sake of my holy **name**,
  which you profaned among the nations to which you came.

persing the people through the countries. Now the prophecy moves stunningly from emphasis on the sin of Israel to the wondrous, healing and transforming actions that God will perform. The repetition of God's promise "I will" is grounds for hope among the exiled people. I will take you, I will gather you, I will bring you, I will sprinkle clean water upon you. The first actions assure the exiles that they will be brought back to their land, and that the sprinkling action of God will cleanse both land and people. Instead of pollution and death, there will be new life. Then God will create

the people anew. I will give you a new heart and a new spirit, God's own spirit placed within them. The final words of God's promise, "You shall be my people and I will be your God," signify a restoration of the covenant made with Israel's ancestors. They will once again, by the power of God's holy name, be God's own people, and the Lord will be their God.

EPISTLE After the last of the readings from the Old Testament, the altar candles are lit, bells are rung, and the Gloria is sung. Such expressions of

joy signal that the story of God's work of salvation has reached a new and joyous phase. The two New Testament readings, first from Paul's Letter to the Romans and then from the Gospel, tell of the astonishing fulfillment of God's ancient promises. It is the inauguration of a new age.

The reading from Paul begins with a question (actually a series of questions, with three others preceding our reading). He uses questions not so much to elicit or develop an intellectual understanding, but to help his audience get involved in the story of salvation. Using the personal pronouns "you" and

Careful with this awkward construction. The phrase about God's name being profaned is repeated twice; heighten the second instance.

God will take charge.

Now God reveals what is in store! Change your tone; slow down and speak with gentleness, as a loving parent.

God not only cleanses us from our past transgressions, but gives us a new heart to draw us closer to God and help us avoid future transgressions.

It's God's own spirit that God gives us!

Here is our destiny.

Lift your head to maintain eye contact with the assembly; speak this last line slowly and with firm conviction.

For meditation and context:

TO KEEP IN MIND
Use inflection (the high or low pitch of your voice) to convey attitude and feeling. High pitch expresses intensity and excitement; low pitch expresses sadness, contrition, or solemnity.

I will prove the **holiness** of my great name, profaned among
    the nations,
    in whose midst you have profaned it.
Thus the nations shall **know** that **I** am the LORD, says the
    Lord GOD,
    when in their sight I prove my holiness through **you**.
For I will take you **away** from among the nations,
    gather you from all the foreign lands,
    and bring you **back** to your **own** land.
I will sprinkle **clean water** upon you
    to **cleanse** you from all your **impurities**,
    and from all your idols I will **cleanse** you.
I will give you a **new** heart and place a new **spirit** within you,
    taking from your bodies your **stony** hearts
    and giving you **natural** hearts.
I will put my spirit **within** you and make you live by my **statutes**,
    careful to observe my **decrees**.
You shall **live** in the land I gave your **fathers;**
    you shall be my **people**, and **I** will be your **God**.

RESPONSORIAL PSALM   Psalm 42:3, 5; 43:3, 4 (2)

R. Like a deer that longs for running streams, my soul longs for you, my God.

Athirst is my soul for God, the living God.
    When shall I go and behold the face
    of God?

I went with the throng
    and led them in procession to the house
    of God,
amid loud cries of joy and thanksgiving,
    with the multitude keeping festival.

Send forth your light and your fidelity;
    they shall lead me on
and bring me to your holy mountain,
    to your dwelling-place.

Then will I go in to the altar of God,
    the God of my gladness and joy;
then will I give you thanks upon the harp,
    O God, my God!

Or:

"we," Paul connects himself to the community, for all have been baptized into Christ, and baptized into his Death. In using forms of the word "baptize," (*baptizo*), Paul refers to the ritual experience of Baptism, and he is likely also using the word *baptizo* in its most basic meaning: to be immersed, submerged, or plunged into. Jesus used *baptizo* with this meaning when he, like Paul, asked a question of his disciples: "Can you drink the cup that that I drink or be baptized with the baptism with which I am

baptized?" (Mark 10:38). Both Jesus and Paul are asking about being immersed into the very Death of Jesus.

Paul explains that believers are plunged into Christ's Death, and also into every dimension of his life. This reality is so new that Paul develops a new vocabulary to describe it. Throughout the passage, he coins a series of compound verbs with the prefix *syn-*, meaning "together," or as a prefix "co-." He says literally that we have been cocrucified, coburied, and that we cogrow

with Christ. If we have died with Christ, we will colive with him.

Paul's opening questions are the catalyst for him to develop an explanation of what the believers have already experienced by baptism—both the ritual and the continued immersion into Christ's life—and how they should live accordingly. The intimate participation of believers who are plunged into Christ, as explained by Paul, has practical implications. The last verse of the reading begins with the word "conse-

For meditation and context:

TO KEEP IN MIND

Be careful not to "swallow" words by mumbling. Articulate carefully so that every word is clearly heard, especially at the end of lines.

RESPONSORIAL PSALM   Isaiah 12:2–3, 4bcd, 5–6 (3)

R. You will draw water joyfully from the springs of salvation.

God indeed is my savior;
    I am confident and unafraid.
My strength and my courage is the LORD,
    and he has been my savior.
With joy you will draw water
    at the fountain of salvation.

Give thanks to the LORD, acclaim his name;
    among the nations make known his deeds
    proclaim how exalted is his name.

Sing praise to the LORD for his glorious
    achievement;
    let this be known throughout all the earth.
Shout with exultation, O city of Zion,
    for great in your midst
    is the Holy One of Israel!

Or:

For meditation and context:

RESPONSORIAL PSALM   Psalm 51:12–13, 14–15, 18–19 (12a)

R. Create a clean heart in me, O God.

A clean heart create for me, O God,
    and a steadfast spirit renew within me.
Cast me not out from your presence,
    and your Holy Spirit take not from me.

Give me back the joy of your salvation,
    and a willing spirit sustain in me.
I will teach transgressors your ways,
    and sinners shall return to you.

For you are not pleased with sacrifices;
    should I offer a holocaust, you would not
    accept it.
My sacrifice, O God, is a contrite spirit;
    a heart contrite and humbled, O God,
    you will not spurn.

TO KEEP IN MIND

Pray the text, using your favorite method of praying with Scripture.

A didactic reading that is full of good news, so proclaim with intensity. You speak to all the baptized in your assembly, but especially to those about to be baptized tonight.

Paul sets up a contrast between life and death, but here death is not a bad thing, because death in Christ leads to life in Christ. A challenging teaching! With each repetition, make the progression from death to life very clear.

Paul makes the point again. Here, emphasize the unity with Christ that Baptism brings.

EPISTLE   Romans 6:3–11

A reading from the Letter of Saint Paul to the Romans

Brothers and sisters:
Are you **unaware** that we who were **baptized** into Christ Jesus
    were baptized into his **death**?
We were indeed **buried** with him through **baptism** into death,
    so that, just as Christ was **raised** from the dead
    by the glory of the **Father**,
    we **too** might live in **newness** of life.

quently," a term that Paul often uses when he moves from theological teaching to exhortation. He tells the community members how they are to live in light of their belief. In the verses following our reading, Paul develops the "consequently," telling the believers in Rome how they are to col-ive in Christ, not as a burden, but as an expression of their intimate relationship with the risen Christ.

The readings from the Old Testament can be heard and interpreted anew in light

of the mystery of Christ as proclaimed by Paul. In Christ there is a new creation, new freedom from enslavement, new release from exile. The transformation proclaimed by Israel's prophets is even greater than they could have hoped for, for the transfor-mation entails a "newness of life" in Christ. Ezekiel's prophecy of a new heart and a new spirit, and the promise "You will be my people and I will be your God," find extraor-dinary, unimaginable fulfillment through the profound intimacy of life with Christ.

GOSPEL The setting for the Gospel is "very early when the sun had risen, on the first day of the week." The day of Sabbath rest is over, and a new day has begun, bringing with it a totally unex-pected and wondrous newness. It is the "first day" of a new creation. Three women who had also witnessed the Death of Jesus bought spices to anoint him at the tomb where he had been buried by Joseph of Arimathea. Shortly before his Death, another woman had anointed Jesus' body

For if we have grown into **union** with him through a **death**
      like his,
   we shall also be **united** with him in the **resurrection**.
We know that our **old** self was **crucified** with him,
   so that our **sinful** body might be done **away** with,
   that we might no longer be in **slavery** to sin.
For a **dead** person has been **absolved** from sin.
If, then, we have **died** with Christ,
   we believe that we shall also **live** with him.
We know that **Christ, raised** from the dead, dies no **more;**
   death no longer has **power** over him.
As to his **death,** he died to sin **once** and for **all;**
   as to his **life,** he lives for **God.**
Consequently, you **too** must think of yourselves as being **dead**
      to **sin**
   and **living** for **God** in Christ **Jesus.**

Paul repeats the point yet again. Slow down.

The good news of this night—we no longer need to fear death!

For meditation and context:

RESPONSORIAL PSALM   Psalm 118:1–2, 16–17, 22–23
R. Alleluia, alleluia, alleluia.

Give thanks to the LORD, for he is good,
   for his mercy endures forever.
Let the house of Israel say,
   "His mercy endures forever."

The right hand of the LORD has struck
      with power;
   the right hand of the LORD is exalted.
I shall not die, but live,
   and declare the works of the LORD.

The stone which the builders rejected
   has become the cornerstone.
By the LORD has this been done;
   it is wonderful in our eyes.

---

in preparation for his burial, and now these three women plan to anoint it after burial. The three are named, unlike so many anonymous men and women: Mary Magdalene, Mary, the mother of James, and Salome. They were among the women who had ministered to Jesus in Galilee, and their desire to anoint him was to be a final ministry to him. Wondering who would roll away the large stone from the tomb entrance, the women see instead that the stone had already been rolled back. On entering the

tomb, to their amazement, they see a young man clothed in white. We can well understand their astonishment, noted by Mark with a strong verb (*exethambethesan*), portraying them as completely amazed, utterly overwhelmed. More than simple surprise at the presence of the young man, theirs is a typical reaction in the face of the divine. The mysterious young man is a heavenly messenger, announcing to them that Jesus has been raised. His use of the passive verb "has

been raised," is a biblical idiom to indicate that that action has been accomplished by God. Although Jesus appeared to be abandoned by God at the Crucifixion, God has not abandoned his Son. Always present and powerful, God has transformed Jesus' Death into life.

   Having told the women that Jesus is not here, the messenger adds that "he is going before you to Galilee." The place where Jesus had begun his ministry is the place where he will again meet the disci-

This narrative is a simple account of an extraordinary event, which we see unfold through the women's eyes. Keep their sense of wonder in your proclamation.

There are three women; make each distinct.

Magdalene = MAG-duh-leen

Salome = suh-LOH-mee

Anxiously.

Curious; something's going on but they're not sure what.
Still confused. Who could move such a large stone?
Slowly; with the women's amazement.

Gently, and perhaps with a smile.

Slowly and with great joy.

Pause at the end of this line.
Pick up your pace; the women have important work to do—they are commissioned to be the first evangelists!
Pause to allow the scene to settle in your assembly's hearts before saying "The Gospel of the Lord."

TO KEEP IN MIND
In a narrative, find an emotion or point of view for each character, keeping in mind that these might change during the reading.

GOSPEL   Mark 16:1–7

A reading from the holy Gospel according to Mark

When the **sabbath** was over,
    Mary **Magdalene**, **Mary**, the mother of James, and **Salome**
    bought spices so that they might go and **anoint** him.
Very **early** when the sun had risen,
    on the **first** day of the week, they came to the **tomb**.
They were saying to one another,
    "**Who** will roll back the **stone** for us
    from the entrance to the **tomb**?"
When they looked **up**,
    they saw that the stone **had** been rolled back;
    it was very **large**.
On **entering** the tomb they saw a **young man**
    sitting on the right **side**, clothed in a **white robe**,
    and they were **utterly** amazed.
He said to them, "Do **not** be amazed!
You seek **Jesus** of **Nazareth**, the **crucified**.
He has been **raised**; he is not **here**.
Behold the place where they **laid** him.
But **go** and **tell** his disciples and Peter,
    'He is going **before** you to **Galilee**;
    there you will **see** him, as he **told** you.'"

---

ples whom he had called in Galilee. These closest disciples had not only deserted Jesus in his suffering, but their leader, Peter, had three times denied him. The messenger is assuring his disciples, through the women, that Jesus has not forsaken them, even mentioning Peter specifically. Jesus had predicted their fall and their scattering, and promised them that he would go before them into Galilee. Now, as the risen Messiah, he will fulfill that promise. No longer scattered in fear and discour-

agement, his disciples will meet Jesus, as utterly amazed as the women at the tomb.

In this Easter Vigil Gospel, we see the empty tomb, but not the appearance of the risen Jesus. On Easter Sunday, the first day of the new creation, we will encounter him, far from the empty tomb, alive among us. E.P.

EASTER SUNDAY OF THE RESURRECTION OF THE LORD

LECTIONARY #42

READING I Acts of the Apostles 10:34a, 37–43

A reading from the Acts of the Apostles

Peter proceeded to **speak** and said:
  "You **know** what has happened all over Judea,
  beginning in Galilee after the **baptism**
  that John preached,
  how God **anointed** Jesus of Nazareth
  with the Holy **Spirit** and **power**.
He went about doing **good**
  and **healing** all those oppressed by the devil,
  for God was **with** him.
We are **witnesses** of all that he did
  both in the country of the Jews and in Jerusalem.
They put him to **death** by hanging him on a **tree**.
This man God **raised** on the **third** day and granted that he
      be **visible**,
  not to **all** the people, but to **us**,
  the witnesses **chosen** by God in advance,
  who **ate** and **drank** with him **after** he **rose** from the dead.
He commissioned us to **preach** to the people
  and **testify** that he is the one appointed by God
  as judge of the living and the dead.
To him all the **prophets** bear witness,
  that everyone who **believes** in him
  will receive **forgiveness** of sins through his **name**."

A didactic reading in the form of a narrative. A summary of the life of Christ and what the early Christian community believed about him.

Although Peter is speaking to a crowd, avoid a preachy tone. Instead, imagine yourself speaking to a friend who has just asked, "So who was this Jesus of Nazareth?"
Judea = joo-DEE-uh

How does Peter feel and sound as he recounts the deeds he witnessed?

There might be a tone of sadness in Peter's voice. Pause.
But death was not to be the last word!

You have inherited this commission as a proclaimer of the Word!

Slow down through the end of this line.
Here's the point of Peter's story. Like every reading we proclaim, this is not a history lesson, but a call to all who hear it to act or be different.

Today, options are given for the readings. Contact your parish staff to learn which will be used.

READING I At the center of the First Reading for Easter Sunday is the proclamation of the Resurrection: "This man God raised on the third day." Taken from Peter's speech given at the house of the Gentile Cornelius, this is the fifth of six discourses by Peter in Acts of the Apostles. Placed at strategic points, the speeches review for a variety of audiences the core of Christian faith: Jesus' Death and Resurrection. Peter's first speech to a largely Jewish audience is given on the day of Pentecost. This one, though to Gentiles, shares features that are common to all the speeches.

Peter begins by making a connection with his audience, with the opening words of this address to Gentiles, unfortunately omitted in today's reading: "In truth, I see that God shows no partiality. Rather, in every nation whoever fears him and acts uprightly is acceptable to him." Before his summary of Jesus' ministry, Peter is assuring his audience that the Good News of Jesus is for them as well as for the Jews. Peter concludes his message with a similarly inclusive statement: "Everyone who believes in him will receive forgiveness of sins through his name." He thereby frames the portrait of Jesus with a sketch of the people for whom he gave his life.

With the Resurrection of Jesus as the climax, Peter tells the story of Jesus, beginning with his ministry in Galilee. Each of the speeches in Acts, those of Peter as well as of Paul and Stephen, is a teaching tool as well as an invitation to conversion. In his

For meditation and context:

TO KEEP IN MIND

Exhortatory texts make an urgent appeal to listeners. They may encourage, warn, or challenge, and often include a call to action. You must convey the urgency and passion behind the words.

An exhortatory reading encouraging your assembly to act like Easter people—a community who has really changed because of the Resurrection. It's brief; take your time.

Colossians = kuh-LOSH-uhnz

Be concerned with things that bring life.

Death is good news here.

Maintain eye contact with your assembly and smile as you share this good news.

TO KEEP IN MIND

Making eye contact with the assembly connects you with them and connects them to the reading more deeply than using your voice alone. This helps the assembly stay with the story and keeps them engaged.

RESPONSORIAL PSALM   Psalm 118:1–2, 16–17, 22–23 (24)

R. This is the day the Lord has made; let us rejoice and be glad. or R. Alleluia.

Give thanks to the Lord, for he is good,
  for his mercy endures forever.
Let the house of Israel say,
  "His mercy endures forever."

"The right hand of the Lord has struck
    with power;
  the right hand of the Lord is exalted.
I shall not die, but live,
  and declare the works of the Lord.

The stone which the builders rejected
  has become the cornerstone.
By the Lord has this been done;
  it is wonderful in our eyes.

READING II   Colossians 3:1–4

A reading from the Letter of Saint Paul to the Colossians

Brothers and sisters:
If then you were **raised** with Christ, seek what is **above**,
    where Christ is seated at the right hand of **God**.
Think of what is **above**, not of what is on **earth**.
For you have **died**, and your life is **hidden** with Christ in **God**.
When Christ your life **appears**,
    then you **too** will appear with him in **glory**.

Or:

---

instruction, Peter explains that in Jesus' entire life "he went about doing good." Then he moves to telling of Jesus' Resurrection, the earliest and most fundamental proclamation, and the heart of each of the speeches. Jesus' acts of "doing good" during his lifetime will continue, Peter explains, now that he has been raised from the dead. He will offer forgiveness to everyone who believes in him. Like the opening words about those who fear God and act uprightly, Peter's final words are an invitation to faith and righteous living in response to the Resurrection of Jesus.

READING II | **Colossians 3:1–4.** Jesus' Resurrection from the dead, the central proclamation of faith, is a foretaste, pattern, and source of the resurrection of those who are immersed into his life. The reading from Colossians looks briefly at the implications of being raised with Christ. Although belief in a future resurrection after death is part of Christian faith, the focus in this reading is not on future resurrection, but on Death and Resurrection that has already happened in the life of believers. "You were raised" and "you have died" are verbs in the perfect

tense, meaning that both actions have already happened; those who have been baptized into Christ have already died and risen with him. In addition to the common verb tense, both verbs have the prefix *syn-*, (together or with) signifying that the baptized have codied and are corisen with Christ. Christ risen from the dead is seated at God's right hand; he is exalted, portrayed as seated on a heavenly throne. Such spatial imagery, above and below, is a common way of expressing the mystery of the earthly realm and the heavenly realm. Psalm 110:1, a frequently cited verse in the

An exhortatory reading. Paul uses the metaphor of a feast to describe the new life of a resurrected people.

Corinthians = kohr-IN-thee-uhnz

Become completely new! Your old ways, even the smallest detail, can keep you from the fullness of life we celebrate today.

The bread of the feast is unleavened.

Now the feast can begin.

This is the way we live as Christians.

For meditation and context:

TO KEEP IN MIND

You can't proclaim what you don't understand. Read the Scripture passage and its commentary in *Workbook*. Then read it from your Bible, including what comes before and after it so that you understand the context.

READING II   1 Corinthians 5:6b–8

A reading from the first Letter of Saint Paul to the Corinthians

Brothers and sisters:
Do you not **know** that a little **yeast** leavens **all** the dough?
Clear out the **old** yeast,
     so that you may become a **fresh** batch of dough,
     inasmuch as you are **unleavened**.
For our paschal **lamb**, **Christ**, has been **sacrificed**.
Therefore, let us **celebrate** the feast,
     not with the **old** yeast, the yeast of **malice** and **wickedness**,
     but with the **unleavened** bread of **sincerity** and **truth**.

SEQUENCE   Victimae paschali laudes

Christians, to the Paschal Victim
     Offer your thankful praises!
A Lamb the sheep redeems;
     Christ, who only is sinless,
     Reconciles sinners to the Father.
Death and life have contended in that
          combat stupendous:
     The Prince of life, who died, reigns
     immortal.

Speak, Mary, declaring
     What you saw, wayfaring.
"The tomb of Christ, who is living,
     The glory of Jesus' resurrection;
Bright angels attesting,
     The shroud and napkin resting.
Yes, Christ my hope is arisen;
     to Galilee he goes before you."
Christ indeed from death is risen,
     our new life obtaining.
     Have mercy, victor King, ever reigning!
     Amen. Alleluia.

New Testament, is likely being alluded to here: "The LORD [God] says to my lord [Christ]: 'Sit at my right hand, while I make your enemies your footstool.'"

Because Christ, risen and ascended, is "above," in the heavenly realm, the baptized should seek and think of that is above. The imperative verbs "seek" and "think" refer not to momentary or one-time actions, but indicate a continuous, ongoing way of life. Seeking implies intensity and determination, directed on the goal of the search. Thinking about what is above adds the notion of sustained focus, not dis-

tracted or being led astray by contrary thoughts and actions. This reading provides the theological underpinning for the kind of life that the baptized are to lead. In the verses immediately after our reading, the author of Colossians makes explicit what seeking and thinking of things above means: "Put to death, then, the parts of you that are earthly," followed by specific actions that are to be put away. Having already codied and corisen, the baptized live in hope that they will ultimately appear with him in glory.

1 Corinthians 5:6b–8. In the reading from 1 Corinthians, Paul uses closely related images from Judaism: yeast, unleavened bread, and paschal lamb, each of them alluding to the feasts of Unleavened Bread and Passover. Originally two separate feasts, by the time of Christ the two celebrations had been joined together as a memorial of God's rescuing the enslaved people from their bondage in Egypt. During the feast, bread that was made without leaven was symbolic of fresh and new life, without any of the contamination of the old year. The unleavened bread used in the

A narrative which may have lost its power to amaze after centuries of repetition. Your job is to return to it a sense of wonder, awe, and astonishment.

Magdala = MAG-duh-luh

This is unexpected.
Quicken your pace to indicate her anxiety.

There should be real fear in your voice.

Out of respect for Peter's position of leadership.

Take your time with this line. This is a clue: if the body had been stolen it's unlikely thieves would have folded the cloth.

He is the first to believe. Your assembly, too, has seen and believed.

TO KEEP IN MIND
Making eye contact with the assembly connects you with them and connects them to the reading more deeply than using your voice alone. This helps the assembly stay with the story and keeps them engaged.

GOSPEL   John 20:1–9

A reading from the holy Gospel according to John

On the **first** day of the **week**,
　　Mary of **Magdala** came to the **tomb** early in the **morning**,
　　while it was still **dark**,
　　and saw the **stone removed** from the **tomb**.
So she **ran** and went to Simon **Peter**
　　and to the **other** disciple whom Jesus **loved**, and told them,
　　"They have taken the **Lord** from the **tomb**,
　　and we don't know where they **put** him."
So **Peter** and the **other** disciple went out and **came** to the tomb.
They both **ran**, but the **other** disciple ran **faster** than Peter
　　and arrived at the tomb **first**;
　　he **bent** down and saw the **burial** cloths there, but did not go **in**.
When Simon **Peter** arrived **after** him,
　　he went **into** the tomb and **saw** the burial cloths there,
　　and the cloth that had covered his **head**,
　　not with the **burial** cloths but rolled up in a **separate** place.
Then the **other** disciple **also** went in,
　　the one who had arrived at the tomb **first**,
　　and he **saw** and **believed**.
For they did not yet **understand** the Scripture
　　that he had to **rise** from the dead.

Passover feast was shared at family tables, along with the paschal lamb. For Paul, as well as for other New Testament sources (for example, John 1:29; 1 Peter 1:19), Christ himself is our sacrificial paschal lamb. Christ's Death was a sacrifice bringing even greater liberation than that from Egypt. Those who share in the feast must put aside everything that is corrupt, like the old leaven that Paul calls "the yeast of malice and wickedness."

The context for Paul's comments is the sexual immorality in the Corinthian community. Not only is such behavior con-

trary to the faith, but some people actually boast about their conduct. Paul uses their boasting (*kauchema*) to connect the situation with the feast of unleavened bread. Like yeast, boasting is a kind of "puffing up" in pride that spreads throughout the whole community. Paul explains, "a little yeast leavens all the dough." The boastful immorality must be removed, like old yeast. The community should rather be unleavened bread, celebrating the feast with the newness of life brought about by the sacrifice of our paschal lamb.

GOSPEL   When the first day of the week had not yet dawned, while it was still dark, Mary Magdalene came to the garden tomb of Jesus. Having stood at the Cross of Jesus, she now comes to his tomb alone, according to John's version of the story. Whether she was bringing spices to anoint his body or simply to mourn Jesus, Mary Magdalene is clearly not expecting his being raised from the dead. Like many Jews of Jesus' day, she likely believed in resurrection at the "last day," a belief that was affirmed by Martha when her brother Lazarus died.

A narrative that suggests how your assembly might meet Jesus today—in the Word, the breaking of the bread, and the stranger. This beloved and powerful story needs careful preparation to make the most of its dialogue, dramatic revelation, and rich insights.

The day of the Resurrection; these disciples have heard the news from the women this morning.

The story has much energy and activity. Keep your pace up.

They can't hide their sadness at Jesus' Death and the confusing events since then.

A bit incredulous. Notice how Jesus, who knows the most about what has happened, allows them to share their story and feelings first.

Jesus wants to meet them where they are.

Try alternating these lines between the two. Change your tone slightly for each.

The first disciple states the facts.

The second gives an interpretation of the facts.

The first jumps in with even more confusing news.

Let their astonishment come through in this description. They still don't know what to make of it all.

"Can you believe it?"

AFTERNOON GOSPEL   Luke 24:13–35

A reading from the holy Gospel according to Luke

That **very** day, the **first** day of the week,
　　two of Jesus' **disciples** were going
　　to a village seven **miles** from Jerusalem called **Emmaus**,
　　and they were **conversing** about all the things that
　　　　had **occurred**.
And it **happened** that while they were **conversing** and **debating**,
　　Jesus **himself** drew near and **walked** with them,
　　but their eyes were **prevented** from **recognizing** him.
He asked them,
　　"What are you **discussing** as you walk along?"
They **stopped**, looking **downcast**.
One of them, named **Cleopas**, said to him in reply,
　　"Are you the **only** visitor to Jerusalem
　　who does not **know** of the **things**
　　that have taken place there in these days?"
And he replied to them, "What **sort** of things?"
They **said** to him,
　　"The **things** that happened to **Jesus** the **Nazarene**,
　　who was a **prophet** mighty in **deed** and **word**
　　before **God** and all the **people**,
　　how our chief **priests** and **rulers both** handed him over
　　to a sentence of **death** and **crucified** him.
But we were **hoping** that **he** would be the one to **redeem** Israel;
　　and **besides** all this,
　　it is now the **third** day since this took place.
Some **women** from our group, however, have **astounded** us:
　　they were at the **tomb** early in the **morning**
　　and did not find his **body**;
　　they came back and reported
　　that they had indeed seen a **vision** of **angels**
　　who announced that he was **alive**.

The notion that one individual would rise before the end was incomprehensible and totally unexpected.

　　When Mary sees that the stone that would have sealed the tomb has been rolled away, she changes course and runs to Simon Peter and the other disciple whom Jesus loved. Now these two disciples show the same urgency that Mary had exhibited as they themselves run to the tomb. Mary had seen the stone removed, they see also the burial cloths. At the raising of Lazarus, he had come forth, still wrapped in the burial linens. Jesus'

Resurrection is altogether different, for even the trappings of death are left behind. For the Beloved Disciple, that is enough: "he saw and believed." Yet belief is not the same as understanding. The Gospel states that they still did not understand the Scripture, a comment that reminds us of another scene in the Gospel of John. When Jesus was in Jerusalem for the celebration of Passover, he had said: "Destroy this temple, and in three days I will raise it up." The evangelist explains that Jesus was speaking of the temple of his body, and that when Jesus was raised form the dead, his disciples

remembered, and "they came to believe the scripture and the word Jesus had spoken." (2:19–22) Yet neither the empty tomb nor the burial cloths give them the understanding of the Scriptures. The risen Jesus himself will provide the understanding.

AFTERNOON GOSPEL Each of the Gospel accounts begins the story of the risen Jesus with an account of the empty tomb. Luke follows this story with the appearance of Jesus to two disciples leaving Jerusalem for the village of Emmaus. He weaves the

The second finishes the story.

What does Jesus feel as he realizes these disciples still don't understand his messiahship? Disappointment, sadness, compassion?

Rather than being frustrated and leaving them in their confusion, Jesus is patient and empathetic.

Jesus will not force himself on anyone; he waits to be invited.

Don't rush these four actions; they echo the Last Supper.

Now quicken your pace.

Convey their excitement!

Don't swallow "at once." The encounter with Jesus impels them to return to the community immediately.

Amazing news!

Keep your voice up through the end of the line.

Then some of those with us **went** to the tomb
    and found things just as the women had **described**,
        but **him** they did not **see**."
And he said to them, "Oh, how **foolish** you are!
How **slow** of heart to believe all that the **prophets** spoke!
Was it not **necessary** that the Christ should **suffer** these things
    and enter into his **glory**?"
Then beginning with **Moses** and all the **prophets**,
    he **interpreted** to them what **referred** to him
    in **all** the **Scriptures**.
As they approached the **village** to which they were **going**,
    he gave the impression that he was going on **farther**.
But they **urged** him, "**Stay** with us,
    for it is nearly **evening** and the day is almost **over**."
So he went in to **stay** with them.
And it **happened** that, while he was with them at **table**,
    he took **bread**, said the **blessing**,
    broke it, and **gave** it to them.
With **that** their **eyes** were **opened** and they **recognized** him,
    but he **vanished** from their **sight**.
Then they **said** to each other,
    "Were not our **hearts burning** within us
    while he **spoke** to us on the way and opened the **Scriptures**
        to us?"
So they set out at **once** and returned to **Jerusalem**
    where they found gathered together
    the **eleven** and those with them who were saying,
    "The Lord has truly been **raised** and has appeared to **Simon**!"
Then the **two** recounted
    what had taken place on the **way**
    and how he was made **known** to them in the **breaking**
        of **bread**.

theme of the journey into this story. The two disciples are making a journey away from the community when Jesus meets them on the road. It is on their journey that he teaches them and corrects their misunderstanding, much as he had done during his ministry. Through the motif of "the way," Luke illustrates that being a disciple of Jesus, not only during his lifetime, but also in his risen life, means to follow him along the road.

In the two parts of the story, we see two ways in which disciples encounter the risen Jesus, first in Word, and then in the

breaking of the bread. Important in Jesus' teaching is the interpretation of Scripture that can only be understood in light of his Death and Resurrection. The misunderstanding of the two Emmaus-bound disciples reflects the misunderstanding and questions of Jesus' first disciples. In his explanation, Jesus reveals for the whole believing community the fulfillment of the Scriptures in his suffering and in his glory.

The second part of the story is more than a simple meal. The breaking of the bread is the evangelist's way of referring to the eucharistic meal that Jesus shared at

the last supper. His actions at both meals are the same. He takes bread, says the blessing, breaks it and gives it to those at the table. In the bread blessed and broken, Jesus is giving his very self. Then, having recognized Jesus in the breaking of the bread, the formerly discouraged and confused disciples proclaim the Good News, retracing their steps back to Jerusalem. E.P.

SECOND SUNDAY OF EASTER (OR SUNDAY OF DIVINE MERCY)

This narrative reading is the classic definition of Christian community. Encourage your assembly to emulate this ideal. Keep that intention uppermost in your mind as you proclaim, "Be of one heart!"

How would you feel being part of such a community? Make a definite choice, and let that feeling show throughout your proclamation.

The oneness of the community is repeated here in different ways: "one heart and mind," "no one," "in common," "all," "no needy person." Heighten each repetition.

Urge your assembly to imagine such a community: "Wouldn't it be wonderful if we were like this?"

For meditation and context:

TO KEEP IN MIND

A *narrative* has characters, dialogue, a setting, and action. Help your listeners see the story unfold, keep characters distinct, and be clear about shifts in setting.

LECTIONARY #44

READING I   Acts of the Apostles 4:32–35

A reading from the Acts of the Apostles

The community of **believers** was of one **heart** and **mind**,
   and **no** one claimed that any of his **possessions** was his **own**,
   but they had everything in **common**.
With great **power** the apostles bore **witness**
   to the **resurrection** of the Lord Jesus,
   and great **favor** was accorded them all.
There was no **needy** person among them,
   for those who owned **property** or **houses** would **sell** them,
   bring the **proceeds** of the sale,
   and put them at the feet of the **apostles**,
   and they were **distributed** to each according to **need**.

RESPONSORIAL PSALM   Psalm 118:2–4, 13–15, 22–24 (1)

R. Give thanks to the Lord, for he is good; his love is everlasting. or R. Alleluia.

Let the house of Israel say,
   "His mercy endures forever."
Let the house of Aaron say,
   "His mercy endures forever."
Let those who fear the LORD say,
   "His mercy endures forever."

I was hard pressed and was falling,
   but the LORD helped me.
My strength and my courage is the LORD,
   and he has been my savior.
The joyful shout of victory
   in the tents of the just.

The stone which the builders rejected
   has become the cornerstone.
By the LORD has this been done;
   it is wonderful in our eyes.
This is the day the LORD has made;
   let us be glad and rejoice in it.

READING I   Acts of the Apostles tells the story of the early Church, beginning in Jerusalem and ending in Rome. In this second volume by Luke, he intersperses recounting of events and speeches with summaries of the Church's growth. The first summary at 2:42–47 is a foundation for the others that follow. Four key elements of this first summary will be important as the Church expands throughout the Mediterranean world: teaching of the Apostles, the communal life, the breaking of the bread, and the prayers.

Today's reading is the second summary, describing how the community continued to grow even after Peter and John had been ordered by the leaders in Jerusalem not to preach in Jesus' name. Luke emphasizes two of the elements from the first summary: communal life and teaching of the Apostles. He begins this summary with a description of the community: they were of one heart and mind. Such unanimity has practical implications, leading the believers to have everything in common as a sign of their fidelity to the communal life. Although the Apostles had

just been ordered not to preach, they boldly bear witness to the Resurrection, a vivid example of apostolic teaching. They also assume the responsibility for distributing the proceeds from sold property to anyone in need. As the Church continues to grow, their fidelity to the essential elements will be tested with pressure both from inside and outside the community.

READING II   In this reading, John addresses the community as beloved, as believers, and as children of God. These three descriptions are intri-

There's a lot here in this didactic reading; take your time and make sure you make the line of reasoning clear.

Good news! We are all children of God!

Note this line refers to our loving *each other* as children of God.

The idea is repeated; more emphatic!

Gently. Keeping commandments is not difficult when you know you are a child of God.

Slowly and deliberately. Make this a statement rather than a question: by our faith, *we* are victors over the world! Pause. Slightly longer pauses at the commas in these lines.

A narrative. For each character—Jesus, Thomas, and the disciples—identify an attitude or intention and let that distinguish them in your proclamation.

This should sound like the surprise that it is!

Immediately, Jesus calms their fears.

READING II   1 John 5:1–6

A reading from the first Letter of Saint John

Beloved:
Everyone who **believes** that Jesus is the **Christ** is **begotten**
      by **God**,
   and everyone who loves the **Father**
   loves also the one **begotten** by him.
In this way we know that we **love** the **children** of God
   when we love **God** and obey his **commandments**.
For the love of God is this,
   that we keep his **commandments**.
And his commandments are not **burdensome**,
   for whoever is begotten by God **conquers** the **world**.
And the **victory** that conquers the world is our **faith**.
Who indeed is the **victor** over the world
   but the one who **believes** that Jesus is the Son of **God**?

This is the one who came through **water** and **blood**, Jesus **Christ**,
   not by water **alone**, but by **water** and **blood**.
The **Spirit** is the one that **testifies**,
   and the **Spirit** is **truth**.

GOSPEL   John 20:19–31

A reading from the holy Gospel according to John

On the evening of that **first** day of the week,
   when the doors were **locked**, where the disciples were,
   for fear of the **Jews**,
Jesus came and stood in their midst
   and said to them, "**Peace** be with you."

cately woven together, for believing and loving are actions that result in becoming children of God. Believing is a major emphasis in this letter, perhaps because of false prophets who are luring people away from the truth and from the covenant bond with God as well as from other believers. To be a believer means to adhere in loving reverence to authentic Christian teaching, and to be faithful to the relationship with God, who is Father, Son, and Spirit.

The opening verse stresses a core dimension of the content of Christian belief: Jesus is the Christ, the anointed one

of God who fulfilled God's promise of anointed descendant of King David. The community also believes that Jesus is Son of God. As God's own Son, Jesus came through water and blood, the water of birth and baptism, and the blood of the Cross. God's own Spirit testifies to this truth, as promised by Jesus himself (John 15:26; 16:13).

Belief in Jesus as Son of God leads to the victory that overcomes "the world," signifying that part of creation associated with darkness. Unlike those in darkness, those who believe love God and love the children

of God. The two expressions are so closely linked that love of God and of neighbor are inseparable. By addressing the community as beloved, John indicates that their very identity is based on the twofold love. The author includes himself in this way of life, uniting himself with his audience in faith and love.

GOSPEL The reading from John's Gospel has two appearances of the risen Jesus. In both scenes, Jesus appears on the first day of the week when his disciples are gathered behind

Let their joy echo in your proclamation.

We are sent by Jesus as he was sent by the Father.

Linger over "breathed." It implies that Jesus is in very close proximity to those present, and evokes the Spirit.

Pause at the end of the line to indicate the passage of time.
Didymus = DID-uh-muhs

This is a joyful exclamation!

Careful not to make Thomas sound too obstinate; he longs for direct experience.

Pause again at the end of the line to separate the scenes.

There is no chiding in Jesus' words. He knows what Thomas needs and gently offers it.

This line is for your assembly. Pause.

Pick up your pace on this conclusion.

Slow down on the last half of this line.

When he had said this, he showed them his **hands** and his **side**.
The disciples **rejoiced** when they saw the Lord.
Jesus said to them **again**, "**Peace** be with you.
As the **Father** has sent me, so **I** send **you**."
And when he had said this, he **breathed** on them and said
      to them,
    "**Receive** the Holy **Spirit**.
Whose **sins** you **forgive** are **forgiven** them,
      and whose sins you **retain** are **retained**."

Thomas, called **Didymus**, one of the **Twelve**,
      was not **with** them when Jesus came.
So the **other** disciples said to him, "We have **seen** the Lord."
But he said to them,
      "Unless I **see** the mark of the **nails** in his **hands**
      and put my **finger** into the nailmarks
      and put my **hand** into his **side**, I will not **believe**."

Now a week **later** his disciples were again inside
      and Thomas **was** with them.
Jesus **came**, although the doors were **locked**,
      and stood in their midst and said, "**Peace** be with you."
Then he said to **Thomas**, "Put your **finger** here and see my **hands**,
      and bring your **hand** and put it into my **side**,
      and do not be **unbelieving**, but **believe**."
Thomas **answered** and said to him, "My **Lord** and my **God**!"
Jesus said to him, "Have you come to **believe** because you have
      seen me?
Blessed are those who have **not** seen and have **believed**."

Now Jesus did many **other** signs in the presence of his disciples
      that are not **written** in this book.
But **these** are written that you may come to **believe**
      that Jesus is the **Christ**, the Son of **God**,
      and that **through** this belief you may have **life** in his name.

locked doors. In both scenes Jesus greets his followers with "Peace be with you," assuring his fearful disciples that he has been victorious over death, and that he has fulfilled the promises he gave to them at their last meal together. He had said then that peace was his farewell gift to them, and that he would come back to them (14:27–28). He also promised that the Spirit of truth, the Advocate, would come to them (16.7–11). Now, breathing on them, he imparts the promised Spirit, and empowers them to forgive sins. He bestows these gifts of peace and the Holy Spirit on the dis-

ciples who had abandoned him during the Passion, thereby revealing his forgiveness and reconciliation with them. Just as Jesus had been sent by the Father, so now he sends his disciples. No longer behind locked doors, they are to continue Jesus' mission of forgiveness.

Between the two appearances of the risen Jesus, Thomas, absent from the first scene, does not believe the disciples who say, "We have seen the Lord." Jesus' next appearance centers on his encounter with Thomas, whose cry of "My Lord and my God" expresses his own faith as well as that

of the believing community. Thomas was able to make his profession of faith when he had seen and touched the risen Lord. The account, however, is not only about Thomas, but also about those who have not seen, whether in the first generation or in the millennia since then. Jesus announces a beatitude for them: "Blessed are those who have not seen and have believed." The final verse of today's Gospel reading attests that the account was written "that you may come to believe . . . [and] may have life in his name." E.P.

THIRD SUNDAY OF EASTER

LECTIONARY #47

An exhortatory reading. What Peter preaches is well known to us, but would have been scandalous to his hearers, who likely still thought of Jesus as a criminal. Knowing this, Peter would have to work even harder to change their hearts. Bring that desire to your proclamation.

Give this first part energy and drive.

Don't rush these phrases.

Abraham = AY-bruh-ham

Isaac = Ī-zik

This is not an accusation. Resist the temptation to stress "you." Rather, stress the verbs. These actions were taken out of ignorance, as Peter says later, but God uses them to bring salvation to fulfillment.

Irony: you asked for one who took a life, but now may receive one who brings life.

Pause after this line.

More slowly and intimately; you are offering a gift.

Slowly.

With encouragement.

TO KEEP IN MIND

Pay attention to the pace of your reading. Varying the pace gives listeners clues to the meaning of the text. The most common problem for proclaimers new to the ministry is going too fast to be understood.

READING I   Acts of the Apostles 3:13–15, 17–19

A reading from the Acts of the Apostles

Peter said to the **people**:
"The God of **Abraham**,
    the God of **Isaac**, and the God of **Jacob**,
    the God of our **fathers**, has **glorified** his servant **Jesus**,
    whom **you** handed over and **denied** in Pilate's presence
    when he had decided to **release** him.
You denied the **Holy** and **Righteous** One
    and asked that a **murderer** be released to you.
The author of **life** you put to **death**,
    but God **raised** him from the dead; of this we are **witnesses**.
Now I **know**, brothers,
    that you acted out of **ignorance**, just as your **leaders** did;
    but God has thus brought to **fulfillment**
    what he had announced **beforehand**
    through the mouth of all the **prophets**,
    that his **Christ** would **suffer**.
Repent, therefore, and be **converted**, that your **sins** may be
    wiped **away**."

READING I   Today's reading is the second speech by Peter in Acts, occurring after Peter and John had healed a crippled man. The opening words, not included in our reading, question: "Why are you amazed at this" (3:12)? Peter's point is that since they are all Israelites, they should know that it isn't by Peter's own power that the man is able to walk. Their common Israelite heritage is the catalyst Peter uses to tell them the story of Jesus: The God of Abraham, the God of their ancestors, "has glorified his servant Jesus." By referring to Jesus as God's ser-

vant, Peter presents him as a loyal Israelite, and his description resonates with the image of Isaiah's suffering servant. In both portraits (Jesus' and the suffering servant's) we see the juxtaposition of being rejected and exalted, of being righteous, though despised.

Peter's message is that the God of Abraham, Isaac, and Jacob acted in Jesus as he had done throughout Israel's history. Jesus had spoken similarly to a Jewish audience of the God of Abraham, Isaac, and Jacob, saying, "He is not God of the dead, but of the living" (Mark 12:27). With a com-

parable point of view, Peter sees Jesus as the "Author of life" in whom the God of life again brings life.

Having announced a prophetic judgment, Peter tells his fellow Jews that they acted in ignorance. He corrects their ignorance. Now they should know that all of Jesus' suffering has brought to fulfillment what God foretold by the prophets. Like other Hebrew prophets, Peter calls his listeners to conversion. And like other speeches in Acts, Peter's call to conversion is centered on Jesus' Death and Resurrection.

For meditation and context:

TO KEEP IN MIND

A *didactic* text makes a point or teaches something. Help your assembly to follow the argument and understand what's being taught.

A didactic reading. This Easter season we hear from John's first letter. John never wavers from his theme that God is love and we love God by loving others. But even if we fail to love, as he notes in today's reading, God forgives us.

Pour all the love you can into the phrase "My children."

Good news! Smile with your voice, eyes, and face.

expiation = ex-spee-AY-shuhn (payment)

Even better news! Pause at the end of the line.

Most especially, for John, the commandment to love.

With a tinge of sadness and disappointment.

Gently, with joy.

A narrative reading. Contrast the calm of Jesus with the fear and confusion of the disciples.

"On the way" to Emmaus (see Luke 24:13–35). Emmaus = eh-MAY-uhs

---

RESPONSORIAL PSALM   Psalm 4:2, 4, 7–8, 9 (7a)

R. Lord, let your face shine on us. or R. Alleluia.

When I call, answer me, O my just God,
   you who relieve me when I am in distress;
   have pity on me, and hear my prayer!

Know that the LORD does wonders for his
      faithful one;
   the LORD will hear me when I call
      upon him.

O LORD, let the light of your countenance
      shine upon us!
   You put gladness into my heart.

As soon as I lie down, I fall peacefully asleep,
   for you alone, O LORD,
   bring security to my dwelling.

READING II   1 John 2:1–5a

A reading from the first Letter of Saint John

My **children**, I am **writing** this to you
   so that you may not commit **sin**.
But if anyone **does** sin, we have an **Advocate** with the Father,
   Jesus **Christ** the **righteous** one.
He is **expiation** for our **sins**,
   and not for **our** sins **only** but for those of the whole **world**.
The way we may be **sure** that we **know** him
   is to keep his **commandments**.
Those who say, "I **know** him," but do **not** keep his
         commandments
   are **liars**, and the **truth** is not **in** them.
But whoever **keeps** his word,
   the love of God is truly **perfected** in him.

GOSPEL   Luke 24:35–48

A reading from the holy Gospel according to Luke

The two disciples **recounted** what had taken place on the way,
   and how Jesus was made **known** to them
   in the **breaking** of **bread**.

READING II   John writes "so that you may not commit sin," coupled with awareness that sin is possible. The Good News is that Jesus is our advocate (*paracletos*), standing by our side to intercede and comfort. In John's Gospel, Jesus had promised that God would send another *paracletos*, the Holy Spirit. During his lifetime, Jesus himself was the advocate, standing by his disciples' side. Here, John says that Jesus remains as *paracletos*. Peter explains further that Jesus is the expiation for our sins. In Judaism, this expiation reestablishes the relationship between God and human persons. It is a sacrifice of blood offered on the Day of Atonement when sins are forgiven and the whole people are reconciled with God. Though the sacrifice is rooted in Judaism, John says that Jesus' expiation benefits the whole world.

Having focused first on Jesus, John shifts focus to the community. He connects knowing Jesus with obeying his commandments. In the Jewish perspective, knowing entails more than cognitive understanding. Knowing is a relational activity, involving intimacy and experience. Thus those who truly know Jesus exhibit their knowledge by obedience to his commandments. Further, obedience means that the love of God has reached perfection. The phrase "love of God" can refer both to the love that God has for us, and the love we have for God. Loving obedience is a sign that this twofold love has been brought to perfection, whole and entire. The exhortation, written "so that you may not commit sin," is a testimony to God's abiding love in Christ for the whole world.

Slowly.

Pick up your pace and energy immediately.
Tenderly and calmly, without accusation.
Jesus understands their fear and, as he did on the road to Emmaus, he meets them where they are.
Articulate carefully the awkward phrase "it is I myself."

With gentleness.

Proclaim this line with the amazement of the disciples—a "ghost" wouldn't eat food.

Don't preach. Jesus is sitting among his disciples in the upper room.

Jesus is clear: his mission is brought to completion through the work of his disciples. Inspire your assembly as Jesus is inspiring his disciples.

A long pause.
Maintain eye contact with the assembly and proclaim this slowly and with great joy.

While they were still **speaking** about this,
   he **stood** in their midst and said to them,
      "**Peace** be with you."
But they were **startled** and **terrified**
   and thought that they were seeing a **ghost**.
Then he **said** to them, "Why are you **troubled**?
And why do **questions** arise in your hearts?
Look at my **hands** and my **feet**, that it is I **myself**.
Touch me and **see**, because a **ghost** does not have flesh and bones
   as you can see I have."
And as he **said** this,
   he **showed** them his hands and his feet.
While they were still incredulous for **joy** and were **amazed**,
   he asked them, "Have you anything here to **eat**?"
They gave him a piece of baked **fish**;
   he took it and **ate** it in **front** of them.

He said to them,
   "These are my words that I spoke to you while I was still
      with you,
   that everything written about me in the law of **Moses**
   and in the **prophets** and **psalms** must be **fulfilled**."
Then he opened their minds to **understand** the Scriptures.
And he said to them,
   "Thus it is written that the Christ would **suffer**
   and **rise** from the dead on the third **day**
   and that **repentance**, for the forgiveness of **sins**,
   would be preached in his name
   to all the **nations**, beginning from **Jerusalem**.
You are **witnesses** of these things."

GOSPEL | The first verses in the Gospel are a transition from the account of Jesus and two disciples on the road to Emmaus and his appearance to his disciples in Jerusalem. The stories have similar features: Jesus appears unexpectedly; he answers their questions through the interpretation of Scripture; he proclaims the Good News of his Resurrection; they share a meal. The two Emmaus disciples tell others what they have seen and heard, and in today's Gospel, Jesus commissions those gathered in Jerusalem to preach to all nations. The common features present essential dimensions of Christian faith: Jesus is present as the risen Messiah; he has fulfilled the Scriptures; the Paschal Mystery is the lens to understand the Scriptures; they will meet him when they gather, particularly in their common meal; they are expected to share the Good News with all people.

In today's scene, Jesus appears to disciples who have just heard their two Emmaus-bound friends tell their story that isn't even finished when Jesus stands in their midst. Luke emphasizes the effect of his appearance: they were startled, terrified, troubled, and questioning. Not recognizing him, they must be reassured that this is the Jesus they had known. He shows them that he is no ghost, for they are able to touch him, and he even eats in their presence. Then he opens their minds to understand how the Scriptures were fulfilled in him. Only after his passing from death to life are they able to grasp how the Scriptures had spoken of him. Then, having opened their minds, Jesus commissions his followers to proclaim repentance and forgiveness in his name to all nations—a commission continued by the Church today. E.P.

FOURTH SUNDAY OF EASTER

LECTIONARY #50

READING I   Acts of the Apostles 4:8–12

A reading from the Acts of the Apostles

Peter, filled with the Holy **Spirit**, said:
  "**Leaders** of the people and **elders**:
  If we are being **examined** today
  about a good **deed** done to a **cripple**,
  namely, by what **means** he was saved,
  then all of **you** and all the people of **Israel** should know
  that it was in the name of Jesus **Christ** the **Nazorean**
  whom you **crucified**, whom God **raised** from the **dead**;
  in **his** name this man stands before you **healed**.
He is *the stone **rejected** by you, the **builders**,*
  *which has become the **cornerstone**.*
There is no **salvation** through anyone **else**,
  nor is there any **other** name under heaven
  given to the human race by which we are to be **saved**."

An exhortatory reading. The Holy Spirit has turned a group of frightened disciples into bold proclaimers of the Gospel

You are filled with that same Spirit, so proclaim with that same boldness! With energy and passion.

The structure of this line is, "If this is the question, then here is the answer." Keep the phrase "If . . . saved" together.
Raise your inflection on "saved" to make it sound like a question.

Nazorean = naz-uh-REE-uhn

Slowly; a restatement of the previous line. Pause.
God turns human judgement upside down! Let your feeling about this come through.

Good news! Don't chide, but offer this gift. Smile with your face, eyes, and voice.

TO KEEP IN MIND
Use inflection (the high or low pitch of your voice) to convey attitude and feeling. High pitch expresses intensity and excitement; low pitch expresses sadness, contrition, or solemnity.

READING I   After the healing of a crippled man, Peter addressed the Jewish crowds in the speech we heard last Sunday. As he was still speaking, the authorities, annoyed at the Apostles' teaching about Jesus' Resurrection, arrested both Peter and John. In their interrogation, the leaders questioned the two: by what power or name had they acted? At issue was the healing as well as their preaching of the Resurrection. Peter's answer to their questioning is another speech—this time to the assembled Jerusalem leaders. By the power of the Spirit, Peter boldly tells his audience that he has healed the man in the name of Jesus Christ. The word that Peter uses for healing (*sozo*) can mean a physical cure, or being made well or whole. It is the word also used in the New Testament to speak of God's ultimate deliverance from sin and death. The physical healing of the crippled man is a sign of God's full, life-giving, saving activity. In the conclusion to his speech, Peter speaks of being saved in this sense. The whole human race receives this salvation through Jesus' name.

At the heart of this speech and the other speeches in Acts, is the *kerygma*, the fundamental proclamation about Jesus' Death and Resurrection. Peter presents a sharp contrast: between the human actions of crucifying Jesus and the divine action of raising him from the dead. Through Jesus, the rejected stone who became the cornerstone, God brings about healing, restoration, and eternal salvation.

READING II   The first word in the reading from 1 John is an imperative: "See." Seeing means more than

For meditation and context:

RESPONSORIAL PSALM   Psalm 118:1, 8–9, 21–23, 26, 28, 29 (22)

R. The stone rejected by the builders has become the cornerstone. or R. Alleluia.

Give thanks to the Lord, for he is good,
  for his mercy endures forever.
It is better to take refuge in the Lord
  than to trust in man.
It is better to take refuge in the Lord
  than to trust in princes.

I will give thanks to you, for you have
  answered me
  and have been my savior.
The stone which the builders rejected
  has become the cornerstone.
By the Lord has this been done;
  it is wonderful in our eyes.

Blessed is he who comes in the name of
  the Lord;
  we bless you from the house of the Lord.
I will give thanks to you, for you have
  answered me
  and have been my savior.
Give thanks to the Lord, for he is good;
  for his kindness endures forever.

An exhortatory reading. Proclaim this short reading to help your assembly really own their true identity as "children of God." Keep the intention "you are God's children" uppermost in your mind as you proclaim.

Let the awesome significance of this love show on your face and in your voice!

Four short words—proclaim slowly and give each word its emphasis.

Pause at the end of this line.

Of course! Pause at the end of the line.

Contrast "now" with "shall be."

Take your time with this line so the thought is clear.

READING II   1 John 3:1–2

A reading from the first Letter of Saint John

Beloved:
See what **love** the Father has bestowed on us
  that we may be called the **children** of **God**.
Yet so we **are**.
The **reason** the world does not **know** us
  is that it did not know **him**.
Beloved, we are God's children **now**;
  what we **shall** be has not yet been **revealed**.
We **do** know that when it **is** revealed we shall be **like** him,
  for we shall **see** him as he **is**.

TO KEEP IN MIND
Words in bold are significant words about which you must make a choice to help their meaning stand out. You may (or may not) choose to stress them.

---

beholding with the eyes; it includes spiritual insight and discernment as well. In exhorting his audience to see, John is telling them that they should be attentive to the reality of God's love that they have experienced themselves. God's love, already revealed through creation and history, took on human flesh in Jesus, God's own Son. The believers have seen and known God's love in Christ. Through him and in him, God has bestowed love so that believers can be called children of God. God's love in Christ is thus life giving and transformative. It brings about a new creation in the believers themselves.

Having received God's love through Christ, the community has such a close kinship with him that the world will not know them any more than it knew Jesus. The world to which John refers is that part of humanity that does not see, know, or accept Jesus. That is the situation that John's audience is facing now. But their present experience is not the whole story; there is more to be revealed. In the eschatological future, the children of God shall be like him, seeing him as he is. The word "see" in this verse points to a deeper awareness than the seeing in the present age. Risen along with Christ, they will see him and know him in glory.

Although John was writing to a first-century audience, the repeated use of first-person plural pronouns (we, us) easily draws us into the reading. We too are God's children who have seen in our own lives the love that God has so richly given. We too wait for the full revelation of seeing him in glory.

An exhortatory reading. Make sure that the great care and love Jesus has for us comes through in your nonverbal expression.

Don't preach. Gently, and with the tenderness of the shepherd.

Don't swallow "wolf."

Pause at the end of this line.

The second time this line appears. Proclaim the whole line slowly and deliberately, and with great love.

Pause at the end of this line.

Pick up your pace.

With joy! Pause.

Emphasize the second half of this line.

Pause at the end of this line.

With a sense of satisfaction.

TO KEEP IN MIND
Pause in order to break up separate thoughts, set apart significant statements, or indicate major shifts. Never pause in the middle of a single thought. Your primary guide for pauses is punctuation.

GOSPEL   John 10:11–18

A reading from the holy Gospel according to John

Jesus said:
  "I am the **good shepherd**.
A **good** shepherd lays down his **life** for the sheep.
A **hired** man, who is **not** a shepherd
    and whose sheep are not his **own**,
    sees a **wolf** coming and leaves the sheep and runs **away**,
    and the wolf **catches** and **scatters** them.
This is because he works for **pay** and has no **concern** for
        the sheep.
I am the **good** shepherd,
    and I know **mine** and mine know **me**,
    just as the **Father** knows **me** and I know the **Father**;
    and I will lay down my **life** for the sheep.
I have **other** sheep that do not **belong** to this fold.
These **also** I must lead, and they will **hear** my voice,
    and there will be **one** flock, **one shepherd**.
This is **why** the Father loves me,
    because I **lay** down my **life** in order to take it **up** again.
No one **takes** it from me, but I lay it down on my **own**.
I have **power** to lay it down, and power to take it **up** again.
This **command** I have received from my **Father**."

GOSPEL   In the Old Testament, sheep and shepherds were so much a part of daily life that they easily became a means of illustrating the relationship between God and Israel. One of the most familiar psalms opens with "The LORD is my shepherd" (Psalm 23:1). In contrast to the Lord, some of Israel's leaders destroyed and scattered the sheep, leaving them as food for wild animals (see, for example, Jeremiah 23:1–4; Ezekiel 34:5–6). Reinterpreting the ancient symbolism, Jesus applies the metaphor of shepherd to himself. Just as the God of Israel was totally dif-

ferent from Israel's unfaithful leaders, Jesus is absolutely different from hirelings who have no concern for the sheep.

In today's reading, part of a longer discourse of Jesus as the shepherd (10:7–18, 27–30), Jesus says twice that he is the Good Shepherd, describing his actions for the flock. First, he lays down his life for the sheep. Such willingness to die for the flock is a loving commitment that goes far beyond Jesus' parable of searching for the lost sheep. When he speaks of laying down his life and taking it up again, he is foretelling his Death and Resurrection. As a Good

Shepherd, he knows those who are his own, and they know him. He likens their mutual knowing to the knowing between himself and his Father, signifying knowledge that is intimate and enduring.

After speaking of those who are already part of his fold, Jesus foresees others who do not yet belong. He will lead them, and they will hear his voice. The little flock during Jesus' lifetime will be greatly increased. All will be brought into one flock under the guidance of one shepherd, Jesus himself. Today we pray for the unity and universality that Jesus promised. E.P.

FIFTH SUNDAY OF EASTER

LECTIONARY #53

READING I   Acts of the Apostles 9:26–31

A reading from the Acts of the Apostles

When **Saul** arrived in **Jerusalem** he tried to join the **disciples**,
but they were all **afraid** of him,
not **believing** that he was a disciple.
Then **Barnabas** took charge of him and brought him
to the **apostles**,
and he **reported** to them how he had seen the **Lord**,
and that he had **spoken** to him,
and how in **Damascus** he had spoken out **boldly** in the name
of Jesus.
He moved about **freely** with them in Jerusalem,
and spoke out **boldly** in the name of the Lord.
He also spoke and debated with the **Hellenists**,
but **they** tried to **kill** him.
And when the brothers **learned** of this,
they took him down to **Caesarea**
and sent him on his way to **Tarsus**.

The **church** throughout all **Judea**, **Galilee**, and **Samaria** was
at **peace**.
It was being built **up** and walked in the fear of the **Lord**,
and with the **consolation** of the Holy **Spirit** it grew
in **numbers**.

A narrative reading which is not a mere history lesson about the early Christian community, but a reminder of how God continually cares for us.

Start quickly and proclaim the anxiety of the disciples.

Saul = sawl

More calmly; Barnabas takes control and brings order and reason to the community.

Barnabas = BAHR-nuh-buhs

With the excitement of Saul.

Damascus = duh-MAS-kuhs

Keep your pace up.

Hellenists = HEL-uh-nist

Don't swallow "kill him."

Caesarea = sez-uh-REE-uh

Tarsus = TAHR-suhs; pause at the end of the line.

Proclaim this conclusion expansively to reflect the growth of the community.

Judea = joo-DEE-uh

Galilee = GAL-ih-lee

Samaria = suh-MAYR-ee-uh

Good news! Smile with your voice, eyes, and face!

READING I   The story of Saul, the fanatical Pharisee who persecuted the Christians, begins with his conversion on the Damascus Road (Acts 9:1–9). Today's reading is an account from the early days of his ministry in Jerusalem, shortly after his conversion. It isn't surprising that the disciples were afraid of him, given his history of violence against the Christians. The one who takes charge of him is Barnabas, who will later be his companion on part of his missionary journeys. In the company of Barnabas, Saul speaks to the Apostles in Jerusalem, and gives them a brief summary of what had happened to him and how he had already begun to preach about Jesus. Here we have the briefest summary of his preaching: he spoke "in the name of Jesus."

Twice in this account, Luke the evangelist says that Saul spoke "boldly" (*parresia*), a term used to stress his prophetic role of speaking with fearless confidence, even in the face of conflict. Just before today's reading, the Jews had conspired to kill him, and now another group, the Hellenists, try to kill him. Whether confronted with the suspicions and rejection of fellow Christians, or the threats of those outside, Saul's characteristic response is to continue to preach with boldness.

After the drama of the first part of today's reading, the conclusion is surprisingly peaceful. One of Luke's many summaries of the growth of the Church, here we have a picture of Spirit-filled tranquility throughout the land of Palestine. There is no violence or division. Typical of other summaries, this one presents an ideal portrait. Scenes both before and after the summary, however, reveal the less-than-ideal reality of the developing Christian communities.

For meditation and context:

RESPONSORIAL PSALM   Psalm 22:26–27, 28, 30, 31–32 (26a)

R. I will praise you, Lord, in the assembly of your people. or R. Alleluia.

I will fulfill my vows before those who fear
    the LORD.
  The lowly shall eat their fill;
they who seek the LORD shall praise him:
  "May your hearts live forever!"

All the ends of the earth
  shall remember and turn to the LORD;
all the families of the nations
  shall bow down before him.

To him alone shall bow down
  all who sleep in the earth;
before him shall bend
  all who go down into the dust.

And to him my soul shall live;
  my descendants shall serve him.
Let the coming generation be told of
    the LORD
  that they may proclaim to a people yet to
    be born
  the justice he has shown.

TO KEEP IN MIND A *didactic* text makes a point or teaches something. Help your assembly to follow the argument and understand what's being taught.	

READING II   1 John 3:18–24

A reading from the first Letter of Saint John

A didactic reading. Make sure you know what John is saying here. His basic message throughout his letter is "love." As long as we love, we obey God's commandments and God lives in us and we in God.
John is a gentle teacher; reflect that in your voice and expression.

Children, let us **love** not in **word** or **speech**
  but in **deed** and **truth**.

Now this is how we shall know that we **belong** to the truth
  and **reassure** our hearts before him
  in whatever our hearts condemn,
  for God is **greater** than our hearts and knows **everything**.

Be careful with the construction of this line. John seeks to reassure us: we all fall short, but as long as we act in love, then we please God who knows we are imperfect.
Pause at the end of this line.

Beloved, if our **hearts** do not **condemn** us,
  we have **confidence** in God
  and **receive** from him whatever we **ask**,
  because we keep his **commandments** and do what
    pleases him.

If we love, we please God and may ask God for whatever we need.

And his commandment is **this**:
  we should **believe** in the name of his **Son**, Jesus **Christ**,
  and **love** one another just as he **commanded** us.

Pause at the end of this line.

Those who **keep** his commandments **remain** in him, and **he**
  in **them**,

Slowly.

  and the way we **know** that he remains in us

Good news!

  is from the **Spirit** he gave us.

READING II   In this reading, John the Presbyter weaves together important themes of his letter: love, truth, believing, and obedience. As a central emphasis of the letter, the word love is a designation for the community itself. They are beloved (*agapetoi*), signifying both their intimate union with God who is love (1 John 4:8,16), and the love they have for one another. In today's verses, John explains how this community of *agapetoi* is to manifest that love: in deed and truth. As he describes acting in truth, John begins by looking at their hearts to discern if their actions are true. His audience would understand the heart as the center of both emotional and intellectual life, the source of moral actions and choices. We belong to the truth, according to John, if our hearts (our consciences) do not condemn us. Even if our hearts do condemn us, we have recourse to God, who knows everything, and will give us whatever we ask.

John moves seamlessly from describing living in truth to keeping God's commandments. Truth must display itself in action, specifically in adhering to a two-pronged commandment: believing in Jesus, and loving one another as he commanded. Believing and loving each flow from the heart. Believing entails adhering to Jesus' teachings, trusting in him, and living faithfully. Loving likewise is a whole way of life. The best way to understand Jesus' commandment to love is to see how he himself loved. His compassion, forgiveness, and seeking out those who are lost are also to be evident in the lives of his followers. God's own Spirit assures that those who keep this commandment remain in Christ and he in them.

An exhortatory reading. Jesus is not making a theological argument, but sharing his desire to be in intimate relationship with us. He is sharing good news, so smile with your voice, eyes, and face.

Don't swallow "vine."

We will bear much fruit!
Set this line apart and take it slowly. This intimacy is almost too much to fathom.
Pick up your pace.

Go slowly again on this line.

Pick up the pace.

Not as punishment, but because they are of no use. There is no life apart from Jesus.

Slowly and deliberately.

GOSPEL   John 15:1–8

A reading from the holy Gospel according to John

Jesus said to his **disciples**:
　"**I** am the **true vine**, and my **Father** is the vine **grower**.
He takes away every **branch** in me that does not bear **fruit**,
　and every one that **does** he **prunes** so that it bears **more** fruit.
You are **already** pruned because of the word that I spoke to you.
Remain in me, as **I** remain in **you**.
Just as a branch cannot bear fruit on its **own**
　unless it remains on the **vine**,
　so neither can **you** unless you remain in **me**.
I am the **vine**, **you** are the **branches**.
Whoever **remains** in **me** and I in **him** will bear **much** fruit,
　because **without** me you can do **nothing**.
Anyone who does **not** remain in me
　will be thrown out like a **branch** and **wither**;
　people will **gather** them and throw them into a **fire**
　and they will be **burned**.
If you **remain** in **me** and my **words** remain in **you**,
　ask for whatever you **want** and it will be **done** for you.
By this is my Father **glorified**,
　that you bear much **fruit** and **become** my **disciples**."

GOSPEL An important theological and verbal link between the reading from 1 John and the Gospel according to John is the word "remain" (*meno*). In the concluding verse of 1 John, we heard that those who keep Jesus' commandments remain in him and he in them. John uses this word more than all the rest of the New Testament combined. In John's writings, *meno* signifies a deeply intimate and constant communion. In this Gospel reading, the evangelist uses the image of a vine and branches to develop the signifi-cance of Jesus remaining in the disciples and the disciples remaining in him.

The metaphor of the vine was already a part of the Jewish tradition, often symbolic of the covenant relationship with God gone awry. God had planted a choice vine, but Israel became a wild, untamed vine instead (Jeremiah 2:21; compare with Isaiah 5:1–7). Whereas the old vine did not produce good fruit, Jesus gives the image new life. He says, "I am the true vine," the last of his "I am" statements in John's Gospel. Along with Jesus' identity as the vine, he says his Father is the vine grower, the one who prunes the branches so they will bear more fruit.

With the vine and branches imagery, Jesus connects his identity with that of his disciples. Precisely because they remain in him, and his words remain in them, his disciples are able to bear fruit. Apart from him they can do nothing. The effects of remaining in Jesus are many: the disciples' prayers will be answered; their ministry will be fruitful; and God will be glorified. E.P.

SIXTH SUNDAY
OF EASTER

LECTIONARY #56

READING I   Acts of the Apostles 10:25–26, 34–35, 44–48

A reading from the Acts of the Apostles

A narrative reading. The text is full of exciting and surprising developments; keep your energy up throughout.

When **Peter** entered, **Cornelius** met him
  and, falling at his **feet**, paid him **homage**.
Peter, however, **raised** him up, saying,
  "**Get** up. I myself am **also** a human being."

Cornelius = kohr-NEEL-yuhs

With a smile.

Then Peter proceeded to speak and said,
  "In **truth**, I see that God shows no **partiality**.
Rather, in **every** nation whoever **fears** him and acts **uprightly**
  is **acceptable** to him."

Peter speaks to himself as much as to those gathered. Express his wonder and pleasure at the generosity of God.

While Peter was still **speaking** these things,
  the Holy **Spirit** fell upon all who were listening to the word.
The **circumcised** believers who had accompanied Peter
  were **astounded** that the gift of the Holy Spirit
  should have been poured out on the Gentiles **also**,
  for they could hear them speaking in **tongues** and
    glorifying **God**.
Then Peter **responded**,
  "Can anyone withhold the water for **baptizing** these people,
  who have received the Holy **Spirit** even as **we** have?"
He **ordered** them to be baptized in the name of Jesus **Christ**.

Good news!

Proclaim this line with the surprise and slight confusion of the Jewish believers.

Pause at the end of this line.

Here is the climax. Who can doubt the inclusivity of God's love and grace now?

With joy!

READING I The story of the Roman centurion Cornelius begins with a vision that leads him to a meeting with Simon Peter. The scene shifts to Joppa where Peter also has a vision, his of unclean animals that he is commanded to eat. When Peter objects, the voice tells him, "What God has made clean, you are not to call profane" (10:15). While Peter is still pondering the meaning of the vision, he receives the messengers from Cornelius inviting him to the centurion's home. Today's reading narrates the initial meeting of Peter and Cornelius. Although ordinarily,

being an observant Jew, Peter would not enter the house of a Gentile, now, the meaning of the vision becomes clear to Peter. In a verse omitted from today's reading he says "God has shown me that I should not call any person profane or unclean" (10:28). Cornelius then recounts his own vision to Peter, who responds with a key theological statement: "I see that God shows no partiality." Peter comes to realize that anyone who fears God and acts uprightly is acceptable to God.

The story illustrates two conversions: Cornelius' to belief in Christ, and Peter's to

openness to the Gentiles. Even as Peter is speaking the Holy Spirit falls upon all who are listening, confirming that Gentiles are to be included in the community. The Holy Spirit had already come upon the assembled Jewish community at Pentecost (2:1–4), and on the Samaritans through the laying on of hands after they heard the Good News from Philip (8:14–17). The Holy Spirit, God's very presence, is the source of unity among the diverse believers. Beginning at Pentecost and continuing in today's reading, Baptism in the name of Jesus Christ brings all into this life-giving communion.

For meditation and context:

RESPONSORIAL PSALM   Psalm 98:1, 2–3, 3–4 (2b)

R. The Lord has revealed to the nations his saving power. or R. Alleluia.

Sing to the LORD a new song,
for he has done wondrous deeds;
His right hand has won victory for him,
his holy arm.

The LORD has made his salvation known:
in the sight of the nations he has revealed
his justice.
He has remembered his kindness and
his faithfulness
toward the house of Israel.

All the ends of the earth have seen
the salvation by our God.
Sing joyfully to the LORD, all you lands;
break into song; sing praise.

TO KEEP IN MIND

Exhortatory texts make an urgent appeal to listeners. They may encourage, warn, or challenge, and often include a call to action. You must convey the urgency and passion behind the words.

An exhortatory reading. Strive to maintain eye contact with the assembly even more than usual in this reading. You are an instrument of God's love as you proclaim; take your time. Let the assembly feel your love for them as well as God's love.

You are urging your assembly to love as they have been loved!

Forms of the word "love" appear ten times in this reading; don't gloss over them.

Slow considerably on the phrase "God is love." Pause.

Pause at the end of this line.

Contrast our love for God (which is good) with God's love for us (which is the source of all love).

TO KEEP IN MIND

Repetition of the same word or phrase over the course of a reading emphasizes a point. Make each instance distinct, and build your intensity with each repetition.

READING II   1 John 4:7–10

A reading from the first Letter of Saint John

Beloved, let us **love** one another,
because **love** is of **God**;
everyone who **loves** is **begotten** by God and **knows** God.
Whoever is **without** love does **not** know God, for **God** is **love**.
In this way the love of God was **revealed** to us:
God sent his only **Son** into the world
so that we might have **life** through him.
In **this** is love:
not that **we** have loved **God**, but that **he** loved **us**
and sent his **Son** as expiation for our **sins**.

READING II   The reading from 1 John is one of the most beautiful of New Testament poems. The purpose and effect of the poetry is not primarily to transmit information, even though it is rich in theological insight. Rather, it draws those who hear it into an experience, specifically into a loving relationship with God. In today's poem, the word "love" is repeated in various forms, creating a rhythmic cadence and resonance, beginning with the opening address to the community as "beloved." Closely associated with love is another repetition: "God" (*theos*), the

source and goal of life and love. The love that is of God is for us and revealed to us, and the divine initiative in loving us is the foundation of our love for one another.

The most personal way that God revealed love to us was by sending his Son into the world so that we might have life through him. The love of God and the life that God gives through Christ are both a present reality, and one still awaited in fullness. We have already been begotten by God, and we already know God. Having revealed love through the Incarnation of his

Son, God sent him "as expiation for our sins," referring to Christ's dying for our sins.

John's poetry is the vehicle for conveying the theology of Christ's Incarnation and Death; both are tangible signs of God's love for us. In John's well-crafted poem, even the prepositions draw us into the experience: the love of God is for us, revealed to us, and coming through Christ. God's love is not static, but forceful and dynamic, and the movement of the poetry is dynamic as well.

An exhortatory reading. This is all good news. How does Jesus feel as he expresses God's love, and his own, for us? Let your proclamation reflect the intensity of his desire to share his love.

Emphasize the repeated parallels Jesus makes between his relationship with God and our relationship with him.
It's very simple.

Don't gloss over "joy."
Pause at the end of this line.
Take your time with these lines. Proclaim with passion!

Pick up your pace.

How would you speak to a friend? Bring that tone to these lines.

Pause at the end of this line.
Slowly and with gentle tenderness.

Pause at the end of this line.
Proclaim this final exhortation slowly and with love, looking directly into the assembly.

TO KEEP IN MIND
Parallelism refers to phrases or sentences that have a similar structure or express a similar idea. Use emphasis and rhythm to make sure any parallelism stands out.

GOSPEL   John 15:9–17

A reading from the holy Gospel according to John

Jesus said to his **disciples**:
"As the **Father** loves **me**, so **I** also love **you**.
Remain in my love.
If you **keep** my **commandments**, you **will** remain in my love,
    just as **I** have kept my **Father's** commandments
    and remain in **his** love.

"I have **told** you this so that my **joy** may be in you
    and your joy might be **complete**.
This is my commandment: **love** one **another** as **I** love **you**.
No one has greater love than **this**,
    to lay down one's **life** for one's **friends**.
You are my friends if you do what **I command** you.
I no longer call you **slaves**,
    because a slave does not **know** what his master is doing.
I have called you **friends**,
    because I have told you **everything** I have heard from my
        Father.
It was not **you** who chose **me**, but **I** who chose **you**
    and **appointed** you to go and bear **fruit** that will **remain**,
    so that **whatever** you ask the Father in my **name** he may
        give you.
This I **command** you: **love** one **another**."

GOSPEL Today's Gospel is a continuation of Jesus' teaching on the vine and branches heard last Sunday. Both segments are from Jesus' last discourse to his disciples in which he prepares them for his coming suffering and Death. Before he leaves them, he wants them to understand how he has loved them, and how they are to love one another. At the meal, he had already given them an example of love when he washed their feet. What he taught through this loving action, he also teaches with words.

Throughout his ministry, Jesus' disciples must have observed the loving relationship between Jesus and his Father. Now Jesus tells them, "As the Father loves me, so I also love you." As the Father's love is unwavering and generous, so too is Jesus' love for his disciples. The love of the Father for Jesus, and the love of Jesus for his friends, illustrates for them how they are to love one another. Jesus explains further that his disciples are to keep his commandment: "Love one another as I love you." Jesus himself sets the pattern: as he was obedient to his Father's commandments, his friends are to keep his commandment. Their obedience is neither fearful nor servile, but expresses their love for Jesus, and will result in joy: Jesus' own joy dwelling in them.

When Jesus tells them that laying down one's life for his friends is the greatest example of love, he is preparing his friends for his ultimate act of love, soon to be accomplished on the Cross. Since his love is a model for their own, they must also be willing to lay down their lives for one another. Love for one another, obedience, and sacrifice are signs of the fruit that will remain. E.P.

THE ASCENSION OF THE LORD

LECTIONARY #58

READING I   Acts of the Apostles 1:1–11

A reading from the Acts of the Apostles

In the **first** book, Theophilus,
  I dealt with all that Jesus **did** and **taught**
  until the day he was taken **up**,
  after giving **instructions** through the Holy **Spirit**
  to the **apostles** whom he had **chosen**.
He presented himself **alive** to them
  by many **proofs** after he had **suffered**,
  appearing to them during **forty** days
  and **speaking** about the kingdom of **God**.
While **meeting** with them,
  he enjoined them not to depart from **Jerusalem**,
  but to **wait** for "the promise of the **Father**
  about which you have heard me **speak**;
  for **John** baptized with **water**,
  but in a few days **you** will be baptized with the Holy **Spirit**."

When they had gathered together they asked him,
  "**Lord**, are you at this time going to restore
  the **kingdom** to Israel?"
He **answered** them, "It is not for **you** to know the **times**
    or **seasons**
  that the Father has established by his own **authority**.
But you will receive **power** when the Holy **Spirit** comes
    upon you,

A narrative reading. There's a lot being recounted in this extraordinary event. Take your time; use pauses at the periods to keep separate thoughts separate.

Theophilus = thee-AWF-uh-luhs

There's a personal and friendly tone to this opening.

Pause slightly after "proofs."

Pause slightly before the quote, and heighten your energy to indicate you are speaking Jesus' words.

Even after all this, the disciples still don't fully understand what sort of Messiah Jesus is.

Jesus' tone is more "Don't worry about this," than "You aren't allowed to know this."

Today, options are given for Reading II. Contact your parish staff to find out which will be used.

READING I   When we speak about the Ascension we distinguish between an event that concluded Jesus' appearances after his Resurrection and the theological meaning of the event. After the last recorded appearances, Jesus was no longer physically present within the Church. Other New Testament passages (for example, John 20:17 and Luke 24:50–51)

imply that the Ascension took place on the same day as the Resurrection. We tend to separate the two mysteries in time, but the theological meaning encompasses both Resurrection and Ascension; it is the glorification of Christ.

Addressing a reader named Theophilus (a name that means the "lover/beloved of God"), the author of Acts reassures him of the Gospel's reliability. He summarizes the closing scenes of the Gospel, spinning back from the Ascension to Jesus' final instructions and the forty-day period of Resurrection appearances.

The mention of forty recalls famous forties in the Bible: among them, the number of days and nights of the flood (Genesis 7:12, 17), the years of the Exodus (Joshua 5:6), and Jesus in the desert preparing his ministry and tempted by the devil (Mark 1:13; Luke 4:2). Now, the gift of the Spirit that distinguished Jesus during his ministry (Luke 3:16.22) is about to be extended to his followers, and Acts of the Apostles will spell out what this promise means for the nucleus of the Church.

Just as Mary of Nazareth was filled with the Holy Spirit at Jesus' conception in

Jesus commissions his disciples with the phrase, "You will be my witnesses."

Judea = joo-DEE-uh

Samaria = suh-MAYR-ee-uh

Slow down on "ends of the earth."

Don't lose "as they were looking on." It establishes them again as witnesses.

Careful not to look toward the sky on this line; rather, look directly at the assembly. Pause after the line.

Quicken your pace with this appearance. These men want to shake the disciples out of their stunned silence and get them moving again. Proclaim with energy!

Pause a little longer than usual at the end to let the men depart.

and you will be my **witnesses** in **Jerusalem**,
throughout **Judea** and **Samaria**,
and to the ends of the **earth**."
When he had said this, as they were **looking** on,
he was **lifted** up, and a cloud **took** him from their **sight**.
While they were looking **intently** at the **sky** as he was going,
suddenly two **men** dressed in white **garments** stood
beside them.
They said, "Men of **Galilee**,
why are you **standing** there looking at the **sky**?
This **Jesus** who has been taken **up** from you into heaven
will **return** in the same way as you have seen him **going**
into heaven."

For meditation and context:

RESPONSORIAL PSALM   Psalm 47:2–3, 6–7, 8–9 (6)

R. God mounts his throne to shouts of joy: a blare of trumpets for the Lord. or R. Alleluia.

All you peoples, clap your hands,
   shout to God with cries of gladness.
For the LORD, the Most High, the awesome,
   is the great king over all the earth.

God mounts his throne amid shouts of joy;
   the LORD, amid trumpet blasts.
Sing praise to God, sing praise;
   sing praise to our king, sing praise.

For king of all the earth is God;
   sing hymns of praise.
God reigns over the nations,
   God sits upon his holy throne.

TO KEEP IN MIND

You can't proclaim what you don't understand. Read the Scripture passage and its commentary in *Workbook*. Then read it from your Bible, including what comes before and after it so that you understand the context.

An exhortatory reading. This is a blessing; pray this for your assembly. Take care with the construction, though, and be sure you understand the thoughts being expressed.

Ephesians = ee-FEE-shuhnz

Look directly at your assembly and let them know this is your prayer for them. Smile with your voice, eyes, and face as you pray for an outpouring of gifts from the Spirit.

READING II   Ephesians 1:17–23

A reading from the Letter of Saint Paul to the Ephesians

Brothers and sisters:
May the **God** of our Lord Jeus **Christ**, the Father of **glory**,
   give you a Spirit of **wisdom** and **revelation**
   resulting in **knowledge** of him.

---

her womb, the Holy Spirit's imminent coming will empower the Church to give birth to Jesus to the larger world. Luke outlines a geographical and missionary program of evangelization, first in Jerusalem, branching out to the surrounding areas within Palestine, and abroad through Paul's missionary travels. Something greater is reserved for the disciples than establishing an earthly realm ("restore the kingdom to Israel"); the Holy Spirit will energize them and they will become witnesses "in Jerusalem, throughout Judea and Samaria, and to the ends of the earth." From now

on, the center of the new world will be wherever the Church witnesses to Jesus in word and act.

READING II | **Ephesians 4:1–13.** Through Baptism the Spirit has fashioned Christians into one body in Christ, one community, belonging to one Lord, and committed to one way of salvation through faith. The unity is manifest in Christ's gifts to individuals that edify his Body, the Church. The one Lord, who brings salvation to his people in Jerusalem, is the source of the gifts. (Verse 8, in italics, quotes Psalm

68:19). Christ, the head of the body, the Church, descended from the heavens in his Incarnation, ascended above the heavens through his Passover, which encompasses his Death, Resurrection, and Ascension, and he is the source of the Church's spiritual gifts.

Ephesians 1:17–23. The prayer, addressed to "the God of our Lord Jesus Christ," recognizes that Jesus, head of the Church, acknowledges the one God, who has accomplished the work of salvation in Christ in whom hope is focused. The phrase "the Father of glory" refers to God,

Keep the structure of this sentence clear. You are blessing your assembly that they may know three things: hope, riches, and power.

Slightly longer pause at comma, then pick up the thought again with the next phrase. Raise your energy slowly from here to the end.

Pause at the end of this line.

Connect the phrases "gave him" and "to the church" so they form one thought.

Slow down and drop your intensity a bit as you conclude.

May the **eyes** of your **hearts** be **enlightened**,
> that you may know what is the **hope** that belongs to his call,
> what are the riches of **glory**
> in his inheritance among the holy ones,
> and what is the surpassing greatness of his **power**
> for us who **believe**,
> in accord with the exercise of his great **might**,
> which he worked in **Christ**,
> raising him from the **dead**
> and seating him at his right hand in the **heavens**,
> far above every **principality**, **authority**, **power**, and **dominion**,
> and every **name** that is **named**
> not only in **this** age but also in the one to **come**.
And he put all things beneath his **feet**
> and gave him as **head** over all things to the **church**,
> which is his **body**,
> the **fullness** of the one who **fills** all things in every **way**.

Or:

READING II   Ephesians 4:1–13

A reading from the Letter of Saint Paul to the Ephesians

Brothers and sisters,
I, a **prisoner** for the **Lord**,
> urge you to live in a manner worthy of the **call** you
>   have received,
> with all **humility** and **gentleness**, with **patience**,
> **bearing** with one another through **love**,
> striving to preserve the **unity** of the spirit
> through the bond of **peace**:
> **one** body and **one** Spirit,
> as you were also called to the one **hope** of your call;

A didactic reading. Paul urges unity in the midst of division. What are the divisions in your community today? Convince your assembly to put those aside and live in peace and unity.

Ephesians = ee-FEE-shuhnz
After all his work evangelizing, the divisions within the Christian community are a source of pain for Paul. Let that hurt come through in his plea for unity.
Bring a sense of urgency to Paul's list of the qualities of true community.

Slight pause; the next line continues and expands Paul's point about living in unity.
Emphasize oneness, which makes apparent division really impossible.

the originator of all that is sublime. The first petition uses different terms—wisdom, revelation, and knowledge—to refer to different kinds of knowledge. The author highlights what comes through revelation, which happens when the interior life is enlightened by what is more profound than the results of scientific investigation. Infused by God's Spirit, knowledge becomes wisdom. The thought stretches toward the future: "the hope that belongs to his call," a "calling" that encompasses the inheritance shared with the saints.

The second part that begins with "which he worked in Christ, raising him from the dead and seating him at his right hand in the heavens" is an often-repeated statement of belief—a creed—(see Acts 3:15; 13:30; Romans 10:9; 1 Thessalonians 1:10). It became customary to apply Psalm 110: 1, "Sit at my right hand," to understand what happened to the risen Christ (for example, in Acts 2:34–35; Romans 8:34; 1 Peter 3:22). The combination of this psalm with Psalm 8 ("all things at his feet") links the idea of Jesus who fulfills God's purpose for humanity as the climax of creation

(Psalm 8:5–7; compare Hebrews 2:6–9), with that of Jesus as David's son receiving a share in God's sovereign rule, which frees humans from fear of the nameless forces that shape existence. That God appointed Christ as "head over all things to the church, which is his body" means that Christ is the head of all reality, and he was given to the Church for her benefit. The concluding phrase, "fullness of the one who fills all things in every way," announces that Christ incorporates the plan of salvation, and his Body, the Church, is where God's presence

We are all one; you can't avoid it!

Pause at the end of this line.

We can't do this on our own—divisions seem part of human nature. But we can do it through the gift of grace!

Christ took on and knows our human nature, and knows how to help us.

Good news! Christ helps us through these ministries to grow in faith. Keep this sentence together, pausing only at the commas.

All have the same purpose.

Be clear that there are three goals to our growth (which is a continual journey): unity, maturity, and full identity with Christ.

Slowly and deliberately.

one **Lord**, one **faith**, one **baptism**;
one **God** and Father of **all**,
who is **over** all and **through** all and **in** all.

But **grace** was given to **each** of us
   according to the measure of Christ's gift.]
Therefore, it says:
   *He **ascended** on high and took prisoners **captive**;*
   *he gave **gifts** to men.*
What does "he **ascended**" mean except that he also **descended**
   into the **lower** regions of the earth?
The one who **descended** is also the one who **ascended**
   far above all the **heavens**,
   that he might **fill** all things.

[And he gave some as **apostles**, others as **prophets**,
   others as **evangelists**, others as **pastors** and **teachers**,
   to **equip** the holy ones for the work of **ministry**,
   for **building** up the body of **Christ**,
   until we all attain to the **unity** of faith
   and knowledge of the Son of God, to mature **manhood**,
   to the extent of the full **stature** of **Christ**.]

[Shorter: Ephesians 4:1–7, 11–13 (see brackets)]

TO KEEP IN MIND
Making eye contact with the assembly connects you with them and connects them to the reading more deeply than using your voice alone. This helps the assembly stay with the story and keeps them engaged.

---

in creation and his love for the world comes to its most eloquent expression.

 GOSPEL In this reading we hear first about the effects of Jesus' Ascension: the eleven Apostles are sent to the whole world, and through their preaching God confers faith and baptism to all peoples. The hearers of the Gospel have a choice, to resist the faith and thereby exclude themselves from salvation, or to believe, be baptized, and saved. Certain signs will accompany those who believe: power over the evil spirits and protection

against the vipers' venom (which recalls the serpent's assault on humanity in paradise); they will be instruments of healing wherever they proclaim the Gospel. Jesus, from his position at God's right hand, will work through them and confirm their evangelization with accompanying signs.

The Ascension embraces the mystery of the moment when Jesus presented our human body in its most perfect state to the Father. Finally, in Jesus, we have experienced a person just like us, but not so superficial. In Jesus we have encountered God in a person like ourselves, but some-

one who had a viable plan for the fullness of life, who spoke with natural and convincing truth. He was so close, so simple that we could touch him. If we turned our backs on him, he did not become annoyed. In spite of our trivialities, God searched us out, found us where and just as we are, and convinced us by his mercy and grace to follow him. The eternal Word of God was present in our flesh; now he has ascended and sits at the Father's right hand. In his whole life that culminates in this mystery, we may be glad that he opens for us the way to glory.

A narrative with exhortatory passages. Vary your pace and energy to convey both the wonder and excitement of these events.

Start strong!

Pause at the end of this line.

Don't run this list together; make each sign distinct. Build your energy on these first four.

Take this last sign slowly and tenderly, with love and care. Pause.

Slowly, with amazement and awe.
Avoid the temptation to look up.

Return quickly to the disciples' action; there is work to be done! Pick up your pace.

With satisfaction.

TO KEEP IN MIND
Pause in order to break up separate thoughts, set apart significant statements, or indicate major shifts. Never pause in the middle of a single thought. Your primary guide for pauses is punctuation.

GOSPEL   Mark 16:15–20

A reading from the holy Gospel according to Mark

Jesus said to his **disciples**:
    "Go into the **whole world**
    and proclaim the **gospel** to every **creature**.
Whoever believes and is **baptized** will be **saved**;
    whoever does **not** believe will be **condemned**.
These **signs** will accompany those who **believe**:
    in my **name** they will drive out **demons**,
    they will speak new **languages**.
They will pick up **serpents** with their **hands**,
    and if they drink any **deadly** thing, it will not **harm** them.
They will lay hands on the **sick**, and they will **recover**."

So then the Lord Jesus, after he **spoke** to them,
    was **taken** up into **heaven**
    and took his **seat** at the right hand of **God**.
But they went **forth** and preached **everywhere**,
    while the Lord **worked** with them
    and **confirmed** the word through accompanying **signs**.

Christ took to himself our flesh, our timid heart, our muddled thoughts and good intentions—everything we are. He assumed it all as his own, this narrow little shack that I am, fragile and barely furnished, with my incessant questions and insecurity. The Son of God adopted as his own this house that we refer to as our human nature; he took it to that place where we might have thought that human nature would disintegrate into nothing at all, and there he transformed it. Where that place is and how things will be there is beyond our imagining, as is what a human

nature might do there for all eternity, except contemplate God and his essence, which is eternally interesting and meaningful. But the important thing is that there will be life as God desires it for us. If at times we find life difficult, human relations strained, social pressures confusing, doubt, fear, and insecurity knocking at our door, we can be sure that in life with Christ, the Blessed Virgin, and the saints, there is no obstacle to happiness. Our faith and consolation are focused on this mystery: that when Christ ascended, he took everything that is ours with him. In the icon of the

Ascension we contemplate the disciples, standing on the Mount of Olives, looking upwards, where they see a cloud separating them from heaven's glory, and just barely poking out of the cloud are our Lord's feet. In those feet we contemplate ourselves and the task we have before us, to become the beautiful feet of Jesus upon the mountain here in the present world, "announcing peace, bearing good news" (Isaiah 52:7) with our attitudes, words, and lives. K.S.

SEVENTH SUNDAY OF EASTER

LECTIONARY #60

READING I Acts of the Apostles 1:15–17, 20a, 20c–26

A reading from the Acts of the Apostles

Peter stood up in the **midst** of the **brothers**
—there was a **group** of about one hundred and twenty persons
in the one place—.
He said, "My **brothers**,
the **Scripture** had to be **fulfilled**
which the Holy **Spirit** spoke beforehand
through the mouth of **David**, concerning **Judas**,
who was the **guide** for those who **arrested** Jesus.
He was **numbered** among us
and was allotted a **share** in this ministry.

"For it is written in the Book of **Psalms**:
*May **another** take his **office**.*

"Therefore, it is necessary that one of the men
who **accompanied** us the whole time
the Lord Jesus came and went among us,
beginning from the baptism of **John**
until the day on which he was taken **up** from us,
become with us a **witness** to his **resurrection**."
So they proposed **two**, **Judas** called **Barsabbas**,
who was also known as **Justus**, and **Matthias**.

A narrative reading. A good example of how the Christian community makes decisions, with the input of the leaders, the community, and most importantly, the Holy Spirit. Share this with your assembly as an example of how they might make decisions in their own lives.

Drop your voice on this parenthetical phrase.

Peter is not preaching. Rather, he is leading the disciples in making a decision about replacing Judas; this should sound more like a meeting than a teaching.
How does Peter feel as he recalls Judas, one of their company who somehow turned out to betray them?

Take your time with this statement. Peter outlines the requirements for being considered one of the Twelve.

Pause at the end of this line.
Note that Judas, Barsabbas (bahr-SAH-buhs), and Justus (JUS-tuhs) all refer to the same person.
Matthias = muh-THĪ-uhs

READING I Judas' defection created a theological problem, not just because of the ecclesial value of the number twelve (Luke 22:30), needed to reconstitute Israel in her integrity, but because of the importance placed on the apostolic office. On Ascension Thursday we heard Luke stress in an earlier verse of Acts that the Apostles were "chosen" by Jesus and taught by him "through the Holy Spirit" (verse 2). Judas' desertion proves that there is no guarantee of fidelity to Jesus, neither being chosen nor the seal of the Holy Spirit. Later, the theologian of Acts, in the episode of Ananias and Sapphira (Acts 5:1–11) illustrates how God punishes treachery against the Spirit, especially in the form of defection inspired by a financial motive. During this critical moment in the early Church, Peter's call for a replacement for Judas, based on an appeal to Scripture, reinforces the group identity, and demonstrates his authority in the apostolic college. In this interim between Jesus' departure and the gift of the Spirit, the assembly of the Church asked God to indicate his choice of a replacement by casting lots to ascertain the divine purpose (compare Proverbs 16:33). The naming of Matthias, bringing the number of Apostles to twelve, shows how the Christian Church is the reconstituted Israel.

READING II The declaration "God is love" is all about the experience of God; the phrase "whoever remains in love remains in God" combines faithfulness to the manifestation of God's love in the Son and charity toward a fellow believer. John stresses that, based on the Father's action in the Son, charity is the believer's calling card and particular trait.

Then they **prayed**,
     "**You**, Lord, who know the hearts of **all**,
     show which **one** of these two you have **chosen**
     to take the place in this apostolic ministry
     from which Judas turned **away** to go to his **own** place."
Then they gave **lots** to them, and the lot fell upon **Matthias**,
     and he was counted with the eleven **apostles**.

RESPONSORIAL PSALM   Psalm 103:1–2, 11–12, 19–20 (19a)
R. The Lord has set his throne in heaven. or R. Alleluia.

Bless the LORD, O my soul;
     and all my being, bless his holy name.
Bless the LORD, O my soul,
     and forget not all his benefits.

For as the heavens are high above the earth,
     so surpassing is his kindness toward
          those who fear him.
As far as the east is from the west,
     so far has he put our transgressions
          from us.

The LORD has established his throne
     in heaven,
     and his kingdom rules over all.
Bless the LORD, all you his angels,
     you mighty in strength, who do
          his bidding.

READING II   1 John 4:11–16

A reading from the first Letter of Saint John

Beloved, if **God** so loved **us**,
     we **also** must love one **another**.
No one has ever **seen** God.
Yet, if we **love** one another, God **remains** in us,
     and his love is brought to **perfection** in us.

This is how we **know** that we remain in **him** and he in **us**,
     that he has given us of his **Spirit**.
Moreover, we have **seen** and **testify**
     that the **Father** sent his **Son** as **savior** of the world.

Slight pause.

Good news! God has provided for the community.

For meditation and context:

TO KEEP IN MIND
Exhortatory texts make an urgent appeal to listeners. They may encourage, warn, or challenge, and often include a call to action. You must convey the urgency and passion behind the words.

An exhortatory reading. All through the Easter season, we've heard John teach about love as the center of the Christian life and identity. This reading summarizes much of that teaching. You may want to review Reading II from prior Sundays for context.

Of course!

John sets up the problem. How can we believe in that which we cannot see?

For one thing, we make God visible in our love for each other.

"This" refers to the second half of the line—we know that God remains in us because we have the Spirit.

Still more evidence that God is with us—we acknowledge Jesus as Son of God.

Our love for one another is the same effective and merciful love with which God loves us in Christ. This distinctive love is proof that we know God who, though invisible, is manifest through those who have been begotten by God and know God. The testimony of the Spirit and that of faith join the testimony of love to confirm our knowledge of God. Christian life is founded on the knowledge of God as love and on his continuing presence, made manifest by our love for one another.

     God has proven his love in the gift of his Son to the world. Christians are urged to continue that pattern and show the same love to others. Our love for one another is the proof of God's action, the evidence that God is with us. Faith and love are united, because faith leads to a life of love in practice. The believer is a person who recognizes that the life of Jesus was an act of God's love for all people, and he or she is called to duplicate that quality of love, to "remain in love." In other words, that we treat each other with the same love with which Jesus loved us. Any other experience of God that does not have this intention is secondary.

GOSPEL   The adjective "holy," here applied to the Father, prepares the reader for what will be said about Jesus' and his disciples' mission. Two imperatives, one at the beginning and one toward the end of this Gospel, punctuate Jesus' prayer for the disciples and their mission: "keep them in your name" and "sanctify" or "consecrate them in the truth." These imperatives encourage the community and contemporary readers who may feel threatened from the outside. The truth comes from the Father through the Son, the mediator and protector. God's Word protected the

Whoever **acknowledges** that Jesus is the **Son** of God,
　God remains in **him** and he in **God**.
We have come to **know** and to **believe** in the love God has for us.

God is **love**, and whoever **remains** in love
　remains in **God** and God in **him**.

GOSPEL　John 17:11b–19

A reading from the holy Gospel according to John

Lifting up his eyes to **heaven**, Jesus **prayed**, saying:
　"Holy **Father**, **keep** them in your name that you have
　　given me,
　so that **they** may be **one** just as **we** are one.
When I was with them I **protected** them in your name that you
　　gave me,
　and I **guarded** them, and **none** of them was **lost**
　except the son of **destruction**,
　in order that the Scripture might be **fulfilled**.
But now I am **coming** to you.
I speak this in the world
　so that they may share my joy **completely**.
I gave them your **word**, and the world **hated** them,
　because they do not **belong** to the world
　any more than **I** belong to the world.
I do not ask that you take them **out** of the world
　but that you **keep** them from the **evil** one.
They do not belong to the world
　any more than **I** belong to the world.
Consecrate them in the **truth**. Your **word** is truth.
As you sent **me** into the world,
　so I sent **them** into the world.
And I **consecrate** myself for them,
　so that they **also** may be consecrated in **truth**."

All this evidence leads to this conclusion.

Slowly and deliberately. This line summarizes all of John's teaching. Smile as you share this good news!

An exhortatory reading. This is a prayer and should sound like one. Make sure your assembly knows this is prayed for them. You pray in Jesus' name on their behalf as you proclaim.

Don't "lift your eyes" lest it appear that you're "portraying" Jesus. Rather, when you look up from the text, look directly into the assembly.

Start slowly.
This line summarizes the whole prayer. Pause.

Pick up your pace a bit.
Drop your voice on this parenthetical phrase (referring to Judas).

Pause at the end of this line.
Slow on this line.

Pick up your pace again.

How does Jesus feel as he prays for our blessing and protection? Make a strong choice (recall that this prayer occurs during the Last Supper), and bring that to your proclamation.
Slow from here to the end.
The parallel between God's relationship with Jesus and Jesus' relationship with us is a favorite theme of John's.

With a sense of satisfaction and fulfillment.

---

disciples, but now the Word of truth sanctifies them. The unity between the Father and the Son is the source of the unity among Jesus and the disciples, an affirmation that echoes the parable of the vine and the branches: "Remain in me, as I remain in you. . . . Whoever remains in me and I in him will bear much fruit, because without me you can do nothing" (John 15:4–5). Jesus protected his own so that "none of them was lost except the son of destruction." Reference to the fulfillment of "the Scripture" (verse 12, reminiscent of Psalm 41:10, and quoted in John 13:18) explains that a disciple could betray his master. Jesus speaks of the joy he has transmitted to his disciples and of the world's hatred; he emphasizes that the disciples share their master's fate in their relationship to the world. The "evil one" to whom Jesus refers, is "the ruler of this world" Jesus has spoken of earlier in this Gospel (12:31; 14:30; 16:33).

In the passage, "Consecrate them in the truth. . . . As you sent me into the world, so I sent them into the world. And I consecrate myself for them, so that they also may be consecrated in truth," the word "consecrate" has two different meanings. The first usage is to "set apart" and "make holy," the second implies a "sacrifice," a "laying down one's life" for their sake (compare to 10:11, 15; 15:13). In John's Gospel, Jesus' Death on the Cross coincides with the hour of the sacrifice of the paschal lambs (on "preparation day,"19:31, 36). K.S.

PENTECOST SUNDAY: VIGIL

LECTIONARY #62

READING I   Genesis 11:1–9

A reading from the Book of Genesis

The whole **world** spoke the same **language**, using the same **words**.
While the people were **migrating** in the east,
    they came upon a valley in the land of **Shinar** and **settled** there.
They **said** to one another,
    "**Come**, let us mold **bricks** and **harden** them with **fire**."
They used bricks for **stone**, and bitumen for **mortar**.
Then they said, "**Come**, let us build ourselves a **city**
    and a **tower** with its top in the **sky**,
    and so make a **name** for ourselves;
    otherwise we shall be **scattered** all over the earth."

The LORD came down to **see** the city and the **tower**
    that the people had built.
Then the LORD said: "If **now**, while they are **one** people,
    all speaking the **same** language,
    they have started to do **this**,
    nothing will **later** stop them from doing whatever they
        presume to do.
Let us then go down there and **confuse** their language,
    so that one will not **understand** what another says."
Thus the LORD **scattered** them from there all over the **earth**,
    and they **stopped** building the city.

A narrative reading that accounts for the varieties of human language, but more importantly, it reminds us that, even today, God is in charge, and God's plans do not go unfulfilled.

The reading starts with no context. Extend the pause before the reading a little longer than usual so the beginning is not so abrupt.

Shinar = SHĪ-nahr

Speak as though you're the person with this idea; be excited about hatching this plan!

bitumen = bih-TYOO-m*n

Another person with an even better idea!

Pause at the end of this line.

Don't speak in anger, but rather with the realization that this could mean trouble.

Pause for a moment, considering what to do.

"Here's an idea."

Today, options are given for the readings. Contact your parish staff to learn which readings will be used.

READING I **Genesis 11:1–9**. The legend of the city of Babel and the tower that the immigrants began to build takes place in the land of Shinar, Mesopotamia (Genesis 10:10). It reminds us of the story of the man and woman dependent on divine providence in paradise (Genesis 3) and their frustrated attempt to rise above the single rule established by

God: to abstain from eating from the tree of the knowledge of good and bad. In the Babel legend, the upward movement of the "tower with its top in the sky" is reversed when God "comes down" to investigate the building attempts of the lowly creatures. Their plan, "let us build ourselves a city," is the counterpoint to God's plan and signals the turning point in the legend: "Let us then go down there and confuse their language, so that one will not understand what another says." The builders are the human population ("the whole world"), and the proposal to "make a name for ourselves"

expresses the universal ambition to attain a preeminence that rivals God, thus erasing the distinction between Creator and creature. The name of the place, Babel, is related to the verb "to mix, scramble, confuse," and is identified with the place name Babylon. An ominous feature is the lack of dialogue between God and humans—in contrast to the conversation that opens the Abraham narrative in the following chapter.

Although God wants humans to live in unity with creation, this project of unity seeks self-preservation and group identity in opposition to the divine will to "fill the

Babel = BAB-*l

Diversity is a hallmark of God's plan for creation.

That is why it was called **Babel**,
     because there the Lord **confused** the speech of all the world.
It was from that **place** that he **scattered** them all over the earth.

Or:

A narrative that details the sealing of the Covenant. There's a lot happening here; take your time.
Exodus = EK-suh-duhs

READING I   Exodus 19:3–8a, 16–20b

A reading from the Book of Exodus

Make this an intimate conversation with Moses, contrasting with the more spectacular, public conversation later.

God's love is the basis of the covenant. Let that love come through in your voice.

How does God sound here?

Pause at the end of this line.

Moses went up the **mountain** to **God**.
Then the Lord **called** to him and said,
     "**Thus** shall you say to the house of **Jacob**;
     tell the Israelites:
     You have seen for **yourselves** how I treated the **Egyptians**
     and how I **bore** you up on **eagle** wings
     and brought you here to **myself**.
Therefore, if you **hearken** to my voice and keep my **covenant**,
     you shall be my **special possession**,
     dearer to me than all **other** people,
     though **all** the earth is **mine**.
You shall be to me a **kingdom** of **priests**, a **holy** nation.
That is what you must tell the **Israelites**."
So Moses went and **summoned** the elders of the people.
When he set before them
     all that the Lord had **ordered** him to tell them,
     the people all answered **together**,
     "**Everything** the Lord has said, we will **do**."

Proclaim "we will do" slowly and with great self-assurance.
Pause at the end of this line.
God now appears to the people in this awesome display. Let it sound awesome!
Raise your intensity on each of these three effects.

On the morning of the **third** day
     there were peals of **thunder** and **lightning**,
     and a heavy **cloud** over the mountain,
     and a very loud **trumpet** blast,
     so that all the people in the camp **trembled**.

---

earth" (Genesis 1:28), God resists their plan, scatters his people, and stirs up diversity. The unity that fosters life succeeds when the community embraces the concerns of the created world of Genesis 1, defined by making distinctions and allowing diversity. Healthy unity is manifest in an ability to live together without conflict and oppression, sharing common objectives in tune with God's purposes for the world. Diversity is part of God's intention for the world, as is evident from the character of the blessing in the long list of Noah's descendants and their settlements in the previous chapter.

In tune with the original intention of creation, God makes a decisive move to foster the richness of diversity and differences in the human race.

At Pentecost, each ethnic group present in Jerusalem heard the message in their native tongue. The gift of the Spirit manifested itself in a linguistic cacophony, but everybody had access to the Good News. The gift was not so much a global language, but a new kind of hearing that transcends language barriers, even as it preserves the differences that language and culture reflect. The gift of the Holy Spirit does not

delete the multiplicity of languages, but gives access to the Gospel for people of different cultures and languages. As a result of their project that promoted uniformity, the peoples were scattered throughout the earth to proclaim the Gospel rather than promote their own interests. Linguistic diversity enriches our understanding of the world bigger than ourselves. But communication is a complex reality in the common life and includes not simply openness to other languages and cultures, but truly accepting others in their unique life situations. Failure to communicate often leads

Contrast the people's fear with Moses' confident leadership.

Drop your voice to a whisper to express the mystery here.

Now raise it again while describing the fire and smoke.

A conversation between trumpets and thunder!

Pause at the end of this line.

Now God invites Moses again into an intimate conversation. Pause a bit longer than usual at the end.

But **Moses** led the people out of the camp to meet **God**,
 and they **stationed** themselves at the **foot** of the mountain.
Mount **Sinai** was all wrapped in **smoke**,
 for the LORD came down upon it in **fire**.
The smoke **rose** from it as though from a **furnace**,
 and the whole mountain trembled **violently**.
The **trumpet** blast grew **louder** and **louder**, while Moses
  was **speaking**,
 and God **answering** him with **thunder**.

When the LORD came **down** to the top of Mount Sinai,
 he **summoned** Moses to the **top** of the mountain.

Or:

READING I   Ezekiel 37:1–14

A reading from the Book of the Prophet Ezekiel

A narrative with exhortatory passages. The vision illustrates the infinite depth of God's desire to bring life to all.

Ezekiel = ee-ZEE-kee-uhl

Convey the quiet sadness in this scene of desolation.

There's absolutely no life in them!

Raise intensity for this first exhortatory passage.

prophesy = PROF-uh-sī

Proclaim as if to someone desperate for God to bring life.

This is good news! Smile with your voice, eyes, and face!

The hand of the LORD came upon me,
 and he **led** me out in the **spirit** of the LORD
 and set me in the center of the **plain**,
 which was now **filled** with **bones**.
He made me **walk** among the bones in every direction
 so that I saw how **many** they were on the surface of the plain.
How **dry** they were!
He **asked** me:
 Son of **man**, can these bones come to **life**?
I answered, "Lord GOD, you **alone** know that."
Then he said to me:
 Prophesy over these bones, and **say** to them:
 Dry **bones**, hear the word of the LORD!
Thus says the Lord GOD to these **bones**:
 See! I will bring **spirit** into you, that you may come to **life**.

to difficulties in relationships, even among persons who share a common language but lack the tolerance or the capacity to comprehend one another.

 Exodus 19:3–8a, 16–20b. The author has sketched a theological event—the theophany or manifestation of God's presence, described in terms drawn from natural phenomena like thunderstorms, earthquakes, and volcanic eruptions—spectacles that point to the indescribable. This narrative portrays the disruptive, cataclysmic upheaval caused by God's entry in history. Its theologian-author portrays awe

and respect in the presence of the Holy One, who is far from photogenic. The sound of the trumpet signals a liturgical assembly. The author identifies two facets of Israel's existence with the phrase a "kingdom of priests, a holy nation." This phrase describes a people dedicated to the service of God, even while it sustains a social and political structure.

 Israel's future is governed by a condition: everything depends on her readiness to listen (Hebrew, *šāma'*; see 15:26) and be faithful to the covenant. Assuming that this condition is met, Israel will occupy a posi-

tion in the world that has sacred significance as well as political authority. The two concepts, "kingdom" and "nation," retain their political references, but their modifiers, "priestly" and "holy," move in the direction of the sacred. Israel (and the Church) are designed to be communities in which government and holiness converge; thus they have a unique vocation, and Sinai, the meeting place between Israel and God, is where that vocation is formulated and received. With concise wording the author voices both an unprecedented purpose that foresees a people, the likes of

sinews = sin-YOOZ

prophesied = PROF-uh-sīd

How does Ezekiel feel as he watches this? Frightened, amazed, maybe a little of both? Bring those emotions to your proclamation.

Let God's excitement come through in the encouragement of Ezekiel.

Demand that the spirit come!

Let the weariness of these bones come through in your voice.

A final exhortatory prophecy expressing God's love and longing for us.

This shouldn't sound like, "Then you'll be sorry!" Rather, "Then you'll know how much I love you!"
At this phrase, look directly at the assembly and fill your voice with love.
These lines restate the same ideas as above; slow down to let them sink in more deeply. How does God sound?
Pause at the end of this line.

Take significant pauses at each comma; slow down on "I will do it," and proclaim with steadfast assurance.

I will put **sinews** upon you, make **flesh** grow over you,
  cover you with **skin**, and put **spirit** in you
    so that you may come to **life** and know that **I** am the LORD.
I, **Ezekiel**, **prophesied** as I had been **told**,
  and even as I was **prophesying** I heard a **noise**;
    it was a **rattling** as the bones came together, **bone** joining **bone**.
I saw the **sinews** and the **flesh** come upon them,
  and the **skin** cover them, but there was no **spirit** in them.
Then the LORD said to me:
vv   Prophesy to the **spirit**, **prophesy**, son of man,
  and **say** to the spirit: Thus says the Lord GOD:
  From the four winds **come**, O spirit,
    and **breathe** into these **slain** that they may come to **life**.
I prophesied as he **told** me, and the spirit **came** into them;
  they came **alive** and stood **upright**, a vast **army**.
Then he said to me:
  Son of **man**, these bones are the whole **house** of **Israel**.
They have been saying,
  "Our bones are **dried up**,
  our hope is **lost**, and we are cut **off**."
Therefore, **prophesy** and **say** to them: **Thus** says the Lord GOD:
  O my **people**, I will open your **graves**
  and have you **rise** from them,
    and bring you **back** to the land of Israel.
Then you shall **know** that I am the LORD,
  when I **open** your graves and have you **rise** from them,
  O my **people**!
I will put my **spirit** in you that you may **live**,
  and I will **settle** you upon your **land**;
    thus you shall **know** that I am the LORD.
I have **promised**, and I will **do** it, says the LORD.

Or:

which has never existed, and a strong condition that affirms that Israel's unique status and holiness always depend on her constant listening to God who directs and counsels. The moment Israel stops listening and being loyal to the covenant, she forfeits her privilege. God released Israel from slavery in Egypt. The destination of their flight from slavery is not the mountain and not even the Promised Land, but the encounter with God.

Ezekiel 37:1–14. Ezekiel is guided around a plain to witness the desiccated bones. He prophesies to the bones, assur-

ing them that God will bring them to life to acknowledge the Lord. The irony is evident. For years Ezekiel prophesied to living Israelites who proved unable to respond as if they were dry bones. Now he prophesies to the bones that come rattling together, while sinews, flesh, and skin grow over them. The prophet calls upon the "spirit" to breathe into the lifeless corpses. When God's Spirit animates the bodies, they stand up and live. God's own Spirit will make possible the Israelites' fidelity to the Lord (compare to Ezekiel 36:27; 39:29). God explained to Ezekiel that the bones are

Israel in its current, hopeless condition (see also 33:10). The image of unburied corpses as parched, scattered bones simultaneously evokes the remains of the Israelites killed in the Babylonian invasions, as well as the unhinged and disoriented victims still living in the land, and the exiles whose hopes have been utterly crushed. God will open these devastated people's graves, restore their life and hope, and bring them home. In this cinematic description of the re-creation of Israel, restoration begins with the remains of the dry bones of old Israel, depicting a hopeless

An exhortatory reading—an exciting vision of what God's spirit can accomplish. Bring that same excitement to your proclamation.

Joel = JOH-*l

Linger over the word "pour," a lavish image.

prophesy = PROF-uh-sī

God's generosity knows no bounds of class or gender.

The world will know the power of God through these signs.

Raise your intensity as you describe these "wonders."

Express the tenderness of God in rescuing all who call on the name of the Lord.

Keep your voice up through the end.

TO KEEP IN MIND
Use inflection (the high or low pitch of your voice) to convey attitude and feeling. High pitch expresses intensity and excitement; low pitch expresses sadness, contrition, or solemnity.

READING I   Joel 3:1–5

A reading from the Book of the Prophet Joel

Thus says the LORD:
I will pour out my **spirit** upon all **flesh**.
Your **sons** and **daughters** shall **prophesy**,
    your **old** men shall dream **dreams**,
    your **young** men shall see **visions**;
even upon the **servants** and the **handmaids**,
    in those days, I will pour out my **spirit**.
And I will work **wonders** in the **heavens** and on the **earth**,
    blood, **fire**, and columns of **smoke**;
the **sun** will be turned to **darkness**,
    and the **moon** to **blood**,
at the coming of the **day** of the LORD,
    the **great** and **terrible** day.
Then everyone shall be **rescued**
    who calls on the **name** of the LORD;
for on Mount **Zion** there shall be a **remnant**,
    as the LORD has said,
and in **Jerusalem survivors**
    whom the LORD shall **call**.

---

situation; the new Israel is an ideal people, inspired and shaped by God's Spirit to be faithful to the covenant and guarantee their life in the land.

Joel 3:1–5. The Hebrew word *rúach*, often translated "spirit," means also "wind" or even "storm-wind," a gust of energy whose effects can be felt and observed. Theologically, this energy is God's life that breathes into a human, enabling him or her to perform extraordinary tasks. Joel prophesies that this divine energy is poured out

"on all flesh," (all humankind) radically changing the mind and conduct of those touched by it. Newly energized, "sons and daughters" will "prophesy," do extraordinary things: old people's dreams will be laden with meaning, and young people's visions will give fresh insight. The social order will be abolished, as everybody, even the servants, will be transformed in mind and behavior. Tremendous cosmic transformations and changed behavior on earth will accompany the outpouring of the

divine energy: "blood, fire, and columns of smoke"; the sun will be eclipsed and the moon will turn to blood. The Lord's "great and terrible day" will bring an end to the world order, as we know it. In the face of this awesome revelation, the prophet gives concrete advice: first, in the face of the disturbances, invoke God's name and trust in the Lord; second, stay in Jerusalem where God will save those whom he chooses.

For meditation and context:

TO KEEP IN MIND
What does the reading ask your
assembly to do or to be after
hearing your proclamation? Focus
on an intention every time you
proclaim.

RESPONSORIAL PSALM   Psalm 104:1–2a, 24, 35c, 27–28, 29bc–30 (30)

R. Lord, send out your Spirit, and renew the face of the earth.
or
R. Alleluia.

Bless the LORD, O my soul!
  O LORD, my God, you are great indeed!
You are clothed with majesty and glory,
  robed in light as with a cloak.

How manifold are your works, O LORD!
  In wisdom you have wrought them all—
the earth is full of your creatures;
  bless the LORD, O my soul! Alleluia.

Creatures all look to you
  to give them food in due time.
When you give it to them, they gather it;
  when you open your hand, they are filled
    with good things.

If you take away their breath, they perish
  and return to their dust.
When you send forth your spirit,
  they are created,
    and you renew the face of the earth.

READING II   Romans 8:22–27

A reading from the Letter of Saint Paul to the Romans

Brothers and sisters:
We **know** that all **creation** is **groaning** in **labor** pains even
    until **now**;
  and not only **that**, but we **ourselves**,
  who have the **firstfruits** of the **Spirit**,
  we **also** groan within ourselves
  as we wait for **adoption**, the **redemption** of our **bodies**.
For in **hope** we were **saved**.
Now **hope** that **sees** is **not** hope.
For who **hopes** for what one **sees**?
But if we hope for what we do **not** see, we wait with **endurance**.

In the **same** way, the Spirit **too** comes to the aid of our **weakness**;
  for we do not know **how** to pray as we **ought**,
  but the Spirit **himself** intercedes with inexpressible **groanings**.

An exhortatory reading. Use this reading as Paul does, to encourage your assembly to be hopeful, as we wait for the fulfillment of God's reign.

Don't lose "all creation." Paul asserts that the whole universe awaits its redemption, not just human beings.

Emphatically.
With the tone of, "Don't you agree?"

What we hope for is worth our patient endurance.

Reassure your assembly. The Spirit knows our longings even when we can't express them.

READING II   Paul writes that the reality of the present world and of human nature is linked with the future that belongs to everyone who believes. Just as we have been marked indelibly by our sinful past, so we are sealed by the future that awaits us—the benefits of redemption and glory. We have every reason to hope, for the harvest of the Spirit's presence is our inheritance. The mother who experiences the first pangs of labor knows that the child in her womb is pressing to be born; we are like that child about to be born in pain, and what awaits us is indescribable joy. Oh, that we might stand on tiptoes like little children, awaiting the good things that our lovely Lord has for us in the gift of the Spirit! While on earth, we enjoy the first pickings of salvation, the Holy Spirit's presence; we are filled with hope, which is an invisible rope that ties us to eternal life with God, hope strengthened by our faith put into practice and our prayer. These are consoling words from Paul: even when we do not know how to pray, the Spirit of God comes to our aid and prays in us.

And the one who searches **hearts**
　　knows what is the **intention** of the Spirit,
　　because he **intercedes** for the **holy** ones
　　according to God's **will**.

GOSPEL　John 7:37–39

A reading from the holy Gospel according to John

On the **last** and **greatest** day of the **feast**,
　　Jesus stood up and **exclaimed**,
　　"Let anyone who **thirsts** come to **me** and **drink**.
As Scripture says:
　　*Rivers of **living** water will flow from **within** him* who
　　　　believes in me."

He said this in reference to the **Spirit**
　　that those who came to **believe** in him were to **receive**.
There was, of course, no Spirit **yet**,
　　because **Jesus** had not yet been **glorified**.

A narrative reading with an exhortatory passage. Although brief, don't rush through the reading.

The setting gives this teaching great importance.

An exhortatory passage. Raise your energy and encourage your assembly to respond to this invitation.

This is us! We have received this spirit!

Drop your voice slightly on this concluding comment.

TO KEEP IN MIND
Use inflection (the high or low pitch of your voice) to convey attitude and feeling. High pitch expresses intensity and excitement; low pitch expresses sadness, contrition, or solemnity.

GOSPEL　Jesus offers living water through the Spirit. He speaks the words in this reading on the last day of the Jewish feast of tabernacles, during which one of the prayers asks that the coming rains fertilize the earth and guarantee life for another year. Jewish documents from the second century tell that on the last day of the feast a grand procession with water from the reservoir of Siloam coursed through the crowded city up to the Temple, and the people celebrated with lights in the women's court. The pilgrims present for the feast, and readers of the Gospel, could easily have associated these ceremonies with Jesus' announcement: "I am the light of the world" (8:12). The believer can drink the water of salvation from Jesus, and the believer who receives this living water treasures it in his or her interior life through the influence of the Spirit. Under that influence the water becomes in the believer "a spring of water welling up to eternal life" (4:14, Jesus speaking to the Samaritan woman at the well). The water at the festival of tabernacles symbolizes the Spirit.

PENTECOST SUNDAY

LECTIONARY #63

READING I   Acts of the Apostles 2:1–11

A reading from the Acts of the Apostles

When the time for **Pentecost** was fulfilled,
    they were all in one place **together**.
And **suddenly** there came from the **sky**
    a noise like a strong driving **wind**,
    and it **filled** the entire **house** in which they were.
Then there appeared to them **tongues** as of **fire**,
    which **parted** and came to **rest** on each **one** of them.
And they were all **filled** with the Holy **Spirit**
    and began to speak in different **tongues**,
    as the Spirit **enabled** them to **proclaim**.

Now there were **devout** Jews from every **nation** under heaven
    staying in Jerusalem.
At this **sound**, they gathered in a large **crowd**,
    but they were **confused**
    because **each** one heard them speaking in his **own** language.
They were **astounded**, and in **amazement** they asked,
    "Are not all these people who are speaking **Galileans**?
Then how does **each** of us hear them in his **native** language?
We are **Parthians**, **Medes**, and **Elamites**,
    inhabitants of **Mesopotamia**, **Judea** and **Cappadocia**,
    Pontus and **Asia**, **Phrygia** and **Pamphylia**,

A narrative reading. Don't proclaim as if this were a news report, but convey all the exciting emotional intensity in the story.

Build your intensity slowly through this line.

Articulate this complex line carefully.

Be amazed at this!

Pause at the end of this line.
Take your time with this line.
Let their astounded amazement come through in your proclamation.
Don't let this list of place names throw you. Practice the pronunciations, but then proclaim as if they were all places you were very familiar with. If you make a mistake, just keep moving.
Parthians = PAHR-thee-uhnz
Medes = meedz
Elamites = EE-luh-mīts
Mesopotamia = mes-uh-poh-TAY-mee-uh
Judea = joo-DEE-uh
Cappadocia = cap-uh-DOH-shee-uh
Pontus = PON-tuhs
Phrygia = FRIJ-ee-uh
Pamphylia = Pam-FIL-ee-uh

Today, options are given for the readings. Contact your parish staff to learn which readings will be used.

READING I | The day of Pentecost is a major feast in the Jewish calendar, taking place fifty days after Passover. Luke's dating and metaphors suggest a theological link between the gift of the Spirit and the Sinai theophany where the covenant between God and Israel was made. The Spirit's descent is described with auditory and visual effects, "a noise

like a strong driving wind . . . tongues as of fire." These images are apt for the Spirit's arrival. Wind, both in Hebrew and Greek, is associated with spirit or breath. The noise of a gust of wind heralds God's new intervention in salvation history. "Tongues as of fire" recalls Exodus 19:18 where fire symbolizes God's presence on Mount Sinai at the formulation of the covenant between God and his people. In today's text the Holy Spirit prepares the Apostles to proclaim the new covenant. The image of fire also links with the Spirit's work of judgment (see Luke 3:16–17), and the metaphor of

"tongues" calls to mind the inspired speech of the Apostles.

In a dramatic change of scenery, the private experience in the "house" moves to the street outside: a large crowd gathers to hear the proclamation of "the mighty acts of God." Some people hear only a confused babble of ecstatic or drunken voices, while others hear them clearly, each in their own language. This miracle of hearing amounts to a reversal of the confusion of tongues at the tower of Babel. Ecstatic prayer and proclamation, recorded as speaking in foreign languages, symbolizes the Church's world-

Libya = LIB-ee-uh

Cyrene = sī-REE-nee

Cretans = KREE-tuhnz

Slight pause after "yet."

Pause a little longer than usual at the end.

Egypt and the districts of **Libya** near **Cyrene**,
as well as travelers from **Rome**,
both **Jews** and **converts** to Judaism, **Cretans** and **Arabs**,
yet we hear them **speaking** in our own **tongues**
of the mighty **acts** of **God**."

For meditation and context:

TO KEEP IN MIND

A *didactic* text makes a point or teaches something. Help your assembly to follow the argument and understand what's being taught.

RESPONSORIAL PSALM   Psalm 104:1, 24, 29–30, 31, 34 (30)

R. Lord, send out your Spirit, and renew the face of the earth. or R. Alleluia.

Bless the LORD, O my soul!
    O LORD, my God, you are great indeed!
How manifold are your works, O LORD!
    The earth is full of your creatures.

If you take away their breath, they perish
    and return to their dust.
When you send forth your spirit,
        they are created,
    and you renew the face of the earth.

May the glory of the LORD endure forever;
    may the LORD be glad in his works!
Pleasing to him be my theme;
    I will be glad in the LORD.

A didactic reading that is familiar, but powerful: regardless of differences in talents, ministries, ethnicity, or class all are one in the Body of Christ.

Corinthians = kohr-IN-thee-uhnz

This is the key; all who believe in Jesus are one in the Spirit.

Put a slight pause before the word "but" in each of these phrases.

Keep these two lines together.

Pause at the end of this line.

Contrast "one" and "many" in this line.

Slow and deliberate.

READING II   1 Corinthians 12:3b–7, 12–13

A reading from the first Letter of Saint Paul to the Corinthians

Brothers and sisters:
No one can say, "**Jesus** is **Lord**," except by the Holy **Spirit**.

There are different kinds of spiritual **gifts** but the same **Spirit**;
    there are different forms of **service** but the same **Lord**;
    there are different **workings** but the same **God**
    who produces **all** of them in **everyone**.
To each individual the **manifestation** of the Spirit
    is given for some **benefit**.

As a body is **one** though it has many **parts**,
    and **all** the parts of the body, though **many**, are **one** body,
    so also **Christ**.

---

wide mission. The elaborate list of towns from which members of the crowd have come evokes the Jewish diaspora, reaching to the borders of the Roman Empire while centered on Jerusalem. The record of faraway place names is a foretaste of the geographical expansion that will dominate the narrative of Acts of the Apostles.

READING II **1 Corinthians 12:3b–7, 12–13**. Paul insists that the varieties of gifts (in Greek *charisma*, meaning "gift of grace") and services can be traced to the same spirit, the same Lord

and God. No single gift is prominent in and of itself and a person cannot play one gift off against others. Despite their diversity, some features are common to all "gifts": they are all graces that are bestowed from outside ourselves. Every gift is a form of service or ministry (Greek, *diakoniai*), a word that expresses purposeful service and the benefit that comes with the gift. All gifts are workings (Greek, *energemata*; note the root of the word energy in this term), because they show God at work for the common good. No one can boast of having a *charisma*, because it is not private

property or the result of personal achievement. The gifts are given not for personal satisfaction or pride, but for community benefit—the common good. Paul uses the metaphor of the body to explain Christ's relationship with believers, and he applies this model to the Church: by Baptism all people, despite the diversity of ethnic or social origins, are integrated into one body. Paul's surprising use of this metaphor highlights the diversity in the Church, even as it argues against distinctions of status, usefulness, or worth. Paul's main point is the combination of diversity and unity—many

For in **one** Spirit we were all **baptized** into **one body**,
  whether **Jews** or **Greeks**, **slaves** or **free** persons,
  and we were **all** given to **drink** of one **Spirit**.

Or:

READING II   Galatians 5:16–25

A reading from the Letter of Saint Paul to the Galatians

Brothers and sisters, **live** by the **Spirit**
  and you will certainly not **gratify** the desire of the **flesh**.
For the **flesh** has desires **against** the Spirit,
  and the **Spirit** against the **flesh**;
  these are **opposed** to each other,
  so that you may **not** do what you **want**.
But if you are guided by the **Spirit**, you are not under the **law**.
Now the works of the flesh are **obvious**:
  immorality, **impurity**, **lust**, **idolatry**,
  sorcery, **hatreds**, **rivalry**, **jealousy**,
  outbursts of **fury**, acts of **selfishness**,
  dissensions, **factions**, occasions of **envy**,
  drinking bouts, **orgies**, and the like.
I **warn** you, as I warned you **before**,
  that those who **do** such things will not **inherit** the kingdom
    of God.
In **contrast**, the **fruit** of the Spirit is **love**, **joy**, **peace**,
  patience, **kindness**, **generosity**,
  faithfulness, **gentleness**, **self-control**.
Against **such** there is **no** law.
Now those who belong to Christ **Jesus** have **crucified** their flesh
  with its **passions** and **desires**.
If we **live** in the Spirit, let us also **follow** the Spirit.

Margin notes (left column):

"So why do you divide yourselves over differences that don't matter?"

An exhortatory reading. Do we live like people who have received the Holy Spirit? Use this reading as Paul does: Exhort your assembly to live so that others see plainly the fruits of the Spirit in our lives!

Galatians = guh-LAY-shuhnz

Start strong! The entire reading is summarized in this one phrase.

Good news!

Be quick and dismissive with this list.

Pause at the end of this line.

Change your tone. Smile, and linger over this list. Be eager to share these fruits!

Pause at the end of this line.

Remind your assembly: you're already dead to the flesh! Live that way!

Slowly. Join with the assembly—"Let's do this!"

---

members in one body. The baptismal formula, "for in one Spirit we were all baptized," admits cultural and social diversity even as it confesses our common access to the Spirit.

Galatians 5:16–25. To "live by the Spirit" and "gratify the desire of the flesh" are opposite orientations in human life, and the phrases could serve as a title for the reading. The two ways of living are "opposed to each other." The Greek term *sarx*, "flesh," problematic for translators, is used several times in this chapter (verses 13, 16, 17, 19, 24, and later in 6:8) in a nega-

tive, ethical sense referring to a person's corrupt nature. The final clause of the sentence, "so that you may not do what you want," baffles interpreters. Paul envisages that the battle between "Spirit" and "flesh" is frustrating even for the believer's best efforts. Now Paul contrasts being "guided by the Spirit" with being "under the law," and sets out a list of "the works of the flesh," followed by a list of virtues that we know as "the fruit of the Spirit." This second category is evocative: "the fruit" is not the result of effort on the believer's part, but rather the result of the Spirit's gift.

After rounding off the list of "the works of the flesh", and warning, "those who do such things will not inherit the kingdom of God," Paul places "love" at the head of the new list of the fruit of the Spirit. He brings his argument to a climax when he states that believers who identify with the Crucifixion of Christ have "crucified their flesh with its passions and desires." How is this possible? By consciously choosing to live by the Spirit. Thus Paul elaborates on what believers are called to do and to be: walk in the Spirit and prove our spiritual

For meditation and context:

TO KEEP IN MIND
Pray the text, using your favorite method of praying with Scripture.

SEQUENCE   Veni, Sancte Spiritus

Come, Holy Spirit, come!
And from your celestial home
 Shed a ray of light divine!
Come, Father of the poor!
Come, source of all our store!
 Come, within our bosoms shine.
You, of comforters the best;
You, the soul's most welcome guest;
 Sweet refreshment here below;
In our labor, rest most sweet;
Grateful coolness in the heat;
 Solace in the midst of woe.
O most blessed Light divine,
Shine within these hearts of yours,
 And our inmost being fill!

Where you are not, we have naught,
Nothing good in deed or thought,
 Nothing free from taint of ill.
Heal our wounds, our strength renew;
On our dryness pour your dew;
 Wash the stains of guilt away:
Bend the stubborn heart and will;
Melt the frozen, warm the chill;
 Guide the steps that go astray.
On the faithful, who adore
And confess you, evermore
 In your sevenfold gift descend;
Give them virtue's sure reward;
Give them your salvation, Lord;
 Give them joys that never end. Amen.
 Alleluia.

A narrative reading. Although brief, take your time. All the emotions—fear, surprise, joy, peace, love—are heightened and need to be fully expressed.

GOSPEL   John 20:19–23

A reading from the holy Gospel according to John

On the evening of that **first** day of the week,
 when the doors were **locked**, where the **disciples** were,
 for fear of the **Jews**,
 Jesus came and **stood** in their midst
 and said to them, "**Peace** be with you."
When he had said this, he showed them his **hands** and his **side**.
The disciples **rejoiced** when they saw the Lord.
Jesus said to them **again**, "**Peace** be with you.
As the **Father** has sent **me**, so **I** send **you**."
And when he had said this, he **breathed** on them and said
 to them,
 "**Receive** the Holy **Spirit**.
Whose sins you **forgive** are **forgiven** them,
and whose sins you **retain** are **retained**."

Or:

This should sound like the surprise that it is!

Immediately, Jesus calms their fears.

Let their joy echo in your proclamation.

As Jesus is sent by the Father, we are sent by Jesus.

Linger over the word "breathed." It implies that Jesus is in very close proximity to those present.

nature by sharing the "fruit of the Spirit" in our lives.

GOSPEL **John 20:19–23.** Jesus appears in Jerusalem on the evening of the first day of the new creation, the day he rose from the dead. The detail of the locked doors emphasizes that the risen Christ is not bound by spatial limitations. It refers to the doors of the room where the disciples were enclosed, as well as to the access to their interior lives, for the disciples had not yet made room for news of the Resurrection. The greeting of

peace prolongs what Jesus had offered in his lengthy farewell discourse at the Last Supper (John 14:27; 16:33). It is the normal greeting in Jewish culture, but its purpose, particularly here, announces the wish for wellbeing, health, happiness, wholeness, and all good things—great news to the formerly broken world now repaired by Christ's Resurrection. The disciples' commission, "As the Father has sent me, so I send you," depends on Jesus' mission and on the gift of the Holy Spirit. In his farewell discourse Jesus had promised that he would send the Advocate. Now the disci-

ples are "baptized" by the risen Christ's Spirit breathed into them, a respiratory gift that recalls Genesis 2:7, when the Genesis author describes how God breathed life into the first human. Just as Adam's life came from God, so now the disciples' new spiritual life comes from God's Son. When Jesus speaks of retaining sins or forgiving them, he links the forgiveness of sins to the gift of the Spirit and the disciples' missionary work.

At Pentecost, the birthday of the Church, we think about gifts that are given and received. When Jesus breathed on his

A didactic reading. Think of someone you know who needs assurance that God is with them through the gift of the Holy Spirit. How would you comfort that person? Proclaim with that same intention and emotion.

Jesus tells the disciples about the Holy Spirit to affirm that he will not abandon them. Bring that tone of reassurance and calm to your proclamation.

The Spirit will banish fear so we can speak out boldly.

Jesus doesn't want to overwhelm the disciples. Be gentle and understanding.

But when the time is right, the Spirit will bring Jesus' teaching to fullness.

We can trust the Spirit just as we trust Jesus.

Emphasize the progression—from the Father to Jesus to us through the Spirit.

TO KEEP IN MIND

Making eye contact with the assembly connects you with them and connects them to the reading more deeply than using your voice alone. This helps the assembly stay with the story and keeps them engaged.

GOSPEL   John 15:26–27; 16:12–15

A reading from the holy Gospel according to John

Jesus said to his **disciples**:
   "When the **Advocate** comes whom I will send you
      from the **Father**,
   the Spirit of truth that **proceeds** from the Father,
   he will **testify** to me.
And you **also** testify,
   because you have been with me from the **beginning**.

"I have much **more** to tell you, but you cannot **bear** it now.
But when he **comes**, the Spirit of **truth**,
   he will **guide** you to **all** truth.
He will **not** speak on his **own**,
   but he will speak what he **hears**,
   and will **declare** to you the things that are **coming**.
He will **glorify** me,
   because he will take from what is **mine** and **declare** it to you.
Everything that the Father has is mine;
   for this reason I told you that he will take from what is **mine**
   and declare it to **you**."

---

disciples grouped together after the Resurrection, the Church received the gift of life.

John 15:26–27; 16:12–15. Because of the intimate association among the Father, the Son, and the Spirit, the "Spirit of truth" acts in relation to Jesus, just as the Father does. The Son has been charged to accomplish the Father's work, and Jesus charges the disciples with testifying to him. Far from being left alone after Jesus' departure, the disciples receive the "Spirit of truth" from the Father and from Jesus, and

it is "the spirit that gives life" (recall Jesus' "bread of life" discourse in 6:63).

At his lengthy Last Supper discourse in the Fourth Gospel Jesus explains the meaning of his Death and Resurrection to the disciples. God has acted in history and thus revealed himself. Now, as the climax of this salvation history, Christ comes as the truth, the final unveiling of God in the mission of Jesus. The Father communicates to us through his Son, who is the Word of God. Jesus' Death and Resurrection has completed the Father's revelation of truth. Now he will send the Spirit—God's power reveal-

ing the fullness of truth in the Church. Thus he will glorify Christ, manifest him in his full impact and meaning. In these terms John describes the roles of the Father, Son, and Spirit in the work of salvation. K.S.

THE MOST HOLY TRINITY

LECTIONARY #165

READING I   Deuteronomy 4:32–34, 39–40

A reading from the Book of Deuteronomy

Moses said to the people:
  "**Ask** now of the days of **old**, before your time,
  ever since God created man upon the earth;
  ask from **one** end of the sky to the **other**:
  Did anything so **great** ever happen **before**?
Was it ever **heard** of?
Did a people ever hear the voice of **God**
  speaking from the midst of **fire**, as **you** did, and **live**?
Or did any god venture to go and take a nation for himself
  from the midst of **another** nation,
  by **testings**, by **signs** and **wonders**, by **war**,
  with strong **hand** and outstretched **arm**, and by great **terrors**,
  all of which the LORD, your God,
  did for **you** in Egypt before your very **eyes**?
This is why you must now **know**,
  and **fix** in your heart, that the **Lord** is **God**
  in the heavens **above** and on earth **below**,
  and that there is no **other**.
You must keep his **statutes** and **commandments** that I **enjoin**
    on you today,
  that **you** and your **children** after you may **prosper**,
  and that you may have **long** life on the land
  which the LORD, your God, is **giving** you **forever**."

An exhortatory reading. Moses reminds the people of the great care God has shown them. Your proclamation will remind your assembly of the same if you keep in mind the intention, "God loves you!" throughout.

Deuteronomy = doo-ter-AH-nuh-mee
With energy. Heighten each phrase.

Keep this line together with the next. "Ask" refers to the question that follows.

These are rhetorical questions but they should still sound like questions; the answer to all of them is "Of course not!"

Share your wonder at God's care for the people.
Incredible! Amazing!

Keep your pace up as you recall God's actions.

Pause at the end of this line.
Slow down—here is the right response to God's grace.

Good news! Smile with your voice, eyes, and face.
Slowly and deliberately through the end.

READING I   Today's reading recalls God's awesome acts in choosing and saving Israel from slavery "with strong hand and outstretched arm." (It might remind us of other triumphal accounts of God's deliverance of Israel from exile, such as Isaiah 45:5–6, 12, 18, 21–22; 46:9–10.) This quick review of creation and salvation builds into a creed: "This is why you must now know, and fix in your heart, that the LORD is God in the heavens above and on earth below, and that there is no other" God's revelation at Mount Horeb in a voice "from the midst of fire" and God's marvelous actions in the Exodus are proof of an exclusive divinity. God's generosity ("long life on the land which the Lord, your God, is giving you forever") guarantees the people's earthly inheritance, so they may honor the One Lord and God. We learn here that it is also the guarantee of our inheritance of life forever with God.

READING II   God's adopted children can address their parent with the same name that Jesus, his beloved Son, uses: Abba—in the Aramaic language, an affectionate word for father (see Mark 14:36). Paul shows that adoption does not imply a second-class birthright; believers are full heirs of God and joint heirs with Christ. By identifying with him, we participate fully in the benefits won by him. By reason of the Spirit's presence within us, baptized Christians enjoy not only life but also a new relationship with God—that of adopted children and heirs through Christ, whose sufferings and glory we share.

TO KEEP IN MIND

You can't proclaim what you don't understand. Read the Scripture passage and its commentary in *Workbook*. Then read it from your Bible, including what comes before and after it so that you understand the context.

An exhortatory reading with exciting news. Encourage your assembly to embrace their true identity as children of God.

The reading is all good news, so keep your voice and energy up throughout.

Amazing!

Raise your voice on the cry "Abba," and make each name distinct. You might proclaim "Father" more quietly and intimately.

Keep this final sentence together, pausing as indicated.

Pause briefly at the end of this line.

Heighten "heirs."

Pause briefly and take a catch-up breath if needed at the end of this line

With joy!

TO KEEP IN MIND

Smile when you share good news in a reading. Nonverbal cues like a smile help your assembly better understand your reading.

RESPONSORIAL PSALM Psalm 33:4–5, 6, 9, 18–19, 20, 22 (12b)

R. Blessed the people the Lord has chosen to be his own.

Upright is the word of the LORD,
  and all his works are trustworthy.
He loves justice and right;
  of the kindness of the LORD the earth
    is full.

By the word of the LORD the heavens
    were made;
  by the breath of his mouth all their host.
For he spoke, and it was made;
  he commanded, and it stood forth.

See, the eyes of the LORD are upon those
    who fear him,
  upon those who hope for his kindness,
to deliver them from death
  and preserve them in spite of famine.

Our soul waits for the LORD,
  who is our help and our shield.
May your kindness, O LORD, be upon us
  who have put our hope in you.

READING II Romans 8:14–17

A reading from the Letter of Saint Paul to the Romans

Brothers and sisters:
Those who are led by the **Spirit** of God are **sons** of God.
For you did not receive a spirit of **slavery** to fall back into **fear**,
  but you received a Spirit of **adoption**,
    through whom we cry, "**Abba**, **Father**!"
The Spirit himself bears **witness** with our spirit
  that we are **children** of God,
  and if children, then **heirs**,
  heirs of God and **joint** heirs with **Christ**,
  if only we **suffer** with him
  so that we may also be **glorified** with him.

GOSPEL This final scene in Matthew's account of the Gospel takes place in Galilee where Jesus' ministry began (4:12), creating a literary arch that spans the Gospel. Having begun in Galilee, Jesus' ministry, now carried on by the Church, will fan out to the whole world. The mountain setting recalls other mountain scenes: the Sermon on the Mount, the Transfiguration, the mountain where Jesus retired to pray, and the Mount of Olives, where Jesus wept over Jerusalem. Matthew's remark, "they worshipped, but they doubted," reminds us of Jesus walking on the water, extending his hands to sinking Peter, and then asking, "why did you doubt?" (14:31–33). Jesus' announcement, "All power in heaven and on earth has been given to me," echoes his statement back in chapter 11: "All things have been handed over to me by my Father" (11:27). In these ways, this Gospel looks back to Jesus' ministry as a whole and forward to the time of the Church, thus linking two periods that have the same Lord and the same mission.

Especially in this parting scene, the author invites the reader to enter into the action. "I am with you always," Jesus reassures, guaranteeing his real though invisible presence and evoking the name Emmanuel (translated "God is with us," 1:23) at the beginning of the Gospel, even as it echoes 18:20, "where two or three are gathered together in my name, there am I in the midst of them." The result is that the believing audience and the ever-present Son of God are intimate friends. And now the mission is expanded to "all nations," whereas earlier it was only to "the lost sheep of the house of Israel" (10:6). The baptismal formula "in the name of the

A narrative that is brief, but full of action and emotion. Keep your energy up, but there's no need to rush.

Their doubt shows that the disciples are human. It's a lot for them to take in!

How does Jesus sound as he gives these last instructions?

Take time with this; be very clear with the commission.

Proclaim the Trinitarian formula as if it's being spoken for the very first time.

Pause.

Be eager to share Jesus' care for your assembly. Make eye contact and proclaim this line with great compassion and reassurance. Take a longer than usual pause at the end.

TO KEEP IN MIND

What does the reading ask your assembly to do or to be after hearing your proclamation? Focus on an intention every time you proclaim.

GOSPEL   Matthew 28:16–20

A reading from the holy Gospel according to Matthew

The **eleven** disciples went to **Galilee**,
    to the mountain to which Jesus had **ordered** them.
When they all **saw** him, they **worshiped**, but they **doubted**.
Then Jesus **approached** and said to them,
    "**All** power in **heaven** and on **earth** has been **given** to me.
Go, therefore, and make **disciples** of all nations,
    baptizing them in the name of the **Father**,
    and of the **Son**, and of the Holy **Spirit**,
    teaching them to **observe all** that I have commanded you.
And **behold**, I am with you **always**, until the **end** of the **age**."

Father, and of the Son, and of the Holy Spirit" is the believer's invitation into the community of the risen Christ, the Church, and it unites the one baptized with the life of the blessed Trinity. "Teaching" recapitulates a central theme of the Gospel and gives the disciples a task that was previously reserved for Jesus.

As elsewhere, Matthew evokes the figure of Moses, the Law-giver, who began and ended his service to the covenanted people on two different mountains—Sinai and the mountain in Nebo where Moses died (Deuteronomy 34). Jesus brings a new Law, expressed in the beatitudes (Matthew 5–7).

Finally, this reading has parallels with the end of Deuteronomy and the beginning of the book of Joshua that describe God, or God through Moses, commissioning Joshua, his successor. In Joshua 1:2–9, Joshua is instructed to "go" and cross the Jordan, to "observe the entire law which my servant Moses enjoined on you," and guarantees his constant presence: "for the Lord, your God is with you wherever you go" (verses 7 and 9). Just as at the close of his life Moses commissioned Joshua to go into the land peopled by foreign nations and to observe all the precepts of the Law, and promised his successor God's abiding presence, so Jesus, at the end of his earthly ministry, commissions his disciples to go into all the world to teach all the commandments, and he guarantees his constant presence. K.S.

THE MOST HOLY BODY AND BLOOD OF CHRIST

LECTIONARY #168

READING I   Exodus 24:3–8

A reading from the Book of Exodus

When **Moses** came to the people
    and related all the **words** and **ordinances** of the LORD,
    they all answered with **one** voice,
    "We will do **everything** that the LORD has **told** us."
Moses then wrote down all the words of the LORD and,
    rising **early** the next day,
    he erected at the foot of the mountain an **altar**
    and twelve **pillars** for the twelve tribes of **Israel**.
Then, having sent certain young men of the Israelites
    to offer **holocausts** and sacrifice young **bulls**
    as **peace** offerings to the LORD,
    Moses took half of the **blood** and put it in large **bowls**;
    the **other** half he splashed on the **altar**.
Taking the book of the **covenant**, he read it **aloud** to the people,
    who answered, "**All** that the LORD has **said**, we will **heed**
      and **do**."
Then he took the **blood** and sprinkled it on the **people**, saying,
    "This is the blood of the **covenant**
    that the LORD has made with you
    in **accordance** with all these words of his."

A narrative reading chosen for today's solemnity because of the blood which seals the covenant. Don't shy away from this visceral image.

Exodus = EK-suh-duhs

Although it seems like this reading tells the same story twice, Moses first asks the people if they will agree to the covenant, then he sets up a ritual to confirm it.

Eagerly.

The ritual of sealing the covenant begins here. See it unfold before you and convey the grandeur of this scene in your voice. Take your time.

Keep your pace steady as the ritual continues.

Quicken your pace slightly and heighten your energy; this exchange of words and blood is the high point of the ritual.

Emphatic.

Slowly and deliberately.

Keep your voice up through to the end or the last phrase will be lost.

READING I   The Sinai narrative concludes with the ceremonial sealing of the alliance between God and his people, who confirm their compliance with the terms of the covenant, "All that the LORD has said, we will heed and do." The people are then consecrated with the blood of the covenant. Several verses after this reading, Moses and a group of elders from the community ascend the mountain to conclude the covenant ceremony with God, and upon seeing him, "they ate and drank" (24:11). That banquet expresses the bond of will and obedience between God and Israel.

It is a eucharistic scene, in which Moses and company eat and drink with God to formalize the alliance. After the people's consent, Moses had built an altar with twelve stones—the ecclesial number twelve is emblematic of the whole of Israel. After complying with the prescribed communion sacrifices and proclaiming the terms of the covenant, Moses had taken the blood, splashed it on the altar—representing the presence of God—and sprinkled the people, thereby forming a family of the same blood. The blood, symbol of life, along with the common meal, expresses the bond

between former slaves and God, their redeemer. The points of contact with the Eucharist are the sacrifice, eating together, and the blood as a ritual sign of communion between God and his people.

The heart of the Eucharist is the sharing in the mystery of Christ's Passion, Death, and Resurrection. The paschal lamb is the sacrament of the old covenant, symbol of God's choice of the people Israel. Just as in Sinai the victim's blood sealed the covenant between God and his people, so in the Eucharist the chalice of "the new covenant in my blood" (1 Corinthians 11:25)

For meditation and context:

TO KEEP IN MIND

You can't proclaim what you don't understand. Read the Scripture passage and its commentary in *Workbook*. Then read it from your Bible, including what comes before and after it so that you understand the context.

A didactic reading. Take care with these long and complex sentences. Make sure you understand the thoughts being conveyed in this teaching.

The main thought in this sentence is "Christ entered the sanctuary with his own blood."

Raise your energy at the top of this phrase; it is the continuation of the main thought.

Keep this phrase together through the comma, in one breath if possible.
heifer = HEF-er

Note the parallel between the cleansing of flesh and the cleansing of our consciences.

Drop your voice slightly on this parenthetical phrase.

Brief pause after "works" to keep these two actions separate.

RESPONSORIAL PSALM   Psalm 116:12–13, 15–16, 17–18 (13)

R. I will take the cup of salvation, and call on the name of the Lord. or R. Alleluia.

How shall I make a return to the Lord
 for all the good he has done for me?
The cup of salvation I will take up,
 and I will call upon the name of the Lord.

Precious in the eyes of the Lord
 is the death of his faithful ones.
I am your servant, the son of your
  handmaid;
 you have loosed my bonds.

To you will I offer sacrifice of thanksgiving,
 and I will call upon the name of the Lord.
My vows to the Lord I will pay
 in the presence of all his people.

READING II   Hebrews 9:11–15

A reading from the Letter to the Hebrews

Brothers and sisters:
When **Christ** came as high priest
 of the **good** things that have come to be,
 passing through the **greater** and more **perfect** tabernacle
 not made by hands, that is, not belonging to **this** creation,
 he entered **once** for **all** into the **sanctuary**,
 not with the blood of goats and calves
 but with his **own** blood, thus obtaining **eternal** redemption.
For if the blood of **goats** and **bulls**
 and the sprinkling of a **heifer's** ashes
 can **sanctify** those who are **defiled**
 so that their flesh is **cleansed**,
 how much **more** will the blood of **Christ**,
 who through the eternal Spirit offered himself **unblemished**
   to God,
 cleanse our consciences from **dead** works
 to **worship** the living God.

---

is shared. The blood of the perfect victim, Jesus, poured out on the Cross, will seal the new covenant between God and all humanity (Luke 22:20; Hebrews 9:12, 15).

 Now our attention shifts to a heavenly sanctuary, where Christ as high priest performs an act that repeats and perfects the annual Jewish ritual of atonement. The first covenant, an indissoluble union between God and his people, is fully consummated when Christ, the definitive mediator, appears before the Father "with his own blood,"

expiates the infidelities of the covenant people, and "through the eternal Spirit," offers himself to God as a sacrifice, thus "obtaining eternal redemption." Jesus' function as both priest and victim of the eternal sacrifice instructs us to put it into practice: "Do this in remembrance of me" (1 Corinthians 11:25).

Religion opens a door and introduces humans into God's presence; worship establishes contact between the people and God. The Temple and its liturgy were meant to do just that, but they are copies of the real tabernacle and its worship,

which give eternal access to God. The sacrificial liturgy of the Old Testament approaches God, but the sacrifices are incomplete and cannot atone for sin once and for all. The author of Hebrews shows that Jesus is the only High Priest who offers a definitive sacrifice that opens the way to God, and that sacrifice is his very self. Old Testament sacrifices consisted of incense offerings, produce of the field, and animals, including, for example, the cleansing sacrifice of the red heifer (Numbers 19:1–9). Hebrews recalls these sacrifices and declares that Jesus' sacrifice is perfect. The

Animal sacrifices were required for atonement under the first covenant.

Good news! We are those who are called! Smile with your voice, eyes, and face.

Hearing this narrative reading outside of the Passion narrative allows us to focus on the Eucharist as the complete self-giving love of Jesus. Strive to show that love to your assembly in your proclamation.

A simple question; don't make it sound foreboding.

A man carrying a water jar (as opposed to a woman) would be an unusual sight.

What might Jesus be feeling as he thinks of this Passover with his friends? It will be a bittersweet occasion.

Convey the disciples' amazement at how events unfold exactly as Jesus described. Pause at the end of this line.

There are four actions; make each one distinct.

Jesus is eager to share himself.

For this reason he is mediator of a **new** covenant:
  since a death has taken place for deliverance
  from transgressions under the **first** covenant,
  those who are **called** may receive the promised
    eternal inheritance.

GOSPEL   Mark 14:12–16, 22–26

A reading from the holy Gospel according to Mark

On the **first** day of the Feast of **Unleavened** Bread,
  when they **sacrificed** the Passover **lamb**,
  Jesus' disciples said to him,
  "**Where** do you want us to go
  and prepare for you to eat the **Passover?**"
He sent two of his disciples and said to them,
  "**Go** into the city and a **man** will meet you,
  carrying a jar of **water**.
Follow him.
Wherever he **enters**, say to the master of the house,
  'The **Teacher** says, "Where is my **guest** room
  where I may eat the Passover with my **disciples?**"'
Then he will show you a **large** upper room furnished and **ready**.
Make the preparations for us **there**."
The disciples then went **off**, **entered** the city,
  and found it **just** as he had told them;
  and they **prepared** the Passover.

While they were eating,
  he took **bread**, said the **blessing**,
  broke it, **gave** it to them, and said,
  "**Take** it; this is my **body**."

"tabernacle not made by hands" is nothing less than the body of Jesus. While the former sacrifices temporarily cleansed a person from uncleanness, Jesus' sacrifice cleansed the person's interior, removing all guilt. In this sacrifice of the new covenant God opens his arms and embraces us with love. It brings eternal redemption and enables humans to become servants of the living God, putting a person right with God once and for all.

GOSPEL ┃ Jesus' last supper is a Passover meal by which he unites his followers with his Passion and Death for the redemption of the world. The covenant he sealed with his blood—the "blood of the covenant"—alludes to the rite of Exodus 24:4–8. This sacrifice constitutes the new covenant established between God and the new people created by God's initiative. When they drink from the cup, the disciples share in all the benefits of the sacrifice and take their places as members of God's new covenant community. The words of institution celebrate the past (the Exodus rite) and foretell the future fullness in the Kingdom of God (the messianic banquet that recalls the imagery of the prophets, as in Isaiah 25:6). Jesus' actions and words institute the new covenant; they are the self-offering of his Body and Blood in anticipation of his Passion and Death.

Again, keep the four actions distinct.

The line is full of Jesus' love for his disciples (and us), first as he generously offers himself so completely . . .

. . . and then with a hint of sadness as he knows this is his last meal with his friends.

Pause at the end of this line.

The meal ends on a celebratory note; don't swallow "hymn."

Then he took a **cup**, gave **thanks**, and **gave** it to them,
    and they all **drank** from it.
He said to them,
    "This is my **blood** of the **covenant**,
    which will be **shed** for **many**.
Amen, I say to you,
    I shall not drink **again** the fruit of the **vine**
    until the **day** when I drink it **new** in the kingdom of **God**."
Then, after singing a **hymn**,
    they went out to the Mount of Olives.

THE 4 STEPS OF *LECTIO DIVINA* OR PRAYERFUL READING

1. *Lectio:* Read a Scripture passage aloud slowly. Notice what phrase captures your attention and be attentive to its meaning. Silent pause.

2. *Meditatio:* Read the passage aloud slowly again, reflecting on the passage, allowing God to speak to you through it. Silent pause.

3. *Oratio:* Read it aloud slowly a third time, allowing it to be your prayer or response to God's gift of insight to you. Silent pause.

4. *Contemplatio:* Read it aloud slowly a fourth time, now resting in God's word.

We were all condemned, and he who came to be one of us offered himself as a victim for our rescue. We were starving, and he who came to be one of us gave his body to nourish us back to health and strength. We were thirsty, and he poured out his blood to quench our thirst. Our garments were indelibly stained with sin and we washed them in his blood, and they came out white as snow. As we celebrate this mystery, as we are wined and dined at the eucharistic table, we, as one body, grow into the likeness of our Risen Lord, who gave himself for us.

We, whose deserts are less precise and more disconcerting than Sinai, hunger and thirst for values more lasting than bodily sustenance. We hunger for meaning in our lives, for joy in our commitments, for mutual consideration, love, and respect in our families and communities. We thirst for a sense of belonging in a world that paradoxically becomes more fragmented even as it boasts of becoming more connected as a global community. Where our people hunger, Jesus offers to feed us; where there is absence, he offers presence. We search for meaning and Jesus gives us, not bread and wine, but his physical presence, his life, and his Spirit: "the one who feeds on me will have life because of me" (John 6:57). It is what we all long for: unlimited reserves of Jesus' presence. K.S.

TENTH SUNDAY IN ORDINARY TIME

A narrative reading that is mostly dialogue. Understand the different intentions and emotions of each character: Adam, Eve, and God.

Start slowly, reminding the assembly where we are in the story.
God begins by asking questions. What response does God really want from Adam and Eve here? What response do you want from your assembly as you proclaim this?
Show Adam's fear in your voice and face.
God sees no shame in their nakedness.

Proclaim God's lines with the feeling of betrayal.

Adam shifts blame from himself to Eve to God.

Is she being honest, or evading blame? Let your choice come through in the proclamation.

Pause before God turns to the serpent; gather your energy before unleashing your anger upon the serpent.

Keep pace and energy up; make eye contact with the assembly.

Make this sound as nasty as it is!

LECTIONARY #89

READING I   Genesis 3:9–15

A reading from the Book of Genesis

After the man, Adam, had **eaten** of the tree,
    the Lord God **called** to the man and asked him, "Where **are** you?"
He answered, "I **heard** you in the garden;
    but I was **afraid**, because I was **naked**,
    so I **hid** myself."
Then he asked, "**Who** told you that you were naked?
You have **eaten**, then,
    from the **tree** of which I had **forbidden** you to eat!"
The man replied, "The **woman** whom **you** put here with me—
    she gave me fruit from the tree, and so I **ate it**."
The Lord God then asked the **woman**,
    "**Why** did you do such a thing?"
The woman answered, "The **serpent tricked** me into it,
    so I **ate it**."

Then the Lord God said to the serpent:
    "Because you have done this, you shall be **banned**
        from all the animals
        and from **all** the wild creatures;
    on your **belly** shall you **crawl**,
        and **dirt** shall you **eat**
        all the days of your **life**.

READING I   The author presents a profound understanding of the Creator's chosen way of relating to his creatures: he does not remain aloof, but strolls in the garden and personally speaks with the humans. Even after their sin God does not leave man and woman alone, but approaches them. The consciousness of their nudity betrays the couple's guilt, and they pretend to escape condemnation by shifting blame. Adam blames Eve, who blames the serpent, who provided incentive for the disobedience. God will punish all three, taking no account of their blame

shifting, and the punishment will be twofold for the humans: the weariness of existence and the perennial battle with the seductive influence of the evil one. Human nature will have to await the coming of Christ who, by the gift of the Holy Spirit, will restore human integrity.

Each of the three punishments—for snake, woman, and man—has a double result: one affecting the individual and the other affecting a basic relationship. The humans' responses can be seen as a consequence of achieving autonomy; the man is afraid, insecure, and ashamed; he tries to

justify himself and deflect the blame onto God for giving him the woman and onto the woman for offering him the fruit. Thus they are alienated from each other. Yet the man admits having eaten. The woman also deflects the responsibility when she lays the blame on the trickery of the serpent, the source of temptation. She too admits having eaten. God proceeds to the sentencing, appropriate to their primary roles in the culture where this text was born, the roles of rank among the animals, female roles of wife and mother, male roles of tiller of the soil and provider of food. The sen-

enmity = EN-mih-tee (mutual hatred)

I will put **enmity** between **you** and the **woman**,
     and between **your** offspring and **hers**;
he will **strike** at your **head**,
     while **you** strike at his **heel**."

Pause longer than usual before the closing dialogue to allow the "storm" to subside and God to disappear from the scene.

For meditation and context:

___

RESPONSORIAL PSALM   Psalm 130:1–2, 3–4, 5–6, 7–8 (7bc)

R. With the Lord there is mercy, and fullness of redemption.

Out of the depths I cry to you, O LORD;
     LORD, hear my voice!
Let your ears be attentive
     to my voice in supplication.

If you, O LORD, mark iniquities,
     LORD, who can stand?
But with you is forgiveness,
     that you may be revered.

I trust in the LORD;
     my soul trusts in his word.
More than sentinels wait for the dawn,
     let Israel wait for the LORD.

For with the LORD is kindness
     and with him is plenteous redemption;
and he will redeem Israel
     from all their iniquities.

TO KEEP IN MIND

Exhortatory texts make an urgent appeal to listeners. They may encourage, warn, or challenge, and often include a call to action. You must convey the urgency and passion behind the words.

An exhortatory reading. Paul encourages us to be faithful to our commitment to please God. Speak this same encouragement directly to your assembly. Take your intention from the reading—Be courageous!—and keep this in the forefront in your mind as you proclaim.
Corinthians = kohr-IN-thee-uhnz
Good news! Keep your energy up throughout.

"I believed . . . spoke" is a quote from what is written. Drop your voice, slow down, and pause slightly before and after the quote.
Raise your voice again. With joy!
Pause at the end of this line.
Make eye contact with your assembly through this line. Make sure they know that this is all for them.
God's bountiful grace gives greater glory and thanksgiving to God!
Resolutely! Here is the key teaching in this reading. How can anyone be discouraged knowing how generous God is?
Be dismissive of this unimportant "outer self"

READING II   2 Corinthians 4:13—5:1

A reading from the second Letter of Saint Paul to the Corinthians

Brothers and sisters:
Since we have the **same** spirit of faith,
     according to what is written, *I **believed**, therefore I **spoke**,*
     we **too** believe and therefore we **speak**,
     knowing that the one who raised the LORD Jesus
     will raise us **also** with Jesus
     and place us **with** you in his presence.
Everything indeed is **for** you,
     so that the grace bestowed in **abundance** on more and
          more people
     may cause the thanksgiving to **overflow** for the glory of God.
Therefore, we are not **discouraged**;
     rather, although our outer self is **wasting** away,
     our **inner** self is being **renewed** day by **day**.

___

tence touches marriage and sexuality; birth and death; work and production; human and nonhuman; human and God. Every relationship has been disrupted. Other outcomes include humiliation, domination, and subordination; conflict, suffering, and struggle—all the fruit of sin. The harmony of the garden has been ruptured and death encroaches on life.

READING II In the verses before this reading, Paul has been speaking about the adversities he experiences in his ministry. He represents the

person who lives between Adam and Christ. Because he identifies his suffering so closely with that of Jesus, he argues that it is for the sake of the Corinthian community he founded and for the sake of his mission. The line "I believed, therefore I spoke," quotes Psalm 116:10 (although translated differently); it links preaching or speaking with the proclamation of faith in the midst of suffering. Paul is forthright about his fragility. The contrast between his outer nature (his visible body) and inner nature (the faith and commitment to Christ) point to the ulti-

mate reality: in the long run, what is eternal weighs more than physical existence.

Earlier Paul had said that Jesus' affliction and Death is constantly at work in us (2 Corinthians 4:10–11), and now he writes of the life-giving effect of the risen Jesus on us and on the Church. With the phrase "and place us with you in his presence," Paul imagines God presenting him and the Corinthian community to Jesus. In a series of contrasts Paul explains the extent of his faith in life, which is not only already present and revealing itself, but is eternal. He writes: "what is unseen is eternal." Ever the

For this momentary **light** affliction
    is producing for us an **eternal** weight of glory beyond **all**
        comparison,
    as we look not to what is **seen** but to what is **unseen**;
    for what is seen is **transitory**, but what is unseen is **eternal**.
For we know that if our **earthly** dwelling, a **tent**,
    should be destroyed,
    we have a **building** from God,
    a dwelling **not** made with hands, **eternal** in heaven.

GOSPEL   Mark 3:20–35

A reading from the holy Gospel according to Mark

Jesus came **home** with his disciples.
Again the crowd gathered,
    making it **impossible** for them even to eat.
When his relatives **heard** of this they set out to **seize him**,
    for they said, "He is out of his **mind**."
The **scribes** who had come from Jerusalem said,
    "He is possessed by **Beelzebul**,"
    and "By the prince of **demons** he drives out **demons**."

Summoning them, he began to speak to them in **parables**,
    "How can **Satan** drive out **Satan**?
If a kingdom is divided against **itself**,
    that kingdom cannot **stand**.
And if a house is **divided** against itself,
    that house will not be able to **stand**.
And if Satan has **risen up** against himself
    and is divided, he **cannot** stand;
    that is the **end** of him.
But **no one** can enter a strong man's house to **plunder** his property
    unless he **first** ties up the strong man.
Then he can plunder the house.

Margin notes

Contrast the insignificance of our current troubles with the glory that they produce.

Stress this final comparison between an easily destroyed tent and a divinely constructed building.

Smile with your voice, eyes, and face!

A narrative reading with two stories, both good news!

Begin calmly, as if this will be a story of welcome and rest. Don't lose "came home."
Quickly pick up your pace and energy; convey the confusion and cacophony of voices—the crowds, his relatives, the scribes.
Not with anger but concern.

Beelzebul = bee-EL-zeh-buhl

Pause at the end of this line.

With wonder and awe as you describe the surprising growth of this "smallest" to "largest."
"Think about it!"

Slowly; make sure the point is understood.
The only one who can conquer a strong person is an even stronger person. Jesus' actions prove that the Holy Spirit is much stronger than Satan.

Pause at the end of this line.

Bottom commentary

teacher, Paul makes his point vivid and concrete by contrasting heavenly existence with fragile, mortal existence, using the imagery of the "earthly dwelling" and "a dwelling not made with hands."

 GOSPEL In this Gospel members of Jesus' family think he is out of his mind and religious authorities accuse him of being possessed by the devil. This is not the first time Mark reports that Jesus meets rejection (see Mark 2:7, 16, 18, 24); there is growing hostility to him because he does not conform to what people expect of

him and his disciples. This represents a closed attitude toward the Good News embodied by Jesus. Resistance to his person is designed to discredit him and anyone who identifies with him—which says a lot about the community that Mark is evangelizing and leading to maturity.

The only argument that the scribes have against Jesus is their own authority, a typical attitude of someone who feels threatened. The family wants to protect him, but in reality what is important for them is what the people might be saying about them. Jesus' argument to the scribes

consists of showing them the absurdity of their reasoning. Jesus uses the occasion of his family's attempt at intervention to redefine the real family of God. He invites his hearers to become a part of that family, the basis of which is an intimate friendship with God and obedience to his will.

The Beelzebul controversy is framed by two halves of the family's visit. Their failure to accept him is akin to the scribes' hostility. As the story progresses Jesus becomes increasingly more isolated as he moves steadily closer to home and one group after another deserts him. The pres-

"Listen up!"

How does Jesus feel about these? They are lost because they don't believe that the Holy Spirit is stronger than sin and Satan; they can't accept forgiveness.

Pause a bit longer than usual before the second story.

The crowd is so large his relatives can't even get into the house.

Urgently.

Look directly into the assembly.

Good news! We are as close to Jesus as his own flesh and blood relatives.

> TO KEEP IN MIND
> Smile when you share good news in a reading. Nonverbal cues like a smile help your assembly better understand your reading.

Amen, I say to you,
  all sins and **all** blasphemies that people utter will be **forgiven**
    them.
But whoever blasphemes against the **Holy Spirit**
  will **never** have forgiveness,
  but is guilty of an **everlasting** sin."
For they had said, "He has an unclean spirit."

His **mother** and his **brothers** arrived.
Standing **outside** they sent word to him and **called him**.
A crowd seated around him told him,
  "Your mother and your brothers and your sisters
  are outside **asking** for you."
But he said to them in reply,
  "**Who** are my mother and my brothers?"
And looking around at those seated in the circle he said,
  "**Here** are my mother and my brothers.
For whoever does the **will of** God
  is my **brother** and **sister** and **mother**."

ent controversy demonstrates the intense hostility from the religious officials (see also 1:22; 2:6), who are "from Jerusalem," a clear indicator of the distinction between Galilee and Jerusalem. (Jerusalem will be the seat of hostility and place of execution.)

The matter in question is Jesus' authority; and the scribes accuse him of using demonic power to cast out demons. Jesus replies in parables based on one principle: a power that battles against itself is bound to collapse. By implication, Satan's kingdom is still operative, so Jesus' power must have another source. In the saying,

"No one can enter a strong man's house to plunder his property unless he first ties up the strong man," Satan is the strong home owner who has been bound and whose property is being plundered by Jesus, whose exorcisms demonstrate the overthrow of Satan's power. The saying about the forgiveness of sins reverts to the issue of Jesus' authority: all sins are forgivable, except blasphemy against the Holy Spirit. Blasphemy against the Holy Spirit is a denial of Jesus' power in his exorcisms, so the implication is that Jesus expels demons by the power of the Holy Spirit (as we see

also in 1:12–13). Refusal to accept this is the unforgivable sin. To the news of the arrival of his family, Jesus responds by showing that not family ties but doing God's will is decisive in the Kingdom. K.S.

ELEVENTH SUNDAY IN ORDINARY TIME

LECTIONARY #92

READING I   Ezekiel 17:22–24

A reading from the Book of the Prophet Ezekiel

Thus says the LORD God:
  I, **too**, will take from the **crest** of the cedar,
    from its **topmost** branches tear off a **tender** shoot,
  and **plant** it on a **high** and **lofty** mountain;
    on the mountain heights of **Israel** I will plant it.
  It shall put forth **branches** and bear **fruit**,
    and become a **majestic** cedar.
  Birds of **every** kind shall **dwell** beneath it,
    every winged thing in the **shade** of its boughs.
  And **all** the trees of the field shall **know**
    that **I**, the **Lord**,
  bring **low** the **high** tree,
    lift **high** the **lowly** tree,
  wither up the **green** tree,
    and make the **withered** tree **bloom**.
  As I, the LORD, have **spoken**, so **will I do**.

An exhortatory reading. Linger over the beautiful imagery of God caring for us as a gardener cares for trees. Though exhortatory, the reading might be best proclaimed with a tender intensity rather than exuberance.

Ezekiel = ee-ZEE-kee-uhl
Imagine speaking this promise to someone you know who is struggling. How would you convey such great love and care in your face and voice?
Gently.
Grandly. See this stately tree rise before you!

Be expansive in your proclamation. The tree is full of life!

Take your time; don't run these powerful images together.

Pause at the end of this line.
With firm conviction.

TO KEEP IN MIND
Use inflection (the high or low pitch of your voice) to convey attitude and feeling. High pitch expresses intensity and excitement; low pitch expresses sadness, contrition, or solemnity.

READING I The Lord will break off a sprig from the top of the cedar and plant it on the high mountain of Israel, Mount Zion. This shoot will branch out, bear fruit, and grow into a towering cedar. The allegory addresses the political situation in the Ezekiel's own time: the lofty cedar is the cowardly king Zedekiah, and the little sprig planted on the mountain is his nephew, Jehoiachin, now in exile in Babylon. God will accomplish what earthly kings attempted, and Israel will thrive under an honest ruler from the line of David. If, in the people's eyes, Israel's destruction frustrated God's power, her restoration will demonstrate God's universal sovereignty. So great will be this tree that "birds of every kind" will nest in its branches. When the prophet announces that "all the trees of the field shall know that I, the Lord, bring low the high tree, lift high the lowly tree," he asserts God's design that Israel and every nation will acknowledge God's sovereignty. This idyllic ending to the allegory, unexpected among oracles of punishment, fits Ezekiel's pattern: God will first destroy and then restore, in order for his sovereignty to be acknowledged.

READING II Paul demonstrates how the consciousness of the last things can affect the way we live in the present. He expresses the tension between present and future with the metaphor of temporary residence in the land. We are like migrants living far from our home, who is the Lord, in whom we believe but have not yet seen. The union with Christ, the final restoration of humans according to Christ's plan, will take place at the end of life as we know it. We are exiles, yet confident that our hope will be fulfilled. Our lives become pleasing to God when we follow

For meditation and context:

TO KEEP IN MIND
Be careful not to "swallow" words by mumbling. Articulate carefully so that every word is clearly heard, especially at the end of lines.

RESPONSORIAL PSALM   Psalm 92:2–3, 13–14, 15–16 (2a)

R. Lord, it is good to give thanks to you.

It is good to give thanks to the LORD,
 to sing praise to your name, Most High,
to proclaim your kindness at dawn
 and your faithfulness throughout
  the night.

The just one shall flourish like the palm tree,
 like a cedar of Lebanon shall he grow.
They that are planted in the house of
  the LORD
 shall flourish in the courts of our God.

They shall bear fruit even in old age;
 vigorous and sturdy shall they be,
declaring how just is the LORD,
 my rock, in whom there is no wrong.

An exhortatory reading. Paul encourages us to be faithful to our commitment to please God. Speak this same encouragement directly to your assembly. Take your intention from the reading—Be courageous!—and keep this in the forefront in your mind as you proclaim.

Corinthians = kohr-IN-thee-uhnz

Start boldly and with energy!

Good news! Smile with your voice, eyes, and face!

Paul repeats the phrase. Proclaim it slowly and with intense conviction.

Remain firm in your conviction that we can face judgement with courage, because we always work to please God.

READING II   2 Corinthians 5:6–10

A reading from the second Letter of Saint Paul to the Corinthians

Brothers and sisters:
We are **always** courageous,
 although we know that while we are at home in the **body**
 we are **away** from the LORD,
 for we walk by **faith**, not by **sight**.
Yet we **are** courageous,
 and we would rather **leave** the body and go **home** to the LORD.
Therefore, we aspire to **please** him,
 whether we are at **home** or **away**.
For we must **all** appear before the judgment seat of Christ,
 so that each may receive **recompense**,
 according to what he did in the **body**, whether **good** or **evil**.

---

the path Christ opened for us. At death we will be faced with the shallowness or depth of our actions and commitments in life.

 GOSPEL This parable stresses the power of the seed to grow in and of itself, mysteriously producing the blade, ear, and finally the ripe grain. Jesus initiates the reign of God by sowing the Word; it sprouts and develops discretely yet assuredly until the harvest at the Last Judgment. The right attitude is to let God act on the seed so that it remains true to itself and its purpose. God's reign begins

with something very small that grows of its own inner strength into something very big and provides a nesting place for birds, an image for the universality of God's reign (a reference to the First Reading). The listeners are invited to apply this parable to their own life situations.

The sower prepares the field, removes rocks, and uproots brush. He sows grain in the field and then gets busy with other chores. After some weeks the observer may calculate that two-thirds of the seed has sprouted. She may observe the patches of weeds and the places where a rainstorm

washed away the seed. As the crop matures, the farmer may enjoy the sight of the whole field rippling in the breeze, reflecting the color spectrum from dusty brown to fresh green to lustrous gold. The late July rains threaten the crop with mildew or make the grains germinate on the stalk. That's the farmer's perspective. But let us consider another angle. If a grain of wheat could speak for herself, how might she recount the adventure of her falling, dying, sprouting, growth, and maturation? A single grain that becomes a blade never enjoys the full view of the sunlit and

A narrative reading. Resist the urge to make these parables sound mysterious. Rather, Mark notes that Jesus speaks in parables so the crowds can understand. He uses parables to make the mysterious accessible.

Pause briefly to set up the parable.

Keep energy and movement in these phrases reflecting the growth of the seed.

Slowly; this is the point of the parable.

Pick up your pace again.

Pause at the end of this line.

With wonder and awe as you describe the surprising growth of this "smallest" to "largest."

Expansively.

Pause at the end of this line.

"There's more than can be told here."

Keep your voice up through the end; don't swallow "in private."

> **TO KEEP IN MIND**
> Always pause at the end of the reading, before you proclaim the closing dialogue ("The Word of the Lord" or "The Gospel of the Lord").

GOSPEL   Mark 4:26–34

A reading from the holy Gospel according to Mark

Jesus said to the crowds:
  "**This** is how it is with the **kingdom** of **God**;
    it is as if a man were to scatter **seed** on the land
    and would **sleep** and **rise night** and **day**
    and through it **all** the seed would **sprout** and **grow**,
    he knows not **how**.
Of its own **accord** the land yields **fruit**,
    first the **blade**, then the **ear**, then the full **grain** in the ear.
And when the grain is **ripe**, he wields the **sickle** at once,
    for the **harvest** has come."

He said,
  "To **what** shall we compare the **kingdom** of **God**,
    or what **parable** can we use for it?
It is like a **mustard** seed that, when it is **sown** in the ground,
    is the **smallest** of all the seeds on the earth.
But once it is **sown**, it **springs** up and becomes the **largest**
      of plants
    and puts forth **large branches**,
    so that the **birds** of the sky can dwell in its shade."
With **many** such parables
    he spoke the word to them as they were able to **understand** it.
Without parables he did not **speak** to them,
    but to his own **disciples** he explained **everything** in **private**.

breeze-swept field. She sends down tenuous root tentacles to absorb the nutrients and moisture of the shared soil. The blade of wheat raises head and hands to catch the light, and may suffer the cramp of neighboring blades growing too close, too fast, too tall. And the weeds and thistles growing in her midst sap her nourishment. A long, dry spell may parch her, or the blight or mildew may threaten her flower and fruit. Finally, she ripens into gold. Yet there is fool's gold in our midst—stalks with little or no grain. But mostly there is the harvest of a generous growing season.

We do not see God's reign from a distance. We, the grains, blades, stalks, and ears of grain, are in the thick of it. From where we are planted we may see just other stalks and blades blocking the view. We consider the weeds and stones from a personal perspective. Or our critical eye may compare our own growth with that of the neighbors. Does the harvest amount to what I alone bear and call my own? Or is it what the farmer God may reap from the whole field?

God enjoys the view from above while I, the grain of wheat, am falling to the ground and dying, and, oh, how I desire my fair share of nutrients, water, and sunlight so that my golden color may be rich and admired! If I could look at the field from God's vantage point, I would see that all the grains are falling and dying, and some at great personal expense, for dying is never easy, for me nor for anyone else. K.S.

THE NATIVITY OF ST. JOHN THE BAPTIST: VIGIL

LECTIONARY #586

A narrative reading. All the emotions are heightened and the stakes are high here, as in an exhortatory reading.

Jeremiah = jer-uh-MĪ-uh
Josiah = joh-SĪ-uh

God has great love for Jeremiah; let that come through in your proclamation.

Although "Ah" is a tiny word, fill it with all Jeremiah's fear and reluctance.

Imagine encouraging a child or a friend afraid of a challenge.

Speak to assure and calm.

Emphasize "I am with you."

Pause at the end of this line.

What does Jeremiah feel as he experiences this? Wonder, fear, confusion?

God gives Jeremiah a preview of his mission: though "only a boy"; he will prophesy to nations and kings in chaotic, dangerous times.

READING I   Jeremiah 1:4–10

A reading from the Book of the Prophet Jeremiah

In the days of King Josiah, the word of the
     Lord came to me, saying:
Before I **formed** you in the **womb** I **knew** you,
     before you were **born** I **dedicated** you,
     a **prophet** to the **nations** I **appointed** you.

"Lord God!" I said,
     "I know not how to **speak**; I am too **young**."
But the Lord answered me,
     Say **not**, "I am too young."
To **whomever** I send you, you shall **go**;
     whatever I **command** you, you shall **speak**.
Have no **fear** before them,
     because I am **with** you to **deliver** you, says the Lord.

Then the Lord extended his **hand** and touched my **mouth**,
     saying,
See, I place my **words** in your **mouth**!
     This day I set you
     over **nations** and over **kingdoms**,
to root **up** and to tear **down**,
     to **destroy** and to **demolish**,
     to **build** and to **plant**.

READING I   John the Baptist, like Jeremiah, was destined to become a prophet before his birth. Jeremiah's call began and remained under the impetus of God's Word. Even before he was born he had been chosen to be the bearer of this Word. God rejected the objections that the young prophet proposed and commissioned him to "root up and to tear down, to destroy and to demolish, to build and to plant"—terms that outline the prophet's basic message and task, and that reappear throughout his book. God appoints him to represent the divine government in negative and positive ways. The verbs for the Lord's constructive work—"to build and to plant"—do not vary, but a more extensive vocabulary describes the task of destruction, with the result that God's work in Jeremiah is often remembered as negative: a prophet of darkness and disaster. This call narrative indicates that impending doom may have a large share in his proclamation, but it also shows that judgment is never the last word in God's dealings with Israel. This prophet was sent to outline God's intention to build and plant new nations and a new people of God—to sow the seed of God's reign. We are invited to look for hope and renewal as well as face the threat of sadness and destruction.

READING II   The "Spirit of Christ" moved the prophets to investigate and prophesy the coming salvation, and impelled the Apostles to preach the fulfillment of salvation that comes with Christ's suffering and glory. The Christian life embodies a paradox. We do not yet possess what is ours by faith. We are acquainted with trials, although we have

For meditation and context:

TO KEEP IN MIND

Pause in order to break up separate thoughts, set apart significant statements, or indicate major shifts. Never pause in the middle of a single thought. Your primary guide for pauses is punctuation.

A didactic reading. Peter speaks directly to your assembly, who has not seen Christ but loves and believes in him. Encourage them with this good news!

Let that "indescribable and glorious joy" show in your voice, eyes, and face!

A complex sentence. The idea expressed is that the prophets of old were inspired by the Spirit of Christ to testify about him. Set the subordinate clauses apart by pausing briefly after "salvation," "yours," "it," "indicated," and "destined for Christ."

RESPONSORIAL PSALM   Psalm 71:1–2, 3–4, 5–6, 15, 17 (6b)

R. Since my mother's womb, you have been my strength.

In you, O LORD, I take refuge;
    let me never be put to shame.
In your justice rescue me, and deliver me;
    incline your ear to me, and save me.

Be my rock of refuge,
    a stronghold to give me safety,
For you are my rock and my fortress.
    O my God, rescue me from the hand of
    the wicked.

For you are my hope, O LORD;
    my trust, O God, from my youth.
On you I depend from birth;
    from my mother's womb you are
    my strength.

My mouth shall declare your justice,
    day by day your salvation.
O God, you have taught me from my youth,
    and till the present I proclaim your
    wondrous deeds.

READING II   1 Peter 1:8–12

A reading from the first Letter of Saint Peter

Beloved:
Although you have not **seen** Jesus Christ you **love** him;
    even though you do **not see** him now
        yet **believe** in him,
    you rejoice with an **indescribable** and **glorious** joy,
    as you attain the **goal** of your faith, the **salvation**
        of your souls.

Concerning this salvation,
    prophets who prophesied about the **grace** that was to be yours
    searched and **investigated** it,
        investigating the **time** and **circumstances**
        that the Spirit of Christ **within** them indicated
        when he **testified** in advance
        to the sufferings **destined** for Christ
        and the glories to **follow** them.

---

every reason to rejoice for our salvation, purchased by Christ, and in which we are assured of fully participating. The virtue of charity already in the present unites believers to Christ. Faith is not simply an inner, subjective conviction; it enables us in the present to possess things yet unseen; faith places us in a true friendship with God even though we do not see him now. In a similar manner, hope is more than just waiting for what might happen. The author writes, "you attain the goal of your faith, the salvation of your souls." The image is from the sports field. To "attain the goal" or win the

prize evokes what runners in the stadium vie for—to reach the finish line. Believers are marathon runners who keep the end of the race in their line of vision, so victory will be theirs. Even as they exert themselves to the utmost, "an indescribable and glorious joy" transfigures them.

GOSPEL   In some ways, this reading seems like a touching family story. By telling us that both Elizabeth and Zechariah belonged to priestly families, however, Luke situates the Gospel in salvation history, and explains further: "Both

were righteous in the eyes of God, observing all the commandments and ordinances of the Lord blamelessly." Fertility was a sign of divine blessing, but "they had no child." What is more foreboding, they did not look forward to having one "because Elizabeth was barren and both were advanced in years." Elizabeth's situation echoes that of other famous biblical mothers: Sarah, Rebekah, Rachel, the nameless wife of Manoah, mother of Samson (Judges 13), and Hannah (the mother of Samuel).

The annunciation of the Baptist's birth took place in the Jerusalem Temple, while

Refocus your attention on the assembly. The good news has been brought to you!

Pause at the end of this line.

Slowly. Imagine—even angels long to receive the good news we have heard!

It was **revealed** to them that they were serving
    not **themselves** but **you**
with regard to the things that have now been
    announced to you
by those who preached the **Good** News to you
through the Holy **Spirit** sent from heaven,
things into which **angels longed** to look.

GOSPEL   Luke 1:5–17

A reading from the holy Gospel according to Luke

A narrative reading in which God turns even an impossible situation like an old, barren couple into a life-giving moment.

Herod = HAYR-uhd
Judea = joo-DEE-uh
Zechariah = zek-uh-RĪ-uh
Abijah = uh-BĪ-juh
Aaron = AYR-uhn

Elizabeth also has inherited priestly qualities.

Let your tone express how you feel about such an upright couple.

Pause at the end of this line.

Drop your voice on this parenthetical phrase.

Raise your intensity with this unexpected appearance.

Let his fear come through in your voice.

In the days of **Herod**, King of Judea,
    there was a priest named **Zechariah**
    of the **priestly** division of Abijah;
    his **wife** was from the daughters of **Aaron**,
    and her name was **Elizabeth**.
Both were **righteous** in the eyes of God,
    observing **all** the commandments
    and ordinances of the LORD **blamelessly**.
But they had no **child**, because Elizabeth was **barren**
    and both were **advanced** in years.
Once when he was serving
    as priest in his division's turn before **God**,
    according to the practice of the priestly service,
    he was chosen by lot
    to enter the **sanctuary** of the LORD to burn incense.
Then, when the whole assembly of the people
    was **praying** outside
    at the hour of the incense offering,
    the **angel** of the LORD **appeared** to him,
    standing at the right of the altar of incense.
Zechariah was **troubled** by what he saw,
    and **fear** came upon him.

Zechariah was serving as priest in the sanctuary. During the daily incense offering the people would gather for prayer and wait in the courtyard while the priest entered the sanctuary and performed the prescribed ritual. It was then that the angel of the Lord appeared to him and Zechariah was troubled. The angel calmed him with the usual phrase "Do not be afraid" (as in Genesis 15:1; Joshua 1:9; Daniel 10:12, 19; Luke 1:30; 2:10), and told him, "your prayer has been heard. Your wife Elizabeth will bear you a son." Was this the answer to Zechariah's personal intention?

He was a priest, offering the evening sacrifice that awaits the coming of the Messiah, and the angel's announcement was God's answer to the prayer of "the whole assembly of the people" that Zechariah was raising toward heaven along with the incense he burned on the altar. The angel was Gabriel (1:19), who had explained to Daniel the events of the end-time and the coming of the Messiah (Daniel 8:16–26). This birth of a child would be joyful news for all God's people in the Temple plaza waiting for Zechariah to give the final blessing. The promised child would not belong to his parents; his father would not choose his name. The child would bear the name God indicated: John, a name that means "The Lord has shown favor," indicating John's role in salvation history. "Great in the sight of the Lord . . . filled with the Holy Spirit even from his mother's womb," he, like Samson and Samuel, would be a Nazirite, set apart for the Lord's service, and thus would abstain from wine and

How would the angel sound relating this happy news?

His birth will bring happiness to the couple and to their community.

This birth is not just to bless his parents but the whole nation!

Elijah = ee-Lī-juh

Pause a little longer than usual before "The Word of the Lord" to let the scene settle.

> TO KEEP IN MIND
> In a narrative, find an emotion or point of view for each character, keeping in mind that these might change during the reading.

But the angel said to him, "Do not be **afraid**, Zechariah,
    because your prayer has been **heard**.
Your wife Elizabeth will bear you a **son**,
    and you shall name him **John**.
And you will have **joy** and **gladness**,
    and many will **rejoice** at his birth,
    for he will be **great** in the sight of the Lord.
John will drink neither **wine** nor strong **drink**.
He will be **filled** with the Holy **Spirit**
    even from his mother's womb,
    and he will turn **many** of the children of Israel
    to the Lord their God.
He will go before him in the **spirit** and **power** of Elijah
      to turn their **hearts** toward their **children** and
the **disobedient** to the understanding
     of the **righteous**,
    to **prepare** a people **fit** for the Lord."

strong drink. "He will go before him in the spirit and power of Elijah."

John, cast in the role of Elijah, is the messenger sent before "the great and terrible day" of the Lord comes" (Malachi 3:1–2,23). The angel specified the promised child's mission: "He will turn many of the children of Israel to the Lord their God," thus embodying the idea of the perfect priest (Malachi 2:6); his mission is akin to that of the great prophet and defined in the same terms. He will preach conversion "to prepare a people fit for the Lord." While Zechariah, like an Old Testament figure, lis-tened to all this in the Temple sanctuary, the people were kept waiting for him to come and give the final blessing, a blessing that the mute priest would be unable to speak, It would be postponed until the end of the Gospel, when Jesus, resurrected and ascending into heaven, would give his blessing to his Apostles for the benefit of the whole Church. In the end it is Jesus, the long-awaited Messiah ushered in by his forerunner, the Baptist, who will be the blessing for all humankind. K.S.

THE NATIVITY OF ST. JOHN THE BAPTIST: DAY

An exhortatory reading. Encourage your assembly to remain faithful to the call they received from God, even when they might feel they are laboring in vain.

Isaiah = ī-ZAY-uh

Call into the distance! Make eye contact with those farthest from you in the assembly and raise your energy to reach them.

Like Isaiah, you have been called to bring good news to your assembly today.

Note the thought rhyme in these lines: God called you to proclaim a "piercing" word, but protects you from harm.

Recall a time when you felt like all your efforts were futile, and proclaim with that feeling.

Now show your confidence in God: It's God's work you're doing, and God will see to its effectiveness.

"For now" introduces something greater. Begin to raise your intensity.

These are tender images, like lost children being restored to their families.

Your glory comes from the work you've been commissioned to do.

Drop your intensity on these lines and dismiss the "smallness" of this work.

LECTIONARY #587

READING I   Isaiah 49:1–6

A reading from the Book of the Prophet Isaiah

Hear me, **O** coastlands,
   listen, O **distant** peoples.
The LORD called me from birth,
   from my mother's **womb** he gave me my **name**.
He made of me a **sharp-edged** sword
   and **concealed** me in the shadow of his arm.
He made me a **polished** arrow,
   in his **quiver** he hid me.
You are my servant, he said to me,
   Israel, through whom I show my **glory**.

Though I thought I had toiled in **vain**,
   and for **nothing**, **uselessly**, spent my strength,
yet my **reward** is with the LORD,
   my **recompense** is with my God.
For **now** the LORD has **spoken**
   who formed me as his servant from the womb,
that Jacob may be brought back to him
   and Israel **gathered** to him;
and I am made **glorious** in the sight of the LORD,
   and my **God** is now my **strength**!

READING I | In this second of the four "servant of the Lord" oracles in Isaiah, the speaker describes how the Lord called him from the womb, as Jeremiah was called. Language used to describe God's relationship to Israel is applied to the individual servant who, in this section of Isaiah, can be identified with the people of Israel. Up to this point, God has called and empowered the servant—"hidden" (protected) and given him effective speech. Despite that commission, this "servant" feels that he has labored in vain. In the face of this discouragement, God clarifies his role and his identity: "It is too little, he says, for you to be my servant, . . . I will make you a light to the nations, that my salvation may reach to the ends of the earth."

READING II | This reading is part of one of Paul's several speeches to Jews in which he proclaims that the way of Jesus Christ is the logical development of pharisaic Judaism; Jesus, the Savior is the descendant of King David. John the Baptist has a special role in God's plan of salvation—he ushers in the era of the Messiah, and the promised kingdom is realized within a repentant Israel. John vehemently denies that he is the Messiah; when speaking of his relationship to Jesus, he states that he is not even worthy to be his servant, to "unfasten the sandals of his feet."

It is too **little**, he says, for you to be my **servant**,
　to raise up the tribes of **Jacob**,
　　and restore the survivors of **Israel**;
I will make you **a light** to the **nations**,
　that my **salvation** may reach to the **ends** of the **earth**.

Here is the climax. Speak these lines slowly and with great joy: you and your community have been chosen to bring light to the whole world!

For meditation and context:

TO KEEP IN MIND

A *didactic* text makes a point or teaches something. Help your assembly to follow the argument and understand what's being taught.

RESPONSORIAL PSALM   Psalm 139:1 – 3, 13 – 14, 14 – 15, (14a)

R. I praise you for I am wonderfully made.

O LORD you have probed me and you
　　know me;
　you know when I sit and when I stand;
　you understand my thoughts from afar.
My journeys and my rest you scrutinize,
　with all my ways you are familiar.

Truly you have formed my inmost being;
　you knit me in my mother's womb.
I give you thanks that I am fearfully,
　　wonderfully made;
　wonderful are your works.

My soul also you knew full well;
　nor was my frame unknown to you
when I was made in secret,
　when I was fashioned in the depths
　　of the earth.

READING II   Acts 13:22–26

A reading from the Acts of the Apostles

In those days, **Paul** said:
"God raised up **David** as king;
　of **him** God testified,
　I have found David, son of Jesse,
　　*a man after my **own** heart;*
　*he will carry out my **every** wish.*

From this man's **descendants** God, according to his **promise**,
　has brought to Israel a **savior**, Jesus.
John **heralded** his coming by proclaiming a **baptism**
　of **repentance**
　to **all** the people of Israel;
　and as John was **completing** his course, he would say,
'**What** do you suppose that I am? **I am not he**.

A didactic reading. Proclaim with the love teachers have for their students or parents have for their children.

Keep your pace up.

Proclaim with God's voice of pleased satisfaction.

Slow down on these lines referring to John. This is why the reading was chosen for today's celebration.

Paul is quoting John. Make sure it doesn't sound like he's referring to himself.

GOSPEL   At John's birth, Elizabeth's neighbors rejoice with her over God's great mercy in granting the child, and on the eighth day, the child is named and incorporated into the people of Israel by the sign of the covenant—circumcision—etched on his body (Genesis 17:1–12). Luke narrates the Baptist's infancy alongside that of Jesus, and the parallel texts are rich in theology. The birth of John to Elizabeth is a prelude to the Messiah's birth; one child announces the presence of another. The boy's name, John, "the Lord has shown favor," foreshadows another name, that of Jesus, "the Lord saves." Elizabeth's maternity prepares for the maternity of the Mother of God. John's mission anticipates and inaugurates Jesus' mission. It is not that the first is characterized by penance and the second by messianic joy. Luke presents a single purpose in two phases, according to God's plan of salvation—two chapters of the same history. Just as early morning darkness makes way for dawn, the precursor opens the path for the Messiah's coming. It is necessary for the darkness to diminish so the day may increase.

Ever since the prophecy of the last of the prophets, Malachi, (some four hundred years) the prophets had been speechless. Nine months before the events of this reading, an angel made his announcement to the priest Zechariah in the Temple, and the incredulous man reasoned with the angel, "How shall I know this? For I am an old

Behold, one is coming **after** me;
   I am not **worthy** to unfasten the sandals of his feet.
      '"My **brothers**, **sons** of the family of Abraham,
   and those **others** among you who **are God-fearing**,
   to **us** this word of salvation has been **sent**."

GOSPEL   Luke 1:57–66, 80

A reading from the holy Gospel according to Luke

When the time arrived for **Elizabeth** to have her **child**
   she gave birth to a **son**.
Her neighbors and relatives heard
   that the LORD had shown his great **mercy** toward her,
   and they **rejoiced** with her.
When they came on the eighth day to **circumcise**
      the child,
   they were going to call him **Zechariah** after his **father**,
   but his **mother** said in reply,
   "**No**. He will be called **John**."
But they answered her,
   "There is **no** one among your relatives
      who has this **name**."
So they made **signs**, asking his **father** what he wished him
      to be called.
He asked for a tablet and wrote, "**John** is his **name**,"
   and **all** were **amazed**.
Immediately his mouth was **opened**, his tongue **freed**,
   and he spoke **blessing** God.

Pause to indicate the end of the quote.

Look directly at the assembly. This message of good news is for us!

A narrative reading. There are three main characters here: Elizabeth, Zechariah, and the neighbors (whom you might imagine as a single, gossipy person). Their emotions and reactions to these events could not be more different, so let your choices for each come through.

A joyous event! Let that happiness shine through.

Zechariah = zek-uh-RĪ-uh

With conviction! Elizabeth is going against the custom of the community.
Express their surprise.

Slow on the phrase, "John is his name."
This break with convention is shocking, especially for a priest of the community.
Let your proclamation ring with his excitement.

---

man, and my wife is advanced in years" (Luke 1:18). The event described in today's story, around the circumcision and naming of the newborn baby, fascinates the parents and instills the fear of God in the neighborhood—two typical reactions before mystery. Zechariah's tongue was tied until he wrote the child's God-given name, "John," on the tablet. Then his silence was broken and (not included in this reading) Zechariah intoned the canticle: "Blessed be the Lord,

the God of Israel, for he has visited and brought redemption to his people" (1:68–79).

Some three months before the birth of John, his mother received the visit from her cousin, who had just received the angel's announcement of the birth of her divine Son. Within Elizabeth's womb the child danced in front of Mary, the Ark of the Covenant, joyful in the Messiah's presence. Later John, with full confidence, will point out the youth from Nazareth and announce that he is the Messiah.

Today's solemnity, which (in the northern hemisphere) occurs near the longest day of the year, just as the daylight is beginning to diminish, is linked to our celebration on December 24–25. Then, just as daylight is at its shortest span, we celebrate the birth of Jesus, the Light of the world. What we celebrate on the cosmic clock, we apply to our own lives. The prophet's voice announces, "he must increase; I must decrease" (John 3:30). The self-absorbed, sacrosanct "I" diminishes, while the life of

Change your emotion again to reflect their confusion and curiosity.

Judea = joo-dee-uh

Lower your voice as if to gossip.

Pause at the end of this line.

Proclaim this line with the pride of Elizabeth and Zechariah.

TO KEEP IN MIND
Proclamation cannot be effective unless it is expressive. As you prepare your proclamation, make choices about emotions. Some choices are already evident in the text.

Then **fear** came upon all their neighbors,
    and all these matters were discussed
        throughout the hill country of Judea.
All who heard these things took them to **heart**, saying,
    "**What**, then, will this child **be**?"
For **surely** the hand of the Lord was **with** him.
The child **grew** and became **strong** in spirit,
    and he was in the **desert** until the day
        of his **manifestation** to Israel.

Christ, the Light of the soul and of the world, grows. Today mercy is born, so that later the Messiah can take possession of souls destined to enjoy an eternal friendship with God. K.S.

THIRTEENTH SUNDAY IN ORDINARY TIME

LECTIONARY #98

An exhortatory reading that is all good news. Keep your voice and energy up throughout.

READING I   Wisdom 1:13–15; 2:23–24

A reading from the Book of Wisdom

God did not make **death**,
  nor does he rejoice in the destruction of the **living**.
For he fashioned **all** things that they might have **being**;
  and the **creatures** of the world are **wholesome**,

Of course not!

and there is not a **destructive** drug among them
  nor any domain of the **netherworld** on earth,
  for justice is **undying**.

Rejoice! This is a God of life!

For God formed man to be **imperishable**;
  the **image** of his own nature he made him.

Note that there is no home for evil on earth.

But by the **envy** of the devil, **death** entered the world,
  and they who belong to his company **experience** it.

Pause at the end of this line.

Slowly, with great joy.

Don't make too much of this; we don't belong to his company.

For meditation and context:

RESPONSORIAL PSALM   Psalm 30:2, 4, 5–6, 11, 12, 13 (2a)

R. I will praise you, Lord, for you have rescued me.

I will extol you, O LORD, for you drew
    me clear
  and did not let my enemies rejoice
    over me.
O LORD, you brought me up from the
    netherworld;
  you preserved me from among those
    going down into the pit.

Sing praise to the LORD, you his
    faithful ones,
  and give thanks to his holy name.
For his anger lasts but a moment;
  a lifetime, his good will.
At nightfall, weeping enters in,
  but with the dawn, rejoicing.

Hear, O LORD, and have pity on me;
  O LORD, be my helper.
You changed my mourning into dancing;
  O LORD, my God, forever will I give
    you thanks.

TO KEEP IN MIND

You can't proclaim what you don't understand. Read the Scripture passage and its commentary in *Workbook*. Then read it from your Bible, including what comes before and after it so that you understand the context.

READING I   The sage (author of the Book of Wisdom) affirms God's project of goodness in the creation of humanity. Physical death, he says, was introduced by a devil jealous to possess human life. A person attains life by loving justice and rejecting injustice that leads to death (physical death being a symbol of spiritual death and definitive separation from God). No destructive drug exists in creation, and Hades has no real power on earth. The alternative to the death brought about by injustice is righteous behavior, and justice is undying. Individuals are free to choose or reject righteousness and thus receive or refuse the gift of immortality.

The author presents a nuanced idea of immortality. Human beings are not created immortal, but we are destined for immortality. In other words, human beings, created in the image of God, project God's identity of immortality through our ethical conduct. Injustice deforms the image of God into the likeness of death that God did not create, death being a total separation from God and the world. The wicked overlook the immortality that God offers. Such an affirmation contradicts the fool's claim that humans came to exist arbitrarily and that after death it will be as though we had never existed. To sustain the claim for immortality, the author appeals to Genesis, which claims that God created humans according to his own likeness and his identity is eternal. Death entered the world through the envy of the adversary, who, like the serpent in Genesis 3, opposes God's generosity. The adversary offers the option of injustice, and those who accept this option experience death.

An exhortatory reading. Paul is asking the community to be generous to those in need, but his intent may not be clear in this excerpt. Your assembly will understand only if you make careful choices about your tone, inflection, and stress.

Corinthians = kohr-IN-thee-uhnz

Indicate with your inflection that "this gracious act" refers to what follows, not what came before.

Emphasize the generosity of one who is rich giving graciously to those who are poor.

Appeal to your assembly's sense of reason and fairness: it makes sense that those with abundance should give to those in need.

Pause at the end of this line.

Stress the parallelism in this line; pause briefly after "much" and "little."

READING II   2 Corinthians 8:7, 9, 13–15

A reading from the second Letter of Saint Paul to the Corinthians

Brothers and sisters:
As you **excel** in **every** respect, in **faith, discourse,**
    knowledge, all **earnestness,** and in the **love** we have for you,
    may you excel in this gracious act **also.**

For you **know** the gracious act of our LORD Jesus Christ,
    that though he was **rich,** for **your** sake he became **poor,**
    so that by his **poverty** you might become **rich.**
Not that **others** should have **relief** while you are **burdened,**
    but that as a matter of **equality**
    your **abundance** at the present time should supply their **needs,**
    so that **their** abundance may also supply **your** needs,
    that there may be **equality.**
As it is written:
    *Whoever had **much** did not have **more,***
        *and whoever had **little** did not have **less.***

A narrative reading with two stories of healing, one interrupting the other.

Jairus = JĪ-ruhs

His actions indicate real anguish. Make sure this shows in your voice and face.

GOSPEL   Mark 5:21–43

A reading from the holy Gospel according to Mark

When Jesus had crossed **again** in the boat
    to the other side,
    a large **crowd** gathered around him, and he stayed close
        to the **sea.**
One of the **synagogue** officials, named **Jairus,** came forward.
Seeing him he **fell** at his **feet** and pleaded **earnestly**
    with him, saying,
    "My **daughter** is at the point of **death.**

READING II   Paul is promoting charity within the context of his theology of the charisms. Now he introduces a sensitive issue—the collection—and he capitalizes on a trademark of his Corinthian flock, who excel in whatever they do. So Paul wants to convince them to use their "excellence" as a benefit for others: to excel in grace which, in the present instance, would amount to their generous giving. He appeals to the example of God's Incarnation in Jesus. Being rich in his preexistence with God, for our sakes Jesus became poor in succumbing to

death, so that we, through his poverty, might become rich.

The challenge of the Corinthians' love and generosity toward others is the measure of God's generosity toward them. Expanding on this, Paul opens a window on his sense of fairness and equity in sharing goods and mutual care among believers. He casts the ideal in economic categories and finds the ground for his counsel in Exodus 16:18: "Whoever had much did not have more, and whoever had little did not have less." Fairness and equity are the guidelines for each individual's contribu-

tion. The Corinthians' current abundance should meet others' need, and on the rebound, other people's abundance will respond to the Corinthians' need. In the Gospel, John the Baptist represents a similar counsel, "Whoever has two tunics should share with the person who has none. And whoever has food should likewise" (Luke 3:11).

GOSPEL   The two scenes in the raising of Jairus' daughter serve as a sandwich for the cure of the hemorrhage victim, and the two stories are

Please, come lay your **hands** on her
    that she may get well and **live**."
He went **off** with him,
    and a large crowd followed him and **pressed** upon him.

There was a **woman** afflicted with **hemorrhages** for **twelve**
    years.
She had suffered **greatly** at the hands of many doctors
    and had spent **all** that she had.
Yet she was not **helped** but only grew **worse**.
She had **heard** about Jesus and came up behind him in the crowd
    and **touched** his **cloak**.
She said, "If I but touch his **clothes**, I shall be **cured**."
Immediately her flow of blood dried **up**.
She felt in her body that she was **healed** of her affliction.
Jesus, **aware** at once that **power** had gone out from him,
    turned around in the crowd and asked, "**Who** has touched
      my clothes?"
But his disciples said to Jesus,
    "You see how the crowd is **pressing** upon you,
    and yet you ask, 'Who **touched** me?'"
And he looked around to **see** who had done it.
The **woman**, realizing what had **happened** to her,
    approached in **fear** and **trembling**.
She **fell** down before Jesus and told him the whole **truth**.
He said to her, "**Daughter**, your **faith** has saved you.
Go in **peace** and be **cured** of your affliction."

While he was still speaking,
    people from the synagogue official's house **arrived** and said,
    "Your daughter has **died**; why **trouble** the teacher any **longer**?"
Disregarding the message that was reported,
    Jesus said to the synagogue official,
    "Do not be **afraid**; just have **faith**."
He did not allow anyone to accompany him inside
    except Peter, James, and John, the brother of James.

Margin notes (left column):

No lengthy pause here; the woman is part of the crowd.

Proclaim with the frustration and humiliation of the woman. (Recall that, as long as she was bleeding, she would be considered unclean.)

With excited hope.

Still excited, but more quietly, as if she were speaking to herself.

Quickly.

Maintain a centered authority as you proclaim Jesus' words and actions. Jesus is neither curious nor accusatory, but concerned that someone is in need.

The disciples are incredulous and frustrated with the crowd.

With gentle love.

Pause at the end of this line.

Quietly, as an aside to Jarius.

Assure him.

---

intertwined. That both females are associated with the number twelve—the age of one and the years of affliction of the other—presents each one in an image of the Church: the people of Israel in the Old Testament, who in one sense are at the point of death and, in another, suffer from chronic impurity. Through physical contact—Jesus taking the hands of the little girl and the woman touching Jesus' garment—the Church is healed and raised from the dead. The detail about giving the girl something to eat is more than simply attention to her enfeebled condition before

having been raised from death; it anticipates the Eucharist and prefigures what will happen in the feedings of the five thousand and of the four thousand in the following chapters, where the whole Church, Jewish and Gentile, will be nourished.

A renowned official rushes toward Jesus, bows, and pleads, "My daughter is at the point of death. Please, come lay your hand on her, that she may get well and live." With such a bold appeal, Jairus confesses his own powerlessness in the face of his daughter's sickness and acknowledges Jesus' power to heal what is beyond

the expertise of a physician. By the time Jesus arrives, the professional mourners have begun their work. Jesus breaks through the confusion and orders them out, "The child is not dead, but asleep." Considering this nonsense, the crowd taunts Jesus. We ask ourselves, what is Jesus really saying here?

The answer is in the story of the other healing. While Jesus was on his way to the house, an anonymous someone approached and secretly touched his robe. A daring woman believed Jesus could do what twelve years of professional doctoring

Quicken your pace to signify the energy of the commotion.

A harsh line. Proclaim with the sneer of the crowd.

Firmly.

Gently. This is a tender family scene.

Talitha koum = tah-lee-thah KOOM or tal-uh-thuh KOOM

Don't make this sound like a command, but like someone waking a child from a nap.

Proclaim with the bystanders' tone of utter astonishment.

This amazing story ends on a very ordinary and practical note.

> TO KEEP IN MIND
> Use inflection (the high or low pitch of your voice) to convey attitude and feeling. High pitch expresses intensity and excitement; low pitch expresses sadness, contrition, or solemnity.

When they arrived at the house of the synagogue official,
  he caught sight of a **commotion**,
  people **weeping** and wailing **loudly**.
So he went in and said to them,
  "**Why** this commotion and weeping?
The child is not **dead** but **asleep**."
And they **ridiculed** him.
Then he put them all **out**.
He took along the child's **father** and **mother**
  and those who were with him
  and entered the room where the **child** was.
He took the child by the **hand** and said to her, "*Talitha koum*,"
  which means, "Little **girl**, I say to you, **arise**!"
The girl, a child of twelve, arose **immediately** and
  walked around.
At that they were utterly **astounded**.
He gave strict orders that **no** one should **know** this
  and said that she should be given something to **eat**.

[Shorter: Mark 5:21–24, 35b–43 (see brackets)]

could not do: cure a chronic illness that stigmatized her interior and social life. The disease legally cut her off from participation in public life and worship. So she furtively touched his robe, and was restored to full health. To this lady who emerged from the crowd and became a memorable Gospel heroine, Jesus declared, "Daughter, your faith has saved you. Go in peace and be cured of your affliction." Our question about Jesus' motive is answered. The father's demand is not unreasonable after all. Faith was the official's access to Jesus, just as faith was the basis of the afflicted woman's claim on Jesus.

Faith does not come easily in any age. It is a gift from God, as basic as life, as necessary as the air we breathe. Faith gives us access to Jesus and his healing power. Not only will it be the conduit of our healing; it will raise us from all that is in communion with death. Faith gives angel's wings with which we can transcend the earthly confines of sin and death, despair, disillusion, and fear. By our intrepid prayer we dare to interrupt and challenge God. K.S.

FOURTEENTH SUNDAY IN ORDINARY TIME

An exhortatory reading. God's desire for a relationship with us will not be thwarted—not by a reluctant prophet or a stubborn people. Bring that sense of urgency to this proclamation.

Ezekiel = ee-ZEE-kee-uhl

Imagine being lifted to your feet and hearing the voice of God! Proclaim with that feeling of awestruck wonder.

How does God feel recalling the actions of these people chosen to be God's own—angry, disappointed, compassionate? Note that God is sending them a prophet so they might repent.

"Your job won't be easy!"

Proclaim the "Thus says . . ." with conviction! The brief phrase stands for all the preaching Ezekiel will be called to do. Pause.

Slowly.

For meditation and context:

TO KEEP IN MIND
Be careful not to "swallow" words by mumbling. Articulate carefully so that every word is clearly heard, especially at the end of lines.

LECTIONARY #101

READING I   Ezekiel 2:2–5

A reading from the Book of the Prophet Ezekiel

As the LORD **spoke** to me, the **spirit** entered into me
  and **set** me on my feet,
  and I heard the one who was **speaking** say to me:
Son of **man**, I am **sending** you to the **Israelites**,
  rebels who have **rebelled** against me;
  they and their ancestors have **revolted** against me
    to this **very day**.
Hard of face and **obstinate** of heart
  are they to whom I am **sending** you.
But you shall **say** to them: **Thus** says the LORD **GOD**!
And whether they **heed** or **resist**—for they are a
  rebellious house—
  they shall **know** that a **prophet** has been **among** them.

RESPONSORIAL PSALM   Psalm 123:1–2, 2, 3–4 (2cd)

R. Our eyes are fixed on the Lord, pleading for his mercy.

To you I lift up my eyes
  who are enthroned in heaven—
as the eyes of servants
  are on the hands of their masters.

As the eyes of a maid
  are on the hands of her mistress,
so are our eyes on the LORD, our God,
  till he have pity on us.

Have pity on us, O LORD, have pity on us,
  for we are more than sated with contempt;
our souls are more than sated
  with the mockery of the arrogant,
  with the contempt of the proud.

READING I God's Spirit, literally wind or breath—a vital energy —enables the prophet to hear God's Word. He cannot rise of his own volition; the Spirit enters and sets him on his feet. "I am sending you . . . and you shall say to them . . . they shall know . . . ," words that express the authorization and essential elements of the prophetic call. The Israelites are "hard of face and obstinate of heart." Whether the "rebellious house" listens or not, "they shall know that a prophet has been among them." Hence, Ezekiel's success does not depend on his audience's

reaction, but on his obedient proclamation of God's Word. Israel will "know"—recognize and acknowledge—that Ezekiel is God's spokesperson only when the prophecies have been fulfilled; the commissioning represents God's concern and involvement in Israel's life, despite her chronic sin and obstinacy.

READING II After his testimony of a mystical experience Paul confesses the "thorn in the flesh" that was given to keep him from becoming too elated by such revelations. The thorn is

variously interpreted as a sickness or physical disability like epilepsy, depression, headaches, or eye problems; it might be a persistent temptation or handicap connected with his personal life or apostolic activity. Since the Hebrew "thorn in the flesh" (Numbers 33:55; Ezekiel 28:24) can refer to persons and echoes the English "a thorn in my side," Paul may refer to an obnoxious opponent. The precise diagnosis is not necessary, and its elusive identity makes it applicable for any reader. Paul appeals insistently, three times, for its removal, like Jesus in Gethsemane, a sign

A didactic reading. Paul uses his own experience to teach about weakness and strength, which have a different value for the Christian than for the rest of the world.

Corinthians = kohr-IN-thee-uhnz

This is a real struggle for Paul; let his anguish come through in your proclamation.

Turn from pain to relief. With God, anything is bearable.

Pick up your pace and energy.

Keep your pace up through this list; none of these things can overwhelm us with Christ in our life.
Pause at the end of this line.

Here is the key teaching. Smile with confidence in Christ who sustains us!

TO KEEP IN MIND

Pay attention to the pace of your reading. Varying the pace gives listeners clues to the meaning of the text. The most common problem for proclaimers new to the ministry is going too fast to be understood.

READING II   2 Corinthians 12:7–10

A reading from the second Letter of Saint Paul to the Corinthians

Brothers and sisters:
That I, **Paul**, might not become **too** elated,
    because of the **abundance** of the revelations,
    a **thorn** in the **flesh** was given to me, an angel of **Satan**,
    to **beat** me, to keep me from being too **elated**.
Three times I **begged** the Lord about this, that it might
      leave me,
    but he said to me, "My **grace** is **sufficient** for you,
    for **power** is made **perfect** in **weakness**."
I will rather **boast** most **gladly** of my **weaknesses**,
    in order that the power of **Christ** may **dwell** with me.
Therefore, I am **content** with **weaknesses**, **insults**,
    hardships, **persecutions** and **constraints**,
    for the sake of **Christ**;
    for when I am **weak**, then I am **strong**.

---

of how intolerable he felt the thorn to be. His petition is denied; relief is withheld for a higher purpose.

    Whatever the thorn was, Paul interprets it as a deterrent prepared by a sinister enemy to remove him from the battle plan. But the effect it has on him is beneficial: it keeps him from being inflated by the gift of private revelations. In this present case, God has co-opted Satan's thorn to help Paul keep perspective and, incidentally, to prove that God is in control. Paul's request that it be removed credits God with the power to remove it, but the denial of

the request helps Paul understand the paradoxical relationship of power and weakness. Jesus affirms that suffering will be accompanied by the grace of endurance, "My grace is sufficient for you." Grace is manifest in the experience of weakness, the Cross. Paul pinpoints the ground for the paradoxical strategy he has adopted in his self-defense, "that the power of Christ may dwell with me." Romans states it directly: as much as sin may abound, God's grace abounds even more (Romans 5:20). In another context, Paul's depiction of humans as earthen vessels into which God

has poured such treasure (2 Corinthians 4:7) shows that the power is from God and not from us. Now, boasting of his weakness, he gives glory to God, the only real power in his life. Christ suffers the ultimate helplessness in his Crucifixion, and he is thus the hallmark of God's power, effective in Jesus raised from the dead.

GOSPEL   "The brother of James . . . Simon": in Semitic usage, the terms "brother" and "sister" are applied to nephews, nieces, cousins, half-brothers, and half-sisters, as well as to chil-

A narrative reading about a very human encounter—one we've likely experienced ourselves. Bring the very real emotions of Jesus and his neighbors to your proclamation so your assembly can connect with the story.

Articulate "his native place" carefully.

Keep your tone hopeful; don't give away the ending yet.

Vary your inflection on these comments; imagine a different person is speaking each one.

Be dismissive: "We know this man! He's nothing special!"

Joses = JOH-seez or JOH-sez

How does Jesus feel—sad, frustrated, disappointed? Make a strong choice and maintain it to the end.

With Jesus' feeling.

Slow your pace on the final line.

TO KEEP IN MIND
Making eye contact with the assembly connects you with them and connects them to the reading more deeply than using your voice alone. This helps the assembly stay with the story and keeps them engaged.

GOSPEL   Mark 6:1–6

A reading from the holy Gospel according to Mark

Jesus departed from there and came to his **native** place, accompanied by his disciples.
When the sabbath came he began to **teach** in the synagogue,
    and many who heard him were **astonished**.
They said, "Where did this man **get** all this?
What kind of **wisdom** has been given him?
What mighty **deeds** are wrought by his hands!
Is he not the **carpenter**, the son of **Mary**,
    and the brother of **James** and **Joses** and **Judas** and **Simon**?
And are not his **sisters** here with us?"
And they took **offense** at him.
Jesus said to them,
    "A **prophet** is not without **honor** except in his **native** place
    and among his own **kin** and in his own **house**."
So he was not able to perform any **mighty** deed there,
    apart from **curing** a few sick people by laying his **hands**
        on them.
He was **amazed** at their lack of faith.

---

dren of the same parents, a usage which is also present in the Greek translation of the Old Testament. Mark demonstrates what comprised the greater part of Jesus' earthly sojourn, the routine of a craftsman who shared the conditions of village life. In this glimpse of Jesus in his hometown we discover the value of daily life as a path to holiness. In his reply "A prophet is not without honor except . . . in his own house", Jesus recalls the prophets the people rejected, and in view of the dishonor he receives from his own townsfolk, he anticipates his eventual rejection by the nation.

In the end, Jesus' healing power in Nazareth could not take effect because of the people's lack of faith. The Gospel informs us that Jesus could not work any miracle there; he just cured some sick persons—a strange observation. On one hand, he could not work any healings in such an environment, and on the other he cured some few. Why some and not all? Is it not the same Jesus for everybody? Perhaps some of those present had reserved a place for God in their lives and approached Jesus not just for the sake of propriety or curiosity, but out of faith, and they enjoyed

a friendship with him, friendship expressed in confidence and prayer. A similar tension exists in our lives. Jesus offers us the miracle of a full life, a miracle that touches persons open to his presence. What is lacking is our confidence and faith for the miracle to take effect in our lives. K.S.

FIFTEENTH SUNDAY IN ORDINARY TIME

A narrative reading. Be sure you understand the context (read 7:10–11). Amos the prophet is being thrown out by Amaziah, the king's priest.

Amos = AY-m*s

Amaziah = am-uh-Zī-uh; Bethel = BETH*l

With real energy. The message is, "Get out of here and stop bothering us!" "Visionary!" is meant to be sarcastic. Judah = joo-duh

prophesying = PROF-uh-sī-ing

prophesy = PROF-uh-sī

With righteous self-importance.

Contrast Amos' humility with Amaziah's haughtiness.

The simple truth.

Urgently; it was a commissioning Amos could not resist.

For meditation and context:

TO KEEP IN MIND

A *narrative* has characters, dialogue, a setting, and action. Help your listeners see the story unfold, keep characters distinct, and be clear about shifts in setting.

LECTIONARY #104

READING I Amos 7:12–15

A reading from the Book of the Prophet Amos

Amaziah, priest of Bethel, said to Amos,
  "**Off** with you, **visionary**, **flee** to the land of Judah!
There earn your bread by **prophesying**,
  but **never** again prophesy in Bethel;
  for it is the **king's** sanctuary and a **royal** temple."
Amos answered Amaziah, "I was no **prophet**,
  nor have I belonged to a **company** of prophets;
  I was a **shepherd** and a dresser of **sycamores**.
The **Lord** took me from following the flock, and said to me,
  Go, **prophesy** to my people Israel."

RESPONSORIAL PSALM Psalm 85:9–10, 11–12, 13–14 (8)

R. Lord, let us see your kindness, and grant us your salvation.

I will hear what God proclaims;
  the LORD—for he proclaims peace.
Near indeed is his salvation to those who
    fear him,
  glory dwelling in our land.

Kindness and truth shall meet;
  justice and peace shall kiss.
Truth shall spring out of the earth,
  and justice shall look down from heaven.

The LORD himself will give his benefits;
  our land shall yield its increase.
Justice shall walk before him,
  and prepare the way of his steps.

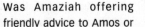 Was Amaziah offering friendly advice to Amos or was he by royal office or his own authority ordering Amos out of the country? His use of the term "visionary" may be demeaning, but nothing else in his language leads one to conclude that he was hostile to the prophet. What is clear is that his authority over the Bethel sanctuary gave him the right to forbid Amos to prophesy there.

Amos reacts to the attempt to classify him as a "prophet-for-hire," exchanging his oracles for payment. To disassociate himself from this kind of professional prophet, he rejects the title *nabi'* ("prophet"). By profession he is an animal herdsman and specialist in the maturation of the "sycamore" fruit (similar to a fig), but God commissioned him to prophesy to Israel. In the performance of his profession God sent Amos to prophesy in the sanctuary; in the end, Amaziah offended God by resisting Amos.

READING II In Greek letter-writing the greeting was usually followed by a thanksgiving and a wish for the health of the recipient. Pauline letters have lengthened the thanksgiving to address the faith of the reader, and in it the Apostle anticipates themes of the letter. In the present blessing Paul praises "God the Father of our Lord Jesus Christ"—such praise being the appropriate response to benefits the Father confers. Paul weaves the function of Christ as heavenly mediator into the praise of God as benefactor.

A series of clauses spells out the promise of salvation: God blessed us in Christ and destined us for adoption in him; redemption is through Christ's blood; knowledge of God's will unites all things in Christ; we are destined to praise God in

An exhortatory reading containing six sentences of praise to God. Let joy show in your voice and face, but vary your tone with each statement. Keep thoughts together by pausing only at commas and periods, except as noted.

Ephesians = ee-FEE-shuhnz

Start strong! Use the top of your range of inflection and keep your pace up.
Slow on "as he chose us in him."

Maintain energy but use a more intimate tone, reflecting the love in this adoptive relationship.

Build slightly. Beyond our adoption, we also have redemption.
Linger over the words "riches" and "lavished."

Build again, with excitement. Even more than redemption, we have wisdom and knowledge.

Brief pause after "will."

Slowly and emphatically. Paul repeats the significance of being chosen.
Return to a normal pace.

Slow again on this phrase, then take a slightly longer pause to set up the final thought.

Look directly into the assembly. Emphasize "In him you also."

With great joy!

Slow to the end.

READING II   Ephesians 1:3–14

A reading from the Letter of Saint Paul to the Ephesians

[**Blessed** be the God and Father of our LORD Jesus Christ,
    who has blessed **us** in Christ
    with **every** spiritual blessing in the heavens,
    as he **chose** us in him, before the foundation of the world,
    to be **holy** and without **blemish** before him.
In **love** he destined us for **adoption** to himself through
        Jesus Christ,
    in accord with the **favor** of his will,
    for the **praise** of the **glory** of his **grace**
    that he granted us in the **beloved**.
In him we have **redemption** by his blood,
    the **forgiveness** of transgressions,
    in accord with the **riches** of his grace that he **lavished**
        upon us.
In all **wisdom** and **insight**, he has made known to us
    the **mystery** of his will in accord with his favor
    that he set forth in him as a plan for the fullness of times,
    to sum up **all** things in **Christ**, in **heaven** and on **earth**.]

In **him** we were also **chosen**,
    destined in accord with the **purpose** of the One
    who accomplishes **all** things according to the intention
        of his **will**,
    so that we might exist for the **praise** of his **glory**,
    we who first **hoped** in Christ.
In **him** you **also**, who have **heard** the word of truth,
    the **gospel** of your salvation, and have **believed** in him,
    were **sealed** with the promised Holy **Spirit**,
    which is the first installment of our inheritance
    toward redemption as God's **possession**, to the **praise**
        of his **glory**.

[Shorter: Ephesians 1:3–10 (see brackets)]

Christ, and through the preaching of the Gospel, Gentiles ("you") are included in this inheritance. That he "chose us" includes Christians along with Israel and places us in the same boat as Jesus' first disciples. Christ's exaltation in the heavens provides the foundation for bringing all of creation into unity under Christ as head. The final words pick up the intent of the whole section, "to the praise of his glory." The election of God's people is universal: we are all called to holiness. As adopted children we have been elected to form part of God's people.

GOSPEL   The mission of the Twelve consists of their exercise of authority in Word and power as representatives of Jesus, anticipating the international mission at the end of the Gospel (16:15–18), which is an extension of Jesus' initial preaching (1:14–15). In the present missionary instructions Jesus exhorted his Apostles to depend on God and on the community for food and shelter. In the list of accessories Jesus permits the use of a walking stick and sandals, and there is no prohibition to enter Samaritan towns or pagan territory. These differences from the other synoptic writers, as well as the prescription of anointing the sick, indicate an adaptation to conditions within and outside Palestine and reflect life in the early Church. One concern arises when the very people to whom the mission is directed reject the missionary: "Whatever place does not welcome you or listen to you, leave there and shake the dust off your feet." Disagreements and frictions frequently happen in our families and communities. Good persons who practice the Gospel values and are deeply committed, at times disagree among themselves or

An exhortatory reading that may look like a narrative, but the urgency of the work of spreading the Gospel gives it the energy and drive of an exhortation. There's still work to do today to build the reign of God, so inspire your assembly with this reading.

Proclaim these instructions with the emotion and intention of Jesus. Keep your pace up throughout. There's no time to lose!

Brief pause.

This is a surprising and unusual instruction, they are to rely completely on God.

The walking stick and sandals indicate how far they will walk to spread the Gospel.

Don't drop your pace or energy.

Pause at the end of this line.
Brief pause after "off."
Good news! Smile with satisfaction as you relate their amazing works.

TO KEEP IN MIND
Pray the text, using your favorite method of praying with Scripture.

GOSPEL Mark 6:7–13

A reading from the holy Gospel according to Mark

Jesus summoned the **Twelve** and began to send them out
   two by **two**
   and gave them **authority** over unclean **spirits**.
He instructed them to take **nothing** for the journey
   but a **walking** stick—
   no **food**, no **sack**, no **money** in their belts.
They were, however, to wear **sandals**
   but not a second **tunic**.
He said to them,
   "Wherever you enter a house, **stay** there until you **leave**.
Whatever place does not **welcome** you or **listen** to you,
   leave there and shake the **dust** off your feet
   in testimony **against** them."
So they went **off** and preached **repentance**.
The **Twelve** drove out many **demons**,
   and they **anointed** with oil many who were **sick** and
   cured them.

meet with rejection. Recall the mission of Amos in the First Reading.

For the first mission of the disciples, the evangelist employs a single word for their preaching: "So they went off and preached repentance"; the content of their preaching, *metanoia* (repentance), refers to a change of attitude.

Why in pairs? With less than two the virtue of charity would not be needed. If two persons respect each other and toler-ate one another's weaknesses of body and spirit; if they are faithful to their promises and collaborate; if they make the effort to understand and listen to each other; if they pardon each other when it is necessary, then they are practicing what they preach, which amounts to a formidable witness to Christian values. In times of persecution Christians could not openly preach Christ, but a contemporary observer, impressed by the concern, tolerance, and mutual understanding among Christians, might observe, "See how they love one another." Alone, one does not have to exert oneself to live the Gospel. There is no sharing of the joys and sorrows, no dialogue, no betrayal nor good counsel, nor anyone with whom to disagree or anyone to pardon, and these are all key factors in the Christian life. K.S.

SIXTEENTH SUNDAY IN ORDINARY TIME

LECTIONARY #107

READING I Jeremiah 23:1–6

A reading from the Book of the Prophet Jeremiah

Woe to the shepherds
    who **mislead** and **scatter** the flock of my pasture,
    says the LORD.
Therefore, **thus** says the LORD, the God of Israel,
    against the shepherds who shepherd my people:
    You have **scattered** my sheep and **driven** them away.
You have not **cared** for them,
    but **I** will take care to **punish** your evil deeds.
I **myself** will gather the **remnant** of my flock
    from **all** the lands to which I have **driven** them
    and bring them **back** to their **meadow**;
    there they shall **increase** and **multiply**.
I will appoint shepherds for them who **will** shepherd them
    so that they need **no longer** fear and tremble;
    and **none** shall be missing, says the LORD.

Behold, the days are **coming**, says the LORD,
    when I will **raise up** a righteous shoot to David;
as king he shall reign and govern **wisely**,
    he shall do what is **just** and **right** in the land.
In his days Judah shall be **saved**,
    Israel shall dwell in **security**.
This is the name they give him:
    "The **Lord** our **justice**."

An exhortatory reading. The first part is addressed to the bad shepherds. The second part is addressed to the sheep—the people of Israel. Be sure your tone changes for each part.

Jeremiah = jayr-uh-MĪ-uh
Start strong and determined! Use "woe" to sound a warning.
Articulate this line carefully.
Keep your pace and energy up.

How does God feel about these misleading shepherds?

Pause at the end of this line.

Slow your pace a bit. Proclaim with a tone of tenderness and love.

See this gentle pastoral scene unfold before your eyes.

Pause at the end of this line.

Quicken your pace. "Behold" announces exciting news!

Smile as you think of the wise and just rule of this king.

Good news!
Pause at the end of this line.

Very slowly; give each word its weight.

READING I Jeremiah's shepherd language draws on the image for kingship in the ancient near East. While many monarchs could, in actuality, be cruel and harsh, ideally the monarch was to be a shepherd who watched over his flock, protected it, kept it together, and took care of any who were injured or sick. That is often what kings failed to do, their failure consisting in their unjust practices and economic oppression. Jeremiah's brief sermon displays the sad state of things. The emphatic construction "It is you who have scattered my flock" accuses the monarchs of misrule,

with the consequence of scattering the flock and causing their exile. Jeremiah predicts that God himself will shepherd the people; he will raise up a new king who will establish justice. In contrast to false rulers, God, the true shepherd, will appoint a worthy ruler from David's line who will rule wisely. The name of the future king, "The LORD our justice" is a play on the name of the last weak king of the Davidic line, Zedekiah, a name that means "the Lord is my righteousness." Unlike this phony, the future monarch will be true to his name.

This prophecy proposes a clear break between the failed past and the promised future. In this announcement, one of the clues to the message of hope is the relational language: my pasture, my people, and my flock. God never cancels the covenant. Another emphatic construction opens the door of hope beyond the exile. God says, "You who have scattered my sheep and driven them away. . . . I myself will gather the remnant of my flock." The theme continues both in the depiction of God's shepherding and in the announcement that he will raise up new shepherds

For meditation and context:

TO KEEP IN MIND
A *didactic* text makes a point or teaches something. Help your assembly to follow the argument and understand what's being taught.

A didactic reading. The "far off" were the Gentiles (read Ephesians 2:11–for context). Who are the "far off" today? Who is missing from our community? Encourage your assembly to put aside divisions as you proclaim.

Ephesians = ee-FEE-shuhnz

The whole reading is good news about God's great love for all. Be sure that love shows in your voice and face throughout.

A long sentence; pause only at the commas except as noted.

No pause after "enmity" (EN-mih-tee).

Slow on the phrase "one new person Man . . . two."

Set apart the phrase "thus establishing peace."

Slowly and broadly to the end of the sentence.

Pause at the end of this line.

Raise your energy and quicken your pace.

Look directly into the assembly on this last line.

RESPONSORIAL PSALM   Psalm 23:1–3, 3–4, 5, 6 (1)

R. The Lord is my shepherd; there is nothing I shall want.

The LORD is my shepherd; I shall not want.
    In verdant pastures he gives me repose;
beside restful waters he leads me;
    he refreshes my soul.

He guides me in right paths
    for his name's sake.
Even though I walk in the dark valley
    I fear no evil; for you are at my side
with your rod and your staff
    that give me courage.

You spread the table before me
    in the sight of my foes;
you anoint my head with oil;
    my cup overflows.

Only goodness and kindness follow me
    all the days of my life;
and I shall dwell in the house of the LORD
    for years to come.

READING II   Ephesians 2:13–18

A reading from the Letter of Saint Paul to the Ephesians

Brothers and sisters:
In Christ Jesus you who once were far **off**
    have become **near** by the blood of Christ.

For he is our **peace**, he who made both **one**
    and broke down the **dividing** wall of **enmity**, through his flesh,
    abolishing the law with its commandments and legal claims,
    that he might create in himself **one** new person in place
        of the **two**,
    thus establishing **peace**,
    and might reconcile **both** with God,
    in **one** body, through the **cross**,
    putting that enmity to **death** by it.
He came and preached **peace** to you who were far **off**
    and **peace** to those who were **near**,
    for through him we **both** have access in **one** Spirit
        to the Father.

true to their name. That basic assurance is in the words "They need no longer fear and tremble"; when God has saved the people, they will have no need for fear.

The hopeful words about the new shepherd become even more specific. God declares his intention to place a descendent of David on the throne different from the previous one. The primary characteristic of the reign of the new ruler will be righteousness—the proof of the proper relationship among God, people, and king. The future king will administer God's rule

by fostering justice and keeping the people safe. Doing justice and defending the rights of the defenseless was the first requisite of the kings at Israel's beginning, and it continues to be the norm here. The safety and security of the people are tied directly to right conduct and defense of the poor.

READING II Paul is teaching here that through Christ's redemptive work on the Cross the religious barriers between Jew and Gentile have been transcended; Jew and Gentile have been recon-

ciled with God and formed into a community, imbued with the same Holy Spirit and worshiping the one Father. Paul alternates between the negative factors that have to be destroyed and the positive outcome of Christ's coming, which is peace. He threads references to Christ throughout: "through his flesh"; "in himself"; "in one body." The negatives are what needs to be dismantled: a barrier, the legalism attached to commandments and decrees, and enmity among peoples. Unity is not just the end of hostility. It

A narrative reading. Encourage your assembly to find balance between work and rest, a message we especially need to hear today.

Proclaim with the Apostles' excitement (see Mark 6:12–13).

With gentleness and care.

How would you feel in this situation? Annoyed, exhausted, overwhelmed?

Quietly. Pause.

Jesus' reaction might be quite different from our own. Proclaim with his compassion.

TO KEEP IN MIND

Always pause at the end of the reading, before you proclaim the closing dialogue ("The Word of the Lord" or "The Gospel of the Lord").

GOSPEL   Mark 6:30–34

A reading from the holy Gospel according to Mark

The **apostles** gathered together with Jesus
    and reported **all** they had **done** and **taught**.
He said to them,
    "Come **away** by **yourselves** to a deserted place and **rest**
        a while."
People were **coming** and **going** in great numbers,
    and they had no opportunity even to **eat**.
So they went off in the boat by themselves to a **deserted** place.
People saw them leaving and many came to **know** about it.
They **hastened** there on foot from all the towns
    and arrived at the place **before** them.

When he **disembarked** and saw the **vast** crowd,
    his heart was **moved** with pity for them,
    for they were like **sheep** without a **shepherd**;
    and he began to **teach** them **many** things.

---

involves reconciliation with God through the Cross. In the end the writer makes a striking point about abolishing hostility in Christ: access for one group does not mean exclusion of others.

GOSPEL Jesus and the disciples attempt to retreat to a "deserted place," but instead they attract a crowd. Mark gives the impression of a great movement of people into that deserted place, reminiscent of the exodus, and Jesus is moved with compassion when he sees them. He satisfies their spiritual hunger by his teaching, thus revealing himself as the true shepherd of the new Israel. This text sets the scene for one manifestation of Jesus in his messianic roles: on two different occasions he will feed the multitude—Jew and Gentile.

In the desert the shepherd was expected to lead God's people in a new exodus and replicate the wonders of the first one. Jesus, the shepherd, is present with the people in the deserted place, echoing God's role as a shepherd leading the flock in the first exodus. As we know from Ezekiel (34:5–6), the Jews expected a new shepherd to come and lead them again after the failure of the official shepherds. So Jesus teaches, gathers the scattered flock, and fulfills his messianic role as provider of wondrous food. K.S.

SEVENTEENTH SUNDAY IN ORDINARY TIME

A narrative reading. We may be accustomed to hearing God's great works described in Scripture, but strive to return to a sense of wonder in this proclamation.

Baal-shalishah = BAY-uhl SHAHL-ih-shuh or BAH-uhl SHAUL-ih shuh

Elisha = ee-LĪ-shuh

Slightly longer pause at this comma so as not to run these phrases together.

Incredulous.

Be careful not to sound angry. Elisha trusts completely in God.

With amazement.

For meditation and context:

TO KEEP IN MIND

In a narrative, find an emotion or point of view for each character, keeping in mind that these might change during the reading.

LECTIONARY #110

READING I   2 Kings 4:42–44

A reading from the second Book of Kings

A man came from Baal-shalishah bringing to **Elisha**,
    the man of **God**,
  twenty barley **loaves** made from the firstfruits,
  and fresh **grain** in the **ear**.
Elisha said, "**Give** it to the people to eat."
But his servant **objected**,
  "How can I set this before a **hundred** people?"
Elisha **insisted**, "**Give** it to the people to **eat**.
For thus says the Lord,
  'They shall **eat** and there shall be some left **over**.'"
And when they had **eaten**, there **was** some left over,
  as the LORD had said.

RESPONSORIAL PSALM   Psalm 145:10–11, 15–16, 17–18 (16)

R. The hand of the Lord feeds us; he answers all our needs.

Let all your works give you thanks, O LORD,
  and let your faithful ones bless you.
Let them discourse of the glory of
  your kingdom
  and speak of your might.

The eyes of all look hopefully to you,
  and you give them their food in
    due season;
you open your hand
  and satisfy the desire of every living thing.

The LORD is just in all his ways
  and holy in all his works.
The LORD is near to all who call upon him,
  to all who call upon him in truth.

READING I Despite the obvious discrepancy between supply and demand, Elisha gives the order to share the bread as he pronounces the oracle from God. From meager provisions comes a great deal, so one hundred hungry men eat their fill and still do not consume all twenty barley loaves. Such theological stories about hunger in the Old Testament encourage solidarity among people, show God's care for his creatures, and give a foretaste of Jesus' multiplication of loaves.

READING II The author's exhortation often opens with the verb *parakaléo*, "I appeal" or "I beg you." After this entreaty comes a brief list of virtues, which then shifts to the main theme of the letter: the unity of the body of Christ. The exhortation to "live in a manner worthy of the call you have received" echoes the Jewish understanding of divine election (being chosen by God). Although Christians are no longer slaves of the Law, the conviction that election leads to a new life remains. The Jewish metaphor for daily conduct is "to walk." The Hebrew word *hal-* *akh* means "walk," and hence, the Jewish legal term *halakah* refers to rules for conduct; this reflects how moral issues normally arise in a person's daily dealings as one walks through life. All of life is a response to the invitation to live for God.

Now the Apostle shifts to the specific focus of this section—unity. A "call" or vocation inevitably means cooperating with others, with all the difficulties, misunderstandings, hurt feelings, and irritation that entails. Paul gives the key to effective cooperation: humility and gentleness (very unmacho characteristics), patience and for-

An exhortatory reading composed of one long sentence; use the punctuation as a guide on where to pause.

Ephesians = ee-FEE-shuhnz

READING II   Ephesians 4:1–6

A reading from the Letter of Saint Paul to the Ephesians

Brothers and sisters:
I, a **prisoner** for the LORD,
    urge you to live in a manner **worthy** of the call
        you have received,
    with all **humility** and **gentleness**, with **patience**,
    bearing with one another through **love**,
    striving to preserve the **unity** of the spirit through the bond
        of **peace**:
    one **body** and one **Spirit**,
    as you were also called to the one **hope** of your call;
    one **LORD**, one **faith**, one **baptism**;
    one **God** and **Father** of **all**,
    who is **over** all and **through** all and **in** all.

Sincerely encourage the assembly.

Smile as you relate these traits of the ideal community.

Pause at the end of this line.

Heighten each successive instance of that which is one, building intensity to the final phrase.

With increasing energy.

Slow slightly through the end of this phrase.

GOSPEL   John 6:1–15

A reading from the holy Gospel according to John

Jesus went across the Sea of Galilee.
A **large** crowd followed him,
    because they saw the **signs** he was performing on the **sick**.
Jesus went up on the **mountain**,
    and there he sat down with his **disciples**.
The Jewish feast of **Passover** was near.
When Jesus raised his **eyes**
    and saw that a large **crowd** was coming to him,
    he said to Philip,
    "Where can we buy enough **food** for them to eat?"
He said this to **test** him,
    because he himself **knew** what he was going to do.

A narrative reading. What do each of the characters want and feel? Make your choices clear in your proclamation.

Galilee = GAL-ih-lee

Quickly, to convey the excitement of the crowd.

Don't gloss over this line. It connects the meal of Passover with the meal about to happen.

Although a "test," this should sound like a legitimate question.

bearance in love, enthusiasm to maintain the unity of the Spirit and "the bond of peace"—Greek *eirēnē*, the gift of the Spirit that goes beyond social interest and absence of strife. "Peace" refers to the salvation that comes from God. Unity is a gift arising from the shared experience of the one Spirit; believers do not create it but we can destroy it! God's peace functions as a bond when there is mutual respect.

Finally, Paul's confession reinforces this unity by recalling its triadic structure—one Spirit, one Lord, one God. By placing "one God" last and attaching to it the "alls"—"the Father of all, who is over all and through all and in all"—the author reminds us that the foundation of Christian unity is God, both in his oneness and in his "allness" as creator. The confession of Christ as "one Lord" echoes the distinctively Jewish emphasis on God as one and reminds us that the principal strains on Christian unity at this time came from including Gentiles in Israel's privileged status. The "one Spirit" unifies the body, both as a shared sexperience and through the manifold workings of grace. The "call" is one, because it is the same for all believers, without deference to rank or ability. The "one faith" recalls one of the earliest baptismal confessions: Jesus is Lord.

GOSPEL   Jesus, the new Moses, now on a different "mountain" from Sinai, takes the initiative. The reference to "the one who is to come into the world" recalls Elijah, whose coming precedes that of the Messiah (Malachi 3:1, 23). In the present chapter the approach of the feast anticipates the final Passover, in which John replaces the words spoken over the bread and wine with the washing of the

Be incredulous!

Tentatively at first, as if this might be a solution, then recognizing how silly it sounds.

Pause at the end of this line.

Slowly; make each action distinct.

Proclaim these lines with the amazement of the disciples.

With excitement and energy!

Let your voice drop (but not inaudibly) to convey his quiet and solitude.

Philip answered him,
    "Two **hundred** days' wages worth of food would not be enough
        for each of them to have a **little**."
One of his disciples,
    Andrew, the brother of Simon Peter, said to him,
    "There is a **boy** here who has five **barley** loaves and two **fish**;
    but what good are these for so **many**?"
Jesus said, "Have the people **recline**."
Now there was a great deal of **grass** in that place.
So the men reclined, about **five thousand** in number.
Then Jesus **took** the loaves, gave **thanks**,
    and **distributed** them to those who were reclining,
    and also as much of the **fish** as they wanted.
When they had had their **fill**, he said to his disciples,
    "Gather the fragments left **over**,
    so that nothing will be **wasted**."
So they **collected** them,
    and filled **twelve** wicker baskets with fragments
    from the five barley loaves
    that had been **more** than they could eat.
When the people **saw** the **sign** he had done, they said,
    "This is **truly** the **Prophet**, the **one** who is to come into
        the world."
Since Jesus knew that they were going to come and carry him off
    to make him **king**,
    he withdrew again to the mountain **alone**.

TO KEEP IN MIND
Pray the text, using your favorite
method of praying with Scripture.

---

disciples' feet. The story begins with Jesus on a mountain, the arrival of the crowd, and the contrast between the measly five barley breads (recalling the Elisha story) and the surplus of food for five thousand people. Jesus' sympathy was kindled at the sight of the crowd, hungry and tired. We may regard the multiplication of the loaves simply as a miracle, but for John it is a sign, a sacramental meal, followed by (not in this reading) Jesus' bread of life discourse about eating his flesh and drinking his blood—which makes the multiplication story eucharistic.

In this story, Philip and Andrew complement each other. Philip calculated the hopeless situation. Andrew put his hand to the task, against all odds. As he had done in the first chapter, Andrew introduced people to Jesus—the boy with the five barley loaves and two fish. In this paltry lunch Jesus found the materials for the sign. What we have to offer may not be much, but Jesus can use it. If we offer the little we have in the service of Christ, there is no calculating what he can do with and through us. We may be shy because we do not have more, but that is no reason for failing to offer what we have. K.S.

EIGTHTEENTH SUNDAY IN ORDINARY TIME

LECTIONARY #113

READING I   Exodus 16:2–4, 12–15

A reading from the Book of Exodus

The **whole** Israelite community **grumbled** against Moses
    and Aaron.
The Israelites said to them,
    "Would that we had **died** at the LORD's hand in the land
        of Egypt,
    as we sat by our **fleshpots** and ate our **fill** of bread!
But **you** had to lead us into this **desert**
    to make the **whole** community die of **famine**!"

Then the **Lord** said to Moses,
    "I will now **rain** down **bread** from **heaven** for you.
Each day the people are to go out and gather their daily **portion**;
    thus will I **test** them,
    to see whether they follow my instructions or **not**.

"I have **heard** the grumbling of the Israelites.
Tell them: In the evening twilight you shall eat **flesh**,
    and in the morning you shall have your fill of **bread**,
    so that you may **know** that I, the LORD, am your **God**."

In the evening **quail** came up and **covered** the camp.
In the morning a **dew** lay all about the camp,
    and when the dew **evaporated**, there on the surface
        of the desert
    were fine **flakes** like **hoarfrost** on the ground.

A narrative reading. Contrast the whining and grumbling of the Israelites with God's gentle compassion. Let the assembly hear the difference in your voice.

Exodus = EK-suh-duhs
The word "grumbled" should sound like what it means.

With real anguish.

Angrily.

God responds calmly.

With compassion.

Pause at the end of this line.

This is not a display of power as much as it is an act of love. Let that love show in your voice, eyes, and face.

READING I In the desert the Israelites' habitual complaining that often precedes a miracle places in relief their lack of faith; in contrast, the author underlines God's attention to their needs. Sometimes he attends to their complaints; at other times he offers the opportunity to change their attitude. The manna is a proof of God's providence. The theologian is not interested in the natural explanation of the miracle; he recounts the episode with a view to what this narrative means for Israel, whose desert sojourn was the extraordinary period when God formed an alliance with his people and demonstrated fidelity and grace as he saved them from slavery. The traditions about the manna, the quail, and water in the wilderness are proof of God's loving care.

READING II Paul contrasts the Ephesians' former existence with the new life they have in Christ, a life that requires every believer to strip off the old garments of vanity and sin and clothe themselves with the new person faithful to Christ. They must reject their former Gentile way of life that does not include God. He reminds them of their earlier instruction, urging them to return to the way "you learned Christ." Notice how he combines two images for conversion: changing clothing and renewal of mind. They must take off vice and put on Christ—thereby transforming the former person into the new. The hope to "be

Amazed.

"See how much the Lord loves you!"

For meditation and context:

TO KEEP IN MIND
Use inflection (the high or low pitch of your voice) to convey attitude and feeling. High pitch expresses intensity and excitement; low pitch expresses sadness, contrition, or solemnity.

An exhortatory reading. Paul sounds a little frustrated here. How do you feel when you have to tell someone the same thing over and over?
Ephesians = ee-FEE-shuhnz

With passion.

Of course not!

Drop your voice on the entire parenthetical thought ("assuming . . . Jesus").

Be dismissive of this "old self."

Smile as you share this better "new self."

Slow on this last line.

On seeing it, the Israelites asked one another, "What **is** this?"
for they did not know what it was.
But Moses told them,
"This is the **bread** that the LORD has given you to **eat**."

RESPONSORIAL PSALM   Psalm 78:3–4, 23–24, 25, 54 (24b)

R. The Lord gave them bread from heaven.

What we have heard and know,
and what our fathers have declared to us,
we will declare to the generation to come
the glorious deeds of the LORD and
his strength
and the wonders that he wrought.

He commanded the skies above
and opened the doors of heaven;
he rained manna upon them for food
and gave them heavenly bread.

Man ate the bread of angels,
food he sent them in abundance.
And he brought them to his holy land,
to the mountains his right hand had won.

READING II   Ephesians 4:17, 20–24

A reading from the Letter of Saint Paul to the Ephesians

Brothers and sisters:
I **declare** and **testify** in the LORD
that you must no longer live as the **Gentiles** do,
in the **futility** of their minds;
that is **not** how you learned Christ,
assuming that you have **heard** of him and were **taught** in him,
as **truth** is in **Jesus**,
that you should put **away** the **old** self of your former way
of life,
corrupted through deceitful desires,
and be **renewed** in the spirit of your minds,
and put on the **new** self,
created in God's way in **righteousness** and **holiness** of truth.

---

renewed in the spirit of your minds" points to the deficiencies of popular reasoning ("futility of their minds"). Ephesians describes the believer as "created in God," a phrase complemented by the attributes of God's newly created person, "in righteousness and holiness of truth."

 GOSPEL   Jesus dialogues with the crowd at Capernaum, and as usual, they misunderstand his meaning. In their previous encounter he had multi-

plied five barley loaves to feed over five thousand hungry mouths. Today, when the crowd approaches, they ask, "Rabbi, when did you get here?" The address "Rabbi" shows that they rallied around him as an outstanding teacher. But they were looking for another miracle that they might exploit for their own ends. Jesus recognized their intentions; his response could be paraphrased as "You look for me because you ate and are full. You have eaten the material bread, but you missed the meaning.

Now listen to the inner meaning of these happenings." Jesus continues (paraphrase), "Do not labor for perishable food and temporal achievement. Strive for food that has value for eternal life. If all your effort, skill, and prayer end in just sustaining your physical existence, life will perish when the body dies. Strive, rather, for bread that nourishes the whole person, food that brings eternal life—food I will give you."

When they ask how to receive this special food, Jesus' answer, "believe in the

A narrative reading that is a dialogue between Jesus and the crowd; think of each exchange as if a different person is speaking within the crowd, each with a different intent and emotion.

Keep your energy up to match the crowd.

Capernaum = kuh-PER-nee-*m

Excited upon finding him.

Don't sound angry; Jesus understands their desires, but wants to show a better way.

What a waste of time!

Sincerely.

This person is more suspicious and challenging than the prior speakers.

A gentle reminder.

GOSPEL   John 6:24–35

A reading from the holy Gospel according to John

When the **crowd** saw that neither Jesus nor his disciples
> were there,
> they **themselves** got into boats
> and came to Capernaum **looking** for Jesus.
And when they **found** him across the sea they said to him,
> "**Rabbi**, when did you **get** here?"
Jesus **answered** them and said,
> "Amen, **amen**, I **say** to you,
> you are looking for me **not** because you saw **signs**
> but because you ate the **loaves** and were **filled**.
Do not work for food that **perishes**
> but for the food that **endures** for eternal **life**,
> which the Son of **Man** will give you.
For on **him** the Father, **God**, has set his seal."
So they said to him,
> "What can we do to **accomplish** the works of God?"
Jesus answered and said to them,
> "**This** is the work of God, that you **believe** in the one
> > he sent."
So they said to him,
> "What **sign** can you do, that we may **see** and **believe** in you?
What can you **do**?
Our ancestors ate **manna** in the desert, as it is written:
> *He gave them bread from heaven to eat.*"
So Jesus said to them,
> "Amen, **amen**, I **say** to you,
> it was not **Moses** who gave the bread from heaven;
> my **Father** gives you the **true** bread from heaven.

one he sent," provokes the crowd's next response. Again, in paraphrase: "In order for us to have faith, we must see a sign. What is your sign? Moses gave our ancestors wonder-manna. Can you perform such a miracle for us?" This attitude recalls the onlookers at the Crucifixion, when they mocked Jesus, saying that if he came down off the Cross they would believe in him (Mark 15:32). That demonstration of power would probably evoke a temporary kind of "belief," but not the kind Jesus wanted.

Jesus responds, saying that Moses did not provide the food from heaven. The Father gave them bread that comes from heaven that gives life to the world. The manna, he explains, is like the miraculous food he'd provided the day before—just a sign of the real food God gives. The audience's misunderstanding of this teaching is like that of the Samaritan woman at the well. They all ask for a constant supply of bread (or water—see John 4:15).

Jesus tries again (paraphrase), "I am the bread of life, the life-giving bread, the bread that is life. No one who comes to me shall ever be hungry or thirsty. Moses was not the giver; the manna was not just bread! God is the constant giver, and I, Christ, am the real food." Here John prods his audience to pay attention to the deeper meaning. It is as if Jesus had said: "You cannot be fulfilled while you are focusing on your stomachs. The earthbound person is only half alive. The person who sees past

Eagerly.

Slowly and deliberately. Jesus knows this teaching will be hard for many to understand. Take your time to make it clear.

For the bread of **God** is that which comes **down** from heaven
     and gives **life** to the world."
So they said to him,
     "Sir, give us this bread **always**."
Jesus said to them,
     "**I** am the bread of life;
     whoever **comes** to me will **never** hunger,
     and whoever **believes** in me will **never thirst**."

THE 4 STEPS OF *LECTIO DIVINA* OR PRAYERFUL READING

1. *Lectio:* Read a Scripture passage aloud slowly. Notice what phrase captures your attention and be attentive to its meaning. Silent pause.

2. *Meditatio:* Read the passage aloud slowly again, reflecting on the passage, allowing God to speak to you through it. Silent pause.

3. *Oratio:* Read it aloud slowly a third time, allowing it to be your prayer or response to God's gift of insight to you. Silent pause.

4. *Contemplatio:* Read it aloud slowly a fourth time, now resting in God's word.

---

the horizon to the stars is truly alive." Of the two kinds of hunger, material food satisfies bodily hunger for a little while, but spiritual hunger is never satisfied; some hungers can only be satisfied by Jesus. Christ alone satisfies the hunger of the human heart and soul. K.S.

NINETEENTH SUNDAY IN ORDINARY TIME

LECTIONARY #116

READING I   1 Kings 19:4–8

A reading from the first Book of Kings

Elijah went a day's journey into the **desert**,
  until he came to a **broom** tree and sat **beneath** it.
He **prayed** for **death**, saying:
  "This is **enough**, O Lord!
Take my **life**, for I am no **better** than my fathers."
He lay down and fell **asleep** under the broom tree,
  but then an **angel** touched him and ordered him to **get** up
    and **eat**.
Elijah **looked** and **there** at his head was a **hearth** cake
  and a jug of **water**.
After he **ate** and **drank**, he lay down **again**,
  but the angel of the Lord came back a **second** time,
  touched him, and ordered,
    "**Get** up and **eat**, else the journey will be too **long** for you!"
He **got** up, **ate**, and **drank**;
  then **strengthened** by that food,
  he walked forty **days** and forty **nights** to the mountain
    of **God**, **Horeb**.

A narrative reading. Think of someone specific you know who is overwhelmed and despondent. Proclaim as if speaking to that person to convey God's compassion.

Elijah = ee-LĪ-juh
Proclaim with tiredness in your voice from the start.
Elijah's exhaustion might be best proclaimed softly, but intensely, with real anguish.

Keep your energy low, then immediately pick it up at the angel's appearance.

With some surprise.

Drop your energy again as Elijah gives up, then pick it up as the angel returns.

Firmly.

Stand up straight and proclaim with Elijah's renewed vigor and confidence in God.

Horeb = HOHR-eb

READING I   Elijah, disillusioned because of the constant opposition his prophetic work had aroused, was ready to give up. But roused and fed by God, he spent forty days and nights retracing the Israelites' forty-year desert trek, going up Mount Horeb to meet God. This story focuses on the breakfast the angel provided under the shrub, a reviving meal that prefigures the Eucharist, Viaticum—provisions for a journey. We pilgrims traveling toward the eternal inheritance are sustained by the Sacrament of the Eucharist. The mountain of God, Horeb, recalls Sinai of the exodus; it is where Elijah met God, who restored his energy to continue his service. All along the wilderness path the prophet was strengthened by food, and so are we. Thus invigorated, we continue our journey to the mountain of God.

READING II   In chapter 4 of the Letter to the Ephesians the author has been expounding on the lifestyle expected of a Christian who receives the grace of the Holy Spirit. In this passage, he outlines the effects of the people's incorporation into the Christian community. The phrase "grieve the Holy Spirit" echoes Isaiah 63:10, speaking of the disobedient Israelites: "they rebelled and grieved his holy spirit." He presents a list of vices to avoid—"bitterness, fury, anger, shouting, and reviling"; all have their root in anger, about which the author has said (several verses before this passage begins): "do not let the sun set on your anger" (4:26). After the list of unacceptable behaviors, this principle is laid down: behave toward one another as God behaves toward you. The Christian's behavior should be kind, compassionate, and forgiving.

For meditation and context:

TO KEEP IN MIND
Exhortatory texts make an urgent appeal to listeners. They may encourage, warn, or challenge, and often include a call to action. You must convey the urgency and passion behind the words.

An exhortatory reading. Make sure Paul's love (and yours) comes through in this short and simple reading.

Ephesians = ee-FEE-shuhnz

Of course you don't want to act this way!

Eagerly.
Pause at the end of this line.

A summary of the whole Christian way of living. Sincerely encourage the assembly with this exhortation.

TO KEEP IN MIND
Be careful not to "swallow" words by mumbling. Articulate carefully so that every word is clearly heard, especially at the end of lines.

RESPONSORIAL PSALM   Psalm 34:2–3, 4–5, 6–7, 8–9 (9a)

R. Taste and see the goodness of the Lord.

I will bless the LORD at all times;
   his praise shall be ever in my mouth.
Let my soul glory in the LORD;
   the lowly will hear me and be glad.

Glorify the LORD with me,
   let us together extol his name.
I sought the LORD, and he answered me
   and delivered me from all my fears.

Look to him that you may be radiant
   with joy,
   and your faces may not blush with shame.
When the afflicted man called out, the
   LORD heard,
   and from all his distress he saved him.

The angel of the LORD encamps
   around those who fear him and
   delivers them.
Taste and see how good the LORD is;
   blessed the man who takes refuge in him.

READING II   Ephesians 4:30—5:2

A reading from the Letter of Saint Paul to the Ephesians

Brothers and sisters:
Do not **grieve** the Holy **Spirit** of God,
   with which you were **sealed** for the day of **redemption**.
All bitterness, **fury**, **anger**, **shouting**, and **reviling**
   must be **removed** from you, along with **all malice**.
And be **kind** to one another, **compassionate**,
   forgiving one another as God has forgiven **you** in Christ.

So be **imitators** of God, as **beloved** children, and live in **love**,
   as **Christ** loved us and handed himself **over** for us
   as a sacrificial **offering** to God for **a fragrant** aroma.

The section concludes with fraternal love and harmony, virtues opposite the divisions caused by anger. When Israel was redeemed from slavery in Egypt, the Passover lamb's blood on their doorposts was the sign of those who would be skipped over and saved from the plague of death. In an analogous way the seal of the Holy Spirit, received in the sacraments of Baptism and Confirmation, is the indelible sign engraved in the soul of those called to salvation by virtue of the redemption in Christ. Be "imitators of God" in forgiving and loving: what a marvelous call—impos-

sible, except for God's grace—to love "as Christ loved us."

What is remarkable is the degree of perfection that is asked of the Christian—to be all things, not in any mediocre way, but in a way that seems impossible for ordinary persons: "forgiving one another as God has forgiven you in Christ." The Eucharist sets before us what we are called to be: a people who live together in peace, a people who choose to act as peacemakers. In celebrating the Eucharist together we assume the task of exercising a peacemaking influence. On this day the Eucharistic Prayer we

pray silently as the celebrant speaks it aloud asks that the individuals gathered for worship be transformed into one people.

GOSPEL   In this passage the audience with whom Jesus dialogues is not the beneficiaries of the multiplication of the loaves but the "Jews" who murmur, as did the Israelites in the desert (Exodus 16:2, 6–12). The people John describes may be Galileans who are familiar with Jesus' background and thus conclude that he is just too ordinary to be the Messiah. Here he says that the Father

A narrative reading ending with an exhortation. Jesus' words are well known to us, but would have been new to the crowd. Take your time.

GOSPEL   John 6:41–51

A reading from the holy Gospel according to John

The Jews **murmured** about Jesus because he said,
  "I am the **bread** that came down from **heaven**,"
  and they said,
  "Is this not **Jesus**, the son of **Joseph**?

These three lines can sound like three different people; convey their "murmurs" with a low, but audible, voice.

Do we not know his **father** and **mother**?
Then **how** can he say,
  '**I** have come down from **heaven**'?"
Jesus answered and said to them,
  "Stop **murmuring** among yourselves.

With emphasis!

The exhortatory passage begins here; make sure Jesus' great love comes through in your voice, eyes, and face.

Take this line slowly.

No one can come to me unless the **Father** who sent me
    draw him,
  and I will **raise** him on the **last** day.
It is written in the prophets:
  They shall all be taught by **God**.
Everyone who **listens** to my Father and **learns** from him **comes**
    to me.
Not that anyone has **seen** the Father
  except the one who is **from** God;
  he has seen the Father.
Amen, **amen**, I say to you,
  whoever **believes** has eternal **life**.
I am the **bread** of life.

Pause at the end of this line.

Good news! Raise your excitement and energy in this section.

Your ancestors ate the **manna** in the desert, but they **died**;
  this is the bread that comes down from heaven
  so that one may **eat it** and **not** die.
I am the **living** bread that came down from heaven;
  whoever eats **this** bread will live **forever**;
  and the bread that **I** will give is my **flesh** for the life
    of the **world**."

Pause at the end of this line.

Proclaim this final section more intimately, with love and tenderness, slowing to the end.

---

draws believers to himself; later (John 12:32), Jesus, elevated on the Cross, draws all people to himself. In the spirit of the Old Testament, does the evangelist also allude to love's power to "draw" (as in Hosea 11:4; Song of Songs 1:4; Jeremiah 31:3)?

This passage shows the reasons why the religious authorities, "the Jews," rejected Jesus, and in rejecting him rejected eternal life. In the first place, they weighed matters by merely human values and market standards. They reacted because Jesus was just a carpenter's son, and they knew of his humble beginnings in Nazareth. How could a tradesman from a plebeian home possibly be God's messenger? Do we reject God's message because we do not care for the messenger? Because God's eloquent message came by means of the Galilean carpenter, the authorities disregarded it.

The religious leaders were so distracted by arguments among themselves that it did not occur to them to refer to God's decision. They were so convinced of their own logical arguments that they ignored the theology. Better to remain quiet and ask God's opinion about what to do. In the end they listened but did not learn. Listening to God consists of silence, hearing beyond the words, and changing one's attitude or, in a word, conversion.
K.S.

THE ASSUMPTION OF THE BLESSED VIRGIN MARY: VIGIL

A narrative reading. See the story unfold before you as you proclaim. Let your face and voice reflect your emotions as you watch.

Chronicles = KRAH-nih-k*ls

This is a big deal! Everyone is there.

Aaron = AYR-uhn

Levites = LEE-vīts

This is a solemn event, but also one of great joy!

Let the excitement of the day come through as you describe the music.

lyres = līrz

You can lower your energy a bit to indicate the mystery unfolding here.

Don't lose the word "blessed." Convey this blessing to your community as well.

LECTIONARY #621

READING I   1 Chronicles 15:3–4, 15–16; 16:1–2

A reading from the first Book of Chronicles

David assembled **all** Israel in Jerusalem to bring the **ark** of the Lord
　　to the place that he had **prepared** for it.
David also called together the sons of **Aaron** and the **Levites**.

The **Levites** bore the ark of God on their **shoulders** with poles,
　　as **Moses** had ordained according to the word of the **Lord**.

David commanded the chiefs of the Levites
　　to appoint their kinsmen as **chanters**,
　　to **play** on musical instruments, **harps**, **lyres**, and **cymbals**,
　　to make a **loud** sound of **rejoicing**.

They brought in the ark of God and set it within the **tent**
　　which David had pitched for it.
Then they offered up burnt **offerings** and **peace** offerings to God.
When David had finished offering up the burnt offerings and
　　peace offerings,
　　he **blessed** the people in the name of the Lord.

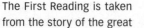 **READING I** The First Reading is taken from the story of the great liturgical procession in which the Ark of the Covenant is installed in the tent set up for it by David in Jerusalem. On this feast of the Assumption of Mary the Church recalls this enthronement of the Ark in Jerusalem and celebrates Mary, the true Ark of the Covenant, the definitive sanctuary of God's presence on earth.

READING II Paul is meditating on the Christian's passage from a mortal to an immortal body. He applies two Scripture quotations, one from Isaiah 25:8, "Death is swallowed up in victory," and a second from the prophet Hosea (13:14), which Paul adapts to his own advantage. Hosea had invited death to wield its sting, but Paul envisions the risen Church speaking these words to taunt death for its ultimate powerlessness: "Where, O death, is your victory? Where, O death, is your sting?" Then, explaining that "the sting of death is sin," he seems to suggest that like a scorpion, sin injects its poison into us and is the cause of death. But through Christ, God gives us the victory.

GOSPEL In this Gospel a woman has called out, "Blessed is the womb that carried you," and Jesus replies, "Rather, blessed are those who hear the word of God and observe it." The beatitude emphasizes that attentiveness to God's Word is more important than a biological relationship to Jesus.

Mary, the Mother of God, is doubly beatified, for her spiritual relationship with God's Word and her physical relationship with his Son. Thus is revealed the fullness of Mary's glory and her significance in the history of salvation. The Mother of God's

For meditation and context:

RESPONSORIAL PSALM   Psalm 132:6–7, 9–10, 13–14 (8)

R. Lord, go up to the place of your rest, you and the ark of your holiness.

Behold, we heard of it in Ephrathah;
   we found it in the fields of Jaar.
Let us enter into his dwelling,
   let us worship at his footstool.

May your priests be clothed with justice;
   let your faithful ones shout merrily for joy.
For the sake of David your servant,
   reject not the plea of your anointed.

For the LORD has chosen Zion;
   he prefers her for his dwelling.
"Zion is my resting place forever;
   in her will I dwell, for I prefer her."

> **TO KEEP IN MIND**
> *Parallelism* refers to phrases or sentences that have a similar structure or express a similar idea. Use emphasis and rhythm to make sure any parallelism stands out.

An exhortatory reading that teaches the central tenet of our faith: life has conquered death through Jesus Christ.
Corinthians = kohr-IN-thee-uhnz

READING II   1 Corinthians 15:54b–57

A reading from the first Letter of Saint Paul to the Corinthians

Brothers and sisters:
When that which is **mortal** clothes itself with **immortality**,
   then the word that is **written** shall come about:

> ***Death*** *is swallowed up in **victory**.*
> ***Where**, **O** death, is your **victory**?*
> ***Where**, **O** death, is your **sting**?*

The **sting** of **death** is sin,
   and the **power** of sin is the **law**.
But **thanks** be to **God** who gives us the **victory**
   through our LORD Jesus **Christ**.

Proclaim with expectant hope!

Paul quotes this song (or poem). You needn't sing, of course, but let your proclamation resound with equal energy and joy.

Slight pause after "But." Take this slowly and look directly into the community.

Son has been elevated to the glory of the elect, where she attests to the victory over death that belongs to everyone who follows Christ, who hears the Word of God and observes it.

In the Byzantine tradition there exists an icon of the "Dormition" of the Mother of God, that represents the mystery of the Assumption. The icon is divided in two panels, top and bottom, which present the same mystery depicted from two angles, the earthly and the heavenly. In the lower panel the Blessed Virgin, asleep in death, is laid out on a pedestal. Anguished, desolate Apostles, mourning her death, surround the bier. One has approached the body and reached out to touch it, when suddenly a sword appears in mid-air and slices off the hands, which are suspended there. In the upper panel of the icon, Jesus appears among angels—the Son of God in glory. He lovingly embraces a little child clothed in white. She is the Blessed Virgin, body and soul, assumed into heaven at the moment of her Passover—her death to the present world and birth into eternity. The persons in the lower panel are not aware of the drama unfolding in heaven, where Christ receives souls, embraces and kisses them in the moment of their death, and presents them to the heavenly choir of angels and saints.

Without the gift of faith human reason tries but cannot comprehend the mystery of death. This effort to grasp death's meaning appears as one person's extended hands, wishing to grasp and retain what must be transferred to the transcendent world, hands now amputated because a person cannot survive intact an incursion into the mystery of death. Suffering, sickness, sin, and death are mysteries that exceed the capacity of our reason. The

A narrative with two exhortations. Short, but don't rush.

Raise your voice and energy. The woman is overcome with excitement and can't help but cry out these words of praise.

Pause at the end of this line.

Don't drop your energy but lower your volume.

Careful not to make Jesus' reply sound like a rebuke. He doesn't negate the woman's blessing of his mother, but offers an even better blessing, available to everyone.

TO KEEP IN MIND

In a narrative, find an emotion or point of view for each character, keeping in mind that these might change during the reading.

GOSPEL   Luke 11:27–28

A reading from the holy Gospel according to Luke

While **Jesus** was speaking,
 a **woman** from the crowd **called** out and said to him,
 "**Blessed** is the **womb** that **carried** you
 and the **breasts** at which you **nursed**."
He replied,
 "**Rather**, **blessed** are those
 who **hear** the word of God and **observe** it."

---

knife in the air that slices off the hands demonstrates how reason is violently cut short in the presence of the sublime mystery of the Virgin's death. We need the eyes of faith, as on the day of the Resurrection of Jesus, when the Beloved Disciple saw and believed; his faith penetrated the Resurrection mystery.

The icon invites us to contemplate two distinct anthropologies: Human life as seen from below, with a limited perspective that responds to the death of the Virgin or of Christ as if it were a period at the end of the sentence of human existence, or human life from the perspective of faith, shown in the upper part of the icon: Jesus in glory as he lovingly embraces his Mother, body and soul, for all eternity. We appreciate here an "anthropology from below," conditioned by doubt, limitation, anguish, sin, and weakness, and marvel before an "anthropology from above," woman and man as God sees and values us, persons capable of perpetual friendship with God.

The Church invites us to contemplate our dignity as God designed it, the image and likeness of that same God, the human being who breathes God's same Holy Spirit, the person who has an excellent worth, a lasting vocation.

THE ASSUMPTION OF THE BLESSED VIRGIN MARY: DAY

LECTIONARY #622

READING I   Revelation 11:19a; 12:1–6a, 10ab

A reading from the Book of Revelation

God's **temple** in heaven was **opened**,
  and the **ark** of his covenant could be seen in the temple.

A **great** sign appeared in the sky, a **woman** clothed with the **sun**,
  with the **moon** under her **feet**,
  and on her **head** a **crown** of twelve **stars**.
She was with **child** and **wailed** aloud in pain as she labored to
    give birth.
Then **another** sign appeared in the sky;
  it was a **huge red dragon**, with seven **heads** and ten **horns**,
  and on its heads were seven **diadems**.
Its tail **swept** away a third of the **stars** in the sky
  and **hurled** them down to the **earth**.
Then the dragon stood before the woman about to give birth,
  to **devour** her child when she gave birth.
She gave birth to a **son**, a **male** child,
  destined to **rule** all the nations with an iron rod.
Her child was **caught up** to God and his **throne**.
The woman herself **fled** into the **desert**
  where she had a place **prepared** by God.

A narrative reading filled with fantastical images; the text demands great energy and passion in its telling.

Start with heightened intensity.

Each part of this image is more amazing than the last!

Your voice can take on a sinister tone, but keep your energy up to convey the ferocity of this creature.

Slow down on "huge red dragon," then return to a normal pace.

Use the words "swept" and "hurled" to show the beast's power.

Pause at the end of this line.

Slow down and lower your intensity a little. This is a moment of joy.

Pick up your pace again; "caught up" and "fled" indicate quick action.

A sense of relief; all will be well. Pause.

READING I The appearance of the Ark of the Covenant represents God's fidelity and portends the victory of Christ and the Church over evil forces. That confrontation takes place in heaven with the fierce dragon's attack against the woman and her son. It signifies that from all eternity God had planned Christ's birth and the devil's powerlessness before his divine person. The woman adorned with the sun, the moon, and the stars symbolizes God's people; she is the Virgin Mother of God, the Church.

The evangelist, Luke, narrating the Annunciation, portrays Mary as the representation of the faithful remnant of Israel: to her the angel addresses the prophet Zephaniah's greeting to the Daughter of Zion ("Do not fear," Zephaniah 3:16). Her pregnancy, prophesied by Isaiah ("The virgin shall conceive, and bear a son, and shall call his name Emmanuel," 7:14), carries within it the suffering of Calvary: Israel of old gave birth to the Messiah and then became the new Israel, the Church, who suffers the dragon's persecution. God will protect the persecuted woman in the des-

ert, as he did the people of God in the exodus—the desert being the traditional place of refuge for the afflicted.

READING II After affirming Christ's Resurrection, Paul explains its positive implications. The "first fruits" is the thanksgiving portion of the harvest offered to God, and it consecrates the rest of the harvest to follow. Christ's Resurrection is the firstfruits that consecrates the harvest of believers that will follow. The union of Christians with Christ is so intimate that his Resurrection is the force of

This is a proclamation of joy.

Then I heard a loud **voice** in heaven say:
"Now have **salvation** and **power** come,
    and the **Kingdom** of our **God**
    and the **authority** of his **Anointed** One."

For meditation and context:

RESPONSORIAL PSALM   Psalm 45:10, 11, 12, 16 (10bc)

R. The queen stands at your right hand, arrayed in gold.

> **TO KEEP IN MIND**
> A *didactic* text makes a point or teaches something. Help your assembly to follow the argument and understand what's being taught.

The queen takes her place at your right hand
   in gold of Ophir.

So shall the king desire your beauty;
   for he is your LORD.

Hear, O daughter, and see; turn your ear,
   forget your people and your father's house.

They are borne in with gladness and joy;
   they enter the palace of the king.

A didactic reading. There's great joy in this teaching; let that come through in your proclamation.

Corinthians = kohr-IN-thee-unz

READING II   1 Corinthians 15:20–27

A reading from the first Letter of Saint Paul to the Corinthians

Brothers and sisters:
Christ has been **raised** from the dead,
   the **firstfruits** of those who have fallen asleep.
For since **death** came through **man**,
   the **resurrection** of the dead came **also** through man.

Paul repeats the same point—that Christ's Resurrection prefigures our own—in different ways.
This should sound self-evident.

For just as in **Adam** all **die**,
   so too in **Christ** shall all be brought to **life**,
   but **each** one in proper order:
   Christ the **firstfruits**;
   then, at his **coming**, those who **belong** to Christ;

What follows is a list of three events.

   then comes the **end**,
   when he **hands** over the Kingdom to his God and Father,
   when he has **destroyed** every **sovereignty**
   and every **authority** and **power**.
For he must reign until he has put all his enemies **under** his feet.
The **last** enemy to be destroyed is **death**,
   for "he subjected **everything** under his feet."

This is good news! The world will be freed from every oppression and evil. Don't make it sound like a terrible Armageddon.

Slight pause after "for" so the final phrase sounds like a quote.

---

our resurrection. Human existence, both natural and supernatural, involves solidarity. In Paul's argument, "In Adam . . . in Christ," Paul presents Adam as a type of Christ. Just as Adam's disobedience resulted in everybody's death, Jesus, the new Adam, ushers in the resurrection from the dead. Salvation culminates in the resurrection of the body at the end of time.

Paul's christological perspective embraces cosmic dimensions, which are evident when he describes the climax of history, "the end." He presents Christ's final relations to his enemies and his Father in both royal and military language: Christ "hands over the kingdom to his God and Father, when he has destroyed every sovereignty" and Paul inserts a proof from Scripture, referring to Psalm 110:1; 8:7. God is the agent and the aim, and we are the beneficiaries of the action. In writing that "the last enemy to be destroyed is death," Paul reflects that death is not just one cosmic power among many but the ultimate effect of sin in the universe. Christ defeats death where it prevails: in our bodies. The destruction of the last enemy is the "coming to life" of "those who belong to Christ."

GOSPEL The *Magnificat*, the Canticle of Mary, ends the cycle of birth annunciations at the beginning of Luke's Gospel account and reveals the greatness of the mystery. It is the Church's thanksgiving hymn for the marvels God accomplished through the mother of his Son, for God's mercy is "on those who fear him in every generation."

But even before that hymn, the greetings exchanged by the two women reveal and celebrate the mystery. "When Elizabeth heard Mary's greeting, the infant leaped in her womb." Elizabeth knew that

A narrative reading with an exhortation. Your tone should be different in each section.

Keep up your pace to indicate Mary's haste.

Judah = JOO-duh

Zechariah = zek-uh-RĪ-uh

Immediately smile with your voice, eyes, and face as you convey Elizabeth's joy.
Let your voice "leap" as well.

There's great excitement in Elizabeth's voice.

She can't contain her excitement.

TO KEEP IN MIND
A *narrative* has characters, dialogue, a setting, and action. Help your listeners see the story unfold, keep characters distinct, and be clear about shifts in setting.

GOSPEL   Luke 1:39–56

A reading from the holy Gospel according to Luke

Mary set out
   and traveled to the hill country in **haste**
   to a town of Judah,
   where she entered the house of **Zechariah**
   and greeted **Elizabeth**.
When Elizabeth **heard** Mary's greeting,
   the infant **leaped** in her womb,
   and **Elizabeth**, **filled** with the Holy Spirit,
   cried out in a loud voice and said,
   "**Blessed** are you among **women**,
   and blessed is the **fruit** of your **womb**.
And how does this happen to **me,**
   that the **mother** of my LORD should come to me?
For at the moment the sound of your greeting reached my ears,
   the infant in my womb **leaped** for **joy**.
Blessed are you who **believed**
   that what was **spoken** to you by the LORD
   would be **fulfilled**."

---

the child, inspired by supernatural joy, leapt in response to Mary's greeting. Because of this "sign," and inspired by the Holy Spirit, Elizabeth's eyes were opened: "And how does this happen to me, that the mother of my Lord should come to me?" Elizabeth reflects on the mystery further when she sings: "Blessed are you who believed that what was spoken to you by the Lord would be fulfilled." In Mary, all the persons of the Old and New Testaments can contemplate with joy and thanksgiving the accomplishment of all that was promised, the fulfillment of their hopes.

To the praise from Elizabeth, the Virgin responds with praise of God. The canticle reveals the depths of her soul and faith and her perfect submission to God's Word and the mission entrusted to her. Interlaced with biblical reminiscences, this song celebrates God's humble servant as the ideal image of the poor, God's beloved. The *Magnificat* expresses an exalted, pure vision of human relations with God as revealed in the Gospel. No one has lived the same experience as Mary, yet the Church appropriates this canticle for herself, for she can see the marvels that God

has done for the faithful throughout the ages. What God has done for the littlest and lost people incites gratitude and unspeakable joy. In these words we can all feel that we have been chosen by God, who shows the initiative to save us out of sheer love. With Mary, "blessed . . . among women," the Church and all the faithful give thanks for the graces received from God.

Mary stands at the center of salvation history: "From this day all ages will call me blessed." But she does not stop with contemplating herself; she marvels at God's works—"Holy is his Name," having "mercy

This song pours from Mary's heart, as if Elizabeth's greeting has banished all fear and anxiety from her, and her pent-up joy overflows into praise. Keep your energy and pace up.

Proclaim as if Mary is speaking directly to Elizabeth—someone she can share her most intimate thoughts with. How do you feel when you're sharing exciting news with a close friend?

These images portray God as the help of the poor and lowly and the vanquisher of the rich and powerful. How do you feel about such a God?

Pause, as if to allow Mary to catch her breath.

Drop your energy slightly and take your time on this last line.

TO KEEP IN MIND
Proclamation cannot be effective unless it is expressive. As you prepare your proclamation, make choices about emotions. Some choices are already evident in the text.

And Mary said:

"My **soul** proclaims the **greatness** of the LORD;
   my spirit **rejoices** in God my **Savior**
   for he has with **favor** on his lowly servant.
From this day **all** generations will call me **blessed**:
   the Almighty has done **great** things for me
   and **holy** is his **Name**.
He has **mercy** on those who **fear** him
   in **every** generation.
He has shown the **strength** of his arm,
   and has **scattered** the **proud** in their **conceit**.
He has **cast** down the mighty from their **thrones**,
   and has **lifted** up the **lowly**.
He has **filled** the hungry with **good** things,
   and the **rich** he has sent away **empty**.
He has come to the **help** of his servant **Israel**
   for he has **remembered** his promise of mercy,
   the promise he made to our **fathers**,
   to **Abraham** and his children for **ever**."

Mary **remained** with her about three months
   and then **returned** to her home.

---

on those who fear him in every generation." The Church joins her voice to Mary's, as she acclaims God's justice, "the strength of his arm," which manifests his faithfulness, his power, and his amazing choices: "He has lifted up the lowly . . . he has remembered his promise of mercy, the promise he made to our fathers." K.S.

TWENTIETH SUNDAY IN ORDINARY TIME

LECTIONARY #119

An exhortatory reading. Help the assembly see the images you describe.

READING I   Proverbs 9:1–6

A reading from the Book of Proverbs

Good news, so smile with your voice, eyes, and face throughout.

> **Wisdom** has built her **house**,
>   she has set up her seven **columns**;
> she has dressed her **meat**, mixed her **wine**,
>   **yes**, she has spread her **table**.
> She has sent out her **maidens**; she **calls**
>   from the **heights** out over the **city**:

Keep your energy up.

> "Let whoever is **simple** turn in **here**";
>   to the one who lacks **understanding**, she says,

"Simple" is not an insult; it refers to those who still seek wisdom.

Maintain eye contact with the assembly and directly invite them, as if you wanted them to get up out of their seats and come forward.

> "**Come**, **eat** of my food,
>   and drink of the **wine** I have mixed!
> Forsake **foolishness** that you may **live**;
>   advance in the way of **understanding**."

For meditation and context:

RESPONSORIAL PSALM   Psalm 34:2–3, 4–5, 6–7 (9a)

R. Taste and see the goodness of the Lord.

I will bless the LORD at all times;
     his praise shall be ever in my mouth.
Let my soul glory in the LORD;
     the lowly will hear me and be glad.

Glorify the LORD with me,
     let us together extol his name.
I sought the LORD, and he answered me
     and delivered me from all my fears.

Look to him that you may be radiant
     with joy,
     and your faces may not blush with shame.
When the poor one called out, the
     LORD heard,
     and from all his distress he saved him.

TO KEEP IN MIND
Exhortatory texts make an urgent appeal to listeners. They may encourage, warn, or challenge, and often include a call to action. You must convey the urgency and passion behind the words.

READING I | The nine-chapter introduction to Proverbs concludes with Lady Wisdom's invitation to share her banquet. The seven columns of the house symbolize the perfection of her home—seven being emblematic of perfection. By design the book is composed of seven collections of proverbs, pointing to the completeness of her wisdom. The banquet offers the teaching of the sages, and the person who listens to Wisdom's teaching and eats at her table assimilates her wisdom. The follower of Wisdom will "advance in the way of understanding."

Wisdom's banquet prefigures the true Bread of Life that God gives, the body of the Word made flesh.

READING II | The new life received in Baptism is characterized by careful consideration, not foolishness. Our aim is to profit from the time God gives to make us holy, to live moderately, and to praise God. This reading summons us to conduct ourselves wisely and to praise God. Together they highlight the purposes for which the new community exists: praise of God's grace and walking in good works.

The warning "Watch carefully how you live" highlights the constant danger that the righteous face in this present age when "the days are evil."

While drunkenness and its resulting lack of control are common in lists of vices to avoid, the blindness or unconsciousness of a drunken humanity also serves as a metaphor for Christians looking forward to eternal life. The antithesis of being "drunk" is to be "filled with the Spirit." Praise and thanksgiving are the appropriate response to what God has accomplished in the life of

An exhortatory reading. Urge your assembly to live consistent with their identity as Christians filled with the Spirit.

Ephesians = ee-FEE-shuhnz

Paul sets up contrasts between the foolish and the wise; be dismissive of the foolish behavior and let your energy rise as you describe the wise.

debauchery = dih-BAW-chuh-ree

Hear the joyful sounds in the scene Paul describes and let that come through in your proclamation.

Slow to the end, but keep your energy up.

TO KEEP IN MIND

You can't proclaim what you don't understand. Read the Scripture passage and its commentary in *Workbook*. Then read it from your Bible, including what comes before and after it so that you understand the context.

READING II   Ephesians 5:15–20

A reading from the Letter of Saint Paul to the Ephesians

Brothers and sisters:
Watch **carefully** how you live,
   not as **foolish** persons but as **wise**,
   making the **most** of the opportunity,
   because the days are **evil**.
Therefore, do not continue in **ignorance**,
   but try to **understand** what is the will of the LORD.
And do not get **drunk** on wine, in which lies **debauchery**,
   but be **filled** with the **Spirit**,
   addressing one another in **psalms** and **hymns** and
     spiritual **songs**,
   singing and **playing** to the LORD in your **hearts**,
   giving thanks **always** and for **everything**
in the name of our LORD Jesus **Christ** to God the **Father**.

---

the believer, and "singing and playing" keeps our hearts focused on the Lord.

GOSPEL This reading has some of the strongest statements from Jesus that can be found. How can we appreciate this tapestry of extraordinary sayings? John the Evangelist is instructing us about the value of the Eucharist. It is offered to us in two ways. The first is from the ambo, the altar of the Word that became flesh (John 1:14); the second is from the altar as bread and wine transformed into the Body and Blood of the

Lamb. The reference to "the bread that came down from heaven" that our "ancestors" ate on the journey from slavery to freedom is eloquent. The manna nourishes us as we travel toward the Promised Land. In this reading Jesus offers the new manna to his community, the Bread of Life in the form of the Word of God. If we understand Jesus' discourse in terms of the Mass, our first communion consists in listening to the Word of God, who enters the ear of our interior life and nourishes us for life. But there is another element to our feast: the altar of sacrifice the Baptist referred to

when he named Jesus "The Lamb of God who takes away the sin of the world."

This discourse of Jesus takes place during the Passover, after the multiplication of the five loaves. We may imagine that it is the Passover Lamb who speaks, or Jesus addressing us from the Cross. The Paschal Lamb invites our contemplation: If you do not share in the Paschal supper, "unless you eat the flesh of the Son of Man [the Lamb] and drink his blood, you do not have life within you." Apart from Holy Communion with Jesus' Passion, Death, and Resurrection, we do not receive life, or

GOSPEL   John 6:51–58

A reading from the holy Gospel according to John

Jesus said to the crowds:
  "**I** am the living **bread** that came down from **heaven**;
  whoever **eats** this bread will live **forever**;
  and the bread that **I** will give
  is my **flesh** for the **life** of the **world**."

The Jews **quarreled** among themselves, saying,
  "How can this man give us his **flesh** to eat?"
Jesus said to them,
  "Amen, **amen**, I say to you,
  unless you eat the **flesh** of the Son of Man and drink his **blood**,
  you do not have **life** within you.
Whoever **eats** my **flesh** and **drinks** my **blood**
  has **eternal** life,
  and I will **raise** him on the **last day**.
For my **flesh** is true **food**,
  and my **blood** is true **drink**.
Whoever **eats** my flesh and **drinks** my blood
  remains in me and **I in him**.
Just as the living Father **sent** me
  and I have life **because** of the Father,
  so also the one who **feeds** on me
  will have life **because** of me.
This is the bread that came down from **heaven**.
Unlike your ancestors who ate and still **died**,
  whoever eats **this** bread will live **forever**."

An exhortatory reading. Although Jesus is preaching to a crowd, he is explaining the depth of the intimacy he wants with us. Convey that intimacy in your tone and energy.

Be excited to share this news; avoid preaching.

Quickly. Express their confusion.

Take this whole section slowly; Jesus knows this is a hard teaching, and conveys it with great love and gentleness.

Good news! Pause.

Our intimacy with Jesus is as close as his is with the Father. Share this insight eagerly with the assembly.

Pause at the end of this line.

Slow your pace but not your energy.

we settle for half a life with little transcendent content outside our own illusions.

So what does Holy Communion really entail? How does the act of communion with the Body and Blood of the Lamb of God who takes away the sin of the world affect us? For believers, communion with Jesus, partaking of his Body and Blood, means receiving the eternal benefits of this food. "Whoever eats my flesh and drinks my blood has eternal life, and I will raise him on the last day." To receive the Body and Blood of Christ is to enter into Holy Communion with the Word made flesh, the Lamb of God who takes away the sin of the world. To enter into communion involves taking a conscious stand on the side of grace and removing ourselves from sin. It entails a decision to approach Christ, receive his very life in our own person, as the dough receives the leaven that ferments the whole loaf. To enter into communion with Christ means that we are not satisfied with sin, but rather we adopt the Death and life of the Lamb as part of our own life. Who of us does not know the face of pain, anguish, and suffering? When we receive communion we share the sacrifice of Jesus, we let his Word and his healing invade, permeate, and save us from ourselves, transforming our very selves into sharers in the sacrifice of Christ for the salvation of the world. K.S.

TWENTY-FIRST SUNDAY IN ORDINARY TIME

LECTIONARY #122

READING I   Joshua 24:1–2a, 15–17, 18b

A reading from the Book of Joshua

Joshua gathered together **all** the tribes of Israel at Shechem,
summoning their **elders**, their **leaders**,
their **judges**, and their **officers**.
When they stood in ranks before **God**,
Joshua addressed all the people:
"If it does not **please** you to serve the **Lord**,
decide **today** whom you will serve,
the gods your **fathers** served beyond the River
or the gods of the **Amorites** in whose country you are
now dwelling.
As for **me** and my **household**, **we** will serve the **Lord**."

But the people answered,
"**Far** be it from us to **forsake** the Lord
for the service of **other** gods.
For it was the LORD, our God,
who brought us and our fathers up **out** of the land of Egypt,
out of a state of **slavery**.
He performed those great **miracles** before our very **eyes**
and **protected** us along our **entire** journey
and among the **peoples** through whom we passed.
Therefore we **also** will serve the LORD, for **he** is our **God**."

A narrative reading. No one is compelled to follow God, who honors our free choice. Urge your assembly to make known their choice today.

Shechem = SHEK-uhm

Propose this question directly to your assembly.

Amorites = AM-her-îtz

Quietly, but with great confidence. Pause before the response.

Quickly and with intensity.

Bump up your energy with this addition.

Raise your energy again. "And furthermore . . . "

Pause at the end of this line.

Slowly and emphatically.

READING I   The Book of Joshua is more than a long report of battles and conquests; it is a theological tract about the faithfulness of God who fulfills his promises. The concluding chapter, from which this passage is taken, includes a call to commitment—an invitation to the people, now taking possession of the Promised Land, to renew the covenant their ancestors made at Sinai. After the prologue that reviews what God has done for his people, Joshua measures their determination to remain faithful. This author understands that God directs history and offers his loyalty to those who are committed to him.

READING II   In this passage Paul lays out a theological foundation for the Ephesians' domestic and community life. His opening instruction, "be subordinate to one another," is a shorthand way of telling them to grow together peacefully. Addressing husbands he writes "love your wives." He develops the motif of the body of Christ, whose self-sacrifice is a model to imitate. Out of Christ's Death was born a Church holy and unblemished. In Christ believers are a single body, the growth of which depends on the well-being of every member.

With this analogy the Apostle encourages married Christians to a steady, mutual love. Basing his idea on the divine institution of marriage in Genesis 2:24, Paul stamps the marriage bond with a new meaning: the intimate relationship between

For meditation and context:

TO KEEP IN MIND

Pay attention to the pace of your reading. Varying the pace gives listeners clues to the meaning of the text. The most common problem for proclaimers new to the ministry is going too fast to be understood.

RESPONSORIAL PSALM   Psalm 34:2–3, 16–17, 18–19, 20–21 (9a)

R. Taste and see the goodness of the Lord.

I will bless the LORD at all times;
    his praise shall be ever in my mouth.
Let my soul glory in the LORD;
    the lowly will hear me and be glad.

The LORD has eyes for the just,
    and ears for their cry.
The LORD confronts the evildoers,
    to destroy remembrance of them from
    the earth.

When the just cry out, the LORD hears them,
    and from all their distress he
    rescues them.
The LORD is close to the brokenhearted;
    and those who are crushed in spirit
    he saves.

Many are the troubles of the just one,
    but out of them all the LORD delivers him;
he watches over all his bones;
    not one of them shall be broken.

A didactic reading that is difficult; read the commentary to understand the context. Work hard to ensure that Paul's love (and yours) for the community comes through.
Ephesians = ee-FEE-shuhnz

READING II   Ephesians 5:21–32

A reading from the Letter of Saint Paul to the Ephesians

[Brothers and sisters:]
Be **subordinate** to one another out of reverence for **Christ**.

Slowly and deliberately. This is a general instruction which applies to all relationships.

Wives should be subordinate to their **husbands** as to the LORD.
For the **husband** is head of his wife
    just as **Christ** is head of the **church**,
    he himself the **savior** of the body.

Emphasize all the parallels with Christ; everyone is to model themselves on the humility and servant-leadership of Christ.

As the church is **subordinate** to Christ,
    so **wives** should be subordinate to their husbands
        in **everything**.
[**Husbands**, **love** your wives,
    even as Christ **loved** the church

With tenderness.

    and **handed** himself over **for** her to **sanctify** her,
    cleansing her by the bath of **water** with the **word**,
    that he might present to himself the church in **splendor**,

With energy and excitement over our splendor as Church.

    without **spot** or **wrinkle** or **any** such thing,
    that she might be **holy** and without **blemish**.
So also husbands should **love** their wives as their own **bodies.**

A key point; slowly.

He who loves his **wife** loves **himself.**]

Christ and the Church. The wife is to serve her husband in the same spirit as the Church represents Christ's interests, and the husband is to care for his wife with the same devotion as Christ cares for the Church. The husband represents Christ, who gave his life for the redemption of the Church, and the wife represents the Church, who is submissive to Christ.

This is a difficult passage to hear today, concerned as we are for women's equal rights. The reading does not promote

a senseless, blind obedience or degrading submission of women to men, and it does not imply the abuse of power of one person over another. The phrase "wives should be subordinate to their husbands in every-thing" does not require wives to accept degrading forms of subjection. The relationship modeled upon Christ's self-sacrificing love indicates the constant concern on the husband's part for her well-being.

This depiction of marriage illustrates the mutual reverence shared among the

members of Christ's body. Christ nourishes and cares for the Church, his body. We, too, nourish and encourage each other. Just as wife and husband are united in the holy bond of marriage, so Christ is one with the Church, and we are one body with each other in Christ.

GOSPEL   The disciples had tasted the fine wine at the Cana wedding; they followed Jesus through unfriendly Samaria and witnessed the conversion of

Good news! We are all nourished by Christ!

For no one **hates** his own **flesh**
   but rather **nourishes** and **cherishes** it,
   even as **Christ** does the **church**,
   because we are **members** of his body.
*For this reason a man shall **leave** his father and his mother
   and be **joined** to his wife,
   and the **two** shall become **one** flesh.*
This is a great **mystery**,
   but I speak in reference to **Christ** and the **church**.

Pause at the end of this line.

Slow on this final point.

[Shorter: Ephesians 5:2a, 25–32 (see brackets). This shorter version
   adds 2a as the first line: "Live in love, as Christ loved us."]

GOSPEL   John 6:60–69

A reading from the holy Gospel according to John

A narrative reading. How does Jesus feel knowing that some will leave him based on what he has taught—sad, disappointed, rejected? Bring your choice to the proclamation.

Many of Jesus' **disciples** who were **listening** said,
   "This saying is **hard**; **who** can accept it?"
Since Jesus knew that his disciples were **murmuring** about this,
   he said to them, "Does this **shock** you?
What if you were to see the Son of Man **ascending**
   to where he was **before**?

In a low voice, to themselves; let their internal struggle come through.

It is the **spirit** that gives life,
   while the **flesh** is of no avail.
The words I have spoken to you are **Spirit** and **life**.
But there are **some** of you who do not believe."

"Don't trust your reason alone; trust in the Spirit."

Jesus **knew** from the beginning the ones who would not believe
   and the one who would **betray** him.
And he said,

Proclaim this line with Jesus' emotion.

   "For this reason I have told you that **no** one can come to me
   unless it is **granted** him by my **Father**."

---

that difficult group; many persons had been healed by Jesus, and the crowd ate and were satisfied by the picnic of the five loaves. Now Jesus tests his disciples, especially Peter.

Jesus is all too familiar with indecisive, volatile human nature; he knows our projects and our best intentions; he also knows that we do what we do not want to do; that we eat what is not good for our health; we think and sin in ways that are not beneficial. Jesus knows that, as long as he fills our

bellies and baskets with his miracles, we will follow him. Such is the force of the gravity of our flesh. But, after filling bellies and reviving hopes, Jesus does not excuse us from the test; he talks to us about the Bread of life, and invites us to renounce any material benefit we might have planned for ourselves. He addresses our spiritual nature. He is the Bread come down from heaven; his flesh is real food and his blood real refreshment.

Many are rejecting Jesus' teaching: "This saying is hard; who can accept it?" Jesus examines us to determine if we follow him for temporal or for eternal values. This test awakens our conscience, and perhaps painfully stirs us to reflect that we have been born not just for life in the present century, but for eternity.

Jesus does not wish to hold anybody by force of the miracles; we are free to follow or to abandon him. He invites us to discover our identity as disciples when he

Slowly, with a tinge of sadness.

Pause at the end of this line.

Let Jesus' real concern come through.

With quiet confidence; this is an intimate scene.

Pause a little longer than usual before "The Gospel of the Lord."

TO KEEP IN MIND

Always pause at the end of the reading, before you proclaim the closing dialogue ("The Word of the Lord" or "The Gospel of the Lord").

TO KEEP IN MIND

Words in bold are significant words about which you must make a choice to help their meaning stand out. You may (or may not) choose to stress them.

As a **result** of this,
      many of his disciples returned to their former way of life
      and **no** longer accompanied him.
Jesus then said to the **Twelve**, "Do you **also** want to leave?"
Simon **Peter** answered him, "**Master**, to **whom** shall we go?
You have the **words** of eternal **life.**
We have come to **believe**
      and are **convinced** that you are the **Holy** One of **God**."

---

asks, "Do you also want to leave?" This question permits Peter to verbalize the supreme love that attracts his heart, "Master, to whom shall we go? You have the words of eternal life." Peter recognized Jesus' distinction between "flesh" and "spirit." "Flesh" is Simon Peter, left to himself, incapable of discerning the things of God. "Spirit" is the Breath of God in the human being, enriching interior life. In this test, when many abandon the teacher, Peter opts for Jesus' words of "Spirit and life."

TWENTY-SECOND SUNDAY IN ORDINARY TIME

An exhortatory reading. Moses is sharing good news with the people. Make sure it sounds that way.

Deuteronomy = doo-ter-AHN-uh-mee

Start boldly and with vigor!

statutes = STACH-oots

Emphasize the rewards of observing the Law: life, land, wisdom, and the closeness of God.

No pause at this comma or the next.

Moses adds his personal advice, like a father to his children.

Be impressed!

Show your pleasure at the justness of God's Law.

LECTIONARY #125

READING I   Deuteronomy 4:1–2, 6–8

A reading from the Book of Deuteronomy

Moses said to the people:
  "**Now**, Israel, **hear** the statutes and decrees
  which I am **teaching** you to observe,
  that you may **live**, and may enter in and take **possession**
    of the land
  which the **Lord**, the God of your fathers, is giving you.
In your observance of the commandments of the Lord,
    your God,
  which I **enjoin** upon you,
  you shall not **add** to what I command you nor **subtract** from it.
Observe them **carefully**,
  for **thus** will you give evidence
  of your **wisdom** and **intelligence** to the nations,
  who will hear of all these statutes and say,
  'This great nation is **truly** a **wise** and **intelligent** people.'
For what great nation is there
    that has gods so **close** to it as the Lord, our God, is to **us**
    whenever we call upon him?
Or what great nation has **statutes** and **decrees**
    that are as **just** as this whole law
    which I am setting before you today?"

READING I   After recalling the desert sojourn from Sinai-Horeb, when God's providence was manifest (the first chapters of Deuteronomy), the author emphasizes the privilege of the Hebrew people, chosen by God from among all peoples to enter into an unprecedented friendship. This passage is part of the prologue, in which the people are urged to fulfill the Law, the history and details of which follow. The main argument for God's might and goodness is his presence among his people. Israel's life, configured by fulfillment of the Law, will be the most eloquent teaching for the other peoples. The Law, with its commandments, customs, and statutes, was understood as the way of life indicated by God for his people. Their life and experience was God's plan for salvation. If Israel will comply with the Law she will receive her inheritance, understood as peaceful life in the land.

READING II   The "Father of lights" designates God as creator of the stars and, in keeping with the symbolism of light, the source of everything good. Christians, engendered by God through "the word of truth," the Gospel, belong to God as his "first-fruits." The author specifies that it is not enough to hear the truth; one must listen and put it into practice. The Christian has been chosen out of the "world"—a term that here takes on pejorative overtones—to belong to the light. God's action, his Word, has done this. This Word-in-action inspires the Christian from Baptism onwards. She or he submits to this Word and work of God, putting it into practice rather than just hearing it. True devotion, fulfilling one's duty to God, is best

For meditation and context:

TO KEEP IN MIND

Pause in order to break up separate thoughts, set apart significant statements, or indicate major shifts. Never pause in the middle of a single thought. Your primary guide for pauses is punctuation.

A didactic reading. When you proclaim, you're giving a gift to the assembly. Let your generosity show.

Take this slowly.

Articulate this complex sentence carefully; pause briefly after "truth."

Urge your assembly to welcome this message.

This is why we proclaim with the intent to get our listeners to respond!

A simple summary of our obligations as Christians.

RESPONSORIAL PSALM   Psalm 15:2–3, 3–4, 4–5 (1a)

R. The one who does justice will live in the presence of the Lord.

Whoever walks blamelessly and does justice;
    who thinks the truth in his heart
    and slanders not with his tongue.

Who harms not his fellow man,
    nor takes up a reproach against
        his neighbor;
by whom the reprobate is despised,
    while he honors those who fear the LORD.

Who lends not his money at usury
    and accepts no bribe against the innocent.
Whoever does these things
    shall never be disturbed.

READING II   James 1:17–18, 21b–22, 27

A reading from the Letter of Saint James

Dearest **brothers** and **sisters**:
All **good giving** and every perfect **gift** is from **above**,
    coming down from the Father of **lights**,
    with whom there is no alteration or shadow caused by **change**.
He willed to give us **birth** by the word of **truth**
    that we may be a kind of **firstfruits** of his creatures.

Humbly **welcome** the word that has been planted in you
    and is able to save your **souls**.

Be **doers** of the word and not **hearers** only, **deluding** yourselves.

Religion that is **pure** and **undefiled** before God and the Father
    is **this**:
    to care for **orphans** and **widows** in their **affliction**
    and to keep oneself **unstained** by the world.

---

expressed in the care of those in need and opposition to the forces of evil.

GOSPEL   Opposite the Pharisees' narrow and legalistic concern about external purification, worship, and observance of the commandments, Jesus emphasizes the moral intent of the Law, going beyond its literal interpretation. The teaching about contamination coming from within cancels the laws about clean and unclean food and opens the way for unity between Jew and Gentile in the Kingdom of God. Mark signals this shift by having Jesus

leave Galilee for Gentile territory in the following episodes of the Gospel.

The Law prescribed certain regulations for cultivating the moral purity necessary to approach God, and the tradition amplified and applied these laws and customs to other matters, like eating. External purity was considered the proof of integrity. The Jerusalem scribes criticize the disciples for not washing their hands properly before eating. Hand washing when returning from the town or market, as well as washing cups, jugs, and kettles, was to cleanse persons and everyday objects from

any accidental legal impurity. The intent is good, but the gesture has meaning only insofar as it expresses the cleansing of the person's interior life. Jesus stresses the importance of purity of heart when he says "from within people, from their hearts, come evil thoughts," pointing to the subconscious that eludes all reason and restriction. Jesus prefers to associate with an amiable, if somewhat untidy, group rather than a clan of critics with clean hands. The scribes' overemphasis on legalism was choking the true sense of friendship with God. Jesus cites Isaiah, "This

A narrative reading. Make the Pharisees and scribes sound like real people. What do they want? What do they fear?

With a suspicious tone, as if they're whispering among themselves.

This section interrupts the narrative to explain the purification rituals. Keep your pace up.

Pause at the end of this line.
Raise your energy as the narrative resumes.

TO KEEP IN MIND
In a narrative, find an emotion or point of view for each character, keeping in mind that these might change during the reading.

GOSPEL   Mark 7:1–8, 14–15, 21–23

A reading from the holy Gospel according to Mark

When the **Pharisees** with some **scribes** who had come from Jerusalem
    gathered around **Jesus**,
    they observed that some of his disciples ate their meals
    with **unclean**, that is, **unwashed**, hands.
—For the **Pharisees** and, in fact, **all** Jews,
    do not eat without **carefully** washing their hands,
    keeping the tradition of the **elders**.
And on coming from the marketplace
    they do not eat without **purifying** themselves.
And there are many **other** things that they have traditionally observed,
    the purification of cups and jugs and kettles and beds.—
So the Pharisees and scribes **questioned** him,
    "**Why** do your disciples not follow the tradition of the elders
    but instead eat a meal with **unclean** hands?"

people honors me with their lips . . . " (Isaiah 29:13), to censure their showy observances—ritual dressed up like divine ordinances. Jesus, the Lord of the Law, declares all food "clean," a profound teaching. The origin of sin and morality is not to be sought in the veneer, but in the interior life.

Jesus knows well the complexity of the person's interior life—that we experience it as a knot of contradictory impulses, desires, and illusions that make us feel bad and, even when we experience some suc-cess or advance, we remain unsatisfied and hunger for more. Jesus knows our frustrations in the face of these contradictions in our interior lives. When he diagnoses a condition as pharisaic, he refers to a surface that masks the abyss of the interior.

This reading raises the question: How can we live with the contradictions of the interior life? How do we correct something so rebellious and stubborn as our interior life? There is no other way than to look directly at our fragile nature, but not to look alone. We need to consider our condition with God's eyes. He knows intimately the human condition. Through his Son's eyes God contemplates human misery. With just one look of true love Jesus heals the wound, raises the fallen, repairs the broken, and untangles the tangles. Jesus looks at the marginalized, at the sinner paralyzed with sin, at the blind, at Peter who has just betrayed him. God knows well our heart and restores it into something beautiful by his tender gaze that heals and saves, an

How does Jesus feel—angry, exasperated, sad? Let your choice come through in his lines.

Set the Isaiah quote apart: "This people . . . precepts."

Change your tone as the audience changes; Jesus is now teaching, not scolding.

"Don't worry so much about this."

The list is not about these specific evils but to show that all evil comes from within. Keep your pace up.

He responded,
   "**Well** did Isaiah prophesy about you **hypocrites**, as it
      is written:
  *This people honors me with their **lips**,*
     *but their **hearts** are **far** from me;*
  *in **vain** do they worship me,*
     *teaching as doctrines **human** precepts.*
You disregard **God's** commandment but cling to
    human tradition."
He summoned the crowd again and said to them,
   "**Hear** me, **all** of you, and **understand**.
Nothing that enters one from **outside** can **defile** that person;
  but the things that come out from **within** are what **defile**.

"From **within** people, from their **hearts**,
  come **evil** thoughts, **unchastity**, **theft**, **murder**,
  adultery, **greed**, **malice**, **deceit**,
  licentiousness, **envy**, **blasphemy**, **arrogance**, **folly**.
All these **evils** come from **within** and **they** defile."

TO KEEP IN MIND
Pay attention to the pace of your reading. Varying the pace gives listeners clues to the meaning of the text. The most common problem for proclaimers new to the ministry is going too fast to be understood.

---

attention that has been entrusted to the Church for every person's good, and in our turn, each one of us becomes a minister of God's loving gaze. One single look of true love of a father for his child, of a spouse, of a person toward the poor and marginalized, replicates the miracle of restoring the life we need so terribly. In the opposite direction, one single look, like that of the Pharisees, can extinguish the hope, happiness, and love of God in humanity.

Jesus clarifies that not everybody who washes his or her hands and takes a place at the table has a pure heart and clean intentions. Even so, Jesus looks at us with love that can restore us, because he looks with compassion. He sees us for who we are and for the best that we can become, and our soiled hands are of little importance to him. Above all, Jesus considers if they got dirty in the service of those who need our help. K.S.

TWENTY-THIRD SUNDAY IN ORDINARY TIME

LECTIONARY #128

READING I   Isaiah 35:4–7a

A reading from the Book of the Prophet Isaiah

Thus says the LORD:
    Say to those whose hearts are **frightened**:
      Be **strong**, fear **not**!
    Here is your **God**,
      he comes with **vindication**;
    with divine **recompense**
      he comes to **save** you.
    Then will the **eyes** of the **blind** be **opened**,
      the **ears** of the **deaf** be **cleared**;
    then will the **lame leap** like a **stag**,
      then the **tongue** of the **mute** will **sing**.
    Streams will burst **forth** in the **desert**,
      and **rivers** in the **steppe**.
    The **burning** sands will become **pools**,
      and the **thirsty** ground, **springs** of **water**.

An exhortatory reading. Do you know someone who needs to hear a message of hope? Imagine speaking this directly to that person.

Isaiah = ī-ZAY-uh

Keep your voice and energy up throughout! Set this short but significant sentence apart.

vindication = vin-dih-KAY-shuhn (clearing from blame)
recompense = REK-uhm-pens (compensation for wrongs suffered)
Pause at the end of this line.

Make the words "leap," "sing," and "burst" sound like what they mean!

steppe = step
Drop your intensity slightly and slow to the end.

> **TO KEEP IN MIND**
> Proclamation cannot be effective unless it is expressive. As you prepare your proclamation, make choices about emotions. Some choices are already evident in the text.

READING I   After depicting the destruction of God's enemies in the previous chapter, now the prophet delivers a message of consolation. Suffering and setback will be followed by salvation as Isaiah presents a vision of Jerusalem restored. God, who protected the exodus generation he had freed from slavery, will replicate the great deeds of that time and open the road to Zion. The people's rejoicing will be reflected in healing the deaf and lame. Later, in messianic times, Jesus' miracles will attest to the redemption announced by the prophets like Isaiah. It is what we all long for, a transformation, a cure of our afflicted society. A desert, where torrents of water transform the landscape that makes life possible. The prophet announces the transformation of our reality that seems tired and resistant to change: light to blind eyes, renewed energies to the worn out, athletic forces to lame legs, sound to deaf ears, and songs from the mute.

READING II   James insists on the practice of the faith; faith simply has no meaning if it is not put into practice. Perhaps incidents had arisen in the Christian communities that prompted this topic: discrimination of persons on the basis of social rank. Such distinctions are not compatible with the life of faith. Jewish Law and the Gospel both condemn discrimination, exemplified by how the person is addressed and in the preferential seating for the rich. James recalls the Church's predilection for the poor. The Christian com-

TO KEEP IN MIND

A didactic reading is usually given out of love for the community. Make sure that love is evident in your proclamation.

RESPONSORIAL PSALM   Psalm 146:6–7, 8–9, 9–10 (1b)

R. Praise the Lord, my soul! or R. Alleluia.

The God of Jacob keeps faith forever,
  secures justice for the oppressed,
  gives food to the hungry.
The Lord sets captives free.

The Lord gives sight to the blind;
  the Lord raises up those who were
    bowed down.
The Lord loves the just;
  the Lord protects strangers.

The fatherless and the widow the Lord
  sustains,
  but the way of the wicked he thwarts.
The Lord shall reign forever;
  your God, O Zion, through all generations.
    Alleluia.

A didactic reading. Don't make the mistake of assuming this teaching doesn't apply to your community. We all have our biases, and need this reminder to be aware and on our guard.

Gently but firmly.

READING II   James 2:1–5

A reading from the Letter of Saint James

My brothers and sisters, show no **partiality**
  as you adhere to the faith in our **glorious** Lord Jesus Christ.
For if a man with gold **rings** and fine **clothes**
  comes into your assembly,
  and a **poor** person in **shabby** clothes **also** comes in,
  and you pay attention to the one wearing the **fine** clothes
  and say, "Sit here, **please**,"
  while you say to the **poor** one, "Stand **there**,"
    or "Sit at my **feet**,"
  have you not made **distinctions** among yourselves
  and become **judges** with evil **designs**?

Listen, my **beloved** brothers and sisters.
Did not God choose those who are **poor** in the world
  to be **rich** in **faith** and **heirs** of the kingdom
  that he promised to those who **love** him?

With great deference.

Make these statements sound like commands.

With love.

A gentle reminder. Smile as you proclaim this good news.

---

munity has no room for favoritism based on status or wealth.

GOSPEL   In the Gospel Jesus generally moves in a region where people believe in one God. He and his disciples travel through Galilee, curing the sick and expelling demons. At first, this region presents no major obstacle to Jesus and the Gospel. But on one occasion Jesus breaks the routine, leaves his homeland, and travels to the distant north. Even the names of the district make us think of a

pagan territory that is deaf to the Gospel. Jesus enters the northern region of Tyre, passes through Sidon, and crosses through the Decapolis—regions that abound in idolatry. That hostile region is where Jesus meets the deaf and the dumb.

Salvation in Jesus makes the deaf hear and the dumb speak—an allusion to Isaiah's image in the First Reading—and Mark shows how Isaiah's words are fulfilled in Christ. The crowd's acclamation ("He has done all things well") shows that the crowd recognizes the fulfillment of what was

expected of the Messiah. He has given speech to the dumb and hearing to the deaf. The Church's Ephphatha Rite, often celebrated before the baptismal liturgy, adopts some of these signs, signifying that Christ opens the ears of the newly baptized to hear and receive the Word of God.

This is the third time Mark records that Jesus tells people not to tell anyone about a healing. The first was a leper (1:44), then the resuscitation of a little girl (5:43), and now a deaf-mute; these will be joined by the blind man (8:26). The silence Jesus

A narrative reading. Keep your energy up. Jesus is generating excitement in the crowd. Can you bring the same excitement to your assembly?

Tyre = tîr

Sidon = SĪ-duhn

Decapolis = dih-KAP-uh-lis

Proclaim with the pleading and hopeful tone of the crowd.

Don't gloss over this earthy image.

Ephphatha = EF-fah-thah; they are alone, so speak with vigor more than volume. Quickly, with amazement.

Pause as they return to the crowd.

With great excitement.

TO KEEP IN MIND
Use inflection (the high or low pitch of your voice) to convey attitude and feeling. High pitch expresses intensity and excitement; low pitch expresses sadness, contrition, or solemnity.

GOSPEL   Mark 7:31–37

A reading from the holy Gospel according to Mark

Again Jesus left the district of **Tyre**
   and went by way of **Sidon** to the Sea of **Galilee**,
   into the district of the **Decapolis**.
And people brought to him a **deaf** man who had a
    speech impediment
   and **begged** him to **lay** his hand on him.
He took him off by himself **away** from the crowd.
He put his **finger** into the man's **ears**
   and, **spitting**, touched his **tongue**;
    then he looked up to heaven and **groaned**, and said to him,
   "Ephphatha!"—that is, "Be **opened**!"—
And **immediately** the man's ears were **opened**,
   his **speech** impediment was **removed**,
   and he spoke **plainly**.
He ordered them not to tell **anyone**.
But the more he ordered them **not** to,
   the more they **proclaimed** it.
They were exceedingly **astonished** and they said,
   "He has done **all** things **well**.
He makes the deaf **hear** and the mute **speak**."

imposes is a reminder that his mission is to be understood not on the basis of miracles, but in the light of the Paschal Mystery, Jesus' Passion, Death, and Resurrection. His saving action makes a person a believer and disciple. Two obstacles to discipleship are the inability to listen and to speak. A person has nothing to say if they cannot listen and assimilate the message. Christ's saving action described in the healing makes this point. He says to the deaf person simply "Be opened," and the effect is that "the man's ears were opened, his speech impediment was removed, and he

spoke plainly." Grace makes it possible for us to hear and understand the Gospel, and Jesus empowers us to testify to that message by word and action.

The deaf cannot hear; the dumb cannot speak. The pagan has no access to the Word of God, nor can he open his mouth to proclaim it. On his own, he does not come to Jesus. Other persons are necessary for such an encounter, and they request a laying on of hands. Jesus removes the afflicted from the people; he opens his ears and looses his tongue. On that day the Gospel arrived to a region previously impervious to it.

Mark narrates how the Gospel entered the regions neighboring Galilee. But there is also a region in the heart so foreign to the Gospel that it resists Jesus and conversion, and places obstacles to grace. The symptoms are deafness, blindness, spiritual paralysis—whatever conditions show that the Good News has not yet penetrated the shadowlands of the interior life. Jesus and his grace enter even the most hostile and rugged regions, open the least sensitive hearts, and loose the tongues of the least probable to proclaim the Gospel. K.S.

TWENTY-FOURTH SUNDAY IN ORDINARY TIME

An exhortatory reading. Maintain a steadfast calm and confidence throughout. Stand up straight and keep eye contact with the assembly.

Isaiah = Ī-ZAY-uh

The prophet names the source of his strength right away.

Careful not to sound weary or put upon.

plucked = tried to pull out

Smile as you recall your relationship with God.

Pause at the end of this line.

"I'm ready to meet anyone who questions that God loves me."

Don't challenge; rather, maintain a centered confidence.

Offer your assembly that same relationship with God.

LECTIONARY #131

READING I   Isaiah 50:5–9a

A reading from the Book of the Prophet Isaiah

The LORD God **opens** my ear that I may **hear**;
and I have **not** rebelled,
     have not turned **back**.
I gave my **back** to those who **beat** me,
     my **cheeks** to those who **plucked** my beard;
my **face** I did not **shield**
     from **buffets** and **spitting**.

The LORD **God** is my **help**,
     therefore I am not **disgraced**;
I have **set** my **face** like **flint**,
     knowing that I shall **not** be put to **shame**.
He is **near** who upholds my **right**;
     if anyone wishes to **oppose** me,
     let us appear **together**.
Who **disputes** my right?
     Let that man **confront** me.
See, the LORD **God** is my **help**;
     who will prove me **wrong**?

READING I   Although this prophecy could also be applied to an individual's experience, the "servant" named here is often interpreted as the community of ancient Israel. In that sense the reading is an expression of the community's understanding of its situation before God. The first part describes the sufferings endured in obedient docility—sufferings the servant has accepted without complaint. Are the people responsible for their unhappy history due to their sins, or are they victims? The preceding verses have spoken of sin and transgression, but here the servant is innocent. The servant has not hidden his face, even though the exposure subjected him to shame and spitting.

In the midst of insult, the servant is confident in the Lord's help, even though the prophet does not specify how it will take place. The last part of the reading stresses the servant's fortitude: silent suffering is not a sign of cowardice; God strengthens him in the face of tormentors. In the end only the servant will continue, while his adversaries will be eclipsed. Christians read this prophecy as fulfilled in Jesus, silently enduring his Passion. It may also be seen as a picture of the Church in the present age.

READING II   Paul wrote that the person is not justified primarily by the works of the Law but by faith and adherence to Jesus. Here James writes that a person is not justified by faith alone. Does this present teaching contradict that of Paul? Paul's works refer to the detailed prescriptions of the Mosaic Law. He holds that a person has to fulfill more than outward observance. James' point is clear: ideological faith, insufficient in itself, must be

For meditation and context:

TO KEEP IN MIND

You can't proclaim what you don't understand. Read the Scripture passage and its commentary in *Workbook*. Then read it from your Bible, including what comes before and after it so that you understand the context.

RESPONSORIAL PSALM Psalm 116:1–2, 3–4, 5–6, 8–9 (9)

R. I will walk before the Lord, in the land of the living. or R. Alleluia.

I love the Lord because he has heard
　my voice in supplication,
because he has inclined his ear to me
　the day I called.

The cords of death encompassed me;
　the snares of the netherworld seized
　　upon me;
　I fell into distress and sorrow,
and I called upon the name of the Lord,
　"O Lord, save my life!"

Gracious is the Lord and just;
　yes, our God is merciful.
The Lord keeps the little ones;
　I was brought low, and he saved me.

For he has freed my soul from death,
　my eyes from tears, my feet from
　　stumbling.
I shall walk before the Lord
　in the land of the living.

A didactic reading. Don't get caught up in the theology here. The teaching is very simple; keep your proclamation the same.

The tone throughout is, "Don't you see?"

Keep your pace up.

Be sincere; it's not the genuineness of the faith that James is challenging but its practical application.

Slow a bit and set this line apart.

Emphasize "from."

READING II James 2:14–18

A reading from the Letter of Saint James

What **good** is it, my brothers and sisters,
　if someone says he has **faith** but does not have **works**?
Can that faith **save** him?
If a brother or sister has nothing to **wear**
　and has no **food** for the day,
　and one of you says to them,
　"Go in **peace**, keep **warm**, and eat **well**,"
　but you do not give them the **necessities** of the body,
　what **good** is it?
So also faith of **itself**,
　if it does not have **works**, is **dead**.

Indeed someone might say,
　"You have **faith** and I have **works**."
Demonstrate your **faith** to me **without** works,
　and **I** will demonstrate my faith to you **from** my works.

translated into action. Needy persons are not aided simply by the good wishes of their fellows; the faith commitment is to be translated into practice.

　Paul argues against those who claim to gain salvation just on the basis of their good deeds, but he understands how true faith leads to a generous life. In this reading James condenses the key idea: faith without works is dead; it cannot save. His example is similar to 1 John 3:17: "If someone who has worldly means sees a brother in need and refuses him compassion, how can the love

of God remain in him?" For James, deeds authenticate the Christian life and give evidence of the truth of faith and charity.

| GOSPEL | Jesus has just given sight to a blind person. Now he will open the eyes of the disciples, a process that spans the following chapters on the road to Jerusalem. This episode when the disciples confess Jesus as the Messiah, is the turning point in his ministry. Popular opinion regards him as a prophet with a stature like that of Elijah, the forerunner of

the Messiah, but the disciples confess him to be the Messiah. Toward the end of Old Testament times, the Messiah was expected to appear as a victorious figure—with no hint of defeat or suffering.

　Jesus now removes any false messianic impressions, explaining that the Messiah will undergo suffering and death. Peter, acting as spokesperson, rebukes Jesus for speaking about such apparent defeat. Jesus' reply is forceful: the plan of salvation requires that the Messiah suffer. Peter, in the role of tempter, represents the limited,

A narrative reading. "Who do you say that I am?" is a question asked of every disciple. Help your assembly reflect on how they might respond by drawing them into this story.

Caesarea Philippi = sez-uh-REE-uh fih-LIP-ī

A sincere question.

Heighten each answer.

Don't make this sound like a test. The crowds may not know him, but he hopes his closest friends do.

Pause before the end of the line.

Don't gloss over this declaration; this would have been shocking news to his disciples. Take it slowly and gently.
Raise your energy suddenly. Make "rebuke" sound like a rebuke. Keep your energy up through Jesus' response.

Pause at the end of this line.

Careful not to make this sound sad. It is a hard truth.

Good news!

GOSPEL   Mark 8:27–35

A reading from the holy Gospel according to Mark

Jesus and his disciples set out
    for the villages of **Caesarea Philippi**.
Along the way he **asked** his disciples,
    "**Who** do people say that I am?"
They said in reply,
    "John the **Baptist**, others **Elijah**,
    still others one of the **prophets**."
And he asked them,
    "But who do **you** say that I am?"
Peter said to him in reply,
    "You are the **Christ**."
Then he **warned** them not to tell **anyone** about him.

He began to **teach** them
    that the Son of Man must suffer **greatly**
    and be **rejected** by the elders, the chief priests, and the scribes,
    and be **killed**, and **rise** after three **days**.
He spoke this **openly**.
Then **Peter** took him aside and began to **rebuke** him.
At this he turned around and, looking at his **disciples**,
    rebuked Peter and said, "Get **behind** me, **Satan**.
You are thinking not as **God** does, but as human **beings** do."

He summoned the **crowd** with his disciples and said to them,
    "Whoever wishes to come **after** me must **deny** himself,
    take up his **cross**, and **follow** me.
For whoever wishes to **save** his life will **lose** it,
    but whoever **loses** his life for **my** sake
    and that of the **gospel** will **save** it."

human viewpoint. Now Jesus confronts the disciples with the paradox of discipleship: the one who undergoes humiliation is exalted; the person who offers his or her life will be saved. Jesus instructs the disciples to embrace the Cross, accept the challenge of self-giving, and renounce the desire to preserve and enrich one's own existence at any cost. Jesus understands his mission as Messiah from God's perspective, and thus, the prediction of his Passion, Death, and Resurrection.

From this point on in the Gospel Jesus will concentrate on the disciples' formation. Three Passion predictions (8:31; 9:31; 10:33–34) identify him as the suffering servant of Isaiah and demonstrate the necessity of the Passion and Death to enter into glory. After the first prediction, Jesus challenges believers to true commitment to him through the renunciation of self and acceptance of suffering, even to the sacrifice of life itself: "Whoever wishes to save his life will lose it, and whoever loses his life . . . will save it" expresses the paradox

of life and its contrasting destiny. "Life" is understood as centered on earthly existence and lived in denial of Christ, an existence that ends in destruction. When lived in union with Christ, despite earthly death, life achieves true and lasting value. K.S.

TWENTY-FIFTH SUNDAY IN ORDINARY TIME

An exhortatory reading. Don't be afraid to sound nasty and vengeful; that's what this text demands. If you proclaim with a flat, indifferent tone, you make it almost impossible for your assembly to understand the reading.

Keep your energy up throughout, but vary your tone, pace, and volume.

Lower your volume to convey collusion. You might suggest wicked delight at your plans.

This is sarcasm; you don't really believe God will deliver him.

Heighten your anger.

Proclaim "gentleness" and "patience" with a mocking tone.

For meditation and context:

TO KEEP IN MIND
Use inflection (the high or low pitch of your voice) to convey attitude and feeling. High pitch expresses intensity and excitement; low pitch expresses sadness, contrition, or solemnity.

LECTIONARY #134

READING I   Wisdom 2:12, 17–20

A reading from the Book of Wisdom

The **wicked** say:
Let us **beset** the just one, because he is **obnoxious** to us;
    he sets himself **against** our doings,
  reproaches us for transgressions of the law
    and charges us with **violations** of our training.
Let us **see** whether his words be **true**;
    let us find out what will **happen** to him.
For if the just one **be** the son of God, God will **defend** him
    and **deliver** him from the hand of his foes.
With **revilement** and **torture** let us put the just one to the **test**
    that we may have **proof** of his **gentleness**
    and **try** his **patience**.
Let us **condemn** him to a **shameful** death;
    for according to his **own** words, **God** will take **care** of him.

RESPONSORIAL PSALM   Psalm 54:3–4, 5, 6–8 (6b)

R. The Lord upholds my life.

O God, by your name save me,
    and by your might defend my cause.
O God, hear my prayer;
    hearken to the words of my mouth.

For the haughty have risen up against me,
    the ruthless seek my life;
    they set not God before their eyes.

Behold, God is my helper;
    the LORD sustains my life.
Freely will I offer you sacrifice;
    I will praise your name, O LORD,
    for its goodness.

READING I   In this reading the author portrays the wicked. They do not tolerate the just person, who is for them a constant reproach. They test and humiliate him to see if God, whom he invokes, will rescue him. If God does not, the wicked believe they are vindicated in their course of action. The ironic expressions of the wicked are echoed in the insults of the leaders and officials against Jesus on the Cross. In the just person, here referred to as "Son of God," we glimpse God's parental care of every just person. In the Book of Wisdom the foolish and bad people typically refuse to acknowledge God's action in the world, even as they test the claims of the just and seek pleasure for its own sake. The sarcastic note in their speech is obvious, for they do not believe the just person has any grounds for trust in God's protection.

READING II   James contrasts the qualities of the wise person with the defects of earthbound wisdom. He addresses the discord among Christians that make the common life difficult, and enumerates the principal causes: the passions of greed and envy, and later he will add the disordered love of worldly things, pride, and arrogance, that breeds bad talk (vv. 4–12).

In the verse following the today's reading, James calls the unwise "adulterers," not referring to interpersonal adultery but to the disordered love of worldly goods that issues in infidelity to God. Christian wisdom is reflected in the community; it means living in sync with God's plan. Group conflict, the result of envy and selfishness, disrupts wisdom, and wisdom shows itself as pure, peaceful, gentle, tolerant, merciful,

A didactic reading. Sincerely urge your assembly to forsake selfishness and seek peace.

Take your time; this line sets up the whole reading, contrasting jealousy and selfishness with wisdom and peace.

List these slowly and give each its emphasis.

Pick up your pace.

Heighten each line.

Pause at the end of this line.

Here is the solution to this conflict; proclaim gently and with love.

READING II   James 3:16—4:3

A reading from the Letter of Saint James

Beloved:
Where **jealousy** and selfish **ambition** exist,
    there is **disorder** and every **foul** practice.
But the **wisdom** from above is first of all **pure**,
    then **peaceable**, **gentle**, **compliant**,
    full of **mercy** and **good** fruits,
    without **inconstancy** or **insincerity**.
And the fruit of righteousness is sown in **peace**
    for those who **cultivate** peace.

Where do the **wars**
    and **where** do the **conflicts** among you **come** from?
Is it not from your **passions**
    that make **war** within your members?
You **covet** but do not **possess**.
You **kill** and **envy** but you cannot **obtain**;
    you **fight** and wage **war**.
You do not **possess** because you do not **ask**.
You **ask** but do not **receive**,
    because you ask **wrongly**, to spend it on your **passions**.

TO KEEP IN MIND
Pause in order to break up separate thoughts, set apart significant statements, or indicate major shifts. Never pause in the middle of a single thought. Your primary guide for pauses is punctuation.

---

constant, and sincere in the quest for truth. Such qualities characterize the believer's life and the healthy community.

GOSPEL   Jesus seeks solitude to instruct the disciples about what awaits them in Jerusalem. Here he teaches the disciples about the Christian community's exercise of authority: not as one who lords over others, but as one who serves. Jesus, the Son of Man, came to serve, not to be served (expressed also in 10:45). Once again the disciples fail to

understand the prediction of Jesus' Passion, Death, and Resurrection.

Like the prediction in the previous chapter, this one is followed by teaching about discipleship. The first part concerns humility and the true meaning of greatness. The disciples' failure to comprehend reflects one of Mark's themes as he unfolds their portrait. The nucleus of this section is the saying about the one who is first being last and the importance of becoming a servant of all. That saying advocates a reversal of values: all that society regards as honorable is called into question, and the disci-

ple, in imitation of Jesus, will adopt the role of the lowest community member.

Mark illustrates the inversion of roles with the saying about the child. Children in the ancient world were not as highly valued as they are in contemporary Western society; they had a lowly status. Jesus presents the child as an example of what the disciples are to strive for: as servants, they are to be attentive even to the least esteemed of society, the children; thus they serve Jesus and, by implication, God himself.

This instruction was necessary, even if perhaps unpalatable, because it demanded

GOSPEL   Mark 9:30–37

A reading from the holy Gospel according to Mark

Jesus and his **disciples** left from there and began a journey
    through **Galilee**,
  but he did not wish anyone to know about it.
He was **teaching** his disciples and telling them,
  "The Son of Man is to be handed **over** to men
  and they will **kill** him,
  and three days after his death the Son of Man will **rise**."
But they did not **understand** the saying,
  and they were **afraid** to question him.

They came to **Capernaum** and, once inside the house,
  he began to ask them,
  "What were you **arguing** about on the way?"
But they remained **silent**.
They had been discussing among themselves on the way
  who was the **greatest**.
Then he sat down, called the Twelve, and said to them,
  "If anyone wishes to be **first**,
  he shall be the **last** of all and the **servant** of all."
Taking a **child**, he placed it in their midst,
  and putting his **arms** around it, he said to them,
  "Whoever receives **one** child such as this in my **name**,
    receives **me**;
  and whoever receives **me**,
  receives not **me** but the One who **sent** me."

Margin notes:

A narrative reading. Jesus repeats his message that he must suffer. Keep his tone gentle; he understands how difficult it is for his disciples (and us) to hear this.

Not too quickly; this is shocking news for his disciples.

With the disciples' confusion.

Pause at the end of this line.

Capernaum = kuh-PER-nee-*m

Without accusation.

Lower your voice; with the disciples' embarrassment.

A very tender image.

---

that the disciples adopt a reversal of commonly accepted values. It required an adjustment in their estimates about salvation and in their way of interacting in community. The believer is to measure his or her greatness in terms of service. A person is considered valuable insofar as he or she puts into practice the role of servant.

From the perspective of the disciples, the news in this Gospel reading seems to have gone from bad to worse: shockingly, the death of the just person (as in the First Reading) is unavoidable in Jesus' understanding of God's plan. The disciples can-

not comprehend Jesus' teaching. They argue about a hypothetical hierarchy among themselves. So Jesus embraces a child in their midst, and with this tender gesture reveals the mystery of God. Amidst power plays and shameless ambition, Jesus unmasks the depth of God's heart. Instead of scolding or rejecting his disciples, God presents a child, who stands in for each one of us.

Without becoming discouraged in the face of our clumsiness, fear, cowardice, or greed, God sets greatness aside and embraces that little child that resides in

every human being. With this gesture, he does more than just give us his attention. God opens our eyes to the absurdity of our ambitions, disagreements, and the torments that unsettle our communities and families. In the disorder engendered by envy and rivalry, Jesus opens the wound and shows us what needs to be healed—as James writes: the cancer of egoism that invades the heart. Jesus demonstrates that God's love approaches and embraces every human being, and thus he engenders in our soul a new birth. K.S.

TWENTY-SIXTH SUNDAY IN ORDINARY TIME

LECTIONARY #137

READING I   Numbers 11:25–29

A reading from the Book of Numbers

The LORD came down in the **cloud** and spoke to **Moses**.
Taking some of the **spirit** that was on Moses,
    the LORD bestowed it on the seventy **elders**;
    and as the spirit came to rest on them, they **prophesied**.

Now **two** men, one named Eldad and the other Medad,
    were not in the gathering but had been left in the **camp**.
They **too** had been on the list, but had not gone out to the **tent**;
    yet the spirit came to rest on them **also**,
    and they **prophesied** in the camp.
So, when a young man quickly told Moses,
    "Eldad and Medad are **prophesying** in the camp,"
    Joshua, son of Nun, who from his youth had been
        Moses' aide, said,
    "Moses, my LORD, **stop** them."
But Moses answered him,
    "Are you jealous for **my** sake?
Would that **all** the people of the LORD were **prophets**!
Would that the LORD might bestow his **spirit** on them **all**!"

A narrative reading. Who is "in" and who is "out" is a source of division even today. Help your assembly put aside such divisions; keep that intention uppermost in your mind as you proclaim.

Keep the story moving.

prophesied = PROF-uh-sĭd
Pause at the end of this line.

Eldad = EL-dad; Medad = MEE-dad

With amazement.

Quickly and with energy. Keep the whole sentence together, pausing briefly at commas.

Indignantly.

Heighten your energy through to the end.
Take a slightly longer pause before "The Word of the Lord."

READING I   The sterling career of Joshua was tarnished by the event narrated in this reading. Seventy elders in Israel had received the spirit of God to prophesy. Two, Eldad and Medad, were absent with the group when the others received the spirit's outpouring, but they were found prophesying in another place. When this was reported, Joshua, who from his youth had been Moses' right-hand man, told his master, "Stop them." What was the motive for the objection? Was it an issue of control, or perhaps a sense of supposed principles of orthodoxy or group solidarity? Whatever the motive, Joshua objected to someone outside the parameters of the group receiving and manifesting the Spirit of God.

READING II   Continuing with the theme of the transitory nature of life, the author of the Letter of James stresses the impending ruin of the godless. The cries of the victims of people who gloat about their wealth and status have reached to heaven and judgment is imminent. The deterioration of costly garments and the corrosion of silver and gold symbolize the worthlessness of wealth and foreshadow the destruction of the possessors. The author does not denounce any specific crime, but he warns against the unfair distribution of goods in society and the harsh treatment of the poor. In a prophetic tone James reproaches the pride, vanity, and avarice of the wealthy and their thoughtless pleasures. He warns them of impending judgment. The obligation to eliminate injustices is a Church doctrine; those who have wealth in abundance are to use it in service of humanity.

For meditation and context:

TO KEEP IN MIND

Proclamation cannot be effective unless it is expressive. As you prepare your proclamation, make choices about emotions. Some choices are already evident in the text.

RESPONSORIAL PSALM   Psalm 19:8, 10, 12–13, 14 (9a)

R. The precepts of the Lord give joy to the heart.

The law of the LORD is perfect,
  refreshing the soul;
the decree of the LORD is trustworthy,
  giving wisdom to the simple.

The fear of the LORD is pure,
  enduring forever;
the ordinances of the LORD are true,
  all of them just.

Though your servant is careful of them,
  very diligent in keeping them,
yet who can detect failings?
  Cleanse me from my unknown faults!

From wanton sin especially, restrain
  your servant;
  let it not rule over me.
Then shall I be blameless and innocent
  of serious sin.

An exhortatory reading. It may be uncomfortable to proclaim this with all the fury and vitriol it requires, but don't hold back, or James' words become meaningless.

Start slowly but strongly; the assembly will not expect this kind of diatribe. Keep your energy up throughout.

Make these "valuable" things sound disgusting.

Lower your volume.

Irony.

Begin to quicken your pace through this section.

Show your contempt for this way of life.

Pause.

A surprising ending; proclaim slowly and with meekness and humility.

READING II   James 5:1–6

A reading from the Letter of Saint James

Come now, you **rich**, **weep** and **wail** over your
    impending **miseries**.
Your wealth has **rotted** away, your clothes have become
    moth-eaten,
  your gold and silver have **corroded**,
  and that corrosion will be a **testimony** against you;
  it will **devour** your flesh like a **fire**.
You have stored up **treasure** for the last days.
Behold, the wages you **withheld** from the workers
  who harvested your fields are **crying** aloud;
  and the **cries** of the harvesters
  have reached the **ears** of the LORD of hosts.
You have lived on earth in **luxury** and **pleasure**;
  you have **fattened** your hearts for the day of **slaughter**.
You have **condemned**;
  you have **murdered** the righteous one;
  he offers you no **resistance**.

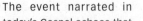 The event narrated in today's Gospel echoes that in the First Reading. The moral of the story denounces factionalism or discrimination in community. Just as faith is a gift and not an achievement (as in 9:24), so what matters is being true to the Gospel, and the exorcist plies his craft in Jesus' name. When John approached Jesus his complaint implied that Jesus should stop the maverick exorcist. We have no idea what motivated John on that occasion, but, given his later performance in company with his brother James, we may deduce the motive.

On that same journey to the Cross Jesus would announce for a third time that he was to suffer, die, and rise (10:33–34). Then John would confess the aspirations of his heart, "that in your glory we may sit one at your right hand and the other at the your left" (10:38). It was only at the Crucifixion, that John realized the irony of his request. He who wanted to be enthroned on the right hand of Jesus, beheld what enthronement with Jesus would entail. Then Jesus' words must have made sense: "Whoever wishes to be great among you will be your

servant; whoever wishes to be first among you will be the slave of all" (10:43–44).

Perhaps in his youthful enthusiasm John wanted to limit the circle of intimacy around Jesus. Presuming to act as Jesus' deputy, John would have excluded the exorcist who used Jesus' name. But Jesus said, "whoever is not against us is for us." And he added what must have stabbed quite deep in John's memory, "If your hand causes you to sin, cut it off." Was John stunned by the accurate aim of Jesus, who insinuated that for the health of his body, the Church, it might be suitable for John,

GOSPEL   Mark 9:38–43, 45, 47–48

A reading from the holy Gospel according to Mark

At that time, **John** said to **Jesus**,
   "**Teacher**, we saw someone **driving** out demons in your **name**,
   and we tried to **prevent** him because he does not **follow** us."
Jesus replied, "Do not **prevent** him.
There is no one who performs a **mighty** deed in my **name**
   who can at the **same** time speak **ill** of me.
For whoever is not **against** us is **for** us.
Anyone who gives you a cup of water to drink
   because you belong to **Christ**,
   amen, I say to you, will surely not lose his **reward**.

"Whoever causes one of these little ones who believe in me
      to **sin**,
   it would be better for him if a great **millstone**
   were put around his neck
   and he were **thrown** into the sea.
If your **hand** causes you to **sin**, **cut** it off.
It is **better** for you to enter into life **maimed**
   than with **two** hands to go into Gehenna,
   into the **unquenchable fire**.
And if your **foot** causes you to sin, **cut** if off.
It is **better** for you to enter into life **crippled**
   than with **two** feet to be thrown into **Gehenna**.
And if your **eye** causes you to sin, **pluck** it out.
Better for you to enter into the kingdom of God with **one** eye
   than with **two** eyes to be thrown into **Gehenna**,
   where 'their worm does not **die**, and the fire is not
      quenched.'"

An exhortatory reading. Jesus' teaching sounds extreme. That's the point—he's using these images for their shock value. Don't try to soften them; match your energy to his words.

Quickly, with excitement.

Gently; don't rebuke.

Pause at the end of this line.
How does Jesus feel about those who support his followers? Let his emotion come through.

And how does he feel about those who cause others to sin?

Pause at the end of this line.
Keep your pace up.

Gehenna = geh-HEN-nah

Raise your energy slightly.

Raise your energy again through to the end.

---

the one who aspired to be Jesus' right hand, to be cut off? And the same would apply to those who aspired to be the eye of the Church, or the foot of the body of Christ. Paul, writing to Corinth, also used the image of eye, hand, and foot in his condemnation of competition among the members of the body (1 Corinthians 12:14–21). "The body is not a single part, but many. If a foot should say, 'because I am not a hand I do not belong to the body,' it does not for this reason belong any less to the body." With such an image Paul exhorts the community to unified thinking and action. Jesus first speaks about hand, foot, and eye, with a similar purpose: if one of the members of the body causes the rest of the body to sin, then for the sake of the health of the whole body, the infected member ought to be amputated. Today's Gospel is the neatest example of Jesus' explicit teaching about what it means to form the body of the Church. To the degree that one member of the body—hand, foot, eye—separates his or her function from the rest of the body, it disables the body. No single member can presume to get along without the others.
K.S.

TWENTY-SEVENTH SUNDAY IN ORDINARY TIME

LECTIONARY #140

READING I   Genesis 2:18–24

A reading from the Book of Genesis

The LORD God said: "It is not **good** for the man to be **alone**.
I will make a suitable **partner** for him."
So the LORD God **formed** out of the **ground**
    various wild **animals** and various **birds** of the air,
      and he **brought** them to the man to see what he would
        call them;
    whatever the man **called** each of them would be its **name**.
The man gave names to all the **cattle**,
    all the **birds** of the air, and all wild **animals**;
    but **none** proved to be the suitable **partner** for the man.

So the LORD God cast a deep **sleep** on the man,
    and **while** he was asleep,
    he took out one of his **ribs** and closed up its place with **flesh**.
The LORD God then built up into a **woman** the rib
    that he had taken from the man.
When he **brought** her to the man, the man said:
    "**This** one, at **last**, is **bone** of my **bones**
      and **flesh** of my **flesh**;
    this one shall be called '**woman**,'
      for out of 'her **man**' this one has been taken."
That is why a man **leaves** his father and mother
    and **clings** to his wife,
    and the **two** of them become **one flesh**.

A narrative reading. Bring a sense of excitement to this well-known story; it's full of unexpected surprises.

Convey the love and concern God has for the man.

Keep your pace up; God is very busy working and creating.

Notice the man is given an important role in creation.

Pause at the end of this line.

With amazement.

Let the man's joy shine through in your voice, eyes, and face.

Don't overemphasize the two syllables in the word "woman"; pronounce it normally.

Pause at the end of this line.

READING I The Creator seeks the creature's good. The author expresses this in anthropomorphic terms, presenting God as a potter who works to perfect his craftsmanship. The creation of the human is not yet concluded: what is needed is to live in union with another human being. Among the animals the human does not find companionship of equal rank, and so God creates the woman from the very cell of the man. Thus there exists complementarity between the two. In this passage we appreciate the interior life of the person who acknowledges his loneliness. Although isolation is presented as a possibility and a fear (more than as a real situation), from the consciousness of his own solitude the human being can appreciate communion with others as a good. The language suggests an affinity between man and woman and a supportive and nurturing relationship between two persons. Such complementarity does not exist in the same way between humans and animals.

The rare Hebrew term translated "deep sleep" refers to a suspended state when a person is open to supernatural incentives (see Genesis 15:2; 1 Samuel 26:12; Job 4:13; 33:15; Isaiah 29:10), as if God suspended the life he had infused in the man to remodel him and embark on the future in a new way: two persons, man and woman, not just one. The story of the formation of the woman from the man's rib teaches that the two are of the same nature and possess equal dignity; both

RESPONSORIAL PSALM   Psalm 128:1–2, 3, 4–5, 6 (5)

R. May the Lord bless us all the days of our lives.

Blessed are you who fear the LORD,
   who walk in his ways!
For you shall eat the fruit of your handiwork;
   blessed shall you be, and favored.

Your wife shall be like a fruitful vine
   in the recesses of your home;
your children like olive plants
   around your table.

Behold, thus is the man blessed
   who fears the LORD.
The LORD bless you from Zion:
   may you see the prosperity of Jerusalem
   all the days of your life.

May you see your children's children.
   Peace be upon Israel!

READING II   Hebrews 2:9–11

A reading from the Letter to the Hebrews

Brothers and sisters:
He "for a little **while**" was made "**lower** than the angels,"
   that by the grace of God he might taste death for **everyone**.

For it was fitting that he,
   for whom and **through** whom all things **exist**,
   in bringing many children to **glory**,
     should make the leader to their salvation perfect
       through **suffering**.
He who **consecrates** and those who are **being** consecrated
   all have one **origin**.
Therefore, he is not ashamed to call them "**brothers**."

GOSPEL   Mark 10:2–16

A reading from the holy Gospel according to Mark

[The **Pharisees** approached Jesus and asked,
   "Is it **lawful** for a husband to divorce his wife?"
They were **testing** him.
He said to them in reply, "What did **Moses** command you?"

Marginal notes (left column)

For meditation and context:

> **TO KEEP IN MIND**
> A *didactic* text makes a point or teaches something. Help your assembly to follow the argument and understand what's being taught.

A didactic reading. Think of someone you know who is suffering. Bring them this message: Jesus is their brother in suffering because he suffered too.

Keep your pace up throughout; if you go too slow the meaning will be lost. Pause very briefly before the two quotes to set them apart.

Drop your voice on this parenthetical phrase.

We have the same origin and have experienced the same suffering as Jesus.

Good news! Smile with your voice, eyes, and face.

A narrative reading. Jesus always teaches out of love, not fear. That distinguishes him from the Pharisees; make sure that distinction comes through in your proclamation.

With suspicion.

Simply.

Bottom commentary

come from the same clay out of which God fashioned the human being.

READING II Suffering, sacrifice, and glory are all designed for humans, because Christ died to make humankind what we are meant to be. He died to rid us of frustration, bondage, and weakness, and to restore our dignity to what it was meant to be from the beginning. The reference to Jesus as "leader" (Greek, *archegos*) is a recurrent theme in

Hebrews: God's people are on pilgrimage to the heavenly sanctuary and final Sabbath rest, following Jesus, the leader, who blazed the trail to perfection through suffering. Now we are to follow him, and this journey includes the way of the Cross. But God makes us perfect through suffering. As our high priest, Jesus consecrates his people. Jesus suffered and died, and because of this, he entered into the glory that is our destiny in Christ.

GOSPEL In the episode before this reading, Jesus had been teaching about the ideals of discipleship; now he is asked about the legitimacy of divorce. Coming from the Pharisees, the question is not sincere, since Jewish Law assumed that divorce was legitimate, and the only point of discussion was the proper grounds for it. Jesus' reply goes behind the legislation of Deuteronomy 24 and settles on the principle found in the creation story. He explains that divorce was instituted as a

They replied,
   "Moses **permitted** a husband to write a bill of divorce
   and **dismiss** her."
But Jesus told them,
   "Because of the **hardness** of your hearts
   he wrote you this commandment.
But from the **beginning** of creation, *God made them male
    and female.*
*For this reason a man shall **leave** his father and mother
   and be **joined** to his wife,
   and the **two** shall become **one** flesh.*
So they are no longer **two** but **one** flesh.
Therefore what **God** has joined **together**,
   no human being must **separate**."
In the house the disciples **again** questioned Jesus about this.
He **said** to them,
   "Whoever **divorces** his wife and marries **another**
   commits **adultery** against her;
   and if **she** divorces her **husband** and marries another,
   she commits adultery."]

And people were bringing **children** to him that he might
    touch them,
   but the disciples **rebuked** them.
When Jesus saw this he became **indignant** and said to them,
   "Let the children **come** to me;
   do not **prevent** them, for the kingdom of God **belongs** to such
    as these.
Amen, I say to you,
   whoever does not **accept** the kingdom of God like a **child**
   will not **enter** it."
Then he **embraced** them and **blessed** them,
   placing his **hands** on them.

[Shorter: Mark 10:2–12 (see brackets)]

Marginal notes (left column):

With no malice.

Marriage is a source of joy! Let that be reflected in Jesus' response.

Pause at the end of this line.
With the puzzlement of the disciples.

Jesus keeps the explanation simple.

Pause at the end of this line.

Smile as you relate this scene, then switch to a tone of rebuke with the disciples' response.

Quicken your pace and raise your energy.

Tenderly; smile again, and slow to the end.

---

concession to weakness and that lifelong, monogamous marriage is the ideal. He reminds the listener of the divine purpose in marriage.

    Mark hands on the words of Jesus, adapted by the Greco-Roman culture of his community some thirty years after the Resurrection. Jewish legislation did not contemplate the possibility of the woman initiating a bill of divorce. Thus, this Gospel adapts Jesus' teaching to an actual community situation, giving evidence of the cultural contexts that can influence interpretation.

    The idea of the child as a model to replicate in the Christian life (a topic that also occurs in the reading of two Sundays ago, in Mark 9:37) is not easy to interpret. Children in ancient societies occupied a low status, and Mark reflects this cultural setting. The Reign of God is for those who are like children, the poor, the hungry, and the dispossessed—persons whose rights and dignity were ignored. Followers of Jesus can only enter and be a part of God's reign if we recognize our dependence on God for all we have and all we are; Jesus invites us to give up all claims to status and rights over others, a theme developed later in this same chapter. Only if disciples become like children can they be received by Jesus and become true followers of the Crucified One. The teaching is firmly in place within the context of the training in discipleship in these chapters. K.S.

TWENTY-EIGHTH SUNDAY IN ORDINARY TIME

LECTIONARY #143

READING I   Wisdom 7:7–11

A reading from the Book of Wisdom

I **prayed**, and **prudence** was given me;
    I **pleaded**, and the spirit of **wisdom** came to me.
I **preferred** her to scepter and throne,
and deemed riches **nothing** in comparison with her,
    nor did I liken any priceless **gem** to her;
because all **gold**, in view of **her**, is a little **sand**,
    and **before** her, **silver** is to be accounted **mire**.
Beyond **health** and **comeliness** I **loved** her,
and I chose to have **her** rather than the **light**,
    because the **splendor** of her never yields to sleep.
Yet **all** good things together came to me in her company,
    and **countless** riches at her hands.

RESPONSORIAL PSALM   Psalm 90:12–13, 14–15, 16–17 (14)

R. Fill us with your love, O Lord, and we will sing for joy!

Teach us to number our days aright,
    that we may gain wisdom of heart.
Return, O LORD! How long?
    Have pity on your servants!

Fill us at daybreak with your kindness,
    that we may shout for joy and gladness all
        our days.
Make us glad, for the days when you
        afflicted us,
    for the years when we saw evil.

Let your work be seen by your servants
    and your glory by their children;
and may the gracious care of the LORD our
        God be ours;
    prosper the work of our hands for us!
    Prosper the work of our hands!

An exhortatory reading. Let the assembly see your delight and maintain that emotion throughout.

Start slowly, with quiet excitement, and build your intensity gradually.

Scoff at the worthlessness of power and wealth.

mire = muck

With real passion. comeliness = beauty

Pause at the end of this line.

Drop your intensity slightly, but don't lose the emotion. Slow to the end.

For meditation and context:

TO KEEP IN MIND
Pay attention to the pace of your reading. Varying the pace gives listeners clues to the meaning of the text. The most common problem for proclaimers new to the ministry is going too fast to be understood.

READING I The model sage, Solomon, did not receive wisdom as a birthright. He requested it in his inaugural prayer as sovereign, desiring wisdom above all other goods: scepters and thrones, material wealth, health, and beauty, and even sunlight. Wisdom is the evidence of God's personal involvement in the created world. More than a blueprint, it is God's saving presence. Because Solomon requested wisdom over the customary perks of royal office, God added to this gift everything Solomon had not requested. In this we hear an echo of Jesus urging us to seek first the Kingdom of God and God's righteousness, and all other good things will be given besides (see Matthew 6:33).

READING II The reading from Hebrews is a continuation of the warning that the "word of God" (which is often used as a title for Jesus Christ and so "Word" is often in upper case) brings judgment as well as salvation. God's Word has been pronounced and cannot be ignored. The Hebrew language has a special idea about words: once pronounced, their effect makes things happen. A spoken word contains within itself a power that does what it says.

God's word-in-action, heard and experienced in the Old Testament, is revealed in its fullness in the life and activity of Jesus, in whom God's Word became a living reality. It is "effective," demanding an active response from us; it is "penetrating" and so incisive that it divides the soul—the life principle—from the spirit—the reason and thought that looks beyond the horizon to God.

Is the author saying that the Word of God tests a person's earthly life and spiritual

READING II   Hebrews 4:12–13

A reading from the Letter to the Hebrews

Brothers and sisters:
Indeed the word of God is **living** and **effective**,
    sharper than any two-edged **sword**,
    penetrating even between **soul** and **spirit**, **joints** and **marrow**,
    and able to discern **reflections** and **thoughts** of the heart.
No creature is **concealed** from him,
    but everything is **naked** and **exposed** to the eyes of him
    to whom we must render an account.

A didactic reading. This text reminds us of the power of the Word we proclaim, and the reason we take care to proclaim it well.

Good news! Share eagerly, but take your time. Keep your voice up at the ends of these phrases.

Don't swallow "heart."

We need not fear; God knows us deeply.

GOSPEL   Mark 10:17–30

A reading from the holy Gospel according to Mark

[As **Jesus** was setting out on a **journey**, a man **ran** up,
    knelt down before him, and **asked** him,
    "Good **teacher**, what must I do to inherit eternal **life**?"
Jesus answered him, "Why do you call me **good**?
No one is good but God **alone**.
You **know** the commandments: *You shall not* **kill**;
    you shall not commit **adultery**;
    you shall not **steal**;
    you shall not bear false **witness**;
    you shall not **defraud**;
    honor your **father** *and your* **mother**."
He replied and said to him,
    "Teacher, **all** of these I have observed from my youth."
Jesus, **looking** at him, **loved** him and said to him,
    "You are lacking in **one** thing.
Go, **sell** what you have, and give to the **poor**
    and you will have **treasure** in heaven; then come, **follow** me."

A narrative reading. Identify and express an emotion for each of the characters; remember, one character may have many emotions in the course of the narrative.

Lively, with the enthusiasm of the man.

Keep your pace up through these commandments; as Jesus says, we know them already.

Slow down, and lower your voice on Jesus' response to reflect the intimacy of the exchange.

existence? The "reflections and thoughts of the heart" are the intellect, conscience, and subconscious. Even our moral and intellectual life is submitted to the scrutiny of the Word. Humans judge according to external conduct and appearances, but God scrutinizes the interior life. In these two verses the theologian formulates a pun with the repetition of specific words: we are confronted with the Word (Greek, *logos*), open to the eyes of him (the *logos*) "to whom we must render an account" (*logos*). We must give a *logos* to him who is the *Logos*.

GOSPEL This story of the wealthy aspirant to eternal life is expanded by sayings about wealth and the difficulty of entering the Kingdom, and then followed by promises about the rewards due to disciples. The inquirer asks about the entrance requirements to eternal life. Jesus' initial reply cites the second half of the Decalogue (replacing "do not covet" with "do not defraud"), focusing on those commandments that concern human relationships. In the Old Testament, wealth and material goods were considered a sign of God's favor. Jesus' reply astonishes the dis-

ciples because it appears to contradict the customary principle. Since wealth, power, and merit generated false security, Jesus rejects them. Achieving salvation is beyond human competence and depends solely on the goodness of God, who offers it as a gift. The inquirer's reply indicates that he agrees that obedience to the letter of the Law is not enough, but his further question—what more must I do?—suggests that he still thinks in terms of achievement.

Jesus' response indicates that no such measuring is appropriate. Discipleship demands absolute attention. The obstacle

With the sadness of the man.
Pause at the end of this line.

How does Jesus feel about the man's response—sad, disappointed, understanding?

With amazement.

With compassion.

Raise your energy; with great anxiety.

Slowly.

How does Jesus feel about his disciples' sacrifices?

Raise your energy and quicken your pace.

The list inserts a caution before naming the most valuable reward, eternal life.

> TO KEEP IN MIND
> Pray the text, using your favorite method of praying with Scripture.

At that statement his face **fell**,
    and he went away **sad**, for he had **many** possessions.

Jesus looked around and said to his disciples,
    "How **hard** it is for those who have **wealth**
    to enter the kingdom of God!"
The disciples were **amazed** at his words.
So Jesus **again** said to them in reply,
    "**Children**, how **hard** it is to enter the kingdom of God!
It is easier for a **camel** to pass through the **eye** of a **needle**
    than for one who is **rich** to enter the kingdom of God."
They were **exceedingly** astonished and said among themselves,
    "Then **who** can be saved?"
Jesus **looked** at them and said,
    "For human beings it is **impossible**, but not for **God**.
All things are possible for God."]
Peter began to say to him,
    "We have given up **everything** and followed you."
Jesus said, "**Amen**, I say to you,
    there is **no** one who has given up house or brothers or sisters
    or mother or father or children or lands
    for **my** sake and for the sake of the **gospel**
    who will not receive a **hundred** times more now in this
        present age:
    houses and brothers and sisters
    and mothers and children and lands,
    with **persecutions**, and eternal **life** in the age to **come**."

[Shorter: Mark 10:17–27 (see brackets)]

---

to the inquirer's total commitment is wealth—a challenge, Jesus implies, that affects everyone, and hence he remarks how hard it is for anyone to enter the Kingdom: "Children, how hard it is to enter the kingdom of God!" He illustrates his statement with the image of a camel being threaded through the eye of the needle. Entry to new life is not a matter of merit. What is eventually a matter of divine grace, entrance into God's reign, is impossible for anyone who banks on his or her own resources. The wealthy person finds that

discipleship is more costly than all the wealth he or she possesses.

Those who give up everything will be rewarded, both in the present life and in the age to come. The reference to the rewards in this life indicates that, even though Christians have given up family and possessions at present, they will experience a new family that is the Church. Christians are assured of their place in a new community. Two features of this new existence are notable. The list of people and things that will be repaid the disciple largely repeats the list of things surrendered; but no

"father" reappears in the list of recompenses, presumably because God is Father and cannot be duplicated; besides, Jesus adds a reference to persecutions. This reflects the situation of Mark's community in Rome threatened with persecution. K.S.

TWENTY-NINTH SUNDAY IN ORDINARY TIME

An exhortatory reading. The good news here is the result of the servant's suffering, not the suffering itself, so convey the emotions very carefully.

Isaiah = ī-ZAY-uh

God does not take pleasure in the suffering, but in the willingness of the servant to bear it for us; don't smile at this line.
Your voice, eyes, and face can hint at the good news God's servant brings to us.

Pick up your pace; the good news is now even more clear.
End on a note of quiet satisfaction.

For meditation and context:

TO KEEP IN MIND

You can't proclaim what you don't understand. Read the Scripture passage and its commentary in *Workbook*. Then read it from your Bible, including what comes before and after it so that you understand the context.

LECTIONARY #146

READING I   Isaiah 53:10–11

A reading from the Book of the Prophet Isaiah

The LORD was pleased
  to **crush** him in infirmity.

If he gives his **life** as an offering for sin,
  he shall see his descendants in a **long** life,
  and the will of the LORD shall be accomplished
    through him.

Because of his **affliction**
  he shall see the **light** in **fullness** of days;
through his **suffering**, my servant shall justify **many**,
  and their **guilt** he shall **bear**.

RESPONSORIAL PSALM   Psalm 33:4–5, 18–19, 20, 22 (22)

R. Lord, let your mercy be on us, as we place our trust in you.

Upright is the word of the LORD,
  and all his works are trustworthy.
He loves justice and right;
  of the kindness of the LORD the earth
    is full.

See, the eyes of the LORD are upon those
    who fear him,
  upon those who hope for his kindness;
to deliver them from death
  and preserve them in spite of famine.

Our soul waits for the LORD,
  who is our help and our shield.
May your kindness, O LORD, be upon us
  who have put our hope in you.

READING I After the exile, Israel saw itself in the persona of the suffering servant depicted in this reading, which describes how the servant's humiliation and suffering will lead to triumph. Rejected and broken, the servant would be revived. His death is a sacrifice in atonement for the sins of all people. The Hebrew term *'āšām* ("reparation offering" or "offering for sin"), frequent in Leviticus, refers to a sacrifice intended as compensation for what is due because of guilt. The writer envisions the suffering servant as comparable to a blameless animal vic-

tim, like the "lamb led to the slaughter" in an earlier verse (7).

One of the striking points is the statement "Through his suffering, my servant shall justify many, and their guilt he shall bear." Here the individual servant and Israel are combined: God's plan of putting things right is to be realized by the community. The term "justify" means to be acquitted or declared innocent. Since the servant bears their iniquity, the act of salvation will be efficacious and not merely legal.

READING II Only here the author calls Jesus our "great high priest." He is acquainted with the tradition of Jesus' temptation and struggle with evil throughout his public life, to which Jesus did not succumb. Jesus is "our great high priest," perfectly in communion with God and humans. He "passed through the heavens," an ambiguous phrase that means that even heaven is too small to hold him; his identity with human nature is total. The author stresses that Jesus was a human being like us. He experienced all that we experience, including temptation in every

270

READING II   Hebrews 4:14–16

A reading from the Letter to the Hebrews

Brothers and sisters:
Since we have a **great** high priest who has passed through
   the **heavens**,
  Jesus, the **Son** of God,
  let us hold **fast** to our confession.
For we do not have a high priest
  who is unable to **sympathize** with our weaknesses,
  but one who has **similarly** been tested in every way,
  yet without **sin**.
So let us **confidently** approach the throne of grace
  to receive **mercy** and to find **grace** for **timely** help.

GOSPEL   Mark 10:35–45

A reading from the holy Gospel according to Mark

James and **John**, the sons of Zebedee, came to **Jesus** and said
   to him,
  "**Teacher**, we want you to do for us **whatever** we ask of you."
He replied, "**What** do you wish me to do for you?"
They answered him, "**Grant** that in your glory
  we may sit one at your **right** and the other at your **left**."
Jesus said to them, "You do not **know** what you are asking.
Can you drink the cup that **I** drink
  or be **baptized** with the baptism with which **I** am baptized?"
They said to him, "We **can**."

Margin notes

An exhortatory reading. A powerful reading, reminding us of the deep connection we have with Jesus.

With energy and eagerness. This is good news!

How does it make you feel to have someone like Jesus who knows our struggles intimately? Bring that emotion to your proclamation.

Slowly and with great assurance; maintain eye contact with the assembly to the end.

A narrative reading. Jesus' definition of leadership is very different from the world's. Make sure this contrast is evident.

Zebedee = ZEB-uh-dee

James and John are acting like children.

Enthusiastically.

With great confidence.

Bottom commentary

way, "yet without sin." Because he never wavered in temptation, we also can be triumphant in our temptations.

Through Jesus, God became so identified with humans as to empathize with us and our suffering; because of the depths of his suffering with us, mercy flows from God's throne. In Jesus, God has visited us in our home, and, now travelling the road before us, he shows us how to forgive. Because he has identified with us in our life struggle, he shows us compassion, mercy, and our better self. His visit to us

brought God to humans, and he brings humans to God.

GOSPEL On three occasions Jesus' Passion prediction is followed by the failure of the disciples to comprehend the implications of Jesus' teaching about his suffering (8:32; 9:33, 10:35–40). In this reading James and John request positions of honor in the coming Kingdom. In reply Jesus asks if they can share his cup and baptism. The images refer to the suffering and death that await him. The "cup" is used in the Old Testament to refer to

divine punishment (Psalm 75:8), and the image may simply refer to the tremendous suffering that falls to Jesus by lot (Mark 14:36). The verb "baptize" can refer to being overwhelmed with catastrophes (Psalm 42:7; Isaiah 43:2 for a similar idea). Here the metaphor of drinking the cup refers to acceptance of the destiny assigned by God, which involves divine judgment of sin that Jesus, the innocent one, is to expiate on behalf of the guilty. His "baptism" will be Crucifixion and Death for the salvation of the human race. James' and John's request for a share in the glory involves a share in

How does Jesus feel about the trials his disciples will undergo?

Angrily.

With increasing disgust at this abuse of power.

Calmly but firmly.

Slow on the end of this line; this is a surprising statement.

Don't gloss over this casually; Jesus is turning human expectations upside down.

TO KEEP IN MIND

Making eye contact with the assembly connects you with them and connects them to the reading more deeply than using your voice alone. This helps the assembly stay with the story and keeps them engaged.

Jesus said to them, "The cup that I drink, **you** will drink,
and with the baptism with which **I** am baptized, **you** will
be baptized;
but to sit at my right or at my left is not **mine** to give
but is for those for whom it has been prepared."
When the ten heard this, they became **indignant** at James
and John.
[Jesus **summoned** them and said to them,
"You know that those who are recognized as rulers over
the Gentiles
Lord it over them,
and their great ones make their **authority** over them felt.
But it shall **not** be so among **you**.
Rather, whoever wishes to be **great** among you will be
your **servant**;
whoever wishes to be **first** among you will be the **slave** of all.
For the Son of Man did not come to be **served**
but to **serve** and to give his life as a **ransom** for **many**."]

[Shorter: Mark 10:42–45 (see brackets)]

Jesus' sufferings, the endurance of trial and suffering for the Gospel. He names his Passion "baptism," a word that indicates his sufferings will be the font of the purification for the whole world. Their fervor makes them give this spontaneous response, "We can," without knowing what they are committing themselves to, but with the hope that in some way they will get what they desire.

Only God assigns places of honor in the Kingdom. To Mark's readers, James' and John's first reply is perhaps an indication of martyrdom. However, Jesus' reply puts their acknowledgment in another light. They accept suffering as a temporary prelude to more assured glory. Jesus assures them that suffering indeed awaits them, but future glory cannot be guaranteed: it is a matter of God's grace. Notice the ironic element: James and John asked to be at Jesus' right and left; Mark's community hears an echo of the two crucified thieves, one on Jesus' right and one on his left.

As earlier, the disciples' failure to understand leads Jesus to teach about service. True greatness lies not in wielding authority over others, but in being the servant or slave of all—a theme that dominates Jesus' teaching. Whatever authority is to be exercised by the disciple must, like that of Jesus, be rendered as service to others rather than for personal aggrandizement. Jesus' service is his Passion and Death for the redemption of the human race. As a clinching argument, Jesus presents himself as an example in his role as Son of Man, who came not to be served but to serve. By implication, any follower of the Son of Man can do no less. K.S.

THIRTIETH SUNDAY IN ORDINARY TIME

LECTIONARY #149

READING I Jeremiah 31:7–9

A reading from the Book of the Prophet Jeremiah

Thus says the Lord:
Shout with **joy** for Jacob,
　　exult at the head of the nations;
　　proclaim your **praise** and say:
The LORD has **delivered** his people,
　　the **remnant** of Israel.
Behold, I will bring them **back**
　　from the land of the north;
I will **gather** them from the **ends** of the world,
　　with the blind and the **lame** in their midst,
the mothers and those with child;
　　they shall **return** as an **immense throng**.
They departed in **tears**,
　　but I will **console** them and **guide** them;
I will lead them to brooks of **water**,
　　on a level road, so that **none** shall stumble.
For I am a **father** to Israel,
　　Ephraim is my **first-born**.

An exhortatory reading. How do you feel knowing how much God cares for us? Bring that emotion to the reading.

Jeremiah = jayr-uh-MĪ-uh
Jubilantly. This is great news! Smile with your voice, eyes, and face through this opening section.

Pause at the end of this line.
God speaks. Lower your volume (but not your energy) and express with tenderness and care.

This gathering requires a gentle touch.

Lift your eyes and see this throng spread before you.

Be eager to show your love.
Slight pause at the end of this line.
With joy and firm conviction.
Ephraim = EE-fray-im or EF-fr*m

READING I Jeremiah describes the future, hoped-for trip home from exile and the people's song: "The LORD has delivered his people, the remnant of Israel." This liturgical refrain provides hope for the community in exile, who await a new exodus, a triumphant return home through the mountainous, desert terrain. Then the prophet announces the divine plan. God will bring them back from where they had been exiled, the land of the north. He will gather the new Israel and lead them by streams of water on pleasant paths, water being a sign of God's attentive love.

Among the companions are the most vulnerable and disabled of the population, the blind, lame, pregnant, and those about to give birth. This procession embodies the whole community, humbled and hurt yet bringing forth new life. God will accompany them on their return as the father of Ephraim, his firstborn, who symbolizes the faithless generation of exiles who have repented and returned.

READING II The Letter to the Hebrews works out the doctrine of the high priesthood of Jesus Christ. We find three essential qualifications of the priesthood described here. (1) A priest, the link between God and humans, was appointed on behalf of humans to deal with the things concerning God. The priest's special function was to offer sacrifice for the people's sins. Sin disturbs the friendship between humans and God and creates a barrier between them. The sacrifice was meant to restore that relationship, and could atone for sins of ignorance. Sacrifice could not atone for the deliberate sin, however. Ignorance is pardonable; presumption is not. Ignorance includes sins committed

For meditation and context:

TO KEEP IN MIND

A didactic reading is usually given out of love for the community. Make sure that love is evident in your proclamation.

A didactic reading. Not a dry, academic treatise, but a teaching about God's care for both the high priest and the people the priest serves.

Don't be dismissive of the high priest. He is recognized as imperfect but still valuable to the community.

Convey the patient understanding of the high priest.

Pause at the end of this line.

With affection.

Show your satisfaction with this great high priest; slow to the end.

Melchizedek = mel-KEEZ-uh-dek

RESPONSORIAL PSALM　Psalm 126:1–2, 2–3, 4–5, 6 (3)

R. The Lord has done great things for us; we are filled with joy.

When the LORD brought back the captives
　　of Zion,
　we were like men dreaming.
Then our mouth was filled with laughter,
　and our tongue with rejoicing.

Then they said among the nations,
　"The LORD has done great things
　　for them."
The LORD has done great things for us;
　we are glad indeed.

Restore our fortunes, O LORD,
　like the torrents in the southern desert.
Those that sow in tears
　shall reap rejoicing.

Although they go forth weeping,
　carrying the seed to be sown,
they shall come back rejoicing,
　carrying their sheaves.

READING II　Hebrews 5:1–6

A reading from the Letter to the Hebrews

Brothers and sisters:
Every high priest is taken from among **men**
　　and made their representative before God,
　　to offer **gifts** and **sacrifices** for **sins**.
He is able to deal **patiently** with the **ignorant** and **erring**,
　　for he **himself** is beset by **weakness**
　　and so, for this reason, must make sin offerings for himself
　　as well as for the people.
No one takes this honor upon **himself**
　　but only when **called** by God,
　　just as Aaron was.
In the **same** way,
　　it was not Christ who glorified **himself** in becoming
　　　high priest,
　　but rather the one who said to him:
　　　You *are my* **son***:*
　　　　this day I have **begotten** *you;*
　　just as he says in **another** place:
　　　You are a priest **forever**
　　　　according to the order of Melchizedek.

---

when a person is swept away by an impulse of anger or passion or mastered by some temptation. The sin of presumption is calculated disobedience of God for which a person is not sorry. The priest could open the way for the sinner to return to God—if the sinner wanted to come back.

(2) The priest was one with humans, toward whom he lived with sympathy. The priest was identified with humans to such an extent that he offered sacrifice for his own sin before offering it for the sins of others. In connection with this the author used a wonderful word, *metriopathein*,

"deal patiently," a term that refers to the ability to sympathize. The Greeks understood *metriopatheia* (the noun) as the mean between excessive grief and indifference. It refers to balanced relations among persons, the ability to bear with them without getting irritated, to not lose one's temper when people are slow or foolish and will not learn but rather do the same thing over and over again. Dealing gently or patiently with others does not condone their faults, nor does it give way to anger with them, but through the patience and

sympathy this virtue implies, it directs persons back to the right way.

(3) A third essential qualification of a priest is that no person appoint himself to the priesthood; his appointment to God's ministry among humans is neither a job nor a career but a calling. A person is able to look at the larger picture and say, "God chose me and gave me this service to offer." Hebrews shows how Jesus fulfills the conditions of the priesthood.

A narrative reading with lots of energy and excitement. Match your nonverbal expression to this tone.

Use your vocal energy to express the movement and bustle of the crowd.
Jericho = JAYR-ih-koh

Bartimaeus = bahr-tih-MAY-uhs

Timaeus = tih-MAY-uhs or tĭ-MEE-uhs

Raise your volume.
Sharply.

Raise your intensity again.
Lower your intensity as Jesus pauses.

Quickly.
More quietly, to convey the intimacy of this one-on-one conversation.
Eagerly.

Keep your voice up; don't swallow "way."

TO KEEP IN MIND
A *narrative* has characters, dialogue, a setting, and action. Help your listeners see the story unfold, keep characters distinct, and be clear about shifts in setting.

GOSPEL   Mark 10:46–52

A reading from the holy Gospel according to Mark

As Jesus was leaving Jericho with his disciples and a siz
    able **crowd**,
  Bartimaeus, a **blind** man, the son of Timaeus,
  sat by the roadside **begging**.
On hearing that it was Jesus of **Nazareth**,
  he began to **cry** out and say,
  "**Jesus**, son of David, have **pity** on me."
And many **rebuked** him, telling him to be **silent**.
But he kept calling out all the **more**,
  "Son of **David**, have **pity** on me."
Jesus **stopped** and said, "**Call** him."
So they called the blind man, saying to him,
  "Take **courage**; get **up**, **Jesus** is calling you."
He **threw** aside his cloak, **sprang** up, and **came** to Jesus.
Jesus said to him in reply, "What do you want me to **do** for you?"
The blind man replied to him, "Master, I want to **see**."
Jesus told him, "Go your **way**; your **faith** has saved you."
Immediately he received his **sight**
  and **followed** him on the way.

GOSPEL Jesus' instruction to his disciples about his Passion and about servanthood are bracketed by the cure of the blind person of Bethsaida (8:22–26) and this reading, the cure of blind Bartimaeus as Jesus leaves Jericho headed for Jerusalem. This narrative represents a parable in action: the physical sight granted to Bartimaeus symbolizes the insight necessary for any disciple. Significant are various informative details about the blind man's condition and attitude toward Jesus: the energy and insistence of his petition, the lack of concern with his wardrobe when Jesus calls him, the faith of the blind man and his simple dialogue with Jesus. The evocative language implies theology: Bartimaeus' faith is said to have saved him—not only healed him physically but brought him salvation—with the result that Bartimaeus follows Jesus "on the way"; that is, on the way to Jerusalem and the Paschal Mystery.

It is significant that, before he is healed, Bartimaeus shouts to Jesus as the "Son of David," a term synonymous with Messiah, which is the term Simon Peter uses in his confession of Jesus' identity (8:29). Neither Peter nor Bartimaeus is aware of the full implications of their use of the term. But the deeper insight into who Jesus really is follows as a divine gift, and Batrimaeus becomes a disciple. As a result of his faith, his condition changes: no longer blind, sitting at the side of the road, he recovers his sight and follows Jesus. His faith, expressed in his petition, has pressed him into action: he leaves behind his cloak, leaps up to approach Jesus, and follows him to Jerusalem. We are called to do the same. K.S.

ALL SAINTS

LECTIONARY #667

READING I Revelation 7:2–4, 9–14

A reading from the Book of Revelation

An exhortatory reading. Don't concern yourself with the allegorical meaning of this fantastical vision; just tell the story as it is, with all its wonder and amazement, so that your community sees it unfolding before them.

Revelation = rev-uh-LAY-shuhn

Don't rush; there's a lot going on.
A scene full of power and energy. Build the intensity slowly to the end.

Begin to raise your volume.

I, **John**, saw another **angel** come up from the East,
    holding the **seal** of the living **God**.
He cried out in a **loud** voice to the four angels
    who were given power to **damage** the land and the sea,
    "Do **not** damage the land or the sea or the trees
    until we put the **seal** on the foreheads of the **servants**
        of our God."
I heard the **number** of those who had been marked with the seal,
    one **hundred** and forty-four **thousand** marked
    from **every** tribe of the children of **Israel**.

Proclaim the number as if it were the biggest number you could imagine.

See the crowd before you; imagine them spilling out of the doors!

After this I had a vision of a great **multitude**,
    which **no** one could count,
    from every **nation**, **race**, **people**, and **tongue**.
They stood before the **throne** and before the **Lamb**,
    wearing white **robes** and holding **palm** branches in
        their hands.
They **cried** out in a loud voice:

    "**Salvation** comes from our **God**, who is seated on the **throne**,
    and from the **Lamb**."

Raise your volume and intensity a bit more here.

All the **angels** stood around the throne
    and around the **elders** and the four living **creatures**.
They **prostrated** themselves before the throne,
    worshiped God, and **exclaimed**:

READING I Our celebration of all the saints includes Revelation's vision of the end-time. The East was considered the entry point of light and the site of paradise (Genesis 2:8). Those bearing the seal belong to God and are protected to serve as the messianic army, which numbers 144,000—the square of twelve (the number of Israel's tribes) multiplied by a thousand, symbolic of the perfect, new Israel. The second innumerable crowd embraces people "from every nation, race, people, and tongue"; they are not just Israelites, but from all nations, thus fulfilling God's promise to Abraham.

This second crowd is standing; their posture and their vesture (the "long white robes"), is a sign of their resurrected status. The palm branches, a symbol of victory, allude to the Passover feast, and remind us of the crowd that welcomed the Messiah-King into Jerusalem. With a loud voice the multitude sings of God's salvation, another link with Jesus' triumphal entry into Jerusalem. Just as the Messiah gains his victory by sacrificial death, so his army is shown to triumph by following him in martyrdom, referred to as "the time of great distress." The washing of robes in the Lamb's blood alludes to the purification mentioned in Daniel 11:35; 12:10, and to their martyrdom in following Jesus. The ultimate triumph to which we are called comes about by faithful witness throughout life, to the time of our death.

READING II The proof of God's love is the gift of his Son—a gift that gives baptized Christians a supernatural dignity and makes us children of God—a present reality and promise of the life to

The climax of the reading; your energy should peak here.

Pause at the end of this line.

Drop your voice now for this more intimate conversation.

A rhetorical question; he's not asking for information.

With a wistful joy as he recounts their suffering and perseverance.

"**Amen**. **Blessing** and **glory**, **wisdom** and **thanksgiving**,
  honor, **power**, and **might**
    be to our God **forever** and **ever**. **Amen**."

Then one of the **elders** spoke up and said to me,
  "Who are these wearing white **robes**, and where did they
    come from?"
I said to him, "My **Lord**, **you** are the one who knows."
He said to me,
  "These are the ones who have **survived** the time
    of great **distress**;
  they have **washed** their robes
  and made them **white** in the **Blood** of the Lamb."

For meditation and context:

RESPONSORIAL PSALM   Psalm 24:1bc–2, 3–4ab, 5–6 (6)

R. Lord, this is the people that longs to see your face.

The LORD's are the earth and its fullness;
  the world and those who dwell in it.
For he founded it upon the seas
  and established it upon the rivers.

Who can ascend the mountain of the LORD?
  or who may stand in his holy place?
One whose hands are sinless, whose heart is clean,
  who desires not what is vain.

He shall receive a blessing from the LORD,
  a reward from God his savior.
Such is the race that seeks him,
  that seeks the face of the God of Jacob.

TO KEEP IN MIND
Use inflection (the high or low pitch of your voice) to convey attitude and feeling. High pitch expresses intensity and excitement; low pitch expresses sadness, contrition, or solemnity.

An exhortatory reading. Reassure your assembly not to be concerned with the future because God's love is destined to win and we will claim our identity as children of God.

Don't bark out "Beloved," but fill it with tenderness.

Linger over this description of God's overflowing love.

Not surprising that we are called what we are!

Convey your care with "Beloved." Contrast "now" with "shall be."

This is not worrisome but exciting!

READING II   1 John 3:1–3

A reading from the first Letter of Saint John

Beloved:
See what **love** the Father has **bestowed** on us
  that we may be called the **children** of God.
Yet so we **are**.
The reason the **world** does not know us
  is that it did not know **him**.
Beloved, we are God's children **now**;
  what we **shall** be has not **yet** been revealed.

---

come. Yet to be gained is knowledge of God, based on our likeness with Christ. Gaining that knowledge requires our constant effort to live in imitation of him. Our hope of seeing God sustains and inspires us along the way to holiness—which is also spelled "wholeness." In that long purification process, hope fortifies us to resist sin.

 GOSPEL The beatitudes offer us promise and consolation. The first half of each beatitude depicts the community's present state; the second half foretells the future. Placing these two con-

ditions in a single verse permits the trials of everyday life to be drawn into contemplation of what awaits us. We are called to become what the beatitudes describe.

The Isaiah prophecy proclaimed by Jesus in his home synagogue provides a helpful key (Isaiah 61:1–2, 7; Luke 4:18–19). It tells of good news for the poor, comfort for all who mourn, and inheriting the land. The beatitudes are uttered by the anointed One of Isaiah's prophecy. The Spirit of the Lord had descended on Jesus at his baptism (Matthew 3:16), and anointed him to bring Good News to the poor, to heal the

brokenhearted, free the captives, and comfort those who mourn. "Blessed are the poor in spirit," like "Blessed are the meek" and "for theirs is the kingdom of heaven" is another way of saying "they will inherit the land." Both beatitudes express a reversal of the present affliction. People without power-status, who depend upon God, will receive the reign of heaven and inherit the earth when things are upended at the judgment.

The first beatitude, "Blessed are the poor in spirit, for theirs is the kingdom of heaven," makes us wonder, who are the "rich in spirit"? If the Kingdom of Heaven is

We **do** know that when it **is** revealed we shall be **like** him,
　for we shall **see** him as he **is**.
Everyone who has this **hope** based on him makes himself **pure**,
　as **he** is pure.

GOSPEL　Matthew 5:1–12a

A reading from the holy Gospel according to Matthew

When Jesus saw the **crowds**, he went up the **mountain**,
　and after he had sat down, his disciples came to him.
He began to **teach** them, saying:

"**Blessed** are the **poor** in **spirit**,
　for **theirs** is the Kingdom of **heaven**.
Blessed are they who **mourn**,
　for they will be **comforted**.
Blessed are the **meek**,
　for they will **inherit** the land.
Blessed are they who **hunger** and **thirst** for **righteousness**,
　for they will be **satisfied**.
Blessed are the **merciful**,
　for they will be shown **mercy**.
Blessed are the **clean** of heart,
　for they will see **God**.
Blessed are the **peacemakers**,
　for they will be called **children** of God.
Blessed are they who are **persecuted** for the sake
　　of **righteousness**,
　for **theirs** is the Kingdom of **heaven**.
Blessed are **you** when they **insult** you and **persecute** you
　　and utter every kind of **evil** against you **falsely** because
　　of **me**.
Rejoice and be **glad**,
　for your **reward** will be **great** in **heaven**."

he = Jesus

An exhortatory reading. Don't let the rhythm lull you into a sleepy, sing-song reading. Make each verse distinct, as if each were a new idea, building up to a complete picture of the community of the faithful.

The surprise in these verses is that the poor, the mourners, and the meek are blessed, whereas most people would consider them cursed.

Make this about your community. Speak directly to the merciful, the clean of heart, the peacemakers in your community.

Note the switch from "blessed are they" to "blessed are you."

Another surprise: we should rejoice when we're persecuted!
Slow down on this final line.

reserved for the poor in spirit, do the rich enjoy their presence and dominion in this present world? If the poor in spirit are those who ask, seek, and knock on the door of divine help, the rich in spirit must be the self-sufficient, who do not give God the time of day. Clearly Jesus is not speaking of destitution, but a poverty of much greater value. He congratulates those who humble themselves, deny themselves, open themselves to God and neighbor. With this beatitude Jesus pulls out at the root the pride of a spirit closed in on itself. The poor in spirit are people who are kind, con-

siderate, open to God and attentive to neighbor. That the Kingdom of Heaven is theirs is no surprise, for through them a bit of heaven has touched the present world.

"Those who mourn" are allied with Christ; they grieve because God has not yet righted the situation. Bad people still prosper; the good suffer. The hunger and thirst for righteousness is expressed in right conduct before God, who is just; this implies that the blessed are not necessarily righteous, but they have right conduct as their conscious goal. The merciful will receive the mercy they have invested in life. Purity

of heart means harmony between intention and deed; it involves singlmindedness and intention to do God's will. Peacemakers, by their lives and actions in tune with Jesus' life, prove they are children of God.

In the last two beatitudes, Jesus focuses us on a lasting reality that gives perspective to current persecution. Those who long for a glorious life with God do not cringe before insults on earth. In this litany Jesus invites his hearers to place their lives and intentions next to his, even as he announces the blessings that have already begun to flow through him to believers. K.S.

THE COMMEMORATION OF ALL THE FAITHFUL DEPARTED (ALL SOULS' DAY)

LECTIONARY #668

READING I   Wisdom 3:1–9

A reading from the Book of Wisdom

The **souls** of the **just** are in the hand of God,
   and no **torment** shall touch them.
They **seemed**, in the view of the **foolish**, to be **dead**;
   and their passing away was thought an **affliction**
   and their going forth from us, **utter** destruction.
But they are in **peace**.
For if before men, indeed, they be **punished**,
   yet is their **hope** full of **immortality**;
chastised a **little**, they shall be **greatly** blessed,
   because God **tried** them
   and found them **worthy** of himself.
As gold in the furnace, he **proved** them,
   and as sacrificial **offerings** he **took** them to himself.
In the time of their **visitation** they shall **shine**,
   and shall **dart** about as **sparks** through **stubble**;
they shall judge **nations** and rule over **peoples**,
   and the LORD shall be their King **forever**.
Those who **trust** in him shall understand **truth**,
   and the **faithful** shall abide with him in **love**:
because **grace** and **mercy** are with his holy ones,
   and his **care** is with his **elect**.

An exhortatory reading. Imagine consoling someone who has just lost a loved one. What tone would you use?

With compassion.

Set this line apart.
Contrast "punished" with "hope," "chastised" with "blessed."

proved = tested; gold is put into fire to harden it so that it will last and shine forever!

They who were thought to be punished will instead appear in glory with the power of God.

Only because of God's great mercy can we be sure of our salvation.

The readings given here are suggestions. Any reading from the Lectionary for the Commemoration of All the Faithful Departed (#668) or the Masses for the Dead (#1011–1015) may be used. Ask your parish staff which readings to prepare.

READING I This reading comes from verses shortly after those we heard on the Twenty-Fifth Sunday in Ordinary Time. In contrast to the terrible death the wicked projected for "the just one" in that reading, the sage (author of the Book of Wisdom) declares here that the just are in God's hand. Besides being treasured by God, they enjoy peace, which is beyond feelings; it is full rest and well-being. From the perspective of the fool, the just have died, and their death was disaster, the result of destruction and even punishment. The sage invites the reader to look beyond the appearances for enduring values.

The idea that God tests his people ("God tried them and found them worthy of himself") is often associated with the Israelites' trials in the desert after the release from Egypt. In Deuteronomy, the desert experience of Israel is a time of trial—an opportunity for learning discipline and gaining knowledge. God's testing of the just who have died is presented with two metaphors of transformation: gold tried and tested in the furnace and sacrificial offerings on the altar. In both, fire causes the transformation. The second one accentuates the union between God and the just, who are likened to a burnt offering that, though consumed by fire, is received by God as a pleasant fragrance. If the metaphor of gold tested in fire stresses transformation and purification,

For meditation and context:

TO KEEP IN MIND

You can't proclaim what you don't understand. Read the Scripture passage and its commentary in *Workbook*. Then read it from your Bible, including what comes before and after it so that you understand the context.

RESPONSORIAL PSALM   Psalm 23:1–3a, 3b–4, 5, 6 (1)

R. The Lord is my shepherd; there is nothing I shall want. or R. Though I walk in the valley of darkness, I fear no evil, for you are with me.

The LORD is my shepherd; I shall not want.
   In verdant pastures he gives me repose;
beside restful waters he leads me;
   he refreshes my soul.

He guides me in right paths
   for his name's sake.
Even though I walk in the dark valley
   I fear no evil; for you are at my side
with your rod and your staff
   that give me courage.

You spread the table before me
   in the sight of my foes;
you anoint my head with oil;
   my cup overflows.

Only goodness and kindness follow me
   all the days of my life;
and I shall dwell in the house of the LORD
   for years to come.

An exhortatory reading that reminds us of God's great love for us in Jesus Christ! Make sure your community knows this is good news from your voice, eyes, and face!

Start strong and full of joy and hope!

Linger over this phrase describing God's overflowing love!

"Ungodly" is a surprise; don't swallow it.

This is an aside; pick up the pace a bit.

Don't stress "proves," as if God's love needs proof; here, it simply means "shows."
God's gift of love is free, for sinner and saint alike. This is indeed good news, so smile with your voice, eyes, and face!
Pause at the end of this line.

READING II   Romans 5:5–11

A reading from the Letter of Saint Paul to the Romans

Brothers and sisters:
Hope does not **disappoint**,
   because the love of God has been **poured** out into our hearts
   through the Holy Spirit that has been **given** to us.
For **Christ**, while we were still **helpless**,
   died at the appointed time for the **ungodly**.
Indeed, only with **difficulty** does one die for a **just** person,
   though **perhaps** for a **good** person
   one might even find **courage** to die.
But God **proves** his love for us
   in that while we were still **sinners** Christ **died** for us.
How much **more** then, since we are now **justified** by his Blood,
   will we be **saved** through him from the wrath.

the burnt offering stresses God's acceptance and communion with the just.

Until "the time of their visitation" (their judgment), the just have been at peace in God's hand. Now they "shall shine and shall dart about as sparks through stubble"; they will govern nations, a reference to their intercessory role. The lines reveal the author's belief in an afterlife, which is guaranteed by God's faithfulness. Grace and mercy rest on the holy ones, and God's providence watches over the elect. Perhaps the most encouraging is this: "the faithful shall abide with him in love."

READING II | **Romans 5:5–11**. Because salvation belongs to the future it is called "hope." Paul's Greek term for hope (*elpís*) does not suggest uncertainty, as in, "I wonder whether God really means it." On the contrary, "hope does not disappoint." The love Paul writes about is God's love for us, manifested by the gift of the Holy Spirit; it is the love that God places in our hearts so we might love. The measure of God's love for us is proven in the "reconciliation" that God worked through the sacrifice on the Cross, when Christ, though innocent, accepted death and

thereby established peace, reconciling us with God.

If Christ manifested this love when we were sinners, how much more so now, once reconciled, can we trust that he will save us. The reconciliation appears with a sharp profile: God was not divorced from the people; we had divorced ourselves from God by our sins. It was not God who had to change his attitude, but humans; even so, God took the initiative by Christ's Death so that humans might return to friendship with him.

Raise your intensity.

> **Indeed**, if, while we were **enemies**,
>   we were **reconciled** to God through the death of his Son,
>   how much **more**, once **reconciled**,
>   will we be **saved** by his **life**.
> Not only **that**,
>   but we also **boast** of God through our Lord Jesus **Christ**,
>   through whom we have now received **reconciliation**.

The best news yet!

We "boast" of our intimacy with God through Christ.

> **Or**:

A didactic reading that is full of good news, so proclaim with intensity.

READING II   Romans 6:3–9

A reading from the Letter of Saint Paul to the Romans

Brothers and sisters:

Are you unaware? = Don't you know?

> Are you **unaware** that we who were **baptized** into Christ Jesus
>   were baptized into his **death**?

Emphasize: we were buried through Baptism.

> We were indeed **buried** with him through baptism into **death**,
>   so that, just as Christ was **raised** from the dead
>   by the glory of the Father,
>   we **too** might live in **newness** of life.

Unity with Christ in death also brings unity in newness of life!

> For if we have grown into **union** with him through a **death**
>   like his,
>   we shall also be **united** with him in the **resurrection**.

Paul makes the point again. Slow down.

> We know that our **old** self was **crucified** with him,
>   so that our **sinful** body might be done **away** with,
>   that we might no longer be in **slavery** to sin.

Our "body" represents not our physical body but our old self.

> For a **dead** person has been **absolved** from sin.

This is self-evident: the dead are no longer subject to sin!

> **If**, then, we have **died** with Christ,
>   we believe that we shall also **live** with him.
> We know that **Christ**, **raised** from the dead, dies **no more**;

Slow down on this final line.

> death no **longer** has power over him.

Romans 6:3–9. When Paul writes about Baptism, he refers to its most basic meaning: persons who are baptized into Christ are baptized into his Death. Jesus spoke of his Death as a baptism, and that meaning is sustained by the exodus connection with baptism that links Jesus' Death to the Passover, interpreting it as the sacrifice of the lamb. The key word is "into": Baptism is into Christ, and hence into his Death. What matters for Paul is the movement of entering "into" the Messiah, our insertion into the mystery of Christ that happens in Baptism. What does it mean to

be baptized into the Messiah's Death? Baptism involves being "coburied" (Greek, *synthaptein*) with the Messiah; it is a rare word that brings out the significance that what happened to the Messiah also happens to those who are "in him" by Baptism. Those who are "in" the Messiah die and are buried with him. The symbolism—the candidate being plunged under water—suggests death and burial. The point is that if the Messiah is Jesus, the Crucified and Risen One, then belonging to the messianic people means being identified with the Cross and Resurrection by dying and rising.

This opens the way for the main theme of the rest of the paragraph. Christ's Resurrection means that those who are "in Christ" now stand, and must walk, on Resurrection ground. The point of the argument is that those who have been baptized no longer belong to the dying world, because they have already died with Christ; Paul does not suppose that one should wait until the bodily resurrection before beginning to "live [in Greek, walk] in newness of life." Walking, with its ethical connotation, points to conduct, the way a person lives. Paul offers a further explanation that liter-

An exhortatory reading. This is all good news, assurance that we belong to Christ and so life is ours. Keep your energy up throughout.

Challenge your community—let us not reject anyone who comes to us!

Remember, you are speaking to an assembly of believers. This gift of life is for them!

How do you feel about this gift? Let your joy come through.

TO KEEP IN MIND
Be careful not to "swallow" words by mumbling. Articulate carefully so that every word is clearly heard, especially at the end of lines.

TO KEEP IN MIND
Words in bold are significant words about which you must make a choice to help their meaning stand out. You may (or may not) choose to stress them.

GOSPEL   John 6:37–40

A reading from the holy Gospel according to John

Jesus said to the crowds:
"**Everything** that the Father **gives** me will **come** to me,
    and I will not reject **anyone** who comes to me,
    because I came down from heaven not to do my **own** will
    but the will of the one who **sent** me.
And **this** is the will of the one who sent me,
    that I should not **lose** anything of what he **gave** me,
    but that I should **raise** it on the last day.
For **this** is the will of my Father,
    that **everyone** who sees the **Son** and **believes** in him
    may have **eternal** life,
    and I shall **raise** him up on the last day."

---

ally reads: "For if we have been united with him in the likeness of his death, we shall also be of his resurrection." The word translated "been united" comes from a rare root that means "grown together." In Baptism, the life of the baptized is intertwined with that of Christ, like two young trees whose trunks grow around one another. Paul may have in mind the Christian practice of the newly baptized being clothed in white, symbolizing their commitment to holiness of life. The statement "we shall also be united with him in the resurrection," indicates, besides the

future life with Christ, that we are united in our present status and behavior. Through Baptism believers share the Death of Christ and escape the grip of sin. The energy to live anew becomes a reality for us in Christ's Resurrection.

GOSPEL | The Son was sent to fulfill the Father's will, which is the guarantee of eternal life and salvation for all persons. The Father desires salvation for all. God's plan thus manifests his unlimited grace and loving attention to every person. In faith we receive the grace of

God's marvelous expression of love: the one who believes in the Son already enjoys eternal life in the present, because he adheres to Jesus, the Resurrection and the life, the only one who can usher us beyond death to life eternal with God. K.S.

THIRTY-FIRST SUNDAY IN ORDINARY TIME

LECTIONARY #152

READING I   Deuteronomy 6:2–6

A reading from the book of Deuteronomy

Moses spoke to the people, saying:
   "**Fear** the LORD, your God,
   and **keep**, throughout the days of your lives,
   all his statutes and commandments which I **enjoin** on you,
   and thus have **long** life.
Hear then, **Israel**, and be **careful** to observe them,
   that you may **grow** and **prosper** the more,
   in keeping with the **promise** of the LORD, the God of your
      fathers,
   to give you a land **flowing** with **milk** and **honey**.

"**Hear**, **O** Israel! The LORD is our God, the LORD alone!
Therefore, you shall **love** the LORD, your God,
   with all your **heart**,
   and with all your **soul**,
   and with all your **strength**.
Take to **heart** these words which I enjoin on you today."

An exhortatory reading. This is a moment of rejoicing for Moses and the people; make sure it sounds that way.

Deuteronomy = doo-ter-AH-nuh-mee
Start strong, with energy.
Emphasize the life that comes from keeping the commandments.

Raise your intensity slightly.

See the beauty of the land before you.

Take this final section slowly and deliberately; Moses ends with a summary of the entire covenant.

Pause at the end of this line.
A final exhortation; maintain eye contact with the assembly and keep your voice up to the end.

TO KEEP IN MIND

You can't proclaim what you don't understand. Read the Scripture passage and its commentary in *Workbook*. Then read it from your Bible, including what comes before and after it so that you understand the context.

READING I This passage, the first part of the Hebrew creed, sums up the basic principle of the Mosaic Law: Since the Lord alone is God, Israel must love God with an undivided heart. Jesus cited this commandment as "the first of all," embracing the whole Law of God, and it is of the utmost importance for the Chosen People's faith and life. Israel's love of God is preceded by God's love for Israel, referred to in the line "in keeping with the promise of the LORD . . . to give you a land flowing with milk and honey." God's love for humanity is a central part of his revelation in the both Testaments, expressed in the affirmation "God is love" (1 John 4:8, 16).

The first Hebrew word, *šema'* ("Hear" or "Listen") signals the disposition that a friend of God is to cultivate. A little capsule, called in Hebrew the *mezuzah*, fixed to the doorjamb of houses and rooms in Jewish homes, contains a little parchment inscribed with Deuteronomy 6:4–9; 11:18–21. As practicing Jews enter or exit through the doorway, they touch this little mezuzah, which they reverence with a kiss as a sign of their profession of faith. God asks for Israel's complete love. Can love be prescribed? What God demands of Israel and of each one of us pertains to the sphere of the will. Our devoted love is to be cultivated consciously, ever more deeply, as will be expressed later in the New Testament: "We love because he first loved us" (1 John 4:19; see also verse 10).

READING II The ancient priesthood consisted of priests who died and had to be replaced, but the priesthood of Jesus is forever. Jesus is the high priest, "higher than the heavens," a priest who has no need to offer sacrifice daily for

For meditation and context:

> **TO KEEP IN MIND**
>
> A *didactic* text makes a point or teaches something. Help your assembly to follow the argument and understand what's being taught.

A didactic reading. The argument is simple to follow, but it will help if you make it clear that this is good news. Consider, how does it make you feel to have such an advocate in Jesus?

Keep your pace up; no need to linger over these details.

levitical = lih-VIT-ih-k*l

Give each characteristic its emphasis.

Lower your voice on the parenthetical phrase ("first . . . people").

This is not a criticism of the priests of the Law; it's just stating facts.

Slow to the end; keep your voice up.

RESPONSORIAL PSALM   18:2–3, 3–4, 47, 51 (2)

R. I love you, O Lord, my strength.

I love you, O LORD, my strength,
    O LORD, my rock, my fortress,
        my deliverer.

My God, my rock of refuge,
    my shield, the horn of my salvation,
        my stronghold!
Praised be the LORD, I exclaim,
    and I am safe from my enemies.

The LORD lives! And blessed be my rock!
    Extolled be God my savior,
you who gave great victories to your king
    and showed kindness to your anointed.

READING II   Hebrews 7.23–28

A reading from the Letter to the Hebrews.

Brothers and sisters:
The **levitical** priests were **many**
    because they were prevented by **death** from remaining in
        office,
    but **Jesus**, because he remains **forever**,
    has a priesthood that does **not** pass away.
Therefore, he is **always** able to save those who **approach** God
        through him,
    since he lives **forever** to make **intercession** for them.

It was **fitting** that we should have such a high priest:
    holy, **innocent**, **undefiled**, **separated** from sinners,
    higher than the **heavens**.
He has no **need**, as did the high priests,
    to offer sacrifice **day** after **day**,
    first for his own sins and **then** for those of the people;
    he did that **once** for **all** when he offered **himself**.
For the **law** appoints men subject to **weakness** to be high priests,
    but the word of the **oath**, which was taken after the law,
    appoints a **son**,
    who has been made **perfect** forever.

---

sins but who offered himself once and for all. The law appointed high priests with human limitations, but the fulfillment of God's oath regarding Melchizedek (Psalm 110:4) makes the Son of God the perfect priest forever. His priesthood will never "pass away," a word that refers to its inalterability. The term *aparabatos* describes what belongs to one person and can never be transferred to anyone else. So Hebrews affirms that Jesus' priesthood can never be taken from him. He is and will always remain the only way to God. The author uses another term when he affirms Christ's

permanence, which connotes that Jesus remains in the capacity of the servant. Wrapped in the phrase is the amazing thought that Jesus is forever at the service of humankind. On earth he served people and gave his life for them; in heaven he intercedes for them. He is the eternal priest, who forever opens the door to friendship with God and is forever the servant of humankind.

The author calls Jesus holy (*hósios*), a word that depicts the person, not so much as he appears before others, but in God's sight. The writer adds that Jesus is "inno-

cent"; he never hurt any person (*ákakos*). The author adds that Jesus is "undefiled" or stainless (*amíantos*), free from any blemish that would separate him from God. The blemished victim cannot be offered, the defiled person cannot approach, but the one who is *amíantos* is fit to enter God's presence. The author writes that Jesus is "separated from sinners," which means that he was different from sinners in that, although he underwent every temptation, he emerged without sin. The difference between Jesus and other persons lies not in the fact that he was not fully human, but

A narrative reading. Not every scribe is trying to trip up Jesus. Make sure your tone shows this is a sincere exchange between teacher and student.

An honest question.

Well-known phrases, but don't rush though them.

Jesus offers more than he was asked; the two commandments cannot be considered apart from each other.

The scribe is not merely repeating Jesus' words, but is demonstrating his own passionate commitment to this way of living.

How does Jesus feel about this wise scribe? Bring that emotion to your proclamation.

Pause at the end of this line.

Drop your volume slightly; proclaim with the admiration of the crowd.

TO KEEP IN MIND
Use inflection (the high or low pitch of your voice) to convey attitude and feeling. High pitch expresses intensity and excitement; low pitch expresses sadness, contrition, or solemnity.

GOSPEL   Mark 12.28-34

A reading from the holy Gospel according to Mark.

One of the **scribes** came to Jesus and asked him,
    "Which is the **first** of all the commandments?"
Jesus replied, "The first is **this**:
    ***Hear, O** Israel!*
    *The **Lord** our God is Lord **alone**!*
    *You shall **love** the Lord your God with all your **heart**,*
    *with all your **soul**,*
    *with all your **mind**,*
    *and with all your **strength**.*
The **second** is this:
    *You shall **love** your **neighbor** as **yourself**.*
There is no other commandment **greater** than these."
The scribe said to him, "**Well** said, teacher.
You are **right** in saying,
    '**He** is **One** and there is no **other** than he.'
And 'to **love** him with **all** your heart,
    with **all** your understanding,
    with **all** your strength,
    and to love your **neighbor** as **yourself**'
is worth **more** than all burnt offerings and sacrifices."
And when Jesus saw that he answered with **understanding**,
    he said to him,
    "You are not **far** from the kingdom of God."
And no one **dared** to ask him any more questions.

---

that he achieved humanity to its highest and best degree. Referring to his exaltation, the author affirms that Jesus is "higher than the heavens." If the previous phrase stresses the perfection of his humanity, this one stresses his divinity. Jesus, a man among humans, is exalted to God's right hand.

 GOSPEL The scribe is friendly when he asks about the first or greatest commandment of the Law. Jesus formulates the double love command, love God and love one's neighbor, two segments taken from the Old Testament Law

(Deuteronomy 6:5; Leviticus 19:18). Love commands are preceded by the words of the *Šema'* (Deuteronomy 6:4), the confession of God's uniqueness. The scribe's response echoes and interprets the *Šema'* by focusing on certain aspects, and adds that this is more important than all offerings and sacrifices.

Love thus becomes the ethical command that far outweighs any cultic rites. Such an attitude to the rites is not foreign to the Old Testament (expressed, for example, in Hosea 6:6) and is at home in Judaism; yet the way this story follows closely on the

incident in the Temple (11:15–19) suggests that here the idea that love "is worth more than all burnt offerings and sacrifices" is aimed to put the institution of the Temple in order. K.S.

THIRTY-SECOND SUNDAY IN ORDINARY TIME

A narrative reading. God cares not only for prophets but for the poor and vulnerable. Encourage your assembly to trust in God's care as well. Keep that intention in mind throughout.

Elijah = ee-LĪ-juh

Zarephath = ZAYR-uh-fath

He's tired after a long journey, and a little abrupt.

Her response at first might sound exasperated.

Now the grief of her situation overtakes her.

Don't swallow "die."

Gently, with real concern.

Confidently and with conviction.

Pause before the woman's response.

Proclaim this miracle slowly, firmly, and with a smile, as if to say to your assembly, "See, you too can trust in God."

LECTIONARY #155

READING I   1 Kings 17:10–16

A reading from the first Book of Kings

In those days, **Elijah** the prophet went to **Zarephath**.
As he arrived at the entrance of the city,
    a **widow** was gathering **sticks** there; he called **out** to her,
    "**Please** bring me a small cupful of **water** to drink."
She **left** to get it, and he called out **after** her,
    "Please bring along a bit of **bread**."
She answered, "As the LORD, your God, lives,
    I have nothing baked; there is only a **handful** of flour in my jar
    and a little **oil** in my jug.
Just now I was collecting a couple of sticks,
    to go in and **prepare** something for **myself** and my **son**;
    when we have **eaten** it, we shall **die**."
Elijah said to her, "Do not be **afraid**.
Go and do as you **propose**.
But **first** make me a little **cake** and **bring** it to me.
Then you can prepare something for **yourself** and your **son**.
For the **Lord**, the God of Israel, says,
    'The jar of flour shall not go **empty**,
    nor the jug of oil run **dry**,
    until the day when the LORD sends **rain** upon the earth.'"
She **left** and **did** as Elijah had said.

READING I   Elijah goes to the city of Zarephath, a Phoenician commercial capital some eight miles south of pagan Sidon, known for its exports, including wine, grain, and oil. The prosperous, idolatrous city is in dire straits because of the drought. Just as God had ordered the ravens to feed Elijah a few verses earlier, so here he ordains a foreigner to feed him. Although she apparently does not know it, this widow is God's instrument for salvation, so she stands in contrast to another important woman in Elijah's story, Jezebel, the Sidonian princess King Ahab married

and who propagated the worship of the pagan god Baal in Israel. It is ironic that God would have a Phoenician, presumably a Baal-worshiper, feed Elijah. That she is a widow means she is part of the unprotected fringes of society, the orphans and the poor; when the prophet comes along she is at the point of death from famine. Yet this widow, who has nothing to spare in a land devastated by drought, is instrumental in God's plan to provide for others. God guarantees that her meager provisions will not be diminished: the jar of meal will not be emptied and the jug of oil will

not fail until God sends rain. Thus God's Word spreads to a foreign territory. Later, Jesus will offer this widow as an example that God freely gives blessings and gifts (in Luke 4:25–26), and not necessarily to persons who suppose they have rights to certain privileges.

READING II   This reading from Hebrews stresses how the sacrifice of Christ is once and for all. In the first place, Christ did not enter a human-made holy place; he entered God's presence. Second, he entered the divine presence not

She was able to eat for **a year**, and he and her son as well;
   the jar of flour did not go **empty**,
   nor the jug of oil run **dry**,
   as the LORD had foretold through **Elijah**.

For meditation and context:

RESPONSORIAL PSALM   Psalm 146:7, 8–9, 9–10 (1b)

R. Praise the Lord, my soul! or R. Alleluia.

The LORD keeps faith forever,
   secures justice for the oppressed,
   gives food to the hungry.
The LORD sets captives free.

The LORD gives sight to the blind;
   the LORD raises up those who were
      bowed down.
The LORD loves the just;
   the LORD protects strangers.

The fatherless and the widow he sustains,
   but the way of the wicked he thwarts.
The LORD shall reign forever;
   your God, O Zion, through all
      generations. Alleluia.

TO KEEP IN MIND

A *didactic* text makes a point or teaches something. Help your assembly to follow the argument and understand what's being taught.

READING II   Hebrews 9:24–28

A reading from the Letter to the Hebrews

A didactic reading. The theme of Christ as high priest continues this week; the teaching will be easier for your assembly to understand if your tone reminds them that this is good news.
Keep your voice and energy up, and keep moving.

Christ did not enter into a sanctuary made by **hands**,
   a **copy** of the true one, but heaven **itself**,
   that he might **now** appear before God on our **behalf**.
Not that he might offer himself **repeatedly**,
   as the high priest enters each year into the sanctuary
   with blood that is not his **own**;
   if **that** were so, he would have had to suffer **repeatedly**
   from the foundation of the world.
But now **once** for **all** he has appeared at the end of the ages
   to take **away** sin by his sacrifice.

Good news!
Pause at the end of this line.

Just as it is appointed that human beings die **once**,
   and after this the **judgment**, so also **Christ**,
   offered **once** to take away the sins of many,
   will appear a **second** time, not to take away **sin**
   but to bring **salvation** to those who eagerly **await** him.

Drop your voice slightly on this parenthetical phrase.

That's us! Show our eagerness in your voice, eyes, and face.

for his own sake but to open the door and intercede for us. Third, besides the intercessory role of the heavenly high priest, the theologian contrasts the single offering of Christ with the perennial offerings of the ordinary high priests. Had he been one of them, he would have had to repeat his sacrifice unceasingly, but he offered the single sacrifice of himself as the final atonement for sin. Just as death is the single act that ends a person's life, so Christ's offering of himself for all is the sacrifice that once and for all achieved redemption.

Thus, Christ's sacrifice clears the highway to God. The fact that humans have always been and always will be sinners does not mean that Christ must go on offering himself repeatedly. Nothing need be added to what he has done to open the way to God's love for sinful people.

Finally, Hebrews draws a parallel between the mortal human life and Christ's life. A mortal dies and is presented for judgment. Christ dies, rises, and comes again—not to be judged but to judge and save the humans depending on him. Now for the believer, whose judge comes as a friend, the Second Coming is a wonderful occasion; if Christ were to come as a stranger or adversary, his coming would be judgment. But as believers we may await Christ's coming with eagerness rather than with apprehension and terror. What makes the difference is how one's heart is with Christ.

| GOSPEL | Jesus censures the scribes and Pharisees for their quest for honor. He does not forbid occupying the reserved places that correspond to persons in office, but he warns the faithful |

A narrative reading. Jesus is not impressed by the trappings of power that might impress us. Encourage your assembly to look beyond their appearances and reflect on their actions.

How does Jesus feel about these scribes? Let his feelings come through in your proclamation.

No doubt there are scribes within the crowd; speak directly to them in these lines.

Pause at the end of this line.

Note that Jesus observes not only what but how the crowd contributes.

Quietly, as an aside to his disciples. Make Jesus' feelings about this widow clear.

Speak of her contribution as if it were worth millions.

TO KEEP IN MIND
Making eye contact with the assembly connects you with them and connects them to the reading more deeply than using your voice alone. This helps the assembly stay with the story and keeps them engaged.

GOSPEL   Mark 12:38–44

A reading from the holy Gospel according to Mark

In the course of his teaching **Jesus** said to the **crowds**,
  "**Beware** of the **scribes**, who like to go around in **long** robes
  and accept greetings in the **marketplaces**,
    seats of **honor** in synagogues,
    and places of **honor** at banquets.
They **devour** the houses of **widows** and, as a **pretext**
  recite **lengthy** prayers.
They will receive a very **severe** condemnation."

[He sat down opposite the treasury
  and **observed** how the crowd put money into the treasury.
Many **rich** people put in **large** sums.
A poor **widow** also came and put in two small **coins** worth
    a few **cents**.
Calling his disciples to himself, he said to them,
  "**Amen**, I say to you, this **poor** widow put in more
  than all the **other** contributors to the treasury.
For they have all contributed from their **surplus** wealth,
  but **she**, from her **poverty**, has contributed **all** she had,
  her **whole** livelihood."]

[Shorter: Mark 12:41–44 (see brackets)]

---

that we should take care to avoid hankering after honors. He also accuses the scribes of exploiting widows financially. Because the care of widows and orphans in Jewish society was of paramount concern, the second charge is a serious one.

Mark contrasts the scribes' behavior with that of a widow who donates to the Temple. Her monetary gift amounts to practically nothing, but it is all she owns, and thus its value in God's eyes is far greater than the donations by wealthier people. Here we see both a negative and a positive example of love and devotion: the scribes' behavior indicates that their service to God is a farce, and in seeking to profit only themselves, they love neither God nor neighbor. Jesus contrasts the scribes' ostentation with the woman's right intention and generous spirit. As she gives the little which is her all, she becomes the model of one who entrusts herself to God. In the phrase "she, from her poverty, has contributed all she had, her whole livelihood," she becomes a christological figure, anticipating the self-emptying of Jesus on the Cross for our salvation. K.S.

THIRTY-THIRD SUNDAY IN ORDINARY TIME

LECTIONARY #158

READING I   Daniel 12:1–3

A reading from the Book of the Prophet Daniel

In those days, **I, Daniel,**
  heard this word of the LORD:
"At that time there shall arise
  Michael, the great **prince**,
  guardian of your people;
it shall be a time **unsurpassed** in distress
  since nations began until that time.
At that time **your** people shall **escape**,
  everyone who is found written in the **book**.

"Many of those who sleep in the dust of the earth shall **awake**;
  some shall live **forever**,
  others shall be an everlasting **horror** and **disgrace**.

"But the **wise** shall shine **brightly**
  like the **splendor** of the **firmament**,
and those who lead the many to **justice**
  shall be like the **stars forever**."

An exhortatory reading. At first glance, this may not seem like good news, but it is. Note how God protects us despite the trials.

Keep your pace up.

Strongly. Your tone should indicate that Michael is not to be feared but is our protector.

With sadness; though we are protected, many others will suffer.

With joy that turns quickly to anguish. Pause.

Raise your energy and see the beauty of those who shine like stars.

Note the thought rhyme; heighten this second part.

READING I | The prophet announces that salvation is to come through the mediation of the guardian angel of Israel, Michael. He will "arise" before a judicial hearing, which is the judgment scene that follows. Michael is summoned because it is a time of distress for the people, and also a time of deliverance. Michael is a comfort. The names of God's people recognized for their fidelity, are inscribed "in the book"; they will survive in the future judgment. The affirmation, "Many of those who sleep in the dust of the earth shall awake; some shall live forever,

others shall be an everlasting horror and disgrace," refers to resurrection and judgment, giving rise to the notion of a separation of the good from the bad in the last days. Daniel's reference to resurrection is reminiscent of Isaiah 26:19—"awake and sing, you who lie in the dust,"—as well as of the reanimation of the bones in Ezekiel 37. The destiny of the good and the bad is for eternity. Greater glory is reserved for "the wise," who have known and taught justice, for the teachers of justice shall be "like the stars forever." Throughout the

Book of Daniel, images of light serve as the main symbol of justice.

READING II | Here Hebrews draws a series of implicit contrasts between the self-sacrifice Jesus offered and the animal sacrifices. Whereas the daily Levitical sacrifices were ineffectual in remitting sin, and there was no end to this process because it left the people conscious of their sin and alienated from God, Jesus' sacrifice was once and for all time, and it won him a permanent place at God's right hand (as in Psalm 110:1). Thus he

For meditation and context:

TO KEEP IN MIND
Use inflection (the high or low pitch of your voice) to convey attitude and feeling. High pitch expresses intensity and excitement; low pitch expresses sadness, contrition, or solemnity.

RESPONSORIAL PSALM   Psalm 16:5, 8, 9–10, 11 (1)

R. You are my inheritance, O Lord!

O LORD, my allotted portion and my cup,
    you it is who hold fast my lot.
I set the LORD ever before me;
    with him at my right hand I shall not
        be disturbed.

Therefore my heart is glad and my soul
        rejoices,
    my body, too, abides in confidence;
because you will not abandon my soul to the
        netherworld,
    nor will you suffer your faithful one to
        undergo corruption.

You will show me the path to life,
    fullness of joys in your presence,
        the delights at your right hand forever.

A didactic reading. Again this week, the comparison is made between the human priest and Christ. Change your tone in each section.

READING II   Hebrews 10:11–14, 18

A reading from the Letter to the Hebrews

Brothers and sisters:
Every priest stands **daily** at his ministry,
    offering **frequently** those same sacrifices
    that can **never** take away sins.
But **this** one offered **one** sacrifice for sins,
    and took his seat **forever** at the right hand of God;
    now he waits until his enemies are made his **footstool**.
For by **one** offering
    he has made perfect **forever** those who are being **consecrated**.

Where there is **forgiveness** of these,
    there is no longer **offering** for sin.

Let the assembly hear the futility of these actions in your voice.

"This one" = Christ

With excitement.

So, we have nothing to fear!

Good news! Smile with your voice, eyes, and face through the end.

Slow to the end.

TO KEEP IN MIND
Exhortatory texts make an urgent appeal to listeners. They may encourage, warn, or challenge, and often include a call to action. You must convey the urgency and passion behind the words.

brought into being in his own person the new covenant prophesied by Jeremiah (Jeremiah 31:33–34). Jesus' sacrifice perfectly shows God's heart, displayed in a life of service and in the depth of love. Jesus is the complete revelation of God and the perfect offering of obedience, which cannot and need not be repeated.

GOSPEL   The signs of the end point to the breakup of the present cosmic order: sun and moon failing and stars falling. The description had been written centuries before in the prophets

(such as Isaiah 13:10; 34:4). The climax is the coming of "the Son of Man, coming in the clouds with great power and glory," gathering the elect from the four corners of the earth. The language is inspired by Daniel's vision, though here the mission of the Son of Man is to gather the faithful (a gathering as in Isaiah 11:11) as the new people of God. What follows are comments on how hearers should behave or react to this event. The tone shifts when Jesus assures his hearer that "this generation will not pass away until all these things have taken place."

The sufferings of believers will lead to the glorious arrival of the Son of Man. With the image of the homeowner Jesus announces the indeterminate nature of his return; it can happen at any time, so the disciple must keep alert. After the final battle, the Son of Man will be triumphant, and the world's destiny is summed up in the glorious moment when Jesus comes to judge the world and save the chosen.

The parable of the fig tree clarifies the message. In winter many trees lose their leaves and to all appearances they are resting, almost as if they were dead. As spring

An exhortatory reading. Jesus teaches not to frighten but out of love. Let that love come through in your proclamation.

Keep your pace up and your energy high.

Drop your volume, but not your energy, and build slowly through to "sky."

Pause at the end of this line.

The tone changes; simply and gently.

Pause at the end of this line.
Firmly.

"So don't worry about it!"

GOSPEL   Mark 13:24–32

A reading from the holy Gospel according to Mark

Jesus said to his disciples:
"In those days after that **tribulation**
　　the sun will be **darkened**,
　　　　and the moon will not give its **light**,
　　and the stars will be **falling** from the sky,
　　　　and the powers in the heavens will be **shaken**.

"And **then** they will see the 'Son of Man **coming** in the clouds'
　　with great **power** and **glory**,
　　and then he will send out the **angels**
　　and gather his **elect** from the four **winds**,
　　from the end of the **earth** to the end of the **sky**.

"Learn a **lesson** from the fig tree.
When its branch becomes **tender** and sprouts **leaves**,
　　you know that summer is **near**.
In the **same** way, when you see **these** things happening,
　　know that **he** is near, at the gates.
Amen, I say to you,
　　this generation will not **pass away**
　　until **all** these things have taken place.
Heaven and **earth** will pass away,
　　but my **words** will **not** pass away.

"But of that day or hour, no one knows,
　　neither the **angels** in heaven, nor the **Son**, but only
　　　　the **Father**."

approaches, the sap rises, the branches of the fig tree become tender, leaves sprout to announce the arrival of summer. Something similar happens to usher in the end of the old world and portend the beginning of the new: the sun and the moon will burn out, the cosmos will be shaken, the Son of Man will arrive on the clouds.

The scene seems incredible for us who have plans and projects for today, tomorrow, and next week, not to mention next year. With reason the disciples ask, "When will all this take place?" Jesus responds with parables that need to be interpreted. When the hardness of the human heart softens, when our short-term estimates about life become long-term, when our attitudes change and divine grace tempers our actions and words, then the Son of man is at the door. The creative Word of God, which is pronounced "mercy," softens the stony heart of judgment, so that the new heart may be fashioned according to God's lovely design—the heart that is converted into a home where God dwells, where his grace enters and leaves freely. On that day, what we recognize as the light of our conscience will become darkness in the knowledge of our God. On that day the human heart of flesh will be transformed, and this transformation will not pass unnoticed in heaven. K.S.

OUR LORD JESUS CHRIST, KING OF THE UNIVERSE

A narrative reading. The story is really a hymn of praise to God. Keep that intention (praising God!) in mind as you proclaim.

Start slowly, with a focused intensity, and build gradually.

Don't swallow "Ancient One."
Keep your inflection up at the comma.

The climax; your volume and energy should be at a high point through the next line.

More intimately.

Slow to the end; with firm conviction.

For meditation and context:

LECTIONARY #161

READING I   Daniel 7:13–14

A reading from the Book of the Prophet Daniel

As the **visions** during the night continued, I saw
   one like a Son of man **coming**,
     on the clouds of **heaven**;
   when he reached the **Ancient** One
     and was **presented** before him,
   the one like a Son of man received **dominion**, **glory**,
     and **kingship**;
   all **peoples**, **nations**, and **languages serve** him.
His dominion is an **everlasting** dominion
   that shall **not** be taken away,
   his **kingship** shall not be **destroyed**.

RESPONSORIAL PSALM   Psalm 93:1, 1–2, 5 (1a)

R. The Lord is king; he is robed in majesty.

The LORD is king, in splendor robed;
  robed is the LORD and girt about
   with strength.

And he has made the world firm,
  not to be moved.
Your throne stands firm from of old;
  from everlasting you are, O LORD.

Your decrees are worthy of trust indeed;
  holiness befits your house,
  O LORD, for length of days.

> **TO KEEP IN MIND**
> A *narrative* has characters, dialogue, a setting, and action. Help your listeners see the story unfold, keep characters distinct, and be clear about shifts in setting.

READING I The Book of Daniel, named not for its unknown author but for its main character, was written in the second century BC to fortify and comfort Jews being forced to accept Greek religious practices. It includes stories and vivid descriptions of visions, a hallmark of apocalyptic literature. The vision described in this reading is classic. It offered to Christian authors, like the author of the Book of Revelation, a way to envision the end-time, especially Christ's Second Coming.

Here, in contrast to the kingdoms opposed to God, represented as beasts, God's reign is portrayed by a human figure: "one like a Son of man." The phrase "Son of Man" was picked up by Christian writers as a title for Jesus, and used particularly in passages dealing with the Second Coming. In today's context, the one who comes on the clouds bears human weakness. He comes to serve and not to be served, yet he has "everlasting dominion."

READING II This reading is the last part of the greeting near the beginning of the Book of Revelation—a greeting purportedly to the "seven churches" with whom John is sharing his vision. He has commended to them peace from Jesus Christ, and so the reading begins with a list of Christ's attributes. The phrase "ruler of the kings of the earth" introduces the notion of Christ's sovereignty, central in the book. The rulers of the earth oppose God's rule until either the King of Kings (17:14; 19:16) defeats them (19:19–21) or they are converted (21:24).

In this poetic description, Christ's redemptive work is understood in terms of a new exodus. The references to "his blood" and "pierced" evoke the Passover

An exhortatory and powerful reading, but if you proclaim it all at the top of your range it will be tiresome; vary your tone as noted.

Good news! Smile with your voice, eyes, and face.

Raise your volume with each phrase.

Pause at the end of this line.

More quietly, but joyfully.

Good news! We only lament those we love!
Firmly, with satisfaction.

Keep this closing simple; you're stating the facts.

An exhortatory and powerful reading, but if you proclaim it all at the top of your range it will be tiresome; vary your tone as noted.

Good news! Smile with your voice, eyes, and face.

Raise your volume with each phrase.

Pause at the end of this line.

More quietly, but joyfully.

Good news! We only lament those we love!
Firmly, with satisfaction.

Keep this closing simple; you're stating the facts.

> **TO KEEP IN MIND**
> Pay attention to the pace of your reading. Varying the pace gives listeners clues to the meaning of the text. The most common problem for proclaimers new to the ministry is going too fast to be understood.

READING II   Revelation 1:5–8

A reading from the Book of Revelation

Jesus **Christ** is the **faithful** witness,
  the **firstborn** of the dead and **ruler** of the kings of the earth.
To him who **loves** us and has **freed** us from our sins by
    his blood,
  who has made us into a **kingdom**, **priests** for his God
    and Father,
  to **him** be **glory** and **power** forever and **ever**. **Amen**.

  Behold, he is **coming** amid the clouds,
    and every eye will **see** him,
    even those who **pierced** him.
  All the peoples of the earth will **lament** him.
    Yes. **Amen**.

"**I** am the **Alpha** and the **Omega**," says the Lord God,
  "the one who **is** and who **was** and who is to **come**,
    the **almighty**."

lamb whose sacrifice resulted in the exodus from Egypt.

The oracle in the last verse again identifies God as sovereign. "The Alpha and the Omega"—the first and last letters of the Greek alphabet—equivalent to "the First and the Last" and "the beginning and the end" (1:17; 2:8; 21:6; 22:13; similar to Isaiah 44:6; 48:12), is here applied to Christ; it suggests the uniqueness of the Creator who precedes all things and the Lord who will bring all things to their fulfillment. The word "almighty" translates the Old Testament phrase "the Lord God of hosts," and stresses God's supremacy over history.

GOSPEL   Jesus accepts the title King of the Jews (given also in 1:49, Nathanael's confession), but with a specific meaning: his royal dignity comes from his Father who sent him to testify to the truth (8:32–47). The title is similar to that of a shepherd to whom the sheep listen (10:16, 27). But Pilate is not of the flock and is skeptical of the truth. He asks a direct question, "Are you the King of the Jews?" From Pilate's political perspective, a king of the Jews was a conspirator against the empire, and, from the Jewish nationalist perspective, the Messiah King was the political-religious liberator who would free a foreign dominated state. The truth of Christ's sovereignty transcends both concepts, which is what Jesus explains to the procurator. His kingship is a reign of truth and justice—eternal values. Christ reigns over persons who accept and live the Truth he reveals, the Father's love.

We conclude the liturgical year with Pilate's question, "Are you the king?" Jesus' affirmation, "My kingdom is not of this

A narrative reading. Proclaim this as a conversation, not a shouting match. Keep the tone intimate, as if they are standing close to each other.

Pilate knows Jesus is no king; there's some sarcasm in his questions.

"Speak for yourself!"

Pilate is intrigued, curious.

Jesus remains calm in his response: kingdoms of this world fight; his kingdom is one of peace.

Don't preach; maintain Jesus' centered intensity.

Invite Pilate—and your assembly—to live in the truth of who they are and who Jesus is.

TO KEEP IN MIND
Use inflection (the high or low pitch of your voice) to convey attitude and feeling. High pitch expresses intensity and excitement; low pitch expresses sadness, contrition, or solemnity.

GOSPEL   John 18:33b–37

A reading from the holy Gospel according to John

Pilate said to **Jesus**,
    "Are you the **King** of the Jews?"
Jesus answered, "Do you say this on your **own**
    or have **others** told you about me?"
Pilate answered, "I am not a **Jew**, am I?
Your own **nation** and the chief **priests** handed you over to me.
What have you done?"
Jesus answered, "My **kingdom** does not belong **to this** world.
If my kingdom **did** belong to this world,
    my attendants would be **fighting**
    to **keep** me from being handed over to the Jews.
But as it **is**, my kingdom is not **here**."
So Pilate said to him, "Then you **are** a king?"
Jesus answered, "**You** say I am a king.
For **this** I was **born** and for **this** I came into the **world**,
    to **testify** to the **truth**.
Everyone who **belongs** to the truth **listens** to my voice."

---

world," disconcerts Pilate, and us. Who speaks? A carpenter from a small town, a preacher whose words and healings disturb people, a pious Passover pilgrim, now arrested, accused, misunderstood by the hierarchy, abandoned by followers.

The incredulous statesman, Pilate, who lives in the human heart, repeats the question and resists the answer. To inhabit Christ's Kingdom brings certain privileges and responsibilities. Besides fulfilling obligations as a citizen in this world, a subject in Christ's reign must pay taxes and live in accord with the principles of his eternal reign. When Jesus accepts the title, he empties the notion of royalty of its customary content and infuses it with the truth, which challenges the habitual schemes of power. The insignia of his office amaze us: his entry into the capital city on a burro is an emblem of peace and humility; his staff is the crosspiece of the Cross; his crown, the bloody wreath of thorns; his throne, the Cross. Later, when the soldiers make fun of him, dress him in purple, and bow down to him, they have no idea that this king is the proprietor of the empty tomb and the organ donor of the transplant of the new heart for our humanity.

Jesus answered Pilate: "You say I am king," and then, "For this I came into the world, to testify to the truth." What is truth? It is the Father's love for every creature, love that Christ the King demonstrates with his Passover—his life, Death, and return to life. The humble service and total sacrifice of Christ the King is the truth that rescues humanity from itself and restores the dignity of the human race. K.S.